Joomla!® Bible

Ric Shreves

WILEY

Wiley Publishing, Inc.

Joomla!® Bible

Published by
Wiley Publishing, Inc.
10475 Crosspoint Boulevard
Indianapolis, IN 46256
www.wiley.com

Copyright © 2010 by Wiley Publishing, Inc., Indianapolis, Indiana

Published by Wiley Publishing, Inc., Indianapolis, Indiana

Published simultaneously in Canada

ISBN: 978-0-470-50957-9

Manufactured in the United States of America

10 9 8 7 6 5 4 3 2 1

For general information on our other products and services please contact our Customer Care Department within the United States at (877) 762-2974, outside the United States at (317) 572-3993 or fax (317) 572-4002.

Wiley also publishes its books in a variety of electronic formats. Some content that appears in print may not be available in electronic books.

Library of Congress Control Number: 2009941923

About the Author

Ric Shreves is a partner at water&stone (www.waterandstone.com), a web development agency focused on open source content management systems. He's been building websites professionally since 1999 and writing about technology for almost as long. He's published several books on open source content management systems, including titles on both the Mambo and Drupal systems. This is his third title with Wiley, having previously released the Mambo Visual Blueprint and the Ubuntu Visual Blueprint.

Ric is an American who has lived in Asia since 1995. He currently resides in Bali, Indonesia, with his wife Nalisa. You can learn more about Ric and his most recent work by visiting his website at http://RicShreves.net.

Credits

Senior Acquisitions Editor
Stephanie McComb

Project Editor
Beth Taylor

Technical Editor
Ed Ventura

Copy Editor
Beth Taylor

Editorial Director
Robyn B. Siesky

Editorial Manager
Cricket Krengel

Production Manager
Tim Tate

Vice President and Executive Group Publisher
Richard Swadley

Vice President and Executive Publisher
Barry Pruett

Associate Publisher
Jim Minatel

Project Coordinator
Patrick Redmond

Graphic and Layout Technician
Jennifer Mayberry

Proofreaders
Cynthia Fields, John Greenough

Indexer
Broccoli Information Management

Acknowledgments

I'd like to thank the Wiley Team for their assistance on this title. No major publication is the work of a single person. In particular, Beth Taylor worked hard to keep this project on track and had a significant impact on the final product. I would like to single out Stephanie McComb who had the vision to champion this subject matter internally at Wiley (this is the first open source CMS title in the Bible series). I would also like to thank Jody Lefevere. While she was not directly involved in this title, she has been instrumental in keeping me involved with Wiley.

Finally, I want to thank my wife Nalisa for her love and support. She kept things running smoothly both at water&stone and at home while I spent many long hours working on this manuscript.

Contents at a Glance

Contents

Contents

Contents

Contents

Contents

Contents

Contents

Contents

Contents

Contents

Contents

Introduction

Welcome to the Joomla! Bible. Like all books in the Bible series, you can expect to find both hands-on tutorials and real-world practical applications, as well as reference and background information that provide a context for what you are learning. This book is a fairly comprehensive resource on the Joomla! open source content management system. By the time you have completed the Joomla! Bible you will be well prepared to build and maintain a Joomla!-based web site.

Joomla! is in the forefront of one of the most dynamic trends in open source software: the rise of open source content management systems (CMS). Historically, a web content management system was a very expensive investment. Open source has changed all that. There are now a number of options that allow site developers and site owners to tap into the power of building CMS-powered web sites.

Of all the options that exist in the market today, perhaps none is more popular than Joomla! — certainly none is growing more quickly than Joomla!. At the time this book was written, Joomla! had just passed the 10 million downloads mark. A truly significant achievement given the relatively short history of the project.

If you are a designer looking to build functional web sites for your clients, Joomla! is an excellent tool. If you are a developer looking for a framework upon which to develop custom functionality, Joomla! can meet your needs. And if you are simply a web site owner who wants to take control of their web site, then you need look no further than Joomla! To all of you: Welcome to the Joomla! Bible.

In keeping with the comprehensive theme of the Bible series, this book seeks to provide a wide range of information suitable to a wide variety of potential readers. While we have strived to present information that is relevant to the largest possible group of users, certain sections of this book are logically more relevant to certain categories of users.

For those looking to take their first steps with an open source content management system, the book progresses logically from the first section of introductory materials through the final sections on customization and site maintenance.

For those who are already familiar with Joomla!, the opening sections will probably add little to your understanding of the system, but the sections that follow will help you unlock the full potential of the system. Joomla! is a fairly complex system, and the middle sections of this book explore in depth how to get the most out of it.

For designers and developers, the middle and final sections will be your focus, as they take you through creating and configuring a Joomla! site and cover the basics of customizing the appearance and functionality of the system.

Finally, for site owners and administrators, this book should serve as a reference work, providing you with an easy-to-use guide to the ongoing ownership of a Joomla! site.

About the Icons

There are many different organizational and typographical features throughout this book designed to help you get the most from the information.

Whenever I want to bring something important to your attention, the information appears in a Tip, Note, Caution, or Cross-Reference. I've also added in important updated information by using the Joomla! 1.6 icon.

Tip

Tips generally are used to provide information that can make your work easier@@mdspecial short-cuts or methods for doing something easier than the norm.

Note

Notes provide additional, ancillary information that is helpful, but somewhat outside of the current presentation of information.

Caution

This information is important and is set off in a separate paragraph with a special icon. Cautions provide information about things to watch out for, whether simply inconvenient or potentially hazardous to your data or systems.

Joomla! 1.6

Information in these notes indicates new features or functions unique to version 1.6 of the Joomla! CMS.

Minimum Requirements

To get the most out of this book you will need access to an installation of the Joomla! CMS. Typically this requires a server running a combination of the Apache web server, the MySQL database, and PHP. Site management is done through a browser with a connection to the server. Full technical requirements and recommendations for optimal versions are discussed in Chapter 2.

In Part IV of the book, where the topics turn to customization, you will also want to have access to your favorite editor for working with the site's code. In Part IV and in several other points in the book, having access to an FTP client will be useful.

Note that this book focuses on versions 1.5.x and 1.6.x of the Joomla! CMS. These releases are significantly different from the older 1.0.x series.

Where To Go From Here

It is our hope that you will take away from this book an increased awareness of the capabilities of the Joomla! system and a higher comfort level when working with sites based on Joomla!

If you spend a bit of time around open source software, you will quickly discover that the rate of change in systems can be impressive (sometimes even a bit daunting). Joomla! is community-driven open source. The community behind it is large, dynamic, and ever changing. New features are developed at a rapid pace and new extensions, tips, tricks, and tools arise even more quickly.

If you want to get the most out of Joomla!, I strongly suggest you make an effort to keep up with the project. In Chapter One of the text we list the official Joomla! project sites. You should bookmark those sites and visit them regularly. The Joomla! Forum is a great place to visit and learn what is new and of interest. Several of the official sites also provide RSS feeds and other easy ways to stay abreast of developments with the project.

If you have feedback on this book, I can be reached directly by visiting my personal web site, RicShreves.net (http://RicShreves.net). There is a contact form on that site that is sent directly to me. You can also visit the official John Wiley & Sons web site (www.wiley.com) if you wish to provide feedback.

Part I

Getting Started with Joomla!

Introducing the Joomla! Content Management System

J oomla! is an award-winning content management system that enables you to easily create and manage the contents of a web site. You don't have to be a programmer to use Joomla!, because you don't need to work with the code to install, set up, or manage a site. To get started all you need is access to a web hosting service and a web browser. Moreover, the Joomla! content management system is open source, free of licensing fees and open for you to modify as needed to meet your requirements. The low cost and ease of use are the primary reasons Joomla! has become so popular, with more than 10 million downloads to date.

This introductory chapter explores the advantages of using Joomla! and open source, and provides basic information about how the Joomla! CMS works.

Discovering Open Source Content Management

A *content management system or CMS*, is a software tool that is installed on a server. A CMS enables you to publish pages on a web site and to manage the web site's features, content, and users through an easy-to-use browser-based interface. Historically, full-featured CMS products were expensive affairs, dominated by major brand names such as Broadvision, Vignette, and Microsoft. Over the last five years, however, this market has begun to shift, as robust open source products have arrived on the scene, supplementing and in some cases supplanting, their commercial brethren.

The appearance of viable open source content management solutions has had a significant impact on the market, essentially democratizing the content management space. Small businesses and individuals that could never before afford a proper CMS can now implement an open source solution and create a web presence that is competitive with much larger firms. As open source systems have increased in stability and functionality, they have also started to find a place in larger firms. Today you can find open source CMS products at every level of business, both public and private. Among the organizations using open source content management systems today are:

NASA

MIT

French Parliament

Nokia

The U.S. Navy

Novell

National Geographic

The Brazilian Government

PBS

Deciding to use a CMS

Content management systems make maintaining a web site more practical and more affordable. In the past, if you wanted to build a web site, you built a set of static HTML pages — that is, you hard-coded each page with your text and images. The problem is that if you build a static web site, you are forever locked into working with page code each time you want to change the site. Changing the contents of a page by manually changing the code on the page is time-consuming and labor-intensive. Managing a static site also locks you into hiring people with coding skills to perform content management tasks. Doing this can be a misuse of resources and is typically not a cost-effective approach to the problem. In contrast, if you use a content management system to power your web site, anyone with basic skills can make changes to the web site . You don't need a programmer to change the text or images on a page. Most systems, including Joomla!, use a content management interface that is largely similar to what you see in common word processing programs, such as Microsoft Word.

With a CMS, you gain significant advantages, including

- Increased control over your web site
- Improved time to market with content changes
- Lower cost per page
- Decreased total cost of ownership for your site

The same arguments that help justify the use of a CMS apply in even greater force to an open source CMS. Open source systems tend to deliver the same high degree of functionality but for a relatively lower cost base. This favorable cost-to-benefit ratio is largely responsible for the success of the systems and helps explain why they have become especially popular for businesses both small and large.

A content management system typically provides the following features:

- Identification of key users and their roles
- Ability to assign roles and responsibilities
- Ability to define workflow
- Ability to schedule and publish content
- Ability to limit access to content and functionality
- Ability to administer the system
- Ability to take the site offline and to perform maintenance tasks
- Ability to add components

Deciding to use open source

Open source is about freedom — not simply the ideal of freedom, but the commercial reality of freedom. Open source software does not carry licensing or subscription fees. Although the initial attraction of open source software may be the fact that it is free of charge, you are likely to find very quickly that the long-term advantage of open source lies in two other characteristics:

- The code is accessible. Unlike many commercial products that not only hide their code but also forbid you from modifying it, open source code is visible and you are free to modify it to suit your needs.
- Open source protects you from being tied to a specific vendor. If you adopt an open source solution, you can partner with the developer of your choice to assist you. If you deploy a system such as Joomla!, which is based on popular and common technologies, you need not dread having to change vendors in the future because finding people who are familiar with the system and have the skills needed to work on it is easy.

Taken together, the initial cost advantage plus the long-term benefits of having access to the code and your choice of vendors create a compelling argument in favor of open source.

However, you should also consider the disadvantages in the course of making your decision. If your firm has existing software deployed on a proprietary system, you may want to continue with those systems rather than introducing different products or platforms into your business. Support can also be an issue with open source products. If your firm requires a high level of support, you need to select an open source vendor that can offer you an appropriate service-level agreement.

Support for Joomla! is typically a self-help scenario. If you need to obtain a commercial support contract with a service-level agreement, you need to search for a developer who can provide this service because Joomla! does not offer commercial support. Although commercial support can be difficult to find, Joomla! does provide numerous community-based support options, including:

- Online documentation
- Community forums
- Online tutorials
- Mailing lists
- RSS feeds
- Developer wiki

Although the software is free of charge, you can expect to pay for a few things, either at the time you build your site or some time during the life of ownership. Common costs include:

- Design services
- Consulting services
- Custom development
- Deployment
- Support
- Hosting services
- Domain names
- Licenses for other related software, for example, certain extensions
- Maintenance

All of these expenses may not be applicable to your project, but you should consider them when calculating the total cost of ownership of an open source system. Even if you plan to manage and maintain the site yourself, don't forget that there is a cost associated with your time. It is a common mistake to underestimate the amount of time it can take to maintain a site. A CMS is a complex piece of software and it can be a target for hackers and others with bad intent. You cannot just build your site and forget it. Across the life of the site you need to install patches and security releases. The more complicated your site, the more time this takes. Don't make the mistake of ignoring this sometimes significant ongoing cost of ownership.

Determining whether open source is right for you

Although open source provides a welcome alternative to commercial software and it will work for the vast majority of people, it is not necessarily the right answer for everyone. Whether open source is right for you depends upon your situation and your tolerance for business risk. The advantages are:

- **Cost.** Open source is cheaper to obtain and studies show that implementation costs can be significantly less than for closed source solutions.

- **Open source can be vendor agnostic.** You are not tied to a single vendor and cannot be held hostage by that vendor.

- **Open source presents less risk.** Studies consistently show that open source development process produces better code and that many eyes make for more secure applications. Moreover, when problems are detected, open source produces patches at an extremely fast rate.

- **Open source is easier to install, configure, and customize.**

- **Open source promises more rapid innovation.**

If you are still not sure, start small. Roll out an open source solution in a limited role in your firm. Try it out. Six months from now evaluate the result and decide whether open source is the right path for you. If you are like many others, you will find that it is not only a viable option, but also an attractive one!

Discovering Joomla!

Joomla! started life in 2005 as a fork of the already popular Mambo open source content management system. The Joomla! community came together around the new project very quickly and helped create prominence and excitement around the new brand. Over the years, the project has gone from success to success and has grown to become one of the largest and most active open source projects.

The features included with the core system include:

- **WYSIWYG Content Editor:** Edit articles with the ease of use of a word processor.
- **Content scheduling:** Set start and stop dates for the publication of your content.
- **Content archiving:** Store old articles for ease of reference.
- **User management:** Create users and assign them to groups.
- **Access control:** Control the users' access to content and functionality.
- **Media manager:** Upload and organize your media files.
- **Language manager:** Add new language packs to enable multi-lingual interfaces for your site.
- **Banner manager:** Upload and run advertisements.
- **Contact manager:** Store contact details of your users and enable contact forms for them.
- **Polls:** Run polls and surveys on the site.
- **Search:** Search the site's content.
- **Web links management:** Create pages containing links to other web sites.
- **Content syndication:** Syndicate your content items with RSS feeds.
- **News feed aggregation and display:** Bring external RSS content into your site.

- **Integrated help system:** View help files from within your admin system.
- **Multiple template management:** Add new templates and assign them to the pages of your site.
- **Cache management:** Manage site performance by controlling the caching of information.
- **Integrated FTP:** Use the system's integrated FTP manager to move files to and from your server.
- **Search engine friendly URLs:** Create search engine friendly URLs to make your site more competitive on the search engines.

Joomla! 1.6

In addition to the core functionalities, Joomla! is extendable. With over 4,000 open source extensions available for little or no charge, you can customize the site to include the functionalities you need.

Deciding to use Joomla!

Why should you use Joomla? The short answer is that Joomla! provides an easy-to-install option for creating and managing a full-featured web site. The system is easy to use, affordable, and flexible enough to grow with you over time.

Who uses Joomla!

Joomla's popularity means that you can find a large number of example sites live on the Web. The system supports everything from small marketing sites to large e-commerce sites. Here's a roundup of some of the better known companies and brands that use Joomla!

Name	URL
Harvard University, Graduate School of Arts and Sciences	http://gsas.harvard.edu/
IHOP Restaurants	http://www.ihop.com/
Nickelodeon	http://www.quizilla.com/
United Nations Regional Information Centre	http://www.unric.org/
U.S. Army Corps of Engineers	http://www.spl.usace.army.mil
Yale University Association of Yale Alumni	http://grad.alumni.yale.edu/
University of Nebraska	http://nebraska.edu/
Olympus (Australia)	http://www.olympus.com.au/
Epson - Research & Development	http://www.erd.epson.com/
Dr. Ruth	http://www.drruth.com
Samuel L. Jackson	http://samuelljackson.com/

Although Joomla! is an excellent solution for many needs, it is not suited to every conceivable use. There are areas where the system excels, and others that present challenges. If you want to be more analytical about Joomla, then you should consider the pros and the cons.

Pros

- **Over 10 million downloads:** This is a healthy and growing project with a large fan base.

- **Over 4,500 extensions available:** The large number of extensions means you can tailor Joomla's functionality for your site.

- **Uses the popular LAMP stack:** It is easy to find hosting and help.

- **Presentation layer is very easy to work with:** You can customize the appearance of the site to match your brand. You aren't restricted to creating a "cookie cutter" web site.

- **Decent e-commerce options:** If you want to sell products online, Joomla! is perfectly capable of delivering all the most common e-commerce functionalities as well as providing usable catalog management.

- **Wide developer support:** It's easy to find help for your Joomla! site. Developers, designers, and other third-party services are readily available.

- **Decent documentation:** The online documentation provided by Joomla! is some of the best in open source. You can also find commercial documentation in a variety of formats.

- **Very active community:** An active and dynamic community means that you can get support in the forums and you can be assured of the ongoing vitality of the project.

- **Affordable development costs:** Competition and a common platform make for a wide range of vendor choices and price points. Given the large number of people providing Joomla! services, you can probably even find someone in your area.

Cons

- **No workflow:** If your site needs to replicate your offline workflow, Joomla! may not be the answer for you. The system does not include a workflow engine.

- **Limited user hierarchies:** The Joomla! 1.5 system includes a limited and fixed hierarchy of users. If you need complex user permissions, you either should choose Joomla! 1.6, or face installing extensions to your site to add this functionality. Be sure to examine the third-party extensions to determine if they will meet your needs in advance of committing to the system.

- **Limited content structure:** The Joomla! 1.5 system includes a limited and fixed content organization structure. If you need to create a site with complex content structures, you should either choose Joomla! 1.6 or face installing extensions to your site to add this functionality. Be sure to examine the third-party extensions to determine if they will meet your needs in advance of committing to the system.

- **Can be tough to maintain customized sites:** If you need to customize the code of your site, you have to be careful with upgrades in order to avoid losing your customizations. So, the greater the amount of customization you need, the greater the amount of work involved in upgrades.

- **SEO is mixed:** Joomla! includes an SEF URLs option, but the default system's configuration options are quite limited. There are, however, a number of third-party extensions you can add to the site to improve this.

- **Extensions vary widely in quality:** While there are a lot of extensions available for the system, they are not of equal quality. Do your homework and check extensions carefully before committing to them.

- **An increasing number of extensions are commercial:** The Joomla! core is free of charge, but a number of extensions for the system are commercial — and some are even encrypted! This troubling trend is a cause for concern and does erode some of the cost advantage of the system. Encrypted extensions also destroy your freedom to modify the code and should be avoided.

The Joomla! open source license

The Joomla! system is released under the GNU General Public License, commonly known as the GNU GPL. Joomla! is governed by Version 2.0 of the license. The GNU General Public License grants users four freedoms:

The freedom to run the program for any purpose.

The freedom to study how the program works and adapt it to your needs.

The freedom to redistribute copies so you can help your neighbor.

The freedom to improve the program and release your improvements to the public, so that the whole community benefits.

As a site owner, this means that the software is free of licensing fees and that you are able to use it for any purpose or any type of site. The only significant restriction is on your ability to resell the system; though it is permissible to sell products that include the code, you must release those products under licensing terms that are consistent with the GNU GPL v.2. This provision essentially takes away the motivation to turn the code into a commercial product because the terms of the license mean that the person who buys the code can distribute it to the public without paying you further for that privilege.

The user's freedom extends to the right to modify the code. You are not only free to use the system however you see fit, but you are also free to customize the code to suit your needs. Although your customizations are modifications of the GPL code, the license does not force you to disclose that modified code to others, unless you decide to release and redistribute the code. In other words, you cannot be forced to release code you have developed but do not wish to release to the public.

The majority of the extensions available for the Joomla! system are also released under the GNU GPL. While some of the extensions are commercial, and a few are even encrypted, a growing impetus exists within the Joomla! community to make sure that extensions are fully GPL-compliant and that the code for the extensions is accessible and can be modified by users.

The Joomla! architecture

Joomla! is designed to run on the popular and widely available LAMP stack, that is, on Linux with the Apache web server, the MySQL database, and the PHP programming language.

In broad terms, Joomla! works like this: When a site visitor requests a page by clicking on a link, Joomla! assembles that page by pulling the contents from the database; it then uses the template files for guidance in how to present that information on the page. The merged information is then sent to the user's browser where it is rendered for the visitor to see.

Unlike other systems that store rendered pages, almost all information in Joomla! is kept in the database and produced on the visitor's screen on demand. The text, images, usernames, and passwords are all kept in the database. Use of caching can change this to a limited extent, but generally speaking everything is dynamically generated. When you are editing content in Joomla!, you are editing information in the database. The Joomla! template files provide the formatting and layout the site visitors see on their screens. A template is actually a collection of files typically containing a mix of CSS, PHP, HTML, XML, and image files. If you want to change the underlying layout of the site's page, then you need to edit the template files.

Programming languages used

Joomla! is primarily written in PHP, though you will find a number of types of files inside the system, including the following:

.css

.html

.ini

.js

.php

.xml

You will also find image files in the following formats:

.gif

.png

.jpg

The database

Joomla! is built to run on the MySQL database. Joomla! 1.5 is compatible with Versions 4.1 and later of MySQL. Joomla! 1.6 requires version 5.0.4 and later.

Official Joomla! sites

The Joomla! team maintains a number of official sites. Some sites are informational in nature, others provide a way to distribute the code, others help promote and market Joomla!

Name	URL
Joomla! (main site)	`http://www.joomla.org/`
JoomlaCode	`http://www.joomlacode.org/`
Joomla! Developer Site	`http://developer.joomla.org/`
Joomla! Extensions Directory	`http://extensions.joomla.org/`
Joomla! Documentation	`http://docs.joomla.org/`
Joomla! Forums	`http://forum.joomla.org/`

Joomla! is an example of a community-driven open source project. This means that unlike corporate- sponsored projects, Joomla! is the work of a loosely affiliated group of individuals working together as a community. It is, in other words, a volunteer effort.

Finding out how the community works

Joomla!, like many of the larger community-backed projects, is supported by a foundation. In the case of Joomla! the foundation is a not-for-profit organization named Open Source Matters. The foundation holds the intellectual property rights to the brand name and related assets and provides legal shelter for the project. The foundation accepts donations of cash and services. The donations go to cover the basic overhead and operating costs such as for the servers, the hosting infrastructure, and promotional expenses. People are not directly paid to work on Joomla!

Open Source systems like Joomla! are offered free of charge for users. Often, people ask how this is possible. How is it that they can afford to give something valuable away for free? That is a complex question and in the case of a community-driven Open Source project, the answer is not always obvious. Community members work for free largely out of a desire for recognition, status, and access to expertise. Some are even more idealistic and participate for the pleasure of being part of something bigger than themselves and to feel like they have given something back to a group that has helped them in some fashion. The Joomla! Team is divided into a set of Working Groups that handle the following responsibilities:

- **Development:** Develops and maintains the Joomla! codeset.
- **Documentation:** Handles the developer and user documentation and maintains the help site.

- **Sites and infrastructure:** Maintains and moderates the forums and takes care of the various official sites.
- **Translation:** Coordinates translation of the interfaces as well as helping produce official announcements in a variety of languages.
- **Foundation:** Handles the more administrative matters related to the project, including marketing, events, and fundraising.

Participating in the community

Volunteers are the lifeblood of Joomla! If you are inclined to get involved with the project, do so. The easiest way to start is by registering on the Joomla! forums and to contribute by helping others in the forums. Many users come to the forums with very basic questions; others with more complex technical issues. The forums always need people who are willing to take the time to answer these questions and help others work their way through problems.

After you have participated in the forums for a while, you will be more familiar with the team members and how things in general work. If you want to do more, you can then approach a team member or the leader of a working group and ask to become involved on a more official level. Open source projects that are the size and scope of Joomla! need all sorts of people. Don't worry about whether you have sufficient technical skills or the right type of knowledge. The most important requirements are a willingness to donate your time and a sincere desire to help others. There are opportunities for everyone who is interested in helping.

Summary

In this introductory chapter, we have taken a look at the basics of Joomla! and open source. You learned the following:

- The advantages of using open source
- The pros and cons of using Joomla!
- How Joomla! works
- The terms of the Joomla! license
- How to get involved in the Joomla! community

Obtaining and Installing Joomla!

G etting started with Joomla! is easy. The open source software is freely available for download and in some cases may already be available as part of your web hosting package. In either case, you usually need to go through a set up process before you can start working on the contents of your web site.

Joomla! includes a wizard-style interface that enables you to create a complete web site installation simply by clicking through a series of steps and providing some information. The installer also includes options that can streamline work in the future and provide assistance to those who are just starting out with Joomla!

This chapter looks at the basics of obtaining the Joomla! files and getting them installed on your server.

Getting the Installation Files

The official Joomla! installation files come bundled together in one compressed archive file. Although downloading this archive from several different sources is possible, I strongly recommend that you only obtain your code from the official Joomla! site for the following reasons:

- By going to the official site, you are assured of downloading the most recent version.

- The official archives are trustworthy and highly unlikely to contain dangerous or malicious code.

- You can be assured that the archive contains a complete set of the official components.

To obtain the files, go to www.joomla.org and look for the download button; it is always displayed prominently on the home page, as shown in Figure 2.1. Clicking the button takes you to a downloads page where you can select the version of the installer that best suits your needs. Note that while the download link is on the main Joomla! site, the actual archive files for the installation are kept on the JoomlaCode.org.

The home page of Joomla.org, showing the download link prominently displayed.

Exploring the JoomlaCode site

JoomlaCode.org is one of the most important of the official Joomla! sites. You can visit the site by pointing your browser to www.joomlacode.org. The site includes a significant number of resources for Joomla! users. First and foremost, it serves as the central storehouse for the official Joomla! files. On the site, you find not only the most recent full release of Joomla!, but also patches and upgrades that allow users running older versions of Joomla! to upgrade to the most recent version.

In addition to the official files, the site also functions as a distribution point for many noncommercial extensions to the Joomla! core. You should take some time to browse the site and explore a bit. As you work more with Joomla! you are very likely to find yourself using the site as a resource to identify and download additional extensions for your site.

At first glance, you may find the site a bit difficult to navigate. JoomlaCode uses an organizational structure that is common to code forges but is not terribly intuitive. If you are not familiar with forge-type sites you may find it a bit confusing at first. Clicking on the Home link at the top right, for example, does not return you to the Home page of JoomlaCode, but instead takes you to a completely different site — Joomla.org. Moreover, browsing by Project can be rather time-consuming unless you already know the name of the extension you seek. The search functionality is also somewhat limited.

Your best bet for browsing JoomlaCode is to use the box labeled Browse Project Topics. The box is located in the right column about halfway down the page. Click on the name of the category you are interested in, and you will be taken to a page displaying a tree-type file directory with a list of files at the bottom, as shown in Figure 2.2. Click on the link labeled Show, next to a directory, to display the contents of the directory. Click on the link labeled Add Filter to restrict the projects shown on the page to only those that fall within the category. For example, clicking on the option Gallery & Multimedia takes you to a page showing a directory tree that has three options: Gallery, Podcasting, and Streaming Media. Below the tree directory is a list of all the projects in the Gallery & Multimedia category. If you click next on the Add Filter link (next to the option labeled Gallery), the page reloads, showing you only those projects that are included in the Gallery subcategory. If you click next on the Add Filter link (next to the Streaming Media option), the page will reload, showing you only those projects that are included in both the Gallery and the Streaming Media subcategories.

Tip

The Joomla! Extensions web site, http://extensions.joomla.org, provides a much more accessible directory of Joomla! extensions. The site also includes comments, ratings, and both commercial and noncommercial extensions. For most users, the Extensions site is a much friendlier option for browsing and searching.

Determining which files you need

Identifying the core files you need involves answering two questions:

> Is this a fresh installation or an upgrade?
>
> Which archive file type is appropriate for your server?

If this is a fresh installation, you simple need to obtain the current full release from the JoomlaCode site. If this is an upgrade of an existing Joomla! site, you need to first identify the version you are running now and then look closely through the list of upgrades on JoomlaCode to find the archive that is intended to be used to upgrade from the version of Joomla! you have on your current site. A complete list of releases, both full versions and upgrades, can be found at `http://joomlacode.org/gf/project/joomla/frs/?action=index`.

Cross-Reference

Patching and upgrading your site is discussed in more detail in Chapter 25.

The official Joomla! releases come in a variety of archive formats, including .zip .tar.gz, and .tar. bz2, as you can see in Figure 2.3. Download the version of your choice; they all contain the same files. The various formats are simply provided as a convenience. The correct choice for you depends on what type of archive file you are able to extract.

FIGURE 2.2

Browsing by Project Topic shows you a list of projects as well as a list of subcategories.

FIGURE 2.3

The JoomlaCode.org site is the home to all the official files.

Technical Requirements

The technical requirements for Joomla! are quite basic. The system is very tolerant of variations in server settings and, generally speaking, runs on the vast majority of commercial services that employ Linux, Unix, or even Windows. This makes installing Joomla! on most commercial web hosts easy and rarely requires additional configuration of the server.

For visitors, the front end is usable by virtually any computer using any browser. For site administrators, the back end supports the most recent versions of all the common browsers.

Many hosts even provide a way for one-click installation of Joomla! on your hosting account. This can be an easy way for beginners to install Joomla! and create the database without having to upload files themselves.

Server requirements

The preferred server setup for Joomla! includes the Apache web server with the MySQL database. Joomla! is primarily written in PHP, so the server must also have PHP installed. The configuration outlined is typical of shared web hosts running the Linux or Unix operating systems. Table 2.1 shows the minimum and preferred technical system requirements for running Joomla! 1.5.x on your web server.

TABLE 2.1

Software Requirements for Joomla! 1.5.x

	Minimum version	Recommended version
Apache web server	1.3	2.x +
MySQL Database	3.23	4.1.x + (but not MySQL 6.x)
PHP	4.3.10	5.2 +

Table 2.2 shows the minimum and preferred technical system requirements for running Joomla! 1.6.x on your web server.

TABLE 2.2

Software Requirements for Joomla! 1.6.x

	Minimum version	Recommended version
Apache web server	1.3	2.x +
MySQL Database	3.23	4.1.x + (but not MySQL 6.x)
PHP	4.3.10	5.2 +

Tip

Although the requirements outline the general configuration, some additional configuration issues exist with the Apache web server. You need to have mod_mysql, mod_xml and mod_zlib enabled. Additionally, if you want to use search engine friendly URLs, you need to the mod_rewrite extension installed.

Note

Although Apache is preferred, it is possible to run Joomla! on the Microsoft IIS web server. Note, however, that Microsoft IIS is not officially supported.

Caution

Problems have been detected with certain PHP versions. Avoid the following versions if at all possible: 4.3.9, 4.4.2, and 5.0.4. Also note that some problems have been reported with versions of the Zend Optimizer.

Site visitor and administrator requirements

The front end of Joomla! is usable by a wide variety of platforms and browsers, including mobile devices. Indeed, the display of the front end is impacted more by the way the site template is coded than by anything inherent in the system itself. Support for JavaScript is recommended, but not required for the default site.

Note

The installation of certain third-party extensions may bring with them additional requirements. You should always check whether the extensions that you install are compatible with the systems you require for your web site visitors.

To administer a Joomla! site you literally need nothing more than a connection to the Internet and a web browser. The back-end admin system is compatible with the recent versions of the most common browsers, including Internet Explorer, Firefox, Safari, and Opera.

Chrome is also a supported browser.

Installing Joomla!

This section covers the installation of Joomla! on either a local server or a remote web host. Installing Joomla! locally allows you to create a testing or development site that can greatly ease your development efforts. Installing Joomla! on a remote web host allows you to create a publicly accessible site that others can see and use. In either event, the process is roughly the same.

Creating a local development site

You can create a Joomla! site on your local computer for testing and development purposes. A local installation makes it faster and easier to work on the creation of a new site. It is a great way to develop a site prior to deploying it on a live server as you can see the impact of your changes immediately without having to move files back and forth from a remote web server. Moreover, if you have only a slow or unreliable Internet connection, a local development installation can save huge amounts of time and frustration.

A local installation can be created on any system — Windows, Mac, or Linux. However, you need to make sure that your machine can function as a server and meets the technical requirements outlined in the preceding section. If you want to obtain and install each of the various components independently you can, but I recommend that you acquire one of several packages that allows you to install all the required software in one click.

- For Windows users, the XAMPP and WampServer packages provide an easy way to install Apache, MySQL, PHP, and related tools.
- Mac users can use either XAMPP or MAMP.
- Linux users can install XAMPP.

Note

You can download XAMPP at `www.apachefriends.org`. **WampServer at** `www.wampserver.com` **and MAMP at** `www.mamp.info`.

Cross-Reference

Installing WampServer is discussed in Appendix C. Installing MAMP is discussed in Appendix D.

After you have installed the underlying package containing all the necessary server components, you are ready to set up Joomla! on your local machine. Installing Joomla! on any of the -AMP packages involves the following steps:

1. **Download the Joomla! core files.**

2. **Open the htdocs directory inside the -AMP folder on your machine.**

3. **Create a new directory for your Joomla! site.** Keep the name simple because you use it for the address in your browser; for example, "joomla15."

   Make sure that you unzip the files in the ROOT of the directory (htdocs). This way, the start page for -AMP will be the ROOT of the directory. The preceding example places the files in a directory named /joomla15 which is one level down from the root directory.

4. **Unzip the Joomla! files and place them inside the new directory.**

5. **Start the servers for your -AMP package. Follow the directions that came with the application.** When the servers start, your browser opens and displays the home page of the -AMP package. What you see should be similar to Figure 2.4.

6. **Click on the link for phpMyAdmin.** The phpMyAdmin interface opens in your browser.

7. **In the text field labeled Create new database, type a name for your database and then click Create.** The system creates a new database.

8. **Point your browser to the directory where you placed your Joomla files.** The Joomla! installation wizard appears.

From this point, you can follow the steps outlined in the "Running the Joomla! Installer" section later in this chapter.

FIGURE 2.4

The start page of MAMP, typical of the -AMP packages.

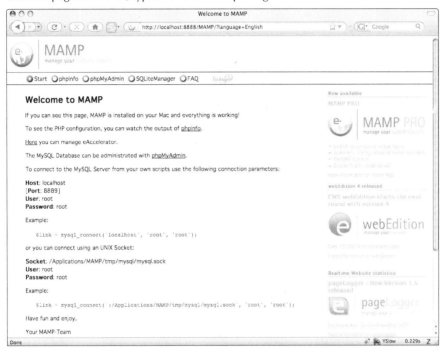

Installing on a web hosting service

Joomla! installation on a remote server typically takes one of two approaches. Some web hosts provide automated installers. The best known of these automated installers is Fantastico. The automated installers allow you to set up Joomla! or other popular systems directly from your web hosting account control panel. If you want to use an automated installer, follow the directions of your web host. Should you need assistance, contact your web host for support.

Note

Occasionally, the use of an automated installer can result in permissions problems in the resulting site. For most users these problems are not an issue, but if you intend to do extensive customization to your site, you are best advised to avoid this whole issue by installing the site files yourself, rather than relying on the automated installer.

Before you begin the install process of Joomla! on the server, you want to create your database with user privileges ahead of time. You need the user and password to finish all the steps in the Joomla! installer.

1. **Download the Joomla! core files.**

2. **Access your web server.**

3. **Create a new directory for your Joomla! site.** Keep the name simple because you use it for the address in your browser; for example, "joomla." If you want to install Joomla! in the root directory, you can skip this step.

4. **Move the archive containing the Joomla! files to the server.** You can do this either by using FTP to transfer the files, or by using the file manager in your Web Hosting control panel. Place the files in the directory where you want the site to appear.

Note
Appendix B shows a listing of the Joomla! files and directories as they should appear on your server.

5. **Extract the Joomla! file archive.** If your web host does not provide the option to extract archive files on the server, you need to extract the archive locally and then move the files up to the server. Note that this can take significantly longer because the number and size of the files are substantial!

6. **Point your browser to the directory where you placed your Joomla files.** The Joomla! installation wizard appears.

From this point, you can follow the steps outlined in the following section, "Running the Joomla! Installer."

Note
The name of the root directory varies from web host to web host. If you're not sure which directory on your web server is the root directory, contact your web hosting support team.

Running the Joomla! installer

Joomla! includes a step-by-step installer with an interface that is similar to many other standard software installation wizards. The installer does the vast majority of the work for you. In most cases, you need to do no more than simply supply information when prompted to do so.

Before you can run the installer, you must follow the steps outlined in the previous two sections, depending on whether you are installing Joomla! locally or on a web host, and then you must point your browser to the address of the Joomla! files on your server. After you load the address of your Joomla! site in the browser, the installation wizard starts automatically, and Step 1 of the installer is displayed on your screen.

Step 1 is to select the language to be used by the Installer, as shown in Figure 2.5. Click the language you prefer and then click the Next button.

FIGURE 2.5

Select the language to be used during the installation process. (Step 1 of the installer.)

Step 2 of the Installer is the Pre-Installation Check, shown in Figure 2.6. Note that two lists appear on this screen: The items listed at the top are requirements that must be met for the system to work properly. The items listed at the bottom are Recommended Settings. If your system fails to support any of these items, you will see a bright red **No** appear next to the item. If any of the items at the top are not supported, you must fix these issues. If your system fails to support any of the items on the bottom list, it is not fatal; the system will function, but the configuration will not be ideal.

If any of the requirements on the top list are not met, you must fix that issue and get a green **Yes** before you can proceed to the next step in the installation process. To have the installer retest your system, click the Check Again button. Repeat as necessary. After all of the required items show a green Yes, click the Next button to move to Step 3.

FIGURE 2.6

You must get all the required elements to show a green Yes before proceeding. (Step 2 of the Installer.)

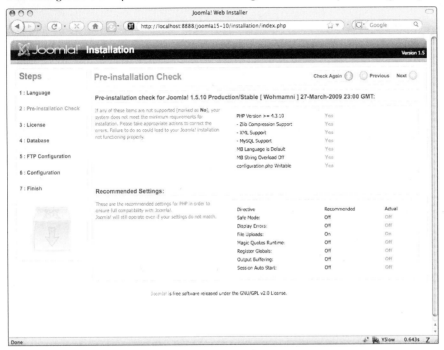

Step 3 of the Installer is the License, as shown in Figure 2.7. Read the terms of the license and then click the Next button. Note that by clicking the Next button you are agreeing to the terms of the license.

Step 4 of the Installer is Database Configuration, as shown in Figure 2.8. You need to complete the information requested on this screen to install Joomla! successfully. If you have manually created the database by using phpMyAdmin, enter that information here. Note, however, that it is not always necessary to manually create the database; in many cases the Joomla! installer is capable of creating the database on its own.

FIGURE 2.7

Read the terms of the License. (Step 3 of the Installer.)

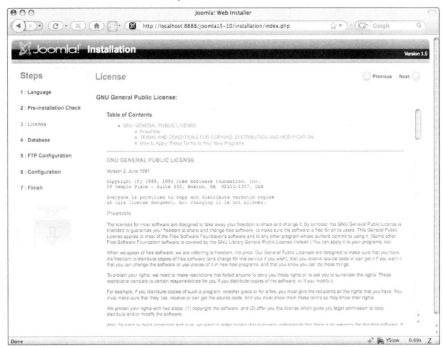

The screen is divided into two sections: Basic Settings and Advanced Settings. All of the following Basic Settings fields are required:

- **Database Type:** For most users the default option, mysql, is correct. If, however, you are using mysqli (MySQL Improved), you should select that option from the combo box.

- **Host Name:** If you are installing Joomla! locally, the odds are you should enter localhost into this field. If you are installing on a web host, use the name they supply.

- **Username:** This field holds the MySQL username. The default name is root. If you or your web host have specified something other than the default value, enter it instead.

- **Password:** Enter the password for your MySQL installation.

- **Database Name:** This is the name you set when you created the database, or if you are relying on the Joomla! Installer to create the database, enter the name you want it to use for your new database.

The Advanced Settings can be viewed by clicking on the name. When you click on the name, the section will fold out, displaying the options in the following list. Note that these options are only applicable if you want to install over an existing Joomla! installation or install multiple instances of Joomla! in one database.

- **Delete existing tables:** Any existing tables are wiped out and replaced with new tables from this installation.

- **Back up Old Tables:** Any existing tables are backed up before the new tables are written.

- **Table Prefix:** The default table prefix is `jos_`. You can set an alternative prefix if you so desire; this setting is most useful when you intend to place multiple installations inside one database. Note that the prefix `bak_` is reserved for use in backups and therefore should not be used.

After you have entered the information, click the Next button. The Installer attempts to connect with your database and if it is successful, it moves on to Step 5. If it is not successful, you will receive an error message explaining where the problem lies. After you have addressed the problem, try clicking the Next button again.

FIGURE 2.8

Showing the Database Configuration fields. (Step 4 of the Installer.)

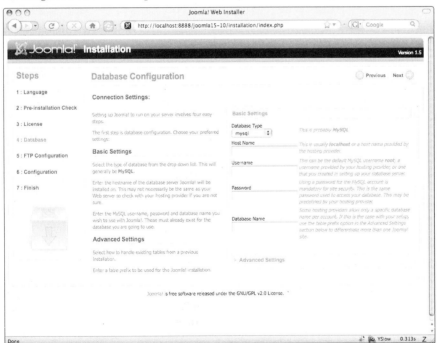

Step 5 of the Installer is the FTP Configuration, as shown in Figure 2.9. The FTP functionality has been included in Joomla! to provide a work-around for situations where the web server prohibits other types of FTP access. If you need this functionality, enable this; if you do not, then skip this step and move to Step 6.

The screen is divided into two sections: Basic Settings and Advanced Settings. All of the following Basic Settings fields are required if you want to enable this feature.

- **Enable FTP file system layer:** The default setting is No. If you want to use this feature, set it to Yes.

- **FTP User:** You must type a name to be used for the FTP access.

- **FTP Password:** You must type a password to be used for the FTP access.

- **FTP Root Path:** Type the FTP root path if you know it; if not you can click the Autofind FTP Path button and let the system attempt to figure this out.

- **Verify FTP Settings:** After you have completed the fields listed above, click this button to verify and test the settings.

The Advanced Settings can be viewed by clicking on the name. When you click, the section folds out, displaying the following options:

- **FTP Host:** The system attempts to determine this value. If it is not correct for your system, type the value you desire.

- **FTP Port:** The system attempts to determine this value. If it is not correct for your system, type the value you desire.

- **Save FTP Password:** Yes/No, the default value is No. Set it to Yes if you want the system to remember the password, rather than prompt you for it when needed.

After you have entered the information, click the Next button. The Installer moves on to Step 6.

Tip

If you want to skip FTP setup during installation, you can always set it up later via the Global Configuration Manager. See Chapter 4 for a discussion of the Global Configuration Manager.

Step 6 of the Installer is the Main Configuration screen, shown in Figure 2.10. A number of important items appear on this screen, including the option to install sample data for your use. First, start off by giving your site a name. Type the name you want to use for your site into the field labeled Site Name. Note that this name will appear on the browser title bar and in a wide variety of circumstances. You can adjust this later through the Global Configuration Manager.

Next, type the e-mail address you want to associate with the administrator account. Type the address in the field labeled Your E-mail. In the field Admin Password, type your choice of password for the default admin account. Type it again to confirm it in the Confirm Admin Password field.

FIGURE 2.9

The optional FTP Configuration. (Step 5 of the Installer.)

Tip

If you want to install sample data for your site, use the Install Sample Data button. If you want an empty site, you can skip this.

Tip

If this is your first time working with Joomla!, I highly recommended that you install the sample data. The Joomla! sample data includes a variety of useful information as well as examples of common site-building techniques. Note that while you can always delete the sample data you cannot easily install it later, so if you think you might want it, install it now!

The Load Migration Script option you see below the Sample Data button is intended for users who want to populate the database of their new site with data from another source, typically from a previous Joomla! site. If this is not applicable to you, skip it and click the Next button to move to Step 7.

FIGURE 2.10

Step 6 of the Installer is the Main Configuration screen, which includes the option to install the sample data or to migrate existing data to the new site.

If, on the other hand, you want to populate your Joomla! site with data from another source, you can do so through this interface, or you can do it later by manually migrating the database content and running the SQL query through phpMyAdmin. Note that the utility provided here is dependent upon the existence of an SQL migration script that is compatible with your version of Joomla!. The best way to achieve this is to use the com_migrator tool to create the migration script.

If you have a compliant script, follow these steps:

1. **Click the radio button to select the option Load Migration Script.**
2. **Enter the old table prefix into the field labeled Old Table Prefix.**
3. **Select the old site's encoding from the combo box.**
4. **Click the Browse button.** The file upload window opens.
5. **Locate the migration script file and then click Upload.** The File Upload window loads and the name of the migration script should appear in the field next to the label Migration Script.
6. **If your script is from a Joomla 1.0 site, click the checkbox labeled This script is a Joomla! 1.0 migration script.**
7. **Click the Upload and Execute button.** The system attempts to populate the database with the script data. If you are successful, a confirmation message appears.

Note

The com_migrator **component is a third-party extension that must be installed on your old site and used to create the migration script. You can find the extension on the JoomlaCode site. Note that** com_migrator **will only migrate your core files. If you have extensions installed on your old site, you need to manage their migration separately. Migration can be the source of a number of problems, due to the wide variations in installation configurations and extensions. For a list of common problems and their solutions, see** http://docs. joomla.org/Common_Migrator_Errors.

Step 7 of the Installer is the Confirmation Screen, as shown in Figure 2.11. There are no required steps here; rather this page provides you with links to both the front end and the back end of your new site, along with a warning that you need to delete your installation directory to avoid problems and security risks.

At this time, you need to access your Joomla! files on the server and delete the directory named installation. After you have deleted the directory, you are ready to go. Click through to either the front end or the back end of your site to close the installer.

FIGURE 2.11

The final Confirmation screen. You're done! (Step 7 of the Installer.)

Sample data

The sample data provided as an option during the installation process is designed to help users new to the system. The topics include tutorials as well as information about the Joomla! project and directions to further help resources. Additionally, when you elect to install the sample data, the system also creates a number of menus and modules that help speed your initial development of the site. Many experienced site developers actually choose to install the sample data because it saves them time creating the most common menus and modules; it's faster to delete what you don't need than to create from scratch all the basic parts.

That said, if you are an experienced developer and you do want the maximum amount of control over your site, you will want to skip the sample data and install a clean site that you can customize to suit your needs exactly.

Summary

In this chapter, we covered the acquisition and installation of Joomla! You learned the following:

- Where to obtain the proper files
- How to install the system on a local host
- How to install the system on a web hosting service
- The various installation requirements and options
- The advantages of using the sample data

Taking a Look at Joomla!

I f you worked through the previous chapter, you should have a complete Joomla! installation, ready to be explored. This chapter goes through Joomla's front-end and back-end interfaces and explains what you see on- screen. This chapter also provides a quick orientation and tour of the Joomla! system.

The references and figures in this chapter all refer to the default site with the sample data installed.

IN THIS CHAPTER

Introducing the front end

Introducing the back end

Introducing the Front End (The Public Interface)

The front end of your Joomla! installation is the interface that is seen by the visitors to the site. The front end is the target for your output and the place where your visitors access the site's content and functionality. By default, access to the front end of a Joomla! site is unrestricted; however, you can restrict the visibility of content and functionality to users who are registered and logged in to the system.

Visitors to the site should be able to see and use the front-end content and functionality with any of a wide range of browsers, both current and older editions. The site is also usable by most common mobile devices.

In terms of the structural functionality of the front end, the key elements you see on-screen, as shown in Figure 3.1 are:

- **Template:** The container for all the output on the page. This defines the look and feel of the page.

- **Articles:** Your content items.

- **Modules:** Provide output and functionality in secondary content areas.

- **Plugins:** Enhance the functionality of your articles, components, and modules.

Understanding content organizational structure

Joomla! organizes content items into a hierarchy comprised of sections, categories, and articles. Sections are the top level parent container. Categories are assigned to sections. Articles can be either assigned to categories or they can be segregated from the hierarchy and grouped into a generic collection called *uncategorized content*.

Looking at the default Joomla! 1.5 site, with the sample data installed, you will find the hierarchy shown in Table 3.1.

Note
All the articles in the sample data content hierarchy are assigned to categories and sections. There are no uncategorized content articles in the default Joomla! 1.5 setup.

FIGURE 3.1

The front end of the default Joomla site with the sample data installed. Note the key output areas.

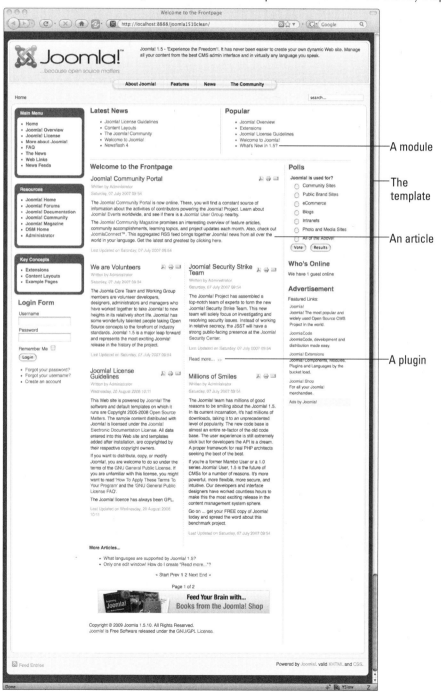

TABLE 3.1

The Content Hierarchy of the Sample Data in Joomla! 1.5.x

Sections	Categories	Articles
About Joomla!		
	The Project	
		Support and Documentation
		Joomla! License Guidelines
		Platforms and Open Standards
	The CMS	
		What's New in 1.5?
		Joomla! Overview
		Extensions
		Joomla! Features
		Content Layouts
	The Community	
		Joomla! Facts
		The Joomla! Community
News		
	Latest	
		Welcome to Joomla!
		Joomla! Community Portal
		Joomla! Security Strike Team
		We are Volunteers
		Millions of Smiles
	Newsflash	
		Newsflash 1
		Newsflash 2
		Newsflash 3
		Newsflash 4
		Newsflash 5
FAQs		
	General	
		Is it possible to change a menu item's Type?
		What is an Uncategorized article?
		How do I install Joomla! 1.5?

Sections	Categories	Articles
		Can Joomla! 1.5 operate with PHP Safe Mode on?
		What are the requirements to run Joomla! 1.5?
		What is the FTP layer for?
		My MySQL database does not support UTF-8. Do I have a problem?
		Why does Joomla! 1.5 use UTF-8 encoding?
	Current Users	
		Where did the Installers go?
		What happened to the local setting?
		How do I upgrade to Joomla! 1.5?
		Only one edit window! How do I create "Read more..."?
		Where did the Mambots go?
		Where is the Static Content Item?
	New to Joomla!	
		What is the difference between Archiving and Trashing an article?
		How do I remove an article?
		Is it useful to install the sample data?
	Languages	
		I installed with my own language, but the back end is still in English.
		What languages are supported by Joomla! 1.5?
		Does the PDF icon render pictures and special characters?
		What is the purpose of the collation selection in the installation screen?
		How do I localize Joomla! to my language?

Cross-Reference

Working with sections, categories, and articles is covered in Chapter 5.

An important point to note here: Any content structures the administrator implements do not translate automatically into the organizational structure that visitors see on the front end of the web site. The content hierarchy is a reflection of how the articles, categories, and sections have been created on the back end of the site. The structure of the menus, discussed in the next section, is primarily responsible for how site visitors experience the content.

Developing your Joomla! vocabulary

Throughout this text I have, with but few exceptions, strived to use terminology that is consistent with that used by the Joomla! team on the documentation site and in the online help files. A quick orientation to Joomla! terms of art can help you develop a clear understanding of discussions both in this book and in Joomla! documentation resources.

- **Access Level:** Access levels provide a way for the site administrator to control access to articles or functionality. Joomla! provides three access levels: Public, Registered, and Special. Setting an item's access level to Public means that anyone can see it. Setting the access level to Registered or Special restricts visibility to the users assigned to specific user groups.

- **Archives:** Articles in Joomla! can be removed from the general content areas of the site and placed in an archive. Archives can be made publicly accessible, but the functionality associated with archived articles is restricted. Archives can also be hidden from public view. Archiving is not the same as moving an article to the trash (see the next term). This is most often used with blog-type sites because the archived articles can be used to organize old articles according to month posted.

- **Article:** An article is a page of content created with Joomla's New Article functionality. Articles are collected inside the Article Manager interface and can be created, edited, deleted, published, unpublished, and archived. Articles can also be created from the front end of the web site when the front-end content management functionality is enabled.

- **Component:** Components are major units of functionality that provide output in the main content area of a page. Components are the most complex individual units in the system, sometimes constituting complete applications in themselves. Each component in the system has its own management interface inside the admin system. A number of components are included in the default system, and you can add more to the system.

- **Core:** The term *core* in this context refers simply to the files included in the default Joomla! distribution.

- **Extensions:** Extension is a generic term that refers to any component, module, plugin, or template that is added to the default system. Extensions can be installed, deleted, or managed through the admin system's Extension Manager. Note that because some extensions are required by Joomla! they cannot be deleted. It's probably a good practice to only delete extensions that you've installed yourself.

- **Menus:** Menus hold the navigation choices for your site. Menus are created, edited, and deleted from within the Menu Manager; menu display, however, is managed from the Module Manager via the Menu Modules. Menus are comprised of menu items.

- **Menu Items:** Menu items are the choices (the links) on a menu. Menu items are created, edited, and deleted from within each of the system's Menu Item Managers. Each menu in the system has one Menu Item Manager.

- **Menu Item Types:** Each menu item is of a specific Menu Item Type. The creation of a new menu item requires the selection of a Menu Item Type for that item. Menu Item Types are very important in Joomla! because they dictate aspects of the appearance of the page that the menu item links to.

- **Module:** Modules typically provide output in the secondary areas of the page, that is, not inside the main content area. Modules are sometimes simply containers that hold text or pictures; at other times, they provide limited functionality, like a login box. Modules are often paired with components to provide an alternative means of displaying output from the component. Modules are collected inside the Module Managers where they can be edited and assigned to various pages and positions. A number of different module types are included in the default system. Modules can be added to the system through the Extensions Manager or created by the site administration from within the Module Manager.

- **Module Positions:** Module positions are places on the page where a module can be assigned to appear. Module positions are created by the template designer who codes into the template the Module Position Holders that define each of the module positions. Modules can also be included in articles by inserting {loadposition NameOfModule} inside the article text.

- **Module Type:** Each module in the system is of a particular module type. When you create a new module manually you must select a Type for the module. The module type dictates aspects of the functionality of the module.

- **News Feeds:** The term *news feed* refers to RSS or similar syndication formats. Joomla! can display news feed data inside the site by using either the News Feed Component or the Feed Display Module. The site can also provide syndication links for your site visitors, turning your content into a news feed for others to view. Do not confuse news feeds with the newsflash functionality (see following term); though the names are similar they are not related in any way.

- **Newsflash:** The Newsflash functionality is a module that displays one or more short items of content on the screen. Do not confuse this functionality with the news feed functionality; they are not related in any way.

- **Plugin:** Plugins are helper applications that enable additional functionality in the site's components, articles, or modules. Plugins are collected in the Plugin Manager. New plugins can be installed through the Extension Manager or created by the site administrator through the Plugin Manager. In previous versions of Joomla!, these were called Mambots.

- **Template:** Templates control the presentation layer of your Joomla! site. They define the interfaces of the site. When you change a template, you change the way the site looks for either the visitors or the administrators. Templates can be added to the system through the Extension Manager. The installed templates are collected inside the Template Manager where they can be edited.

- **Translations and Language Packs:** Translations are the language files of your Joomla! site. In this text the collection of translated language files for a single language is called *Language Packs*, as that name is rather more descriptive and less confusing than the generic term *Translations*. New Language Packs can be added through the Extension Manager and installed Language Packs are collected inside the Language Manager.

- **Trash:** The trash functionality in Joomla! provides a temporary holding area for articles and menu items that have been removed from use on the site and are pending permanent deletion. In Joomla! 1.5, articles and menu items are the subject of two separate Trash Managers that allow you to restore or permanently delete the articles or items. In Joomla! 1.6, the multiple Trash Manager functionalities have been merged into the manager interfaces for the various items.

Understanding menu structure

The default Joomla! installation, with the sample data in place, contains thirty-one menu items organized into seven menus. The menus are visible in the Menu Manager; the menu items are in the Menu Item Managers of each menu. Table 3.2 shows a list of all the menus in the default system with the sample data installed, including the number of menu items in each menu and the access level settings.

TABLE 3.2

Summary of the Default Menu Structure

Menu Name	Number of Items	Access Level
Main Menu	9	Public
User Menu	4	Registered & Special
Top Menu	4	Public
Resources	7	Public
Example Pages	4	Public
Key Concepts	3	Public

Note that all of the menus and their menu items are set to the public access level, except for the User Menu. The User Menu has a mix of items assigned to either the registered or special access levels. The result is that the User Menu only appears on the page when a site visitor is registered and authenticated. Certain items on that menu are visible by registered users; others are only visible by users that are assigned to higher user groups, for example, authors, editors, or publishers.

Menu placement on the page is controlled by the assignment of the menu modules to specific module positions, as shown in Figure 3.2.

Cross-Reference

Working with menus and menu items is covered in Chapter 8.

Modules and module positions

The default Joomla! installation with the sample data installed includes a large number of modules. Some of the modules are published and visible, others are not. Module visibility depends upon

- Whether the module is enabled, that is, whether it is published
- Whether the module is assigned to the page you are viewing
- Whether the viewer has sufficient access privileges to view the module

FIGURE 3.2

The site's default menus, showing the placement of each menu on the page.

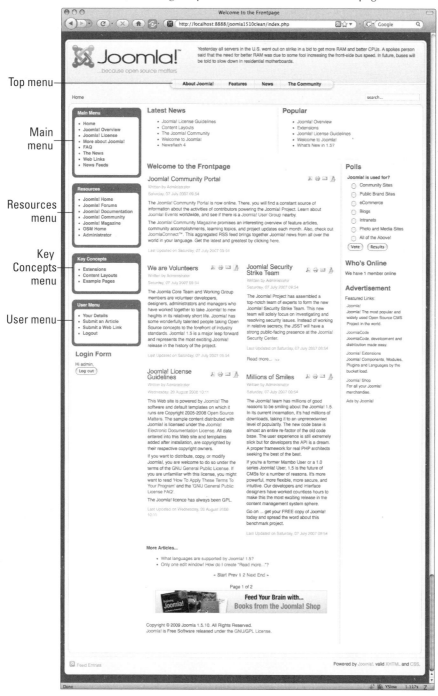

The module assignment, visibility, and access levels are set by editing the module from the Module Manager. See Figure 3.3.

FIGURE 3.3

A typical page from the default site with the sample data installed, showing various modules as they appear to front-end site visitors.

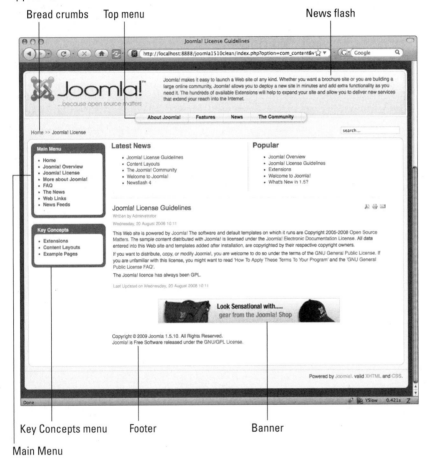

In addition to the modules you see on the default site, the sample data in Joomla 1.5.x includes other modules that are not published, including:

- Statistics
- Archive
- Sections

- Related Items
- Wrapper
- Feed Display

If you want to see these in action, go to the Module Manager and enable them. Note that some require additional configuration for the output to be meaningful.

Modules are placed on the page by assigning them to module positions. The module positions are coded into the template by the template designer. Figure 3.4 shows the same page you saw in Figure 3.3, but with the names of the module positions overlaid.

FIGURE 3.4

A page showing an overlay that indicates the names of the available module positions. Note this information is specific to this particular template. Module positions vary from template to template.

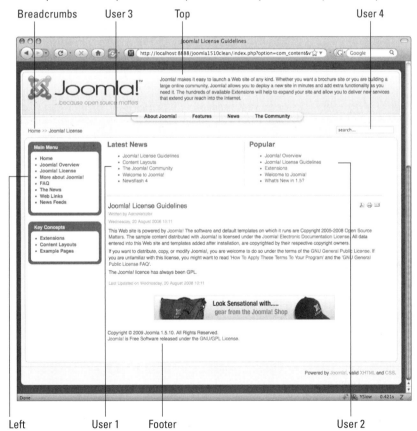

Note

Joomla! classifies modules into two categories: Site modules and Administrator modules. The Site modules are visible on the front end of the site. The Administrator modules are only visible on the back end of the site. To view and manipulate the Site modules, access the Module Manager.

Cross-Reference

Site modules are discussed in Chapter 17. Administrator modules are covered in Chapter 18.

Introducing the Back End (The Admin Interface)

The back end of your Joomla! site is the administration interface where the majority of your site management activities occur. Access to the admin system is controlled by a login form and is restricted to only those users who are assigned to user groups higher than publisher. By default the admin login page is always located at /administrator, for example, www.yourdomain.com/administrator.

Note

Back-end users should access the system with only more recent versions of Internet Explorer, Firefox, or Safari to assure maximum accessibility to all the admin functions. Older or more obscure browsers may not function optimally.

Exploring the admin interfaces

Three primary types of interfaces are in the admin system: the Control Panel, the manager pages, and the workspace pages. I cover each of these interfaces in the following sections.

Control Panel

The first page you see when you log into the admin system is the Control Panel, as shown in Figure 3.5. You can also return to this page at any time by selecting the option Control Panel under the Site Menu.

The Control Panel is designed to provide administrators with quick access to the most frequently used tasks and tools as well as a summary of useful information.

FIGURE 3.5

The Control Panel is the first page you see when you log in to the back-end admin system.

At the top left of the page is the main navigation menu. Click on the choices to access the various areas of the admin system. At the top right of each page is a set of tools that provides you with the following functionality:

- **Preview:** Click to open a preview of the front end of the site.

- **Mail icon (no label):** This shows you the number of unread messages in the admin system's Private Messaging center. Click to open the Private Messaging Manager.

- **People icon (no label):** The number shown here indicates the number of users logged in to the site.

- **Logout:** Click this icon to log out of the admin system.

On the left side of the page, below the main navigation bar, are the shortcut icons. The icons are simply provided as a convenience; they are accelerators that repeat functionality that can be found under the menus at the top of the main navigation page. Click on any icon to open the functionality in the browser.

On the right side of the page is the Welcome Message, along with various information concerning the current state of the site. In addition to the Welcome Message, the options visible in Joomla! 1.5.x are:

- **Logged in Users:** A list of all users currently logged in to the system.
- **Popular:** A list of the most frequently viewed articles on the site.
- **Recent Added Articles:** A list of the most recently modified articles on the site.
- **Menu Stats:** A list of all the menus with a count of the Items assigned to each.
- **Joomla! Security Newsfeed:** This tab shows the RSS news feed from the Joomla! Security Team. This is provided as a convenience to help keep you informed of alerts and notifications of upgrades and vulnerabilities.

Tip

The output you see on the Control Panel page is created by various Administrator modules. You can customize the appearance of this page somewhat to suit your needs by re-ordering or disabling Modules.

Manager pages

All of the various manager interfaces in the admin system are largely similar. The pages are structured consistently, though the data displayed may vary. Click on any of the manager links in the shortcut icons on the Control Panel or use the links under the main admin nav bar to see a manager page similar to what is shown in Figure 3.6.

Manager pages are designed to handle large numbers of items and to display key information. In the chapters that follow, this book looks at each of the managers and explains the controls and the information that you see on that page.

Workspace pages

Once you click through from the manager page to perform a specific task, in the vast majority of cases you are taken to a page with a workspace layout. All workspace pages are largely similar, with elements laid out consistently.

Typically a workspace page displays the key elements you see in Figure 3.7 including

- A toolbar at the top right
- The primary information fields at the top left, below the title
- A text field, where necessary, at the bottom left
- Parameters fields on the right side of the page

FIGURE 3.6

A typical Manager page interface, in this case the Article Manager in Joomla 1.5.x.

In the following chapters, this book looks at each of the various workspaces and explains the controls and the information that you see on those pages.

Tip

Although the Joomla! admin interface is designed to work just fine on a wide variety of screen display settings, the workspace pages really benefit from having your display set to a resolution greater than 1024 x 768.

FIGURE 3.7

A typical Workspace Page interface, in this case the Article Editing Dialogue in Joomla 1.5.x.

The Site menu

Clicking on the Site option on the admin main nav displays the following options:

- **Control Panel:** Click to return to the Control Panel.
- **User Manager:** Click to open the User Manager.
- **Media Manager:** Click to open the Media Manager.
- **Global Configuration:** Click to open the Global Configuration Manager.
- **Logout:** Click to log out of the admin system. Note this is redundant with the Logout icon on the top right of each admin page.

The Menus menu

Clicking on the Menus option on the admin main nav displays the following options:

- **Menu Manager:** Click to open the Menu Manager.
- **Menu Trash:** Click to open the Menu Trash Manager.
- **Main Menu:** Click to open the Main Menu's Menu Item Manager.
- **User Menu:** Click to open the User Menu's Menu Item Manager.
- **Top Menu:** Click to open the Top Menu's Menu Item Manager.
- **Resources:** Click to open the Resources Menu's Menu Item Manager.
- **Example Pages:** Click to open the Example Pages Menu's Menu Item Manager.
- **Key Concepts:** Click to open the Key Concepts Menu's Menu Item Manager.

Joomla! 1.6

The Menu Trash option does not appear in this location in Joomla! 1.6; instead it is integrated into the toolbar at the top right of each Menu Manager.

The Content menu

Clicking on the Content option on the admin main nav displays the following options:

- **Article Manager:** Click to open the Article Manager.
- **Article Trash:** Click to open the Article Trash Manager.
- **Section Manager:** Click to open the Section Manager.
- **Category Manager:** Click to open the Category Manager.
- **Front Page Manager:** Click to open the Front Page Manager.

Joomla! 1.6

The Content menu does no t exist in Joomla! 1.6; instead you can access the content articles from under the Articles option on the Components menu.

The Components menu

Clicking on the Components option on the admin main nav displays the following options:

- **Banner:** Click to go to the Banner Component. Sub-nav choices here let you jump directly to the Banner Manager, the Banner Client Manager, and the Banner Category Manager.
- **Contacts:** Click to access the Contacts Component. Sub-nav choices here let you jump directly to the Contacts Manager and the Contacts Category Manager.
- **News Feeds:** Click to access the News Feed Component. Sub-nav choices here let you jump directly to the Feeds Manager and the News Feeds Category Manager.

- **Polls:** Click to open the Polls Component.
- **Search:** Click to access the Search Statistics.
- **Web Links:** Click to access the Web Links Component. Sub-nav choices here let you jump directly to the Links Manager and the Web Links Category Manager.

Joomla! 1.6

The Components menu in Joomla! 1.6 includes a number of differences. First, the menu includes the option articles, which give access to the Articles Manager. Second, the menu does not include the Polls option, as the Polls component is not included in the Joomla! core in version 1.6.x. Finally, the menu does not include the Search option, as that functionality has been removed.

The Extensions menu

Clicking on the Extensions option on the admin main nav displays the following options:

- **Install/Uninstall:** Click to go to the Install/Uninstall Extensions functionality.
- **Module Manager:** Click to open the Module Manager.
- **Plugin Manager:** Click to open the Plugin Manager.
- **Template Manager:** Click to open the Template Manager.
- **Language Manager:** Click to open the Language Manager.

Joomla! 1.6

The Extensions menu in Joomla! 1.6 includes only one small difference: The option Install/Uninstall has been renamed to Extension Manager.

The Tools menu

Clicking on the Tools option on the admin main nav displays the following options:

- **Read Messages:** Click to access the admin system Private Messaging Manager.
- **Write Message:** Click to write a message using the admin system's Private Messaging Manager.
- **Mass Mail:** Click to send mail to the site's users.
- **Global Checkin:** Click to force all items currently open for editing to close.
- **Clean Cache:** Click to open the Cache Manager.
- **Purge Expired Cache:** Click to open the Cache Manager's Purge Cache function.

Joomla! 1.6

The Tools menu in Joomla! 1.6 includes one additional function: Redirect. Clicking on the Redirect option opens the Redirect Manager, which allows you to redirect specific URLs to specific pages.

The Help menu

Clicking on the Help option on the admin main nav displays the following options:

- **Joomla Help:** Click to open an index of the help topics available from the Joomla! help system.
- **System Info:** Click to view information about your server system and your Joomla! installation.

Summary

In this chapter, we have taken a quick tour of both the front end and the back end of the default Joomla! installation. You learned the following:

- How the content is organized
- How the menus and menu items are structured
- How to access the admin system
- How the Admin interfaces are organized
- The contents of each of the menus on the main admin navigation bar

Getting the Most from Site Configuration

The first task most users undertake after installing Joomla! is setting the site's global configuration options. To assist with this important process, Joomla! provides the Global Configuration Manager that enables you to set many of the site's configuration options in one place.

As the name implies, the options you set in the Global Configuration Manager are applied to your site as a whole. Although many of the settings contained in the Global Configuration Manager are set once and not touched again, some of the options can be overridden by the parameter options provided for individual items.

In this chapter, I explain the options that are available in the Global Configuration Manager and provide tips on how you can set the configuration options to achieve the best effect.

Exploring the Global Configuration Manager

You can access the Global Configuration Manager in two ways: Click on the Global Configuration icon on the Control Panel or select the option Global Configuration under the Site Menu. After the Global Configuration Manager loads in your browser, note that it is divided into three separate screens, labeled Site, System, and Server. I cover all three of these tabs in the following sections.

The toolbar at the top of the Global Configuration Manager includes the following functions:

- **Save:** Click to save any changes you've made. After saving, the system exits the Global Configuration Manager and returns you to the Control Panel.
- **Apply:** Click to save any changes without exiting the Global Configuration Manager.
- **Close:** Click to exit the Global Configuration Manager without saving your changes.
- **Help:** Click to access the online help files related to the active screen.

Below the toolbar and above the workspace are three text links used for changing between the three screens of the Global Configuration Manager.

Working with the Site Tab

The Site tab is the default landing page for the Global Configuration Manager. This tab contains basic site options, such as the site name and the site's metadata and URL structures. You can view the Site tab at any time by clicking on the text link labeled Site. The contents of the Site tab loads in your browser window, as shown in Figure 4.1.

FIGURE 4.1

Using the Site tab of the Global Configuration Manager.

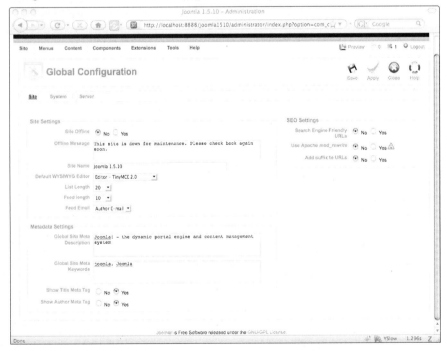

The workspace of the Site tab is broken into three areas: Site Settings, Metadata Settings, and SEO Settings. I detail each area in the next sections.

Site settings

The Site Settings area of the Site tab contains a mix of options that relate to the basic characteristics of your site. Two of the most important controls on this tab relate to your ability to take the site offline and to set the name of the site. You can also apply the following options:

- **Site Offline:** Click Yes to hide your site from public view, showing visitors instead the message you enter in the field below. This option is most useful when you are installing site upgrades and patches, because it avoids the possibility of visitors seeing your site in an incomplete or nonfunctional state.

Note

Taking the site offline means that only the front end is blocked from access; the admin system will remain accessible.

- **Offline Message:** In this field, type the message you want visitors to see if they visit your site during periods in which you have set it to be offline. This control is related to Site Offline.

- **Site Name:** In this field, type the name you want to use for the site. The choice of a name for your site has several implications beyond merely acting as a label for the site itself. The name is displayed in numerous places, including in e-mails and RSS feeds generated by the site, so choose something appropriate and practical. The e-mail from name can be overridden on the Server tab.

- **Default WYSIWYG Editor:** The combo box to the right of this control displays a list of all the editor options for your site — either a WYSIWYG editor or the No Editor option. Select one to be the default choice for your users. Note that the list of WYSIWYG editors is determined by which are installed and enabled.

Cross-Reference

See Chapter 19 for information on enabling additional WYSIWYG Editors.

- **List Length:** Select a value from the combo box to set the default length of lists of items that appear in the admin system. The default value is 20.

Note

Setting the control to a higher value results in more options appearing on the page and less use of the pagination controls, but may also result in the admin system being slightly slower due to the increased page loading times.

- **Feed Length:** Select a value from the combo box to set the number of items displayed in the RSS feeds. The default value is 10.

- **Feed Email:** The RSS feeds generated by your Joomla! site include with each item the name of the author and an e-mail address. Use the combo box to select the e-mail address to be displayed. Author E-mail and Site E-mail are the only two options. The default is Author E-mail.

Note

The Feed Email option was new in Version 1.5.10. This option may not be desirable to all because it publicizes e-mail addresses and potentially makes them accessible to spammers. Unfortunately, there is no way to disable this option without altering the related code.

Metadata settings

The metadata for your web site appears in the head area of the page code. Metadata is not visible to your visitors, but it is indexed by the search engines. This area of the workspace enables you to specify metadata options that are applied to the site as a whole. Some of these options can be overridden for individual articles or by the installation of third-party extensions. The following options are available:

- **Global Site Meta Description:** In this text field, type the information you want to appear in the description metadata field of your pages. Doing this sets the description metadata for the site as whole.
- **Global Site Meta Keywords:** In this text field, type the information you want to appear in the keywords metadata field of your pages. Doing this sets the keywords metadata for the site as whole.

Note

Both the Description and Keywords options can be overridden on individual articles by specifying different values in the article's Metadata Information Parameters field.

- **Show Title Meta Tag:** Click Yes to include the title metadata field in your pages. The contents of the field are taken from the page titles.
- **Show Author Meta Tag:** Click Yes to include the author metadata field in your pages. The contents of the field are taken from the name of the author you specify in the article's Metadata Information Parameters field.

SEO settings

The default URLs generated by Joomla! are not considered to be optimal for search engine marketing purposes. The default URLs frequently include query strings and additional characters that may cause the search engine spiders difficulties. Additionally, the URLs tend to be hard to remember and unfriendly for humans as well.

For example, a default system URL may look like this:

```
http://www.yoursite.com/index.php?option=com_
content&view=article&id=27:the-joomla-community&catid=30:the-
community&Itemid=30
```

The SEO settings area of the Site tab allows you to toggle options that enable search engine friendly URLs that help overcome this problem. In contrast with the preceding example, if you enable the search engine friendly URLs options, the page URL will look like this:

```
http://www.yoursite.com/the-community.html
```

- **Search Engine Friendly URLs:** Click Yes to enable the system to display search engine friendly URLs. The default setting is No.
- **Use Apache mod_rewrite:** Click Yes to use Apache's mod_rewrite function in the creation of search-engine-friendly URLs. The default setting is No. Note that this is only applicable if you are using the Apache web server and only relevant if you have set the preceding control, Search Engine Friendly URLs, to Yes.

Note

To use the Apache mod_rewrite option, you must use the .htaccess file supplied with your Joomla! site. The default Joomla! distribution includes in the root a file named htaccess.txt. You will need to rename this file to .htaccess for this feature to work properly.

- **Add suffix to URLs:** Set to Yes to add to the end of all URLs the suffix .html. The default setting is No.

Tip

For security, it is best to set this to add the suffix .html instead of leaving the URL open-ended.

If you are using the Apache web server, you can enable search engine friendly URLs by following these steps:

1. Access the root of your web server.
2. Find the file htaccess.txt and rename the file .htaccess.

Note

On some servers, when you change the name of the file from htaccess.txt to .htaccess, the file will appear to disappear. It actually did not disappear, but some servers hide from view files that start with a period.

3. Log in to the admin system of your site.
4. **Click on the option Global Configuration under the Site Menu.** The Global Configuration Manager loads in your browser.
5. **Set the option Search Engine Friendly URLs to Yes.**
6. **Set the option Use Apache mod_rewrite to Yes.**
7. **Click the Save icon on the toolbar.** Your system now displays search engine friendly URLs.

Using the System Tab

The System tab includes a number of important controls that enable you to specify the conditions relating to user registration, the permissible file types for uploads to your system, and the cache and session settings. The System tab of the Global Configuration Manager is accessed by clicking on the text link labeled System, on the top left side of the page. Figure 4.2 shows the workspace of the System tab.

FIGURE 4.2

The System tab of the Global Configuration Manager in Joomla 1.5.x.

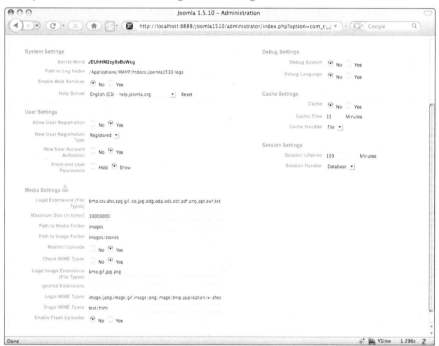

The workspace of the System tab is broken into six areas; each area is discussed in the following sections.

System settings

The system settings are largely populated automatically by your Joomla! system. Several of these values cannot, or should not, be changed.

- **Secret Word:** The *Secret Word* is unique to every Joomla! site and is used by the system as the basis for creating tokens and for encrypting user passwords. The Secret Word is automatically created by the system during installation. This cannot be changed.

- **Path to Log folder:** This field shows the location of the log files on your server. This information is supplied automatically by Joomla! during installation.

- **Enable Web Services:** Click Yes to enable Remote Procedure Calls (RPC) using HTTP and XML. There is no need to change this setting unless it is specifically called for by a third party extension. The default value is No.

- **Help Server:** The URL of the site used to supply the information your administrators see when they click on the Help icons in the admin interface. By default this is set to the official Joomla! site.

User settings

The settings in this area of the workspace relate to the ability of users to register on your site and are only relevant if your site does permit user registration from the front end. The settings are:

- **Allow User Registration:** Click Yes to allow site visitors to apply to become registered users of your site. Note that you must have the user registration form published for public visitors or there is no point in enabling this option. The default value is Yes.

- **New User Registration Type:** Select from the combo box the level that you want assigned automatically to new users. This selection can always be overridden on a case-by-case basis by the site administrator through the User Manager. The options here are limited to Registered, Author, Editor, and Publisher. The default value is Registered.

- **New User Account Activation:** Set this value to Yes to require the system to send all new users a confirmation e-mail that the user must act upon to validate and activate his account; until the user validates the account, it cannot be used. Setting this to No means that user accounts will be immediately active without the need for the user to take further action. The default value is Yes.

- **Front-end User Parameters:** Set to Show to permit users to set certain preferences that are specific to their account. The options include the ability to set preferences for language, editor, and help site. This is only applicable to registered users and the options will only be available on the user's page. The default value is Show.

Cross-Reference

Managing users and user registration is discussed in more detail in Chapter 10.

Media settings

The controls in this section relate to the permissible and forbidden file types for your system. These limitations apply to yours, or your users', ability to upload new files to the system for use in the content and components of your site. The controls in this area also allow you to specify the location where the uploaded files will be stored. You can adjust the following settings:

- **Legal Extensions (File Types):** The field contains a list of permitted file types, shown by their extensions. You can add new types or delete existing ones. The default values are: bmp, csv, doc, epg, gif, ico, jpg, odg, odp, ods, odt, pdf, png, ppt, swf, txt, xcf, and xls.

- **Maximum Size (in bytes):** Sets a limit on the size of files that can be uploaded. The value is expressed in bytes. The default value is 100,000,000 — that is, 100 MB.

- **Path to Media Folder:** Shows the destination for all uploaded nonimage media files. You can change this to whatever path you prefer. The default value is images.

- **Path to Image Folder:** Shows the destination for all uploaded image files. You can change this to whatever path you prefer. The default value is images/stories.

Caution

You can set alternative paths for either the media or the image files, but do not move the system-created images **directory or the files or directories that are located inside the** images **folder. The system needs files located inside those directories, and moving them will break the links to those files.**

- **Restrict Uploads:** When set to Yes, this imposes the restrictions on the file uploads. The default setting is Yes.

- **Check MIME Types:** Leave this set to Yes to have the system check the file's MIME type against the filenames to make sure that what is actually being uploaded is what the name says it is. The default setting is Yes.

- **Legal Image Extensions (File Types):** The field contains a list of permitted image file types, shown by their extensions. You can add new types or delete an existing one. The default values are: bmp, gif, jpg, and png.

- **Ignored Extensions**: Enter here the extensions of any files you want to exempt from restrictions, including the confirmation of MIME type. By default, no file types are exempted.

- **Legal MIME Types:** By default, this field contains a list of permitted file extensions with their related MIME types. The default values are image/jpeg, image/gif, image/png, image/bmp, application/x-shockwave-flash, application/msword, application/excel, application/pdf, application/powerpoint, text/plain, and application/x-zip.

- **Illegal MIME Types:** Contains a list of the blocked MIME types. The default value is text/html.

- **Enable Flash Uploader:** Set to Yes to enable the Flash Uploader in the Media Manager. The Flash Uploader allows you to easily upload multiple files at one time. The default value is No.

Joomla! 1.6

Joomla! 1.6 includes an additional option here: Minimum User Level for Media Manager. The combo box contains a list of the user groups on the site and allows you to restrict the use of the Media Manager to only those users who belong to the selected group, or higher.

Cross-Reference
The Media Manager is discussed in detail in Chapter 6.

Debug settings

You can use the Debug Settings during development or if you are having problems with your site. The settings should not be enabled for a live site, because the output will be visible to site visitors at the bottom of the pages. This section only includes two options:

- **Debug System:** Set to Yes to enable the debugging system. The tool provides you with diagnostic information as well as language translations and the output of SQL errors. By default this is set to No.

- **Debug Language:** Set to Yes to enable debugging of language files. This control does not work unless the preceding control, Debug System, is set to Yes. By default this is set to No.

Cache settings

Use these controls to enable and configure the system-wide caching. The options available here include the following:

- **Cache:** Set this to Yes to enable systemwide caching.

- **Cache Time:** Type an integer value to set the number of minutes that the cache contents are kept before being dumped and refreshed. The default value is 15 minutes. This setting is dependent upon the control above, Cache, being set to Yes.

- **Cache Handler:** This setting has only one option, so there are no options here for you to set.

Session settings

The Session settings enable you to choose how to handle a logged-in, but inactive, user. The two controls are:

- **Session Lifetime:** Set an integer value to specify the number of minutes the user can be inactive before the system forces them to log out. The default value is 15 minutes.

- **Session Handler:** Select from the combo box how the session data will be maintained. The default setting is Database.

Note
Longer session values are more convenient for the users and the administrator, but excessively long values can be a security threat to your site, as they open up the possibility that a user who does not log out properly will leave an active open session which might be used by an unauthorized user. During development, however, very long session times are extremely convenient when working on the site contents.

Managing Server Tab Options

The Server Tab provides a collection of settings that relate to the way your system interacts with the server upon which is it hosted. Settings here cover not only the web server, but also the Database, FTP, and Mail systems. The Server tab of the Global Configuration Manager is accessed by clicking on the text link labeled Server, on the top-left side of the page. Figure 4.3 shows the workspace.

FIGURE 4.3

The Server tab of the Global Configuration Manager.

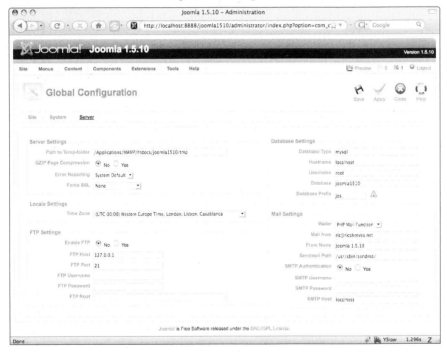

The workspace of the Site tab is broken into five areas; each area is discussed in the following sections.

Server settings

The following settings discussed relate to your general server configuration.

- **Path to Temp-folder:** This field shows the path to the directory where the system's temporary files are kept. The value for this field is created automatically by Joomla! during installation.

- **GZIP Page Compression:** Set this to Yes if your server supports GZIP page compression. Doing this improves site performance, but note that it only works if this feature is provided by your server.

- **Error Reporting:** Select a value from the combo box to set the level of error reporting you want the system to use. The options available are System Default, None, Simple, and Maximum. The default setting is System Default, which allows the level of error reporting to be determined by the settings in the server's php.ini file.

Note

The output from the error reporting is displayed at the bottom of all pages and is visible to both front-end and back-end users.

- **Force SSL:** Choose from the combo box to select whether the system requires the use of SSL for connections. The options are None, Administrator Only, and Entire Site. The default is None. Note that this control depends upon whether your server supports SSL.

Locale settings

The Locale setting allows you to adjust the time settings to suit your site, regardless of the server's default time setting — Time Zone: Select your preferred time zone from the combo box.

FTP settings

Joomla! has a built-in FTP function that will assist you with moving files to the server without having to resort to a third party piece of software. The settings in this area of the workspace allow you to set up this feature. If you wish to use traditional FTP or your web site file manager, there is no reason to enable the following:

- **Enable FTP:** Set to Yes to use Joomla's FTP function.

- **FTP Host:** Type the FTP URL of the host server. There is likely to be a value already in this field; it is Joomla's best guess at the proper FTP URL and is likely to be correct.

- **FTP Port:** Type an integer value for the port number where FTP is accessed. The default value is 21.

- **FTP Username:** Type the username that Joomla! can use to access the server via FTP.

- **FTP Password:** Type the password that goes with the FTP username.

- **FTP Root:** Type the name of the directory where the files should be uploaded.

Database settings

The values in the fields in the Database Settings area are initially created during the installation of your site. The information in this section should not be modified, except under exceptional circumstances, for example, moving your site to a new server. The fields provided are:

Caution

Changing any of these values can result in your site crashing and being inaccessible.

- **Database Type:** This field shows the type of database being used by your system. This value is determined during the installation of your site.

- **Hostname:** This field shows the hostname for your database. This value is determined during the installation of your site.

- **Username:** This field shows the username used to access your database. This value is determined during the installation of your site.

- **Database:** This field shows the name of your database. This value is determined during the installation of your site.

- **Database Prefix:** This field shows the prefix used by your database tables. This value is determined during the installation of your site.

Note

If you are running multiple Joomla! installations on one database, you need to set unique Database Prefixes for each site.

Mail settings

Your Joomla! site can send e-mails to users under a variety of circumstances. The settings in this section of the workspace control the mail server configuration, as the following list describes:

- **Mailer:** Select from the combo box the mailer you wish to use. This is normally determined during installation.

- **Mail from:** This field contains the e-mail address that will show in the e-mails sent by the system. This value in this field is set during installation but can be altered at any time here.

- **From Name:** This field contains the name that will show in the Mail from field of e-mail sent by the system. By default, this is the site name, as input in the Site tab.

- **Sendmail Path:** Enter in this field the path to the server's SendMail program. This is only used if the Mailer control is set to SendMail.

- **SMTP Authentication:** Set this to Yes if the SMTP server requires authentication. This is only used if the Mailer control is set to SendMail.

- **SMTP Username:** This field contains the username for the SMTP server. This is only used if the Mailer control is set to SendMail.

- **SMTP Password:** This field contains the password for the SMTP server. This is only used if the Mailer control is set to SendMail.

- **SMTP Host:** This field contains the hostname of the SMTP server. This is only used if the Mailer control is set to SendMail.

Summary

In this chapter, we went over how to use the system's Global Configuration options. You learned the following:

- How to use the Site configuration options
- How to use the System configuration options
- How to use the Server configuration options

Part II

Working with Content and Users

Managing Content

The management of content is at the very core of the Joomla! CMS. Not surprisingly, the content management options in the system include a wide variety of possibilities. This chapter documents the key concepts and features associated with the creation, organization, and management of content in your Joomla! site.

Getting the most out of the system requires gaining an understanding of the way the sections, categories, and articles work together to create a hierarchy of items. Logical structuring of content not only makes the site easier to use for your visitors, but also enhances the efficient management of the site. This chapter covers the most common approaches to handling content organization challenges as well as the various parameters that enable you to tailor the system to your needs.

Understanding the Joomla! Content Hierarchy

Like most content management systems, Joomla! allows you to organize your content inside of a hierarchy. Joomla! was built with the capacity to handle large and complex sites, which can be good and bad. The capacity is an advantage when you need the flexibility to manage large amounts of content, but it can be a challenge where you have a small amount of content, as improper use of the system can result in a site that is confusing to manage and needlessly complex. Still, that said, it is all quite manageable if you keep a few simple things in mind — and don't get confused by the terminology.

To get the most out of the system, you need to understand the relationship between three items: articles, categories, and sections.

- The most basic level of the content hierarchy is the article.
- Articles can either stand alone as uncategorized content, or they can be grouped together inside of categories.
- Each category belongs to a parent grouping called a section.

Joomla! 1.6

There are significant differences between Joomla! 1.5.x and Joomla! 1.6 in the way articles are organized. Joomla! 1.6 has significantly more flexibility and the administrator is not restricted to the fixed hierarchy of articles, sections, and categories.

The Joomla! 1.5.x system includes dedicated management tools for handling both sections and categories; these managers can be found under the content navigation menu. The number of sections you can create is limitless, and there is no limit to the number of categories that can be contained in any one section. It is important to remember that the imposition of the sections and categories hierarchy creates sets and subsets of your articles and that this can impact significantly the display of information, the ease of navigation, and the ease of administration. Sloppy use of the hierarchy can result in sites that are both hard for visitors to navigate and hard to administer. It is best to plan before building as it can be time-consuming exercise to have to move things around later (but not impossible if that need arises).

Note

The organization of articles inside of categories and categories inside of sections has no bearing on the actual URL display of the web site. It is simply an organization of your articles in the back end.

The tools collected under the content menu are all designed to help you find and manipulate your content pages. The various content managers, as they are called, allow you to create, edit, organize, and archive your content. You can also control the Front Page component from this menu.

Cross-Reference

Working with the Front Page Manager is the subject of Chapter 9.

Joomla! 1.6

The Joomla! 1.6 article management tools are located under the Articles option of the Components menu. There are dedicated managers for articles, categories, and featured articles only; there are no sections in Joomla! 1.6.

Creating Content Hierarchies

In all but the most basic sites you will want to create sets and subsets of content, that is, a content hierarchy. Joomla! 1.5.x is, unfortunately, restricted to presenting content in a maximum of three levels. This section is concerned with working inside of that restriction and making the most of the restrictions in Joomla 1.5.x.

Working with sections and categories

Sections and categories are critical organizational structures. Joomla! provides you with dedicated tools for managing both. The Section Manager and the Category Manager are located under the Content menu on the main admin navigation bar.

Overview of the Section Manager

The Section Manager is your workspace for creating, editing, and deleting the sections in your site. It can be reached either from the Section Manager icon on the Control Panel, or by clicking the option labeled Section Manager under the Content Menu on the main admin nav bar. Clicking either choice brings up a screen that contains a list of all the sections, as shown in Figure 5.1. You can accomplish a number of tasks directly from this screen, all related to managing your sections.

In the default system, with the sample data loaded, you can see that three sections have already been created:

- About Joomla!
- News
- FAQ

You can either choose to work with the existing sections, rename them and edit them to suit your needs, or you can delete them and start afresh.

The toolbar at the top of the Section Manager provides quick access to the following functions:

- **Publish:** Select one or more sections from the list and then click this icon to publish them.
- **Unpublish:** Select one or more sections from the list and then click this icon to unpublish them.
- **Copy:** Select one or more sections from the list and then click this icon to make copies of them, including their contents.
- **Delete:** Select one or more sections from the list and then click this icon to delete them.
- **Edit:** Select a section from the list and then click this icon to edit the section's details.
- **New:** Click to add a new section.
- **Help:** Click to access the online Help files related to the active screen.

FIGURE 5.1

The Section Manager interface.

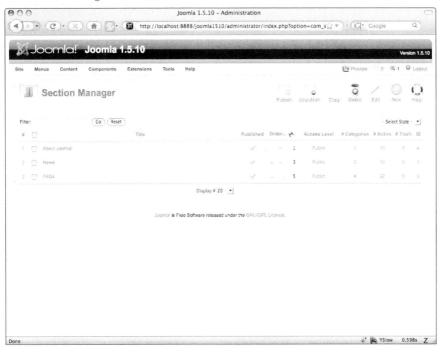

Below the toolbar and above the list of sections are two sorting and searching tools to help you manage long lists of sections:

- The Filter field on the left works like a search box. Type a word or phrase into the field and then click Go. The page reloads and displays the results of the search. To clear the screen and return to a full listing, click the Reset button.

- The Select State filter on the far right allows you to filter and display the sections according to whether they are published or unpublished. This provides an easy way to identify all sections that are currently active on the site. To reset this filter, change the combo box back to the default setting.

The main content area of the screen contains a list of all the sections in your Joomla! site. The columns provided are:

- **#** : An indexing number assigned by Joomla! This cannot be changed.

- **Checkbox (no label):** Click a checkbox to select a section; this is needed if you want to use several of the toolbar options.

- **Title:** This field displays the full name of the section. Click the name to edit the section's details.

- **Published:** A green check mark in this column indicates that the section is published. A red circle with an X in it indicates the Section is unpublished. Click the icon to toggle between the two states.

- **Order:** The number indicates the order of the section relative to the other sections. You can reorder the sections by either clicking the green arrows to move an item up or down in the order, or by entering numbers for the order and then clicking the Save icon at the top of the column.

- **Access Level:** Shows the access level set for that section. The options are Public, Registered, and Special. Click the word to change between the three options. The default setting is Public.

- **# Categories:** Shows the number of categories assigned to the section.

- **# Active:** Shows the number of articles that are active within the categories of the section.

- **# Trash:** Indicates how many articles inside the categories in the section are currently in the Article Trash Manager.

- **ID:** The system-generated user ID number. This is used internally by the system and cannot be changed by the user.

At the bottom of the screen, below the content area, is the Display # option. Change the value in the combo box control to alter the number of sections that are displayed on the page. The default value can be altered by changing the List Length option on the Global Configuration Manager.

Adding new sections

New sections can be created as needed by using the New option on the toolbar of the Section Manager. Clicking the New icon opens the New Section dialogue, as shown in Figure 5.2.

The toolbar at the top of the New Section dialogue provides quick access to the following functions:

- **Save:** Click this icon to save your work, create a new section, and exit the New Section dialogue.

- **Apply:** Click this icon to save you work without exiting from the New Section dialogue.

- **Cancel:** Cancels the task and exits the New Section dialogue.

- **Help:** Click to access the online help files related to the active screen.

FIGURE 5.2

The New Section dialogue.

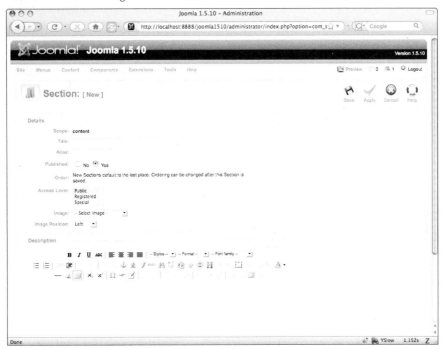

The workspace is divided into two areas. At the top of the workspace, immediately below the title, is the Details area. The fields available are:

- **Scope:** The value — content — is supplied by the system and cannot be changed.
- **Title:** Type a name for your section in this field. This field is the only required field.
- **Alias:** This field holds the internal name for the section. If left blank, the system uses your section's title. This field only accepts lowercase letters and the hyphen (dash) character. No spaces are allowed. In some situations, the alias may appear as part of the URL string.
- **Published:** Click Yes to publish the section.
- **Order:** New sections automatically default to the last place in the order of sections. This cannot be altered at the time the section is created but it can be changed after the section is saved.
- **Access Level:** Set the access level applicable to the section. The options are Public, Registered, and Special. The default value is Public.

- **Image:** If you want to associate an image with this section, select one from the combo box. You can use your own images by uploading them to the `images/stories` directory.

- **Image Position:** Set the alignment of the image by selecting an alignment value from the combo box.

Below the Details area in the workspace is the Description area. This area contains only one field, the text field used to enter the description of the section. Note that in the default configuration, the description field includes the TinyMCE editor and it also includes the Insert Image button below the text field.

Note

Whether the Section description shows on any pages is determined by the values set in the Parameters field of the Menu Item Type used to display the pages.

To create a new section, follow these steps:

1. **Log in to the admin system of your site.**

2. **Access the Section Manager by clicking the Section Manager option under the Site menu on the admin nav bar.** The Section Manager loads in your browser.

3. **On the Section Manager interface, click the New icon on the toolbar at the top of the Section Manager.** When you click that icon, the New Section Dialogue opens. (Refer to Figure 5.2.)

4. **In the Title field, enter a name for the section.** This field is required.

5. **Complete any other fields you want; all other fields are optional.**

6. **Click the Save icon on the toolbar at the top right to save your new section.** The dialogue closes and returns you to the Section Manager.

Copying sections

The Joomla! Section Manager provides the option to create copies of sections. Technically, you are not copying a section but rather copying all the contents of an existing section and moving the copies of the items into a new section. The distinction is meaningful because one of the characteristics of the process is that you can select multiple sections and by using the Copy command, you can merge the copies of the contents into a single new section. The Copy Section dialogue is shown in Figure 5.3.

Caution

The merging of section content is sometimes problematic, with the system creating multiple new sections, all of the same name, but containing varying numbers of categories and articles. Given this bug in the system, if you want to merge sections, the better course is to do it by moving the categories one at a time.

FIGURE 5.3

The Copy Section dialogue, showing the name of the sections being copied together with a list of all the categories and articles to be copied.

To copy a section, follow these steps:

1. **Open the Section Manager.**

2. **Click the select box next to the section you want to copy.**

3. **Click the Copy icon on the top right toolbar.** The Copy Section opens. (Refer to Figure 5.3.)

4. **Type a name for New Section.**

5. **Click the Copy icon on the top-right toolbar.** The system creates a new section and returns you to the Section Manager.

Editing and deleting sections

Existing sections can be edited from the Section Manager. To edit a section, either click the Section name in the Section Manager, or click the checkbox next to the section and then click the Edit icon on the Section Manager toolbar. Regardless of which method you use, the system opens the Edit Section dialogue.

The Edit Section dialogue is identical to the New Section dialogue, with the same fields and requirements.

To make changes to a section, simply alter the desired fields in the Edit Section dialogue and then click the Save or Apply icon on the toolbar. Any changes you have made are applied immediately.

Complete Ssection deletion can be achieved through the Section Manager. Deletion via the Section Manager bypasses the Trash Manager and deletes all the elements immediately. Deleting a section results in the removal of the section itself, the categories assigned to the section, and also the articles assigned to those categories.

To delete a section, follow these steps:

1. **Open the Section Manager.**
2. **Click the checkbox next to the name of the section you want to delete.**
3. **Click the Delete icon on the top-right toolbar.** The system deletes the section, along with its contents and then returns you to the Section Manager.

Caution

You cannot delete a section that contains categories. Categories must be deleted first and then the section can be removed. Note also that deletion does not require a confirmation; the deletion is instantaneous and the contents are removed from the system permanently.

Also you can not delete a category that has articles in it. They need to be moved or deleted first.

Overview of the Category Manager

Clicking on this navigation choice brings up a screen containing a list of all the categories. You can accomplish a number of tasks directly from this screen, all related to managing your categories. This interface is shown in Figure 5.4.

In the default system, with the sample data loaded, you find the following nine categories:

- The Project
- The CMS
- The Community
- General
- Current Users
- New to Joomla!
- Languages
- Latest
- Newsflash

FIGURE 5.4

The Category Manager interface.

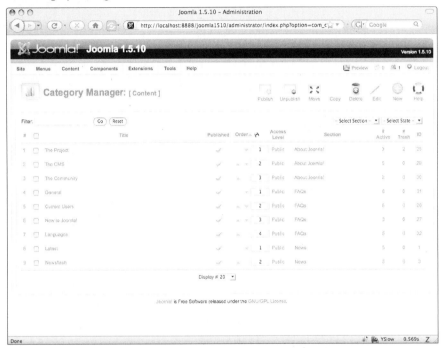

The toolbar at the top of the Category Manager provides quick access to the following functions:

- **Publish:** Select one or more categories from the list and then click this icon to publish them.

- **Unpublish:** Select one or more categories from the list and then click this icon to unpublish them.

- **Move**: Select one or more categories from the list and then click this icon to move the items in the category into a different category.

- **Copy:** Select one or more categories from the list and then click this icon to make copies of them, including their contents.

- **Delete:** Select one or more categories from the list and then click this icon to delete them.

- **Edit:** Select a category from the list and then click this icon to edit the Category's details.

- **New:** Click to add a new category.

- **Help:** Click to access the online Help files related to the active screen.

Below the toolbar and above the list of categories are three sorting and searching tools to help you manage long lists of categories:

- The Filter field on the left works like a search box. Type a word or phrase into the field and then click Go. The page reloads and displays the results of the search. To clear the screen and return to a full listing, click the Reset button.

- The Select Section filter allows you to filter and display the categories according to the section to which they are assigned. To reset this filter, change the combo box back to the default setting.

- The Select State filter on the far right allows you to filter and display the categories according to whether they are published or unpublished. This provides an easy way to identity all categories that are currently active on the site. To reset this filter, change the combo box back to the default setting.

The main content area of the screen contains a list of all the categories in your Joomla! site. The columns provided are:

- **#** : An indexing number assigned by Joomla! This cannot be changed.

- **Checkbox (no label):** Click a radio button to select a category; this is needed if you want to use several of the toolbar options.

- **Title:** This field displays the full name of the category. Click the name to edit the category's details.

- **Published:** A green checkmark in this column indicates that the category is published. A red circle with an X in it indicates the category is unpublished. Click the icon to toggle between the two states.

- **Order:** The number indicates the order of the category, relative to the other categories. You can reorder the categories by either clicking the green arrows to move an item up or down in the order, or by entering numbers for the order and then clicking the Save icon at the top of the column.

- **Access Level:** Shows the access level set for that category. The options are Public, Registered, and Special. Click the word to change between the three options.

- **Section:** Shows the name of the section to which the category is assigned. Click the name of the section to open the Section Editing dialogue.

- **# Active:** Indicates how many articles are assigned to this category and are active.

- **# Trash:** Shows the number of articles in this category that are currently in the trash.

- **ID:** The system-generated user ID number. This is used internally by the system and cannot be changed by the user.

Finally, at the bottom of the screen, below the content area, is the Display # option. Change the value in the combo box control to alter the number of categories that are displayed on the page. The default value can be altered by changing the List Length option on the Global Configuration Manager.

Adding new categories

New categories can be added to your site at any time by using the New icon on the toolbar of the Category Manager. Clicking the New icon opens the New Category dialogue, as shown in Figure 5.5.

The New Category dialogue.

The toolbar at the top of the New Category dialogue provides quick access to the following functions:

- **Save:** Click this icon to save your work, create a new category, and exit the New Category dialogue.

- **Apply:** Click this icon to save your work without existing from the New Category dialogue.

- **Cancel:** Cancels the task and exits the New Category dialogue.

- **Help:** Click to access the online Help files related to the active screen.

The workspace on this dialogue is broken into two areas. At the top of the workspace, immediately below the title, is the Details area. The available fields are:

- **Title:** Type a name for your category in this field. This field is the only required field.

- **Alias:** This field holds the internal name for the category. If left blank, the system will use your category's title. This field only accepts lowercase letters and the hyphen (dash) character. No spaces are allowed. In some situations, the alias may appear as part of the URL string.

- **Published:** Click Yes to publish the category.

- **Section:** Select the section to which you want to assign the category. By default the system selects the first section on the list.

- **Category Order:** New Categories automatically default to the last place in the order of sections. This cannot be altered at the time the category is created but it can be changed after the category is saved.

- **Access Level:** Set the Access Level applicable to the category. The options are Public, Registered, and Special. The default value is Public.

- **Image:** If you want to associate an image with this category, select one from the combo box. You can use your own images by uploading them to the `images/stories` directory.

- **Image Position:** Set the alignment of the image by selecting an alignment value from the combo box.

Below the Details area in the workspace is the Description area. This area contains only one field, the text field used to enter the description of the Category. Note that in the default configuration, the description field includes the TinyMCE editor and the Insert Image button below the text field.

Note

Whether the category description shows on any pages is determined by the values set in the Parameters field of the Menu Item Type used to display the pages.

To create a new category, follow these steps:

1. **Log in to the admin system of your site.**

2. **Access the Category Manager by clicking on the Category Manager option under the Site menu on the admin nav bar.** The Category Manager loads in your browser.

3. **On the Category Manager interface click the New icon on the toolbar at the top of the Category Manager.** When you click that icon, the New Category Dialogue opens. (Refer to Figure 5.5.)

4. **In the Title field, enter a name for the category.** This field is the only required field.

5. **Complete any other fields you want; all other fields are optional.**

6. **Click the Save icon on the toolbar at the top right to save your new category.** The dialogue closes and returns you to the Category Manager.

Copying categories

The Joomla! Category Manager enables you to create copies of categories, together with all their articles. Copying a category results in the creation of an exact copy of the category and all of its articles. During the process you are asked to select the section to which the new category will be assigned.

The new category will be automatically named "copy of [name of original Category]" and it will inherit the published state and access level of the original category. It is possible to copy more than one category at a time, but the new categories must all be assigned to the same section.

To copy a category, follow these steps:

1. **Open the Category Manager.**

2. **Click the select box next to the category you want to copy.**

3. **Click the Copy icon on the top-right toolbar.** The Copy Category dialogue opens, as shown in Figure 5.6.

FIGURE 5.6

The Copy Category dialogue, showing the name of the category being copied together with a list of all the items in that category.

4. Select the section to which you want the category to be assigned.

5. **Click the Save icon on the top-right toolbar.** The system creates a new category and returns you to the Category Manager.

Moving categories

The Move option in the Category Manager allows you to move one or more categories to a different section. The Move option moves the categories selected, together with all their articles.

To move a category, follow these steps:

1. **Open the Category Manager.**

2. **Click the select box next to the category you want to copy.**

3. **Click the Move icon on the top-right toolbar.** The Moving Category dialogue opens, as shown in Figure 5.7.

FIGURE 5.7

The Moving Category dialogue.

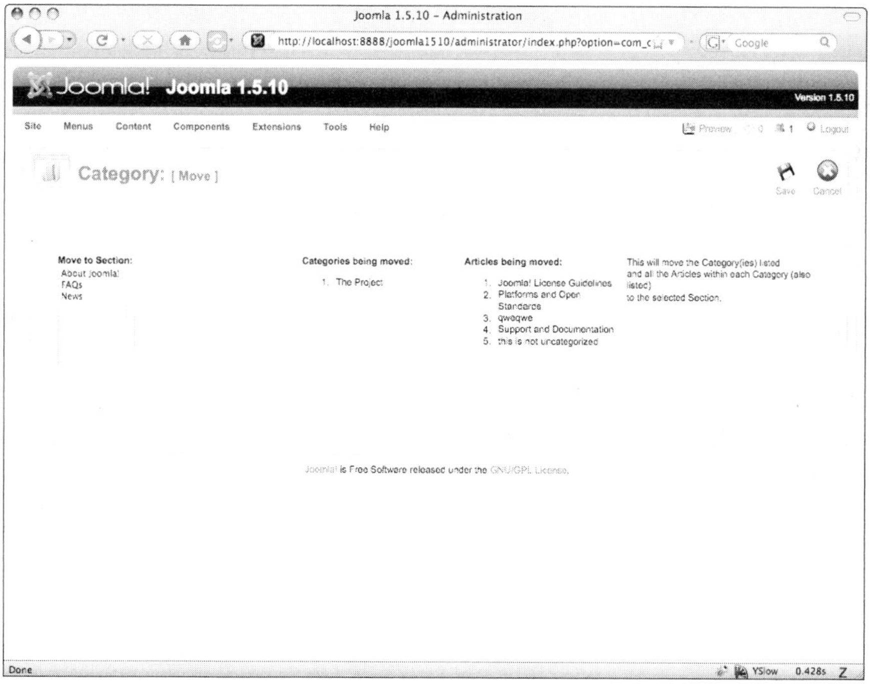

4. Select the section to which you want to move the category.

5. **Click the Save icon on the top-right toolbar.** The system moves the category to the new section and returns you to the Category Manager.

Editing and deleting categories

Existing categories can be edited from the Category Manager. To edit a category, either click the category name in the Category Manager, or select the category and then click the Edit icon on the Category Manager toolbar. Regardless of which method you use, the system opens the Edit Category dialogue.

The Edit Category dialogue is identical to the New Category dialogue, with the same fields and requirements as discussed in the previous section.

To make changes to a category, simply alter the desired fields in the Edit Category dialogue and then click the Save or Apply icon on the toolbar. Any changes you have made are applied immediately.

Complete category deletion can be achieved through the Category Manager. Deletion from the Category Manager bypasses the Trash Manager and deletes the category immediately. Categories must be emptied of both active and trashed articles before the deletion can occur.

To delete a category, follow these steps:

1. **Open the Category Manager.**

2. **Select the category you want to delete.**

3. **Click the Delete icon on the top right toolbar.** The system deletes the category and then returns you to the Category Manager.

Caution

Note also that deletion does not require a confirmation; the deletion is instantaneous and the contents are removed from the system permanently.

Joomla! 1.6

As there are no sections in Joomla! 1.6, the creation of a nested hierarchy is managed through the Category Manager. The Category Manager is accessed from the Components menu, under the Articles option, and the subheading Categories. The manager allows you to create an unlimited number of categories and then nest them as you see fit. This is significantly more flexible than Joomla! 1.5.x, and enables you to create whatever structure you need to organize your content logically.

Understanding the role of uncategorized content

During the creation of new article, you have the option to assign the article to either an existing category or to leave it uncategorized. As the name implies, an article that is uncategorized is outside the system's hierarchy.

Note

Prior to Joomla 1.5, uncategorized articles were known as static content items.

Assigning an article to the uncategorized group has several implications. First and most importantly, the article will not be shown in any page that displays the contents according to the articles membership in section or category. Second, uncategorized articles do not show up in the list of latest articles that are displayed by Joomla!'s Latest News module. In all other regards, uncategorized articles are similar to any other article. Unlike the old static content items, uncategorized articles can be assigned to the site's front page.

Creating typical content structures

Three of the most common content structures are flat sites, multilevel sites, and blog sites. In this section I look at ways to efficiently organize content to create all three of these content structures.

Flat site structures

A *flat site structure* is an organizational structure that does not rely upon multiple levels of nested articles, and is most appropriate for smaller sites. If you are planning to build a basic site that has little content, a flat structure may be right for you.

Flat site structures can be created with or without using the typical section and category structure to hold your articles. Indeed, if you so want, you could build the entire site out of uncategorized articles. If you are using Joomla 1.5.x and you choose to use sections and categories for a flat site structure, you may want to create only one section and inside that section only one category, into which you place all the articles. Although placing the pages in more than one section or category is possible, there is likely to be little advantage to that approach and may, in fact, complicate administration.

Joomla! 1.6

The same logic can be applied if you are using Joomla 1.6 and you wish to use categories to create a flat site; create one master category and assign all you articles to that category in order to keep the site management simple.

Note

If you intend to use the Latest News module to display your articles, then you will not want to create the entire structure out of uncategorized articles, as noted in the previous section.

Multilevel content structures

The Joomla! system makes it easy to create multilevel content structures, within certain limitations. The content hierarchy of Joomla! is fixed and limited to only three levels: sections, categories, and articles. In Joomla 1.5, it is essentially impossible to create a site with more than three levels (without the addition of third-party extensions).

The content hierarchy in action

Perhaps the best way to grasp the Joomla! 1.5.x content hierarchy is by looking at an example. Let's say you want to create an organizational scheme for the articles on your Recipes web site. Your site lists recipes by their place in the order of a meal, so you have decided to organize recipes into three courses that reflect a typical meal. The three courses are:

- Entrees
- Main Courses
- Desserts

And let's say that within the Entrees area of the site, you want to cover two different types of recipes:

- Appetizers
- Salads

And let's say that within the Main Courses area of the site you want to organize the recipes into four different groups:

- Fish
- Meat
- Fowl
- Vegetarian

And let's say that within the Desserts area of the site you want to cover three different types of desserts:

- Cookies
- Cakes
- Pastries

Here's how this translates into a Joomla! Content Hierarchy:

First, create the top level of the hierarchy as sections. To do this, follow these steps:

1. Access the Section Manager.
2. Click the New icon. The New Section dialogue loads.
3. Create a new section named Entrees.
4. Repeat for the other two main content division: Main Courses and Desserts.

Next, create the second tier of content structure as categories. To do this, follows these steps:

1. Access the Category Manager.
2. Click the New icon. The New Category dialogue loads.
3. Create a new category named Appetizers.
4. Assign the Appetizers category to the section named Entrees.
5. Repeat the process to create a new category named Salads, and assign it to the Entrees Section.
6. Repeat the process to create four new categories named Fish, Meat, Fowl and Vegetarian, assigning each to the Main Courses section.

7. Repeat the process one more time to create three new categories named Cookies, Cakes, and Pastries, assigning each to the Desserts section.

Your content structure should now look something like this:

1. Entrees (a section)

    a. Appetizers (a category)

    b. Salads (a category)

2. Main Courses (a section)

    a. Fish (a category)

    b. Meat (a category)

    c. Fowl (a category)

    d. Vegetarian (a category)

3. Desserts (a section)

    a. Cookies (a category)

    b. Cakes (a category)

    c. Pastries (a category)

Now you have everything you need to start building pages and grouping items together within the hierarchy.

Now let's take one section and complete the process by creating the articles for specific recipes. Let us expand on the Main Courses section: If you want to create individual articles with recipes for Beef Brisket and Lamb Shank — both recipes belonging to the Main Courses section, you will group them together under the Meat category.

When you create the two articles for the recipes, you will assign them to the Main Courses section and to the Meat category.

Logically then, your hierarchy all fits together neatly like this:

1. Main Courses (a Section)

    a. Meat (a Category)

        i. Beef Brisket (an Article)

        ii. Lamb Shank (an Article)

Now, when you create your site navigation you have many options. You can:

- Create a Content Section link to all Main Courses, which will pull up everything in the Main Courses Section
- Create a Content Category link to all Meat, which will pull up everything in the Meat Category
- Create a Content Item link to an individual article, like the Beef Brisket page or the Lamb Shank page

The net result of an organized approach like this is that you have a logical structure on the front end for clients to navigate and on the back end you have an organizational scheme for your content that is intuitive and easy for your administrators to use.

The content hierarchy imposes a parent-child relationship on sections, categories, and articles. Menu item creation allows you to display an organizational hierarchy to your site visitors via the navigation menus by creating parent-child relationships between menu items, or through the creation of menus and submenus. While the content structure is limited to three levels, menus do not suffer from this limitation; it is possible to create multitiered menus that are much deeper than three levels. Therefore, if your need is only to display a complex hierarchy through the menus of your site, you can achieve more flexibility.

However, several complications result from the creation of menu items tiered deeper than three levels. First, the site's breadcrumb trail will reflect the section, category, and article organization of your content, regardless of the menu structure. Therefore, you run the risk of rendering the breadcrumbs feature useless. Second, using the multitiered menu structure means that you will be limited in your ability to use the system's section and category list views, as the content logic they display may be inconsistent with the menu item logic. When you put this all together, adopting a multitiered menu approach to a complex content structure most likely means that you will forego the use of the breadcrumbs feature and will also look to a combination of uncategorized articles and, if appropriate, sections and categories for some of the site's articles. So, while this can be done, the end result can be a site that is less than optimal in usability and more complex than you might like for the administrators.

Cross-Reference
Menus, Menu Items, and Menu Item Types are discussed in detail in Chapter 8.

Joomla! 1.6
The creation of a multitiered content hierarchy is significantly easier with Joomla! 1.6. The site administrator simply needs to create all the categories needed, and then nest them as desired. The nesting of categories is handled inside the Category Manager. To make one category a subcategory of another, simply select the name of the desired parent category from the combo box named Parent. Once the structure is created, you can assign your articles to the desired categories by editing the articles and choosing the name of the category from the combo box of the same name.

Blog sites
Blog sites typically have a home page that contains numerous articles that span the width of the page and are ordered chronologically, with the newest items first. The default Front Page layout of Joomla! follows a different page format, with only a single article spanning the page, followed by articles laid out in two columns.

You can achieve a more traditional blog site layout by altering the menu item parameters for the home page. The default Front Page is created with the Menu Item Type named Front Page Blog Layout. The basic parameters for the Menu Item Type include the options for controlling the number of items, their display, and the number of columns.

To achieve a traditional blog layout for your front page in Joomla! 1.5.x, follow these steps:

1. **Log into the admin system of your site.**

2. **Select the Main Menu option from under the main nav option labeled Menus.** The Main Menu's Menu Item Manager opens in your web browser.

3. **Click the name of the menu item labeled Home.** The Menu Item Editing dialogue opens.

4. **Under the Basic Parameters on the right side of the page, set the Columns to 1.**

5. **Set the # Leading Parameter to zero.**

6. **Set the # Intro Parameter to the maximum number of items you want to show on the page.**

7. **Set the # Links Parameter to the number of links you want to display at the bottom of the page.**

8. **Click the Save icon.** The system saves the changes, closes the Menu Item Editing dialogue, and returns you to the Menu Item Manager.

Working with Articles

Articles are the essence of your site. Articles hold your text content, together with any pictures or media files you have attached. The look and feel of your web site is largely influenced by your site administrator's fluency with the Article Manager and the associated parameters.

Using the Article Manager

The Article Manager provides access to all the articles in your system, as well as the tools to create new articles and to copy, move, edit, delete, and archive them. Taken all together, this is one of the most powerful and most important screens in your Joomla! system.

To view the Article Manager, either click the icon of the same name on the control panel, or select Article Manager under the Content menu on your main admin nav bar. In either event, the Article Manager opens in your web browser, as shown in Figure 5.8.

The toolbar at the top of the Joomla 1.5.x Article Manager provides quick access to the following functions:

- **Unarchive:** Select one or more archived articles from the list and then click this icon to unarchive them.

- **Archive:** Select one or more active articles from the list and then click this icon to archive them.

- **Publish:** Select one or more articles from the list and then click this icon to publish them.

- **Unpublish:** Select one or more articles from the list and then click this icon to unpublish them.

- **Move:** Select one or more articles from the list and then click this icon to move the items into a different category.

- **Copy:** Select one or more articles from the list and then click this icon to make copies of them.

- **Trash:** Select an article from the list and then click this icon to move the article to the Trash.

- **Edit:** Select an article from the list and then click this icon to edit the article details.

- **New:** Click to add a new article.

- **Parameters:** Click to edit the Global Article parameters.

- **Help:** Click to access the online Help files related to the active screen.

FIGURE 5.8

The Article Manager interface in Joomla! 1.5.x, showing the default sample data installed.

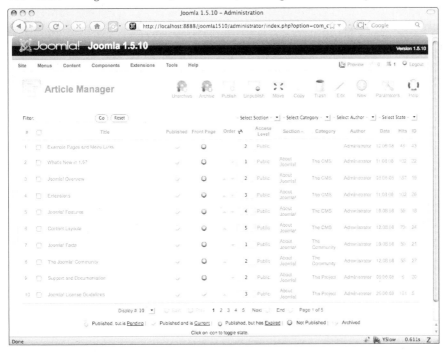

Below the toolbar and above the list of articles are five sorting and searching tools to help you manage long lists of articles:

- The Filter field on the left works like a search box. Type a word or phrase into the field and then click Go. The page reloads and displays the results of the search. To clear the screen and return to a full listing, click the Reset button.

- The Select Section filter enables you to filter and display the articles according to the section to which they are assigned. To reset this filter, change the combo box back to the default setting.

- The Select Category filter lets you to filter and display the articles according to the category to which they are assigned. To reset this filter, change the combo box back to the default setting.

- The Select Author filter enables you to filter and display the articles according to the author associated with them. To reset this filter, change the combo box back to the default setting.

- The Select State filter on the far right allows you to filter and display the articles according to whether they are published or unpublished. The filter provides an easy way to identity all articles that are currently active on the site. To reset this filter, change the combo box back to the default setting.

The main content area of the screen contains a list of all the articles in your Joomla! site. The columns provided are:

- **#** : An indexing number assigned by Joomla! This cannot be changed.

- **Checkbox (no label):** Click a radio button to select an article; this is needed if you wish to use several of the toolbar options, referenced in the preceding list.

- **Title:** This field displays the full name of the article. Click the name to edit the article.

- **Published:** A green checkmark in this column indicates the publication state of the article. As indicated by the legend that appears at the very bottom of the Article Manager, the icon that is displayed indicates the publication state. You can click the icon to publish or unpublish the article, depending on its state:

  - A yellow dot beside an Article icon indicates the article is approved and scheduled for publication but is pending.

  - A green checkmark beside an Article icon indicates the article is currently published.

  - A red circle with an X beside an Article icon indicates the article was published but has expired.

  - A red circle with an X in it (without an Article icon) indicates the article is neither published nor scheduled for publication.

  - A gray circle with a crossbar (without an Article icon) indicates the article is archived.

Tip

If you hover the cursor over the Published icon, the system displays the article's start and stop publication dates.

- **Front Page:** A green checkmark in this column indicates that the article is assigned to appear on the front page of the site. A red circle with an X in it indicates the article is not assigned to the front page. Click the icon to toggle between the two states.

- **Order:** The number indicates the order of the article, relative to the other articles. You can reorder the articles by either clicking the green arrows to move an item up or down in the order, or by entering numbers for the order and then clicking the save icon at the top of the column.

- **Access Level:** Shows the access level set for that article. The options are Public, Registered, and Special. Click the word to change between the three options.

- **Section:** Shows the name of the section to which the article is assigned. Click the name of the section to open the section editing dialogue.

- **Category:** Shows the name of the category to which the article is assigned. Click the name of the category to open the category editing dialogue.

- **Author:** Shows the name of the author of the article. Click the name of the author to open the User editing dialogue for the author.

- **Date:** Shows the date the article was created.

- **Hits:** Shows the number of times the article has been viewed.

Tip

You can change the result shown in the hit counter by changing the value in the parameter in the Article Edit dialogue.

- **ID:** The system-generated user ID number. This is used internally by the system and cannot be changed by the user.

Finally, at the bottom of the screen, below the content area, is the Display # option. Change the value in the combo box control to alter the number of articles that are displayed on the page. The default value can be altered by changing the List Length option on the Global Configuration Manager.

Creating articles

New articles are created by clicking the New icon on the toolbar at the top right of the Article Manager. Clicking the New icon opens the New Article dialogue, as shown in Figure 5.9.

The toolbar at the top of the New Article dialogue provides quick access to the following functions:

- **Preview:** Click to open a lightbox showing how the article will appear to a site visitor. Note that the article does not appear inside your site's page template; the only way to see the article inside your site template is to publish it and view it from the front end.

- **Save:** Click this icon to save your work, create a new article, and exit the New Article dialogue.

- **Apply:** Click this icon to save you work without exiting from the New Article dialogue.

- **Cancel:** Cancels the task and exits the New Article dialogue.

- **Help:** Click to access the online Help files related to the active screen.

The fields in the workspace are:

- **Title:** Type in this field a name for the article. The value in this field will be used as the article's title. This field is required.

- **Alias:** Enter an alias for the system to use internally for this article. Note that this field only accepts lowercase letters without spaces. If you leave this field blank, the system will modify the article's title for use as the alias. Note that in some cases the alias may appear as part of the URL strings when SEF URLs are enabled.

- **Section:** Select a section for the article. This field is required.

- **Published:** Set to Yes to publish the article.

- **Front Page:** Set to Yes to display this article on the site's front page.

- **Category:** Select a category for the article from the combo box.

- **Text field (no label):** Enter your content for the article in this box. This field is required.

At the top right of the workspace, immediately below the icons, is a summary of key article information, including the article's state, the number of hits it has received, the number of revisions, the creation date, and the date modified. At the time of article creation, much of this information will be blank.

FIGURE 5.9

The New Article dialogue in Joomla 1.5.x.

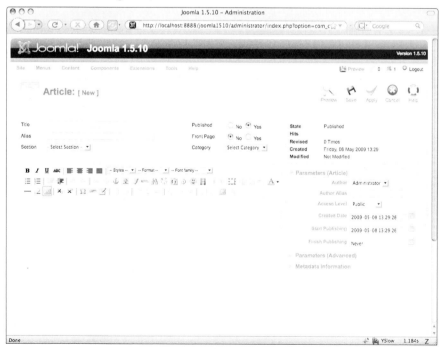

Below the article summary are the article parameters, which I discuss later in this chapter.

To create a new article, follow these steps:

1. **Log in to the admin system of your site.**

2. **Access the Article Manager by clicking on the Article Manager option under the Content menu on the admin nav bar.** The Article Manager loads in your web browser.

3. **On the Article Manager interface, click the New icon on the toolbar at the top of the Article Manager.** The New Article dialogue opens. (Refer to Figure 5.9.)

4. **In the Title field, type a name for the article.** This field is required.

5. **From the combo box labeled Section, select either a section for the article or the Uncategorized option.** This field is a required

6. **Type some text for the article.** This field is required.

7. **Complete any other fields you wish; all other fields are optional.**

8. **Click the Save icon on the toolbar at the top right to save your new article.** The dialogue closes and returns you to the Article Manager.

Setting the parameters

Articles in Joomla! include parameters that you can use to affect the article display and behavior. Note that many of the parameter options are repeats of the same choices available in the Global Article parameters, or in the Menu Item Type parameters. The settings you indicate in the Article parameters will take precedence over other parameter settings, thereby allowing you to tailor the display of individual articles.

Global parameters

The Global Article parameters are accessed by clicking the Parameters icon on the Article Manager toolbar. Clicking the icon causes a menu to appear, as shown in Figure 5.10. Set the options you wish; then click the Save button to set the changes and close the pop-up window.

Options set through the Global parameters controls apply to all articles in the system, unless they are overridden by the individual article's parameters.

Note

Where there is a conflict between the Global Article Parameters and the individual article parameters, the settings in the article parameters are applied by the system.

FIGURE 5.10

The Global Article Parameters pop up in Joomla! 1.5.x.

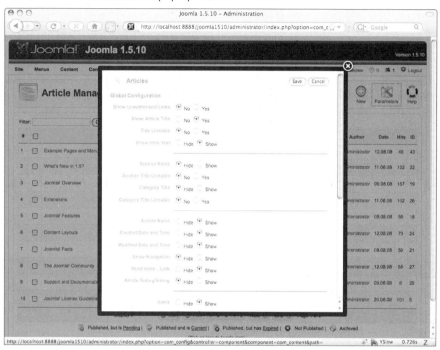

The following parameters are included here:

- **Show Unauthorized Links:** This control determines whether users are shown links to content for which they lack sufficient access privileges to view. If set to Yes, the links appear, but when a user without sufficient privileges clicks on the link, they will be prompted to log in; if they do not log in, they will not be able to view the article. The default state is No.

- **Show Article Title:** Whether the article title is displayed along with the content. The default state is Yes.

- **Title Linkable:** Set this parameter to Yes if you want the article title to be hyperlinked to the full article. The default state is No.

- **Show Intro Text:** Determines whether intro text, if any, is displayed both as a teaser and with the full article. Set this to Hide to display the full article without the intro text, in other words, the teaser will not be shown in the full article view. The default state is Show.

- **Section Name:** Determines whether the section name is shown. The default state is Hide.

- **Section Title Linkable:** Set this parameter to Yes to hyperlink the section title to a list of the section contents. The default state is No. Linkable titles can be good for SEO

- **Category Title:** Determines whether the category name is shown. The default state is Hide.

- **Category Title Linkable:** Set this Parameter to Yes to hyperlink the category title to a list of the category's contents. The default state is No.

- **Author Name:** When set to Show, the name of the author of the article will appear on the article. The default state is Show.

- **Created Date and Time:** When set to Show, the Article's creation date and time will appear on the article. The default state is Show.

- **Modified Date and Time:** When set to Show, the date and time the article was last modified appears on the article. The default state is Show.

- **Show Navigation:** Determines whether navigation options, such as the next and previous controls, appear on the article. The default state is Hide.

- **Read more... Link:** Determines whether the Read more. . . text will appear on the article intro text. The default state is Show.

- **Article Rating/Voting:** Set this parameter to Show to display the rating option on the articles. The default state is Hide.

- **Icons:** Controls whether the PDF, Print, and E-mail Icons are displayed on the articles. This can be overridden by the controls that follow, or by the settings on the articles.

- **PDF Icon:** Show or Hide the PDF Icon on the articles.

- **Print Icon:** Show or Hide the Print Icon on the articles.

- **E-mail Icon:** Show or Hide the E-mail Icon on the articles.

- **Hits:** Show or Hide the Hit count for each article.

- **For each feed item show**: If there is a feed item displayed, this parameter controls whether the full item, or only the intro text, appears.

- **Filter groups:** Select one or more groups for applying the content filtering. You can select multiple groups by holding down the Control key while clicking.

- **Filter type:** Select from one of three options: Black List, White List, or No HTML. The default is Black List.

- **Filter tags:** If the Filter type parameter is set to Black List, terms typed in this text field are added to the default list of Black List tags. If the Filter type parameter is set to White List, the tags typed in this field become the White List terms.

- **Filter Attributes:** If the Filter type parameter is set to Black List, terms typed in this text field are added to the default list of Black List attributes. If the Filter type parameter is set to White List, the attributes typed in this field become the White List terms.

Content filtering

Any time you provide an opportunity for users to input HTML into your site, you create the possibility that harmful, or even malicious, code can find its way into your system. In order to help prevent this from happening, Joomla! has added content filtering to the system. The filtering works by assessing the HTML that is input by the users and checking it against a black list to see if the code is permitted.

Joomla! provides content filtering in the default system and applies it to all users except for the Super Administrator. The default settings can be overridden by the Filter parameters contained in the Global Article Parameters, discussed previously.

The default Joomla! system includes a pre-determined Black List that contains the following tags: `applet`, `body`, `bgsound`, `base`, `basefont`, `embed`, `frame`, `frameset`, `head`, `html`, `id`, `iframe`, `ilayer`, `layer`, `link`, `meta`, `name`, `object`, `script`, `style`, `title`, and `xml`. The Black List also excludes the following attributes by default: `action`, `background`, `codebase`, `dynsrc`, `lowsrc`.

Through the Global parameters, you can either add new terms to the Black List or you can create a White List that specifically allows certain elements to be used. The parameters also give you a way to specify which users will be subject to the controls. Note that setting a control for one user group automatically sets that control for all children user groups.

Article parameters

Individual Article parameters (shown in Figure 5.11) are accessed via the Article Editing dialogue.

The Article parameters section of all articles contains the following options:

- **Author:** The combo box next to this field contains a list of users; select from this box to specify the author of the article and override the default setting.

- **Author Alias:** This field is normally left blank; enter text here if you wish to display a name other than the name associated with the user in the system.

- **Access Level:** Sets the access level for this article. Select from one of three options: Public, Registered, or Special. The default is Public.

- **Created Date:** The default value is the date and time the article is created. Click the calendar icon to the right of the field to override the default date to specify one of your choosing.

- **Start Publishing:** By default, articles are scheduled to begin publishing immediately; use this field to specify a publication date in the future.

- **Finish Publishing:** Click the calendar icon to the right of this field to select a stop date for the publication of this article. The default value is Never.

FIGURE 5.11

The Article parameters.

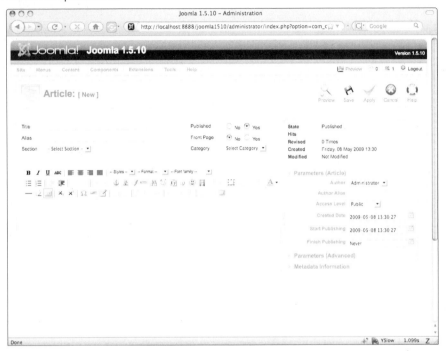

Advanced parameters

Like the Article parameters, the Advanced parameters are accessed via the Article Editing dialogue, as shown in Figure 5.12.

The Advanced parameters section of all articles contains the options outlined below. Note that the default value for all parameters is Use Global, which specifies that the system will apply the values set in the Global Article parameters. Setting a contrary value will override the Global parameter setting:

- **Show Title:** Whether the article title is displayed along with the content.
- **Title Linkable:** Set this Parameter to Yes if you want the article title to be hyperlinked to the full article.

- **Intro Text:** Determines whether intro text, if any, is displayed both as a teaser and with the full article. Set this to Hide to display the fill article without the intro text, in other words, the teaser will not be shown in the full article view.

- **Section Name:** Determines whether the section name is shown.

- **Section Title Linkable:** Set this parameter to Yes to hyperlink the section title to a list of the section contents.

- **Category Title:** Determines whether the category name is shown.

- **Category Title Linkable:** Set this parameter to Yes to hyperlink the category title to a list of the category's contents.

- **Article Rating:** Set this parameter to Show to display the rating option on the articles.

- **Author Name:** When set to Show, the name of the author of the article appears on the article.

- **Created Date and Time:** When set to Show, the article's creation date and time appears on the article.

- **Modified Date and Time:** When set to Show, the date and time the article was last modified will appear on the article.

- **PDF Icon:** Show or hide the PDF Icon on the articles.

- **Print Icon:** Show or Hide the Print Icon on the articles.

- **E-mail Icon:** Show or Hide the E-mail Icon on the articles.

- **Content Language:** Articles are normally displayed in the default system language; that can be overridden by selecting another language from the combo box. The contents of the combo box are determined by which language packs have been installed.

- **Key Reference:** Enter a value in this field if you wish to provide an alternative method for accessing the article. The Key Reference allows you to call this item without using the Article ID in the query string. This is normally used by the system to provide an alternative reference that can be tied to an external resource, for example, to provide the appropriate Joomla! Help files for a particular page.

- **Alternative Read more: text:** This field can be used to specify the text that appears with the Read more link. By default the field is blank, in which case the system will use the article's title.

FIGURE 5.12

The Advanced parameters.

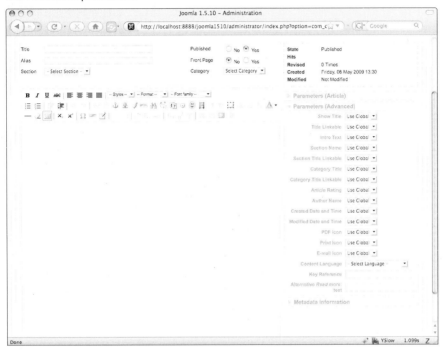

Article metadata

In addition to the global site metadata, Joomla! allows you to specify metadata specific to individual articles. Information entered into any of these fields will override and replace any contrary values specified in the Global Configuration Manager.

The Article Metadata fields discussed below are located below the parameters in the Article Editing dialogue, as shown in Figure 5.13.

- **Description:** Enter into the text field any information you want to appear in the meta Description field for this article.

- **Keywords:** Enter into the text field any key words you want to appear in the meta Keyword field for this article. Separate multiple keywords with commas.

- **Robots:** Enter into this text field the commands you want to specify for the meta Robots field for the article.

- **Author:** Enter into this text field the information you want to appear in the meta Author field for the article.

FIGURE 5.13

The Metadata Information screen for articles.

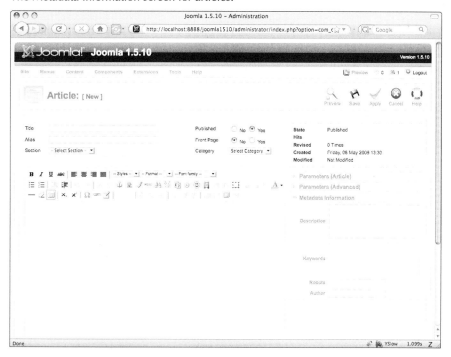

Controlling intro text

Intro text provides a teaser view of Joomla! articles. By using the parameters and the content editing controls you can create articles that appear either with or without the intro text.

Designating the intro text inside an article is a simple matter of inserting a Read more. . . break in the text. The Read more button, located at the bottom of the Article editing window, will automatically insert the break when you click it. The button's position is shown in Figure 5.14.

The text you want to use for intro text should be placed at the very beginning of your article. Remember that you have the choice to show the full article text either with or without the intro text, as discussed next. Regardless of whether you want it to show in the full article, however, you must enter it first and in the same box as the full text.

FIGURE 5.14

The Read more. . . button is located below the Article editing window, next to the Pagebreak button.

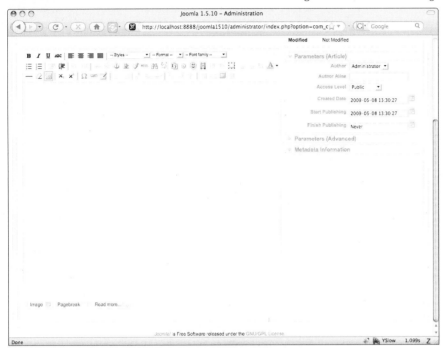

To set the Intro Text for an article follow these steps:

1. Open the Article Editing dialogue.

2. Type the intro text, followed by the full article text.

3. Place the cursor at the end of the intro text.

4. Click the Read more button at the bottom of the content editing window. A dotted red line appears, as shown in Figure 5.15.

Tip

If you are editing articles without the assistance of the Read more button, you can define the selection of the intro text in the article by inserting the following HTML tag where you want to separate the intro text from the balance of the Article:

```
<hr id="system-readmore" />.
```

FIGURE 5.15

The Article editing screen showing the intro text divider in the text area.

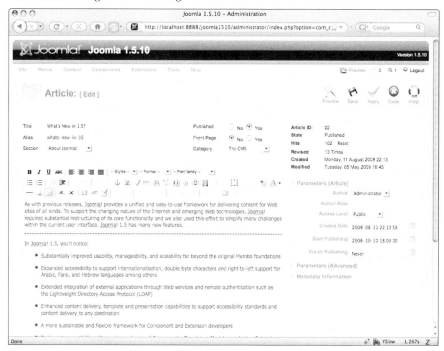

Creating multipage articles

By default, all articles created in Joomla are presented as a single page. Multipage articles are, however, only a click away. The Pagebreak button is used to divide a single-page article into multiple pages. The button is located at the bottom of the Article editing window. (Refer to Figure 5.14.)

Clicking the Pagebreak button opens a pop-up window that contains two text fields: Page Title and Table of Contents Alias, as shown in Figure 5.16. Anything you type in the Page Title field is shown at the top of the visitor's browser when they view the article. The Table of Contents Alias serves as the text for the link to the individual pages of the article in the Table of Contents.

In the default Joomla! system, breaking an article into multiple pages results in the appearance of a Table of Contents on each of the new pages, as shown in Figure 5.17. The Table of Contents provides links to all the pages in the article. You can also navigate between the pages by clicking on the Prev - Next text links that appear at the bottom of each of the new pages.

FIGURE 5.16

The Pagebreak pop-up window.

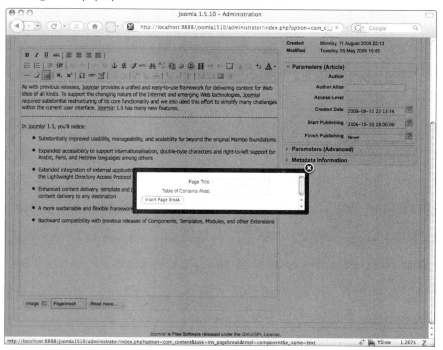

To split a single page article into multiple pages, follow these steps:

1. Access the Article Editing dialogue.

2. Place the cursor where you want to split the article.

3. Click the Pagebreak button. The Pagebreak window opens.

4. Type a Page Title for the new page.

5. Type a Table of Contents Alias for the page.

6. **Click Insert Page Break.** The window closes and returns you to the Article Manager, where you will note a gray dashed line now appears in the article at the place where you clicked.

Note

The display of the Table of Contents is controlled by the Content - Pagebreak plugin. The plugin contains several parameters that allow you to alter the display or to hide completely the table of content. The plugin is discussed in more detail in Chapter 19.

FIGURE 5.17

This Joomla! article from the sample data has been split into multiple pages. Note the Table of Contents to the right of the article and the text navigation links below the article.

Managing Existing Articles

If you site is large or active, the management of the existing articles on your site can take up a considerable amount of your time. In this section, I cover the most common tasks you will perform.

Publishing and unpublishing articles

Articles can be published and unpublished in any of three ways:

- You can access the Article Manager and click the icon in the Published column; clicking the icon toggles between published and unpublished.

- You can click the checkbox next to the article's name in the Article Manager and then click the Publish or Unpublish icon on the toolbar at top right.

- You can edit an article and modify the control marked published.

If you want to publish or unpublish more than one item at a time, you may do so by clicking the checkbox next to each article in the Article Manager and then clicking the Publish or Unpublish icon on the main toolbar at the top right.

Publication normally begins immediately and lasts indefinitely. You can, however, set an article to start and stop publication on specific dates. The start and stop publishing controls are located on the Article Parameters tab inside the Article Editing dialogue.

Note

The ability to publish an article depends on the user's privileges. Users belonging to user groups below the level of Publisher have no say in publication. Articles created by lower-level users must be published by higher level users.

Cross-Reference

Publishing articles from the front end of the web site is discussed in Chapter 7.

Modifying articles

An existing article can be edited at any time by accessing the Article Manager and either by clicking the article name, or by clicking the checkbox next to the article name and then clicking the Edit icon on the Article Manager toolbar. Changes made to articles are applied to the article immediately when you click either the Save icon or the Apply icon.

Note

Joomla does not support Article versioning, that is, maintaining a record of changes to the articles. There are, however, third-party extensions that provide limited functionality in this area.

Copying articles

The Article Manager enables you to create copies of articles. When you copy an article, the system makes an exact duplicate, changing only the article name. During the copy process you are given the chance to assign the new article to whatever section and category you desire, as shown in Figure 5.18. The new article will inherit the old article's publication state and access level.

You can copy more than one article at a time, but when you select multiple articles to copy they must all be assigned to the same section and category.

FIGURE 5.18

The Copying Article dialogue in Joomla! 1.5.x.

To copy an article, follow these steps:

1. **Access the Article Manager.**

2. **Select the article you want to copy by clicking the checkbox next to the article's title.**

3. **Click the Copy icon on the Article Manager toolbar.** The Copying Article dialogue opens.

4. **Assign the article to the section and category you desire.**

5. **Click the Save icon on the toolbar at the top right to save your new article.** The dialogue closes and returns you to the Article Manager.

Moving articles

You can move articles between categories by using the Move command in the Article Manager, or by editing the article and reassigning it to a different section and category. The end result of both processes is the same, but working from the Article Manager is faster and also allows you to move multiple articles simultaneously.

To move an article, follow these steps:

1. **Access the Article Manager.**

2. **Select the article you want to move by clicking the checkbox next to the article's title.**

3. **Click the Move icon on the Article Manager toolbar.** The Move Articles dialogue opens, as shown in Figure 5.19.

4. **Assign the article to the section and category you desire.**

5. **Click the Save icon on the toolbar at the top right to save the change.** The dialogue closes and returns you to the Article Manager.

FIGURE 5.19

The Move Articles dialogue in Joomla! 1.5.x.

Deleting articles

The deletion of articles in Joomla! is a two-step process. The first step involves moving the article to the Trash, where it is held until you take the second step and permanently delete the article. Articles held in the Trash Manager can be restored at any time prior to deletion.

Overview of the Articles Trash Manager

The Trash Manager feature of Joomla! provides you with a way to clean up and remove articles from the general admin areas of the site. Sending an article to the Trash will result in the article being removed from the Article Manager and moved to the Articles Trash Manager.

Articles moved to the Articles Trash Manager are held there indefinitely. The items can be restored or deleted at the option of the administrator. Restored items are moved back to their original locations, but deleted items are permanently removed from the system and cannot be restored.

Note

Though articles can be left in the Trash Manager indefinitely, the Article Trash is distinctly different from the Archive Manager. Moving articles to the Trash Manager should not be confused with archiving articles, as discussed in the following section.

In Joomla! 1.5.x, you can view the contents of the Trash Manager at any time by clicking the option named Article Trash under the Content Menu. Clicking that option displays the Article Trash Manager in your browser, as shown in Figure 5.20.

The toolbar at the top of the Articles Trash Manager provides quick access to the following functions:

- **Restore:** Select one or more articles from the list and then click this icon to restore them and remove them from the Trash.
- **Delete:** Select one or more articles from the list and then click this icon to delete the items permanently.
- **Help:** Click to access the online Help files related to the active screen.

Below the toolbar and above the list of articles is the Filter field. The Filter works like a search box. Type a word or phrase into the field and then click Go. The page reloads and displays the results of the search. To clear the screen and return to a full listing, click the Reset button.

FIGURE 5.20

The Article Trash Manager interface in Joomla! 1.5.x.

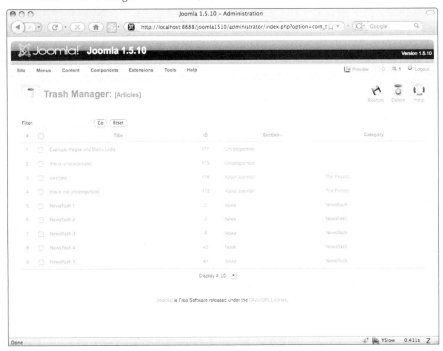

The main content area of the screen contains a list of all the articles in the Trash Manager. The columns provided are:

- **#** : An indexing number assigned by Joomla! This cannot be changed.
- **Checkbox (no label):** Click a checkbox to select a menu; this is needed if you want to use several of the previously referenced toolbar options.
- **Title:** This field displays the name of the article.
- **ID:** This is a system-generated ID number for the item and cannot be changed.
- **Section:** The section that the article is assigned to.
- **Category:** The category that the article is assigned to, if any.

Finally, at the bottom of the screen, below the content area, is the Display # option. Change the value in the combo box control to alter the number of articles that are displayed on the page. The default value can be altered by changing the List Length option on the Global Configuration Manager.

To move an article to the Trash, follow these steps:

1. **Click the Article Manager option under the Content menu.** The Article Manager opens in your browser.

2. **Click in the checkboxes next to the articles you want to remove.**

3. **Click the Trash icon on the top-right toolbar.** The system removes the articles to the Trash Manager.

Note

Any articles moved to the Trash will be instantly unpublished and not visible to site visitors.

Restoring articles from the Trash

Articles moved to the Trash are held there indefinitely until further action is taken by the administrator. Any article can be restored at any time. The process of restoring an item is simple and the result instantaneous: the article is removed from the Trash Manager and returned to where it was located when it was moved to the Trash.

Articles restored from the Article Trash are moved back to the section and category where they were located at the time they were moved to the Trash. The articles are returned to the previous location but will be unpublished and will be moved to the bottom of the order of articles. To manage the articles, access them under the Article Manager.

To restore an article from the Trash, follow these steps:

1. **Access the Article Trash Manager by clicking the option Article Trash under the Content menu.** The Article Trash Manager loads in your browser.

2. **Click the checkbox next to the article you want to restore.**

3. **Click the Restore icon on the top right toolbar.** The Restore Confirmation dialogue opens, as shown in Figure 5.21.

4. **Check the information; if correct, click the Restore button, or click the Cancel icon.** A confirmation window opens.

5. **Click OK.** The system removes the article from the Trash, restores it to its previous location, and then returns you to the Trash Manager.

FIGURE 5.21

The Restore Confirmation dialogue.

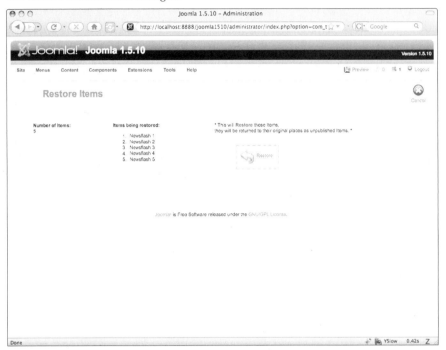

Permanently deleting articles

Articles and menu items held in the Trash Manager can be removed from the system by deleting them. Deleting an item from the Trash Manager results in the item's permanent removal from the system; it cannot be restored once deleted.

To permanently delete an article or menu item from the Trash, follow these steps:

1. **Click the checkbox next to the article or item you want to delete.**

2. **Click the Delete icon on the top-right toolbar.** The Delete Confirmation dialogue opens, as shown in Figure 5.22.

3. **Check the information; if correct, click the Delete button, or click the Cancel icon.** The system removes the article or item from the Trash, restores it to its previous location, and returns you to the Trash Manager.

FIGURE 5.22

The Delete confirmation dialogue.

Archiving articles

If you want to remove an article from the primary content area of your site, but do not want to delete it, you can move it to the Article Archive. By default, archived articles are not shown in the front end of the web site. You can, however, make archived articles accessible by publishing the Archive Module.

Archived articles are stored in the Article Manager, though the color of the listing changes from the default blue to a light gray, and the published icon changes to indicate archived content, as shown in Figure 5.23.

FIGURE 5.23

The Article Manager, showing at the top of the list a number of Archived Articles.

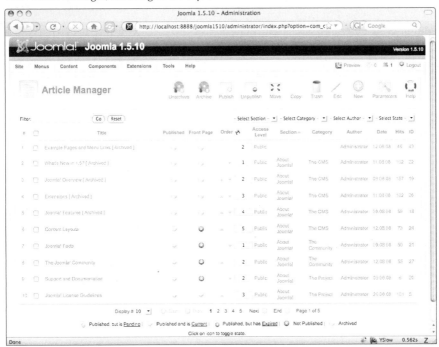

To archive an article, follow these steps:

1. **Access the Article Manager.**

2. **Click the checkbox next to the articles you want to archive.**

3. **Click the Archive icon on the top-right toolbar.** The system immediately moves the article to the archive and removes it from the general content area of the site.

Note

Archived articles cannot be edited. If you want to modify the content of an Archived Article you must unarchive it, edit it, and then archive it again.

Unarchiving articles

Articles that have been moved into the archive can be restored to the general content area of your site by unarchiving the article. Note that unarchived articles are restored unpublished.

To unarchive an article, follow these steps:

1. **Access the Article Manager.**

2. **Click the checkbox next to the articles you want to unarchive.**

3. **Click the Unarchive icon on the top-right toolbar.** The system immediately unarchives the article.

The Archive module

Articles that have been archived are not accessible to front-end site visitors unless the Archive module is published. The Archive module contains links to the articles, organized for view by date. The Archive module is, by default, unpublished. You will need to publish the module and assign it to the position and pages you desire before it can be used by the site visitors. This module is most often used in blog layouts where you want to group articles according to month published. Figure 5.24 shows the output of the Archive module.

FIGURE 5.24

The Archive module in action.

Cross-Reference

The Archive module is discussed in more detail in Chapter 17.

Global Check-in

When articles are in use by another user, or when an article has been left open in an editing window or improperly closed, Joomla! prevents another user from editing the article. This feature is designed to prevent users from overwriting each others' work and creating conflicts between editors.

Articles that are blocked from editing produce an error message when you try to access them from the admin system. If you need to access a blocked article for editing, you will need to force it to close. In Joomla!, the process of forcing an article to close is achieved by selecting the Global Check-in option under the Tools menu. Once you click on Global Check-in, all articles that are currently open and blocked for editing are forced to close.

Caution

The Global Check-in feature is necessary, but it also presents the possibility for problems. If your site has multiple administrators, be careful with this command because executing Global Check-in will check in all the articles; if someone else is working on an article at that time it can cause them to lose their unsaved work.

Summary

In this chapter, we have covered the various tasks associated with managing the articles on your site. You learned the following:

- How the Joomla! content hierarchy works
- How to create, edit, and delete articles
- How to create various site content structures
- How to configure the article parameters
- How to schedule and control publishing
- How to work with the Article Trash Manager
- How to work with archived content

Working with Editors and Media

To create attractive and usable articles in Joomla!, you need to have an understanding of the various Editor and Media Management options. Joomla! provides a number of article-editing choices. The system is bundled with a very good WYSIWYG editor, TinyMCE. Alternatively, you can choose to download and install the XStandard Lite editor. Finally, for those who prefer to work without an editor, you can also create content directly in HTML with only a text editor interface.

In addition to the editing tools, Joomla! is also bundled with a Media Manager that enables you to add and manage the media files in your web site without having to use an FTP folder. By using the editors in conjunction with the Media Manager, you can add images or other files to your articles quickly and easily, as I explain later in this chapter.

Using WYSIWYG Editors

WYSIWYG is an acronym for What You See Is What You Get. The term is used to describe content-editing tools that let you view your text formatting as you work. The interface for most of these tools is similar to what you might find in a typical desktop word processing tool, such as Microsoft Word.

WYSIWYG editors are easy to use and one of the most popular features of content management systems. Joomla! creators recognized the importance of the WYSIWYG editor and installed an excellent open source editor known as TinyMCE. Joomla! 1.5.x also includes an alternative: the XStandard Lite editor. Although XStandard Lite requires an additional download and a change in configuration, for some users it is the preferred option. Both editors are discussed in the following sections.

Using the TinyMCE editor

TinyMCE is a full-featured WYSIWYG editor with a number of configuration options that allow the site administrator to tailor the interface to suit the particular needs of the site. As you can see in Figure 6.1, the interface with its multiple toolbars above the content window is not dissimilar to what you might see in a desktop word processer. The tool works exactly the same as a desktop word processing application and enables you to view your work as you go.

TinyMCE is enabled in the default configuration.

FIGURE 6.1

The default TinyMCE editor interface. In the default system, the editor is in Advanced mode.

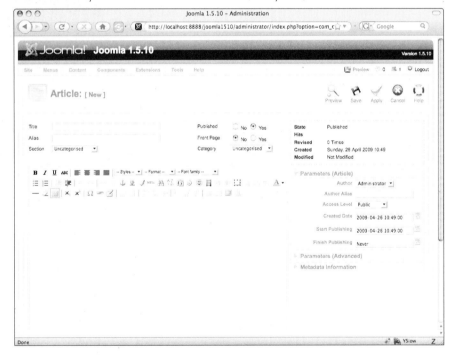

Top row controls

In the default configuration, the top row of the editor bar includes a set of controls focused on font formatting, styles, and alignment. The bar includes the following controls:

- **Bold:** Format text bold.
- **Italic:** Format text italic.
- **Underline:** Format text underline.
- **Strikethrough:** Format text strikethrough.
- **Align Left:** Align paragraph to the left.
- **Align Center:** Align paragraph to the center.
- **Align Right:** Align paragraph to the right.
- **Align Fully:** Fully align paragraph.
- **Styles:** Click to view and apply available styles.
- **Format:** Click to view and select HTML formatting.
- **Font Family:** Click to view and select font.

Middle row controls

In the default configuration, the middle row of the editor bar includes a set of controls focused on the insertion and formatting of various elements. The bar includes the following controls:

- **Bullet List:** Click to convert text to bulleted list.
- **Numbered List:** Click to convert text to numbered list.
- **Decrease Indent:** Click to decrease paragraph indentation.
- **Increase Indent:** Click to increase paragraph indentation.
- **Undo:** Click to undo the last action.
- **Re-do:** Click to re-apply the previous action.
- **Link:** Click to insert a link. Opens a pop-up window that allows you input the URL and set parameters and attributes.
- **Unlink:** Click to remove a link.
- **Insert Anchor:** Click to insert an anchor point in the text. Opens a pop-up window that allows you input parameters and attributes.

Note

Anchors are used to mark places inside an article that can be hyperlinked. This allows you to add accelerators to an article, providing a way for the user to jump to a specific place in the article by clicking on a link.

- **Insert Image:** Click to open the Insert Image dialogue, which allows you to add an image to an article. Discover the path information for your image file by using the Media Manager.
- **Cleanup Code:** Click this button and the system will attempt to clean up the HTML code for the text in the window. This is generally used where you have copied the code into the window from another source, like Microsoft Word. Copying formatted text from other

applications often leads to unnecessary code appearing in your article; this tool helps avoid that problem by eliminating the unnecessary code.

- **Toggle HTML Mode:** Click to switch from the WYSIWYG interface to a straight text editor, allowing you to edit the content and formatting in plain HTML. Click again to return to the WYSIWYG editor.

- **Find:** Click to open a window containing the Find and the Find and Replace controls. This control opens the same window as the Find and Replace control , but its shows a different tab on the resulting window.

- **Find and Replace:** Click to open a window containing the Find and the Find and Replace controls. This control opens the same window as the Find control , but its shows a different tab on the resulting window.

- **Insert Date:** Click to insert the current date.

- **Insert Time:** Click to insert the current time.

- **Insert Smilie:** Click to open a pop-up window containing an assortment of smilies you can add to your article.

- **Insert Embedded Media:** This control enables the easy insertion of embedded media files, such as Flash, Quicktime, Shockwave, Windows Media, and Real Media. Click the button to open the insertion dialogue. Click on the Advanced tab in the pop-up window to see additional controls used for Flash files.

- **Left to Right:** Select some text and this control becomes active. Click it to change the text orientation to Left to Right.

- **Right to Left:** Select some text and this control becomes active. Click it to change the text orientation to Right to Left.

- **Insert New Layer:** Click to insert a new layer. Click and drag the shape to alter the height and width. You can also edit the new layer by clicking on the HTML button and then changing the CSS for the layer directly. The order of the layer can be changed by using the next two controls.

- **Move to Front:** Click on a layer and then click this button to move the layer to the front of the order.

- **Move to Back:** Click on a layer and then click this button to move the layer to the back of the order.

- **Absolute Position:** Click to toggle absolute positioning of the elements in the article. This control is most useful for controlling the formatting of articles that contain multiple layers.

- **Select Font Color:** Click to open a palette window that allows you to select the color for the font.

Bottom row controls

In the default configuration, the bottom row of the editor bar includes a set of controls focused on tables and other miscellaneous controls. The bar includes the following controls:.

- **Insert Horizontal Rule:** Click to insert a horizontal rule at the location of the cursor in the text. The rule is created with the HTML tag HR and can be controlled by the styling set for that tag. Note that this tool is very similar to the Insert Horizontal Rule control.

- **Remove Formatting:** Highlight a segment of text and then click this icon to clear all formatting associated with that text.

- **Toggle Guidelines:** If your article is using any invisible elements, for example, multiple layers, click this icon to make the boundaries of the object visible and allow you to work with the object more easily.

- **Subscript:** Select text and click this icon to transform the text into lowered subscript.

- **Superscript:** Select text and click this icon to transform the text into raised superscript.

- **Insert a Custom Character:** Click to open a window containing a list of the custom characters available in the system. Click on a character in the pop-up window to insert it into the article.

- **Insert Horizontal Rule**: Click to open a window that allows you to specify the width, height, and styling of a horizontal rule. Note that this tool is very similar to the Horizontal Rule control.

- **Insert a New Table:** Click to insert a table into the article. A pop-up window opens that allows you to define the basic characteristics of the table. If you want to edit an existing table, click on the table and then click on this button to open the pop-up window for editing.

- **Table: Row Properties:** Click in a table cell and then click on this button to open a pop-up window that allows you to edit the characteristics of the row where the cell is located.

- **Table: Cell Properties:** Click in a table cell and then click on this button to open a pop-up window that allows you to edit the characteristics of the table cell.

- **Table: Insert Row Before:** Click in a table cell and then click on this button to insert a new row of empty cells above the row where the cell is located.

- **Table: Insert Row After:** Click in a table cell, then click on this button to insert a new row of empty cells below the row where the cell is located.

- **Table: Delete Row:** Click in a table cell and then click on this button to delete the row where the cell is located.

- **Table: Insert Column Before:** Click in a table cell and then click on this button to insert a new column of empty cells before the column where the cell is located.

- **Table: Insert Column After:** Click in a table cell and then click on this button to insert a new column of empty cells after the column where the cell is located.

- **Table: Delete Column:** Click in a table cell and then click on this button to delete the column where the cell is located.

- **Table: Split Cells:** Click in a merged table cell and then click on this button to split the cell into its original cells.

- **Table: Merge Cells:** Select more than one table cell and then click this button to merge the cells into one.

- **Toggle Full Screen Mode:** Click this button to open the editing window in full screen mode for easy editing.

- **Edit CSS Style:** Click to open a set of controls that let you tailor the styling of the text.

Cross-Reference

A number of the options outlined above can be turned off by editing the settings in the TinyMCE Plugin. The Plugins are discussed in Chapter 19.

Optional features

The TinyMCE Editor is powered by a plugin. The plugin is named Editor - TinyMCE 2.0 and can be accessed under the Plugin Manager. The plugin includes a number of parameters that dictate in part what controls are visible to the users of the editor. In addition to the controls discussed previously, several more are hidden in the default configuration.

Under the Plugin Advanced Parameters tab several optional features can be turned on for users:

- **XHTMLxtras:** Clicking the Show option for this Parameter adds to the Editor's toolbar six additional windows, including:

  - **Citation:** You can specify the styling for a citation.

  - **Abbreviation:** You can specify the styling for an abbreviation.

  - **Acronym:** You can specify the styling for an acronym.

  - **Insertion:** You can mark a change to the article as an insertion and add a date and other relevant information.

  - **Deletion:** You can mark a change to the article as a deletion and add a date and other elegant information.

  - **Insert Attributes:** You can add attributes to an object or text.

- **Template:** If the Parameter is set to Show, the users can choose from a set of predefined content templates for use in the article. Note that no default templates are in the system, so if you want to use this feature you must also define the templates.

- **Element Path:** Toggling the Element Path Parameter to On adds an accessibility feature to the editor. When Element Path is active, the bottom bar below the editing window shows the name of the HTML elements as you move the cursor in the article. This is intended as an aid to those using keyboard navigation.

Note

If you want to enable the templates feature in your TinyMCE editor, take a look at the documentation for that feature, as it is rather involved. Visit

    http://wiki.moxiecode.com/index.php/TinyMCE:Plugins/template.

Simple Mode

Simple Mode is an optional setting for the TinyMCE Editor. In Simple Mode, the editor interface includes only nine buttons: Bold, Italic, Underline, Strikethrough, Undo, Re-do, Cleanup Code, Bullet List, and Numbered List.

Figure 6.2 shows the Simple Mode interface.

FIGURE 6.2

The TinyMCE Editor interface in Simple Mode. Note that by default, the Simple Mode toolbar appears below the editing window.

Using the XStandard editor

The XStandard editor is an optional WYSIWYG editor for use in Joomla! 1.5.x. XStandard strives to provide an editor that is simple to use and fully accessibility-compliant. The XStandard editor generates code that is clean and complies with the XHTML Strict standard. The markup also meets the stringent requirements of the most common accessibility standards. Unfortunately, to use the editor, you must download and install the XStandard application on each machine that you want to use to edit your Joomla! site content. The XStandard Lite interface is shown in Figure 6.3.

FIGURE 6.3

The XStandard Lite editor interface.

Joomla! 1.6

Joomla! 1.6 does not come preconfigured to support the XStandard editor. Although it is possible to install it, you will need to do a complete manual installation, following the instructions on the developer's web site: http://www.xstandard.com/.

Installing XStandard

To install the XStandard editor in Joomla! 1.5.x, follow these steps:

1. Log in to the admin system.

2. Click on the option **Plugin Manager** under the **Extensions** menu. The Plugin Manager loads.

3. Click to enable the plugin names **Editor - XStandard Lite 2.0**.

4. Access the **Global Configuration Manager** by clicking the option **Global Configuration** under the **Site** menu. The Global Configuration Manager loads in your browser.

5. Select the option Editor - XStandard Lite 2.0 from the combo box by the option Default WYSIWYG Editor, located on the Site tab.

6. Click Save.

7. **Download the XStandard Lite component from the developer's web site and install it on the machine you plan to use for editing your Joomla! site.** Note that you must install the version relevant to your local machine's OS. Visit `http://xstandard.com` to download the editor's files.

The XStandard controls

The control and formatting options for the XStandard Lite are simpler than those for the TinyMCE editor. All controls are laid out in two rows at the top of the editing window.

Top row controls

The bar includes the following controls:

- **Styles:** Opens a combo box containing a list of styles. Apply a style by selecting the text first and then clicking to select the style.
- **Separator:** Inserts the HTML <HR> tag.
- **Hyperlink:** Inserts a hyperlink to a web address.
- **Attachment:** Inserts a link to a file for the user to download.
- **Directory:** Opens a dialogue that allows you to insert articles and special characters.
- **Edit:** Click to edit the HTML source code in a text editor format.
- **View Source:** Click to view the source of the article.
- **Screen Reader Preview:** Opena a preview of the article showing Screen Reader view.
- **Expand:** Expand the editing window to full screen.

Bottom row controls

The bar includes the following controls:

- **Bold:** Format text bold.
- **Italic:** Format text italic.
- **Underline:** Format text underline.
- **Strikethrough:** Format text strikethrough.
- **Align Left:** Align paragraph to the left.
- **Align Center:** Align paragraph to the center.
- **Align Right:** Align paragraph to the right.
- **Add Long Quotation:** Click to indent the text.
- **Remove Long Quotation:** Click to outdent the text.

- **Numbered List:** Click to insert a numbered list.
- **Bulleted List:** Click to insert a bulleted list.
- **Undo:** Undo a command.
- **Redo:** Redo a command.
- **Insert Layout Table:** Click to open a dialogue that enables you to set the properties of a table and inset it into the article.
- **Insert Data Table:** Click to open a dialogue that enables you to set the properties of a table and inset it into the article.
- **Draw Layout Table:** Click to draw a table by dragging the mouse to indicate the desired number of rows and columns.
- **Draw Data Table:** Click to draw a table by dragging the mouse to indicate the desired number of rows and columns.

Configuration options

The XStandard Editor is powered by a plugin named Editor - XStandard Lite 2.0 that includes a parameter that allows you to switch between different configuration modes. The default mode provides the WYSIWYG editor interface and the toolbars previously outlined. Two other options are available:

- **Source:** When this option is selected, the users of the editing window see a very different toolbar with a source editing window. The Source toolbar includes only nine options, many of them concerned with the visibility of the source in the editing window.
- **Screen Reader:** Select the Screen Reader option to start the editor with the Screen Reader launched. Note the toolbars displayed in this configuration option are the same as those shown in the default setting.

Working with the No Editor option

It is possible to work directly with the HTML source behind the article by selecting the HTML editing option on either of the WYSIWYG editors, or by selecting the option No Editor in the Global Configuration Manager. In any event, the result is a plain text-editing window that enables you to type HTML formatting tags directly into the window, as shown in Figure 6.4.

The choice to work with or without the WYSIWYG tools is largely a matter of personal preference. Although a slight performance improvement can be seen when working with the configuration set to No Editor, it will not be an issue for the vast majority of users. For most, the convenience of having the easy-to-use WYSIWYG formatting options far outweighs the inconvenience of a slight delay in loading times.

FIGURE 6.4

The article editing interface shown in Joomla! 1.5.x with Global Configuration set to No Editor.

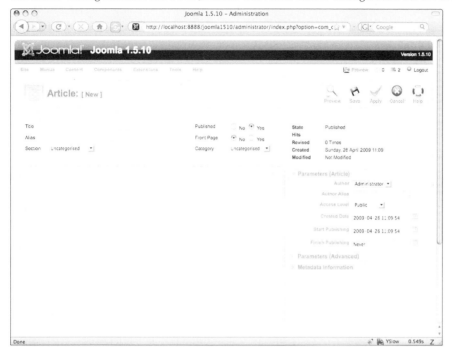

Tip

If you have multiple content contributors, I recommend that you enable at least one of the WYSIWYG editors and set it to the default role. Those users who prefer to work with the HTML code can always toggle the view to show the HTML editing window. Also, do not forget that it is possible to allow registered users to select which editor they can use and therefore it may be desirable to enable more than one. This ability only applies to users assigned to the group Authors or higher.

Cross-Reference

Enabling the ability for users to select their preferred editor is discussed in Chapter 11.

Overview of the Media Manager

The Media Manager provides Joomla! site administrators with the ability to add images and other media files to the system and to help keep those files organized. After you have added the files to the system, you can use the Media Manager to preview images and discover the paths to files so that you can insert them into the articles on your site.

Although it is possible to manage your media files via FTP, the helpful interface and features of the Media Manager make it an attractive alternative. For those who lack FTP access to their server, the Media Manager is indispensable.

Either method results in the display of the Media Manager interface, as shown in Figure 6.5.

FIGURE 6.5

The Media Manager interface shown in the default Thumbnail View with the sample data loaded.

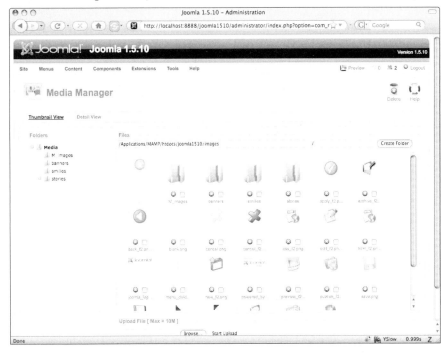

The toolbar at the top of the Media Manager provides quick access to the Delete and Help functions:

- **Delete:** Select one or more items from the list and then click this icon to delete the items permanently.
- **Help:** Click to access the online help files related to the active screen.

Below the toolbar and above the list of items are two text links used for changing the view shown in the Media Manager. The default view is Thumbnail View, which shows a larger image and less information. The Detail View, in contrast, shows a smaller image but more information about each file, as shown in Figure 6.6.

In either view, the workspace of the screen contains a list of all the items in the Media Manager and the controls to view them.

FIGURE 6.6

The Menu Media Manager interface shown in Detail View with the sample data loaded.

Note

By default, the Media Manager shows you the contents of the /images directory. The contents are not affected by the decision whether to install the sample data.

The Folders area on the left of the workspace displays a directory tree that shows all the Media folders in your system. The folders shown are the contents of the /images directory on your server. In addition to the images files located in the root directory, the default system includes the following directories:

- **M_images:** Contains small images commonly used for controls and field labels that appear on pages.

- **banners:** The default Joomla! banner ads that are loaded into the Banner Manager Component.

- **smilies:** A set of generic smilies (also known as *emoticons*).

- **stories:** Images used to illustrate sections, categories, and articles. There are two sub-directories here, food and fruit. The sub-directories contain sample images that can be used in articles.

Clicking on the names of any of the directories in the Folders area displays the contents of the directory in the Files area on the right of the workspace. At the top of the Files area, the path of the directory is displayed. Underneath the path is a set of thumbnails representing the contents of the active directory. The green arrow at the top left of the set of thumbnails is a navigation tool that lets you move up to a higher directory, where one exists. The other thumbnails in the Files area show the sub-directories inside the active directory, if any, and the media files, if any.

Note

Inside the default Media Manager installation there is a directory named /smilies that contains a set of graphical smilies, or "emoticons." Note that the emoticons in the smilies folder are different from the ones you see in the TinyMCE WYSIWYG editor. The emoticons shown under the WYSIWYG editor's Insert emotion control are not managed by the Media Manager, instead they are located at /plugins/editors/tinymce/jscripts/tiny_mce/ plugins/emotions/images.

Where the thumbnails indicate image files, clicking on the thumbnail causes the image to open in a light box for you to view. You can close the light box by clicking anywhere on the screen. Where the thumbnail represents other types of media files, for example, a PDF or a PowerPoint document, you cannot open a view of the file, and the thumbnail that is shown is a generic image used to represent the file type.

Below each thumbnail you can see a red circle with an x inside and a checkbox. Clicking the red circle with the x deletes the file. Clicking inside the checkbox selects the file, which enables you to select multiple items and delete them all simultaneously by using the Delete icon on the top-right toolbar. At the very bottom is the name of the file. You can click on the name to view the file inside the workspace, without a pop-up window.

Two other controls appear on the page. At the top right of the Files area is a blank text field next to a button labeled Create Folder. You use this control to add new sub-directories to the system. Below the Files area is the Upload File function, which enables you to add additional media files to the system. Both are discussed later in this chapter.

Clicking the Detail View text link changes the view of the Media Manager, shown in Figure 6.6. This view option changes the format of the Files area to display the following columns:

- **Preview:** Opens a light box view of the image. Note this only functions if the file is an image file.
- **Image Name:** The name of the file. Though the column is labeled Image Name, it shows the name of all media files, regardless of whether they are in fact images.
- **Dimensions:** The width and height of the image in pixels. This is only relevant where the file is an image file.
- **Size:** The size of the file. This is expressed in bytes or kilobytes (Kb).
- **Delete:** Click either the red circle to delete the file immediately or click the checkbox and then the Delete icon on the top toolbar.

Working With Media Files

The primary purpose of the Media Manager is to move files onto the server so that you can use them on your site. To enable this ability, you want to preview images, obtain file dimensions and sizes, and eventually obtain the paths to the files so that they can be added to your site articles. All of these functions are possible within the Media Manager.

Viewing file information

The Detail view (refer to Figure 6.6) provides the most information at a glance. You can preview files, find the filenames or discover the file paths in either Thumbnail or Detail view. If you need the file dimensions or size, you can find that information easiest with Detail view.

Uploading files

Additional media files can be added to your system either by accessing the server directly via FTP or by using the upload function in the Media Manager. Although FTP may be preferable in situations where you need to move large numbers of files, the default uploader function in the Joomla! Media Manager is fast and convenient for single file uploads.

In addition to the default uploader, the system also includes an optional Flash uploader that can be enabled through the Global Configuration Manager. The Flash uploader enables you to designate multiple files for upload and then upload them all simultaneously. If you are looking to move large numbers of files into your system and do not want to use FTP, or if you plan to frequently upload more than one file at a time, you should consider enabling the Flash uploader because it will save you time over the default uploader. The Flash Uploader is shown in Figure 6.7.

Cross-Reference

The Global Configuration Manager is discussed in Chapter 4.

To add a new file to your system using the Media Manager, follow these steps:

1. **Log in to the admin system of your site.**

2. **Access the Media Manager by clicking on the option Media Manager under the Site menu.** The Media Manager opens in your browser.

3. **Click the Browse button on the Upload File area at the bottom of the Media Manager interface.** A pop-up window opens.

4. **Navigate through the pop-up window to locate the file you want to upload and then click the Open button on the pop-up window.** The name of the file appears in the text field to the left of the Browse button.

5. **Click the Start Upload button.** The system uploads the file to the active directory and return to the Media Manager. A confirmation message and a thumbnail for the file should be visible in the Media Manager.

FIGURE 6.7

The optional Flash Uploader in action.

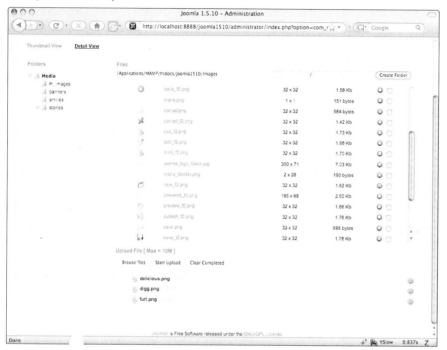

Note

By default, the system accepts not only all common image file types but also other common file types, including Flash files, PowerPoint files, and various document formats. The maximum file size in the default system is set to 10MB. Permissible file types and maximum file sizes can be modified by changing the settings in the System section of the Global Configuration Manager.

Alternatively, if you want to add media files via FTP, place the files inside the /images directory on your server. Any files placed inside the directory will show up in the Media Manager. Similarly, if you use FTP to create any sub-directories inside /images, your new directories will show up in the Media Manager. Files and directories uploaded via FTP to those locations can thereafter be managed by the Media Manager without limitation.

Organizing files

By default, the files included in the default system are organized into the directories you see in the Folders area of the Media Manager. You can create new sub-directories and upload new files to any of the directories in the Media Manager. It is also possible to delete files and directories from within the Media Manager.

Unfortunately, files in the system cannot be easily moved from one directory to another. The only way around this limitation is to download the file and then upload it again to the directory of your choosing. Although a download option is not included in the Media Manager you can easily download image files in the system by following these steps:

1. **Access the Media Manager and find the image file you want to download.**

2. **Click on the file's name.** The file appears alone in the Files area of the Media Manager.

3. **Right click on the file.** A menu appears.

4. **Select the Save File As option.** A dialogue window opens.

5. **Navigate to where you want to save the file on your local computer and then click Save.** The system downloads the file to your local machine and then returns you to the Media Manager.

After the file is on your local machine, you can upload it to the directory of your choice by using either the uploader in the Media Manager or by using FTP, as discussed in the preceding section.

Deleting one or more files is easy to do. To delete files one at a time, simply click the red circle with the x that appears on each file. To delete multiple files, click the checkboxes next to the files and then click the Delete icon on the top-right toolbar.

Caution

Be cautious deleting files. Deletion is instantaneous — there is no confirmation or warning dialogue. Deletion is also permanent — files are removed from the system, not moved to the Trash Manager.

New directories can be added to the system using the Create Folder control on the Media Manager. Each new directory will be a sub-directory of the /images folder. To create a new sub-directory to hold your media files, follow these steps:

1. **Access the Media Manager.**

2. **In the Folders area of the Media Manager, click the name of the directory you want to be the parent directory.** The contents displays in the Files area.

3. **Type a name for the new sub-directory in the text field next to the Create Folder button.**

4. **Click Create Folder.** The system creates a new directory. The new directory appears in the Folders area of the Media Manager.

Adding files to articles

The most common reason for adding files to a system is to make them available for use in the site's articles. Although getting files into the Media Manager takes care of one important task, that is, adding files to your Joomla! system, it does not enable you to automatically place the files inside your site's articles.

Depending on what you are trying to accomplish, you want to either insert the file into the article or simply display a link to the file. To make an image visible, for example, you want to insert it into the article. If, on the other hand, you wish to enable visitors to download a file, you can insert into the article a link to the file. In either event, you must first discover the path the file. After you know the path to the file, you can use the WYSIWYG editor of your choice to insert the file or the URL.

To obtain the path to an image file, simply right-click on the file's name in the media manager and copy the link. Typically, this is done by selecting from the right-click menu the option Copy Link Location. You can now either paste the link into the appropriate place in the WYSIWYG editor or into an external document for later reference.

To obtain the path to a non-image file type, you need to look at the path information at the top of the Files area and append to the end of that path the name of the file.

Summary

In this chapter, we have covered the use of the system's various default Editor options and the use of the Media Manager. You learned the following:

- How to use the TinyMCE editor
- How to use the XStandard Lite editor
- How to edit Articles without a WYSIWYG editor
- How to view files with the Media Manager
- How to upload files to the Media Manager
- How to organize files in the Media Manager
- How to delete files from the Media Manager
- How to add files in the Media Manager to articles

Employing Advanced Content Management Techniques

I n previous chapters, I discuss the basics of Joomla! content management. In this chapter, I take a look at some of the more advanced techniques that help you create a richer content experience for your visitors and also look at the tools that enable you to set up alternative content management work flows.

The modules included with the default system provide numerous options for displaying content on your site. Additionally, functions like the Newsfeeds component, the Feed Display module, and the wrappers allow you to bring external content into your site. This chapter discusses how to integrate these options into your site and make them part of the content mix.

Joomla! also enables you to allow visitors to submit articles to your site and to create a workflow around content contributed from the front end. The system provides a number of tools to enable this functionality, thereby giving you another way to add interactivity to your site and build community with your users. This chapter examines front-end content management in depth.

Using Content Display Modules

The modules included with your Joomla! site provide a variety of options for displaying content on the pages of your site. Although a number of the modules only provide links to your articles, such as the Latest News or the Sections module, others actually display content items on the page. This section looks at the two key Joomla! modules that provide content display: the Custom HTML module and the Newsflash module. Later in this chapter I also look at the Feed Display module you can use to show Newsfeed output on your pages.

Using the Custom HTML module

The Custom HTML module is a blank canvas that you can use to display content of your choosing. It is nothing more than an empty container designed to hold text, images, or a mix of the two. The module provides no content of its own, rather it gives you an empty text box and a WYSIWYG editor that allows you to create and edit the content as you see fit. You can either copy and paste content into the module or create it from scratch, complete with full formatting.

Cross-Reference

The Custom HTML module is discussed in more detail in Chapter 17.

One of the most common uses for this module is to create a short excerpt or synopsis of an article or another feature on your site, together with a link to the full article or feature. When used in this fashion, the module functions as a teaser that encourages people to click and explore your site further. Although it is not possible to automatically display an article or its intro text inside of the module, the Custom HTML module enables you to manually create this. Simply copy and paste part of the article into a module, add a link to the full article; then publish the module where you want the teaser to appear.

To make your own teaser module, follow these steps:

1. **Log in to the admin system of your site.**
2. **Click on the option Article Manager, under the Content menu.** The Article Manager loads in your browser.
3. **Click on the name of the article you want to use as the subject of your teaser module.** The article editing window opens.
4. **Copy the portion of the text you want to use as the teaser content in the module.**
5. **Click the Cancel icon.** The Article Editing dialogue closes and returns you to the Article Manager.
6. **Click the option Module Manager under the Extensions menu.** The Module Manager opens.
7. **Click the New icon on the top-right toolbar.** The New Module dialogue opens.
8. **Click the option Custom HTML. Select the Next icon.** The next step of the New Module dialogue opens.
9. **Give your new module a name.**
10. **Select a position for the module.**
11. **Set the pages upon which the module appears by selecting the menu items from the Menu Selection combo box.**
12. **Paste the text you copied from the article into the text box.**
13. **Enter a hard return at the end of the text and then add the words Read more. . .**

14. **Hyperlink the words Read more. . . to the full article.**

15. **Click the Save icon on the top-right toolbar.** The system creates and save your new module and exit the Module editing window, returning you to the Module Manager.

The Newsflash Module provides a different way to reach a similar result.

Using the Newsflash module

The Newsflash module is used to display the first few sentences of one or more articles. If you've loaded the sample data with your Joomla! site, you can see the Module in action, because it is used to display random article content at the top of the pages. Figure 7.1 shows the output as it appears on the default Joomla! site.

FIGURE 7.1

The Newsflash Module's output, shown here as it is implemented in the default site with the sample data installed.

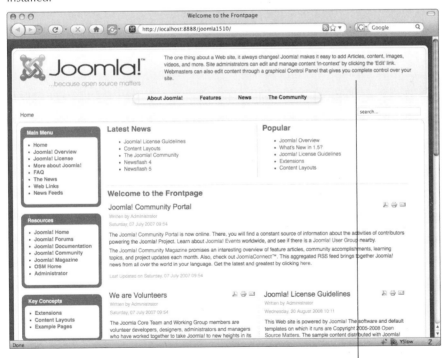

Outupt of the Newsflash Module

Cross-Reference

See Chapter 17 for more information on the Newsflash module.

The ability to display at random the first few sentences from articles in a specific content category is only one way that this module can be used. It can also be configured to show part of a single article or part of a group of articles drawn from a specific section and category.

The module is configured through the module parameters. The parameters can be set to display any of the following:

- The introductory sentences from articles chosen at random from a specific category. The article shown changes each time the page is reloaded. (This configuration is used in the default site.)

- The introductory sentences from a specific article, with a read more link to the full article. This configuration is similar to the teaser module used as an example in the previous section.

- The introductory sentences from a specific article, without a read more link.

- The introductory sentences from multiple articles in a specific category, with read more links to the full articles.

- The introductory sentences from multiple articles in a specific category, without read more links.

If you elect to use the randomization feature, you will only see one article at a time, in a fixed layout. However, if you want to show multiple articles, you can set the number of articles shown and whether they are shown in a horizontal or a vertical layout.

Note

There are a couple of important limitations that you need to keep in mind when using this module. You cannot set the amount of text that is shown; this is set by the system. Also note that the order of the articles shown is based on their order within the category; if you need to re-order the display in the module, you have to change the order of the articles inside the category; depending on how your site is configured; this may impact the display of content in other areas of the site.

Cross-Reference

See Chapter 5 for more information on reordering articles within a category.

Placing modules inside articles

Ordinarily, module output is confined to the spaces around the main content area of your page — the left or right sides, or above or below the main content area. The placement of the modules is defined by their assignment to the Module Position Holders that have been specified in the site's template.

Cross-Reference

See Chapter 20 for more information on working with the Module Position Holders inside template files.

In some cases, however, you may want to place a module inside of the content area of a page. If that page contains an article, you can do so. Joomla! makes it possible to put a module directly inside an article; all you need to do is type a bit of code into the text of the article. The result appears similar to what you see in Figure 7.2.

FIGURE 7.2

The text area in the editing window shows a Module Position holder embedded in an article, in this case creating a Module Position Holder named "insidearticle."

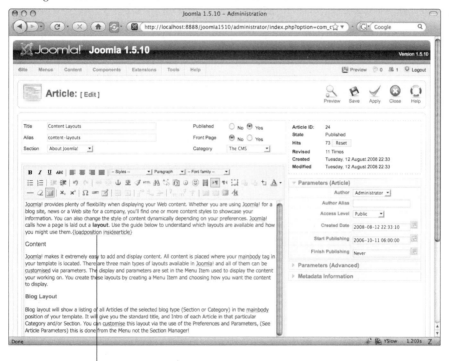

Module position holder code

To insert a module inside of the content area of an article, open the Article Editing dialogue and then follow these steps:

1. **Place the cursor where you want the module output to appear.**

2. **Type the following code {loadposition modulepositionname}, where "modulepositionname" is the name you want to use for this specific Module Position Holder.**

3. **Click the Save icon at the top right.** The system saves the article with the new Module Position Holder in place and exits the Article Editing dialogue, returning you to the Article Manager.

4. **Click the Module Manager option, under the Extensions menu.** The Module Manager loads.

5. **Click the name of the module you want to place inside the article.** The Module Editing dialogue opens.

6. **In the Position field, type the name you gave the Module Position inside the article;** in this example, that name would be modulepositionname.

7. **Click the Save icon at the top right.** The system saves you changes and the Module Editing dialogue closes and returns you to the Module Manager.

Note

Take special note of the syntax used by the code: {loadposition xxx}, where xxx is the name of the Module Position Holder. You can use any name you want for the Module Position Holder, as long as it is not in use elsewhere.

As a general rule, it is better not to use a common name for Module Position Holders placed inside of articles. A unique and distinctive name for the Module Position Holder avoids confusion with traditional Module Position Holders and avoids the necessity to make sure that there is a menu selection for the page; you can simply set the module's Menu Assignment to All, without fear that the module will show on undesired pages or positions.

Tip

The capability to place modules inside articles is enabled by the Joomla! Plugin named Content - Load Module. By default, the Content - Load Module Plugin is enabled, but if for some reason it is not, then you need to enable it from the Plugin Manager before you can use this technique.

Cross-Reference

The Plugin Manager and the Content - Load Module plugin are discussed in more detail in the Chapter 19.

Bringing External Content into Your Site

Creating content for a site and then keeping that content maintained is one of the biggest challenges of site ownership. Joomla! provides a variety of tools that enable you to bring external content into your site, thereby providing you with fresh and updated content created by others. The various tools and techniques available in the default system are covered in the following sections.

Using wrappers

A wrapper is an iFrame that allows you to display a web page inside of either a module or the content area of a page. The wrapper essentially creates a page within a page, where the embedded page can be either from your own site, or from an external source. The page that is being wrapped maintains all its functionality, including navigation and other features.

Wrappers are used most frequently to perform one of the following tasks:

- Display another page from your Joomla! site — a form, for example.
- Display a non-Joomla! page that is located on your server.
- Display a page that is located on a different server.
- Display output from an application that is located on your server.

Caution

Although wrappers provide an easy way to display third-party content inside your site, care must be taken to avoid infringing on the intellectual property rights of others. Unless you have the permission of the site owner, displaying the content of other sites inside your site is not appropriate, especially if doing so gives others the impression that the content is yours.

To create a wrapper inside of the content area of a page, use the Wrapper Menu Item Type. To wrap a web page and display it inside of a module position, use the Wrapper module. In either case, you can use the configuration options to gain limited control over the appearance of the wrapper. Note, however, that generally you have very little control over what happens within a wrapper unless you also control the web page that is being wrapped.

Cross-Reference

See Chapter 8 for details on the Wrapper Menu Item Type, and go to Chapter 17 for more information on the Wrapper module.

Displaying syndicated content

Syndicated content — RSS feeds, Atom feeds, and the like — provide a convenient source of ready-to-use content. Joomla! gives you two methods for bringing syndicated content into your site.

To display news feed content within the content area of the page, use the Newsfeed component in conjunction with the Single Feed Layout Menu Item Type. Though the Newsfeed component is most commonly used to aggregate multiple syndicated news feeds and display them based upon categories, you can also use the Menu Item Type named Single Feed Layout to display the contents of a single feed within the content area of a page, as shown in Figure 7.3.

Cross-Reference

See Chapter 8 for more information on the Newsfeed component.

Alternatively, if you want to display feed content in a module position, use Joomla!'s Feed Display module. The Feed Display module is independent of the Newsfeed component. Instead of drawing content from one of the news feeds contained in the Newsfeed component, you input the URL of the news feed into the module parameters.

FIGURE 7.3

The result of creating a Single Feed Layout Menu Item Type to display the content of the Joomla! Announcements newsfeed.

Cross-Reference

Turn to Chapter 17 to find out more about the Feed Display module.

Managing Content from the Front End

While the vast majority of site administrators manage their site content exclusively through the administration interface, Joomla! does provide the option to manage content from the front end. The technique has limitations, but it is a useful option that some will find attractive. In the following sections I discuss the pros and cons and how this option can be structured effectively.

Understanding advantages and limitations

One of the more under-used and under-documented features of Joomla! is the front-end content management functionality. The system is set up by default to allow certain classes of users to be able to submit, edit, and publish content from the front end of the web site. This functionality is intended to give administrators the option to open the site up for community contribution without having to give users access to the admin system of your Web site.

With proper planning, you can make this functionality useful and practical; however this feature is neither obvious nor intuitive and it does require a bit of explanation. To use front-end content management, you need to configure the site properly and publish the right tools for the users (see Figure 7.4). You also need to pay particular attention to creating the proper user accounts to create a practical workflow. The various user categories carry different privileges and you must decide what is optimal for your site.

Front-end content management has several significant limitations:

- It is not possible to create or manage sections, categories, or menu items from the front end.

- Authors cannot edit their own articles prior to publication of the article.

- You must consider carefully the suitability of the site template. While the back end is tailored to handling the content-editing window and the WYSIWYG editor, front-end content management has to be done inside a site template.

- The system lacks a proper alert system to automatically notify higher-level users when content has been added to the system or is waiting to be edited or published.

Tip

You may want to consider installing a clean and fast template with a wide content area on your site. You can then assign that template specifically to the Submit an Article Menu Item. Doing this gives your content contributors a suitable workspace. Note, however, that this technique provides a suitable interface for article creation, but it does not help you with editing content from the front end; published articles use the template to which the articles are assigned. See Chapter 20 for a discussion of installing and assigning templates.

Though submitting content from the front end is useful for providing your site visitors with a way to contribute to your site, as a site administrator you are unlikely to want to manage your content from the front end. Front-end content management is generally slower and more difficult than working from within the admin system because the admin system content management interface provides more tools and a greater range of options. For the same reason, the users that you assign to edit the articles may prefer to work through the admin system. You can decide whether your site security concerns outweigh the practical advantages of granting back-end access.

Enabling user-created content

The first step to setting up front-end content management is to create users with the necessary privileges. To contribute or edit content on the front end, a user must have privileges higher than a Registered User (Author status or higher). The Special access level is specifically designed to help set up front-end content management.

The front-end Submit an Article page, shown here as it is seen by a user with Author level privileges.

You also want to make sure that all the necessary tools your contributors need are set to the appropriate access level. The access level named Special is intended to help enable front-end content management. Only users assigned to the Author group or higher are able to view items that have been set to Special; therefore you will want to set the access levels of the menu items intended for your content contributors to Special in order to limit their access.

The article submission form is the key to content creation. By default, the system has included in the User menu a menu item named Submit an Article; this is the article submission form. Clicking on the Submit an Article link takes the user to a page containing a blank article form, thereby allowing the user to create a new article and assign it to a section and category.

Editing is enabled by default; whenever a user with appropriate access levels is logged in, an edit icon appears on each article, as shown in Figure 7.5. Clicking on the editing icon opens an editing dialogue inside the current template, thereby allowing the user to make and save their changes.

Tip

If you do not want to use the default User menu, you will need to provide some other way for users to access the content submission form. There is a dedicated Menu Item Type that provides this functionality: Article Submission Layout.

FIGURE 7.5

The Article Editing icon, as seen by an authenticated front-end user with sufficient access privileges.

Editing icon

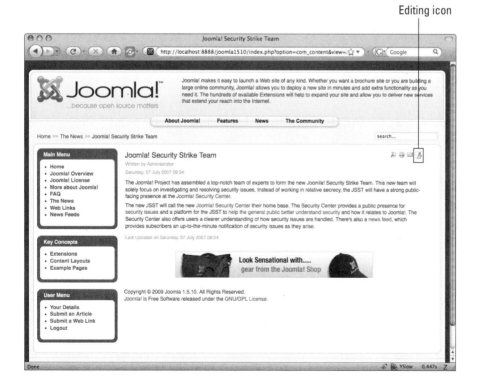

Cross-Reference

Managing menus and creating new menu items is covered in Chapter 8.

Workflow options

The three user groups focused on front-end content management are Authors, Editors, and Publishers. Each of the three has different capabilities and privileges. Having an awareness of the varying roles enables you to create a usable and practical workflow for your site's front-end content management.

Authors

Of all the user groups that are useful for front-end content management, Authors enjoy the fewest privileges and the most restrictions. Authors can perform a limited set of front-end content management tasks. They can:

- Create new articles.
- Assign the article to a section and category.
- Schedule the an article (though it will not publish until approved by someone with at least Publisher access).
- Assign the article to the front page.
- Create article metadata.
- Change the section or category assignment of their own published articles.
- Edit their own published articles.

Authors cannot publish their articles, nor can they edit the work of others. Also, unlike Editors and Publishers, Authors cannot edit unpublished articles — not even their own. Figure 7.6 shows an unpublished article ready to be edited or published.

Caution

As Authors lack the ability to edit unpublished articles, once an Author clicks the Save button on their article, they lose the ability to edit the article! This problem can be significant because it means that the Author must create the article and do any revisions on it before he clicks the Save button. When it is saved, it goes into the queue where it has to be approved by a higher level user. After the article is approved and published, the Author can edit it.

Editors

Editors are able to perform the following tasks:

- Create new articles.
- Assign the article to a Section and category.

- Schedule the article (though it will not publish until approved by someone with at least Publisher access).

- Assign the article to the front page.

- Create article metadata.

- Change the section or category assignment of articles.

- Edit any article, published or unpublished.

The key difference between an Author and an Editor is that an Editor can make changes to any article, regardless of who wrote it or its publication state.

FIGURE 7.6

The highlighted article at the top of this page shows an unpublished article, which can be edited by clicking on the edit icon.

Publishers

The Publisher user group is by far the most useful of the three dedicated front-end content management user groups. Publishers can perform all the key functions necessary to create and publish content on a site:

- Create new articles.
- Assign the article to a section and category.
- Schedule the article.
- Assign the article to the front page.
- Create article metadata.
- Change the section or category assignment of articles.
- Edit any article, published or unpublished.
- Publish or unpublish an article.

Although the Publisher user group has significant privileges, there are several key content management functions that they lack; Publishers cannot perform the following tasks:

- Create new sections.
- Create of new categories.
- Copy, move, or delete sections or categories.
- Create, modify, or delete sections of menus.
- Create, modify, or delete menu items.

All the tasks listed immediately above require back-end admin system access.

Tip

The Manager user group is another option to consider. Managers are the lowest level user granted back-end admin system access. The privileges they enjoy are not dramatically greater than those enjoyed by Publishers. Not only can they manage Sections Categories and menu Items, but they also have access to the more powerful and easy-to-use content management tools located in the admin system. As a result, you may want to consider granting one or more users Manager level access as an alternative to Publisher access.

One approach to improving workflow in Joomla! 1.5.x

If you decide that the three-tier front-end content management system is needed for your site, you may want to consider employing the following suggestion as a way to improve the workflow.

As noted earlier, one of the limitations of the system is the lack of an automatic notification system. The more complex your front-end content management structure, the more important this limitation becomes. As Authors contribute articles, the Editors have to be notified, and then the Editors have to find the contributed articles and edit them. Once the articles are edited, the Editors need to notify the Publisher who again has to find the articles and publish them.

An effective workaround for this problem is to create a dedicated section with two categories for the use of the front-end content team. Set up the following:

1. Create a new section, name it Submissions.

2. Set the access level for the section named Submissions to Special.

3. Create two new categories inside the new section. Name the categories To be Edited and To be Published.

4. Create a new menu item on the User menu. Select the Menu Item Type Category List Layout. Name the new item To be Edited, and select in the Basic Parameters the category To be Edited.

5. Create another new menu item on the User menu. Select the Menu Item Type Category List Layout. Name the new item To be Published, and select in the Basic Parameters the category To be Published.

All the tools are in place; now you need to instruct your team to use them.

- Instruct the Authors to assign all new articles to the category To be Edited.

- Instruct the Editors to check the To be Edited menu item when they log in. After they complete their edits on the articles, the Editors must re-assign the articles to the category To be Published.

- Instruct the Publishers to check the To be Published menu item when they log in. The Publishers can then assign the articles to the proper sections and categories and publish the articles.

This approach has the added advantage of allowing you to set a specific template to the entire front-end content management workflow. As discussed earlier in this chapter, you may want to use a template that is tailored to front-end content management tasks. A wide template makes it easier to use the editing window, and a clean template without unnecessary graphics or module assignments can also speed your work.

Syndicating Your Articles

You can syndicate the primary content from your Joomla! site through the use of RSS. The Syndication module enables this functionality. In the default configuration, there is one Syndication module enabled and published at the bottom left of the front page of the site, inside the Syndicate Module Position, as shown in Figure 7.7.

The RSS syndication icon shown published on the Front Page of the default site.

Users who click on the Syndication icon that appears on the page are taken to a page that contains the content, formatted for RSS. Users can copy this link and paste it into their favorite news reader (feed reader) application so stay abreast of changes to the front page of your site.

Tip

The default Joomla! Syndication module always shows the text Feed Entries next to the icon, even when you delete the module title from the module. To work around this bug, enter a space, surrounded by double quotes (" ").

Summary

In this chapter, we covered the various advanced tasks associated with managing the content on your site. You learned the following:

- How to use the system's content display modules
- How to display modules inside of content items
- How to bring external content into your site using wrappers and news feeds
- How to set up and use front-end content management
- How to enable RSS syndication of your content items

Working with the Menu System

M enus are used to create the principal navigation links on the pages of your web site. Joomla! provides a number of tools for creating and controlling your menus. The constituent parts of Joomla's menu system are the menu items, which are grouped together into menus that are displayed on the page through the use of menu modules. Mastering the menu system means gaining an awareness of how these parts are created and managed.

The Menu Manager enables the creation of the menus. Each individual menu is the subject of a dedicated Menu Item Manager and one or more menu modules. The Menu Item Manager handles the creation and configuration of the items on the menu, while the module handles the actual display of the menu on the page. You control the placement of the menus by assigning the various modules to the desired module positions.

In this chapter, I go through the creation and management of menu and menu items.

Introducing the Menu Manager

The Menu Manager is a standard Joomla! component and is included with the default Joomla! system. You will use the Menu Manager to create and manage all the menus on your Web site. To access the Menu Manager, select the option named Menus on the admin navigation bar, and then select the option Menu Manager. The Menu Manager interface loads in your browser. Figure 8.1 shows the Menu Manager as it appears in Joomla! 1.5.x with sample data installed.

FIGURE 8.1

The Joomla! 1.5.x Menu Manager interface.

The toolbar at the top of the Menu Manager provides quick access to the following functions:

- **Copy:** Select a menu from the list and then click this icon to publish it.
- **Delete:** Select a menu from the list and then click this icon to delete the menu.
- **Edit:** Select a menu from the list and then click this icon to edit the menu details.
- **New:** Click to add a new menu.
- **Help:** Click to access the online Help files related to the active screen.

The main content area of the screen contains a list of all the menus in your Joomla! site. The columns provided are:

- **#:** An indexing number assigned by Joomla! This number cannot be changed.
- **Radio Button** (no label): Click a radio button to select a menu; this is needed if you wish to use several of the toolbar options, referenced above.
- **Title:** This field displays the full name of the menu. Click the name to edit the menu's details.

- **Type:** This field displays the system name for the menu. The creator of the menu sets this.
- **Menu Item(s):** This icon is a link to the Menu Item Manager for each particular menu. Click to jump to that screen.
- **# Published:** Shows the number of menu items published on the menu.
- **# Unpublished:** Shows the number of menu items unpublished on the menu.
- **# Trash:** Shows the number of menu items currently in the trash.
- **# Modules:** Indicates how many menu modules are associated with this menu.
- **ID:** The system-generated user ID number.

Finally, at the bottom of the screen, below the content area, is the Display # option. Change the value in the combo box control to alter the number of menus that are displayed on the page. The default value can be altered by changing the List Length option on the Global Configuration Manager.

Joomla 1.6

The Joomla! 1.6 Menu Manager interface is slightly different in appearance from the Joomla! 1.5.x Menu Manager, but the functionality is almost exactly the same.

Creating and Managing Menus

All the front-end menus in the system are created and managed through the Menu Manager. The sample data included with the Joomla! 1.5.x system includes a number of different menus, including the Main menu, the User menu, the Top menu, the Resources menu, Example Pages, and Key Concepts menus. Those menus can be edited to change their contents to suit your needs, or you can create a new menu from scratch, using the New option on the Menu Manager.

Understanding the relationship between menus and modules

As I mention previously, the Menu Manager and the Menu Items Manager are used to manage the menu contents, but the display of the menu is controlled by the menu module. Every menu in the system has associated with it at least one menu module. When a new menu is created, a new menu module is typically created by the system to enable the display of the menu.

During the process of creating a new menu, the system prompts you to enter Module Title, which will be used to name the menu module for the menu. If you leave this field blank, the system creates the menu, but no module, resulting in the menu not being visible on the front end of the site. All Menu modules are of the module type `mod_mainmenu`.

Note

It is possible to create multiple menu modules for a single menu. This technique is used primarily to create sub-menus, as discussed later in this chapter.

Creating a new menu

To create a new menu, click the New icon on the toolbar at the top of the Menu Manager. Figure 8.2 shows the New Menu dialogue.

FIGURE 8.2

The Joomla! 1.5.x New Menu dialogue.

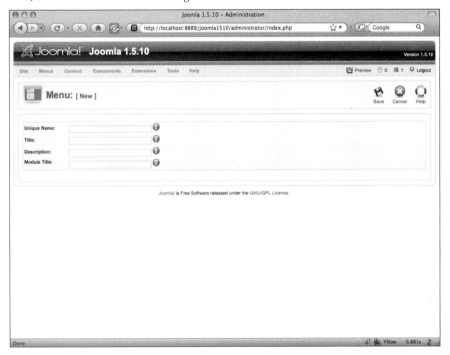

The toolbar at the top of the Menu Manager provides quick access to the following functions:

- **Save:** Click this icon to save your work, create a new menu, and exit the New Menu dialogue.

- **Cancel:** Cancels the task and exits the New Menu dialogue.

- **Help:** Click to access the online help files related to the active screen.

The fields in the workspace are:

- **Unique Name:** The value entered into this field will serve as the system name for the menu. This field accepts only lowercase letters with no spaces. This field is required.

- **Title:** Enter into this field a name for the menu. This field is required.

- **Description:** Type a description for the menu. This field is optional.

- **Module Title:** If you want to create a parallel menu module at this time, enter the name in this field. This is an optional field, but without it, you must first create a Menu module through the Module Manager in order to display the menu items on the front-end of the web site.

Cross-Reference

Creating new Site modules is discussed in Chapter 20.

To create a new menu, follow these steps:

1. **Log in to the admin system of your site.**

2. **Access the Menu Manager by clicking on the Menu Manager option under the Menus option on the admin nav bar.** The Menu Manager loads in your browser.

3. **On the Menu Manager interface, click the New icon on the toolbar at the top of the Menu Manager.** The New Menu dialogue opens. (Refer to Figure 8.2.)

4. **In the Unique Name field, enter a machine-readable name for the menu.** This field permits only lowercase letters with no spaces. This field is required.

5. **In the Title field, type a name for the menu.** This field is required.

6. **Complete any other fields you wish; all other fields are optional.**

7. **Click the Save icon on the toolbar at the top right to save your new menu.** The dialogue closes and returns you to the Menu Manager.

Joomla 1.6

The Joomla! 1.6 New Menu Dialogue interface is slightly different in appearance from the Joomla! 1.5.x New Menu Dialogue, but the functionality is the same.

Copying a menu

You can create an exact copy of an existing menu, complete with its menu items. Using the Copy function in the Menu Manager, the system will automatically create a copy of the menu, the menu items, and the menu's associated module. The new menu module will be assigned to the same module position as the original module and with the same access level.

To copy a menu, click the copy icon at the top right of the Menu Manager. The Copy Menu dialogue loads in your browser, as shown in Figure 8.3.

FIGURE 8.3

The Copy Menu dialogue, showing the name of the menu being copied together with a list of all the menu Items on that menu.

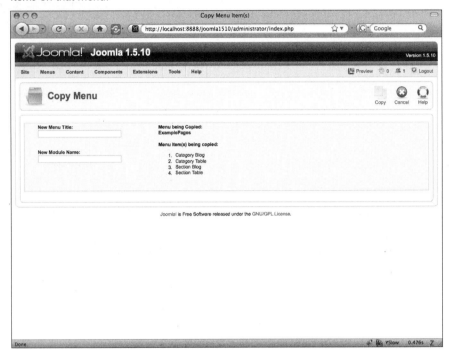

Caution

Copying an existing menu will result in a new menu module that is published by default - even if the original menu module was not enabled!

To copy a menu, follow these steps:

1. Open the Menu Manager.

2. Click the select box next to the Menu you want to copy.

3. Click the Copy icon on the top-right toolbar.

   The Copy Menu dialogue opens. (Refer to Figure 8.3.)

4. Type a name for New Menu Title.

5. Type a name for the New Module Name.

6. Click the Copy icon on the top-right toolbar. The system creates a new menu and a new menu module and returns you to the Menu Manager.

Editing and deleting menus

Existing menus can be edited from the Menu Manager. To edit a menu, either click the menu name in the Menu Manager or select the menu and then click the Edit icon on the Menu Manager toolbar. Regardless of which method you use, the system opens the Edit Menu dialogue.

The Edit Menu dialogue is identical to the New Menu dialogue, with the same fields and requirements as discussed in the preceding section.

To make changes to a menu, simply alter the desired fields in the Edit Menu dialogue, and then click the Save or Apply icon on the toolbar. Any changes you have made will be applied immediately.

Complete menu deletion can be achieved through the Menu Manager. Deletion from the Menu Manager bypasses the Trash Manager and deletes all the elements immediately. Deleting a menu results in the removal of the menu itself, the items assigned the menu, and also the menu's module.

Note
While it is possible to delete a menu module without deleting the related menu, it is not possible to delete a menu without deleting the associated module.

To delete a menu, follow these steps:

1. **Open the Menu Manager.**
2. **Select the menu you want to delete.**
3. **Click the Delete icon on the top right toolbar.** The Delete Menu dialogue opens.
4. **Review the list of items to be deleted and then click the Delete icon on the toolbar.** The system deletes the menu, the menu items, and the related menu module and then returns you to the Menu Manager.

Caution
Deleting a menu also deletes the menu items associated with that menu and the related menu module. Note that the menu items are not moved to the Trash — rather, they are deleted completely!

Caution
Do not delete the menu containing your site's default menu item! In the standard configuration, that is the Main menu, which includes the home page. In the default configuration, the home page link is the default menu item. If you delete the menu containing the default menu item, your site will not function.

Introducing the Menu Item Manager

Where Joomla!'s Menu Manager is designed for handling the menus, the Menu Item Manager provides the interface for managing the individual items on each of the menus, as shown in

Figure 8.4. Unlike the Menu Manager, there is no link on the administrator menus to a choice labeled Menu Item Manager. Because there are individual Menu Item Managers for each of the menus, you access this feature by clicking on the name of the menu you want to edit. The list appears under the menu labeled Menus on the admin interface main navigation bar.

FIGURE 8.4

The Joomla! 1.5.x Menu Item Manager interface, showing the Main menu.

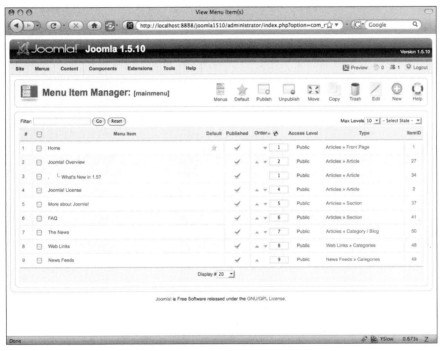

The toolbar at the top of the Menu Item Manager provides quick access to the following functions:

- **Menus:** Click this icon to jump to the Menu Manager.
- **Default:** Select of the items from the list and then click this icon to set this item as the site's default (home) page.
- **Publish:** Select one or more menu items from the list and then click this icon to publish them.
- **Unpublish:** Select one or more menu items from the list and then click this icon to unpublish them.
- **Move:** Select one or more menu items from the list and then click this icon to move the items to a different menu.

- **Copy:** Select one or more menu items from the list and then click this icon to makes copies of them.

- **Trash:** Select one or more menu items from the list and then click this icon to move the items to the Menu Trash.

- **Edit:** Select a menu item from the list and then click this icon to edit the menu item details.

- **New:** Click to add a new menu item.

- **Help:** Click to access the online Help files related to the active screen.

Below the toolbar and above the list of menus are three sorting and searching tools to help you manage long lists of menus:

- **The Filter field** on the left works like a search box. Type a word or phrase into the field and then click Go. The page reloads and displays the results of the search. To clear the screen and return to a full listing, click the Reset button.

- **The Max Levels filter field** is located on the right, next to the Select State filter. Select a value from this list to limit the view to menu items that contain no more levels than the value selected. In this context, levels is used to mean sub navigation choices, or to put it another way, those parent items with a certain number of children items. After you select the value, the page will reload and display the items that match the criteria.

- **The Select State filter** on the far right allows you to filter and display the menus according to whether they are published or unpublished. This provides an easy way to identify all menus that are currently active on the site. To reset this filter, change the combo box back to the default setting.

The main content area of the screen contains a list of all the menu items in this particular menu. The columns provided are:

- **#:** An indexing number assigned by Joomla! This cannot be changed.

- **Checkbox (no label):** Click in a checkbox to select a menu; this is needed if you want to use several of the toolbar options.

- **Menu Item:** This field displays the full name of the menu item. This is the name as it will appear on the menu— the label that will be visible to your site visitors. Click the name to edit the item's details.

- **Default:** A yellow star in the column indicates that the item is the site's default page (home page). There can only be one default item on the site.

- **Published:** A green checkmark in this column indicates that the menu item is active. The field will show a red X if the menu item is disabled. Note that this is only one of several settings that are needed for a menu item to be visible. The item must be published, but so also must the menu itself and the related menu module. Administrators can toggle between enabled and disabled by clicking the icon shown.

- **Order:** The order of appearance of the items on the menu. You can change the ordering either by clicking the up and down arrows or by typing numerical values into the text field, and then clicking the Save icon.

- **Access Level:** Indicates the access level associated with this menu item. The options are Public, Registered, and Special. Administrators can toggle between the three levels by clicking on the word.

- **Type:** Indicates the menu item type assigned to the menu item. This can be changed by editing the menu item.

- **ID:** The system-generated user ID number. This cannot be changed.

Note

The order in which the menu items appear can also be controlled from the menu item's Advanced parameters. The choices made on the parameters option will override any ordering choices made from the Menu Item Manager screen.

Finally, at the bottom of the screen, below the content area, is the Display # option. Change the value in the combo box control to alter the number of menus that are displayed on the page. The default value can be altered by changing the List Length option on the Global Configuration Manager.

Joomla 1.6

The Menu Item Manager has been revised in Joomla! 1.6, but the changes are largely cosmetic and intended to enhance the usability of the interface. The functionality is essentially the same.

Creating and Managing Menu Items

From the perspective of your site visitors, menu items simply provide the choices seen listed on the menus. For the site administrator, however, menu items are far more important. The decisions made during the process of creating menu items have implications for the way the resulting page is shown on the screen.

New items are created from within the Menu Item Manager. Existing items are edited from the same location, either by clicking on the name of the menu item or by selecting Edit from the Menu Item Manager toolbar. The Menu Item Manager also provides controls to copy items or to move them to the trash for later deletion.

Creating new menu items

The Menu Item Manager includes a wizard-type process for the creation of new menu items. The wizard is initiated by clicking the New icon on the top right toolbar. During the process of creating a new item, you must select a menu item type, specify the name and target of the item, and configure the various parameter options.

There are numerous menu item types included in the Joomla! system. The various options are detailed in the following list. Adding other extensions into your Joomla! installation may result in more menu item types being available to you.

Note

Take a moment to become fluent in the various menu item types as they vary widely according to the content and functionality with which they are associated. Remember that the choice to use one type over another will have significant impact on the layout of the resulting page.

To create a new menu item, follow these steps:

1. **Under the admin menu option labeled Menus, select the name of the menu to which you want too add a new item.** The Menu Item Manager opens.

2. **Select the New icon from the top-right toolbar.** The first page of the New Menu Item wizard opens in your browser. Figure 8.5 shows the first page of the wizard.

FIGURE 8.5

The first page of the Joomla! 1.5.x New Menu Item wizard.

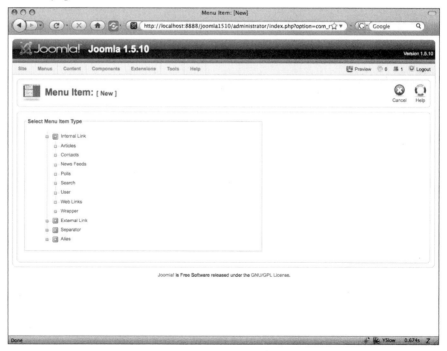

3. **Select the desired menu item type.** The second page of the New Menu Item wizard opens in your browser. Figure 8.6 shows the second page of the wizard.

FIGURE 8.6

The second page of the Joomla! 1.5.x New Menu Item wizard, showing a typical workspace.

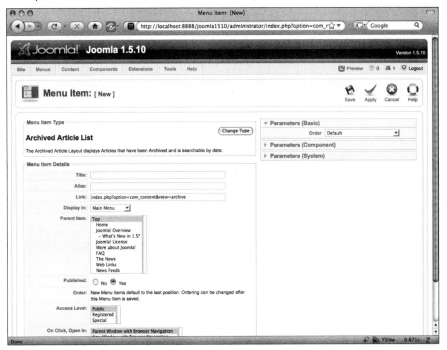

4. **Type a title for the menu item.** This field is required and provides the label that appears on the menu.

5. **Complete the other fields as needed, and configure the parameter options as you desire; these options will vary by menu item type, as discussed in the section that follows.**

6. **Click the Save icon.** The system creates the new menu item and return you to the Menu Item Manager.

The toolbar at the top of the dialogue provides quick access to the following functions:

- **Save:** Click this icon to save your work, add a new menu item, and exit the New Menu Item dialogue.

- **Apply:** Click this icon to save your work and create a new item without exiting from the New Menu Item dialogue. This option lets you save without exiting the screen and it useful in case you are interrupted or you otherwise want to save yet keep working on this screen.

- **Cancel:** Click this icon to cancel the task and exit the Menu Item Manager.

- **Help:** Click this icon to display the Help files related to the active screen.

The Menu Item Details section of a typical menu item workspace contains the following fields:

- **Title:** This is the name of the menu item as it will appear on the menu as an option for your site visitors and on the Menu Item Manager.

- **Alias:** This is the internal name of the item and the name that will be used if you have selected the option to display SEF URLs. Note that this field only accepts lowercase letters with no spaces. If you do not provide a value for this field, the system will use the label you have specified for the title, converting it as needed to comply with the system naming requirements.

- **Link:** The system attaches the link to the menu item. When visitors click the menu item, they are taken to the linked page.

- **Display in:** The menu where this menu item appears.

- **Parent Item:** Sets the level of the menu item, that is, whether it is a top level item or a submenu item. Select Top to make this item a top level item. If you want to create a new submenu item, select a parent item from the list.

- **Published:** Select Yes to publish the item.

- **Order:** Sets the order of this item relative to others on the same menu.

- **Access Level:** Sets the access level for the menu item. There are three options here: Public, Registered, and Special.

- **On Click, Open in:** This control provides the option for specifying whether clicking on the menu item opens the target in the same window or uses a new browser window.

Joomla 1.6

The creation of menu items has been changed significantly in Joomla! 1.6. Gone is the Step Creation wizard. In Joomla! 1.6, you need only click the New icon and then complete the fields in the dialogue that appears in your browser. Menu item types are controlled by the Type field, which functions by opening a pop-up menu from which you select the menu item type you want to apply.

Also new in Joomla! 1.6 is the ability to set metadata in association with menu items and the ability to control module assignment directly from within the New Menu Item dialogue.

Menu item types

The Joomla! menu item types provide options for creating various layouts on your pages. By choosing one type over another, you are able to show content or functionality in a variety of styles. The parameters associated with each menu item type allow you to tailor the result more closely to your needs.

Although menu item types are set when you create a new item, they can also be modified after the item is created. To change the item type of an existing menu item, simply edit the menu item and choose the Change Type button at the top of the workspace.

The menu item types are divided into four groups:

- Internal Link
- External Link
- Separator and
- Alias

Each of the types within a specific group shares a number of common parameters, but they also frequently have unique parameters. In the following sections, I go through all the various menu item types in the default Joomla! 1.5.x system and note the parameters involved. If you have installed additional extensions, you may see even more menu item types in your system.

Joomla 1.6

The extent of the changes to the menu item types in Joomla! 1.6 was unclear at the time of the writing of this text.

Internal Link - Articles

The Internal Link group of menu item types contains the largest number of options. This category includes the links to all internal content and functionality. The grouping is divided into eight sub-groupings:

- Articles
- Contacts
- News Feeds
- Polls
- Search
- User
- Web Links
- Wrapper

The menu item types located in the group labeled Internal Link - Articles share common component parameters and system parameters, as shown in Figure 8.7. Individual item types, however, often have specific advanced parameters. Each is discussed in turn in the following text.

FIGURE 8.7

The Internal Link - Articles menu type parameters.

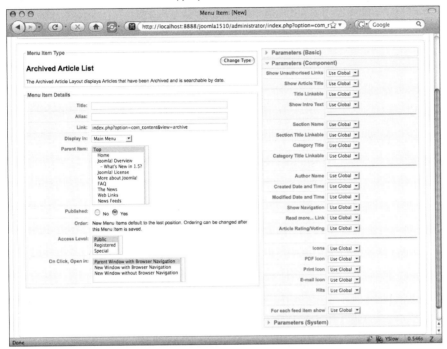

The Component parameters section of all the Internal Link - Articles menu types contains the following options:

- **Show Unauthorised Links:** Determines whether the visitor can see links to which they do not have access. If set to Yes, then all links will show, regardless of whether the user has sufficient access privileges to view them. If users click a link that they cannot access, the system shows them an error message and prompts them to log in.

- **Show Article Title:** Hide or show the article title.

- **Title Linkable:** Whether the article title in the teaser view is hyperlinked to the full article text.

- **Show Intro Text:** Whether to show the article in teaser view.

- **Section Name:** Hide or show the section name.

- **Section Title Linkable:** Whether the section title will be hyperlinked to the section page.

- **Category Title:** Hide or show the category title.

- **Category Title Linkable:** Whether the category title will be hyperlinked to the category page.

- **Author Name:** Hide or show the author's name on the article.

- **Created date and time:** Hide or show the date and time the article was created.

- **Modified Date and Time:** Hide or show the date and time the article was last modified.

- **Show Navigation:** Whether to hide or show the page navigation controls.

- **Read more... Link:** Hide or show the Read more... link on the article teaser.

- **Article Rating/Voting:** Whether to enable the article rating functionality.

- **Icons:** This control governs how the PDF, print, and e-mail options, discussed later, are displayed on the screen. Setting this to hide causes the links to be displayed as text; setting it to show forces the links to use icons. Note that this control has no effect if the PDF, print, and e-mail options are disabled.

- **PDF Icon:** Hide or show the PDF link.

- **Print Icon:** Hide or show the Print link.

- **E-mail Icon:** Hide or show the E-mail link.

- **Hits:** Hide or show the number of views the article has reviewed.

- **For each feed item show:** This control relates to the display of the output of feeds. If set to Intro Text, only the intro text will be shown; the visitor has to click to read the rest of the entry. If set to Full text, the entire text of the feed item is displayed.

The hierarchy of article and item parameters

In addition to the parameters contained in the menu item types, the articles in your Joomla! system are also subject to two other groups of parameters: Article Manager parameters, and the Advanced parameters section of the Article Editing dialogue. It is important to understand the hierarchical relationship between these three sets of parameters to avoid undesired results caused by entering contradictory settings.

The system works as follows: First, the system examines the settings in the Advanced parameters of the Article Editing dialogue. If a specific Yes/No, Show/Hide value is set, then those values are applied to the article and no further checking is done. However, if the values are set to Use Global, then the system looks next to the Component parameters set in the menu item type. If a specific Yes/No, Show/Hide value is set, then those values are applied to the article and no further checking is done. However, if the values are set to Use Global, then the system looks finally to the Article Manager parameters.

The System parameters section of all the Internal Link - Articles menu types contains the following options:

- **Page Title:** Enter the text you want to show in the title bar of the browser when the visitor views the page. If no value is entered, the system will use the menu title. This option can also be used to control the display of the Page Title on the article itself, where the control, Show Page Title, is enabled.

- **Show Page Title:** Enable this control to show the Page Title specified in the field above on the article. If the option is set to Yes but no text is entered in the Page Title parameter, then the Menu Title is used. Note also that this control has no effect on the Article, Section Table, and Category Table menu item types.

- **Page Class Suffix:** Enter a text value here to create a suffix that will be added to all CSS classes related to the page. This allows you to add specific styling tailored to specific pages.

- **Menu Image:** Select an image from the combo box to be associated with the menu item. Note that you can add your own images by uploading them to the directory `images/stories`.

- **SSL Enabled:** Elect whether this page should use SSL and the Secure Site URL.

Archived Article List

The Archived Article List format is used to create a page containing a list of the site's archived content items, as shown in Figure 8.8. The items are typically searched by date. You can control the display order of the items using the options in the Basic parameters section.

Cross-Reference

A discussion of archiving articles can be found in Chapter 5.

The Basic parameters section contains only the Order option. This option sets the display order of the items on the page. The default order is most recent first. Note also that the option named Order follows the display order set in the order column of the Article Manager.

FIGURE 8.8

Example of the Archived Article List menu type in action.

Article Layout

The Article Layout menu item type is used to display a single article on a page, as shown in Figure 8.9. This is probably the most commonly used menu item type, as it is the basis for the display of the majority of a typical site's content items.

FIGURE 8.9

Example of the Article Layout menu item type in action.

The Basic parameters section contains only the Select Article option. Click the Select button to display a list of the site's content items. Click the name of the content item you want to display. This field is required.

Article Submission Layout

The Article Submissions Layout is a specialty menu item type used to create a page specifically for the purpose of allowing front-end visitors to add content, as shown in Figure 8.10. This menu item type is only relevant to users assigned to the User Group Author or higher.

FIGURE 8.10

Example of the Article Submission Layout menu type in action.

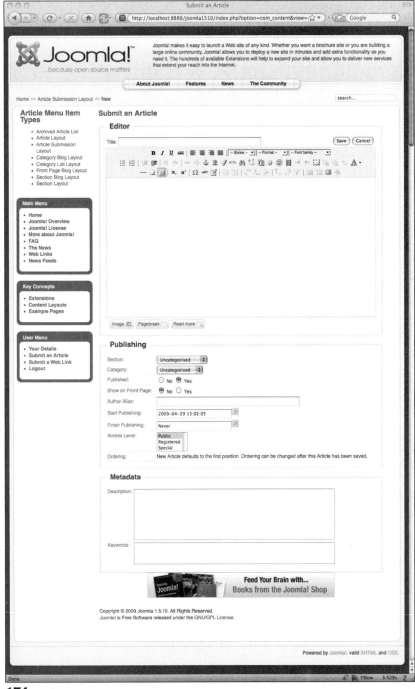

There are no basic parameters for this menu item type.

Tip

If your site does not employ the front-end content creation process, there is no reason to create items of this type.

Category Blog Layout

This menu item type displays all of the articles in a category, laid out in a blog-type format.

In Joomla!, a blog-type layout divides the content area of the page into three sections. At the top are one or more lead articles. Lead articles span the width of the page. Below the lead articles are the intro articles, which are typically displayed in multiple columns. At the bottom of the content area of the page is a links area which shows a list of links to additional articles. The number of articles, the number of columns, and the number of links can all be controlled through the basic parameters.

Figure 8.11 shows a Category Blog Layout in the default configuration, that is, with one leading article, two intro articles displayed in two columns, and with a list of four links at the bottom.

This menu item type includes both Basic and Advanced parameters options. The Basic parameters are the following:

- **Category:** Select the name of the category you want to display from the combo box. This is field required.

- **Description:** If set to Yes, the system displays the category description. The descriptions are set in the Category Edit dialogues.

- **Description Image:** If set to Yes, the system displays the category image. The image is set in the Category Edit dialogues.

- **# Leading:** Enter an integer value to set the number of leading articles displayed.

- **# Intro:** Enter an integer value to set the number of intro articles displayed.

- **Columns:** Enter an integer for the number of columns to be used for the intro articles. Note the only valid values here are 1, 2, and 3. If set to 1, then the intro articles will span the width of the page, the same as the leading articles.

- **# Links:** Enter an integer for the number of links to be used in the Links section of the layout.

FIGURE 8.11

Example of the Category Blog Layout menu type in action.

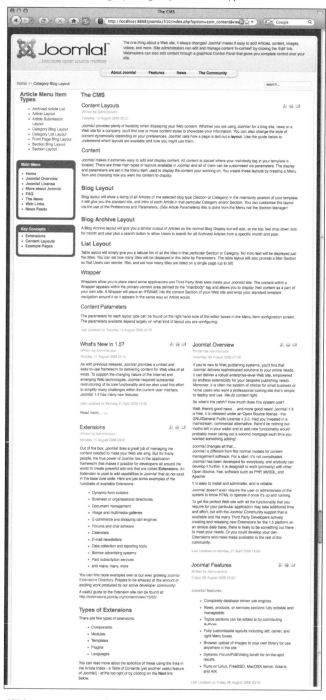

FIGURE 8.11 *(continued)*

Components

A Component is the largest and most complex of the Extension types. Components are like mini-applications that render the main body of the page. An analogy that might make the relationship easier to understand would be that Joomla! is a book and all the Components are chapters in the book. The core Article Component (com_content), for example, is the mini-application that handles all core Article rendering just as the core registration Component (com_user) is the mini-application that handles User registration.

Many of Joomla!'s core features are provided by the use of default Components such as:

- Contacts
- Front Page
- News Feeds
- Banners
- Mass Mail
- Polls

A Component will manage data, set displays, provide functions, and in general can perform any operation that does not fall under the general functions of the core code.

Components work hand in hand with Modules and Plugins to provide a rich variety of content display and functionality aside from the standard Article and content display. They make it possible to completely transform Joomla! and greatly expand its capabilities.

Modules

A more lightweight and flexible Extension used for page rendering is a Module. Modules are used for small bits of the page that are generally less complex and able to be seen across different Components. To continue in our book analogy, a Module can be looked at as a footnote or header block, or perhaps an image/caption block that can be rendered on a particular page. Obviously you can have a footnote on any page but not all pages will have them. Footnotes also might appear regardless of which chapter you are reading. Similarly Modules can be rendered regardless of which Component you have loaded.

Modules are like little mini-applets that can be placed anywhere on your site. They work in conjunction with Components in some cases and in others are complete stand-alone snippets of code used to display some data from the database such as Articles (Newsflash) Modules are usually used to output data but they can also be interactive form items to input data for example the Login Module or Polls.

Modules can be assigned to Module positions which are defined in your Template and in the back-end using the Module Manager and editing the Module Position settings. For example, "left" and "right" are common for a 3 column layout.

Displaying Modules

Each Module is assigned to a Module position on your site. If you wish it to display in two different locations you must copy the Module and assign the copy to display at the new location. You can also set which Menu Items (and thus pages) a Module will display on, you can select all Menu Items or you can pick and choose by holding down the control key and selecting multiple locations one by one in the Modules [Edit] screen.

Note: Your Main Menu is a Module! When you create a new Menu in the Menu Manager you are actually copying the Main Menu Module (mod_mainmenu) code and giving it the name of your new Menu. When you copy a Module you do not copy all of its parameters, you simply allow Joomla! to use the same code with two separate settings.

Newsflash Example

Newsflash is a Module which will display Articles from your site in an assignable Module position. It can be used and configured to display one Category, all Categories, or to randomly choose Articles to highlight to Users. It will display as much of an Article as you set, and will show a *Read more...* link to take the User to the full Article.

The Newsflash Component is particularly useful for things like Site News or to show the latest Article added to your Web site.

Plugins

One of the more advanced Extensions for Joomla! is the Plugin. In previous versions of Joomla! Plugins were known as Mambots. Aside from changing their name their functionality has been expanded. A Plugin is a section of code that runs when a pre-defined event happens within Joomla! Editors are Plugins, for example, that execute when the Joomla! event onGetInsertAreas occurs. Using a Plugin allows a developer to change the way their code behaves depending upon which Plugins are installed to react to an event.

Languages

New to Joomla! 1.5 and perhaps the most basic and critical Extension is a Language. Joomla! is released with multiple installation Languages but the base Site and Administrator are packaged in just the one Language en-GB - being English with GB spelling for example. To include all the translations currently available would bloat the core package and make it unmanageable for uploading purposes. The Language files enable all the User interfaces both Front-end and Back-end to be presented in the local preferred language. Note these packs do not have any impact on the actual content such as Articles.

More information on languages is available from the http://community.joomla.org/translations.html

The Advanced parameters for this menu item type are the following:.

- **Category Order:** This control has no effect on the Category Blog Layout menu item type.
- **Primary Order:** Sets the order of articles within categories. The Default option shows the most recent items first. Note that the option named Order will follow the display order set in the Order column of the Article Manager.
- **Multi-Column Order:** If you have set the Columns parameter to show your intro articles in multiple columns, this control allows you to determine whether the articles are sequenced by column and row or by row only.
- **Pagination:** Show or hide the pagination controls at the bottom of the page.
- **Pagination Results:** Show or hide in the pagination the current page number and the total number of pages.
- **Show a Feed Link:** This allows users to subscribe to an RSS feed for the contents of this page.

Category List Layout

The Category List Layout menu item type displays a list of all the articles in a particular category, as shown in Figure 8.12.

This menu item type includes both Basic and Advanced parameters options.

- **Category:** Select from the combo box the name of the category you want to display. This field is required.
- **# Links:** Use the combo box to select the number of links to appear.
- **Table Headings:** Hide or show the table headings above the list of links.
- **Date Column:** Hide or show the date the item was created.
- **Date Format:** Set the date format. Note this field uses the PHP `strftime` command format.
- **Filter:** Hide or show the filters for your visitor's' use. These are displayed at the top of the page.
- **Filter Field:** Add an additional filter field for your visitors' use. Select from Title or Author.

The Advanced parameters section contains the following options:

- **Primary Order:** Set the order of display of the links. The default is most recent first. Note that the option named order follows the display order set in the Order column of the Article Manager.
- **Pagination:** Show or hide the pagination controls at the bottom of the page.
- **Display Select:** Show or hide the Display Select combo box that allows users to set the number of items visible per page.
- **Show a Feed Link:** Show or hide an RSS feed link. This allows users to subscribe to an RSS feed for the contents of this page.

FIGURE 8.12

Example of the Category List Layout menu type in action.

Front Page Blog Layout

This menu item type displays all of the articles that are currently assigned and published to the Front Page. This is the menu type that is used by the default system for the front page of the site. The articles are laid out in a blog-type format.

In Joomla!, a blog-type layout divides the content area of the page into three sections. At the top are one or more lead articles. Lead articles span the width of the page. Below the lead articles are the intro articles, which are typically displayed in multiple columns. At the bottom of the content area of the page is a links area which shows a list of links to additional articles. The number of articles, the number of columns, and the number of Links can all be controlled through the Basic parameters.

Figure 8.13 shows a Front Page Blog Layout in the default configuration, that is, with one leading article, two intro articles displayed in two columns, and with a list of four links at the bottom.

FIGURE 8.13

Example of the Front Page Blog Layout menu type in action.

This menu item type includes both Basic and Advanced parameters options.

- **# Leading:** Enter an integer value to set the number of leading articles displayed.
- **# Intro:** Enter an integer value to set the number of intro articles displayed.

- **Columns:** Enter an integer for the number of columns to be used for the intro articles. Note the only valid values here are 1, 2, and 3. If set to 1, then the intro articles span the width of the page, the same as the leading articles.

- **# Links:** Enter an integer for the number of links to be used in the Links section of the layout.

The Advanced parameters section contains the following options:

- **Category Order:** Whether to order the articles without consideration of the categories to which they belong. The No, Order by Primary Order Only option disregards the articles' category association and looks to the setting of the Primary Order parameter.

- **Primary Order:** Sets the order of articles within categories. The Default option shows the most recent items first. Note that the option named Order follows the display order set in the Order column of the Article Manager.

- **Multi-Column Order:** If you have set the Columns parameter to show your intro articles in multiple columns, this control allows you to determine whether the articles are sequenced by column and row or by row only.

- **Pagination:** Show or hide the pagination controls at the bottom of the page.

- **Pagination Results:** Show or hide in the pagination the current page number and the total number of pages.

- **Show a Feed Link:** This allows users to subscribe to an RSS feed for the contents of this page.

Section Blog Layout

This menu item type displays all of the articles from a specific section, laid out in a blog-type format.

In Joomla!, a blog-type layout divides the content area of the page into three sections. At the top are one or more lead articles. Lead articles span the width of the page. Below the lead article are the intro articles, which are typically displayed in multiple columns. At the bottom of the content area of the page is a Links area which shows a list of links to additional articles. The number of articles, the number of columns, and the number of links can all be controlled through the Basic parameters, as discussed in the following text.

Figure 8.14 shows a Section Blog Layout in the default configuration, that is, with one leading article, two intro articles displayed in two columns, and a list of four links at the bottom.

FIGURE 8.14

Example of the Section Blog Layout menu type in action.

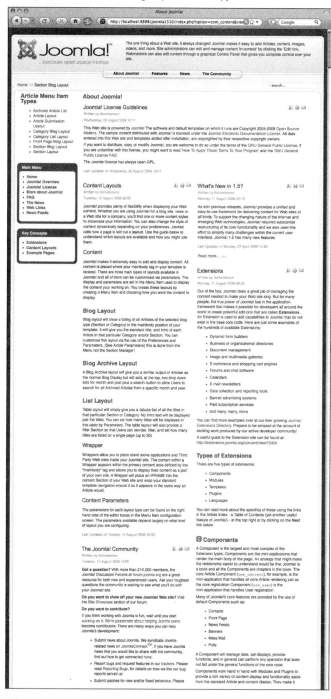

FIGURE 8.14 *(continued)*

read Reporting Bugs, for details on how we like our bug reports served up.

- Submit patches for new and/or fixed behaviour. Please read Submitting Patches, for details on how to submit a patch.
- Join the developer forums and share your ideas for how to improve Joomla. We're always open to suggestions, although we're likely to be sceptical of large-scale suggestions without some code to back it up.
- Join any of the Joomla Working Groups and bring your personal expertise to the Joomla community.

These are just a few ways you can contribute. See Contribute to Joomla for many more ways.

Last Updated on Tuesday, 12 August 2008 16:50

Components work hand in hand with Modules and Plugins to provide a rich variety of content display and functionality aside from the standard Article and content display. They make it possible to completely transform Joomla! and greatly expand its capabilities.

Modules

A more lightweight and flexible Extension used for page rendering is a Module. Modules are used for small bits of the page that are generally less complex and able to be seen across different Components. To continue in our book analogy, a Module can be looked at as a footnote or header block, or perhaps an image/caption block that can be rendered on a particular page. Obviously you can have a footnote on any page but not all pages will have them. Footnotes also might appear regardless of which chapter you are reading. Similarly Modules can be rendered regardless of which Component you have loaded.

Modules are like little mini-applets that can be placed anywhere on your site. They work in conjunction with Components in some cases and in others are complete stand alone snippets of code used to display some data from the database such as Articles (Newsflash) Modules are usually used to output data but they can also be interactive form items to input data for example the Login Module or Polls.

Modules can be assigned to Module positions which are defined in your Template and in the back-end using the Module Manager and editing the Module Position settings. For example, "left" and "right" are common for a 3 column layout.

Displaying Modules

Each Module is assigned to a Module position on your site. If you wish it to display in two different locations you must copy the Module and assign the copy to display at the new location. You can also set which Menu Items (and thus pages) a Module will display on, you can select all Menu Items or you can pick and choose by holding down the control key and selecting multiple locations one by one in the Modules [Edit] screen

Note: Your Main Menu is a Module! When you create a new Menu in the Menu Manager you are actually copying the Main Menu Module (mod_mainmenu) code and giving it the name of your new Menu. When you copy a Module you do not copy all of its parameters, you simply allow Joomla! to use the same code with two separate settings.

Newsflash Example

Newsflash is a Module which will display Articles from your site in an assignable Module position. It can be used and configured to display one Category, all Categories, or to randomly choose Articles to highlight to Users. It will display as much of an Article as you set, and will show a *Read more...* link to take the User to the full Article.

The Newsflash Component is particularly useful for things like Site News or to show the latest Article added to your Web site.

Plugins

One of the more advanced Extensions for Joomla! is the Plugin. In previous versions of Joomla! Plugins were known as Mambots. Aside from changing their name their functionality has been expanded. A Plugin is a section of code that runs when a pre-defined event happens within Joomla!. Editors are Plugins, for example, that execute when the Joomla! event onGetEditorArea occurs. Using a Plugin allows a developer to change the way their code behaves depending upon which Plugins are installed to react to an event.

Languages

New to Joomla! 1.5 and perhaps the most basic and critical Extension is a Language. Joomla! is released with multiple installation Languages but the base Site and Administrator are packaged in just the one Language **en-GB** - being English with GB spelling for example. To include all the translations currently available would bloat the core package and make it unmanageable for uploading purposes. The Language files enable all the User interfaces both Front-end and Back-end to be presented in the local preferred language. Note these packs do not have any impact on the actual consent such as Articles.

More information on languages is available from the http://community.joomla.org/translations.html

Last Updated on Monday, 27 April 2009 14:55

More Articles...

- Platforms and Open Standards
- Joomla! Facts
- Support and Documentation
- Joomla! Overview

« Start Prev 1 2 Next End »

Page 1 of 2

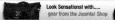
Look Sensational with.....
gear from the Joomla! Shop

Feed Entries

Powered by Joomla!, valid XHTML and CSS.

Done

This menu item type includes both Basic and Advanced parameters options. The Basic parameters options are the following:

- **Section:** Select the name of the section you want to display from the combo box. This field is required.

- **Description:** If set to Yes, the system displays the Section description. The description is set in the Section Edit dialogues.

- **Description Image:** If set to Yes, the system displays the Section image. The image is set in the Section Edit dialogue.

- **# Leading:** Enter an integer value to set the number of leading articles displayed.

- **# Intro:** Enter an integer value to set the number of intro articles displayed.

- **Columns:** Enter an integer for the number of columns to be used for the intro articles. Note the only valid values here are 1, 2, and 3. If set to 1, then the intro articles will span the width of the page, the same as the leading articles.

- **# Links:** Enter an integer for the number of links to be used in the Links section of the layout.

The Advanced parameters section contains the following options:

- **Category Order:** Whether to order the articles without consideration of the categories to which they belong. The option No, Order by Primary Order Only disregards the articles' category association and looks to the setting of the Primary Order parameter.

- **Primary Order:** Sets the order of articles within categories. The default option shows the most recent items first. Note that the option named Order will follow the display order set in the Order column of the Article Manager.

- **Multi- Column Order:** If you have set the Columns parameter to show your intro articles in multiple columns, this control allows you to determine whether the articles are sequenced by column and row or by row only.

- **Pagination:** Show or hide the pagination controls at the bottom of the page.

- **Pagination results:** Show or hide in the pagination the current page number and the total number of pages.

- **Show a Feed Link:** This allows users to subscribe to an RSS feed for the contents of this page.

Section Layout

The Section Layout menu item type lets you place on a page the name of a section, together with a list of all categories and articles within that section. The parameters allow you to tailor the view in various manners.

Figure 8.15 shows the Section Layout with the default configuration options.

FIGURE 8.15

Example of the Section Layout menu type in action.

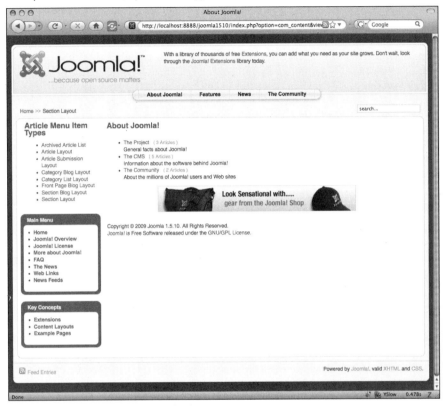

This menu item type includes both Basic and Advanced parameters options.

The Basic parameters section contains the following options:

- **Section:** Select the name of the section you want to display from the combo box. This field is required.

- **Description:** If set to Yes, the system displays the section description. The description is set in the Section Edit dialogues.

- **Description Image:** If set to Yes, the system will display the section image. The image is set in the Section Edit dialogue.

- **Category List - Section:** Show or hide the list of categories in the section.

- **Empty Categories in Section:** Show or hide empty categories.

- **# Category Items:** Show or hide a count of the number of items inside in a category.
- **Category Description:** Show or hide the category description text. This text is set in the Category Edit dialogue.

The Advanced parameters section contains the following options:

- **Category Order:** Whether to order the articles without consideration of the categories to which they belong. The option No, Order by Primary Order Only disregards the articles' category association and looks to the setting of the Primary Order parameter.
- **Article Order:** Sets the order of articles within categories. The default option shows the most recent items first. Note that the option named Order follows the display order set in the Order column of the Article Manager.
- **Show a Feed Link:** This allows users to subscribe to an RSS feed for the contents of this page.

Internal Link - Contacts

The Internal Link - Contacts group of menu item types contains only two options: Contact Category Layout and Standard Contact Layout. Both menu item types in this group relate to the display of contacts on your pages. The two types in this grouping share common Component and System parameters, as shown in Figure 8.16.

Cross-Reference

The creation and editing of contacts is done through the Contact Manager component. Working with Contacts is discussed in Chapter 15.

The Component parameters section contains the following options:

- **Icons/Text:** Whether to display icons or text next to the Contacts fields. You can also select to display neither by choosing none from the combo box.
- **Address Icon:** Select from the combo box the icon you want to display by the Address field. Only relevant if the icon display is enabled.
- **E-mail Icon:** Select from the combo box the icon you want to display by the E-mail field. Only relevant if the icon display is enabled.
- **Telephone Icon:** Select from the combo box the icon you want to display by the Telephone field. Only relevant if the icon display is enabled.
- **Mobile Icon:** Select from the combo box the icon you want to display by the Mobile field. Only relevant if the icon display is enabled.
- **Fax Icon:** Select from the combo box the icon you want to display by the Fax field. Only relevant if the icon display is enabled.
- **Miscellaneous Icon:** Select from the combo box the icon you want to display in the Miscellaneous field. Only relevant if the icon display is enabled.

- **Show Table Headings:** Whether to show the table column headings on pages showing the data in tabular form.

- **Show Contact's Position:** Show or hide the Position field.

- **Show E-mail Address:** Show or hide the E-mail field.

- **Show Telephone Number:** Show or hide the Telephone field.

- **Show Mobile Number:** Show or hide the Mobile Number field.

- **Show Fax Number:** Show or hide the Fax Number field.

- **Enable vCard:** Whether to enabled vCard support for the contacts.

- **Banned E-mail:** Any e-mail addresses containing any of the terms listed in this field will be banned from the site. Enter a list of terms separated by semicolons.

- **Banned Subject:** Any e-mail subject lines containing any of the terms listed in this field will be banned from the site. Enter a list of terms separated by semicolons.

- **Banned Text:** Any e-mail message text containing any of the terms listed in this field will be banned from the site. Enter a list of terms separated by semicolons.

- **Session Check:** When set to Yes this option will limit e-mail access to only those users who have cookies enabled in their browsers.

FIGURE 8.16

The Internal Link - Contacts menu type parameters.

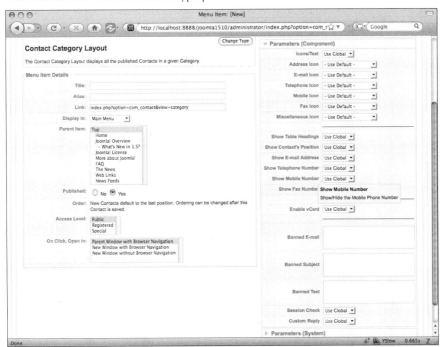

The System parameters section contains the following options:

- **Page Title:** Enter the text you want to show in the title bar of the browser when the visitor views the page. If no value is entered, the system will use the menu title. This option can also be used to control the display of the page title on the article itself, where, Show Page Title is enabled.

- **Show Page Title:** Enable this control to show the page title specified in the field above on the article. If the option is set to Yes, but no text is entered in the Page Title parameter, then the menu title is used. Note also that this control has no effect on the Article, Section Table and Category Table menu item types.

- **Page Class Suffix:** Enter a text value here to create a suffix that will be added to all CSS classes related to the page. This allows you to add specific styling tailored to specific pages.

- **Menu Image:** Select an image from the combo box and it will be associated with the menu item. Note that you can add your own images by uploading them to the directory `images/stories`.

Contact Category Layout

This menu item type enables you to display on a page all the published contacts from a given category, as shown in Figure 8.17.

The Contact Category Layout menu item type contains several options under the Basic parameters heading.

- **Select Category:** Select the Contacts category to be displayed. If none is selected, all are shown.

- **# Links:** Select from the combo box the number of items you want to display.

- **Contact Image:** Select from the combo box an image to display.

- **Image Align:** If an image is selected in the previous option, use this control to set the image alignment.

- **Limit Box:** Show or hide the limit box, which allows visitors to set the number of items shown per page.

- **Show a Feed Link:** This allows users to subscribe to an RSS feed for the contents of this page.

FIGURE 8.17

Example of the Contact Category Layout menu type in action.

Standard Contact Layout

This menu item type shows a single contact's details on a page, as shown in Figure 8.18.

The Basic parameters section contains several options.

- **Select Contact:** Use the combo box to select a contact to display.
- **Dropdown:** Show or hide a combo box that lets user view other contacts from the same category.
- **Show the Category in Breadcrumbs:** Show or hide the category name in the breadcrumb trail.

FIGURE 8.18

Example of the Standard Contact Layout menu type in action.

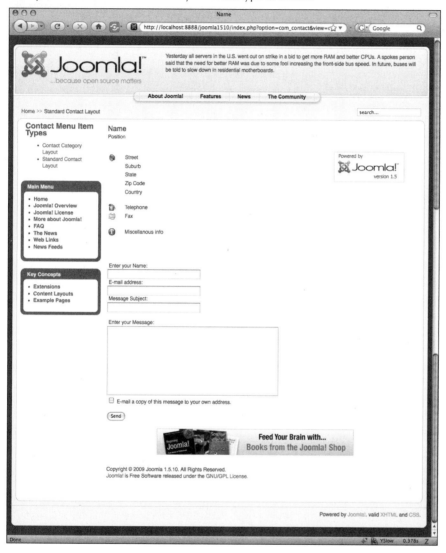

Internal Link - News Feeds

The Internal Link - News Feeds group of menu item types enables you to display news feeds in list form, by category, or individually, as shown in Figure 8.19. The types share common Component and System Parameters; individual types, however, have specific Basic parameters.

FIGURE 8.19

The News Feeds menu type parameters.

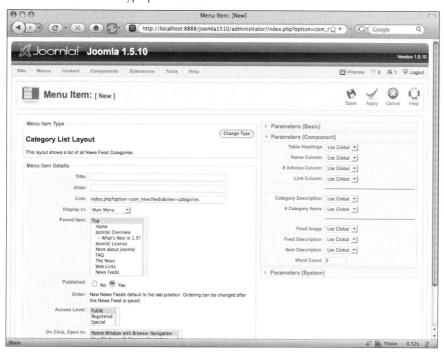

The Component parameters section contains the following options:

- **Table Headings:** Show or hide the table column headings on the display.

- **Name Column:** Show or hide the feed name column.

- **# Articles Column:** Show or hide the number of items in the feed.

- **Link Column:** Show or hide the link to the news feed.

- **Category Descriptions:** Show or hide the description for the category. The description text is managed from the News Feed Category Edit dialogue.

- **# Category Items:** Show or hide the number of items in the category.

- **Feed Image:** Whether to show the news feed image, if any is supplied by the source of the feed.

- **Feed Description:** Whether to display the description supplied by the source of the news feed.

- **Item Description:** Show or hide the intro text for an item.

- **Word Count:** Type an integer value to limit the display to a certain number of words per news feed item. Leave this field blank to display the entire feed item.

The System parameters section contains the following options:

- **Page Title:** Enter the text you want to show in the title bar of the browser when the visitor views the page. If no value is entered, the system will use the menu title. This option can also be used to control the display of the page title on the article itself, where the control below, Show Page Title, is enabled.

- **Show Page Title:** Enable this control to show the page title specified in the field above on the article. If the option is set to Yes, but no text is entered in the Page Title parameter, above, then the menu title is used. Note also that this control has no effect on the Article, Section Table, and Category Table menu item types.

- **Page Class Suffix:** Enter a text value here to create a suffix that will be added to all CSS classes related to the page. This allows you to add specific styling tailored to specific pages.

- **Menu Image:** Select an image from the combo box and it will be associated with the menu item. Note that you can add your own images by uploading them to the directory `images/stories`.

- **SSL Enabled:** Elect whether this page should use SSL and the Secure Site URL.

Category List Layout

This menu item type enables the display of a list of the news feed categories, as shown in Figure 8.20. Each of the category names listed is hyperlinked to a separate page that shows the items from the feeds in the category.

The menu type includes several options in the Basic parameters section.

- **Show Limit Box:** Select whether to display the limit box, which allows visitors to set the number of items shown per page.

- **Description:** Whether to display the text entered in the Description Text field. The text appears below the title on the page.

- **Description Text:** Enter any text you want to display on the page with the news feed. Note the visibility of the text is controlled by the Description parameter.

- **Image:** Select an image to display with the news feed. Note that you can add your own images by uploading them to the directory images/stories.

- **Image Align:** Set the image alignment. This option is only meaningful if an image has been selected in the parameter above.

FIGURE 8.20

Example of the Category List Layout List menu type in action.

Category Layout

Enables you to display on a page the list of news feeds from a specific category, as shown in Figure 8.21.

There are two parameters associated with this menu item type.

- **Category:** Select the category you want to display. This field is required.
- **Show Limit Box:** Select whether to display the Limit Box, which allows visitors to set the number of items shown per page.

FIGURE 8.21

Example of the Category Layout menu type in action.

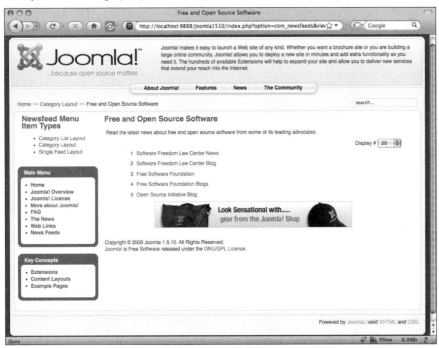

Single Feed Layout

This Menu item type displays the contents of a single news feed on a page, as shown in Figure 8.22.

One parameter is unique to this menu item type: Feed. This allows you to select from the combo box the name of the news feed you want to display. This field is required.

FIGURE 8.22

Example of the Single Feed Layout menu type in action.

Internal Link - Polls

The Internal Link - Polls group of menu item types includes only one item: Poll Layout. This menu item type is used to display poll results in the main content area of a page, as shown in Figure 8.23. The output shows the results of the poll voting, as well as providing additional information and a combo box link to other poll results, if any.

Cross-Reference

The Polls component and the Polls module are the subject of Chapter 15.

FIGURE 8.23

Example of the Poll Layout menu item type in action.

This menu item type includes both Basic and System parameters, as shown in Figure 8.24.

The Basic parameters section contains only one option: Poll. Select from the combo box the name of the poll you want to display. This field is required.

FIGURE 8.24

The Poll Layout menu type parameters.

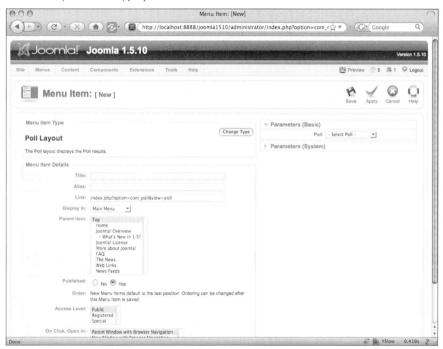

The System parameters section contains the following options:

- **Page Title:** Enter the text you want to show in the title bar of the browser when the visitor views the page. If no value is entered, the system will use the menu title. This option can also be used to control the display of the page title on the article itself, where the following control, Show Page Title, is enabled.

- **Show Page Title:** Enable this control to show the page title specified in the field above on the article. If the option is set to Yes, but no text is entered in the Page Title parameter above, then the menu title is used. Note also that this control has no effect on the article, section table, and category table menu item types.

- **Page Class Suffix:** Enter a text value here to create a suffix that will be added to all CSS classes related to the page. This allows you to add specific styling tailored to specific pages.

- **Menu Image:** Select an image from the combo box and it will be associated with the menu item. Note that you can add your own images by uploading them to the directory `images/stories`.

- **SSL Enabled:** Elect whether this page should use SSL and the Secure Site URL.

Internal Link - Search

The Internal Link - Search group contains only on menu item type: Search. The item type makes it possible to display the search form and the search results in the content area of the page, as shown in Figure 8.25. Note that the search form displayed has more features than the basic search form typically used in a module position. The parameters allow some control over these features.

FIGURE 8.25

Example of the Search menu type in action.

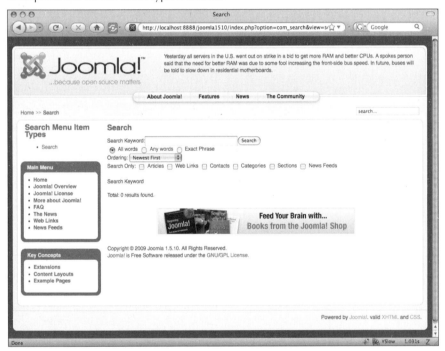

This menu item type has Basic, Component, and System parameters, as shown in Figure 8.26.

FIGURE 8.26

The Search menu type parameters.

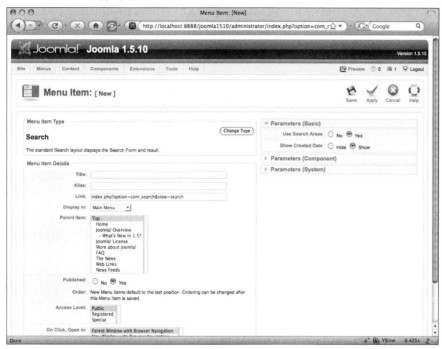

The Basic parameters section contains the following options:

- **Use Search Areas:** If set the Yes, the form will include a set of checkbox filters the visitors can use to refine the search.

- **Show Created Date:** Whether search results will show the date and time the articles were created.

The Component parameters section contains the following options:

- **Gather Search Statistics:** Set this parameter to Yes if you want the system to gather statistics on the usage of the search form.

- **Show Created Date:** Whether search results will show the date and time the articles were created.

The System parameters section contains the following options:

- **Page Title:** Enter the text you want to show in the title bar of the browser when the visitor views the page. If no value is entered, the system will use the menu title. This option can also be used to control the display of the page title on the article itself, where the control below, Show Page Title, is enabled.

- **Show Page Title:** Enable this control to show the page title specified in the field above on the article. If the option is set to Yes, but no text is entered in the Page Title parameter above, then the menu title is used. Note also that this control has no effect on the Article, Section Table, and Category Table menu item types.

- **Page Class Suffix:** Enter a text value here to create a suffix that will be added to all CSS classes related to the page. This allows you to add specific styling tailored to specific pages.

- **Menu Image:** Select an image from the combo box and it will be associated with the menu item. Note that you can add your own images by uploading them to the directory `images/stories`.

- **SSL Enabled:** Elect whether this page should use SSL and the Secure Site URL.

Internal Link - User

There are six different menu item types in the group Internal Link - User. The types all relate to content and functions specific to user accounts, including the login, registration, and various reminder and reset forms. All the menu types in this group share the same System parameters, as shown in Figure 8.27, though a number have unique Basic parameters.

Cross-Reference

For more information on managing users and the related functions, see Chapter 11.

Note

A number of the parameters relevant to this menu item type relate to the ability to customize system messages, for example, the greeting users see when they log in. While you can modify the settings for these items using the parameters discussed later, an alternative exists: Modify the default system messages themselves. The language you see in the default system messages is stored an .ini file located in the language directory on your server. The file can by identified by its suffix: `com_user.ini`. For example, if your site is using the English (Great Britain) language file, you would need to edit `language/en-GB/en-GB.com_user.ini`.

FIGURE 8.27

The User menu type parameters.

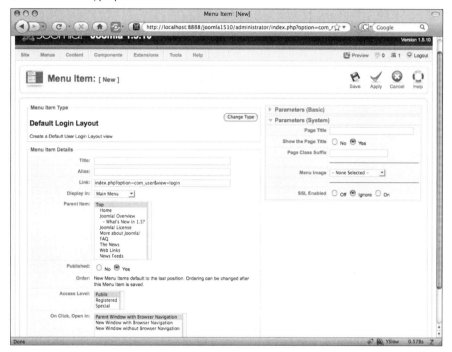

The System parameters section contains the following options:

- **Page Title:** Enter the text you want to show in the title bar of the browser when the visitor views the page. If no value is entered, the system will use the menu title. This option can also be used to control the display of the page title on the article itself, where the control, Show Page Title, is enabled.

- **Show Page Title:** Enable this control to show the page title specified in the field above on the article. If the option is set to Yes, but no text is entered in the Page Title parameter, then the menu title is used. Note also that this control has no effect on the article, Section Table, and Category Table menu item types.

- **Page Class Suffix:** Enter a text value here to create a suffix that will be added to all CSS classes related to the page. This allows you to add specific styling tailored to specific pages.

- **Menu Image:** Select an image from the combo box and it will be associated with the menu item. Note that you can add your own images by uploading them to the directory `images/stories`.

- **SSL Enabled:** Elect whether this page should use SSL and the Secure Site URL.

Default Login Layout

The Default Login Layout menu item type enables you to display a login form in the content area of a page, as shown in Figure 8.28. Note that this page will be used both for login and logout; accordingly, the parameters for this menu item type allow you to tailor the output for either function.

Example of the Default Login Layout menu type in action.

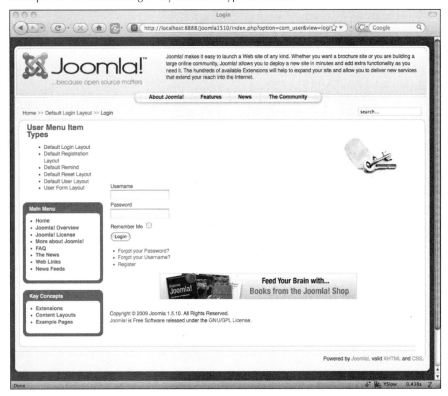

This menu item type contains a number of Basic parameters.

- **Show Login Page Title:** Show or hide the Login Page Title, as defined in the parameter below.

- **Login Page Title:** Enter the name you want to be used as the Page Title; if left blank the title of the menu item will be used. Note that if the previous parameter is set to Hide, this field is meaningless.

- **Login Redirection URL:** By default, Joomla! will redirect the user to the home page after log in. If you want to direct them to another URL, enter it here.

- **Login JS Message:** Choose show for a pop-up welcome message to be displayed to the user upon log in.

- **Login Description:** Show or hide the Login Description text. The text is created in the parameter immediately following.

- **Login Description Text:** Enter the text you want to be used as the Login Description; if left blank the default system message will be used. Note that if the previous parameter is set to Hide, this field is meaningless.

- **Login Image:** Select from the combo box the image you want to display on the Login Page. Note that you can add your own images by uploading them to the directory `images/stories`.

- **Login Image Align:** If you have selected an image to display in the previous parameter, use this parameter to set the image alignment.

- **Show Logout Page Title:** Show or hide the Logout Page Title, as defined in the following parameter.

- **Logout Page Title:** Enter the name you want to be used as the Logout Page title; if left blank the title of the menu item will be used. Note that if the previous parameter is set to Hide, this field is meaningless.

- **Logout Redirection URL:** By default, Joomla! redirects users to the home page after log out. If you want to direct them to another URL, enter it here.

- **Logout JS Message:** Choose Show for a pop-up welcome message to be displayed to the user upon log out.

- **Logout Description:** Show or hide the logout description text. The text is created in the following parameter.

- **Logout Description Text:** Enter the text you want to be used as the Logout Description; if left blank the default system message will be used. Note that if the parameter above is set to hide, this field is meaningless.

- **Logout Image:** Select from the combo box the image you want to display on the Logout Page. Note that you can add your own images by uploading them to the directory `images/stories`.

- **Logout Image Align:** If you have selected an image to display in the parameter above, use this parameter to set the Image Alignment.

Default Registration Layout

Use this menu item type to assign the User Registration Form to its own page, as shown in Figure 8.29.

There are no Basic parameters for this menu item type.

FIGURE 8.29

Example of the Default Registration Layout menu type in action.

Default Remind

This menu item type enables you to place the Forget Your Username? form on a page, as shown in Figure 8.30.

There are no Basic parameters for this menu item type.

FIGURE 8.30

Example of the Default Remind menu type in action.

Default Reset Layout

This menu item type enables you to place the Forgot Your Password? form on a page, as shown in Figure 8.31.

There are no Basic parameters for this menu item type.

FIGURE 8.31

Example of the Default Reset Layout menu type in action.

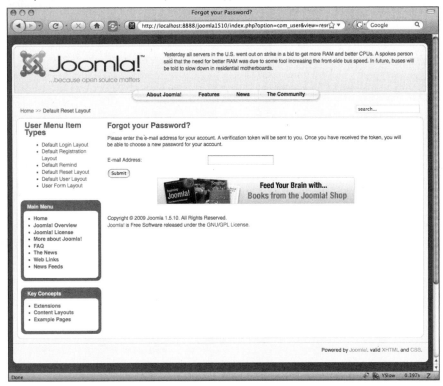

Default User Layout

The system provides the Default User Layout menu item type to enable administrators to create a welcome page to greet users upon login, as shown in Figure 8.32.

This menu item type contains only one Basic parameter, Welcome Description. Enter into this text field the welcome message you want the user to see. To use this menu item type effectively, you need to take the following steps:

1. Create the menu item, setting the access level to Registered.
2. Save the menu item.
3. Go to the Module Manager, under the Extensions menu.
4. Edit the Login Module to set the Login Redirection Page to your newly created menu item.
5. Save the Login module.

FIGURE 8.32

Example of the Default User Layout menu type in action.

Note

Given the limitations of this menu item type, it is probably simpler to create a new article and use it for your Login Redirection Page. If you create the article, you can control the contents easily through the Article Editing dialogue.

User Form Layout

The User Form Layout menu item type provides users with a page where they can manage their account details and set options for their use of the site, including the language and time zone settings, as shown in Figure 8.33.

There are no Basic parameters for this menu item type.

FIGURE 8.33

Example of the User Form Layout menu type in action.

Internal Link - Web Links

The Internal Link - Web Links group contains three menu item types. All three types are concerned with the display of content from the Web Links component. All three types share the same Component and System parameters. These parameters are shown in Figure 8.34.

Cross-Reference

The Web Links component is detailed in Chapter 18.

FIGURE 8.34

The Web Links menu type parameters.

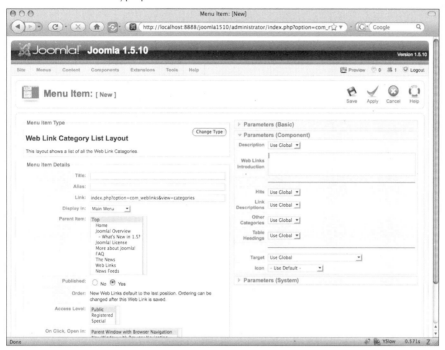

The Component parameters section contains the following options:

- **Description:** Show or hide the Web Links Introduction text. The text is controlled by the parameter immediately below.

- **Web Links Introduction:** Type any text here you want to appear at the top of the page. Note that the previous parameter, Description, must be set to Show for the text to appear.

- **Hits:** Show or hide the number of times each web link has been viewed.

- **Link Descriptions:** Show or hide the link description text for each link. The description text is controlled in the Web Link Editor dialogue.

- **Other Categories:** This parameter has no function for this menu item type.

- **Table Headings:** Show or hide the table headings above each column in the display.

- **Target:** Specify the target for the URL; that is, where the page will open. The options are Parent Window with Browser Navigation, New Window with Browser Navigation, and New Window Without Browser Navigation.

- **Icon:** Select from the comb box an image to display. Note, you can add your own images by uploading them to the `images/M_images` directory on your server.

The System parameters section contains the following options:

- **Page Title:** Enter the text you want to show in the title bar of the browser when the visitor views the page. If no value is entered, the system will use the menu title. This option can also be used to control the display of the page title on the article itself, where the control below, Show Page Title, is enabled.

- **Show Page Title:** Enable this control to show the page title specified in the field above on the article. If the option is set to Yes, but no text is entered in the Page Title parameter above, then the menu title is used. Note also that this control has no effect on the Article, Section Table, and Category Table menu item types.

- **Page Class Suffix:** Enter a text value here to create a suffix that will be added to all CSS classes related to the page. This allows you to add specific styling tailored to specific pages.

- **Menu Image:** Select an image from the combo box and it will be associated with the menu item. Note that you can add your own images by uploading them to the directory `images/stories`.

- **SSL Enabled:** Elect whether this page should use SSL and the Secure Site URL.

Web Link Category List Layout

This menu item type can be used to display a list of the web links categories on a page. The category names are clickable and will display a list of all links in the category, as shown in Figure 8.35.

The Basic parameters of this menu item type contain several options.

- **Image:** Select from the combo box an image to appear on the page. Note that you can add your own images by uploading them to the directory `images/stories`.

- **Image Align:** If you have selected an image in the previous parameter, use this parameter to set the alignment of the image relative to the text.

- **Show a Feed Link:** This allows users to subscribe to an RSS feed for the contents of this page.

Example of the Web Link Category List Layout menu type in action.

Category List Layout

This menu item type displays on a page a list of all the web links in a single category, as shown in Figure 8.36.

This menu item type has two Basic parameters.

- **Category:** Select the name of the category you want to display.
- **Show a Feed Link:** This allows users to subscribe to an RSS feed for the contents of this page.

FIGURE 8.36

Example of the Category List Layout menu type in action.

Web Link Submission Layout

Use this menu item type when you want to enable front-end users to submit web links to your site, as shown in Figure 8.37. This privilege is only available to users with an access level of Special, that is, authors and above. If this menu item is shown to users who lack the proper permissions, they will see an error message when they click on the menu item.

There are no Basic parameters for this menu item type.

FIGURE 8.37

Example of the Web Link Submissions Layout menu type in action.

Internal Link - Wrapper

The Internal Link - Wrapper group contains only one menu item type. This type enables you to create a link to an iFrame, which can be used to display a page inside your site that shows external content, as shown in Figure 8.38.

This menu item type includes Basic, Advanced, and System parameters, as shown in Figure 8.39.

FIGURE 8.38

Example of the Wrapper menu type in action.

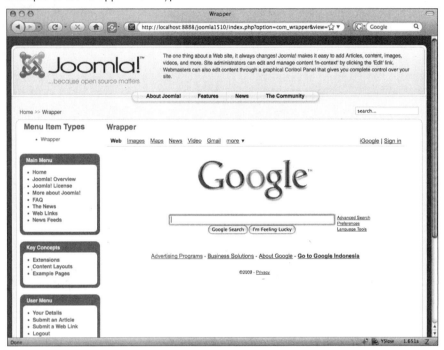

The Basic parameters section contains the following options:

- **Wrapper URL:** Enter in this field the full URL of the page you want to wrap.

- **Scrollbars:** Decide whether to show scrollbars when the size of the content being displayed inside the iFrame is larger than the space provided.

- **Width:** Specify the width of the iFrame. The width can be specified either in pixels or as a percentage. To specify a pixel value, simply enter an integer. To specify a percentage value, enter an integer followed by the percentage symbol (%).

- **Height:** Specify the width of the iFrame. The height can be specified either in pixels or as a percentage. To specify a pixel value, simply enter an integer. To specify a percentage value, enter an integer followed by the percentage symbol (%).

FIGURE 8.39

The Wrapper menu type parameters.

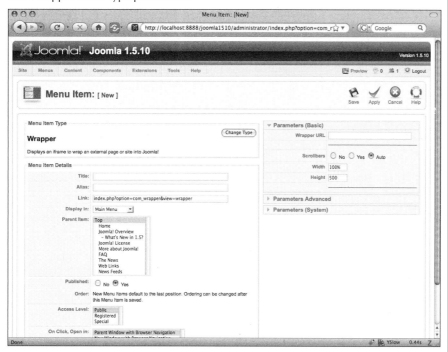

The Advanced parameters section contains the following options:

- **Auto Height:** Select Yes to have the system automatically adjust the height of the iFrame in response to the sixe of the page being wrapped.

- **Auto Add:** Select Yes to have the system automatically add the http:// prefix to the URL you enter in the Basic parameters URL field.

The System parameters section contains the following options:

- **Page Title:** Enter the text you want to show in the title bar of the browser when the visitor views the page. If no value is entered, the system will use the menu title. This option can also be used to control the display of the page title on the article itself, where the following listed control, Show Page Title, is enabled.

- **Show Page Title:** Enable this control to show the Page Title specified in the field above on the article. If the option is set to Yes, but no text is entered in the Page Title parameter above, then the menu title is used. Note also that this control has no effect on the Article, Section Table, and Category Table menu item types.

- **Page Class Suffix:** Enter a text value here to create a suffix that will be added to all CSS classes related to the page. This allows you to add specific styling tailored to specific pages.
- **Menu Image:** Select an image from the combo box and it will be associated with the menu item. Note that you can add your own images by uploading them to the directory `images/stories`.
- **SSL Enabled:** Elect whether this page should use SSL and the Secure Site URL.

External links

The External Link menu item type is used to add to your Joomla! site a link to an external web site. There is only one menu type in this group.

Note that this is the only menu item type that requires you to specify the link in the Menu Item Details. The Link field is provided for you to input the URL that the menu item will link to, as shown in Figure 8.40.

FIGURE 8.40

The External Links menu type parameters.

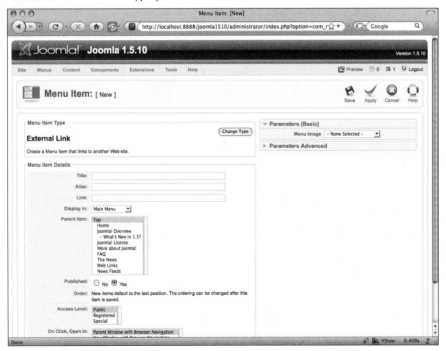

The Basic parameters section contains the option Menu image. Select from the combo box an image to display with the menu item. Note that you can add your own images by uploading them to the directory images/stories.

Note

Though an Advanced parameters heading appears on the workspace, in reality there are no advanced parameters for this menu item type.

Separator

This Menu item type is used to add to a menu a visual separator. Separators provide a break in long lists of menu items and enable you to group menu items visually. There is no other functionality associated with this type.

This Menu item type contains only one parameter, as shown in Figure 8.41. It is Menu Image. You can select from the combo box an image to display with the menu item. Note that you can add your own images by uploading them to the directory images/stories.

FIGURE 8.41

The Separator menu type parameter.

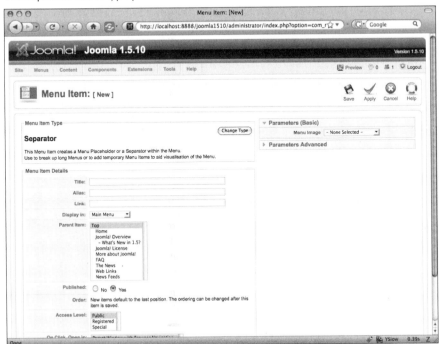

Note

Though an Advanced parameters heading appears on the workspace, in reality there are no advanced parameters for this menu item type.

Menu Alias

The Menu Alias menu item type is designed to allow you to create duplicates of menu items for those situations in which you want to have a menu item appear on more than one menu on the page. By way of example, if you want to have a choice on both the header and the footer of the page, you could either create two standard menu items and place one on each of the menus at the top and bottom of the page or you could create one standard menu item that you assign to one menu and then create a menu alias that you assign to the other menu. The alias will mirror the settings of the original menu item. If you change the original item, then the alias will be modified as well; this simplifies menu item management.

There is only one parameter to this menu item type, Menu Image. You can select from the combo box the menu item you want to link to. This parameter is shown in Figure 8.42.

FIGURE 8.42

The Menu Alias menu type Parameters.

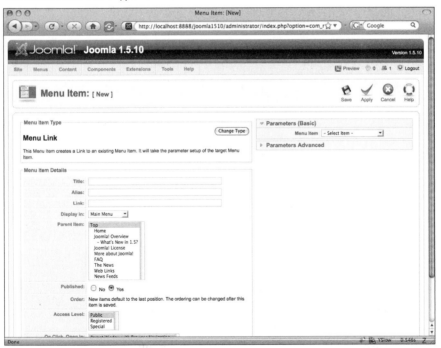

Note

Though an Advanced parameters heading appears on the workspace, in reality there are no advanced parameters for this menu item type.

Creating multitiered menus

The default Joomla! system gives you two methods for creating menus that contain multiple levels of menu items. In short, you can either place all levels of items in one menu or create multiple menus to hold individual levels.

Adding all the items to a single menu can be done with the Menu Item Manager alone, but if you want to split the items by level to display them in multiple menus, you will need to work with both the Menu Item Manager and the Module Manager. In either event, you are creating a parent-child relationship between different menu items and this establishes the hierarchy of the menu items.

The two formatting options allow you a significant degree of flexibility in displaying your menu items. To make the most of the menu options, however, you will need to configure the items properly and you will need some ability to modify the styling of the menus and items.

To create one menu with multiple levels of items, follow these steps:

1. **Access the menu you want to modify by clicking the name of the menu under the option Menus on the main admin navigation.** The Menu Item Manager opens in your browser.

2. **Click the New icon to create a new menu item or click the name of an existing menu item.** The Menu Item Editing dialogue opens.

3. **In the field marked Parent, select a menu item to be the parent of the item you are editing.**

4. **Complete any other fields you want to modify.**

5. **Click the Save icon.** The system saves your changes to the item and returns you to the Menu Item Manager.

This process can be repeated as needed to create multiple levels of menu items, where each child item is attached to a parent. In this case, all the parents and their children appear inside one menu.

If, on the other hand, you want to display the various menus and submenus in separate menu modules, you can do so by following these steps:

1. **Assign your menu items to parent/child relationships.**

2. **Click on Module Manager, under the Extensions menu.** The Module Manager loads in your browser.

3. **Click the name of the menu you want to divide into multiple modules.** The Module Editing dialogue opens in your browser.

   4. Set the Start Level to zero.

   5. Set the End Level to 1.

   6. **Click the New icon at the top right of the page.** Page one of the New Module dialogue opens.

   7. **Select the module type Menu and then click the Next icon.** Page 2 of the New Module dialogue appears in your browser.

   8. **Type a name for the module in the Title field.**

   9. **Select from the Menu Name combo box under the Module parameters, the name of the menu that contains your submenu items.**

   10. Set the Start Level to 1.

   11. Set the end Level to 2.

   12. Set any other options you desire.

   13. Click the Save icon.

   14. **The system creates the new menu module and returns you to the Module Manager.**

The new Menu module now displays only when the parent menu item is clicked. This approach to creating multi-tier menus enables you to create separate subnavigation menus that appear only when active.

Note

The options to control whether the menu is expanded to display all the levels by default, or is closed by default and expands only when clicked, are contained in the parameters of each individual menu's module.

Cross-Reference

See Chapter 23 for a discussion of menu styling. See Chapter 25 for a discussion of extensions that can be added to your site to enhance the menu functionality.

Editing and deleting menu items

Existing menu items can be edited from the Menu Item Manager. To edit a menu item, either click the menu item name in the Menu Item Manager, or select the menu item and then click the Edit icon on the Menu Item Manager toolbar. Regardless of which method you use, the system opens the Edit Menu Item dialogue.

The Edit Menu Item dialogue is identical to the New Menu Item dialogue, with the same fields and requirements as previously discussed .

To make changes to a menu item, simply alter the desired fields in the Edit Menu Item dialogue, then click the Save or Apply icon on the toolbar. Any changes you have made will be applied immediately.

The Menu Trash Manager

The Trash Manager feature of Joomla! 1.5.x provides you with a way to clean up and remove menu items from the general admin area of the site. Sending a menu item to the trash will result in the menu item being removed from the Menu Item Manager and moved to the Menu Trash Manager.

Menu items moved to the Trash Manager are held there indefinitely. The items can be restored or deleted at the option of the administrator. Restored items are moved back to their original locations; deleted items are permanently removed from the system and cannot be restored.

Joomla! 1.5's Menu Trash Manager interface is shown in Figure 8.43.

FIGURE 8.43

The Menu Trash Manager interface.

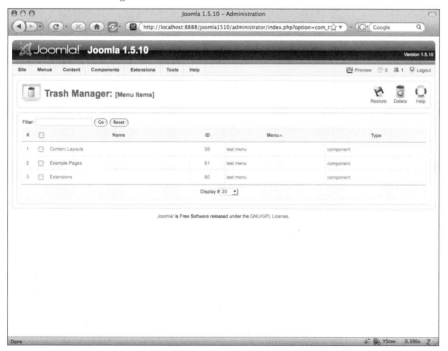

The toolbar at the top of the Trash Manager provides quick access to the following functions:

- **Restore:** Select one or more menu items from the list and then click this icon to restore them and remove them from the trash.

- **Delete:** Select one or more menu items from the list and then click this icon to delete the items permanently.

- **Help:** Click to access the online help files related to the active screen.

Below the toolbar and above the list of menu items is the Filter field. The filter works like a search box. Type a word or phrase into the field and then click Go. The page reloads and displays the results of the search. To clear the screen and return to a full listing, click the Reset button.

The main content area of the screen contains a list of all the menu items in the Trash Manager. The columns provided are:

- **#** : An indexing number assigned by Joomla! This cannot be changed.
- **Checkbox (no label):** Click in a checkbox to select a menu item; this is needed if you want to use several of the toolbar options.
- **Name:** This field displays the name of the menu item.
- **ID:** This is a system-generated ID number for the item and cannot be changed.
- **Menu:** The name of the menu where this item was located when it was moved to the Trash.
- **Type:** Displays the menu item type of the item.

Finally, at the bottom of the screen, below the content area, is the Display # option. Change the value in the combo box control to alter the number of menu items that are displayed on the page. The default value can be altered by changing the List Length option on the Global Configuration Manager.

To move a menu item to the trash, follow these steps:

1. **Access the Menu Item Manager containing the menu items you want to remove.** To do this, go to this Menus option on the admin navigation bar and click the name of the menu where the items are located. The Menu Item Manager opens in your browser.

2. **Click the checkboxes next to the items you want to remove.**

3. **Click the Trash icon on the top-right toolbar.** The system removes the items to the Trash Manager.

Note

Any menu items moved to the trash will be instantly unpublished and not visible to site visitors.

Caution

Deleting a menu item involves moving the Item to the trash, then deleting it permanently from the Trash Manager. Note that there is no confirmation dialogue prior to moving an Item to the trash. Alternatively, you can delete an entire menu and its items simultaneously from the Menu Manager dialogue.

Restoring items from the trash

Menu items moved to the trash are held there indefinitely until further action is taken by the administrator. Any menu item can be restored at any time. The process of restoring an item is simple and the result instantaneous: The item is removed from the Trash Manager and returned to where it was located when it was moved to the trash.

Menu items restored from the menu trash are moved back to the menu where they were located at the time they were moved to the trash. Menu items restored from the menu trash will be unpublished and pushed to the bottom of the order of items on the menu. To manage the items, access the Menu Item Manager.

To restore a menu item from the trash, follow these steps:

1. **Click the checkbox next to the item you want to restore.**

2. **Click the Restore icon on the top-right toolbar.** The Restore Confirmation dialogue opens, as shown in Figure 8.44.

FIGURE 8.44

The Restore Confirmation dialogue.

3. **Check the information; if correct, click the Restore button; otherwise click the Cancel icon.** A confirmation window opens.

4. **Click OK.** The system removes the item from the trash, restores it to its previous location, and returns you to the Trash Manager.

Permanently deleting items

Menu items held in the Trash Manager can be removed from the system by deleting them. Deleting an item from the Trash Manager results in the item's permanent removal from the system; it cannot be restored once deleted.

To permanently delete a menu item from the trash, follow these steps:

1. **Click the checkbox next to the item you want to delete.**

2. **Click the Delete icon on the top-right toolbar.** The Delete Confirmation dialogue opens, as shown in Figure 8.45.

FIGURE 8.45

The Delete confirmation dialogue.

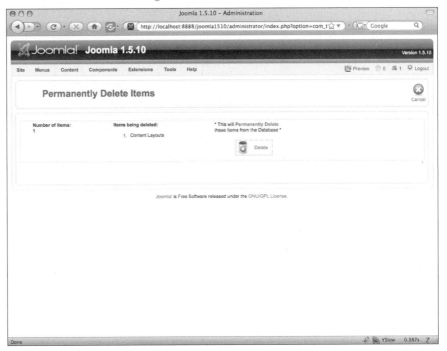

3. **Check the information; if correct, click the Delete button; otherwise click the Cancel icon.** The system removes the item from the trash, restores it to its previous location, and returns you to the Trash Manager.

Controlling Access to Menus and Menu Items

Both menus and menu items are subject to access level controls. The visibility of menus and menu items can be controlled either in tandem or individually, given certain logical constraints. As a general rule, where there is a conflict between the access level settings of a menu and those of an item on that menu, the more restrictive access level will be applied.

By way of example: If the access level of the items of a particular menu are set to Public, but the access level of the menu itself is set to Restricted, nonauthenticated users (Public users) will not be able to see either the menu or the individual menu items. In contrast, if the access level of the menu is set to Public, but the access levels of the items are set to Restricted, the menu will be visible, but the menu items will not.

Menu access levels are set via the relevant menu module. To set access to a menu as a whole, follow these steps:

1. **Click Module Manager, under the Extensions menu.** The Module Manager loads.
2. **Identify the menu module that provides the menu you want to edit.**
3. **Click the name of the relevant menu module.** The Module Editing dialogue opens in your browser.
4. **Change the access level control to suit your needs — Public, Registered, or Special.**
5. **Click the Save icon.** The system saves the changes and returns you to the Module Manager.

Menu item access levels are set inside the Menu Item Edit dialogue. To set access to a menu item, follow these steps:

1. **Under the menus option on the admin navigation bar, select the name of the menu that contains the item you want to edit.** The Menu Item Manager opens in your browser.
2. **Click the name of the item you want to edit.** The Menu Item Editing dialogue appears in your browser.
3. **Change the access level control to suit your needs — Public, Registered, or Special.**
4. **Click the Save icon.** The system saves the changes and returns you to the Menu Item Manager.

Note
The access levels for articles and many other functionalities can also be set via the parameters specific to that article or functionality. This means you may in some cases have a third level of access controls that you must consider. Regardless, the general rule remains the same: Where there is a conflict, the more restrictive access level applies.

Summary

In this chapter, we have covered the use of both the Menu component and the Menus module. You learned the following:

- How to create, edit, and delete menus
- How to configure the Menus Manager to work in concert with the Menus module
- How to create and edit a menu module
- How to create and edit menu items
- How to create multitiered menus
- How to control access to menus and menu items

Managing the Front Page of Your Site

The front page of your web site is your first impression to visitors. Because the front page has such an important role, Joomla! creators have provided site owners with dedicated tools for managing the page and the contents that appear on it. Gaining command of those tools is the goal of this chapter.

Using the tools in the admin system, you can assign articles to your front page, as well as component output and module output. Although controlling the contents that appear on the page is the easiest way to make your front page effective, you can also work with the layout of the page to achieve more variety. The controls on the Menu Item and Article parameters give you a measure of control over the layout, and if you want to do even more, you can assign a unique template to provide the front page with its own distinct look and feel.

Controlling Front Page Layout

Your default Joomla! site comes with only one Menu Item Type tailored for use as the front page of your site. That Menu Item Type, named Front Page Blog Layout, has several options that allow you to customize the appearance of the front page to suit your needs. The Menu Item Type options, together with the parameters associated with the articles that are displayed on the page, give you basic content layout control.

Note

In addition to content items, modules assigned to the front page also impact your site's appearance. The options in this area are limited by the availability of module position holders in the particular template that you are using for the front page. Publishing modules to the front page is discussed later in this chapter.

Understanding the default content layout options

The front page you see in the default Joomla! installation is created from the Menu Item Type named Front Page Blog Layout, as shown in Figure 9.1. As noted, this is the only Menu Item Type provided specifically for the front page. The unique nature of the Front Page Blog Layout Menu Item Type is a key factor, because the front page management tools in the system are all dependent upon your use of the Front Page Blog Layout Menu Item Type. In other words, if you select an alternative Menu Item Type for your front page, the Front Page Manager and the option to assign articles to the front page via the Article Manager are not available to you. Although the loss of those tools is not fatal to successful management of your site, they are convenient to use and you should think twice before foregoing these useful utilities. In the following section, we focus on how to get the most out of the default system by using the default Front Page Blog Layout.

Cross-Reference

See Chapter 8 for a complete discussion of the layout choices available for Joomla's many Menu Item Types. The chapter also includes screen shots showing the impact of each of the options.

To view the key parameters that contribute to the layout you see in the default site, access the menu item that controls the front page by following these steps:

1. **Click on the Main Menu option under the man nav choice named Menus.** The Main menu Menu Item Manager opens in your browser.

2. **Click on the menu item named Home.** The Menu Item Editing dialogue opens in your browser.

The basic parameters on the Menu Item Editing dialogue, shown in Figure 9.2, provide the key layout options that impact the layout you see on your default front page. The four parameters here set the number of items displayed, the number of columns used to hold the articles, and the number of links shown at the bottom of the screen.

FIGURE 9.1

The default Joomla! Front Page in Joomla! 1.5.x. This shows the sample data installed.

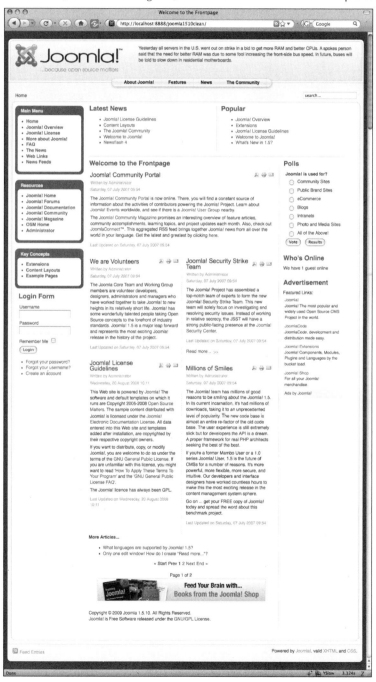

FIGURE 9.2

The default Joomla! Front Page in Joomla! 1.5.x. This shows the sample data installed with callouts.

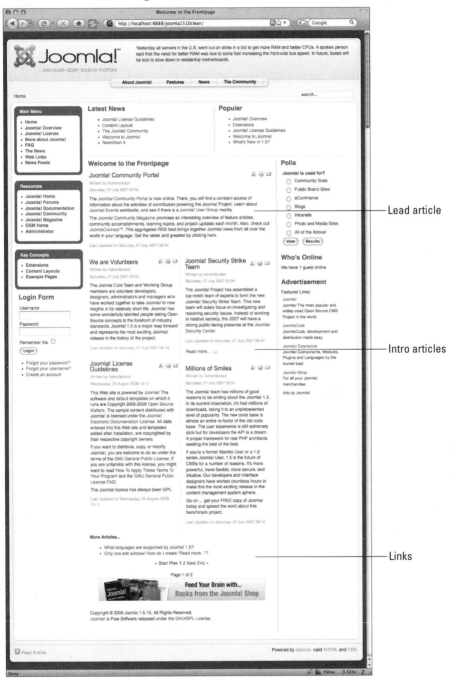

In the default configuration, the front page is configured to show one leading article, four intro articles, two columns, and four links. Here's how that translates into the display you see in Figure 9.1.

- **# Leading:** A leading article is positioned at the top of the content area and spans the width of the content area. In the default configuration, the value of this parameter is set to one. The leading article is not impacted by the setting of the Columns parameters. If you set this value to zero, then no leading article is used and the first articles that appear are the intro articles.

- **# Intro:** The value in this parameter sets the number of articles that appear after the leading articles. Note that the intro articles are subject to the settings in the Columns parameter. If you set this value to zero, no intro articles are shown.

- **Columns:** Controls the number of columns used to display the intro articles. Note that the value needs to be set between one and three.

- **# Links:** Controls the number of links that are shown at the bottom of the content area of the page. Set the value to zero if you do not want to use this feature.

As a content manager, one of the issues that you have to be aware of is the need to keep track of the number of articles that you have assigned to the front page at any point in time. Regardless of your settings in the Menu Item parameters, the system does not automatically limit the number of items that can be assigned to the front page. For example, in the default configuration with the sample data installed, the settings in the Menu Item Type parameters provide for the display of no more than five articles on the front page. However, the default sample data in the system has seven articles assigned to the front page. As a result, the default site shows five articles on the front page, and then creates a second page to hold the additional two articles. When this happens, the front page displays pagination controls at the bottom of the Front Page (refer to Figure 9.1). While the ability to push articles onto additional pages may be desirable in a blog-type site, you may not want this format on your site.

A different issue arises if you fail to publish a sufficient number of articles to the front page. Looking again at the default configuration, if you publish fewer than five articles to the front page, the layout may not be so pleasing to the eye. You can see the impact of this on the second page where the additional front page items are displayed, as shown in Figure 9.3. The system shows two items on this page, which leaves a blank spot in the layout where a third article would appear in the second column.

Single-column layout

If you prefer for your site to use a single-column layout (see Figure 9.4), you can apply two different approaches to create this look with the default Menu Item Type. One option is to set the Columns parameter to a value of 1, in which case you can use both the #Leading and #Intro to control the number of articles shown. Alternatively, you can set the Intro Articles parameter to the value zero and use only the Leading Articles parameter to set the number of articles displayed. No matter which option you choose, the visual output on the front page is the same.

FIGURE 9.3

The second front page that shows in the default installation. Because only two articles are on this page, the layout is not as pleasing.

FIGURE 9.4

Creating a single-column layout.

Multicolumn layout

The default system uses a hybrid layout, with a single column leading article followed by the intro articles displayed in two columns. Common variations to this layout include using one or more of the following modifications to the parameters:

- Use more than one leading article

- Change the number of intro articles

- Change the Columns parameter to display three columns

Alternatively, if you want to create a multicolumn layout throughout the front page content area, you can do so by setting the value of the #Leading parameter to zero. This configuration results in only the intro articles being displayed. You can then set the Columns parameter to display the intro articles in either two or three columns.

Tip
The Advanced parameters for this Menu Item Type include options to control the order of multiple columns — either ordering them down or across.

Using a distinct template for the front page

Although the default Joomla! system uses only one template to display all the pages on the site, you can easily change this and assign a distinct template to serve as your front page. Many sites employ more than one template, often for the purpose of providing a unique look and feel for the front page. Because the front page of your web site sets the tone and provides the first impression for your visitors, creating a template that is specifically designed to present the Front Page in the most optimal fashion is often judged to be worthwhile. A separate template, or templates, can then be used for the internal pages.

The assignment of templates to pages is handled by Joomla!'s Template Manager. To set a separate template for the front page, follow these steps:

1. Log in to the admin system of your Joomla! site.

2. **Click on the Template Manager option, located under the Extensions menu on the main admin nav.** The Template Manager loads in your browser.

3. **Click the radio button next to the name of the template you want to assign to the front page of your site.**

4. **Click the Edit icon on the top-right toolbar.** The Template Editing dialogue opens in your browser.

5. **Click the radio button Select From List.**

6. **Select from the Menu Selection combo box the menu link that identifies your front page.** For many sites, and in the default installation, that option is named Home.

7. **Click the Save icon on the top-right toolbar.** The system now associates the template with the front page, closes the Template Editing dialogue, and returns you to the Template Manager.

FIGURE 9.5

A completely multicolumn layout, in this case created by setting the #Leading parameter to zero.

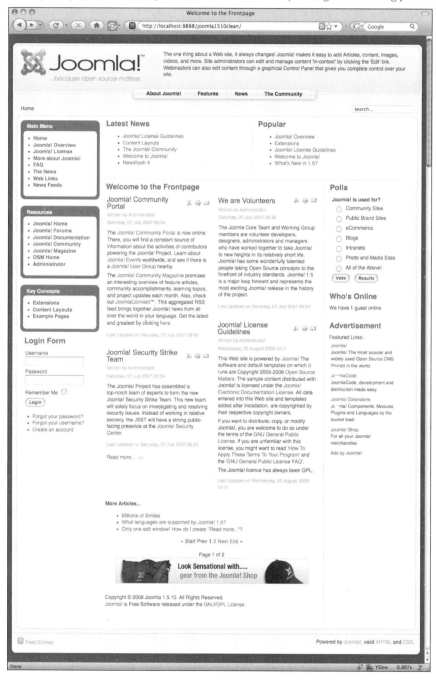

Note

Before you can begin, you must move the template files to your server, by using either FTP, your hosting service's file manager, or the Install function in Joomla's Extensions Manager. After the template files are on your server, you can complete the process.

Cross-Reference

To find out how to add more templates to your system, see Chapter 20.

Publishing Articles on the Front Page

If you are using the default front page features, you can control the articles that appear on your front page via the Article Manager and the Front Page Manager. The Article Manager gives you the ability to assign pages to the front page. The Front Page Manager allows you to manage the articles assigned to the front page.

Joomla! 1.6

Joomla! 1.6 does not include the Front Page Manager feature, instead providing for the management of the front page items via the Featured Article Manager. The new Featured Article Manager functions in essentially the same fashion as the old Front Page Manager and can be found under the Components menu, under the sub-heading articles. Setting an article as Featured will result in that article appearing on the front page and also appearing inside the Featured Article Manager.

Working with the Front Page Manager

The Front Page Manager holds only those articles that you have assigned to the Front Page. When an article is unassigned to the Front Page, you can remove it from the Front Page Manager. The Manager enables you to see all the articles assigned to the Front Page in one place and to perform basic management tasks, such as reordering the articles or moving them to the Article Archive.

Cross-Reference

Working with articles and the Article Manager are discussed in Chapter 5. Article Archives are covered in Chapter 2.

The Front Page Manager is located under the Content menu on the main admin navigation bar; clicking on that option opens the Front Page Manager in your browser, as shown in Figure 9.6.

FIGURE 9.6

Joomla! 1.5.x's Front Page Manager interface.

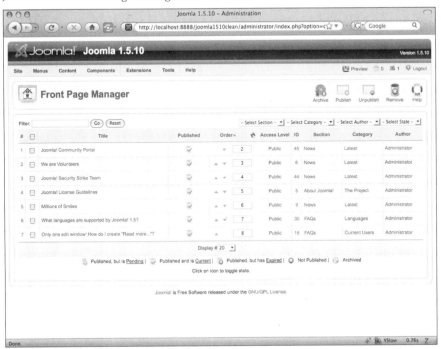

The toolbar at the top of the Front Page Manager provides quick access to the following functions:

- **Archive:** Select one or more active articles from the list and then click this icon to archive them.

- **Publish:** Select one or more articles from the list and then click this icon to publish them.

- **Unpublish:** Select one or more articles from the list and then click this icon to unpublish them.

- **Remove:** Select one or more articles from the list and then click this icon to remove them from the front page.

- **Help:** Click to access the online Help files related to the active screen.

Below the toolbar and above the list of articles are five sorting and searching tools to help you manage long lists of articles:

- **The Filter field** on the left works like a search box. Type a word or phrase into the field and then click Go. The page reloads and displays the results of the search. To clear the screen and return to a full listing, click the Reset button.

- **The Select Section filter** allows you to filter and display the articles according to the section to which they are assigned. To reset this filter, change the combo box back to the default setting.

- **The Select Category filter** allows you to filter and display the articles according to the category to which they are assigned. To reset this filter, change the combo box back to the default setting.

- **The Select Author filter** allows you to filter and display the articles according to the author associated with them. To reset this filter, change the combo box back to the default setting.

- **The Select State filter** on the far right allows you to filter and display the articles according to whether they are published or unpublished. This provides an easy way to identify all articles that are currently active on the front page. To reset this filter, change the combo box back to the default setting.

The main content area of the screen contains a list of all the articles that are currently assigned to the Front Page of your Joomla! site. The columns provided are:

- **#** : An indexing number assigned by Joomla! This number cannot be changed.

- **Checkbox (no label):** Click a radio button to select an article; do this if you want to use several of the toolbar options.

- **Title:** This field displays the full name of the article. Click on the name to edit the article.

- **Published:** A green checkmark in this column indicates the publication state of the article. As indicated by the legend that appears at the very bottom of the Article Manager, the icon that is displayed indicates the publication state. You can click on the icon to publish or unpublish the article, depending on its state:

  - A yellow dot against an article icon indicates the article is approved and scheduled for publication but is pending.

  - A green checkmark against an article icon indicates the article is currently published.

  - A red circle with an X against an article icon indicates the article was published but has expired.

  - A red circle with an X in it (without an article icon) indicates the article is neither published nor scheduled for publication.

  - A gray circle with a crossbar (without an article icon) indicates the article is archived.

Tip

If you hover the cursor over the Published icon, the system displays the article's start and stop publication dates.

- **Order:** The number indicates the order of the article, relative to the other articles. You can reorder the articles either by clicking on the green arrows to move an item up or down in the order, or by entering numbers for the order and then clicking the save icon at the top of the column.

- **Access Level:** Shows the access level set for that article. The options are Public, Registered, and Special. Click the word to change between the three options.

- **ID:** The system-generated user ID number. This number is used internally by the system and cannot be changed by the user.

- **Section:** Shows the name of the section to which the article is assigned. Click on the name of the section to open the Section editing dialogue.

- **Category:** Shows the name of the category to which the article is assigned. Click on the name of the category to open the Category editing dialogue.

- **Author:** Shows the name of the author of the article. Click on the name of the author to open the User editing dialogue for the author.

Finally, at the bottom of the screen, below the content area, is the Display # option. Change the value in the combo box control to alter the number of articles that are displayed on the page. The default value can be altered by changing the List Length option on the Global Configuration Manager.

Working without the Front Page Manager

If you have chosen for your Front Page a Menu Item Type other than Front Page Blog Layout, you will not be able to manage the contents with the Front Page Manager; you need to manually control your front page content.

The method for managing the Front Page content depends upon the Menu Item Type chosen for the front page. For example, if you have chosen to display a single article on the front page and have done so by designating as your front page the Menu Item Type named article layout, you will control the contents of the front page directly from the Basic Parameters of the Article Layout Menu Item dialogue. In contrast, if you have chosen to display for your home page the contents of a section or a category, you can manage the order and appearance of the articles from the Section or Category Manager.

The key here is that if you do not use the default option, you can forget about controlling your front page in the default fashion; assigning articles to the front page has no impact on the front page, and the Front Page Manager is rendered useless. Given these disadvantages, most people think twice before exploring options other than the default front page setup.

Tip

Chances are you can achieve your goals for the front page without abandoning the Front Page Menu Item Type. Before you decide to abandon the default setup, explore thoroughly the results that can be achieved through a combination of the options built into the system, including parameter settings, block assignments, and template assignment. Proper, perhaps even creative, use of the default options allows you to retain all the system's functionality and thereby ease the burden of maintaining the site over time.

Publishing Component Output on the Front Page

The default components in your Joomla! system are capable of displaying output either through modules or on a page. Displaying component output in the content area of a page requires the creation of a menu item that links directly to the component. In the case of the front page, however, this option is not available if you are using the default front page setup.

In the default system, it is possible to use the output of the following components as the site's front page: contacts, news feeds, polls, and web links. In all cases, this is done by creating a menu item of the appropriate Menu Item Type and then setting the menu item as the front page. (I discuss this earlier in this chapter.)

Although the display of component output on the front page is unlikely to be an issue for most site owners, it is more likely to arise if you are using third-party components to provide more advanced functionality to your site. The good news is that many third-party components that supply significant output also provide options for getting it on the front page. If all else fails, you can explore options for getting the output on the front page through the use of modules, as I discuss in the following section.

Publishing Modules on the Front Page

Modules can be published on any page, including the front page, if Module Position Holders are available in the active template. In the default system, much of the output you see on the front page of the site is provided by modules, as shown in Figure 9.7.

One of the advantages to using modules to place content on your pages is the fact that you can show modules on specific pages and in specific positions; this gives you the ability to provide your site with a great deal of variety simply through creative use of module assignments. In most templates, the Module Position Holders fold up and disappear from sight when nothing is assigned to them. This feature has many practical advantages. In addition to avoiding the appearance of blank spots or holes on your page when a module is unpublished, you can also use module assignments to control whether a page displays one, two, or three columns. For example, in the default system, the front page uses a three-column layout. You can change that easily into a two-column layout simply by hiding all the modules on one side of the page, thereby allowing the content area to expand and fill the space previously occupied by the modules, as shown in Figure 9.8.

FIGURE 9.7

The front page of the default Joomla! 1.5.x site, with the modules marked.

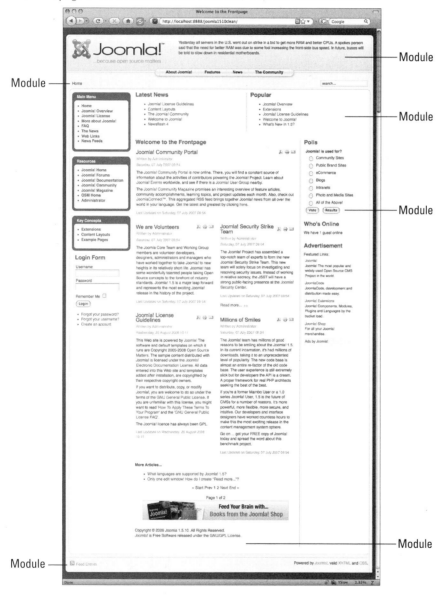

FIGURE 9.8

The front page of the default Joomla! 1.5.x. site, in this case with the modules on the right side of the page unpublished, which allows the content area to expand and create a two-column layout.

Tip

Modules provide many options for content display. When there are Module Position Holders placed at the top or bottom of the content area, you can assign component output or additional content to those module positions. This provides you with alternative content areas that can be managed independently and without reliance on the Front Page Manager. Additionally, as discussed in Chapter 7, you can insert modules inside of articles, thereby giving you even more flexibility.

Summary

In this chapter, we have covered the various tasks associated with managing the front page of your site. You learned the following:

- How to assign articles to the front page
- How to control front page layout
- How to use the Front Page Manager
- How to configure the default system to give you variety on your front page
- Alternatives to the default system's approach to front page management
- Working with component and module output on the front page.

Working with the User Manager

Effective command of user privileges and access controls is essential to the creation of a successful web site. Users are the lifeblood of any site and proper user management is needed to both inspire repeat visitors and to protect the integrity of the site. Joomla! provides several tools that enable user privileges and access; the most important of these tool is the User Manager.

In this chapter, I take a detailed look at the Joomla! User Manager and how it is used to create and manage the registered users on your Web site. I also examine the connection between the various Joomla! User Groups and the Access Level controls that are associated with the site's many content items, components, modules, and plugins.

Introducing the User Manager

The User Manager handles the creation and management of all registered users in the Joomla! system. The User Manager is located inside the Joomla! admin system. After you have logged in to the admin system, you can access the User Manager in two ways: either by clicking on the User Manager icon on the Control Panel or by selecting the User Manager option from the Site menu. Figure 10.1 shows the default User Manager in Joomla! 1.5.x.

FIGURE 10.1

The Joomla! 1.5.x User Manager interface, showing the default administrator account (logged in) and one front-end user (not logged in).

The toolbar at the top of the User Manager provides quick access to the following functions:

- **Logout:** Select one or more users from the list and then click this icon to manually log the users out of the system.

- **Delete:** Select one or more users from the list and then click this icon to delete the user account(s).

- **Edit:** Select a user from the list and then click this icon to edit the user's account details.

- **New:** Click to create a new user account.

- **Help:** Click to access the online Help files related to the active screen.

Three sorting and searching tools to help you manage long lists of users are below the toolbar. They are:

- **The Filter field** on the left works like a search box for the User Manager. Type a word or phrase into the field and then click Go. The page reloads and displays the results of the search. To clear the screen and return to a full listing, click the Reset button.

- **The Select Group filter** on the right side allows you to display only those users that have been assigned to a specific group. Note that the combo box lists all of the user groups provided by Joomla!, regardless of whether any users are assigned to those groups. In other words, you can filter by a group that has no members, in which case the system will return no results. To reset this filter, change the combo box back to the default setting.

- **The Select Log Status filter** on the far right allows you to filter and display the users according to whether they are presently logged in to the system. This provides an easy way to identify all users that are currently active on the site. To reset this filter, change the combo box back to the default setting.

The main content area of the screen contains a list of all the registered users in your Joomla! site. The columns provided are:

- **#** : An indexing number assigned by Joomla! This number cannot be changed.

- **Checkbox (no label):** Click in a checkbox to select a user account; this is needed if you want to use several of the toolbar options.

- **Name:** This field displays the full name of the user. Click on the name to edit the user's details.

- **Username:** The name displayed in this field is the username needed for login.

- **Logged In:** A checkmark in this column indicates that the user is currently logged in to the system. This field is blank if the user is not logged in.

- **Enabled:** A green checkmark in this column indicates that the account is active. The field shows a red X when the user account is disabled. A user account may be disabled for one of two reasons: Either the user has been blocked by an administrator, or the user has failed to confirm and activate a new account. Administrators can toggle between the two settings by clicking on the icon shown.

- **Group:** The group to which the user is assigned.

- **Email:** The e-mail address associated with this user account. Click the address to send the user an e-mail.

- **Last Visit:** This column displays the date and time the user last logged in to the site.

- **ID:** The system-generated user ID number.

Finally, at the bottom of the screen, below the content area, is the Display # option. Change the value in the combo box control to alter the number of users that are displayed on the page. The default value can be altered by changing the List Length option on the Global Configuration Manager.

Cross-Reference

See Chapter 4 to find out more about the Global Configuration Manager.

Joomla! 1.6

Significant changes to the User Manager functionality in Joomla! 1.6 have been planned, however at the time of writing this chapter the final version of Joomla! 1.6 was not yet available for review.

Understanding the Joomla! User Hierarchy

The Joomla! 1.5.x system provides a fixed user hierarchy consisting of seven different levels. User access levels are called groups in Joomla! The seven groups are divided between users with only front-end access, and those with access to both the front end and the back end of the site. Each group has different privileges in the system. Higher-level groups always include all the privileges of lower-level groups as shown in Figure 10.2

One of the unfortunate limitations of the Joomla! 1.5.x system is a lack of flexibility in relation to users access levels. User Group privileges are fixed and cannot be modified. Moreover, you cannot create new groups, or assign to individual users privileges that are inconsistent with the group to which they belong. If you have a compelling need for greater flexibility in your user access levels, you must install a third-party extension to enhance the default system.

FIGURE 10.2

The Hierarchy of User Privileges.

	Front-end Groups				Back-end Groups		
	Registered	Author	Editor	Publisher	Manager	Administrator	Super Administrator
view Public content	✓	✓	✓	✓	✓	✓	✓
view Registered content	✓	✓	✓	✓	✓	✓	✓
view Special content	X	✓	✓	✓	✓	✓	✓
create new Articles	X	✓	✓	✓	✓	✓	✓
edit own Articles	X	✓	✓	✓	✓	✓	✓
edit all Articles	X	X	✓	✓	✓	✓	✓
publish Articles	X	X	X	✓	✓	✓	✓
access Admin system	X	X	X	X	✓	✓	✓
manage Menu Items	X	X	X	X	✓	✓	✓
manage Menus	X	X	X	X	X	✓	✓
manage Users	X	X	X	X	X	✓	✓
manage Components, Modules, Plugins	X	X	X	X	X	✓	✓
manage Templates	X	X	X	X	X	X	✓
manage Language Packs	X	X	X	X	X	X	✓
access Global Configuration Manager	X	X	X	X	X	X	✓

Classifying public front-end users

Four different groups are classified as public front-end users. The groups are named Registered, Author, Editor, and Publisher. The users assigned to these groups have a limited access to only the front end of the site. Although they can log in to the front end and perform tasks, they do not have the ability to log into the back end of the site. This limited form of access is useful both for providing control to content and for setting up a workflow that allows users to add content to the site.

Registered

Registered users are the most basic and the most limited access group. A user in this group can view pages and menus where the access level has been set to either Public or Registered. This user group has no ability to add or edit content items. Typically this user group is concerned with access to content, not with administration privileges. This group allows you to recognize and distinguish certain users from general public viewers of the web site and to allow your Registered site visitors to see more items and do more things than a general public visitor.

Author

The Author group is one step up the hierarchy from a Registered visitor. Authors cannot only access restricted content items and menus, but can also access pages and menus where the access level has been set to Special. The most important privilege that users in this group enjoy is the ability to add content to pages from the front end.

The Author group is typically used by administrators to create a front-end content management workflow. An Author can add content to pages and edit content they have created. Authors cannot, however, edit the pages of other users. Additionally, Authors cannot schedule or publish content items and they cannot create content structures, such as sections or categories. As such, this group is typically part of a larger work flow process that includes other user groups that complete the publication cycle. In the default configuration, members of the Author group are also able to submit web links from the front end of the site, though this can be modified by the site administrator.

Editor

Users assigned to the Editor group enjoy the same privileges as authors, plus the ability to edit the content items created by other users. Editors are part of a front-end content management workflow, but because they are unable to schedule or publish pages, Editors are normally part of a larger schema involving other user groups.

Publisher

The Publisher group is the highest level of public front-end users. Publishers enjoy the same privileges as Editors, plus they can create pages, edit the pages of other users, and schedule and publish pages.

Classifying public back-end users

Three groups are classified as Public back-end users: Manager, Administrator, and Super Administrator. Users assigned to these groups are able to log in to the back-end administration system of your site; accordingly, care should be taken to only grant this level of access to trusted users.

Manager

In terms of privileges, Managers are more concerned with content management than with system administration. Users assigned to the Managers group enjoy rights very similar to those of Publishers, but with the added ability to create content structures, such as sections and categories and the ability to work with the site's menus. Unlike Publishers, Managers are able to use the admin interface to edit and otherwise manage pages. Because the admin interface is typically more user-friendly for editing pages than the front end, the ability to access the back end is a considerable advantage.

Administrator

The Administrator group has significant system administration privileges. Users in this group enjoy all the rights of a Manager, plus the ability to work with the site's users, modules, and components.

Super Administrator

The Super Administrator Group is the Joomla! equivalent of a Super User. This user group is the most powerful in the system, with no limits on the user's ability to perform tasks with the system. Key privileges, such as access to the Global Configuration Manager and the ability take the site offline make this group suitable for only the most trusted users. As a general rule, you can restrict membership to this group to the fewest number of persons possible.

Tip

A Super Administrator account cannot be directly deleted, but it can be downgraded to a lower level group and then deleted.

Adding Users to the System

You can add an unlimited number of users to your system. You can create new users in one of two ways: by a site administrator via the User Manager, or by the users themselves via the front-end user registration process.

In this section, we discuss adding users through the admin system, because this way is the most common and the most powerful approach to user creation. Note that if you want to create a user account with more than just the most basic of user permissions and privileges, then you must create the account from inside the back-end User Manager.

Later in this chapter, you find out about enabling user registration in order to allow users to create their own accounts.

Creating a new user

A Super Administrator can add new users to your Joomla! system from inside the User Manager. To create a new user, follow these steps:

1. Log in to the back-end admin system.

2. **Click the User manager icon in the Control Panel or select the option User Manager under the Site menu.** The User manager loads in your browser window.

3. **Click the New icon on the User manager toolbar.** The New User dialogue opens.

4. Type the user's name in the Name field.

5. Assign a username by typing in the field marked Username.

6. Type the user's e-mail address in the field marked E-mail.

7. Assign the user a password in the New Password field.

8. Type the password again in the Verify Password field.

9. Assign the user to a group by clicking in the Group field.

10. Set any additional parameters you wish.

11. **Click Save.** The new user account will be created and the system will return you to the User manager.

Caution

Note that the system allows you to create a user account without a password; however, the user will not be able to access the account. So, although the system does not prompt you for a password, it is essentially a required field and should always be set.

Working with the New User dialogue

When you click the New icon on the User Manager toolbar, the New User dialogue loads in your browser window, as shown in Figure 10.3.

At the top of the page, the New User toolbar includes the following icons:

- **Save:** Click to save your work, create a new user account, and exit the New User dialogue.

- **Apply:** Click to save your work and create a new user account without exiting from the New User dialogue. This option lets you save without exiting the screen and it useful in case you are interrupted or you otherwise wish to save yet keep working on this screen.

- **Cancel:** Cancels the task and exits the New User dialogue.

- **Help:** Displays the Help files related to the active screen.

FIGURE 10.3

The New User dialogue in Joomla! 1.5.x.

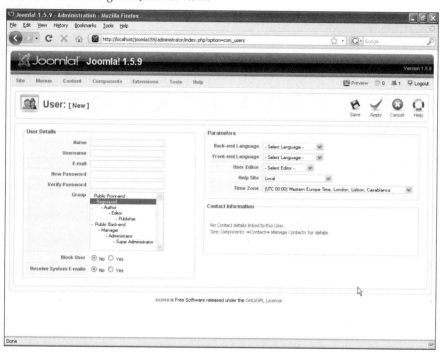

The workspace of the New User dialogue is broken down into three areas:

- User Details
- Parameters
- Contact Information

Each is discussed in more detail in the following sections.

User Details

The User Details section of the New User dialogue includes the following fields, some of which are required to create a new user account:

- **Name:** This field is typically used to hold the user's real name. This field is required
- **Username:** The user uses this name to log in to the system. This field is required.
- **E-mail:** A valid e-mail address for contacting the user. All system e-mails, including the Username Reminder and Password Reset notifications are sent to this address. This field is a required.

- **New Password:** Create a password for the user account in this field.

- **Verify Password:** This field is to confirm the password. The value typed into this field must be identical to the value typed into the New Password field.

- **Group:** Select the Group membership for the user. The default Group is Registered.

- **Block User:** Set to Yes to prevent the user from accessing the system.

- **Receives System E-mails:** Set to Yes if the user is to receive administrative notifications from the Joomla! system. Note this is really only appropriate for users with some administration role in the site.

Parameters

The Parameters section contains a set of optional fields that can be used to tailor the user's account to their language and locale preferences. The fields are:

- **Back-end language:** Select the language you want this user to see when they access the back end of the system. By default, this is set to the language you have designated in the Global Configuration Manager. The choices in the combo box are limited to the language packs you have installed in your system. Also note that if this user is assigned to a group that does not have access to the back end, the settings for this field have no impact on the user.

- **Front-end language:** Select the language you want this user to see when they access the front end of the system. By default, this is set to the language you have set in the Global Configuration Manager. The choices available in the combo box will reflect the language packs you have installed in your system.

- **User editor:** Select an editor for this user. By default, this is set to the editor you have designated in the Global Configuration Manager. Note that the choices in the combo box reflect the editors you have installed in your system.

- **Help site:** This determines where the user is directed when they click the Help icon. Use this control to direct the user to a specific Help site. The default setting is the Help site selected in the Global Configuration Manager.

- **Time zone:** Sets the time zone for the user. The default setting is the time zone specified in the Global Configuration Manager.

Contact Information

This section indicates whether contact details are linked to the user. When a new user is created, this is blank. If you want to add contact details and link a contact form to the user, you must first create the user and then go through the process of creating a new contact with the Contact Manager component.

Cross-Reference

See Chapter 13 for more information on the Contact Manager component.

Managing account notification e-mails

By default, the Joomla! system automatically sends e-mail notifications to users in several circumstances. When a new account is created, the system sends a new account notification e-mail to a user at the e-mail address input into the New User dialogue. Similarly, when the user clicks the Username Reminder or Password Reset links, the system sends an e-mail to the user with details about how to regain access to their account.

The text for the various notification e-mails is contained in the system's language files. The specific file for handling the user e-mail notification ends with _user.ini, for example, if you are using the default language settings you will find the desired language in the file language>en-GB>en-GB.com_user. ini. You can modify the wording in the e-mail notifications by downloading the file, locating the appropriate line in the file, and then changing the portions you desire. After you have made your changes, upload the file to your server, overwriting the original.

Managing Users

In addition to enabling the creation of new user accounts, the User Manager provides the interface for managing your existing users. You can update user details, create new passwords, or change a user's Group affiliation, giving them greater or lesser privileges.

Editing user accounts

The accounts of existing users can be edited from the User Manager. To edit a user account either click the user's name in the User manager, or select the account and then click the Edit icon on the User manager toolbar. Regardless of which method you use, the system opens the Edit User dialogue, shown in Figure 10-4.

Although the toolbar and many of the fields in the Edit User dialogue are identical to those seen in the New User dialogue explained earlier in this chapter, there are small differences. First, the Edit User dialogue provides information about the user account. At the bottom of the User Details section two fields tell you the date of creation of the account and the date of the user's last activity. Second, the fields displayed in the Parameters section vary according to the group to which the user has been assigned. If the user is a member of Public front-end group, then the parameters section will not display the Back-end Language field. Additionally, if the user is a member of the Registered group, the Parameters section will display neither the Back-end Language field nor the User Editor field.

To make changes to a user's account, simply alter the desired fields in the Edit User dialogue and then click the Save or Apply icon on the toolbar. Any changes you have made are applied immediately.

FIGURE 10.4

The Edit User dialogue in Joomla! 1.5.x.

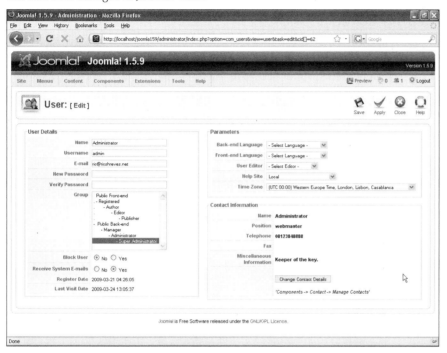

Deleting users

To delete one or more users, follow these steps:

1. Open the User manager.
2. Select the accounts of one or more users.
3. Click the Delete icon.

Caution

Deleting a user account is permanent and cannot be undone. Moreover, there is not a confirmation dialogue. Clicking the Delete icon immediately deletes the user account!

Forcing a user to log out

Situations may occur in which an administrator needs to force a user to log out of the system. This is typically done as a preventative measure to stop abuse or to deny access to a particular user due to their conduct on the site. Joomla! gives you two ways to force logout.

A tab labeled Logged In Users is located on the right-hand side of the Joomla! control panel. Clicking on that tab opens a list of all the users who are currently logged in to the system. In the right hand column, next to each user's name is a red checkmark under the column header Logout. Forcing Log Out from the control panel is shown in Figure 10.5.

Clicking the red icon in Log Out column immediately logs out the user from the system.

A second method for forcing log out is available from the User Manager interface. Viewing the User Manager shows you all users who are currently logged in to the system. To force any of those users to log out, you need only to select the account and then click the Logout icon on the User Manager toolbar.

Caution

Forcing a user to log out does not prevent the user from gaining access to the system — they can always log in again. If you want to block the user's access, see the next section.

FIGURE 10.5

Forcing Log Out from the control panel.

Blocking users

The Super Administrator can block the access of any user. If you have a problem user or you simply need to shut down an account temporarily, blocking access is the only certain way of keeping the user out of the system.

Note
Blocking a user only denies the user access to their account; it does not prevent them from visiting or viewing the site.

To block access, follow these steps:

1. Access the User Manager.
2. Click on the user's name to open the Edit User dialogue.
3. Beside the field Block User, click the option Yes.
4. Click either the Save or the Apply icon.

Blocking a user does not delete the user's account. If the issue with the user is resolved, the Super Administrator need only change the option Block User back to No, and the user's account becomes fully active.

Caution
Blocking a user effectively can be difficult if your site allows user registration, because blocking one account does not prevent the user from obtaining a new account by re-registering under a new name or e-mail address.

Creating User Registration

By default, user registration is active in the Joomla! system. A site visitor can register and create his own account by clicking on the Create an Account link on the Login Form. You can use alternatives to the default approach, however. The User Registration settings can be manipulated by the administrator via the Global Configuration Manager.

Using the Login module

The Login module contains several elements: The login form itself, links to the Username Reminder and Password Reset functions, and a link to the Create an Account function. The latter is optional and can be de-activated, depending upon the settings in your Global Configuration Manager. Note the links below the form in the image, shown in Figure 10.6.

FIGURE 10.6

The Default Login Form module.

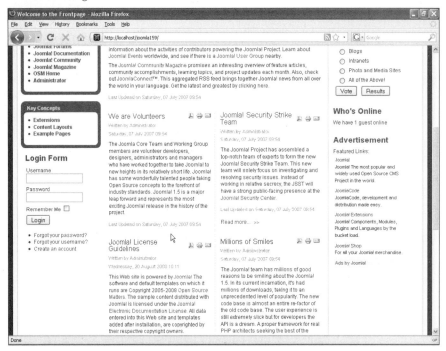

Configuring user registration

Although your Joomla! site has User Registration enabled by default, you can use several possible alternative settings. The default setting allows casual visitors to register, but access to the site is not automatic. After the user registers, the system sends a confirmation e-mail to the address entered during the registration process. The new user must then click on a link in that confirmation e-mail to validate and activate the account. Only after successful validation will the username and password grant access to the site.

By coupling the self-registration process with a validation procedure, site security is enhanced. The confirmation e-mail process helps protect you from automated registration routines, or from people who try to register without giving a valid e-mail address. The default approach to user registration is commonly used and for many sites it is sufficient. However, if you are concerned about automated bots or spammers setting up accounts on your site, you should require a more rigorous registration process. It is possible to configure the site to use either more secure or less secure approaches to the registration process.

To create a more secure registration process, you can remove the possibility that a user can create a new account without action on the part of the administrator. You can do this by completely disabling the ability of users to register on the site. Though more secure, this approach is also more inconvenient because you must rely solely upon a Super Administrator to create new accounts.

To disable front-end user registration, follow these steps:

1. **Log in to the back-end admin system.**

2. **Access the Global Configuration Manager by clicking the Global Configuration icon on the Control Panel, or by clicking the option Global Configuration on the Site menu.** The Global Configuration Manager loads in your browser window.

3. **On the Global Configuration Manager, click the System tab.** After you click, the tab comes to the front.

4. **In the section labeled User Settings, change the setting labeled Allow User Registration from Yes to No.**

5. **Click the Save icon on the toolbar when you are finished.**

If, on the other hand, you feel that your site can operate safely with a less secure user registration process, you can allow user registration without the need for the user to first receive and click on a link in a validation e-mail; this approach allows the user to access the site immediately after registration.

To enable registration without confirmation, follow these steps:

1. **Log in to the back-end admin system.**

2. **Access the Global Configuration Manager by clicking the Global Configuration icon on the Control Panel, or by clicking the option Global Configuration on the Site menu.** After you click, the Global Configuration Manager loads in your browser window.

3. **On the Global Configuration Manager, click the System tab.**

   After you click, the tab comes to the front.

4. **In the section labeled User Settings, change the control labeled New User Account Activation from Yes to No.**

5. **Click the Save icon on the toolbar when you are finished.**

The Username Reminder function

As a convenience to users, Joomla! comes with a built-in Username Reminder function. If a user visits the site and has forgotten their username, they can click on the link Forgot Your Username? and then enter their registered e-mail address. If they have entered the correct e-mail address, the system will send the user their username by e-mail. The process is entirely automatic. The Username Reminder link is typically located underneath the form in the Login Form module. Note that this function only works when the user has correctly entered the e-mail address that is registered with the account.

As an alternative you can create a direct link to the Username Reminder page by using the Menu Manager. To link directly to the Username Reminder page, follow these steps:

1. **Log in to the back-end admin system.**

2. **On the menu named Menus, select the menu where you want the link to the Login page to appear.** The Menu Item Manager loads in your browser window.

3. **On the Menu Item Manager, click the icon marked New on the toolbar.** The New Menu Item dialogue opens in your browser.

4. **Click the option User.** The option expands to list several choices.

5. **Select the option named Default Remind.** A new page loads in your browser.

6. **Type a name for the link in the field marked Title.**

7. **Click the Save icon on the toolbar when you are finished.**

Note that the Username Reminder link is hard-coded into the Login Form module. If you display the Login Form module, you must also display the link. The only way to remove this link is to edit the module code to remove or otherwise hide the link.

Cross-Reference
Modifying the default modules is discussed in Chapter 24.

The Password Reset function

Similar to the Username Reminder function is Joomla's Password Reset tool. An existing user who has forgotten her password can request the system to assist her with regaining access. Unlike the Username Reminder, which simply sends the data to the user, the Password Reset process requires additional steps. When a user clicks on the link Forgot your Password? a new page opens and prompts the user to input their registered e-mail address. If the address is input correctly, the system sends a verification e-mail to the user. The e-mail contains a token and a link to a page on the web site. The user must copy the token, and then visit the web page. On the web page, the user pastes the token into the space provided and clicks the Submit button. The system opens yet another page where the user enters a new password which can then be used to access the site.

To create an alternative to the Password Reset function in the Login module, you can create a direct link to the Password Reset page with the Menu Manager. To create a direct link to the Password Reset page, follow these steps:

1. **Log in to the back-end admin system.**

2. **On the menu named Menus, select the menu where you wish the link to the Login page to appear.** After you click, the Menu Item Manager loads in your browser window.

3. On the Menu Item Manager, click the icon marked New on the toolbar. The New Menu Item dialogue opens in your browser.

4. Click the option User. The option expands to list several choices.

5. Select the option named Default Reset Layout. A new page loads in your browser.

6. Type a name for the link in the field marked Title.

7. Click the Save icon on the toolbar when you are finished.

Note

The Password Reset link is hard-coded into the Login Form module. If you display the Login Form module, you will also display the link. The only way to remove this link is to edit the module code to remove or otherwise hide the link.

Cross-Reference

See Chapter 21 for more information on modifying the default modules.

Creating a Login page

The Login Form module is the most commonly used method for providing a login functionality for Joomla! sites, but it is not the only way; the Login Form can also be displayed as a page, where the form will be located in the main content area. To create a Login page, you can use the Menu Manager to create a link to log in by following these steps:

1. Log in to the back-end admin system.

2. On the menu named Menus, select the menu where you wish the link to the Login page to appear. After you click, the Menu Item manager loads in your browser window.

3. On the Menu Item manager, click the icon marked New on the toolbar. The New Menu Item dialogue opens in your browser.

4. Click the option User. The option expands to list several choices.

5. Select the option named Default Login Layout. A new page loads in your browser.

6. Type a name for the link in the field marked Title.

7. Click the Save icon on the toolbar when you are finished.

Cross-Reference

See Chapter 8 for a detailed discussion of the Parameters and other options available for Menu Items.

Redirecting users after login or logout

It is possible to automatically redirect users to particular pages upon login or logout. This is a useful feature of the system that helps you channel users into particular content, or allows you the option to set up landing pages with content tailored to a user who is entering or exiting the restricted areas of your site. One of the most effective uses of this feature is to create a landing page that greets members upon login. The page usually carries a welcome message to site members and highlights what is new or being featured on the site.

If you are using the Login Form module, the Login and Logout Redirection Page options are contained in the Parameters section of the Login Form Module Editing dialogue. In Figure 10.7 you can see both controls.

To set the Login Redirection Page from the Login module, follow these steps:

1. **Log in to the back-end admin system.**

2. **On the menu named Extensions, click the option Module manager.** The Module manager will load in your browser window.

3. **In the Module manager, click on Login Form.** The Login Form editing dialogue opens in your browser.

4. **Click the combo box control next to the label Login Redirection Page.** Select from the list the page that you want the users too see.

5. **Click the Save icon on the toolbar.**

If, on the other hand, you are using the Login page rather than the Login module, you must set this up in a different fashion:

1. **Log in to the back-end admin system.**

2. On the menu named Menus, click on the name of the menu that contains the link to your Login page. The Menu Item Editing dialogue loads in your browser window. In the right-hand column you can see the Parameters section. The Parameters (Basic) tab contains the redirection options.

3. **Type the URL of the page you want the users to see in the field labeled Login Redirection URL.**

4. **Click the Save icon on the toolbar.**

Note

The Login page option contains more flexibility than the Login Form module. Although the module restricts your redirection options to only the site's sections, categories, and menu items, the Login page carries no such restriction — you can literally enter any URL you like, even that of another site or a page outside of the Joomla! system.

FIGURE 10.7

The Login Form Redirection Parameters.

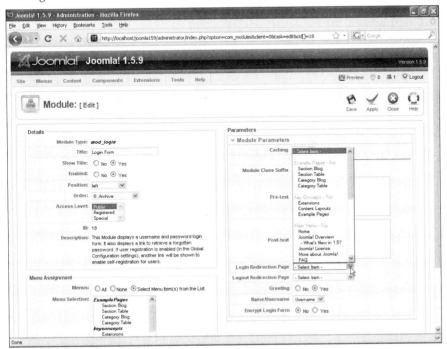

Controlling Access to Content and Functionalities

The essential reason for creating user groups is to control access to content and functionalities. As discussed at the outset of this chapter, the Joomla! system's seven user classes are designed to give you varying levels of privileges; however, those user Groups do not dictate access to content or functionality. Controlling access requires an understanding of the Access Level parameters in Joomla! and how those relate to the user Groups.

Default access levels

Items can be assigned to any one of three access levels: Public, Registered, or Special. Table 10.1 shows how the access levels impact the users' ability to view content and functionality.

Squeezing the most out of three access levels

In this sidebar, I show you two examples of how you can manage access levels to create content hierarchies for the front-end of your Joomla! 1.5.x Web site.

First, let's assume you want to have both unrestricted content for the general public and some items that users must register to view. Let's also assume that you need to implement front-end workflow for the creation and editing of content items. In this case, your options are limited. For the unrestricted items, you must set the Access Level to Public. For the items you wish to be limited to your registered users, you must set the Access Level to Registered. Note that you may need to restrict access to both Pages and to Menu Items to cleanly separate the options available to your Public and Registered users. Finally, since you are enabling front-end content management, you will have to use the Special Access Level to restrict access Menu Items that are needed to implement the content submission and editing options. In other words, in this example, you are only able to achieve two levels of visitor access to your content (Public and Registered), as the third level (Special) must be reserved for the User Groups needed to implement front-end content management.

Now, let's look at a different example: Assume that you do not need to use front-end content management workflow; that you are going to manage all your content from the back end. In this situation, you can actually dedicate all three access levels to controlling content on the front end of your site and thereby create three different levels of access for your site visitors.

A concrete example makes this easier to understand. Let's assume you are building a site for your local sports league. You have three different types of users: general public visitors, team members, and coaches and officials. The general public members need to see information about game schedules and news items. The team members need a higher level of access as they need to be able to read league announcements. The last group, coaches and officials, need a still higher level of access to view internal management and policy items.

Initially it may seem like this is impossible to achieve without installing an additional extension to expand the user group functionality, but in fact it can be done by using the three default Access Levels. Set the general public items to Public. Set the team member items to Registered. Set the coaches and officials items to Special.

The Access Levels are only one part of what you need to do to implement this schema. You must also group the users and the content accordingly. Assign the team members to the Registered Group. Assign the Coaches and the Officials to the Author Group. As for the content items, assign them to the access level you need to control their visibility.

One more step and you are finished. By default, the system assumes you are using front-end content management and will automatically show Author, Editor, and Publisher links on the User Menu that enables page submission and editing. Let's disable those by going to the User Menu and unpublishing the options Submit an Article and Submit a Web Link.

That's it; you're done. Your front-end pages and menu items can now be displayed to any one of the three groups through use of the Access Level controls, and assignment of the users to the proper Groups.

TABLE 10.1

How Access Levels Impact Visibility

Access Level	Description
Public	An unrestricted item. Can be viewed or used by any visitor to your site.
Registered	A limited access item. Can be viewed or used only by registered users. Public visitors, that is, unauthenticated visitors, will not be able to see or use the item.
Special	A limited access item. Can be viewed or used only by registered users that have been granted at least Author level group membership. Public visitors and members of the Registered user group cannot see or use the item.

The three access levels effectively divide your site visitors into three groups: Those who can only access Public items, those who can access both Public and Registered items, and those who can access any item. Note that this distinction is only meaningful on the front end of the site; back-end access is restricted to only those users who are assigned to the Manager, Administrator, and Super Administrator Groups. By definition, users in those Groups have unfettered access to all front-end content and functionality.

Cross-Reference

Working with front-end content management work flow is discussed at length in Chapter 5.

Restricting access to content items

You can control access to sections, categories, and articles, as shown in Table 10.2. By limiting access to a section or a category you limit access to the items within that content grouping. Although access levels for individual articles can be set to create exceptions, they can only be used to create more restricted access, not less restricted access. In other words, if you set a section's access levels to Registered, then setting the categories or articles in that section to Public will have no effect — the more restricted access of the parent grouping (the section) prevails. In contrast, if you set the parent grouping to Public, then you can make access to any child items more restricted. For example, you can set access to a section to Public and set access to an article in that section to Registered with no problem.

TABLE 10.2

Managing content access levels in Joomla! 1.5.x

Item	To change Access Levels, visit...
Section	Section manager and click on Access Level, or edit the Section item
Category	Category manager and click on Access Level, or edit the Category item
Article	Article manager and click on Access Level, or edit the Article item

Restricting access to menus and menu items

Joomla! allows you to control access to both entire menus and to individual menu items. Limiting access to a menu also limits access to the items on that menu, as shown in Table 10.3. In contrast, it is possible to set more restrictive access levels on menu items.

TABLE 10.3

Managing Menu Access Levels in Joomla! 1.5.x

Item	To change Access Levels, visit...
Menu	Module Manager and click on the menu module's Access Level, or edit the Module
Menu Item	Menu Item Editing dialogue and click on Access Level, or edit the Menu Item

Restricting access to components, modules, and plugins

Access Level settings can be managed for all modules and plugins in the system, but a number of the Joomla! default components lack individual access level controls. Of the components, only the contact, news feeds, and web links components offer the access level option. Moreover, while individual contacts can be managed, only the categories associated with news feeds and web links are given access level settings; you cannot set access levels for individual news feeds or web links Table 10.4 summarizes the options for Joomla! 1.5.x.

Although not all the components are associated with access level settings, you can always apply access restrictions to the menu items that link to those components if you need greater control than is offered by the Component Manager.

TABLE 10.4

Managing access levels for components, modules, and plugins in Joomla! 1.5.x

Item	To change Access Levels, visit...
Contact Component	Contact Manager and click on the contact's Access Level, or edit the contact
News Feeds Component (Category only)	News Feed manager and click on News Feed Category Access Level, or edit the news feed category
Web Link Component (Category only)	Web Link manager and click on the Web Link Category's Access Level, or edit the web link category
Module	Module manager and click on the module's Access Level, or edit the module
Plugin	Plugin Manager and click on the plugin's Access Level, or edit the plugin

Caution

Exercise caution when you restrict access to plugins. If you limit the access to a plugin, it may result in the failure of functionalities that are dependent upon the plugin.

Summary

In this chapter, we have covered the Joomla! User Manager in depth. You learned the following:

- How to create, edit, and delete users
- The fixed Joomla! User Hierarchy and the privileges associated with each group
- Various options for managing User Registration
- Options for the Login Form module and how to create a login page
- The connection between groups and access levels
- How to control access to content and functionality by using the groups together with the access level controls

Working with the Language Manager

The Language Manager makes it possible for you to add additional languages to your site and manage them with ease. All of the site controls, warning messages, prompts, and notifications are controlled by the language packs and can be administered via the Language Manager. Although the Joomla! installation package is delivered with only one language installed, over 80 translations of Joomla! are available. Through the use of the language packs and the Language Manager, you can tailor both the front-end and the back-end interfaces of your site to suit your needs, in almost any language you choose.

In addition to global language settings, the system also supports the use of separate languages for the front end and the back end and even separate languages for particular users or articles. This chapter looks at all of the various configurations that are available in the default system.

The Function of the Language Manager

The Language Manager serves two important functions: First, it enables you to manage multiple language packs, or translations, and secondly, it allows you to set the language used by the front-end and back-end interfaces of your web site.

To access the Language Manager, log in to the admin system of your web site and go to the menu item extensions; click on the option named Language Manager. The Language Manager loads in your browser window, as shown in Figure 11.1.

FIGURE 11.1

The Language Manager interface.

The toolbar at the top of the Language Manager contains only two controls:

- **Default:** Select a language from the list and then click this icon to set the language as the site's default language.
- **Help:** Click to access the online Help files related to the active screen.

Below the toolbar there are two text links. The link labeled Sites shows you the Site Language Manager; the Administrator link displays the Administrator Language Manager. The controls and fields on each are the same, so I have combined the discussion of them.

The main content area of the screen contains a list of all the language packs installed on your Joomla! site. The columns provided are:

- **# :** An indexing number assigned by Joomla! This cannot be changed.
- **Radio Button (no label):** Click a radio button to select a menu; this is needed if you want to use the default option on the toolbar, referenced above.
- **Language Name:** This field displays the full name of the language packs installed on the site.
- **Default:** A yellow star in this column indicates that the language is selected as the site's default language.

- **Version:** The version number of the language pack.

- **Date:** The creation date of the language pack.

- **Author:** The name of the author of the language pack.

- **Author E-mail:** A contact e-mail for the author of the language pack.

Finally, at the bottom of the screen, below the content area, is the Display # option. Change the value in the combo box control to alter the number of language packs that are displayed on the page. The default value can be altered by changing the List Length option on the Global Configuration Manager (see Figure 11.2).

Note

Having multiple language packs installed on your site does not automatically enable the display of multilingual content. Language packs only control the language used for the display of system elements, for example, controls and warning messages. If you want to display articles in multiple languages and give users the ability to easily switch languages, then you need to install a third-party extension to enable this functionality. Multilingual site extensions are discussed in Chapter 22.

FIGURE 11.2

The front end of the default site with the French language pack installed and set as the front-end default language.

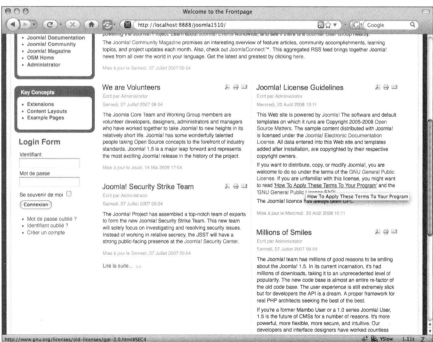

Installing New Language Packs

If your Joomla! site does not use your preferred language, or you want to add an additional translation for the site's interface, then you can download and install one or more additional language packs. The language packs are available on the Joomla! Extensions web site. Each pack contains complete translations of all the various text strings used for both the front end and the back end of the site.

Note

Some language packs contain only slightly different contents to allow for regional variations, for example, British English versus American English.

To install a new language pack, download the language pack and then follow these steps:

1. **Log in to the admin system of your Web site.**

2. **Click on the option Install/Uninstall on the Extensions menu of the main admin nav bar.** The Extension Manager loads in your browser window.

3. **Click the Browse button inside the Upload Package File box.** The File Upload dialogue opens in your browser.

4. **Navigate to the location of your downloaded language pack.** Click once to select the language pack and then click the Open button.

   The File Upload dialogue closes and returns you to the Extension manager, where you should see the name of the language pack in the Package File text field.

5. **Click the button labeled Upload File & Install.** The system attempts to install the language pack and if successful, will display a confirmation message on the Extension Manager.

After you have installed the language pack, you see it listed in the Language Manager.

Note

You can find a list of all the available language packs and download the ones of your choosing from the Joomla! Extensions directory at

```
http://extensions.joomla.org/extensions/languages/translations-for-joomla.
```

Caution

You delete language packs the same way that you delete other extensions. However, you should take care not to delete the default language because it will cause errors on the web site. Deleting extensions is discussed in Chapter 22.

Modifying a Language Pack

The system's language packs specify the language strings that are used throughout the site. The strings cover everything from basics such as Read more. . . , to error messages, to instruction text for common core functionalities. If you want to change the wording used in any of these strings you have two options. You can edit the language files on the server or you can create your own language pack.

Editing the default language files

The language pack files are organized inside of directories, one directory for each language. The individual language pack directories are kept on the server inside the main `language` directory.

The files that contain the language strings in a language pack are primarily `.ini` files. If you want to change a word or a phrase, you must locate the appropriate `.ini` file containing the word or phrase, open it, edit it, and save it to overwrite the original file.

For example, assume that you want to change the Password Reminder text that appears on the Login module. That text in the default installation reads "Forgot your password?" You can change it to the more conversational "Have you forgotten your password?" To do so, follow these steps:

1. **Access your Joomla! installation on your server.**
2. **Find the directory language/en-GB and open the file en-GB.mod_login.ini. You can open and edit this file with a text editor.**
3. **Search for the phrase "Forgot your password."**

   You will find this: `FORGOT_YOUR_PASSWORD=Forgot your password?`
4. **Edit the last part of that line of code. Change the code to read FORGOT_YOUR_ PASSWORD=Have you forgotten your password?**
5. **Save the file, overwriting the original. If you check your site you can see the change in the Login module.**

Cross-Reference

See Appendix B for a list of all the key files you may want to modify, including the language files.

Creating a new language pack

Creating a new language pack is more complicated than simply editing the core language pack files, but it has the advantage of creating a distinct set of files that you can maintain independently of the Joomla! core. If you plan to make numerous changes to the individual language files, it is probably easier in the long run to create your own language pack instead of modifying and then maintaining all the various language files. Don't forget that changes made to the Joomla! core run the risk of being overwritten when you do an upgrade to the system. If you have created your own language pack, you can always reinstall it when you upgrade your site instead of having to go through and modify numerous language files.

The easiest way to create a new language pack is to copy an existing language pack and rename the files. In this way you get all of the elements and save yourself a great deal of time. Assume that you want to make a number of changes to the default en-GB language pack and have decided to create your own variation to hold the changes. Follow these steps:

1. Access the Joomla! installation on your server.

2. Duplicate the existing language/en-GB directory.

3. Change the name of all directories and files from "en-GB" to "en-ME." Don't forget to update the tag field in the en-GB.xml file.

4. Make your changes to the language strings inside the files of your new en-ME Language Pack.

5. Access the Language Manager and set your new language pack as the default language.

Cross-Reference
Changing the default language is discussed in the following section.

Specifying the Language Used

The default setting for Joomla! has one language assigned to both the front end and the back end. The Language Manager allows you to specify the default language used for either the front end, the back end, or both. In addition to the global Language control you get from the Language Manager, you can configure the site to allow users to choose their preferred language and you can also override the global language settings for individual articles.

Changing the default language

To change the default language used, follow these steps:

1. Log in to the admin system of your web site.

2. Click on the option Language Manager under the Extensions menu. The Language Manager loads in your browser.

3. When you access the Language Manager, you will be shown the front-end languages. If you want to change the back-end default language, click the Administrator link at the top of the Language Manager.

4. Click the radio button next to the language you want to set as the default.

5. Click the Default icon on the toolbar. The system sets your chosen language as the default language and if successful, displays a yellow star in the Default column next to the name of the chosen language, as shown in Figure 11.3.

FIGURE 11.3

The Language Manager interface, showing the French translation set as the default language for the front-end of the site.

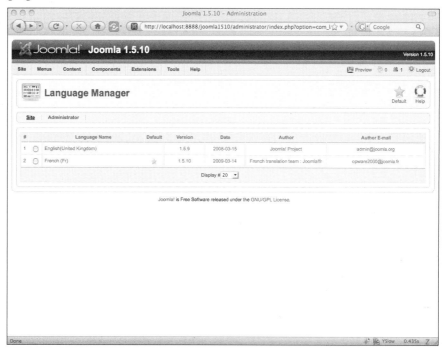

Note

The front-end and the back-end language selections are independent of each other. Changing one does not impact the other. If you want to change both, you must repeat the process above, once for the front end and once for the back end.

Setting the language for users

The site administrator can set a specific front-end or back-end language for a user. The parameters associated with the user account include options for selecting a front-end language and if the user is authorized to access the back end, they also include a parameter for the back-end language. The options available correspond to the language packs installed on the site. If no selection is made, the system will apply the default language set in the Language Manager.

Cross-Reference

Chapter 10 covers creating and editing User accounts.

Administrators can also give users the chance to select their preferred language. To enable this functionality, you need to publish for the User Form page for the users. To set this up, follow these steps:

1. **Log in to the admin system of your Web site.**

2. **Access the Menu Item Manager for the User menu by clicking on the option User menu, located under the Menus menu on the main admin nav bar.** The User menu Menu Item Manager opens.

3. **Click the New icon the top-right toolbar.**

   The first step of the New Menu Item dialogue opens.

4. **Select the Menu Item Type named User Form Layout.**

5. **Click the Next button.**

   The final step of the New Menu Item dialogue appears.

6. **Name the Menu Item.**

7. **Set the Access Level to Registered.**

8. **Click Save.** The system creates the new menu item. The New Menu Item dialogue closes and returns you to the Menu Item Manager.

The new menu item now appears on the User menu and is visible to authenticated users. When they click on this menu item, they are taken to a page that allows them to manage their account details and set the choice of language. If they have access to the back end, the language options include both the front end and the back end. The options available to the user are limited to the language pack installed on the site.

Cross-Reference

See Chapter 8 for more discussion on managing menus and menu items.

Setting the language for specific articles

It is possible to display articles in languages other than the default language, without the necessity of installing third-party extensions. This is most useful when you want to show only a limited number of pages in other languages, rather than creating a truly multilingual site.

Tip

If your goal is to create a truly multilingual site, you should download and install an additional extension that gives you all the proper tools you need for managing the content and for giving the users easy access to the content in the various languages.

If, however, you do not need or do not want to create a fully multilingual site, you can set specific articles to use languages other than the default language. The language option is included in the advanced parameters of the Article Editing dialogue. Simply edit the article and select the language you desire from the combo box. The options in the combo box are limited to the language packs installed on your site. Note that you need to do this for each individual article for which you want to use an alternative language.

Cross-Reference
See Chapter 5 for more information on creating and editing articles.

Summary

In this chapter, we covered the various advanced tasks associated with managing the language packs on your site. You learned the following:

- The function of the Language Manager
- How to install new language packs
- How to edit a language pack
- How to create a new language pack
- How to change the default language
- How to set the language for a user
- How to set the language for an article

Part III

Working with Components, Modules, and Plugins

Using the Banner Manager

Joomla!'s Banner Manager component is responsible for handling the advertising space on your web site. Although the name implies that it is only suitable for banner ads, it can be used for the display of graphical content in any shape or size; the only limitation you face comes from what fits comfortably into your page layout.

The Banner Manager works in conjunction with the Banners module. The component handles the management of the banners and the clients, while the module handles the actual display of the banners. You control the placement of the banners by assigning the module into the relevant module position. The component, in contrast, serves as an interface that lets you organize banners into categories and associate them with clients, as well as set the limitations on display.

Introducing the Banner Manager

To get started placing ads on your site, first you must add the files to the system and then organize them using the Banner Manager component. To access the component, go to the Components menu and select the Banner option. The Banner Manager interface loads in your browser. Figure 12.1 shows the Banner Manager as it appears with the Joomla! sample data installed in Joomla! 1.5.x.

Note

On the Components menu, the option labeled Banner leads to the same screen as the Banner submenu labeled Banners. Despite the names, there is no difference between these two navigation choices.

FIGURE 12.1

The Banner Manager interface.

The toolbar at the top of the Banner Manager provides quick access to the following functions:

- **Publish:** Select one or more banners from the list and then click this icon to publish them.

- **Unpublish:** Select one or more banners from the list and then click this icon to unpublish them.

- **Copy:** Select a banner from the list and then click this icon to create a copy of the banner.

- **Delete:** Select one or more banners from the list and then click this icon to delete the banner(s).

- **Edit:** Select a banner from the list then click this icon to edit the banner details.

- **New:** Click to add a new banner.

- **Parameters:** Click this to view the parameters available for this component.

- **Help:** Click to access the online Help files related to the active screen.

Below the toolbar there are three links: Banners shows you the Banner manager, Clients shows you the Banner Clients manager, and Categories shows you the Banner Categories manager. The Banner Clients manager and the Banner Categories manager are discussed in the sections that follow.

Below the three links and above the list of banners are three sorting and searching tools to help you manage long lists of banners:

- **The Filter field** on the left works like a search box. Type a word or phrase into the field and then click Go. The page reloads and displays the results of the search. To clear the screen and return to a full listing, click the Reset button.

- **The Select a Category filter** on the right allows you to display only those banners that have been assigned to a specific category. To reset this filter, change the combo box back to the default setting.

- **The Select State filter** on the far right allows you to filter and display the banners according to whether they are published or unpublished. This provides an easy way to identity all banners that are currently active on the site. To reset this filter, change the combo box back to the default setting.

The main content area of the screen contains a list of all the banners in your Joomla! site. The columns provided are:

- **Checkbox (no label):** Click in a checkbox to select a banner; this is needed if you want to use several of the toolbar options.

- **Name:** This field displays the full name of the banner. Click the name to edit the banner's details.

- **Client:** The name displayed in this field is the client to whom the banner is assigned.

- **Category:** The name displayed in this field is the category to which the banner is assigned.

- **Published:** A green checkmark in this column indicates that the banner is active. The field shows a red X if the banner is disabled. Note that both the banner and the Banners module must also be published for your banners to appear on the site. Administrators can toggle between the two settings by clicking on the icon shown.

- **Order:** The numbers in this field affect the ordering of the banners on this list. Change the numbers and click the Save icon at the top of the column to reorder the banners.

- **Sticky:** Indicates whether the banner has been marked as sticky. You can use your Banner module settings to prioritize sticky banners. Sticky banners always show in the position. They do not rotate impressions with other banners.

- **Impressions:** This field indicates two items: First it shows the number of times the banner has appeared on the site (known as "impressions"); second it indicates whether the administrator has set a limitation on the number of impressions of the banner. If no limit has been set on the impressions, the field indicates "Unlimited."

- **Clicks:** Indicates the number of times the banner has been clicked on by visitors to the site.

- **Tags:** Shows any Tags associated with each of the banners. Tags can be used to set conditions on the display of Banners.

- **ID:** The system-generated user ID number.

Finally, at the bottom of the screen, below the content area, is the Display # option. Change the value in the combo box control to alter the number of banners that are displayed on the page. The default value can be altered by changing the List Length option on the Global Configuration Manager.

Understanding Banner Parameters

Global options for the Banner Manager component can be configured by means of the parameters option. The parameters are viewed and modified by clicking the Parameters icon on the Banner Manager toolbar. Clicking the icon causes a lightbox to be superimposed on top of the page. Inside the lightbox are the parameter variables that are available.

The Banner Manager includes a very limited number of parameters:

- **Track Banner Impression Times:** Set the option to Yes to track the number of impressions per banner per day.

- **Track Banner Click Times:** Set the option to Yes to track the number of clicks on each banner each day.

- **Tag Prefix:** Set a prefix to be used for the Tag matching function. This improves the performance of the Banners module.

After you have set the parameters you desire, click the Save button at the top right to save your changes or click Cancel to close the parameters window without saving the changes.

Managing Clients

Clients are created by the administrator for the purpose of grouping banners. Every banner must be assigned to a client. Although clients provide one unit of organization for banners, another level of organization is available — Banner categories. Before you can add your first banner you must have at least one banner client and one banner category.

To view the clients in your system, click on the Clients link at the top of the Banner Manager.

Tip

If you have no need for multiple clients, simply create a single client and assign all your banners to that client.

Exploring the Banner Client Manager

The Banner Client Manager displays a list of all the clients that exist in the system. You can use this interface to add new clients and to review and edit existing clients. Figure 12.2 shows the Banner Client Manager.

The toolbar at the top of the Banner Client Manager provides quick access to the following functions:

- **Delete:** Select one or more clients from the list and then click this icon to delete the client(s).
- **Edit:** Select a client from the list and then click this icon to edit the client details.
- **New:** Click to create a new client.
- **Help:** Click to access the online Help files related to the active screen.

FIGURE 12.2

The Banner Client Manager.

Below the three links and above the list of Clients is the Filter field. The Filter works like a search box. Type a word or phrase into the field and then click Go. Click the Reset button to clear the filter and display all the entries.

The main content area of the screen contains a list of all the banner clients in your Joomla! site. The columns provided are:

- **#:** An indexing number assigned by Joomla!
- **Checkbox (no label):** Click in a checkbox to select a client; this is needed if you want to use several of the toolbar options.
- **Client Name:** The name given to the client.
- **Contact:** The contact associated with this client.
- **# Banners:** The number of banners associated with the client.
- **ID:** The system-generated user ID number.

Finally, at the bottom of the screen, below the content area, is the Display # option. Change the value in the combo box control to alter the number of banner clients that are displayed on the page. The default value can be altered by changing the List Length option on the Global Configuration Manager.

Creating clients

Clients are created from the New Banner Client dialogue, as shown in Figure 12.3. To access the New Banner Client dialogue, click the New icon on the toolbar at the top of the Banner Client Manager.

The toolbar at the top of the New Banner Client dialogue provides quick access to the following functions:

- **Save:** Click this icon to save your work, create a new client, and exit the New Client dialogue.
- **Apply:** Click to save your work and create a new client without exiting from the New Banner Client dialogue. This option lets you save without exiting the screen and is useful in case you are interrupted or otherwise want to save yet keep working on this screen.
- **Cancel:** Cancels the task and exits the New Banner Client dialogue.
- **Help:** Displays the Help files related to the active screen.

Three links are located below the toolbar: Banners shows you the Banner Manager, discussed in the previous section. Clients shows you the Banner Client Manager. Categories shows you the Banner Categories Manager, discussed in the next section.

FIGURE 12.3

The New Banner Client dialogue.

To create a new banner client, follow these steps:

1. **Access the Banner Client Manager. To do so, go to the Components menu and select the Clients option from the submenu under the heading Banners.** The Banner Client Manager loads in your browser.

2. **Click the New icon on the toolbar at the top of the Banner Client Manager.** The New Banner Client Dialogue opens. Refer to Figure 12.3.

3. **In the Client Name field, type the name of the client.** This field is required.

4. **In the Client Contact field, type the name of the person who will be your contact for this client.** This field is required.

5. **In the Contact E-mail field, type the Client's Contact's e-mail address.** This field is required.

6. **Add any notes you like in the Extra Information text box; this field is optional.**

7. **Click the Save icon on the toolbar at the top right to save your new banner client.** The dialogue closes and returns you to the Banner Client Manager.

Editing and deleting clients

Existing banner clients can be edited from the Banner Client Manager. To edit a client, either click on the client name in the Banner Client Manager, or select the client and then click the Edit icon on the Banner Client Manager toolbar. Regardless of which method you use, the system opens the Edit Client dialogue.

The Edit Client dialogue is identical to the New Client dialogue, with the same fields and requirements as discussed in the previous section.

To make changes to a client, simply alter the desired fields in the Edit Banner Client dialogue and then click the Save or Apply icon on the toolbar. Any changes you have made are applied immediately.

To delete one or more clients, follow these steps:

1. Open the Banner Client Manager.
2. Select one or more clients.
3. Click the Delete icon.

Caution

Deleting a banner client is permanent and cannot be undone. Moreover, there is no confirmation dialogue — clicking the Delete icon immediately deletes the client! Note, however, that a client cannot be deleted if banners are assigned to that client. If you want to delete the client, first delete or re-assign any banners assigned to that client.

Managing Categories

Categories, like clients, are an organizational tool for grouping banners. Every banner must be assigned to a category. Categories are independent of the clients grouping, that is, a banner can belong to any combination of the category and client fields.

Tip

If, in your system, there is no need for multiple categories, simply create a single category and assign all your banners to that category.

Exploring the Banner Category Manager

Categories are created and edited through the Banner Category Manager. The Banner Category Manager is accessed by clicking on the Banner option under the Components menu. After the Banner Manager loads, click the link labeled Categories to access the Category manager. Figure 12.4 shows the Category Manager as it appears with the Joomla! 1.5.x sample data in the system.

FIGURE 12.4

The Banner Category Manager.

The toolbar at the top of the Banner Category Manager provides quick access to the following functions:

- **Publish:** This option is not relevant to banner categories. Note that while this will change the category's publication state in the Published column, it has no impact on the front end of the site.

- **Unpublish:** This option is not relevant to banner categories. Note that while this will change the category's publication state in the Published column, it has no impact on the front end of the site.

- **Delete:** Select one or more categories from the list and then click this icon to delete the category(s).

- **Edit:** Select a category from the list and then click this icon to edit the category details.

- **New:** Click to create a new category.

- **Help:** Click to access the online Help files related to the active screen.

Three links are below the toolbar. Clicking on the Banners link takes you to the Banner Manager. The Clients link takes you to the Banner Client Manager. The Categories link leads to the Banner Categories Manager. The Banner Manager and the Banner Client Manager are discussed in previous sections of this chapter.

Below the three links and above the list of categories are two sorting tools. On the left side of the screen is the Filter field. The Filter works like a search box. Type a word or phrase into the field and then click Go. Click the Reset button to clear the filter and display all the entries.

On the right side of the screen is the Select State filter — a combo box that lets you filter the list by whether the category is published or unpublished. Returning the Select State filter to its default position resets the control and displays all the banner categories in the system.

Note
Although the Banner Category dialogue displays the Published field and a filter is provided for this field, it has no applicability to banner categories.

The main content area of the screen contains a list of all the banner categories in your Joomla! site. The columns provided are:

- **Checkbox (no label):** Click in a checkbox to select a category; this is needed if you want to use several of the toolbar options.
- **Title:** This field displays the name given to the category. Click on the title to edit the category details.
- **Published:** This field is not applicable to the banner categories.
- **Order:** Controls the ordering of the categories on the page. Change the integer values and then click the Save icon to reorder the items on the screen.
- **Access Level:** This field is not applicable to the banner categories.
- **ID:** The system-generated user ID number.

Finally, at the bottom of the screen, below the content area, is the Display # option. Change the value in the combo box control to alter the number of categories that are displayed on the page. The default value can be altered by changing the List Length option on the Global Configuration Manager.

Creating categories

New categories can be created from within the Banner Category Manager. Figure 12.5 shows the New Category dialogue. Remember, you need at least one category on the system before you can begin adding banners to your site.

FIGURE 12.5

The New Category dialogue.

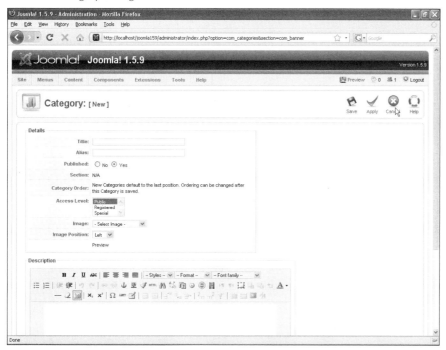

The toolbar at the top of the New Banner Category dialogue provides quick access to the following functions:

- **Save:** Click this icon to save your work, create a new category, and exit the New Category dialogue.

- **Apply:** Click to save your work and create a new category without exiting from the New Banner Category dialogue. This option lets you save without exiting the screen and it useful in case you are interrupted or you otherwise want to save yet keep working on this screen.

- **Cancel:** Cancels the task and exits the New Banner Category dialogue.

- **Help:** Displays the Help files related to the active screen.

The workspace on this dialogue has two sections, labeled Details and Description.

The Details section of the New Banner Category dialogue includes the following fields:

- **Title:** This field is used to assign the category a name. This field is the only required field.

- **Alias:** The alias is the internal name for the item. If you leave this field blank, the system will automatically use your title for the alias, with any spaces converted to hyphens. Note that if you want to add a value to this field, it only takes lowercase letters with no spaces.

- **Published:** This field is not applicable to the banner categories.

- **Category Order:** Sets the order of the appearance of this category in the list of categories in the Banner Category Manager. This can be altered directly from the Banner Category Manager.

- **Access Level:** This field is not applicable to the banner categories.

- **Image:** This field is not applicable to the banner categories.

- **Image Position:** This field is not applicable to the banner categories.

The Description area at the bottom of the dialogue provides a free text field into which you can add a description of the banner category. Note that this is provided for the benefit of the administrators and does not appear on the front end of the site. The Image button below the description field is really of no use for banner categories.

To create a new banner category, follow these steps:

1. **Access the Banner Category Manager. To do so, go to the Components menu and select the Categories option from the submenu under the Banners heading.** The Banner Category Manager loads in your browser.

2. **Click the New icon on the toolbar at the top of the Banner Category Manager.** When you click on that icon, the New Banner Category Dialogue opens. Refer to Figure 12.5.

3. **In the Title field, type the name you want to use for the category.** This field is the only required field.

4. **Select and complete any other fields you wish; all other fields are optional.**

5. **Click, the Save icon on the toolbar at the top right to save your new banner category.** The dialogue closes and returns you to the Banner Category Manager.

Editing and deleting categories

Existing banner categories can be edited from the Banner Category Manager. To edit a category, either click on the category title in the Banner Category Manager or select the category and then click the Edit icon on the Banner Category Manager toolbar. Regardless of which method you use, the system opens the Edit Category dialogue.

The Edit Category dialogue is identical to the New Category dialogue, with the same fields and requirements as discussed in the previous section.

To make changes to a category, simply alter the desired fields in the Edit Banner Category dialogue and then click the Save or Apply icon on the toolbar. Any changes you have made are applied immediately.

To delete one or more categories, follow these steps:

1. Open the Banner Category Manager.

2. Select one or more categories.

3. Click the Delete icon.

Caution

Deleting a banner category is permanent and cannot be undone. Moreover, there is no confirmation dialogue — clicking the Delete icon immediately deletes the category! Note, however, that a category cannot be deleted if there are banners assigned to that category. If you want to delete the category, first delete or reassign any banners assigned to that category

Managing Banners

Creating, copying, editing, and deleting banners are all tasks performed from within the confines of the Banner Manager. The only additional resource you need is the artwork for the banner itself.

Note

The advertising banner files must be created outside the Joomla system. Typically these files are .gifs, .jpgs, or other artwork formats. You cannot actually create the ads themselves inside Joomla!, you can only add existing graphic files to Joomla!

Creating banners

Adding banners to the Joomla! system is called creating banners, although, you are not actually creating the ads; you are merely adding them to the system. To get started, click the New icon on the toolbar at the top of the Banner Manager. Figure 12.6 shows the New Banner dialogue.

The toolbar at the top of the New Banner dialogue provides quick access to the following functions:

- **Save:** Click this icon to save your work, create a new banner, and exit the New Banner dialogue.

- **Apply:** Click to save your work and create a new banner without exiting from the New Banner dialogue. This option lets you save without exiting the screen and is useful if you are interrupted or you otherwise want to save yet keep working on this screen.

- **Cancel:** Cancels the task and exits the New Banner dialogue.

- **Help:** Displays the Help files related to the active screen.

FIGURE 12.6

The New Banner dialogue.

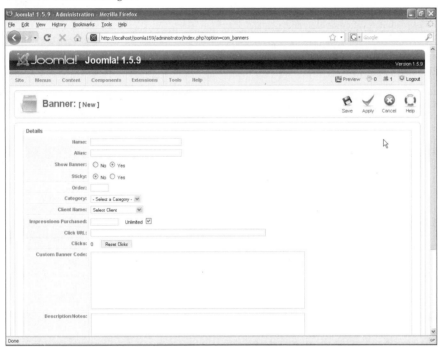

The Details section of the New Banner dialogue includes the following fields, some of which are required to create a new banner:

- **Name:** This field is used to give the banner a name. This field is required.

- **Alias:** The alias is the internal name for the item. If you leave this field blank, the system automatically uses your title for the alias, with any spaces converted to hyphens. Note that if you want to add a value to this field, it only takes lowercase letters with no spaces.

- **Show Banner:** This setting determines whether the banner is visible on the site. Set it to Yes to make the banner visible. The default value is Yes.

- **Sticky:** Gives this banner preference in the rotation of multiple banners. A sticky banner will appear more often than a nonsticky banner. The default value is No. This is only applicable where the Banner module is set to give preference to sticky banners.

- **Order:** Use this control to set the display order of the banner. This is only applicable where the Banner module is set to display the banners in order.

- **Category:** This field allows you to assign the banner to a category. This field is required.

- **Client Name:** This field allows you to assign the banner to a client. This field is required.

- **Impressions Purchased:** Use this field to set a limit on the number of times the banner will appear. Click the checkbox marked Unlimited to remove the restrictions. The default value is Unlimited.

- **Click URL:** This field determines where the user will be taken when they click on the banner.

- **Clicks:** Indicates how many times the banner has been clicked on by site visitors. For a new banner this value will be 0. Use the Reset Clicks button to return the value of this field to 0.

- **Custom Banner Code:** This field is used to add additional code to the banner, for example, if the banner is part of an affiliate scheme and you need to add an affiliate tracking code.

- **Description/Notes:** This field is used for the administrators to add notes or comments for their internal use.

- **Banner Image selector:** This combo box lists the contents of the directory images/ banners in your Joomla! installation. Select the image you want to use as your banner. Add new images to the directory with the Media Manager.

- **Width:** This field has no effect on this dialogue.

- **Height:** This field has no effect on this dialogue.

- **Banner Image:** An image of the banner you have selected appears here for the convenience of the administrators.

- **Tags:** Use this field to associate tags with a banner. The tags can be used to trigger the display of the banner on content pages where the tags appear in association with the content items. This is only applicable if the Banner module is set to search for matching tags.

To create a new banner, follow these steps:

1. **Upload an image to use for the banner to the images/banner directory.**

2. **Access the Banner Manager by clicking on the Banner option under the Components menu.** The Banner Manager loads in your browser.

3. **On the Banner Manager interface, click on the New icon on the toolbar at the top of the Banner Manager.** When you click on that icon, the New Banner dialogue opens. Refer to Figure 12.6

4. **In the Name field, type the name you wish to use for the banner.** This field is required.

5. **Select a category for the banner.** This field is required.

6. **Select a client for the banner.** This field is required.

7. **Select an image from the Banner Image Selector.**

8. **Complete any other fields you want; all other fields are optional.**

9. **Click the Save icon on the toolbar at the top right to save your new banner.** The dialogue closes and returns you to the Banner Manager.

Cross-Reference

Turn to Chapter 13 for more on managing files with the Media Manager.

Copying banners

You can create exact copies of existing banners very quickly. The copy includes the same settings as the original. This is a quick and easy way to create multiple Banner modules. To make a copy, follow these steps.

1. **Access the Banner Manager by clicking on the Banner option under the Components menu.** The Banner Manager loads in your browser.

2. **Select the banner you want to copy by clicking in the select box to the left of the banner name.**

3. **On the Banner Manager interface, click on the Copy icon on the toolbar at the top of the Banner Manager.** When you click on that icon, a copy will be made and will appear in the Banner Manager with the name "Copy of (original Banner name)."

Editing and deleting banners

Existing banners can be edited from the Banner Manager. To edit a banner, either click on the banner name in the Banner Manager or select the banner and then click the Edit icon on the Banner Manager toolbar. Regardless of which method you use, the system opens the Edit Banner dialogue.

The Edit Banner dialogue is identical to the New Banner dialogue, with the same fields and requirements as discussed in the previous section.

To make changes to a banner, simply alter the desired fields in the Edit Banner dialogue, then click the Save or Apply icon on the toolbar. Any changes you have made are applied immediately.

Tip

If you've set limits on the number of impressions for a banner and need to reset the counter, access the Banner Edit dialogue and click the Reset Clicks button.

To delete one or more banners, follow these steps:

1. Open the Banner Manager.

2. Select one or more banners.

3. Click the Delete icon.

Caution

Deleting a banner is permanent and cannot be undone. Moreover, there is no confirmation dialogue — clicking the Delete icon immediately deletes the banner!

Using the Banners Module

The Banners module works hand-in-hand with the Banner component to control the display of ads on your web site. Although the Banner component is used to set up your clients and organize your banners, it is the Banners Module that is responsible for the placement of the ads on the page. The component and the module work together to control campaigns and the settings in one can affect the other. Appreciating the interaction between these two items is key to running ads effectively on your site.

The Banners module, like all other modules in your system, is accessed from the Module Manager. To reach your Banners module, click on the option Module Manager under the Extensions menu. Find the link labeled Banners in the Modules Names column and click on it to view the settings for the Banners module. Figure 12.7 shows the default Banners module, with the Joomla! sample data loaded.

FIGURE 12.7

The Banners module interface.

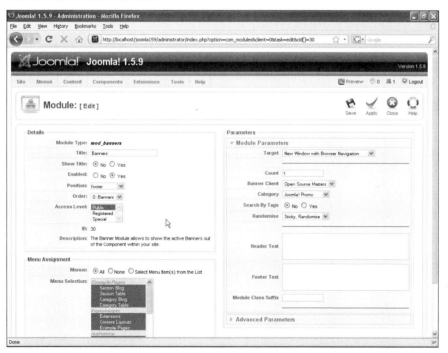

The toolbar at the top of the Banners module dialogue provides quick access to the following functions:

- **Save:** Click this icon to save changes made to the module and exit the Banners module dialogue.
- **Apply:** Click to save your work without exiting from the Banners module dialogue. This option lets you save without exiting the screen and is useful in case you are interrupted or you otherwise want to save yet keep working on this screen.
- **Cancel:** Cancels the task and exits the Banners module.
- **Help:** Displays the Help files related to the active screen.

The workspace on this dialogue has three sections labeled Details, Menu Assignment, and Parameters.

The Details section of the Banners module includes the following fields:

- **Module Type:** This field is determined by the system and is not editable. The label mod_ banners tells you that this is a Banners module.
- **Title:** The name of the module.
- **Show Title:** If this control is set to Yes, the Module Title will appear wherever the module appears on the front end of the web site. Generally speaking, for a Banner module, you will want to set this control to No.
- **Enabled:** Set this control to Yes if you want the module to appear on the front end of your site.
- **Position:** The combo box control is used to assign the module to one of the template's module position holders.
- **Order:** This field is only applicable if there is more than one module assigned to the same module position, in which case this is used to control the ordering of the modules.
- **Access Level:** Set the control for Public, Registered, or Special, depending upon which User Groups you want to be able to see the module.
- **ID:** This internal ID field is set automatically by the system and cannot be edited.
- **Description:** The description text is supplied by the system and cannot be edited.

The Menu Assignment area, at the bottom left of the dialogue, shows a list of all the menus and menu items in the system. This control allows you to designate the pages where the module will appear.

Module parameters

On the right hand side of the Banners module dialogue is the parameters section. The controls here work closely in combination with the settings assigned in the Banner component to control the behavior of the banners on the page.

The controls available are broken into two groups, Module parameters and Advanced parameters. The Module parameters are:

- **Target:** This control specifies what happens when a site visitor click on a banner that is associated with a URL. The combo box includes three options: Window with Browser Navigation, New Window with Browser Navigation, and New Window without Browser Navigation. Note that if the banner is not associated with a URL (that is, if clicking on the banner will not open a new web page), then this control has no effect.

- **Count:** Set the number of banners to display.

- **Banner Client:** Use this control to display banners belonging to a specific client. This control can be used in combination with the Category control.

- **Category:** Use this control to display banners belonging to a specific category. This control can be used in combination with the Banner Client control.

- **Search by Tags:** Set this control to Yes to enable the system to match tags in content with tags assigned to banners to determine which banners to display. Note that you must associate tags with content items and with banners for this to work.

- **Randomize:** Determines whether banners are displayed sequentially or randomly.

- **Header Text:** Type text you want to display on the page immediately before the banner.

- **Footer Text:** Type text you want to display on the page immediately after the banner.

- **Module Class Suffix:** Use this field to add a suffix to the CSS classes that relate to this module; this enables you to provide styling that affects only this specific module.

The Advanced parameters are:

- **Caching:** Set this control to specify whether this module follows the Global Caching settings (set in the Global Configuration Manager).

- **Cache Time:** If you want to cache the contents of this module, enter an integer value here. The value represents the time, in seconds.

Creating additional Banner modules

You may want to run more than one Banner module, or, if you have not installed the sample data, you may need to create your first Banner module. In either case, Joomla! makes it easy to create Banner modules for your system.

Running multiple Banner modules is a common solution to the need to show more than one ad on a page, or to show ads in different positions on different pages. Clever use of multiple Banner modules, coupled with appropriate configuration of the modules and the Banner component, will allow you to give your site variety and will make your available advertising space more flexible and effective.

To create an additional Banner module, follow these steps:

1. **Access the Module Manager by clicking on the selection of the same name under the Extensions menu.** The Module Manager loads in your browser window.

2. **Click on the New icon at the top right toolbar.** The New Module wizard opens.

3. **Select the option Banner and then click the Next button.** The Module Editing dialogue opens.

4. **Type a name for the Module in the Title field.** This is a required field.

5. **Select the option No for the field Show Title.**

6. **Select either a client or a category, or both, to determine which banners will display.** This is necessary for your ads to appear.

7. **Select other options as you see fit; all other options are optional.**

8. **Click the Save icon to create your module and return to the Module Manager.**

Summary

In this chapter, we have covered the use of both the banner component and the banners module. You learned the following:

- How to create, edit, and delete banners
- How to create, edit, and delete banner clients
- How to create, edit, and delete banner categories
- How to configure the Banner Manager to work in concert with the Banners module
- How to create a Banner module

Working with the Contact Manager

J oomla! includes the Contacts component to allow the administrator to easily manage contact information for each of the users of the web site. If your site allows membership, the Contact Manager becomes an essential tool for staying in touch with the membership. Even if you do not allow membership and your only users are the site administrators, the Contact Manager is useful, as it maintains the contact details for your administrators.

The Contact Manager is also the key to the creation of Contact forms in Joomla!. The system automatically creates the forms, but it needs to link the forms to an existing contact. In this chapter I go through contact creation, management, and the creation of contact forms.

Introducing the Contact Manager

The Contact Manager is the essential tool for working with the contact details for the users of your web site. The manager allows for the creation, grouping, editing, and deletion of user contact information. You access the Contact Manager by going to the Components menu and clicking on the option Contacts. The Contact Manager interface will load in your browser, as shown in Figure 13.1.

FIGURE 13.1

The Contact Manager interface.

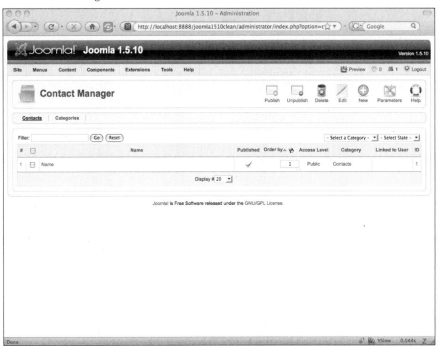

The toolbar at the top of the Contact Manager provides quick access to the following functions:

- **Publish:** Select one or more contacts from the list and then click this icon to publish them.

- **Unpublish:** Select one or more contacts from the list and then click this icon to unpublish them.

- **Delete:** Select one or more contacts from the list and then click this icon to delete the banner(s).

- **Edit:** Select a contact from the list then click this icon to edit the banner details.

- **New:** Click to add a new contact.

- **Parameters:** Click to view the parameters available for this component.

- **Help:** Click to access the online Help files related to the active screen.

Two links are below the toolbar: Contacts shows you the Contact Managerand Categories shows you the Contact Categories Manager.

Below the two links and above the list of contacts are the following three sorting and searching tools to help you manage long lists of contacts:

- **The Filter field** on the left works like a search box. Type a word or phrase into the field and then click Go. The page reloads and displays the results of the search. To clear the screen and return to a full listing, click the Reset button.

- **The Select a Category filter** on the right side allows you to display only those contact that have been assigned to a specific category. To reset this filter, change the combo box back to the default setting.

- **The Select State filter** on the far right allows you to filter and display the banners according to whether they are published or unpublished. This provides an easy way to identify all contacts that are currently active on the site. To reset this filter, change the combo box back to the default setting.

The main content area of the screen contains a list of all the contacts in your Joomla! site. The columns provided are:

- **#:** An indexing number assigned by Joomla! This number cannot be changed.

- **Checkbox (no label):** Click in a checkbox to select a contact. Do this if you want to use several of the toolbar options.

- **Name:** This field displays the full name of the contact. Click on the name to edit the banner's details.

- **Published:** A green checkmark in this column indicates that the contact is active. The field shows a red X if the banner is disabled. Note that both the banner and the Contact module must also be published for your contact to appear on the site. Administrators can toggle between the two settings by clicking on the icon shown.

- **Order by:** The numbers in this field affect the ordering of the contacts on this list. Change the numbers and click the Save icon at the top of the column to reorder the banners.

- **Access Level:** Set the control for Public, Registered, or Special, depending upon which User Groups you want to be able to see the contact.

- **Category:** Displays the Contact Category the contact has been assigned to.

- **Linked to User:** If this contact has been linked to a user, the user's name shows here.

- **ID:** The system-generated user ID number.

Finally, at the bottom of the screen, below the content area, is the Display # option. Change the value in the combo box control to alter the number of contacts that are displayed on the page. The default value can be altered by changing the List Length option on the Global Configuration Manager.

Setting Contact Parameters

Global options for the Contacts component can be configured by means of the Parameters icon located on the top-right toolbar of the Contacts Manager. Clicking the icon causes a lightbox to be superimposed on top of the page. Inside the lightbox are the Global parameters available to this component. Note that these parameters can be overridden for individual contacts by setting alternative values in the Contact parameters, discussed later in this chapter.

The Contacts Manager includes the following Global parameters:

- **Icons/Text:** Choose what to show next to the Contact fields on the page. The options are Icon, Text, and None.
- **Address icon:** Select the icon from the combo box to show next to the Address field. This option is only applicable if you have chosen to display Icons in the Icons/Text parameter.
- **E-mail icon:** Select the icon from the combo box to show next to the E-mail field. This option is only applicable if you have chosen to display icons in the Icons/Text parameter.
- **Telephone icon:** Select the icon from the combo box to show next to the Telephone field. This option is only applicable if you have chosen to display Icons in the Icons/Text parameter.
- **Mobile icon:** Select from the combo box the icon to show next to the Mobile field. This option is only applicable if you have chosen to display icons in the Icons/Text parameter.
- **Fax icon:** Select from the combo box the icon to show next to the Fax field. This option is only applicable if you have chosen to display icons in the Icons/Text parameter.
- **Miscellaneous icon:** Select from the combo box the icon to show next to the Miscellaneous field. This option is only applicable if you have chosen to display icons in the Icons/Text parameter.
- **Show Table Headings:** Show or hide the labels for the table headings when contacts are displayed in table view.
- **Show Contact's Position:** Show or hide the contact's position.
- **Show E-mail Address:** Show or hide the contact's e-mail address.
- **Show Telephone Number:** Show or hide the contact's telephone number.
- **Show Mobile Number:** Show or hide the contact's mobile number.
- **Show Fax Number:** Show or hide the contact's fax number.
- **Enable vCard:** Select Yes to display a link to download the Contact's information in vCard format.

After you have set the parameters you desire, click the Save button at the top right to save your changes or click Cancel to close the Parameters window without saving the changes.

Cross-Reference
Parameters set here can be overriden by the Menu Item Type parameters. See Chapter 8.

Contact parameters

Each individual contact includes the following optional Contact parameters; any values set here that are in conflict with the settings in the Global parameters will take precedence:

- **Name:** Show or hide the contact's name.
- **Contact's Position:** Show or hide the contact's position.
- **E-mail:** Show or hide the contact's e-mail address.
- **Street Address:** Show or hide the contact's street address.
- **Town/Suburb:** Show or hide the contact's town/suburb.
- **State/County:** Show or hide the contact's state/county.
- **Postal/Zip Code:** Show or hide the contact's postal/zip code.
- **Country:** Show or hide the contact's country.
- **Telephone:** Show or hide the contact's telephone.
- **Mobile Phone Number:** Show or hide the contact's mobile phone number.
- **Fax:** Show or hide the contact's fax.
- **Web URL:** Show or hide the contact's web URL.
- **Miscellaneous Information:** Show or hide the contact's miscellaneous information.
- **Contact Image:** Show or hide the contact's image.
- **vCard:** Show or hide the contact's name. The Enable vCard parameter in the Global Parameters must be set to Yes for this to work.

Advanced parameters

Each individual contact includes the following optional advanced parameters; any values set here that are in conflict with the settings in the Global parameters will take precedence:

- **Icons/Text:** Choose what to show next to the Contact fields on the page. The options are Icon, Text, and None.
- **Address Icon:** Select the icon from the combo box to show next to the Address field. This option is only applicable if you have chosen to display icons in the Icons/Text parameter.
- **E-mail icon:** Select the icon from the combo box to show next to the E-mail field. This option is only applicable if you have chosen to display icons in the Icons/Text parameter.
- **Telephone icon:** Select the icon from the combo box to show next to the Telephone field. This option is only applicable if you have chosen to display icons in the Icons/Text parameter.

- **Mobile icon:** Select the icon from the combo box to show next to the Mobile field. This option is only applicable if you have chosen to display icons in the Icons/Text parameter.

- **Fax icon:** Select the icon from the combo box to show next to the Fax field. This option is only applicable if you have chosen to display icons in the Icons/Text parameter.

- **Miscellaneous Icon:** Select the icon from the combo box to show next to the Miscellaneous field. This option is only applicable if you have chosen to display icons in the Icons/Text parameter.

E-mail parameters

Each individual contact includes the following optional e-mail parameters; any values set here that are in conflict with the settings in the Global parameters take precedence:

- **E-mail form:** Show or hide an e-mail form that allows site visitors to send an e-mail directly to the contact.

- **Description text:** Enter description text to accompany the e-mail form. This option is only applicable if the E-mail Form parameter is set to Show.

- **E-mail copy:** Show or hide the option for the user to e-mail themselves a copy of the mail they sent to the contact. This option is only applicable is the E-mail Form parameter is set to show.

- **Banned e-mail:** To control SPAM, enter any terms you want to be banned from the e-mail form. If any e-mail address includes any of the banned terms, the form submission will be blocked. Separate multiple terms with semicolons. This is only applicable if the E-mail Form parameter is set to Show.

- **Banned subject:** To control SPAM, enter any terms you want to be banned from the e-mail form subject lines. If any e-mail subject line includes any of the banned terms, the form submission will be blocked. Separate multiple terms with semicolons. This is only applicable if the E-mail Form parameter is set to Show.

- **Banned text:** To control SPAM, enter any terms you want to be banned from the e-mail form text. If any e-mail address includes any of the banned terms, the form submission will be blocked. Separate multiple terms with semicolons. This is only applicable if the E-mail Form parameter is set to Show.

Managing Contacts and Categories

Categories are created by the administrator for the purpose of grouping contacts. Every contact must be assigned to a category.

To view the categories available in your system, click on the Categories link at the top of the Contacts Manager. The Contacts Category Manager loads in your browser, as seen in Figure 13.2.

FIGURE 13.2

The Contacts Category Manager.

The toolbar at the top of the Contact Category Manager provides quick access to the following functions:

- **Publish:** Select one or more categories from the list, and then click this icon to publish them.

- **Unpublish:** Select one or more categories from the list, and then click this icon to unpublish them.

- **Delete:** Select one or more categories from the list, and then click this icon to delete the category(s).

- **Edit:** Select a category from the list and then click this icon to edit the category's details.

- **New:** Click to create a new category.

- **Help:** Click to access the online Help files related to the active screen.

Two links are below the toolbar. The Contacts link shows you the Contact Manager. The Categories link shows you the Contact Categories Manager.

Below the two text links and above the list of categories are two sorting and searching tools to help you manage long lists of categories:

- **The Filter field** on the left works like a search box. Type a word or phrase into the field and then click Go. The page reloads and displays the results of the search. To clear the screen and return to a full listing, click the Reset button.

- **The Select State filter** on the far right allows you to filter and display the categories according to whether they are published or unpublished. This provides an easy way to identify all categories that are currently active on the site. To reset this filter, change the combo box back to the default setting.

The main content area of the screen contains a list of all the Contact categories. The columns provided are:

- **#:** This field is an indexing number set automatically by Joomla! You cannot alter this field.

- **Checkbox (no label):** Click in a checkbox to select a category; do this if you want to use several of the toolbar options, referenced previously.

- **Title:** This field displays the full name of the category. Click on the name to edit the category's details.

- **Published:** A green checkmark in this column indicates that the category is published. The field shows a red X if the category is not published. Administrators can toggle between the two settings by clicking on the icon shown.

- **Order:** The numbers in this field affect the ordering of the categories on this list. Change the numbers and click the Save icon at the top of the column to reorder the categories.

- **Access Level:** Indicates the access levels assigned to the category. You can toggle between the options Public, Registered, and Special by clicking on the words.

- **ID:** The system-generated user ID number.

Finally, at the bottom of the screen, below the content area, is the Display # option. Change the value in the combo box control to alter the number of categories that are displayed on the page. The default value can be altered by changing the List Length option on the Global Configuration Manager.

Creating a new category

Categories are created from within the Contact Category Manager by clicking the New icon on the toolbar. Category data is entered into the New Contact Category dialogue, shown in Figure 13.3

FIGURE 13.3

The New Contact Category dialogue.

The toolbar at the top of the New Contact Category dialogue provides quick access to the following functions:

- **Save:** Click this icon to save your work, create a new category, and exit the New Contact Category dialogue.

- **Apply:** Click to save your work and create a new category without exiting from the New Contact Category dialogue. This option lets you save without exiting the screen and is useful in case you are interrupted or you otherwise want to save yet keep working on this screen.

- **Cancel:** Cancels the task and exits the New Contact Category dialogue.

- **Help:** Displays the Help files related to the active screen.

The workspace in this dialogue is broken down into two sections, Details and Description. The Details section contains the following fields:

- **Title:** Type into this field a title for the Contact category. This field is the only required field.

- **Alias:** The alias is an internal label for the category. The alias is also used in the creation of a search engine friendly path for the category. This field only accepts small case letters, with no spaces. Note that if you leave this blank, the system automatically uses the value you entered into the title field.

- **Published:** A green checkmark indicates that the category is published. A red X means it is not published. You can click on the icon to toggle the state.

- **Section:** This field is not applicable to the Contact category, and as a result the system displays only n/a.

- **Category order:** This field cannot be controlled when a new category is created. New categories always default to last on the list. The order can be changed from the Contact Category Manager or by editing the category.

- **Access Level:** This field is not used for Contact categories.

- **Image:** Provides the option to display a small image next to the category name on pages listing the categories. This is optional. The Image Position control is related to this option. Note that the image you want to select must be located in the folder `images/stories`.

- **Image position:** Controls placement of the image relative to the category name. The choices are limited to left or right. Left is selected by default. Note that this control is only applicable if an image is selected from the Image control.

The Description field at the bottom of the screen provides c a place to add a description of the category. The description will not appear on any pages on the front end of the site; this description is purely for your information. The text box enables you to use images and formatting for the description. The Image button at the bottom of the Description field gives you easy access to controls for inserting an image into the description, if you so desire.

To create a new category, follow these steps:

1. **Log in to the admin system on your site.**

2. **Access the Contacts Category Manager.**

    To do so, go to the Components menu and select the Categories option from the submenu under the heading Contacts. The Contacts Category Manager will load in your browser.

3. **Click the New icon on the toolbar at the top of the Contacts Category Manager.**

    The New Contacts Category Dialogue opens.

    (Refer to Figure 13.3.)

4. **In the Title field, type a name for this category.**

    This is the only required field.

5. Add additional information or optional settings as you see fit.

6. Click the Save icon on the toolbar at the top right to save your new Contact Category. The dialogue closes and returns you to the Contact Category Manager.

Editing and deleting categories

Existing contact categories can be edited from the Contact Category Manager. To edit a category, either click the category name in the Contact Category Manager or select the category on the list and then click the Edit icon on the Contact Category Manager toolbar. Regardless of which method you use, the system opens the Edit Category dialogue.

The Edit Category dialogue is identical to the New Category dialogue, with the same fields and requirements as discussed in the previous section.

To make changes to a category, simply alter the desired fields in the Edit Category dialogue and then click the Save or Apply icon on the toolbar. Any changes you have made are applied immediately.

To delete one or more categories, follow these steps:

1. Open the Contact Category Manager.

2. Select one or more categories.

3. Click the Delete icon.

Caution

Deleting a contact category is permanent and cannot be undone. Moreover, there is no confirmation dialogue— clicking the Delete icon immediately deletes the category! Note, however, that a category cannot be deleted if contacts are assigned to that category. If you want to delete the category, you need to first delete or move any contacts to another category.

Adding a new contact

To add a new contact to your site, visit the Contact Manager and click the New icon on the toolbar. The New Contact dialogue opens in your browser, as shown in Figure 13.4.

The toolbar at the top of the New Contact dialogue provides quick access to the following functions:

- **Save:** Click this icon to save your work, add a new contact, and exit the New Contact dialogue.

- **Apply:** Click this icon to save your work without exiting from the New Contact dialogue.

- **Cancel:** Cancels the task, exits the New Contact dialogue, and returns you to the Contact Manager.

- **Help:** Displays the Help files related to the active screen.

FIGURE 13.4

The New Contact dialogue.

The workspace is divided into three areas: details, information, and parameters. The Details section of the workspace contains the following fields:

- **Name:** Type into this field the full name of the contact. This field is required.

- **Alias:** The Alias field is an internal identifier for your contact. This is used in some cases to create search engine friendly URLs for the item. You can specify the contents of this field if you want, but note that it only takes lowercase letters with no spaces. If you do not specify the contents of this field, the system will automatically create the alias based on the contact's name.

- **Published:** Select Yes to publish the contact. The default state is Yes.

- **Category:** Assign the contact to a category using the combo box. This field is required.

- **Linked to User:** Use the combo box to link the contact to a registered user on the site. If you do not want to link it to a user, select the value No User.

- **Order:** Note that this control is not available for a new contact. New items are placed by default in the last position on the list. After you add your contact, you can adjust the list position from either the Contact Manager or by editing the contact item.

- **Access Level:** Set the access level to control the visibility of the contact. The options are Public, Registered, and Special. The default is Public.

The Information section of the workspace contains the following fields:

- **Contact's Position:** Type the contact's position into this field.

- **E-mail:** Type the contact's e-mail address into this field.

- **Street Address:** Type the contact's street address into this field.

- **Town/Suburb:** Type the contact's town/suburb into this field.

- **State/County:** Type the contact's state/county into this field.

- **Postal Code/ZIP:** Type the contact's Postal Code/ZIP into this field

- **Country:** Type the contact's country into this field.

- **Telephone:** Type the contact's phone number into this field.

- **Mobile Phone Number:** Type the contact's mobile phone number into this field.

- **Fax:** Type the contact's fax number into this field.

- **Web URL:** Type the contact's web site address into this field.

- **Miscellaneous Information:** Type into this field any additional information you want to display with the contact.

- **Contact Image:** Select from the combo box an image to display with this contact. Images are drawn from the `images/stories` directory. You can add your own images by using the Media Manager.

To add a new contact, follow these steps:

1. **Log in to the Admin system on your site.**

2. **Access the Contacts Manager. To do so, go to the Components menu and select the Contacts option.** The Contact Manager loads in your browser.

3. **Click the New icon on the toolbar at the top of the Contacts Manager.** The New Contact dialogue opens. (Refer to Figure 13.4.)

4. **In the Name field, type a name for the contact.** This is a required field.

5. **Select a Category for the contact from the Category combo box.** This is a required field.

6. Select any additional options you wish; all other fields are optional.

7. **Click the Save icon on the toolbar at the top right to save your new contact.** The dialogue closes and returns you to the Contacts Manager.

Editing and deleting contacts

Existing contacts can be edited from the Contacts Manager. To edit a contact, either click the contact name in the Contacts Manager or select the contact and then click the Edit icon on the Contact Manager toolbar. Regardless of which method you use, the system opens the Edit Contact dialogue.

The Edit Contact dialogue is identical to the New Contact dialogue, with the same fields and requirements as discussed in the previous section.

To make changes to a contact, simply alter the desired fields in the Edit Contact dialogue, and then click the Save or Apply icon on the toolbar. Any changes you make are applied immediately.

To delete one or more contacts, follow these steps:

1. Open the Contacts Manager.

2. Select one or more contacts.

3. Click the Delete icon.

Caution

Deleting a contact is permanent and cannot be undone. Moreover, there is no confirmation dialogue — clicking the Delete icon immediately deletes the contact as well as any cached content of the feed.

Creating Contact Forms

The Contact Manager is the key to setting up contact forms for your web site. Creating a generic contact form for your site visitors to use is a two-stage process. The first stage is to create a specific contact to receive the output of the form. Creating a new contact is discussed previously. The second stage is to create a new menu item of the type Standard Contact Layout, making sure that you enable the form functionality for the menu item. Associate the menu item with the contact you have created to receive the form output

Cross-Reference

Creating a new menu item and a discussion of the Menu Item Types is discussed in Chapter 8.

Summary

In this chapter, we covered the Contacts Manager. You learned the following:

- How to create new contacts
- How to edit and delete contacts
- How to create contact categories
- How to edit and delete contact categories
- How to create a generic contact form for your site

Using the News Feeds Component

The News Feeds component is an RSS aggregation tool. The component allows you to add syndicated RSS and Atom feeds (referred to in Joomla! by the generic name "news feeds") to your site and to group them into categories. You can then display the content on your pages by creating menu items that link to the component's output.

The News Feeds component provides all the parameters needed to manage the aggregation of multiple feeds and, to a lesser extent, the individual feed items. You can control the number of items gathered and the frequency of the updates. The feed items gathered by the News Feeds component can then be channeled into the site to display in a variety of manners.

Although, as I discuss elsewhere in this book, you can use other ways to bring syndicated content into your site, the News Feeds component makes it easy to manage and display a large number of feeds and to create groups of feed items that update automatically on your site.

Introducing the News Feeds Manager

To get started adding news feeds to your site, you need to access the News Feeds Manager, which is the interface to the component. Go to the Components menu and select the News Feeds option. The News Feeds Manager interface loads in your browser.

Figure 14.1 shows the News Feeds Manager as it appears with the Joomla! sample data installed.

FIGURE 14.1

The News Feeds Manager.

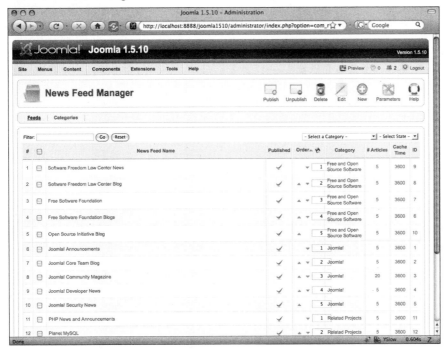

Note

On the Components menu, the option labeled News Feeds leads to the same screen as the News Feeds sub-menu option labeled Feeds. Despite having different names, these two navigation choices lead to the same page — the News Feeds Manager.

The toolbar at the top of the News Feeds Manager provides quick access to the following functions:

- **Publish:** Select one or more news feeds from the list, and then click this icon to publish them.

- **Unpublish:** Select one or more news feeds from the list, and then click this icon to unpublish them.

- **Delete:** Select one or more news feeds from the list, and then click this icon to delete the news feeds.

- **Edit:** Select a news feed from the list, and then click this icon to edit the news feed's details.

- **New:** Click to add a new news feed.

- **Parameters:** Click this to view the parameters available for this component.

- **Help:** Click to access the online Help files related to the active screen.

Two text links are located below the toolbar. The link labeled News Feeds shows you the News Feeds Manager. The Categories link takes you to the News Feeds Category Manager, which is discussed in following text.

Below the two links and above the list of news feeds are three sorting and searching tools to help you manage long lists of News Feeds. Try the following:

- **Filter field** on the left works like a search box. Type a word or phrase into the field and then click Go. The page reloads and displays the results of the search. To clear the screen and return to a full listing, click the Reset button.

- **Select a Category filter** on the right side allows you to display only those news feeds that have been assigned to a specific category. To reset this filter, change the combo box back to the default setting.

- **Select State filter** on the far right allows you to filter and display the news feeds according to whether they are published or unpublished. The Select State filter provides an easy way to identity all news feeds that are currently active on the site. To reset this filter, change the combo box back to the default setting.

Tip

The Select a Category filter and the Select State filter can be combined to further refine the view of the list of news feeds.

The main content area of the screen contains a list of all the news feeds in your News Feeds component. The columns provided are:

- **# :** An indexing number assigned by Joomla! This number cannot be changed.

- **Checkbox (no label):** Click in a checkbox to select a news feed; this is needed if you want to use several of the toolbar options, referenced previously.

- **News Feed Name:** This field displays the full name of the news feed. Click on the name to edit the news feed's details.

- **Published:** A green checkmark in this column indicates that the news feed is published. The field shows a red X if the news feed is not published. Administrators can toggle between the two settings by clicking on the icon.

- **Order:** The numbers in this field affect the ordering of the news feeds on this list. Change the numbers and click the Save icon at the top of the column to reorder the news feeds.

- **Category:** The name of the category to which the news feed has been assigned. You can click on the category name to open the Category Editing dialogue. I cover how to edit categories in the next section.

- **# Articles:** How many items have been gathered from this feed and are available for display.

- **Cache Time:** How long the contents of the news feed are kept locally before the list is refreshed.

- **ID:** The system-generated user ID number.

At the bottom of the screen, below the content area, is the Display # option. Change the value in the combo box control to alter the number of news feeds that are displayed on the page. The default value can be altered by changing the List Length option on the Global Configuration Manager.

Caution

At the very bottom of the page, underneath the Display # option, Joomla! provides an indication of whether the cache directory is writeable. This information is provided for your reference. If the cache is not writeable, the News Feeds component will not work properly, because it will be unable to cache feed output. If this indicator shows the directory is unwriteable, you need to adjust the privileges on the indicated directory.

Understanding News Feed Parameters

Global options for the News Feeds component can be configured by means of the Parameters options. The parameters are viewed and modified by clicking the Parameters icon on the News Feeds Manager toolbar. Clicking the icon causes a lightbox to be superimposed on top of the page. Inside the lightbox are the parameters available to this component.

The News Feeds Manager includes the following parameters:

- **Table Headings:** The settings chosen here are only visible on pages where the feeds are displayed in category view. This control relates to the display characteristics of the table holding the lists of feeds. Select Yes if you want the columns of the table to include descriptive headings.

- **Name Column:** The settings chosen here are only visible on pages where the feeds are displayed in category view. This control relates to the display characteristics of the table holding the lists of feeds. Select Yes if you want to display a column showing the feed's Name in the table.

- **# Articles Column:** The settings chosen here are only be visible on pages where the feeds are displayed in category view. This control relates to the display characteristics of the table holding the lists of feeds. Select Yes if you want to display in the table a column showing the number of articles in the feed.

- **Link Column:** The settings chosen here are only visible on pages where the feeds are displayed in category view. This control relates to the display characteristics of the table holding the lists of feeds. Select Yes if you want to display a column showing a link to the source of the feed in the table.

- **Category Description:** The settings chosen here are only visible on pages where the feeds are displayed in category view. Select yes if you want to display on the page listing the feeds the category description. The category description is set by the administrator when a News Feed Category is created.

- **# Category Items:** The settings chosen here are only visible on pages where the feeds are displayed in category view. Select Yes if you want to display on the page listing the feeds the number of News Feeds in each News Feed category.

- **Feed Image:** Select Yes if you want to display the feeds that the Feed Image provided by the source of the feed on the page listing.

- **Feed Description:** Select Yes if you want to display on the page listing the feeds the Feed Description set by the source of the feed.

- **Item Description:** Select Yes if you want to display on the page listing the feeds a short description of the item. The description is taken from the first few words of the item. Note that this parameter works in conjunction with the Word Count control below, which dictates the length of the description displayed.

- **Word Count:** An integer value that determines the size of the Item description, in words. Set the value of this field to zero to display the entire feed item.

After you have set the parameters you desire, click the Save button at the top right to save your changes or click Cancel to close the Parameters window without saving the changes.

Managing Feeds and Categories

Categories are created by the administrator for the purpose of grouping news feeds. Every news feed must be assigned to a category.

Note
Before you can add your first news feed you must have at least one category in the system.

To view the categories available in your system, click on the categories link at the top of the News Feeds Manager. The News Feeds Category Manager loads in your browser, as shown in Figure 14.2.

FIGURE 14.2

The News Feeds Category Manager.

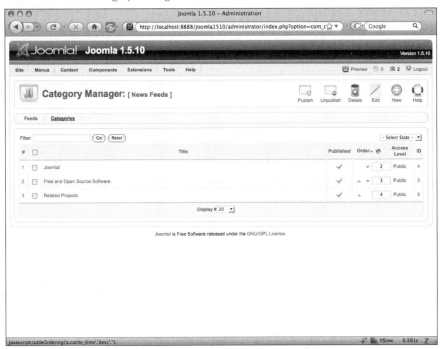

The toolbar at the top of the News Feeds Category Manager provides quick access to the following functions:

- **Publish:** Select one or more categories from the list and then click this icon to publish them.

- **Unpublish:** Select one or more categories from the list and then click this icon to unpublish them.

- **Delete:** Select one or more categories from the list and then click this icon to delete the category(s).

- **Edit:** Select a category from the list and then click this icon to edit the category's details.

- **New:** Click to create a new category.

- **Help:** Click to access the online Help files related to the active screen.

Two text links are below the toolbar. The Feeds link shows you the News Feeds Manager, discussed earlier in this chapter. The Categories link displays the News Feeds Category Manager.

Below the two text links and above the list of categories are two sorting and searching tools to help you manage long lists of categories:

- **The Filter field** on the left works like a search box. Type a word or phrase into the field and then click Go. The page reloads and displays the results of the search. To clear the screen and return to a full listing, click the Reset button.

- **The Select State filter** on the far right allows you to filter and display the categories according to whether they are published or unpublished. This provides an easy way to identity all categories that are currently active on the site. To reset this filter, change the combo box back to the default setting. (- select state -)

The main content area of the screen contains a list of all the News Feeds categories. The columns provided are:

- **#:** This field is an indexing number set automatically by Joomla! You cannot alter this field.

- **Checkbox (no label):** Click in a checkbox to select a category. The checkbox is needed if you want to use several of the toolbar options, referenced previously.

- **Title:** This field displays the full name of the category. Click on the name to edit the category's details.

- **Published:** A green checkmark in this column indicates that the category is published. The field will show a red X if the category is not published. Administrators can toggle between the two settings by clicking on the icon shown.

- **Order:** The numbers in this field affect the ordering of the categories on this list. Change the numbers and click the Save icon at the top of the column to reorder the categories.

- **Access Level:** Indicates the access levels assigned to the category. You can toggle between the options Public, Registered, and Special by clicking on the words.

- **ID:** The system-generated user ID number.

Finally, at the bottom of the screen, below the content area, is the Display # option. Change the value in the combo box control to alter the number of categories that are displayed on the page. The default value can be altered by changing the List Length option on the Global Configuration Manager.

Creating a new category

Before you can add news feeds to your system, you must create at least one category. Categories are created from within the News Feed Category Manager, by clicking the New icon on the toolbar. Category data is entered into the New News Feed Category dialogue, shown in Figure 14.3.

FIGURE 14.3

The New News Feed Category dialogue.

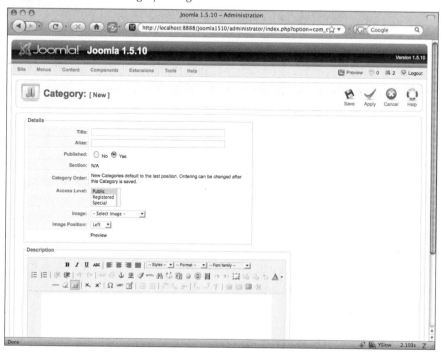

The toolbar at the top of the New News Feed Category dialogue provides quick access to the following functions:

- **Save:** Click this icon to save your work, create a new category, and exit the New News Feed Category dialogue.

- **Apply:** Click to save your work and create a new category without exiting from the New News Feed Category dialogue. This option lets you save without exiting the screen and it is useful in case you are interrupted or you otherwise want to save yet keep working on this screen.

- **Cancel:** This option cancels the task and exits the New News Feed Category dialogue.

- **Help:** This option displays the Help files related to the active screen.

The workspace in this dialogue is broken into two sections, Details and Description. The Details section contains the following fields:

- **Title:** Type a title for the News Feed Category into this field. This field is the only required field.

- **Alias:** The alias is an internal label for the category. The alias is also used in the creation of a search engine friendly path for the category. This field only accepts small case letters, with no spaces. Note that if you leave this blank, the system will automatically use the value you entered into the Title field.

- **Published:** A green checkmark indicates the category is published. A red X means it is not published. You can click on the icon to toggle the state.

- **Section:** This field is not applicable to the News Feed category, and as a result the system displays only n/a.

- **Category Order:** This field cannot be controlled when a new category is created. New categories always default to last on the list. The order can be changed from the News Feed Category Manager or by editing the category.

- **Access Level:** Sets the access level restrictions for the category and its contents. The options Registered, Public, or Special appear in this column. You can click the names to toggle the level. If no value is chosen, the system defaults to Public.

- **Image:** Provides the option to display a small image next to the category name on pages listing the categories. This is optional. The Image Position control is related to this option. Note that the image you want to select must be located in the folder images/stories.

- **Image Position:** Controls placement of the image relative to the category name. The choices are limited to Left or Right. Left is selected by default. Note that this control is only applicable if an image is selected from the Image control.

The Description field at the bottom of the screen provides you with a place to add a description of the category. The description appears on pages where the categories are listed. The text box allows you to use images and formatting for the description. The Image button at the bottom of the Description field gives you easy access to controls for inserting an image into the description.

To create a new category, follow these steps:

1. **Log in to the admin system on your site.**

2. **Access the News Feeds Category Manager. To do so, go to the Components menu and choose the Categories option from the submenu under the heading News Feeds.** The News Feeds Category Manager loads in your browser.

3. **Click the New icon on the toolbar at the top of the News Feeds Category Manager.** The New News Feeds Category dialogue opens. Refer to Figure 14.3.

4. **In the Title field, type a name for this category.** This is the only required field.

5. **Add additional information or optional settings as you see fit.**

6. **Click the Save icon on the toolbar at the top right to save your new News Feed Category.** The dialogue closes and returns you to the News Feed Category Manager.

Editing and deleting categories

You can edit existing News Feed categories from the News Feed Category Manager. To edit a category, do either of the following

- Click on the category name in the News Feed Category Manager.
- Select the category on the list and then click the Edit icon on the News Feed Category Manager toolbar.

Regardless of which method you use, the system opens the Edit Category dialogue.

The Edit Category dialogue is identical to the New Category dialogue, with the same fields and requirements as discussed in the section above.

To make changes to a category, simply alter the desired fields in the Edit Category dialogue and then click the Save or Apply icon on the toolbar. Any changes you have made are applied immediately.

To delete one or more categories, follow these steps:

1. Open the News Feed Category Manager.
2. Select one or more categories.
3. Click the Delete icon.

Caution

Deleting a Ne⁻ ᵢ Feed category is permanent and cannot be undone. Moreover, there is no confirmation dialogue — click ..g the Delete icon immediately deletes the category! However, a category cannot be deleted if there are News Feeds assigned to that category. If you want to delete the category, you need to first delete or reassign any news feeds assigned to that category.

Adding a new feed

To add a new news feed to your site, visit the News Feeds Manager and click the New icon on the toolbar. The New News Feed dialogue opens in your browser, as shown in Figure 14.4.

The toolbar at the top of the New News Feed dialogue provides quick access to the following functions:

- **Save:** Click this icon to save your work, add a new News Feed, and exit the New News Feed dialogue.
- **Apply:** Click to save your work and add a new News Feed without exiting from the New News Feed dialogue. This option lets you save without exiting the screen, and it useful in case you are interrupted, or you otherwise want to save yet keep working on this screen.
- **Cancel:** This option cancels the task and exits the New News Feed dialogue.
- **Help:** This option displays the Help files related to the active screen.

FIGURE 14.4

The New News Feed dialogue.

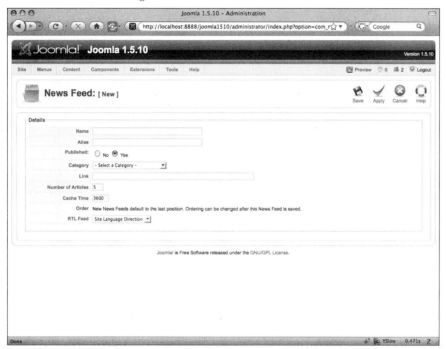

The Details section of the workspace contains the following fields:

- **Name:** Use this field to give a name to your news feed. This is a required field.

- **Alias:** The alias field is an internal identifier for your news feed. An alias is used in some cases to create search engine friendly URLs for the item. You can specify the contents of this field if you want, but note that it only takes lowercase letters with no spaces. If you do not specify the contents of this field the system automatically creates the alias based on the item's name.

- **Published:** Select Yes to publish the news feed. The default state is Yes.

- **Category:** Assign the news feed to a category using the combo box. This field is required.

- **Link:** Enter into this field the URL for the source of the news feed. This field is required. Note that this should normally begin with `http://`.

- **Number of Articles:** This field requires an integer value to specify the number of items that will be cached. The default is 5.

- **Cache Time:** This field requires an integer value to specify the length of time the items are cached; after this period the system attempts to refresh the news feed items from the source of the news feed. This value is in seconds. The default is 3600 (one hour).

- **Order:** Note that this control is not available for a new news feed. New items are placed by default in the last position on the list. After you add your news feed, you can adjust the list position from either the News Feed Manager or edit the News Feed item.

- **RTL Feed:** If your site uses right-to-left text orientation, use this control to specify the text direction of the feed's contents.

Note

Supported feed formats include: RSS 0.91, RSS 1.0, RSS 2.0, Atom 0.3, and Atom 1.0.

To add a new news feed, follow these steps:

1. **Log in to the admin system on your site.**

2. **Access the News Feeds Manager. To do so, go to the Components menu and select the News Feeds option.** The News Feeds Manager loads in your browser.

3. **Click the New icon on the toolbar at the top of the News Feeds Manager.** The New News Feed Dialogue opens. Refer to Figure 16.4.

4. **In the Name field, type a name for the feed.** This field is required.

5. **Select a category for the feed from the category combo box.** This field is required.

6. **Type the address for the feed source in Link field.** Normally this begins with `http://`. This field is required.

7. **Select any additional options you want; all other fields are optional.**

8. **Click the Save icon on the toolbar at the top right to save your new news feed.**

   The dialogue closes and returns you to the News Feeds Manager.

Displaying news feeds on your site

After you bring news feeds into your system with the News Feed Manager, the question becomes how to display the news feeds on your site. Adding feeds to the Manager does not automatically translate into displaying feed output on your site.

There are two common ways to display news feed content on your site: use either a page or a module

By linking your menus to the News Feed component, you can display feeds or categories of feeds as content items on your site. For a discussion of how to add news feeds to the pages on your site through the creation of Menu Items, see Chapter 8.

Alternatively, you can bypass the News Feeds component completely and create a new module to hold a single news feed. Modules can be used to aggregate and display individual news feeds and are not dependent in any way upon the News Feed component. Chapter 20 covers adding news feed content inside of a module on your site.

Editing and deleting feeds

Existing news feeds can be edited from the News Feeds Manager. To edit a news feed, either click on the news feed name in the News Feeds Manager or select the news feed and then click the Edit icon on the News Feeds Manager toolbar. Regardless of which method you use, the system opens the Edit News Feed dialogue.

The Edit News Feed dialogue is identical to the New News Feed dialogue, with the same fields and requirements as discussed in the preceding section.

To make changes to a news feed, simply alter the desired fields in the Edit News Feed dialogue and then click the Save or Apply icon on the toolbar. Any changes you have made are applied immediately.

To delete one or more news feeds, follow these steps:

1. **Open the News Feeds Manager.**
2. **Select one or more news feeds.**
3. **Click the Delete icon.**

Caution

Deleting a news feed is permanent and cannot be undone. Moreover, there is no confirmation dialogue — clicking the Delete icon immediately deletes the news feed as well as any cached content of the feed.

Summary

In this chapter, we cover the use of the News Feed Component. You learned the following:

- How to configure the News Feeds component
- How to create, edit, and delete news feeds
- How to create, edit, and delete News Feed categories

Using the Polls Component

J oomla! 1.5.x includes a Polls component that enables you to create and run polls and surveys for your site. The Poll Manager allows for the creation of single question polls with up to 12 answer choices. You can create and run multiple polls and you can view the results from one or more polls in an easy- to- read chart format.

The Polls component works in conjunction with the Polls module. The component handles the creation of the Poll content, while the module handles the actual display of the polls. You control the placement of the polls on the page by assigning the module to the desired module position.

Introducing the Poll Manager

The Poll Manager is the interface to the component. You can use the Poll Manager to create and manage all the polls on your web site. To access the manager, go to the Components menu and select the Polls option. The Poll Manager interface loads in your browser. Figure 15.1 shows the Poll Manager as it appears with the Joomla! sample data installed.

Joomla! 1.6
There is no Polls component in Joomla! 1.6.

FIGURE 15.1

The Poll Manager interface in Joomla! 1.5.

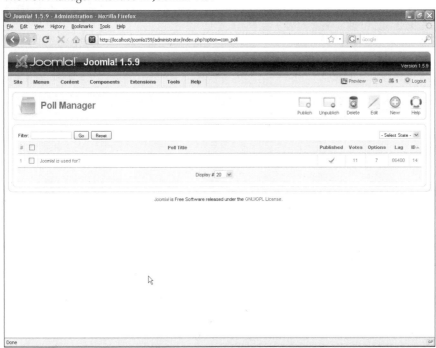

The toolbar at the top of the Poll Manager provides quick access to the following functions:

- **Publish:** Select one or more polls from the list and then click this icon to publish them.

- **Unpublish:** Select one or more polls from the list and then click this icon to unpublish them.

- **Delete:** Select one or more polls from the list and then click this icon to delete the poll(s).

- **Edit:** Select a poll from the list and then click this icon to edit the poll details.

- **New:** Click to add a new poll.

- **Help:** Click to access the online Help files related to the active screen.

Below the toolbar and above the list of polls are two sorting and searching tools to help you manage long lists of polls:

- **The Filter field** on the left works like a search box. Type a word or phrase into the field and then click Go. The page reloads and displays the results of the search. To clear the screen and return to a full listing, click the Reset button.

- **The Select State filter** on the far right allows you to filter and display the Polls according to whether they are published or unpublished. This provides an easy way to identify all polls that are currently active on the site. To reset this filter, change the combo box back to the default setting.

The main content area of the screen contains a list of all the polls in your Joomla! site. The columns provided are:

- **#** : An indexing number assigned by Joomla! This number cannot be changed.
- **Checkbox (no label):** Click in a checkbox to select a poll; this is needed if you want to use several of the toolbar options, referenced above.
- **Poll Title:** This field displays the full name of the poll. Note that Joomla! uses the question being asked in the poll as the name of the poll. Click on the name to edit the poll's details.
- **Published:** A green checkmark in this column indicates that the poll is active. The field will show a red X if the poll is disabled. Note that both the individual poll and the page or module containing the poll must be published for the poll to appear to site visitors. Administrators can toggle between the two settings by clicking on the icon shown.
- **Votes:** A running count of the number of responses to each poll.
- **Options:** Indicates how many options, that is, answer choices, the poll contains.
- **Lag:** Use this field to limit the number of times the same visitor can respond to the poll during a specific time period. The integer value in this field indicates how long a visitor must wait before submitting an additional response to the poll time measured in seconds
- **ID:** The system-generated user ID number.

Finally, at the bottom of the screen, below the content area, is the Display # option. Change the value in the combo box control to alter the number of polls that are displayed on the page. The default value can be altered by changing the List Length option on the Global Configuration Manager.

Creating and Managing Polls

All polls content is created and managed through the Poll Manager. The sample data included with the default system includes one poll entitled "Joomla! is used for?" That Poll can be edited to change the content for your use, or you can create a new poll from scratch by using the New option on the Poll Manager.

Creating polls

To create a new poll, click the New icon on the toolbar at the top of the Poll Manager. Figure 15.2 shows the New Poll dialogue.

FIGURE 15.2

The New Poll dialogue.

The toolbar at the top of the New Poll dialogue provides quick access to the following functions:

- **Preview:** Click this icon to view how your poll will appear to site visitors. The poll appears in a lightbox on top of your browser page.

- **Save:** Click this icon to save your work, create a new poll, and exit the New Poll dialogue.

- **Apply:** Click to save your work and create a new poll without exiting from the New Poll dialogue. This option lets you save without exiting the screen and it useful in case you are interrupted or you otherwise want to save yet keep working on this screen.

- **Cancel:** Cancels the task and exits the New Poll dialogue.

- **Help:** Displays the Help files related to the active screen.

The Details section of the New Poll dialogue includes the following fields:

- **Title:** This field is used to create the question for the poll; this field is also used as the Poll's name inside the Poll Manager interface. This field is required.

- **Alias:** The alias is the internal name for the item. This field only accepts lowercase letters. Spaces are not permitted. If you leave this field blank, the system automatically uses your title for the alias, after modifying it to fit the system formatting requirements.

- **Lag:** Input an integer value to specify how long a visitor must wait before responding to the poll again. The time is calculated in seconds. The default value is 86,400.

- **Published:** Set the control to Yes to publish the poll. Note that setting the poll to Publish is only half of what is needed to make it visible to site visitors; you also must display the Poll module.

The Options section of the New Poll dialogue includes a set of fields that are used to input the answer choices for the poll. The system supports up to 12 answer options. Although you can create a poll without filling in any of the Option fields, the result would be a poll with no answer choices; therefore, for all practical purposes this section requires at least two entries.

To create a new poll, follow these steps:

1. **Access the Poll Manager by clicking on the Polls option under the Components menu.** The Poll Manager loads in your browser.

2. **On the Poll Manager interface, click the New icon on the toolbar at the top of the Poll Manager.** The New Poll Dialogue opens. Refer to Figure 15.2.

3. **In the Title field, type the question you wish to pose in the Poll.** This field is required.

4. **Set the Published option to Yes.**

5. **Enter the answer choices in the Options fields.**

6. **Complete any other fields you wish; all other fields are optional.**

7. **Click the Save icon on the toolbar at the top right to save your new poll.** The dialogue closes and returns you to the Poll Manager.

Editing and deleting polls

Existing polls can be edited from the Poll Manager. To edit a poll, either click on the poll name in the Poll Manager or select the poll and then click the Edit icon on the Poll Manager toolbar. Regardless of which method you use, the system opens the Edit Poll dialogue.

The Edit Poll dialogue is identical to the New Poll dialogue, with the same fields and requirements as discussed in the preceding section.

To make changes to a poll, simply alter the desired fields in the Edit Poll dialogue and then click the Save or Apply icon on the toolbar. Any changes you have made are applied immediately.

To delete one or more polls, follow these steps:

1. **Open the Poll Manager.**

2. **Select one or more polls.**

3. **Click the Delete icon.**

Caution

Deleting a poll is permanent and cannot be undone. Moreover, there is no confirmation dialogue — clicking the Delete icon immediately deletes the poll!

Displaying Polls

Although the poll component is used to set up and organize your polls, you must take additional steps to place the polls on the page. The question with the answer choices is displayed to front-end site visitors through the use of the Polls module. A summary of the results of one or more polls can be displayed inside the content area of pages by using the Poll Layout Content Item option under the Menu Item Manager.

Cross-reference

The creation of new menu items and the various Menu Item Types are discussed in Chapter 8.

Using the Polls module

The Polls module, like all other modules in your system, is created and controlled from within the Site Module Manager. A new Polls module can be created by clicking on the New icon on the toolbar or, if you have installed the Joomla! sample data, you can modify the existing Polls module to suit your needs.

Cross-Reference

Turn to Chapter 20 for more information on creating and managing the various Site Modules.

Figure 15.3 shows the default Polls module, with the Joomla! sample data loaded.

The toolbar at the top of the Polls module dialogue provides quick access to the following functions:

- **Save:** Click this icon to save changes made to the module and exit the Polls Module dialogue.

- **Apply:** Click to save your work without exiting from the Polls module dialogue. This option lets you save without exiting the screen and it useful in case you are interrupted or you otherwise want to save yet keep working on this screen.

- **Cancel:** Cancels the task and exits the Polls module.

- **Help:** Displays the Help files related to the active screen.

FIGURE 15.3

A poll displayed using the Polls module, shown here in the default configuration with the Joomla! sample data.

The workspace on this dialogue has three sections labeled Details, Menu Assignment, and Parameters. The Details section of the Polls module includes the following fields:

- **Module Type:** This field is determined by the system and is not editable. The label **mod_poll** tells you that this is a Polls module.

- **Title:** The name of the module.

- **Show Title:** If this control is set to Yes, the module title appears wherever the module appears on the front end of the web site.

- **Enabled:** Set this control to Yes if you want the module to appear on the front end of your site.

- **Position:** The combo box control is used to assign the module to one of the template's module position holders.

- **Order:** This field is only applicable if more than one module is assigned to the same module position, in which case this is used to control the ordering of the modules.

- **Access Level:** Set the control for Public, Registered, or Special, depending upon which User Groups you want to be able to see the module.

- **ID:** This internal ID field is set automatically by the system and cannot be edited.

- **Description:** The description text is supplied by the system and cannot be edited.

The Menu Assignment area, at the bottom left of the dialogue, shows a list of all the menus and menu items in the system. This control allows to you designate the pages where the module will appear.

Module parameters

On the right hand side of the Polls module dialogue is the parameters section. The controls here work closely in combination with the settings assigned in the Polls component to control the behavior of the polls on the page.

The controls available are broken into two groups: Module parameters and Advanced parameters. The Module parameters are:

- **Poll:** This control allows you to select the poll that will be displayed by the module. The list of polls reflects the polls created by the Polls component; it will only display those polls marked as published in the Polls component.

- **Module Class Suffix:** Use this field to add a suffix to the CSS classes that relate to this module; this enables you to provide styling that affects only this specific module.

The Advanced parameters are:

- **Caching:** Set this control to specify whether this module follows the Global Caching settings (set in the Global Configuration Manager).

- **Cache Time:** If you want to cache the contents of this module, enter an integer value here. The value represents the time, in seconds.

Displaying multiple polls

If you have created more than one poll with the Polls component, you can display them by using multiple modules. A Polls module displays one poll at a time, so displaying multiple polls requires having multiple modules. Running multiple modules allows you to match polls to appropriate page content or functionality or to show the same poll in different positions on different pages.

Displaying poll results

The results of a poll are shown in the content area of your site's pages. The results of the current poll can be viewed by a site visitor by clicking on the results button on the Polls module. Clicking the results button takes the viewer to a page that shows the poll results in a graphical summary view. If there is more than one poll active on the site, the visitor will also see on the results page a combo box control that allows the visitors to switch between poll results.

FIGURE 15.4

Poll results are displayed inside of the content area.

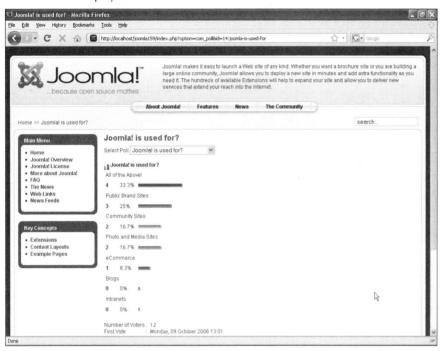

You can also link directly to the poll results page by creating a new Menu Item and selecting the Poll Layout Content Item option. Figure 15.4 shows the poll output.

To link directly to the poll results page from a menu, follow these steps:

1. **Under the Menus menu, click the name of the menu where you want the link to the poll to appear.** The Menu Item Manager loads in your browser.

2. **Click the New icon on the toolbar.** The New Menu Item dialogue opens.

3. **Select the option Poll Layout from under the polls choice.** The second page of the New Menu Item dialogue opens.

4. **Give the item a Title.** This field is required.

5. **On the Poll parameters, select the name of the poll whose results appear by default.** This field is required.

6. **Select any other options you desire; all other fields are optional.**

7. **Click Save.** The system creates the new menu item, closes the dialogue, and returns you to the Menu Item Manager.

Note

If your system contains multiple polls, the results of all will be available to viewers. There is no way to restrict the view to the results of only certain polls. The output will always display all published polls.

Summary

In this chapter, we covered the use of both the Polls component and the Polls module. You learned the following:

- How to create, edit, and delete polls
- How to configure the Poll Manager to work in concert with the Polls module
- How to create a Polls module

Using the Web Links Component

The Web Links component enables you to add a links page showing URLs to other web sites and online resources. This component also makes it easy to organize those links and to track the number of times users have clicked on the links.

The Web Links component provides all the parameters needed to control the appearance and behavior of the links. The link items gathered by the Web Links component can then be displayed on the pages of your site. Although you can use other ways to bring links into your site, the Web Links component makes it easy to manage and display a large number of links on your site by grouping them into categories.

Introducing the Web Link Manager

To get started adding links to your site, go to the Web Links component. To access the component, log in to the admin system; then go to the Components menu and select the option Web Links. The Web Link Manager loads in your browser window.

Figure 16.1 shows the Web Link Manager as it appears with the Joomla! sample data installed.

Note
On the Components menu, the option labeled Web Links leads to the same screen as the Web Links submenu option labeled Links. Despite having different names, these two navigation choices lead to the same page — the Web Link Manager.

FIGURE 16.1

The Web Link Manager.

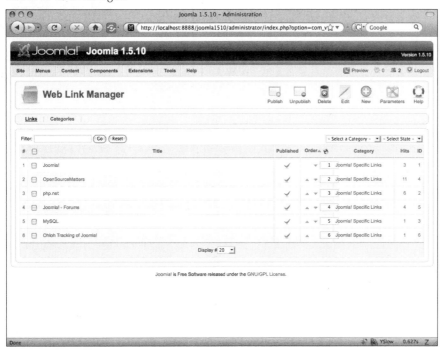

The toolbar at the top of the Web Link Manager provides quick access to the following functions:

- **Publish:** Select one or more Web Links from the list and then click this icon to publish them.

- **Unpublish:** Select one or more Web Links from the list and then click this icon to unpublish them.

- **Delete:** Select one or more Web Links from the list and then click this icon to delete the Web links.

- **Edit:** Select a Web link from the list and then click this icon to edit the Web link details.

- **New:** Click to add a new Web link.

- **Parameters:** Click this to view the parameters available for this component.

- **Help:** Click to access the online Help files related to the active screen.

Two text links are located below the toolbar: the link labeled Web Links shows you the Web Links Manager. The Categories link takes you to the Web Links Category Manager, which is discussed later in this chapter.

Located below the two text links and above the list of Web Links are three sorting and searching tools to help you manage long lists of Web Links. Try the following:

- **Filter field** on the left works like a search box. Type a word or phrase into the text box and then click Go. The page reloads and displays the results of the search. To clear the screen and return to a full listing, click the Reset button.

- **Select a Category** filter on the right side allows you to display only those Web Links that belong to a specific category. To reset this filter, change the combo box back to the default setting.

- **Select State** filter on the far right allows you to filter and display the Web Links according to whether they are published or unpublished. The Select State filter provides an easy way to identify all Web Links that are currently active on the site. To reset this filter, change the combo box back to the default setting.

Tip

The Select a Category filter and the Select State filter can be combined to further refine the view of the list of Web Links.

The main content area of the screen contains a list of all the Web Links in your Web Links component. The columns provided are:

- **#** : An indexing number assigned by Joomla! This number cannot be changed.

- **Checkbox (no label):** Click in a checkbox to select a Web Link; this is needed if you want to use several of the toolbar options previously referenced.

- **Title:** This field displays the full name of the Web Link. Click on the name to edit the Web Link's details.

- **Published:** A green checkmark in this column indicates that the Web Link is published. The field shows a red X if the Web Link is not published. Administrators can toggle between the two settings by clicking on the icon.

- **Order:** The numbers in this field affect the ordering of the Web Links on this list. Change the numbers and click the Save icon at the top of the column to reorder the Web Links.

- **Category:** Shows the name of the category to which the Web Link has been assigned. You can click on the category name to open the Category Editing dialogue. Editing categories is discussed in the next section.

- **Hits:** How many times the Web Link has been clicked by visitors to your site.

- **ID:** The system-generated user ID number.

At the bottom of the screen, below the content area, is the Display # option. Change the value in the combo box control to alter the number of Web Links that are displayed on the page. The default value can be altered by changing the List Length option on the Global Configuration Manager.

Setting Web Links Parameters

Global options for the Web Links Component can be configured by means of the parameters options. The parameters are viewed and modified by clicking the Parameters icon on the Web Link Manager toolbar. Clicking the icon causes a lightbox to be superimposed on top of the page. Inside the lightbox are the parameters available to this component.

The Web Link Manager includes the following parameters:

- **Description:** Choose whether to show or hide the Web Links Introduction text, set below. The default setting is Show.

- **Web Links Introduction:** Type in any text you want to appear above the list of links on the Web Links page in this box.

- **Hits:** Show or hide the number of hits each Web Link has received from site visitors. The default setting is Show.

- **Link Descriptions:** Choose whether to show or hide the description data for the Web Link. Description data is input when you create a Web Link. This control determines whether it is shown to visitors. The default setting is Show.

- **Other Categories:** This control has no application to the Web Links component.

- **Table Headings:** Hide or show the column headings for the Web Links list when viewed as a table. The default setting is Show.

- **Target:** Select from the combo box to set the target for the Web Links URLs. This gives you control over how the browser responds when a visitor clicks a link. The three options are: Parent Window with Browser Navigation, New Window with Browser Navigation, and Window without Browser Navigation.

- **Icon:** This field is optional; it allows you to set an icon to appear next to the link name when the links are shown in a list.

Tip

Parent window means the same window as your site. If you set the target option to Parent window, the user will be taken away from your site when they click on the link. Opening the link in a new window simply puts a new window on top of your site. Although the visitor can see the target of the link, your site remains in the browser window behind. The browser navigation options refer to whether the window is shown with or without navigation controls. If you choose to open the link in a new window without browser navigation, the user is essentially restricted to viewing the content on the link and using the navigation that is on that web page.

After you have set the parameters you desire, click the Save button at the top right to save your changes or click Cancel to close the parameters window without saving the changes.

Managing Links and Categories

Categories are created by the administrator for the purpose of grouping Web Links. In Joomla!, every Web Link must be assigned to a category. The Web Link categories are managed by way of the Web Links Category Manager, shown in Figure 16.2.

Note
Before you can add your first Web Link you must have at least one category in the system.

To view the categories available in your system, click on the Categories link at the top of the Web Links Manager.

The toolbar at the top of the Web Links Category Manager provides quick access to the following functions:

- **Publish:** Select one or more categories from the list and then click this icon to publish them.
- **Unpublish:** Select one or more categories from the list and then click this icon to unpublish them.
- **Delete:** Select one or more categories from the list and then click this icon to delete the category(s).
- **Edit:** Select a category from the list then click this icon to edit the category's details.
- **New:** Click to create a new category.
- **Help:** Click to access the online Help files related to the active screen.

Two text links are below the toolbar. The Links link shows you the Web Links Manager, discussed earlier in the chapter. The Categories link displays the Web Link Category Manager.

Below the two text links and above the list of categories are two sorting and searching tools to help you manage long lists of categories:

- **The Filter field** on the left works like a search box. Type a word or phrase into the field and then click Go. The page reloads and displays the results of the search. To clear the screen and return to a full listing, click the Reset button.
- **The Select State filter** on the far right allows you to filter and display the categories according to whether they are published or unpublished. This provides an easy way to identify all categories that are currently active on the site. To reset this filter, change the combo box back to the default setting.

FIGURE 16.2

The Web Links Category Manager.

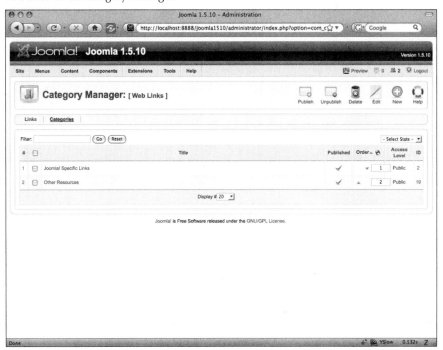

The main content area of the screen contains a list of all the Web Link Categories. The columns provided are:

- **#:** This field is an indexing number set automatically by Joomla! You cannot alter this field.

- **Checkbox (no label):** Click in a checkbox to select a category; this is needed if you want to use several of the toolbar options, referenced earlier.

- **Title:** This field displays the full name of the category. Click on the name to edit the category's details.

- **Published:** A green checkmark in this column indicates that the category is published. The field shows a red X if the category is not published. Administrators can toggle between the two settings by clicking on the icon shown.

- **Order:** The numbers in this field affect the ordering of the categories on this list. Change the numbers and click the Save icon at the top of the column to reorder the categories.

- **Access Level:** Indicates the Access Levels assigned to the category. You can toggle between the options Public, Registered, and Special by clicking on the words.

- **ID:** The system-generated user ID number.

Finally, at the bottom of the screen, below the content area, is the Display # option. Change the value in the combo box control to alter the number of categories that are displayed on the page. The default value can be altered by changing the List Length option on the Global Configuration Manager.

Creating a new category

Before you can add Web Links to your system, you must create at least one category. Categories are created from within the Web Link Category Manager, by clicking on the New icon on the toolbar. Category data is entered into the New Web Link Category dialogue, shown in Figure 16.3

FIGURE 16.3

The New Web Link Category dialogue.

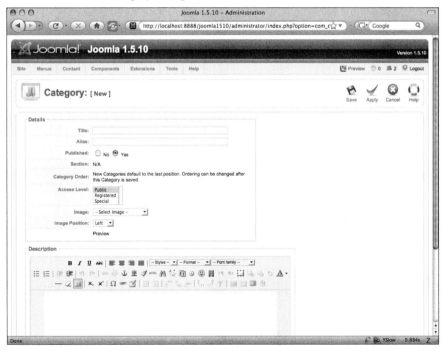

The toolbar at the top of the New Web Link Category dialogue provides quick access to the following functions:

- **Save:** Click this icon to save your work, create a new category, and exit the New Web Link Category dialogue.

- **Apply:** Click to save your work and create a new category without exiting from the New Web Link Category dialogue. This option lets you save without exiting the screen and it useful in case you are interrupted or you otherwise want to save yet keep working on this screen.

- **Cancel:** Cancels the task and exits the New Web Link Category dialogue.

- **Help:** Displays the Help files related to the active screen.

The workspace in this dialogue is broken down into two sections, Details and Description. The Details section contains the following fields:

- **Title:** Type into this field a title for the Web Link category. This field is the only required field.

- **Alias:** The alias is an internal label for the category. The alias is also used in the creation of a search engine friendly path for the category. This field only accepts lowercase letters, with no spaces. Note that if you leave this blank, the system will automatically use the value you entered into the Title field.

- **Published:** Click Yes to publish the item. No icons on this screen, only yes/no radio buttons.

- **Section:** This field is not applicable to the Web Link category, and as a result the system displays only n/a.

- **Category Order:** This field cannot be controlled when a new category is created. New categories always default to last on the list. The order can be changed from the Web Link Category Manager or by editing the category.

- **Access Level:** Sets the access level restrictions for the category and its contents. The options Registered, Public, or Special appear in this column. You can click on the name to toggle the level. If no value is chosen, the system defaults to Public.

- **Image:** Provides the option to display a small image next to the category name on pages listing the categories. This is optional. The Image Position control is related to this option. Note that the image you want to select must be located in the folder `images/stories`.

- **Image Position:** Controls placement of the image relative to the category name. The choices are limited to left or right. Left is selected by default. Note that this control is only applicable if an image is selected from the Image control.

The Description field at the bottom of the screen provides you a place to add a description of the category. The description will appear on pages where the Web Links from a specific category are listed. The text box allows you to use images and formatting for the description. The Image button at the bottom of the Description field gives you easy access to controls for inserting an image into the description.

To create a new category, follow these steps:

1. **Log in to the admin system on your site.**

2. **Access the Web Links Category Manager. Go to the Components menu and select the Categories option from the submenu under the heading Web Links.** The Web Links Category Manager loads in your browser.

3. **Click the New icon on the toolbar at the top of the Web Links Category Manager.** The New Web Links Category Dialogue opens. Refer to Figure 16.3.

4. **In the Title field, type a name for this category.** This field is the only required field.

5. **Add additional information or optional settings as you see fit.**

6. **Click the Save icon on the toolbar at the top right to save your new Web Link category.** The dialogue closes and returns you to the Web Link Category Manager.

Editing and deleting categories

Existing Web Link categories can be edited from the Web Link Category Manager. To edit a category, do either of the following:

- Click on the category name in the Web Link Category Manager.
- Select the category on the list and then click the Edit icon on the Web Link Category Manager toolbar.

Regardless of which method you use, the system opens the Edit Category dialogue.

The Edit Category dialogue is identical to the New Category dialogue, with the same fields and requirements as discussed in the preceding section.

To make changes to a category, simply alter the desired fields in the Edit Category dialogue and then click the Save or Apply icon on the toolbar. Any changes you have made are applied immediately.

To delete one or more categories, follow these steps:

1. Open the Web Link Category Manager.
2. Select one or more categories.
3. Click the Delete icon.

Caution

Deleting a Web Link Category is permanent and cannot be undone. Moreover, there is no confirmation dialogue — clicking the Delete icon immediately deletes the category! Note, however, that a Category cannot be deleted if Web Links are assigned to that category. If you want to delete the category, you need to first delete or reassign any Web Links assigned to that category.

Adding a new link

To add a new Web Link to your site, visit the Web Link Manager and click on the New icon on the toolbar. The New Web Link dialogue opens in your browser, as shown in Figure 16.4.

The toolbar at the top of the New Web Link dialogue provides quick access to the following functions:

- **Save:** Click this icon to save your work, add a new Web Link, and exit the New Web Link dialogue.
- **Cancel:** Cancels the task and exits the New Web Link dialogue.
- **Help:** Displays the Help files related to the active screen.

The workspace is divided into three areas: Details, Parameters, and Description. The Details section of the workspace contains the following fields:

- **Name:** Use this field to give a name to your Web Link. This field is required.
- **Alias:** The alias field is an internal identifier for your Web Link. This is used in some cases to create search engine friendly URLs for the item. You can specify the contents of this field if you want, but note that it only takes lowercase letters with no spaces. If you do not specify the contents of this field the system will automatically create the alias based on the item's name.
- **Published:** Select Yes to publish the Web Link. The default state is Yes.
- **Category:** Assign the Web Link to a category using the combo box. This field is required.
- **URL:** Enter into this field the URL for the source of the Web Link. This field is required field. Note that this should normally begin with `http://`.
- **Order:** This control is not available for a new Web Link. New items are placed by default in the last position on the list. After you add your Web Link, you can adjust the list position from either the Web Link Manager or by editing the Web Link item.

The Parameters section offers only one choice, the Target option. The option provides you with the ability to override the Global Target parameter set from the Web Links Manager's Parameter controls. The default option is Use Global settings. Optional settings include Parent window with Browser Navigation, New window with Browser Navigation, New window without Browser Navigation. Setting this option controls the browser behavior when the user clicks on a Web Link.

The Description field allows you to enter a brief text description that appears underneath the Web Link for your site visitors.

To add a new Web Link, follow these steps:

1. **Log in to the admin system on your site.**
2. **Access the Web Link Manager.** To do so, go to the Components menu and select the Web Links option. The Web Link Manager loads in your browser.
3. **Click the New icon on the toolbar at the top of the Web Links Manager.** The New Web Link Dialogue opens. See to Figure 16.4.

FIGURE 16.4

The New Web Link dialogue.

4. **In the Name field, type a name for the link.** This is a required field.

5. **Select a category for the link from the Category combo box.** This field is required.

6. **Type the address for the link source in URL field.** Normally this begins with `http://`. This field is required.

7. **Select any additional options you want; all other fields are optional.**

8. **Click the Save icon on the toolbar at the top right to save your new Web Link.** The dialogue closes and returns you to the Web Links Manager.

Editing and deleting Web Links

Existing Web Links can be edited from the Web Link Manager. To edit a Web Link, either click the Web Link name in the Web Link Manager or select the Web Link and then click the Edit icon on the Web Link Manager toolbar. Regardless of which method you use, the system opens the Edit Web Link dialogue.

The Edit Web Link dialogue is identical to the New Web Link dialogue, with the same fields and requirements as discussed in the preceding section.

To make changes to a Web Link, simply alter the desired fields in the Edit Web Link dialogue and then click the Save or Apply icon on the toolbar. Any changes you make are applied immediately.

To delete one or more Web Links, follow these steps:

1. **Open the Web Link Manager.**

2. **Select one or more Web Links.**

3. **Click the Delete icon.**

Caution

Deleting a Web link is permanent and cannot be undone. Moreover, there is no confirmation dialogue — clicking the Delete icon immediately deletes the Web Link as well as any cached content of the feed.

Displaying Web Links on your site

After you bring Web Links into your system with the Web Link Manager, the question becomes how to display the Web Links on your site. Adding links to the Manager does not automatically translate into displaying links on your site.

By linking a menu item to the Web Link Component, you can display links or categories of links as content items on your site. For a discussion of various layout options that are available to display Web Links content on the pages on your site, see Chapter 8.

The Web Links component and SEO

The Web Links component is not ideal for the creation of links pages intended for the purpose of building reciprocal link exchanges. The tracking function that enables the hit count "hides" the actual URL from the search engine spiders. Unfortunately, this function cannot be disabled and as a result, links added to the Web Links component are not indexed by search engines.

To you as an Administrator this is typically only an issue in cases where you are trying to build a reciprocal link exchange. Link exchange partners are unlikely to grant a link exchange in this situation because it means that they cannot gain a search engine benefit from your link to their site.

To address this situation you need to either bypass the Web Links component entirely and build your links page as a content item —a page— or look at a third-party extension to use for links management.

Summary

In this chapter, we cover the use of the Web Links component. You found out about the following:

- How to configure the Web Links component
- How to create, edit, and delete Web Links
- How to create, edit, and delete Web Links categories

Working with the Site Modules

J oomla! uses modules to display content and functionality on areas of the page other than the main content area. Modules often appear in sidebars, at the top or bottom of a layout, and on the edges of or even surrounding the main content area of the page. Modules are critical for designing compelling sites with good functionality. The system includes both front-end modules and back-end modules. The modules for the front end of the system are called Site modules.

The Site Modules Manager provides an interface for controlling the system's numerous Site modules. The Joomla! system includes 20 different Site module types. Several of the module types are closely related to and dependent on the core components; others are independent, self-contained units. All share a similar process for the creation, copying, and deletion of modules. The difference between the modules is largely in the parameters that are available for each module. Mastery of the parameters enables you to tailor the modules to your needs.

In this chapter, I introduce the module manager and all of the default Joomla! 1.5.x Site modules.

Reviewing the Module Manager

All the Joomla! modules are controlled through the Module Manager. The manager contains all the system modules, together with any third-party modules you may install. To access the Site Module Manager, log in to the admin system, and then go to the Extensions menu and select the option Module Manager. The Module Manager loads in your browser window, as shown in Figure 17.1.

FIGURE 17.1

The Module Manager, showing the Site Module Manager with sample data installed.

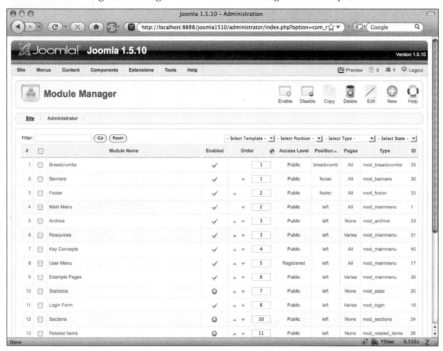

The toolbar at the top of the Module Manager provides quick access to the following functions:

- **Enable:** Select one or more modules from the list and then click this icon to enable them.

- **Disable:** Select one or more modules from the list and then click this icon to disable them.

- **Copy:** Select a module and then click this icon to make an exact copy of the module.

- **Delete:** Select one or more modules from the list and then click this icon to delete the module.

- **Edit:** Select a module from the list and then click this icon to edit the module's details.

- **New:** Click to add a new module.

- **Help:** Click to access the online Help files related to the active screen.

Two text links are located below the toolbar. The link labeled Sites shows you the Site Module Manager. The Administrator link takes you to the Administrator Modules Manager, which is discussed later in this chapter.

Located below the two text links and above the list of modules are five sorting and searching tools to help you manage long lists of modules:

- **The Filter field:** Works like a search box. Type a word or phrase into the text box and then click Go. The page reloads and displays the results of the search. To clear the screen and return to a full listing, click the Reset button.

- **Select Template:** Shows a list of the available templates. Select a template name from the combo box to restrict the search to that template.

- **Select Position:** Shows the position the module has been assigned to.

- **Select Type:** Filter the list by the module type.

- **The Select State filter:** Allows you to filter and display the modules according to whether they are published or unpublished. This provides an easy way to identify all modules that are currently active on the site. To reset this filter, change the combo box back to the default setting.

Tip

The Select Position, Type, and State filters can be combined to further refine the view of the list of modules.

The main content area of the screen contains a list of all the modules in your Site Modules Manager. The columns provided are:

- **# :** An indexing number assigned by Joomla! This number cannot be changed.

- **Checkbox (no label):** Click in a checkbox to select a module; this is needed if you want to use several of the toolbar options.

- **Module Name:** This field displays the full name of the module. Click on the name to edit the module's details.

- **Enabled:** A green checkmark in this column indicates that the module is published. The field shows a red X if the module is not published. Administrators can toggle between the two settings by clicking the icon.

- **Order:** The numbers in this field affect the ordering of the modules on this list. Change the numbers and click the Save icon at the top of the column to reorder the modules.

- **Access Level:** Displays the access level that has been specified for the module. You can click on the label toggle between Public, Registered, and Special, or you can modify this by editing the module.

- **Position:** The module position to which the module is assigned. A single module can only be assigned to a single position.

- **Pages:** An indicator of which pages the module has been assigned to. The only options here are All, meaning to all pages on the site; None, which means the module has not been assigned to any pages; and Varies, which means the module is assigned to some but not all the pages. To change these setting, edit the module.

- **Type:** The module type of the module. Each module can be of only one type.

- **ID:** The system-generated user ID number.

At the bottom of the screen, below the content area, is the Display # option. Change the value in the combo box control to alter the number of modules that are displayed on the page. The default value can be altered by changing the List Length option on the Global Configuration Manager.

Creating new modules

New modules can be created from within the Module Manager. Simply click the New icon at the top toolbar, and the system loads a new window in the browser, as shown in Figure 17.2. The new window requires you to specify the module type you want to create.

Select one of the 20 module type choices and click the Next icon; the page reloads and displays the next step in the module creation process, as shown in Figure 17.3.

The module types all share common elements, but each also has unique parameters that must be considered.

FIGURE 17.2

The default module type options for Site modules.

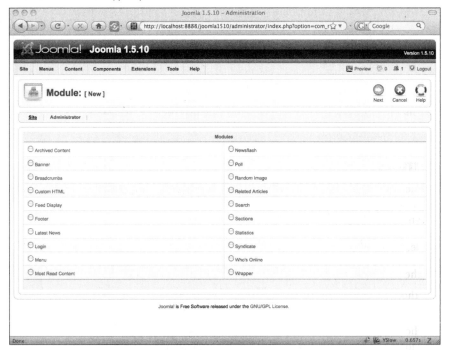

FIGURE 17.3

The second step in the New Module creation process. This shows the screen for a new Newsflash module.

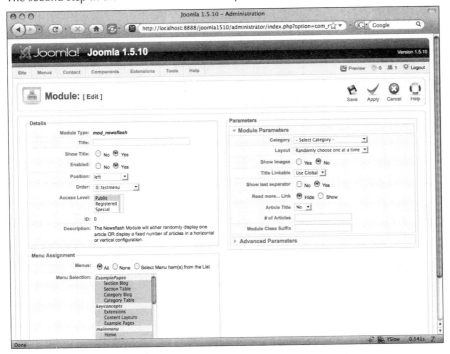

Note

If you have installed additional extensions to your site, it is possible you may also see additional module types that allow for the creation of new modules beyond the system defaults.

Copying modules

You can make exact copies of modules by using the Copy command on the Module Manager. This function is very useful if you need to run multiple instances of the same module type because the Copy function can save you time configuring your new modules.

To copy a module, follow these steps:

1. **Open the Module Manager.**

2. **Select the module you want to copy by clicking in the select box next to the module name.**

3. **Click the Copy icon.** The system immediately makes a copy of the module and places it in the Module Manager with the name Copy of (original module's name).

Editing and deleting modules

Existing modules can be edited from within the Module Manager. To edit a module, either click the module name in the Module Manager or select the module on the list and then click the Edit icon on the Module Manager toolbar. Regardless of which method you use, the system opens the Edit Module dialogue. The Edit Module dialogue is identical to the New Module dialogue, with the same fields and requirements.

To make changes to a module, simply alter the desired fields in the Edit Module dialogue and then click the Save or Apply icon on the toolbar. Any changes you have made are applied immediately.

To delete one or more modules, follow these steps:

1. Open the Module Manager.
2. Select one or more modules.
3. Click the Delete icon.

Caution

Deleting a module is permanent and cannot be undone. Moreover, there is no confirmation dialogue — clicking the Delete icon immediately deletes the module! As a safety measure, it might be better to just unpublish a module if you are unsure if you will need it in the future.

Introducing the Site Modules

The workspace of each Site Module dialogue is divided into three areas: Details, Menu Assignments, and Parameters, as shown in Figure 17.4. The Details and Menu Assignments portions of all the module types are identical; the differences lie in the Parameters area.

The toolbar at the top of the module dialogue provides quick access to the following functions:

- **Save:** Click this icon to save your work, add a new module, and exit the New Module dialogue.

- **Apply:** Click to save your work and create a new category without exiting from the New Module dialogue. This option lets you save without exiting the screen and is useful if you are interrupted or you otherwise wish to save yet keep working on this screen.

- **Cancel:** Cancels the task and exits the Module Manager.

- **Help:** Displays the Help files related to the active screen.

FIGURE 17.4

A typical module dialogue, in this case, the Archived Content module.

The Details section of the workspace contains the following fields:

- **Module Type:** This identifier is set by the system and tells you the type of module being created. The module type cannot be changed.

- **Title:** Use this field to give a name to your module. This field is required.

- **Show Title:** This controls the visibility of the module's title for the front-end visitor. Set the control to Yes if you want the module title to appear when the module appears. The title appears immediately above the module. The default state is Yes.

- **Enabled:** Select Yes to publish the module. The default state is Yes.

- **Position:** Controls the placement of the module on the page. Use the combo box to select from the list of eligible module positions. This field is required.

- **Order:** Sets the order of the module relative to other modules assigned to the same position. Has no effect where there is only one module assigned to a position.

- **Access Level:** Set the module to appear for all or only select categories of users. The three options here are Public, Registered, and Special. The default setting is Public.

- **ID:** A system-assigned identification number. This cannot be changed.

- **Description:** Joomla! provides this description text to help users understand the use of the module.

Cross-Reference

For a discussion of placing modules inside the content area of your site's articles, please see Chapter 7.

The Menu Assignment area of the workspace is used to assign the module to appear on only certain pages of your site. You have the option to assign the module to no pages, to all pages, or to only certain pages. If you want to assign the module selectively, choose the option Select Menu Item(s) From the List and then pick the appropriate choices from the multiselect box; to select more than one choice, hold down the Option key (the Command key on a Mac) while you click.

The parameters section varies for each module. Details on the parameters for each module are discussed in the sections that follow.

Archived Content module

The Archived Content module provides access to archived articles. It is, essentially, a navigation menu for archived content items, as shown in Figure 17.5. When activated, the module displays a list of months for which there are archived content items. Clicking on the name of the month takes the user to a page listing all the archived items for that time period.

Cross-Reference

Working with archived content is dealt with in Chapter 5.

This module is not enabled in the default configuration. However, if you have installed the sample data, an Archived Content module does appear in the Module Manager under the name archive. Because the module is not enabled, it is not visible on the front end of the site.

Note

The system name for this module type is mod_archive.

The Parameters section is divided into two sections: Module parameters and Advanced parameters. Figure 17.6 shows the Module parameters.

FIGURE 17.5

The Archived Content module viewed from the front end of the site.

The Archive Module

The Module parameters section contains two controls:

- **Count:** This field contains an integer value which determines the number of items displayed by the module. The default is 10.

- **Module Class Suffix:** This field allows you to specify a suffix that will be automatically appended to all CSS styles that affect this module. The use of a specified suffix makes it possible for you to style this module individually.

The Advanced parameters section contains only one option: Caching. This control allows you to exempt a specific module from the site's caching, as set in the Global Configuration. Select the option No Caching to prevent the contents of this module from being cached. The default setting is Use Global.

FIGURE 17.6

The Archived Content Module parameters.

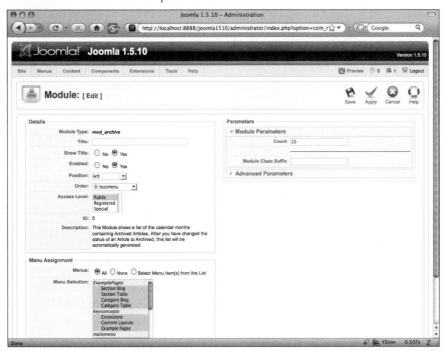

To add an Archive module to your site, follow these steps:

1. **Go to the Extensions menu and select the Module Manager option.** The Module Manager loads in your web browser.

2. **Click the New icon on the toolbar at the top of the Module Manager.** The New Module dialogue opens. Refer to Figure 17.2.

3. **Select the option Archived Content, and then click the Next button.** The Archived Content dialogue loads in your web browser.

4. **In the Title field, type a name for the module.** This field is required.

5. **Set the Enabled option to Yes.**

6. **Set the Position control to assign the module to a position on the page.**

7. **Set the Menu Assignment to specify the pages upon which the module will appear.**

8. **Select any additional options or parameters you wish; all other fields are optional.**

9. **Click the Save icon on the toolbar at the top right to save your new module.** The system creates the module, closes the dialogue, and returns you to the Module Manager.

Tip

The Archived Content module is a necessity if you employ Joomla's content-archiving functionality. The module provides the links to give your site visitors easy access to archived content. The links are organized chronologically and cannot be controlled by the administrator; the only option you have is to control the number of items displayed in the module.

Banner module

The Banner module controls the placement of banners on your site, as shown in Figure 17.7. As discussed previously in the book, this module works in conjunction with the Banner component.

Cross-Reference

The use of the Banner component and a further discussion of the Banner module can be found in Chapter 12.

FIGURE 17.7

The output of the Banner module, viewed from the front end of the site, seen here in the Footer module position.

If you have installed the sample data, you will find two Banner modules in your system. The two modules are named Banners and Advertisement. The Banners option is assigned to the Footer position and Advertisement to the Right position. The two Banner modules are used to control the banner ads that are part of the sample data included with the Banner Component.

The Parameters section is divided into two sections: Module parameters and Advanced parameters, as shown in Figure 17.8.

Note
The system name for this module type is mod_banner.

The Module parameters section contains the following controls:

- **Target:** This control allows you to specify the browser's behavior when a user clicks on a Banner that is linked to another web page. By default, the system opens the link in a New Window with Browser Navigation. You can, however, select from two other options: Parent Window with Browser Navigation or New Window without Browser Navigation.

- **Count:** An integer value that specifies the number of different banners that will be shown by this module. The default value is 1.

- **Banner Client:** This optional parameter allows you to restrict the module to showing only those banners belonging to a specific Banner client. The available clients are listed in the combo box. If set to the default position, the module will show banners from all clients.

- **Category:** This optional parameter allows you to restrict the module to showing only those banners belonging to a specific Banner category. The available categories are listed in the combo box. If set to the default position, the module shows banners from all categories.

- **Search by Tags:** Choose Yes to enable the system to control banner display by matching banner keywords with content keywords. The default value is No.

- **Randomize:** This control determines the order in which the banners are displayed inside the module. If you chose the option Sticky, Ordering, the system will display the banners in order with those marked as Sticky in the Banner Manager showing first. If you chose the option Sticky, Randomize, the system displays the banners randomly with those marked as Sticky in the Banner Manager showing first.

- **Header Text:** Enter into this box any text you want to appear above the banner in the module position.

- **Footer Text:** Enter into this box any text you want to appear below the banner in the module position.

- **Module Class Suffix:** This field allows you to specify a suffix that will be automatically appended to all CSS styles that affect this module. The use of a specified suffix makes it possible for you to style this module individually.

FIGURE 17.8

The Banner module parameters.

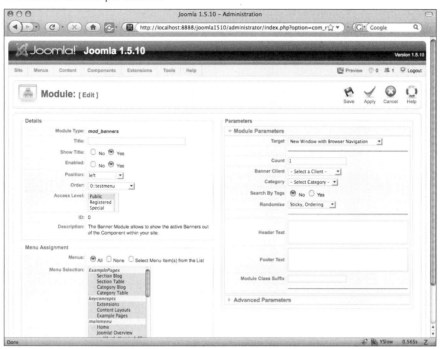

Cross-Reference

The creation and management of Banner Clients and Banner Categories, and the upload of Banner graphics, is discussed at length in Chapter 12.

The Advanced parameters section contains two options:

- **Caching:** This control allows you to exempt a specific module from the site's caching, as set in the Global Configuration. Select the option No Caching to prevent the contents of this module from being cached. The default setting is Use Global.

- **Cache Time:** The time, in minutes, you want the contents to be cached. Enter an integer value here. The default value is 900 minutes, meaning that after 900 minutes the system will re-create, or refresh this module. Note this control is only meaningful if the caching for the module is enabled.

To add a Banner module to your site, follow these steps:

1. **Go to the Extensions menu and select the Module Manager option.** The Module Manager loads in your web browser.

2. **Click the New icon on the toolbar at the top of the Module Manager.** The New Module dialogue opens. Refer to Figure 17.2.

3. **Select the Banner option and then click the Next button.** The Banner dialogue loads in your web browser.

4. **In the Title field, type a name for the module.** This field is a required.

5. **Set the option Enabled to Yes.**

6. **Set the Position control to assign the module to a position on the page.**

7. **Set the Menu Assignment to specify the pages upon which the module appears.**

8. **Select any additional options or parameters you wish; all other fields are optional.**

9. **Click the Save icon on the toolbar at the top right to save your new module.** The system creates the module, closes the dialogue, and returns you to the Module Manager.

Tip

Sites frequently employ more than one instance of this module, because running multiple Banner modules allows you to run ads in different positions and on different pages. With the available parameters and the ability to run multiple instances, it is possible to get quite a bit of variation out of this module. Copying an existing Banner module is the fastest way to create multiple modules.

Cross-Reference

See Chapter 12 for information on implementing the Banner module.

Breadcrumbs module

The Breadcrumbs module of your Joomla! system is responsible for the display of the breadcrumbs trail on your web site's pages, as shown in Figure 17.9. A *breadcrumb trail* is a position marker, in the sense that it shows users where they are in the site, and provides a way for users to navigate back or up to higher levels in the site's hierarchy.

Note

The system name for this module type is mod_breadcrumbs.

The Parameters section is divided into two sections: Module parameters and Advanced parameters, as shown in Figure 17.10.

The Breadcrumb module's output, viewed from the front end of the site.

The Breadcrumb module

The Module parameters section contains the following options:

- **Show Home:** Choose whether the breadcrumb always includes a link back to the home page. The default setting is Yes.

- **Text for Home entry:** Type the label you want to appear for the home page entry in the breadcrumb trail in this field. The default setting is Yes. Note this control is dependent upon the previous, Show Home. Where Show Home is set to No this field has no function.

- **Show Last:** Choose whether the breadcrumb always includes the current page. The default setting is Yes.

- **Text Separator:** Select a keyboard symbol to be used to separate entries on the breadcrumb trail. If this is left blank the system uses the default separator, ">>."

- **Module Class Suffix:** This field allows you to specify a suffix that will be automatically appended to all CSS styles that affect this module. The use of a specified suffix makes it possible for you to style this module individually.

FIGURE 17.10

The Breadcrumbs module parameters.

The Advanced parameters section contains only one option, Caching, and it is permanently set to Never. This option cannot be changed.

To add a Breadcrumb module to your site, follow these steps:

1. **Go to the Extensions menu and select the Module Manager option.** The Module Manager loads in your web browser.

2. **Click the New icon on the toolbar at the top of the Module Manager.** The New Module dialogue opens. Refer to Figure 17.2.

3. **Select the option Breadcrumbs and then click the Next button.** The Breadcrumb Module dialogue loads in your browser.

4. **In the Title field, type a name for the module.** This field is required.

5. **Set the option Enabled to Yes.**

6. **Set the Position control to assign the module to a position on the page.**

7. Set the Menu Assignment to specify the pages upon which the module will appear.

8. Select any additional options or parameters you wish; all other fields are optional.

9. Click the Save icon on the toolbar at the top right to save your new module. The system creates the module, closes the dialogue, and returns you to the Module Manager.

Tip

While the Breadcrumbs module is an easy way to improve the navigation and usability of your site, if you are using third-party components, you should check your Breadcrumb output because some components may not produce the result you expect.

Breadcrumb output can also be a bit confusing where you use your menu items to link to pages deep inside your site. In that case, the user with one click may penetrate several layers inside your site. The result will be a long and complex breadcrumb trail that may be confusing to some users.

Custom HTML module

The Custom HTML module allows you to create modules that contain HTML code and then position those on your pages. This useful option allows you to integrate outside functionality, like an affiliate link, or a PayPal button or to display content in a sidebar or other module position.

Note

The system name for this module type is mod_archive.

The Custom HTML module dialogue varies from other module types. The important difference is the presence of an additional section on the workspace, as shown in Figure 17.11. The section is labeled Custom Output, and it provides you with a field for inputting whatever you want this module to display.

Note that you can add to this module type text, images, or pure HTML. If you have a WYSIWYG Editor enabled on your site, the Custom Output section will display the WYSIWYG toolbars.

Tip

Some WYSIWYG Editors, including Tiny MCE, restrict your ability to enter certain HTML tags. Accordingly, if you want to work in HTML unhindered by restrictions, you should visit the Global Configuration Manager and set the option for the control Default WYSIWYG Editor to No Editor. After you have saved your module, you can switch the WYSIWYG Editor back on.

The Parameters section contains only the Module Class Suffix control, which allows you to specify a suffix that will be automatically appended to all CSS styles that affect this module. The use of a specified suffix makes it possible for you to style this module individually.

FIGURE 17.11

The Custom HTML module dialogue. Note this module dialogue includes a unique section labeled Custom Output. In this example, the TinyMCE WYSIWYG Editor is enabled.

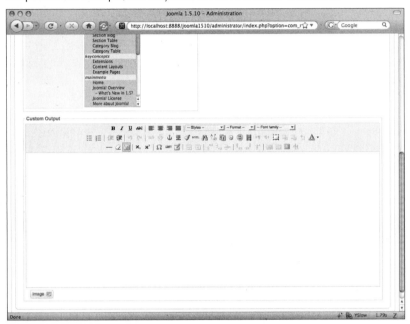

To add a Custom HTML module to your site, follow these steps:

1. **Go to the Extensions menu and select the Module Manager option.** The Module Manager loads in your web browser.

2. **Click the New icon on the toolbar at the top of the Module Manager.** The New Module dialogue opens. Refer to Figure 17.2.

3. **Select the option Custom HTML and then click the Next button.** The Custom HTML Module dialogue loads in your web browser.

4. **In the Title field, type a name for the module.** This field is required.

5. **Set the option Enabled to Yes.**

6. **Set the Position control to assign the module to a position on the page.**

7. **Set the Menu Assignment to specify the pages upon which the module will appear.**

8. **Enter your content in the field marked Custom Output.**

9. **Select any additional options or parameters you wish;** all other fields are optional.

10. **Click the Save icon on the toolbar at the top right to save your new module.** The system creates the module, closes the dialogue, and returns you to the Module Manager.

Tip

This module type should be thought of as simply the custom content module. Despite the name, entering custom HTML is only one thing you might do with this module type. This is a catchall module category that has quite a bit of utility for a site administrator who needs to create placeholders for a variety of content that does not fit neatly into one of the other module types. If you use your site actively, you will mostly likely find that you will use this Module one or more times.

Cross-Reference

Chapter 7 contains a discussion of using modules to display content on a site.

Feed Display module

The Feed Display module type is used to create a module that contains content obtained from an RSS feed, as shown in Figure 17.12. The module allows you to input a feed URL and specify the output for the front end of your web site. You select from the available module positions to display the contents on the front end of the site. The system automatically retrieves and refreshes the feed data. Note that this module is independent in functionality and not associated with the News Feed Component.

FIGURE 17.12

The output from a Feed Display module.

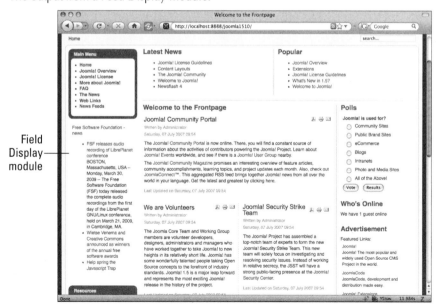

Field
Display
module

If you have installed the Joomla! sample contents, you will find a module named Feed Display. The module is linked to the Joomla! Community blog, but it is unpublished.

Note

The system name for this module type is mod_feed.

The Parameters section is divided into two sections: Module parameters and Advanced parameters, as shown in Figure 17.13.

The Module parameters section contains the following controls:

- **Module Class Suffix:** This field allows you to specify a suffix that will be automatically appended to all CSS styles that affect this module. The use of a specified suffix makes it possible for you to style this module individually.
- **Feed URL:** The address of the feed. Typically this begins with http://. This field is required.
- **RTL Feed:** If your feed reads right to left, set this option to Yes.
- **Feed Title:** Controls whether to display the title of the feed, as supplied by the source of the feed.
- **Feed Description:** Controls whether to display the description of the feed, as supplied by the source of the feed.
- **Feed Image:** Controls whether to display the image associated with the feed, as supplied by the source of the feed.
- **Items:** Specify an integer value to control the number of feed items that will be displayed in the module. The default is 3.
- **Item Description:** Controls whether to display the description of the feed item, as supplied by the source of the feed.
- **Word Count:** Specify an integer value to control the length of the feed item shown. Set the value to zero to show the entire item.

The Advanced parameters section contains caching options for the module:

- **Caching:** This control allows you to exempt a specific module from the site's caching, as set in the Global Configuration. Select the option No Caching to prevent the contents of this module from being cached. The default setting is No Caching.
- **Cache Time:** Specify an integer value for the number of minutes the system will store the module contents before refreshing.

To add a Feed module to your site, follow these steps:

1. **Go to the Extensions menu and select the Module Manager option.** The Module Manager loads in your browser.
2. **Click the New icon on the toolbar at the top of the Module Manager.** The New Module dialogue opens. Refer to Figure 17.2.

3. **Select the option News Feed and then click the Next button.** The Feed Module dialogue loads in your web browser.

4. **In the Title field, type a name for the module.** This is a required field.

5. **Set the option Enabled to Yes.**

6. **Set the Position control to assign the module to a position on the page.**

7. **Set the Menu Assignment to specify the pages upon which the module will appear.**

8. **Specify the address of the feed source in the field labeled Feed URL.**

9. **Select any additional options or parameters you want; all other fields are optional.**

10. **Click the Save icon on the toolbar at the top right to save your new module.** The system creates the module, closes the dialogue, and returns you to the Module Manager.

Tip

The use of modules to hold feed data is a common and effective technique for displaying feed content on your web site. You can set up multiple modules to pull content from multiple sources and then match the module placement to pages that contain relevant content.

FIGURE 17.13

The Feed Display module parameters.

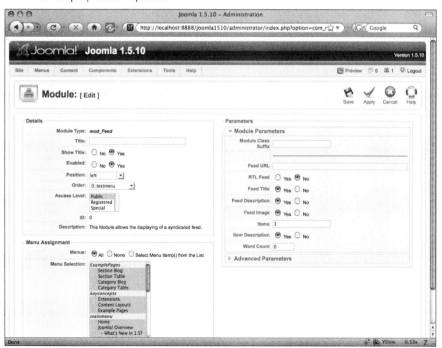

Cross-Reference

I cover the use of modules to bring external content into your site in more detail in Chapter 7. The News Feeds component is covered in Chapter 14.

Footer module

The Footer module type serves no purpose other than to generate and display a Joomla! copyright notice, as shown in Figure 17.14. The module cannot be controlled other than to limit its display to particular positions or pages.

The default Joomla! installation comes with a Footer module, published in the Footer module position on each page.

Note

The system name for this module type is mod_footer.

The Parameters section contains only one option: Caching, as shown in Figure 17.15. This control allows you to exempt a specific module from the site's caching, as set in the Global Configuration. Select the option No Caching to prevent the contents of this module from being cached. The default setting is Use Global.

FIGURE 17.14

The Footer module, viewed from the front end of the site.

FIGURE 17.15

The Footer module parameters.

To add an Archive module to your site, follow these steps:

1. **Go to the Extensions menu and select the Module Manager option.** The Module Manager loads in your web browser.

2. **Click the New icon on the toolbar at the top of the Module Manager.** The New Module dialogue opens. Refer to Figure 17.2.

3. **Select the option Footer and then click the Next button.** The Footer Module dialogue loads in your web browser.

4. **In the Title field, type a name for the module.** This field is required.

5. **Set the option Enabled to Yes.**

6. **Set the Position control to assign the module to a position on the page.**

7. **Set the Menu Assignment to specify the pages upon which the module will appear.**

8. **Select any additional options or parameters you wish; all other fields are optional.**

9. **Click the Save icon on the toolbar at the top right to save your new module.** The system creates the module, closes the dialogue, and returns you to the Module Manager.

Tip

If you want to display your own footer content, unpublish this module and then create a new Custom HTML module containing your own content. Assign your new Footer module to the Footer module position.

Latest News module

The Latest News module displays a list of the most recent articles on the site, as shown in Figure 17.16. Using the parameters, you can control the content selected for display, showing for example, only those articles belonging to a particular section, category, or author.

The default Joomla! installation comes with a Latest News module, published in the User1 module position on several pages.

Note

The system name for this module type is mod_latestnews.

The parameters section is divided into two sections: Module parameters and Advanced parameters, as shown in Figure 17.17.

FIGURE 17.16

The front-end output of the Latest News module. In this case the module is assigned to the template's User1 module position where it is showing a list of articles from the Joomla! sample data.

FIGURE 17.17

The Latest News module parameters.

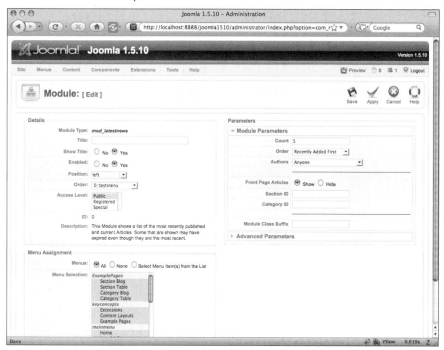

The Module parameters section contains the following options:

- **Count:** Specify an integer value to control the number of items displayed by this module. The default value is 5.

- **Order:** The setting of this control allows you to specify what the system considered to be the latest: either the most recently added, or the most recently modified. The default is Recently Added First, meaning the module will display the most recently created items.

- **Authors:** This field provides a filter to select articles by author. The options here are Anyone, Added or Modified by Me, Not Added or Modified by Me.

- **Front Page Articles:** Set this filter to determine whether the module includes articles that are also assigned to the Front Page.

- **Section ID:** Enter a Section's ID number to limit the display to articles of a particular section. You can list multiple Section IDs, separating them with commas.

- **Category ID:** Enter a category's ID number to limit the display to articles of a particular category. You can list multiple category IDs, separating them with commas.
- **Module Class Suffix:** This field allows you to specify a suffix that will be automatically appended to all CSS styles that affect this module. The use of a specified suffix makes it possible for you to style this module individually.

Tip

To find a section's ID number, view the section in the Section Manager. To find a category's ID number, view the category in the Category Manager. In both cases the ID number appears in the far right column, labeled ID.

The Advanced parameters section contains two caching controls:

- **Caching:** This control allows you to exempt a specific module from the site's caching, as set in the Global Configuration. Select the No Caching option to prevent the contents of this module from being cached. The default setting is Use Global.
- **Cache Time:** The time, in minutes, you want the contents to be cached. Enter an integer value here. The default value is 900 minutes, meaning that after 900 minutes the system will re-create, or refresh this module. Note this control is only meaningful if the caching for the module is enabled.

To add a Latest News module to your site, follow these steps:

1. **Go to the Extensions menu and select the Module Manager option.** The Module Manager loads in your web browser.

2. **Click the New icon on the toolbar at the top of the Module Manager.** The New Module dialogue opens. Refer to Figure 17.2.

3. **Select the option Latest News and then click the Next button.** The Latest News Module dialogue loads in your web browser.

4. **In the Title field, type a name for the module.** This is a required field.

5. **Set the option Enabled to Yes.**

6. **Set the Position control to assign the module to a position on the page.**

7. **Set the Menu Assignment to specify the pages upon which the module will appear.**

8. **Select any additional options or parameters you wish; all other fields are optional.**

9. **Click the Save icon on the toolbar at the top right to save your new module.** The system creates the module, closes the dialogue, and returns you to the Module Manager.

Login module

The Login module provides a Login Form to give site users a way to log in to the system and gain access to additional articles or functionality, as shown in Figure 17.18. In addition to the Login Form, the module also displays links to the password reminder and the username reminders. If the site is configured to allow users to register, the module will also display a link to the create a new user account function.

Note
The system name for this module type is mod_login.

The Login module's administration interface is shown in Figure 17.19.

FIGURE 17.18

The front-end output of the Login module, seen here displayed in the Left module position and with the system configured to allow User Registration.

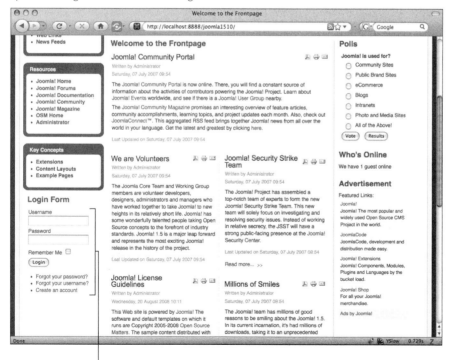

The Login module

FIGURE 17.19

The Login module, as it appears in the admin system.

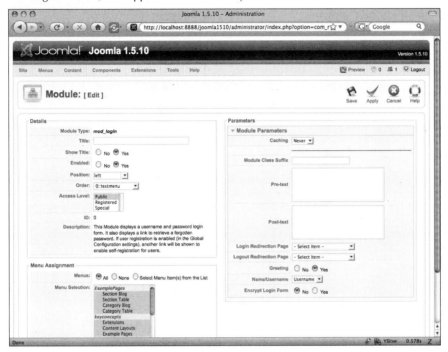

The Module parameters section contains the following controls:

- **Caching:** This control allows you to exempt a specific module from the site's caching, as set in the Global Configuration. Select the option No Caching to prevent the contents of this module from being cached. The default setting is Use Global.

- **Module Class Suffix:** This field allows you to specify a suffix that will be automatically appended to all CSS styles that affect this module. The use of a specified suffix makes it possible for you to style this module individually.

- **Pre-text:** Text entered into this box appears above the Login Form.

- **Post-text:** Text entered into this box appears below the Login Form.

- **Login Redirection Page:** If you want to redirect the user to a new page after they log in, you can select the page from the combo box beside this control.

- **Logout Redirection Page:** If you want to redirect the user to a new page after they log out, you can select the page from the combo box beside this control.

- **Greeting:** Controls whether the system uses a greeting for users upon login. The default is Yes, which results in the greeting being printed in the module position after login. The default greeting is "Hi, username."

- **Name/Username:** This control determined whether the greeting shows the username or the real name of the user. This control is only relevant if the Greeting parameter is set to yes.

- **Encrypt Login Form:** If the value Yes is selected, the system will encrypt the form using SSL. The default value is No.

Warning

Do not select the option to Encrypt Login Form unless your site is SSL-enabled and URLs with the `https://` prefix are accessible.

To add a Login module to your site, follow these steps:

1. **Access the Module Manager. To do so, go to the Extensions menu and select the Module Manager option.** The Module Manager loads in your web browser.

2. **Click the New icon on the toolbar at the top of the Module Manager.** The New Module dialogue opens. Refer to Figure 17.2.

3. **Select the option Login and then click the Next button.** The Login Module dialogue loads in your browser.

4. **In the Title field, type a name for the module.** This field is required.

5. **Set the option Enabled to Yes.**

6. **Set the Position control to assign the module to a position on the page.**

7. **Set the Menu Assignment to specify the pages upon which the module will appear.**

8. **Select any additional options or parameters you wish; all other fields are optional.**

9. **Click the Save icon on the toolbar at the top right to save your new module.** The system creates the module, closes the dialogue, and returns you to the Module Manager.

Cross-Reference

More detailed information about creating user registration functionality can be found in Chapter 10.

The Menu modules

The Menu modules play a key role in the system and are closely tied to the Menu Manager. Each menu in the system has its own module. The Menu Modules are automatically created by the system each time a menu is created in the Menu Manager. A typical Menu module output is shown in Figure 17.20.

Cross-Reference

The Menu Manager is dealt with in detail in Chapter 8.

FIGURE 17.20

The front-end output of the Menu module. This example shows the default Main menu assigned to the Left module position.

Menu module

Though the menu module's main purpose is to control menu placement, visibility, and access, it also impacts certain aspects of the menu's appearance. The parameters include a number of options for assisting in the styling of the menu, as shown in Figure 17.21.

In the default system with the sample data installed, you find six menu modules named: Main menu, Resources, Key Concepts, User Menu, Example Pages and Top Menu. All of the default modules are assigned to the left module position, except for the top menu, which is assigned to the User3 position.

Note

The system name for this module type is mod_mainmenu.

The Parameters section of the Menu module is one of the most complicated module interfaces. The workspace is divided into three sections: Module parameters, Advanced parameters, and Other parameters.

FIGURE 17.21

The Menu module parameters.

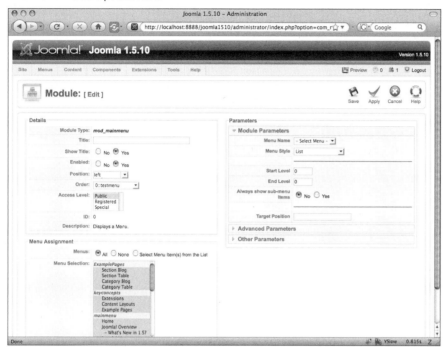

The Module parameters section contains the following options:

- **Menu name:** Select the menu you want to control from the combo box.

- **Menu style:** Select the formatting for the menu -- the menu layout. The default style is List, but other options include Legacy - Vertical, Legacy - Horizontal, and Legacy - Flat List.

- **Start Level:** This control is used in conjunction with the End Level control to turn one menu into multiple menus by separating the menu items into hierarchical groupings. This is optional and if you do not intend to separate your menu items into multiple menus, then set the value for this control (and the End Level control as well) to zero. This item has no impact where the menu uses a flat hierarchy.

- **End Level:** This control is used in conjunction with the Start Level control to turn one menu into multiple menus by separating the menu items into hierarchical groupings. This is optional and if you do not intend to separate your menu items into multiple menus, then set the value for this control (and the End Level control as well) to zero. This item has no impact where the menu uses a flat hierarchy.

- **Always show submenu items:** This control sets the visibility of submenu items. Set this control to Yes to display all submenu items, even when the parent item is not selected. The default setting is No. This control has no impact if there are no submenu items.

- **Target position:** This field allows you to specify the placement of any drop-down or pop-up submenus. This is an optional field and has a particular syntax that must be followed. A proper entry for this field will specify the position of the submenu in terms of position and size, for example, `top=20,left=20,width=100,height=200`.

Note

The menu style options include three Legacy modes. These Legacy options are intended primarily for site owners who are upgrading to Joomla 1.5.x from the old Joomla 1.x. The Legacy styles are intended to help you keep your pre-Joomla 1.5 formatting and they use different CSS classes than the default Joomla 1.5.x menus. The default style, List, is specifically intended for Joomla 1.5.x sites and is employed by all the menus in the default installation.

The Advanced parameters section contains the following:

- **Show whitespace:** Setting this option to No results in the code relating to the menu to compress through the elimination of unnecessary whitespace in the code. Setting the option to Yes keeps the whitespace in place, which renders the code easier to read. Setting this option to Yes while in development is helpful; set it to No for a live site to improve performance.

- **Caching:** This control allows you to exempt a specific module from the site's caching, as set in the Global Configuration. Select the No Caching option to prevent the contents of this module from being cached. The default setting is Use Global.

- **Menu Tag ID:** Set an integer value in this field and it will be appended to the UL tag for this menu. This enables you to create unique styling for the Menu UL tag.

- **Menu class suffix:** This field allows you to specify a suffix that will be automatically appended to all CSS styles that affect this menu. The use of a specified suffix makes it possible for you to style this menu individually.

- **Module class suffix:** This field allows you to specify a suffix that will be automatically appended to all CSS styles that affect this module. The use of a specified suffix makes it possible for you to style this module individually.

- **Maximum menu depth:** Set an integer value in this field to control the maximum number of levels the menu can have. The default value is 10.

Cross-Reference

I discuss the formatting of menus and the creation of submenus in Chapter 8.

The Other Parameters section contains the following:

- **Show menu images:** Set to Yes if you want to show images for the menu items. This control is the trigger for the Image options that follow in this section.

- **Menu image alignment:** Select to align the images to the left or the right. This option is dependent upon the Show Menu Images control being set to Yes.

- **Menu image link:** Set to Yes to have the image itself function as a link to the item. This option is dependent upon the Show Menu Images control being set to Yes.

- **Expand menu:** Set this control to Yes to show submenu items expanded.

- **Activate parent:** Set this control to Yes to make the parent items active whenever the child item is active.

- **Full active highlighting:** Set this control to Yes to make all parts of the full menu item active.

- **Indent image:** Use this control to specify what indent image, if any is used. The default setting is template, meaning the system should use the indent items specified by the template. Set to the option Joomla! default images to use the system defaults rather than the template images. Setting the control to None results in no indent images being used. The final option, Use Parameters below, activates the following six Indent Image controls.

- **Indent Image 1-6:** When the Indent Image parameter is set to Use Parameters below, this control is active. Use it to select the image to be used for the first level of indentation.

- **Spacer:** Use this field to specify a character to be used for the spacer between horizontal menu items.

- **End spacer:** Use this field to specify a character to be used for the spacer at the end of the horizontal menu.

To add a Menu module to your site, follow these steps:

1. **Log in to the admin system of your site.**

2. **Go to Extensions menu and select the Module Manager option.** The Module Manager loads in your browser.

3. **Click the New icon on the toolbar at the top of the Module Manager.** The New Module dialogue opens. Refer to Figure 17.2.

4. **Select the Menu option and then click the Next button.** The Menu Module dialogue loads in your browser.

5. **In the Title field, type a name for the module.** This field is required.

6. **Set the option enabled to Yes.**

7. **Set the Position control to assign the module to a position on the page.**

8. **Set the Menu Assignment to specify the pages upon which the module will appear.**

9. **Select the name of the menu you wish to control from Menu Name combo box under Module parameters.**

10. **Select any additional options or parameters you wish; all other fields are optional.**

11. **Click the Save icon on the toolbar at the top right to save your new module.** The system creates the module, closes the dialogue, and returns you to the Module Manager.

Tip

The menu modules are among the most important in the system. Fluency in menu styling requires an awareness of not only the parameters, but also the underlying CSS styles that affect the menus. Tools like Firebug or the Web Developer Toolbar for the Firefox browser can make the task of styling menus much easier by exposing the styling and making it easy to identify exactly which styles impact which items. You can download the Firebug or Web Developer extensions from

`http://addons.mozilla.org.`

Most Read Content module

The Most Read Content module allows you to place on the page a list of the most popular articles on the site, as judged by the number of views the article has received. The module displays a list of the items with links to the pages, as shown in Figure 17.22.

In the default installation with the sample data installed there is one Most Read Content Modules; it is named Popular and is assigned to various pages in the User2 module position.

FIGURE 17.22

The front-end output of the Most Read Content module; in this case the module named Popular in the default installation, shown here assigned to the User3 module position on the front page.

The Parameters section is divided into two sections: Module parameters and Advanced parameters. Figure 17.23 shows the Module parameters.

Note
The system name for this module type is mod_mostread.

The Module parameters section contains the following controls:

- **Module class suffix:** This field allows you to specify a suffix that will be automatically appended to all CSS styles that affect this module. The use of a specified suffix makes it possible for you to style this module individually.

- **Front page articles:** Determines whether the front page articles are included in the list.

- **Count:** Specify an integer value to control the number of items displayed by this module. The default value is 5.

- **Category ID:** Enter a Category's ID number to limit the display to articles of a particular category. You can list multiple Category IDs, separating them with commas.

- **Section ID:** Enter a section's ID number to limit the display to articles of a particular section. You can list multiple Section IDs, separating them with commas.

FIGURE 17.23

The Most Read Content module parameters.

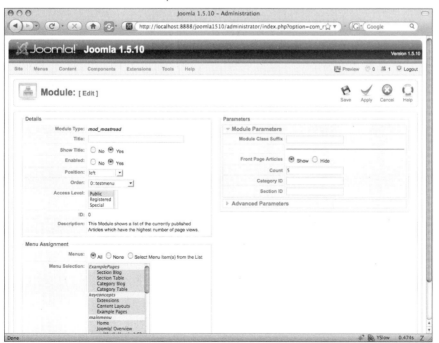

Tip

The Advanced parameters section contains caching options:

- **Caching:** This control allows you to exempt a specific module from the site's caching, as set in the Global Configuration. Select the option No Caching to prevent the contents of this Module from being cached. The default setting is Use Global.

- **Cache Time:** The time, in minutes, you want the contents to be cached. Enter an integer value here. The default value is 900 minutes, meaning that after 900 minutes the system will re-create, or refresh this module. Note this control is only meaningful if the caching for the module is enabled.

To add a Most Read Content module to your site, follow these steps:

1. **Log in to the admin system of your site.**

2. **Go to the Extensions menu and select the Module Manager option.** The Module Manager loads in your browser.

3. **Click the New icon on the toolbar at the top of the Module Manager.** The New Module dialogue opens. Refer to Figure 17.2.

4. **Select the option Most Read Content and then click the Next button.** The Most Read Content Module dialogue loads in your browser.

5. **In the Title field, type a name for the module.** This is a required field.

6. **Set the option called Enabled to the value Yes.**

7. **Set the Position control to assign the module to a position on the page.**

8. **Set the Menu Assignment to specify the pages upon which the module will appear.**

9. **Select any additional options or parameters you wish; all other fields are optional.**

10. **Click the Save icon on the toolbar at the top right to save your new module.** The system creates the module, close the dialogue and return you to the Module Manager.

Tip

Newsflash

The Newsflash module provides a way for you to insert into a module position a fixed or rotating content item. The content displayed can be drawn from either a dedicated category or from existing content categories. This feature is a useful because it enables you to place, typically, a small piece of text that rotates to display news, announcements, or any other items you want to attract the visitors' attention, as shown in Figure 17.24.

In the default installation, with the sample data installed, there is one Newsflash module enabled and published. The module is called simply Newsflash and it is assigned to the Top module position on all pages of the default site.

Note

The system name for this module type is mod_newsflash.

The Parameters section is divided into two sections: Module parameters and Advanced parameters, as shown in Figure 17.25.

FIGURE 17.24

The front-end output of the default Newsflash module with the sample data loaded. Here the module is shown in the Top module position of the default template.

FIGURE 17.25

The Newsflash module parameters.

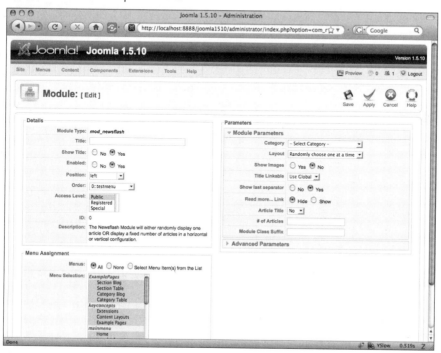

The Module parameters section contains the following controls:

- **Category:** Use this control to select a content category for display by the module. If you do not designate a specific category, the module will display items from all categories.

- **Layout:** The label for this control is a bit deceptive. The combo box contains three options: Randomly choose one at a time, Horizontal, and Vertical. The last two do indeed impact the layout, but they also specify that the module does not randomize article, but rather shows a fixed display of articles. In contrast, the default choice, Randomly choose one at a time, randomizes the articles selected and displays them one at a time. Note that this parameter is also related to the # of Articles parameter, below.

- **Show Images:** Decide whether the module shows images associated with the content item. The default setting is No.

- **Title Linkable:** Decide whether the article title will; function as a clickable hyperlink that leads to the article. This control provides you with the option to break with the Global Configuration setting for this parameter. The options here are: Use Global, No and Yes. The default is Use Global.

- **Show last separator:** Set this to Yes if you want to show a separator in the module immediately after the last article.

- **Read more... Link:** Elect to show or hide the read more link at the end of each article.

- **Article Title:** Show or hide the article's title.

- **# of Articles:** Set the number of articles to be displayed or randomized. If this is left blank the system will display five articles.

- **Module Class Suffix:** This field allows you to specify a suffix that will be automatically appended to all CSS styles that affect this module. The use of a specified suffix makes it possible for you to style this module individually.

Tip
The ordering of the appearance of the items in the Newsflash is dictated by the order in which the articles are displayed within the Category Manager in the Article Manager.

The Advanced parameters section contains caching options:

- **Caching**: This control allows you to exempt a specific module from the site's caching, as set in the Global Configuration. Select the No Caching option to prevent the contents of this module from being cached. The default setting is Use Global.

- **Cache Time**: The time, in minutes, you want the contents to be cached. Enter an integer value here. The default value is 900 minutes, meaning that after 900 minutes the system will re-create, or refresh this module. Note this control is only meaningful if the caching for the module is enabled.

To add a Newsflash module to your site, follow these steps:

1. **Log in to the admin system of your site.**

2. **Access the Module Manager.** To do so, go to the Extensions menu and select the Module Manager option. The Module Manager will load in your browser.

3. **Click the New icon on the toolbar at the top of the Module Manager.** The New Module dialogue opens. Refer to Figure 17.2.

4. **Select the option Newsflash and then click the Next button.** The Newsflash Module dialogue loads in your browser.

5. **In the Title field, type a name for the module.** This field is required.

6. **Set the Enabled option to Yes.**

7. **Set the Position control to assign the module to a position on the page.**

8. **Set the Menu Assignment to specify the pages upon which the module appears.**

9. **Select any additional options or parameters you wish; all other fields are optional.**

10. **Click the Save icon on the toolbar at the top right to save your new module.** The system creates the module, closes the dialogue, and returns you to the Module Manager.

Tip

This module is useful for both showing short news items and announcements and for displaying short versions — teasers — of articles. In the sample data you can see what is probably the most common use, that is, the Newsflash is assigned to a prominent module position, and then configured to display short content items drawn from a dedicated category. In the case of the Joomla! 1.5.x sample data, the dedicated category is named Newsflash and is part of the News section.

Poll

The Polls module allows you to display polls created in the Polls component inside module positions, as shown in Figure 17.26. The module is tied closely to the Polls component and cannot display content other than that generated by the component.

Cross-Reference

The Polls component and module are discussed in more detail in Chapter 15.

FIGURE 17.26

The front-end output of the Polls module, showing the poll from the sample data.

Poles module

The default system with the sample data installed shows one Polls module in use. The module is named Polls and is assigned to the right module position holder on various pages where it displays the Joomla! Is Used For? item from the Polls component.

Note

The system name for this module type is mod_polls.

The Parameters section is divided into two sections: Module parameters and Advanced parameters, as shown in Figure 17.27.

The Module parameters section contains two controls:

- **Poll:** Select one of the Polls created in the Polls Component. This is a required field.
- **Module Class Suffix:** This field allows you to specify a suffix that will be automatically appended to all CSS styles that affect this module. The use of a specified suffix makes it possible for you to style this module individually.

FIGURE 17.27

The Poll module parameters.

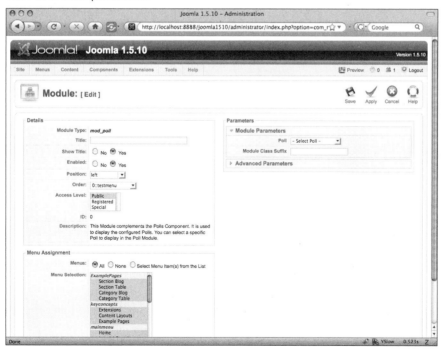

The Advanced parameters section contains caching options:

- **Caching:** This control allows you to exempt a specific module from the site's caching, as set in the Global Configuration. Select the No Caching option to prevent the contents of this module from being cached. The default setting is Use Global.

- **Cache Time:** The time, in minutes, you want the contents to be cached. Enter an integer value here. The default value is 900 minutes, meaning that after 900 minutes the system will re-create, or refresh this module. Note this control is only meaningful if the caching for the module is enabled.

To add a Polls module to your site, follow these steps:

1. **Log in to the admin system of your site.**

2. **Access the Module Manager. To do so, go to the Extensions menu and select the Module Manager option.** The Module Manager loads in your browser.

3. **Click the New icon on the toolbar at the top of the Module Manager.** The New Module dialog box opens. Refer to Figure 17.2.

4. **Select the option Polls and then click the Next button.** The Polls Modules dialog box opens in your browser.

5. **In the Title field, type a name for the module.** This is a required field.

6. **Set the Enabled option to Yes.**

7. **Set the position control to assign the module to a position on the page.**

8. **Set the Menu Assignment to specify the pages upon which the module appears.**

9. **Choose a poll to display using the Poll parameter.**

10. **Select any additional options or parameters you wish; all other fields are optional.**

11. **Click the Save icon on the toolbar at the top right to save your new module.** The system creates the module, closes the dialog box, and returns you to the Module Manager.

Random Image

The Random Image module displays a selection of images in a module position, according to the parameters you set, as shown in Figure 17.28. Images are drawn from a single directory that you designate in the configuration parameters. The display of the images is randomized. There are few options for controlling this module.

FIGURE 17.28

The front-end output of the Random Image module.

Note that the default system with the sample data installed includes a Random Image module, but the module is neither published nor assigned to any pages. The default module is named Random Image.

Note

The system name for this module type is mod_random_image.

The Parameters section is divided into two sections: Module parameters and Advanced parameters, as shown in Figure 17.29.

FIGURE 17.29

The Random Image module parameters.

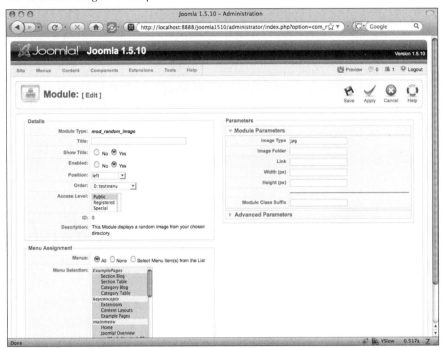

The Module parameters section contains the following options:

- **Image Type:** Enter file extensions in this blank to filter the images that will be displayed by the module. You can enter multiple file types, separated by commas. Note that you do not need the leading "." as in ".jpg." The default setting for this Parameter is jpg.

- **Image Folder:** Specify the address of the directory that contains the images you want to display. The path you enter here should relative to the site's URL.

- **Link:** If you want to hyperlink the images to a specific URL, enter the full URL here.

- **Width (px):** Enter an integer value to force the image to a specific width, as measured in pixels (px). If you do not specify a value here the system will use the original file's dimensions.

- **Height (px):** Enter an integer value to force the image to a specific width, as measured in pixels (px). If you do not specify a value here the system will use the original file's dimensions.

- **Module Class Suffix:** This field allows you to specify a suffix that will be automatically appended to all CSS styles that affect this module. The use of a specified suffix makes it possible for you to style this module individually.

The Advanced parameters section contains caching options:

- **Caching:** This control allows you to exempt a specific module from the site's caching, as set in the Global Configuration. Select the option No Caching to prevent the contents of this module from being cached. The default setting is Use Global.

- **Cache Time:** The time, in minutes, you want the contents to be cached. Enter an integer value here. The default value is 900 minutes, meaning that after 900 minutes the system will re-create, or refresh this Module. Note this control is only meaningful if the caching for the Module is enabled.

To add a Random Image module to your site, follow these steps:

1. **Log in to the admin system of your site.**

2. **Access the Module Manager.** To do so, go to the Extensions menu and select the Module Manager option. The Module Manager will load in your browser.

3. **Click the New icon on the toolbar at the top of the Module Manager.** The New Module dialogue opens. Refer to Figure 17.2.

4. **Select the option Random Image and then click the Next button.** The Random Image Module dialog box opens in your browser.

5. **In the Title field, type a name for the module.** This field is required.

6. **Set the Enabled option to Yes.**

7. **Set the position control to assign the module to a position on the page.**

8. **Set the Menu Assignment to specify the pages upon which the module appears.**

9. **Enter the path to the directory containing the images in the module parameter named Image Folder. This field is required.**

10. **Select any additional options or parameters you want;** all other fields are optional.

11. **Click the Save icon on the toolbar at the top right to save your new module.** The system creates the Module, closes the dialogue, and returns you to the Module Manager.

Tip

The Random Image module is useful but is rather lacking in features. Given the inability to control the display time, order, or re-sizing of the images, many administrators who desire this feature resort to a third-party extension. A quick review of the Joomla! Extensions site shows that a number of alternatives to using the core Random Image module exist.

Related Articles

The Related Articles module displays a list of links to articles that are considered to be related to the article the user is viewing. The front-end output of the Related Articles module is shown in Figure 17.30. The criteria for selection of Related Articles is keyword matching, and is based upon the keyword tags associated with the articles. To employ this feature, articles must be tagged with keywords.

Cross-Reference

Tagging articles is discussed in Chapter 5.

The default system with the sample data installed includes a Related Articles module. The module, however, is neither published nor assigned to any pages. The module is named Related Items.

Note

The system name for this module type is mod_related_items.

The Parameters section is divided into two sections: Module parameters and Advanced parameters, as shown in Figure 17.31.

FIGURE 17.30

The front-end output of the Related Articles module.

Related Articles module

FIGURE 17.31

The Related Articles module, as it appears in the admin system.

The Module parameters section contains two controls:

- **Show Date:** Set this option to Show if you wish to display in the list of articles the date of publication along with article names. The default setting is Hide.

- **Module Class Suffix:** This field allows you to specify a suffix that will be automatically appended to all CSS styles that affect this module. The use of a specified suffix makes it possible for you to style this module individually.

The Advanced parameters section contains caching options:

- **Caching:** This control allows you to exempt a specific module from the site's caching, as set in the Global Configuration. Select the option No Caching to prevent the contents of this module from being cached. The default setting is Use Global.

- **Cache Time:** The time, in minutes, you want the contents to be cached. Enter an integer value here. The default value is 900 minutes, meaning that after 900 minutes the system will re-create, or refresh this module. Note this control is only meaningful if the caching for the module is enabled.

To add a Related Articles module to your site, follow these steps:

1. **Log in to the admin system of your site.**

2. **Access the Module Manager.** To do so, go to the Extensions menu and select the Module Manager option. The Module Manager loads in your browser.

3. **Click the New icon on the toolbar at the top of the Module Manager.** The New Module dialogue opens. Refer to Figure 17.2.

4. **Select the option Related Articles, and then click the Next button.** The Related Articles Module dialogue loads in your browser.

5. **In the Title field, type a name for the module.** This field is required.

6. **Set the Enabled option to Yes.**

7. **Set the Position control to assign the module to a position on the page.**

8. **Set the Menu Assignment to specify the pages upon which the module will appear.**

9. **Select any additional options or parameters you wish; all other fields are optional.**

10. **Click the Save icon on the toolbar at the top right to save your new module.** The system creates the module, closes the dialogue, and returns you to the Module Manager.

Tip

To get the most out of the Related Articles module, you need to not only tag your articles, but you need to tag them consistently and accurately. The key to getting good results with this module is solely determined by the integrity of the underlying tag schema.

Search

The Search module makes it possible for you to place a site search box on any page inside of a module position. Site indexing is handled automatically and all you need to do is enable and publish this module to allow visitors to search the site with ease. There are few configuration options; all parameters related to this module are focused on the appearance of the search form.

The default system includes a Search module. The module, named simply Search, is published on all pages and assigned the module position named user4, as shown in Figure 17.32.

Note

The system name for this module type is mod_search.

The Parameters section is divided into two sections: Module parameters and Advanced parameters, as shown in Figure 17.33.

FIGURE 17.32

The front-end output of the Search module in the default Joomla! system. The module is shown here in the user4 position of the default template.

FIGURE 17.33

The Search module parameters.

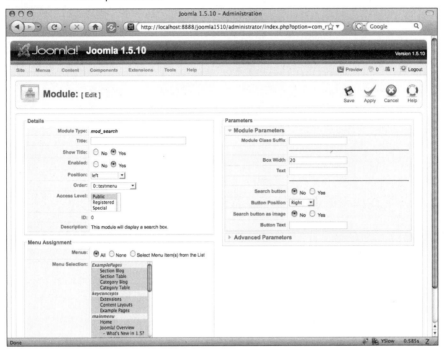

The Module parameters section contains two controls:

- **Module Class Suffix:** This field allows you to specify a suffix that will be automatically appended to all CSS styles that affect this module. The use of a specified suffix makes it possible for you to style this module individually.

- **Box width:** Enter an integer value here to set the width of the text field for the search form.

- **Text:** Enter text here to set a default message inside the search text field. The text you enter here displays in the search field until the user clicks in the text box to type their query. Typically this is used to hold a prompt such as, "Search this site."

- **Search button:** Hide or display a search button on the form. In either event, the user can initiate the search by pressing the Return key on their keyboard, but with the button present they also have the option to click on the button to start the search.

- **Button position:** Position the button relative to the search text field. The options are Right, Left, Top, and Bottom with the default option being to the right of the search form.

- **Search button as image:** Select whether button will be drawn using CSS or with an image. If yes, you must make sure you have an image file named `searchButton.gif` saved to the `images/M_images` directory on your server.

- **Button text:** Specify any text you want to appear on the Search button. If this is left blank the system will use the default search string specified in the language file.

The Advanced parameters section contains caching options:

- **Caching:** This control allows you to exempt a specific module from the site's caching, as set in the Global Configuration. Select the option No Caching to prevent the contents of this module from being cached. The default setting is Use Global.

- **Cache Time:** The time, in minutes, you want the contents to be cached. Enter an integer value here. The default value is 900 minutes, meaning that after 900 minutes the system will re-create, or refresh this module. Note this control is only meaningful if the caching for the module is enabled.

To add a Search module to your site, follow these steps:

1. **Access the Module Manager. To do so, go to the Extensions menu and select the Module Manager option.** The Module Manager loads in your browser.

2. **Click the New icon on the toolbar at the top of the Module Manager.** The New Module dialogue opens. Refer to Figure 17.2.

3. **Select the option Search and then click the Next button.** The Search Module dialogue loads in your browser.

4. **In the Title field, type a name for the module.** This field is required.

5. **Set the Enabled option to Yes.**

6. **Set the Position control to assign the module to a position on the page.**

7. **Set the Menu Assignment to specify the pages upon which the module will appear.**

8. **Select any additional options or parameters you wish; all other fields are optional.**

9. **Click the Save icon on the toolbar at the top right to save your new module.** The system creates the module, closes the dialogue, and returns you to the Module Manager.

Tip

Site search in Joomla! is enabled by the search plugins. Some of the settings for the plugins can be used to configure your search, for example, by specifying what is or what is not included in the search results. To learn more about configuring the search plugin, see Chapter 19.

Sections

The Sections module provides a list of links to the content sections of your site. The module is primarily intended to function as a navigation block and has very limited configuration options. The default Joomla system with sample data installed has a single Sections module; however it is neither published nor assigned to any page. The module is named Sections and is shown in Figure 17.34.

FIGURE 17.34

The Sections module as it appears on the front end of the site.

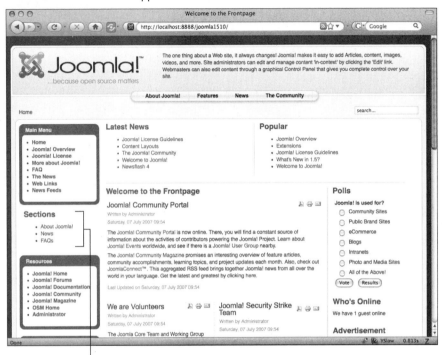

Sections module

Note

The system name for this module type is mod_sections.

The Parameters section is divided into two sections: Module parameters and Advanced parameters, as shown in Figure 17.35.

The Module parameters section contains two controls:

- **Count:** Type an integer value into this field to specify the maximum number of sections that will be shown in the module. The default value is 5.
- **Module Class Suffix:** This field allows you to specify a suffix that will be automatically appended to all CSS styles that affect this module. The use of a specified suffix makes it possible for you to style this module individually.

FIGURE 17.35

The Sections module parameters.

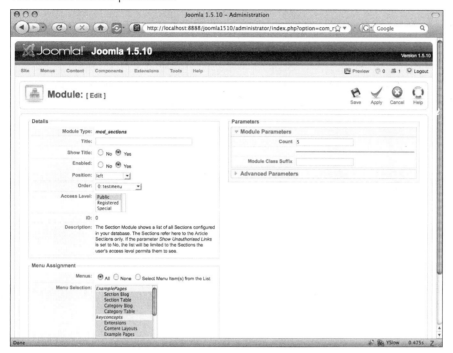

The Advanced parameters section contains caching options:

- **Caching:** This control allows you to exempt a specific module from the site's caching, as set in the Global Configuration. Select the option No Caching to prevent the contents of this module from being cached. The default setting is Use Global.

- **Cache Time:** The time, in minutes, you want the contents to be cached. Enter an integer value here. The default value is 900 minutes, meaning that after 900 minutes the system will re-create, or refresh this module. Note this control is only meaningful if the caching for the module is enabled.

To add a Sections module to your site, follow these steps:

1. **Log in to the admin system of your site.**

2. **Access the Module Manager. To do so, go to the Extensions menu and select the Module Manager option.** The Module Manager loads in your browser.

3. **Click the New icon on the toolbar at the top of the Module Manager.** The New Module dialogue opens. Refer to Figure 17.2.

4. **Select the option Sections and then click the Next button.** The Sections Module dialogue loads in your browser.

5. **In the Title field, type a name for the module.** This field is required.

6. **Set the Enabled option to Yes.**

7. **Set the position control to assign the module to a position on the page.**

8. **Set the Menu Assignment to specify the pages upon which the module will appear.**

9. **Select any additional options or parameters you want; all other fields are optional.**

10. **Click the Save icon on the toolbar at the top right to save your new module.** The system creates the module, closes the dialogue, and returns you to the Module Manager.

Tip

Sections, as the term is used by this module, refers to only content sections, not to any other kind of section that may exist in your system. Note as well that your content sections are subject to the access level control settings you gave them. If you have restricted access to any sections, links in the Sections module may not be visible to all users. If you are having problems with the display of this module, check both the access level settings for the sections and the Section parameter named Show Unauthorized Links.

Statistics

The Statistics module displays information about your site and hosting environment in a module position. The module is configurable and can be set to display basic information about your server, your site visitor traffic and information on the contents of your site, including the number of articles and web links. The default system with the sample data includes a Statistics module but it is neither enabled nor assigned to any pages. The module is named simply Statistics and is shown in Figure 17.36.

Note

The system name for this module type is mod_stats.

The Parameters section is divided into two sections: Module parameters and Advanced parameters, as shown in Figure 17.37.

The Module parameters section contains five controls. For example to display on your site, at least one of the first three controls must be set to Yes.

- **Server Info:** Set this to Yes to display basic information about your server, including the OS, the Time, whether Caching or Gzip are enabled, and the version number of your PHP and MySQL installations. The default setting for this control is No.

- **Site Info:** Set this to Yes to display basic information about your site and its contents, including the number of members, Content items, and web links. The default setting is No.

- **Hit Counter:** Set this to Yes to display how many views your content items have received. The default setting is No.

- **Increase Counter:** Enter an integer value here to increase the number of hits shown on the Hits counter.

- **Module Class Suffix:** This field allows you to specify a suffix that will be automatically appended to all CSS styles that affect this module. The use of a specified suffix makes it possible for you to style this module individually.

The Advanced parameters section contains only one option: Caching. This control allows you to exempt a specific Module from the site's caching, as set in the Global Configuration. Select the option No Caching to prevent the contents of this module from being cached. The default setting is Use Global.

FIGURE 17.36

The front-end output of the Statistics Module.

Statistics module

FIGURE 17.37

The Statistics module parameters.

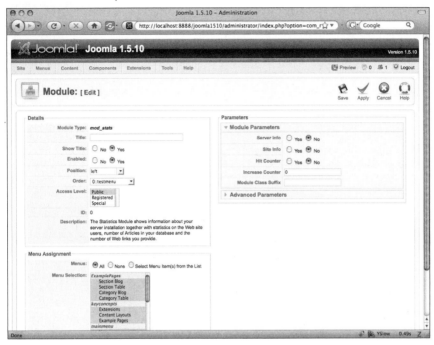

To add a Statistics module to your site, follow these steps:

1. **Log in to the admin system of your site.**

2. **Access the Module Manager. To do so, go to the Extensions menu and select the Module Manager option.** The Module Manager loads in your browser.

3. **Click the New icon on the toolbar at the top of the Module Manager.** The New Module dialogue opens. Refer to Figure 17.2.

4. **Select the option Statistics and then click the Next button.** The Statistics Module dialogue loads in your browser.

5. **In the Title field, type a name for the module.** This field is required.

6. **Set the Enabled option to Yes.**

7. **Set the position control to assign the module to a position on the page.**

8. **Set the Menu Assignment to specify the pages upon which the module will appear.**

9. Select any additional options or parameters you want; all other fields are optional.

10. **Click the Save icon on the toolbar at the top right to save your new module.** The system creates the module, close the dialogue and return you to the Module Manager.

Tip

Although the Statistics module is a convenient way to add a bit of extra content to your site— content that you don't have to maintain — you may want to think twice before exposing information about your server configuration to the world.

Syndicate

The Syndicate module displays an RSS feed icon that is automatically linked to the RSS feed for the page upon which it appears. The module is used when you want visitors to know they can subscribe the content of a particular page. There are no filters that allow you to refine this functionality; it always links to the feed for the page contents. There is a Syndicate module included in the default site's setup. It is assigned to the Syndicate module position on all pages. The Module is named Syndicate, as shown in Figure 17.38.

FIGURE 17.38

The front-end output of the Syndicate module, shown here in the default system in the Syndicate module position of the default template.

Syndication module

Note

The system name for this module type is mod_syndicate.

The Parameters section includes only four module parameters, as shown in Figure 17.39

- **Caching:** The only option for this module is Never. This cannot be changed.
- **Text:** Set the text label you want associated with the icon. Leave it blank for none.
- **Format:** Select the format of the feed. Joomla! supports both RSS 2.0 and Atom 1.0.
- **Module Class Suffix:** This field allows you to specify a suffix that will be automatically appended to all CSS styles that affect this module. The use of a specified suffix makes it possible for you to style this module individually.

To add a Syndicate module to your site, follow these steps:

1. **Log in to the admin system of your site.**
2. **Access the Module Manager. To do so, go to the Extensions menu and select the Module Manager option.** The Module Manager loads in your browser.
3. **Click the New icon on the toolbar at the top of the Module Manager.** The New Module dialogue opens. Refer to Figure 17.2.
4. **Select the option Syndicate and then click the Next button.** The Syndicate Module dialogue loads in your browser.
5. **In the Title field, type a name for the module.** This field is required.
6. **Set the Enabled option to Yes.**
7. **Set the position control to assign the module to a position on the page.**
8. **Set the Menu Assignment to specify the pages upon which the module will appear.**
9. **Select any additional options or parameters you want; all other fields are optional.**
10. **Click the Save icon on the toolbar at the top right to save your new module.** The system creates the module, closes the dialogue, and returns you to the Module Manager.

Tip

While the default system has the Syndicate module assigned to all the pages of the site, this is unlikely to be the preferred choice for most people. The module provides visitors access to a feed for every page on which it appears — a feature that is unlikely to be needed for most sites. The better choice is to show the module on only those pages where it is relevant. To do so, use the Menu Assignment option in the Syndicate module dialogue to assign the module to the desired pages.

The Syndicate module parameters.

Who's Online

The Who's Online module is a way of showing activity levels on your site. The module displays the number of members online at any time, and can also be configured to list their names as well. The default system with the sample data installed includes one Who's Online module. The module is assigned to the Right module position and configured to show only a count of users. The module name is Who's Online, as shown in Figure 17.40.

Note

The system name for this module type is mod_whosonline.

The Parameters section includes only three module parameters, as shown in Figure 17.41.

- **Caching:** The only option for this module is Never. This cannot be changed.

- **Display:** Select what you want the module to display. The options are # of Guests / Members, Member Names, and Both.

- **Module Class Suffix:** This field allows you to specify a suffix that will be automatically appended to all CSS styles that affect this module. The use of a specified suffix makes it possible for you to style this module individually.

FIGURE 17.40

The front-end output of the Who's Online module, shown in the default configuration in the Right module position. The module is configured to show only the number of Guests and Members.

Who's Online module

To add a Who's Online module to your site, follow these steps:

1. **Log in to the admin system of your site.**

2. **Access the Module Manager. To do so, go to the Extensions menu and select the Module Manager option.** The Module Manager loads in your browser.

3. **Click the New icon on the toolbar at the top of the Module Manager.** The New Module dialogue opens. Refer to Figure 17.2.

4. **Select the option Who's Online, and then click the Next button.** The Who's Online module dialogue loads in your browser.

5. **In the Title field, type a name for the module.** This field is required.

6. **Set the Enabled option to Yes.**

7. **Set the Position control to assign the module to a position on the page.**

8. **Set the Menu Assignment to specify the pages upon which the module will appear.**

9. Select any additional options or parameters you want; all other fields are optional.

10. Click the Save icon on the toolbar at the top right to save your new module. The system creates the module, closes the dialogue, and returns you to the Module Manager.

Note

The Who's Online module dialogue says "Guests," but it means "users who are not logged in." When the dialogue refers to "Members," it means "authenticated users."

FIGURE 17.41

The Who's Online module parameters.

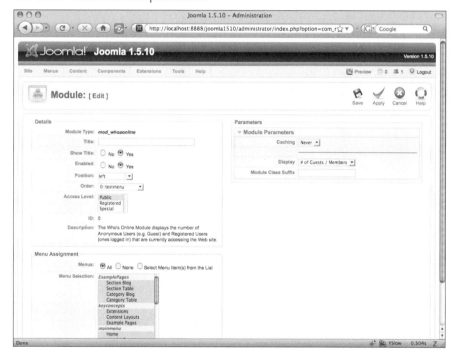

Wrapper

The Wrapper module provides you with a way to display external web pages in your site. A Wrapper is just another name for an iFrame, which can be configured to display an external URL, as shown in Figure 17.42. The parameters associated with this module relate to the URL content, the appearance, and the size of the iFrame.

There is no Wrapper module included in the default Joomla! installation.

FIGURE 17.42

The front-end output of the Wrapper module, shown here wrapping an external web site (in this example, Google), inside the Footer module position.

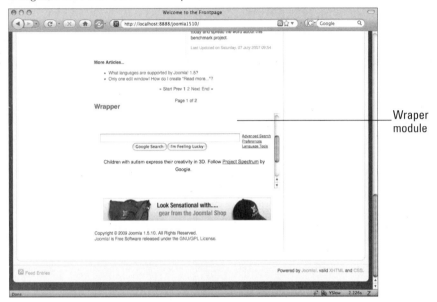

Wraper module

Note

The system name for this module type is mod_wrapper.

The Parameters section is divided into two sections: Module parameters and Advanced parameters, as shown in Figure 17.43.

The Module parameters section contains the following controls:

- **Module Class Suffix:** This field allows you to specify a suffix that will be automatically appended to all CSS styles that affect this module. The use of a specified suffix makes it possible for you to style this module individually.

- **URL:** The address of the web page you want to display inside the Wrapper.

- **Scroll Bars:** Set the control to No to hide scrollbars, to Yes to show them. Setting the control to Auto means that the system will only display scrollbars when they are needed to display the entire page.

- **Width:** Specify the width of the iFrame in either pixels or as a percentage.

- **Height:** Specify the width of the iFrame in either pixels or as a percentage.

- **Auto Height:** Setting this control to Yes will result in the iFrame sizing itself automatically to match the web page being displayed.

- **Auto Add:** Set this to Yes to automatically append the prefix `http://` to the URL. Set the control to No to disable this feature.

- **Target Name:** Specify a name for the iFrame. This is optional and only needed where you are using the iFrame as a target for opening a URL.

The Advanced parameters section contains caching options:

- **Caching:** This control allows you to exempt a specific module from the site's caching, as set in the Global Configuration. Select the option No Caching to prevent the contents of this module from being cached. The default setting is Use Global.

- **Cache Time:** The time, in minutes, you want the contents to be cached. Enter an integer value here. The default value is 900 minutes, meaning that after 900 minutes the system will re-create, or refresh this module. Note this control is only meaningful if the caching for the module is enabled.

FIGURE 17.43

The Wrapper module, as it appears in the admin system.

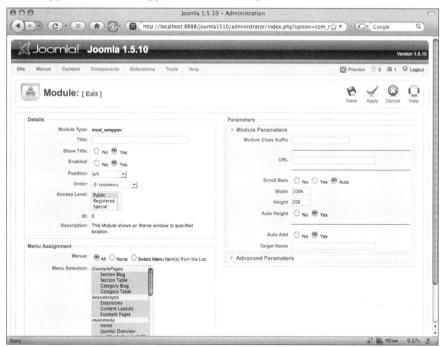

To add a Wrapper module to your site, follow these steps:

1. **Log in to the admin system of your site.**

2. **Access the Module Manager.** To do so, go to the Extensions menu and select the Module Manager option. The Module Manager loads in your browser.

3. **Click the New icon on the toolbar at the top of the Module Manager.** The New Module dialogue opens. Refer to Figure 17.2.

4. **Select the option Wrapper and then click the Next button.** The Wrapper Module dialogue loads in your browser.

5. **In the Title field, type a name for the Module.** This field is required.

6. **Set the Enabled option to Yes.**

7. **Set the Position control to assign the module to a position on the page.**

8. **Set the Menu Assignment to specify the pages upon which the Module appears.**

9. **Specify the URL of the web page in the Module parameters URL field.**

10. **Select any additional options or parameters you want; all other fields are optional.**

11. **Click the Save icon on the toolbar at the top right to save your new module.** The system creates the module, closes the dialogue, and returns you to the module Manager.

Tip

The Wrapper module is typically used in module positions located in, above, below, or inside the main content area, as the sidebar columns are typically too small for the wrapper to work effectively. If you intend to use the wrapper in the side columns, be aware that the scrollbars can take up a lot of space when they are active. If you have control over the web page that is being displayed, this can be accounted for. If, however, the web page you want to display is not controlled by you, then the wrapper display may be more difficult to control. Placing the wrapper at the top or bottom of the content area, in contrast, give you a much wider area to work with, plus the ability to expand the height without completely breaking your page layout.

Summary

In this chapter, we have covered the use of the Site modules. You learned the following:

- How to use the Site Module Manager
- The nature and uses of the core Site modules
- How to create, copy, edit, and delete Site modules

Working With the Administrator Modules

T he Joomla! system includes both Site modules and Administrator modules. The former provide output for the site visitors, and the latter help create the administration interface and provide the back end of the site with useful functionality.

Because they tend to supply critical functionality, Administrator modules are rarely touched by programmers and system administrators. The vast majority of people use the default configuration. However, a closer examination of the modules shows that some benefits can be gained from learning to manage your site's Administrator modules.

Reviewing the Module Manager

All the Joomla! modules are controlled through the Module Manager. The manager contains all the default Joomla! modules, together with any third-party modules you may have installed. To get started, go to the Extensions menu and select the option Module Manager. The Module Manager loads in your browser window, as shown in Figure 18.1.

IN THIS CHAPTER

Reviewing the Module Manager

Reviewing the Administrator modules

FIGURE 18.1

The Joomla! 1.5.x Module Manager, showing the Administrator modules.

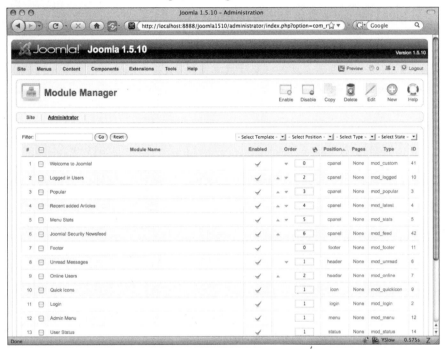

The toolbar at the top of the Module Manager provides quick access to the following functions:

- **Enable:** Select one or more modules from the list, then click this icon to enable them.
- **Disable:** Select one or more modules from the list, then click this icon to disable them.
- **Copy:** Select a module then click this icon to make an exact copy of the module.
- **Delete:** Select one or more modules from the list, then click this icon to delete the module.
- **Edit:** Select a module from the list then click this icon to edit the module's details.
- **New:** Click to add a new module.
- **Help:** Click to access the online Help files related to the active screen.

Below the toolbar are two text links: the link labeled Site shows you the Site Module Manager, discussed previously. The Administrator link displays the Administrator Module Manager.

Located below the two links and above the list of modules are five sorting and searching tools to help you manage long lists of modules:

- **The Filter field** on the left works like a search box. Type a word or phrase into the text box and then click Go. The page reloads and displays the results of the search. To clear the screen and return to a full listing, click the Reset button.

- **Select Template:** Shows a list of the available templates. Select a template name from the combo box to restrict the search to the modules associated with that template. Note that for the administrator system, there is only one template in the default installation.

- **Select Position:** Sort and display the modules according to the position they are assigned to.

- **Select Type:** Filter the list by the module type.

- **The Select State filter** on the far right allows you to filter and display the modules according to whether they are published or unpublished. The Select State filter provides an easy way to identify all modules that are currently active on the site. To reset this filter, change the combo box back to the default setting.

Tip

The Select Position, Type, and State filters can be combined to further refine the view of the list of modules.

The main content area of the screen contains a list of all the modules in your Administrator Modules Manager. The columns provided are:

- **# :** An indexing number assigned by Joomla! This number cannot be changed.

- **Checkbox (no label):** Click in a checkbox to select a module; this is needed if you want to use several of the toolbar options, referenced above.

- **Module Name:** This field displays the full name of the module. Click on the name to edit the module's details.

- **Enabled:** A green checkmark in this column indicates that the module is published. The field shows a red X if the module is not published. Administrators can toggle between the two settings by clicking the icons.

- **Order:** The numbers in this field affect the ordering of the module on this list. Change the numbers and click the Save icon at the top of the column to reorder the module. You can also click the up and down arrows to reorder the list.

- **Position:** The module position to which the module is assigned. A single module can only be assigned to a single position.

- **Pages:** An indicator of which pages the module has been assigned to. The only options here are

  All, meaning to all pages in the administration system,

  None, which means the module has not been assigned to any pages and

  Varies, which means the module is assigned to some but not all the pages.

  To change these settings, edit the module.

- **Type:** The module type of the module. Each module can be of only one type.
- **ID:** The system-generated user ID number.

Tip

The information you see on the Control Panel screen is provided by various Administrator modules. On the right side of the Control Panel, the Welcome to Joomla! message, Logged in Users, Popular, Recent added Articles, Menu Stats, and Joomla! Security Newsfeed are all created by Admin modules. The ordering control on the Administrator Module Manager interface makes it possible for you to unpublish or reorder these elements. For example, you may want to unpublish the Welcome to Joomla! message, or move the Joomla! Security Newsfeed to the top of the list where it is always visible.

At the bottom of the screen, below the content area, is the Display # option. Change the value in the combo box control to alter the number of modules that are displayed on the page. The default value can be altered by changing the List Length option on the Global Configuration Manager.

Creating new modules

All modules are created from the Module Manager. Simply click the New icon at the top toolbar, and the system loads a new window in the browser. The new window requires you to specify the module type you want to create. Select one of the 20 choices and the page reloads, showing you the proper module creation dialogue, like the one in Figure 18.2. The module types all share common elements, as discussed next, but each also has unique parameters that must be considered.

Note

If you have in..alled additional extensions to your site, it is possible you may also see additional module types that allow for the creation of new modules beyond the system defaults.

Copying modules

You can make exact copies of modules by using the Copy command on the Module Manager. This function is very useful if you need to run multiple instances of the same module type; in this case the Copy function can save you time configuring your new modules.

To copy a module, follow these steps:

1. Open the Module Manager.
2. Select the module you want to copy by clicking in the select box next to the Module Name.
3. Click the Copy icon. The system makes a copy of the module and places it in the Module Manager with the name "Copy of (original module's name)."

FIGURE 18.2

The New Module Dialogue, in this case, for creation of an Administrator module. This shows the default system options.

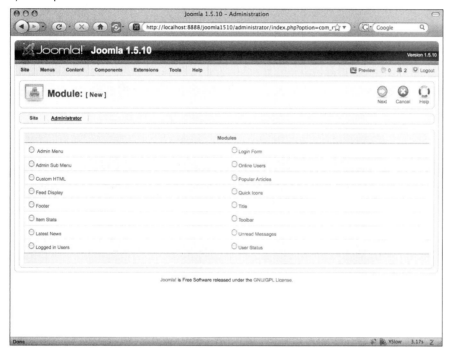

Editing and deleting modules

Existing modules can be edited from the Module Manager. To edit a module, either click the module name in the Module Manager, or select the module on the list and then click the Edit icon on the Module Manager toolbar. Regardless of which method you use, the system opens the Edit Module dialogue. The Edit Module dialogue is identical to the New Module dialogue, with the same fields and requirements.

To make changes to a module, simply alter the desired fields in the Edit Module dialogue and then click the Save or Apply icon on the toolbar. Any changes you make are applied immediately.

To delete one or more modules, follow these steps:

1. Open the Module Manager.
2. Select one or more modules.
3. Click the Delete icon.

Caution

Deleting Admin modules is rarely appropriate. All the existing module types provide functional output in the default system. Some of the modules are essential, and the deletion of the module may make administering the site difficult. Note that the Login module cannot be disabled or deleted. In general, you should be cautious about deleting modules because there is no confirmation dialogue — clicking the Delete icon immediately deletes the module!

Reviewing the Administrator Modules

The workspace of each Administrator Module dialogue is divided into three areas: Details, Menu Assignment, and Parameters, as shown in Figure 18.3. The Details and Menu Assignment portions of all the module types are identical. Unlike the site modules, the Administrator modules cannot be assigned to specific pages, hence the Menu Assignment area serves no function. Moreover, there are few options associated with the Administrator modules, and those few that exist are found in the parameters area of the module dialogue.

FIGURE 18.3

A typical Administrator Module dialogue, in this case, the Logged In Users module.

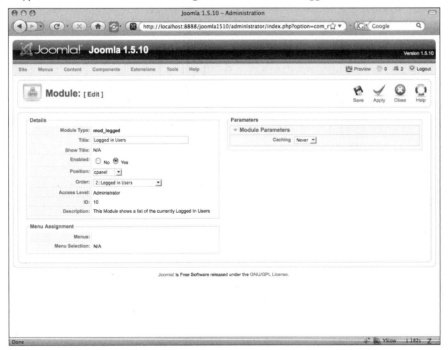

The toolbar at the top of the module dialogue provides quick access to the following functions:

- **Save:** Click this icon to save your work, add a new module, and exit the New Module dialogue.

- **Apply:** Click to save your work and create a new module without exiting from the New Module dialogue. This option lets you save without exiting the screen and is useful in case you are interrupted or you otherwise want to save yet keep working on this screen.

- **Cancel:** Cancels the task and exits the Module Manager.

- **Help:** Displays the Help files related to the active screen.

The Details section of the workspace contains the following fields:

- **Module Type:** This identifier is set by the system and tells you the type of module being created. This cannot be changed.

- **Title:** Use this field to give a name to your module. This field is required.

- **Show Title:** This control is not active and has no impact on Administrator modules.

- **Enabled:** Select Yes to publish the module. The default state is Yes.

- **Position:** Controls the placement of the module on the page. Use the combo box to select from the list of eligible module positions. This field is required.

- **Order:** Sets the order of the module relative to other modules assigned to the same position. Has no effect if only one module is assigned to a position.

- **Access Level:** This field is set to Administrator and cannot be changed.

- **ID:** A system-assigned identification number. This cannot be changed.

- **Description:** Joomla! provides this description text to help users understand the use of the module.

Cross-Reference

For more information about working with the administrator template, see Chapter 23.

The Menu Assignment area of the workspace serves no purpose for Administrator modules. Admin modules cannot be assigned to particular pages. The modules appear on only the pages of Administrator section. Outside of the Control Panel, all pages show the same modules.

The Parameters section varies for each module. Details on the parameters for each module are discussed in the sections that follow.

Working with Khepri

The administrator template distributed with Joomla! 1.5.x is named Khepri. The template provides module position holders that are applicable to all the admin pages. The Control Panel page, however, is different from the other pages in the Admin system. Though it uses the Khepri template and hence has the same module position holders as the other admin pages, it also has additional Admin modules placed inside the content area of the page. Those module position holders are named Cpanel and Icon and are only active on the Control Panel page. Cpanel is positioned on the right side of the page and Icon is on the left. Neither is visible on the other admin pages.

The Login module position appears on yet another page, the admin entry page. The page holds only the Login Form for gaining access to the admin system. The Login position does not accept any new module assignments.

The Khepri template includes only five module position holders: Menu, Submenu, Status, Title, and Toolbar. So, although the Position combo box shows a larger assortment of available positions, only the five positions are available outside of the Control Panel. Assigning your module to either Cpanel or Icon results in the module output being hidden on the internal admin pages.

Admin Menu module

The Admin Menu module is responsible for the navigation menu that shows at the top left of each Administrator page, as seen in Figure 18.4. Unlike the site modules, the administrator modules are not linked to the Menu Manager. Modifying the options on the Admin Menu is not possible, (aside from hacking the core files).

The default system includes one example of the Admin Menu module, which is located in the Menu Module position at the top of the admin pages.

Note
The system name for this module type is mod_menu.

The Parameters section is divided into two sections: Module parameters and Advanced parameters. The Module parameters section contains no controls, and the Advanced parameters section contains only one option: Caching. This control enables you to exempt a specific module from the site's caching, as set in the Global Configuration. Select the option No Caching to prevent the contents of this module from being cached. The default setting is Use Global.

To add an Admin Menu module to your site, follow these steps:

1. **Log in to the admin system of your site.**
2. **Access the Module Manager. To do so, go to the Extensions menu and select the Module Manager option.** The Module Manager loads in your browser.
3. **Click the Administrator link.** The Administrator Module Manager loads in your browser.

4. **Click the New icon on the toolbar at the top of the Module Manager.** The New Module dialogue opens. (Refer to Figure 18.2.)

5. **Select the option Admin Menu, and then click the Next button.** The Admin Menu Module dialogue loads in your browser.

6. **In the Title field, type a name for the module.** This is a required field.

7. **Set the option Enabled to Yes.**

8. **Set the position of the module.**

9. **Select any additional options you wish; all other fields are optional.**

10. **Click the Save icon on the toolbar at the top right to save your new module.** The dialogue closes and returns you to the Administrator Module Manager.

Note

Although it is possible to add multiple menu modules to your Administration system, there is no point in doing so because Joomla! recognizes only one menu module at a time.

FIGURE 18.4

The output of the Admin Menu module, shown here assigned to the default Menu module position.

Admin Menu module

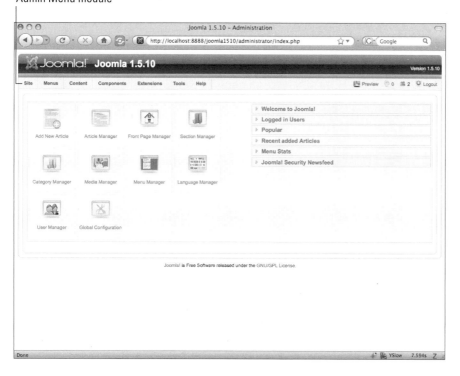

Admin submenu

The Admin submenu appears on some pages of the admin system, immediately below the title, but above the filters. You can see this menu in action, for example, on the Module Manager screen where it holds the text links Site and Administrator, as shown in Figure 18.5.

Like the Admin menu, this menu is not part of the normal Joomla! Menu Manager scheme; the module is not related to and cannot be controlled by the Menu Manager.

There is one Admin SubMenu module in the default Joomla! installation. It is assigned to the SubMenu module position.

Note

The system name for this module type is mod_submenu.

The module parameters section contains only one option, Caching, and it is permanently set to Never. This option cannot be changed.

The Admin SubMenu module in action; here you can see it on the Module Manager interface.

Admin Submenu module

To add an Admin SubMenu module to your site, follow these steps:

1. **Log in to the admin system of your site.**

2. **Access the Module Manager.** To do so, go to the Extensions menu and select the Module Manager option. The Module Manager loads in your browser.

3. **Click the link Administrator.** The Administrator Module Manager loads in your browser.

4. **Click the New icon on the toolbar at the top of the Module Manager.** The New Module dialogue opens. (Refer to Figure 18.2.)

5. **Select the option Admin SubMenu and then click the Next button.** The Admin SubMenu module dialogue loads in your browser.

6. **In the Title field, type a name for the module.** This field is required.

7. **Set the option Enabled to Yes.**

8. **Set the position of the module.**

9. **Select any additional options you wish; all other fields are optional.**

10. **Click the Save icon on the toolbar at the top right to save your new module.** The dialogue closes and returns you to the Administrator Module Manager.

Custom HTML module

The Custom HTML module is designed to allow you to enter the content of your choosing and to that end, provides a large text editing box and a WYSIWYG Editor. The module enables you to enter text, images, or HTML code and then display the output in a module position in the admin system. Use this module type to create blocks of text inside the admin system and to provide information and messages to the administrators, as shown in Figure 18.6.

In the default configuration, the Joomla! system uses a Custom HTML module to present the Welcome to Joomla! content that greets administrators on the Control Panel. The Custom HTML module in the default system is named Welcome to Joomla! and is assigned to the Cpanel module position. Note that this module position is one of the two that appears only on the Control Panel page; if you want to use the Custom HTML module on internal admin pages, you will need to use a different module position.

Note

The system name for this module type is mod_custom.

The module parameters section contains only one control: the Module Class Suffix. This field allows you to specify a suffix that will be automatically appended to all CSS styles that affect this module. The use of a specified suffix makes it possible for you to style this module individually.

FIGURE 18.6

The Custom HTML module in action on the Control Panel. The module is assigned to the Cpanel module position.

To add a Custom HTML module to your site, follow these steps:

1. **Log in to the admin system of your site.**

2. **Access the Module Manager. To do so, go to the Extensions menu and select the Module Manager option.** The Module Manager loads in your browser.

3. **Click the link Administrator.** The Administrator Module Manager loads in your browser.

4. **Click the New icon on the toolbar at the top of the Module Manager.** The New Module dialogue opens. (Refer to Figure 18.2.)

5. **Select the option Custom HTML and then click the Next button.** The Custom HTML module dialogue loads in your browser.

6. **In the Title field, type a name for the module.** This field is required.

7. **Set the option Enabled to Yes.**

8. **Set the position of the module.**

9. **Input the text, or the HTML code, you desire into the Custom Output field.**

10. Select any additional options you wish; all other fields are optional.

11. Click the Save icon on the toolbar at the top right to save your new module. The dialogue closes and returns you to the Administrator Module Manager.

Tip

The default system's Custom HTML module can be unpublished to give your Admin Control Panel a nice clean appearance. Alternatively, the default Welcome to Joomla! message included in the module can be replaced with content of your own choosing, such as a branding message, instructions, or other notices that need to be brought to the attention of the site administrators.

Feed Display module

The Feed Display module enables the gathering of RSS feed output and the display of that output inside a module position in the admin system, as shown in Figure 18.7. Although you can use this module to display content from any newsfeed, the default Joomla! system uses a Feed Display module to gather the output of the Joomla! Security Announcements newsfeed and to display that on the Control Panel page.

FIGURE 18.7

The Feed Display module, shown here in the default configuration: Assigned to the Cpanel position on the Control Panel.

The default Feed Display module is named Joomla! Security Newsfeed and it is assigned to the Cpanel module position. Note that the default module is assigned to a position that only appears on the Control Panel; if you want the module to be viewable on other admin pages, you will need to assign it to a different position.

Note

The system name for this module type is mod_feed.

The parameters section is divided into two sections: Module parameters and Advanced parameters. The module parameters section contains two controls:

- **Caching:** This control allows you to exempt a specific module from the site's caching, as set in the Global Configuration. Select the No Caching option to prevent the contents of this module from being cached. The default setting is No Caching.

- **Cache Time:** Specify an integer value for the number of minutes the system will store the module contents before refreshing.

- **Module Class Suffix:** This field allows you to specify a suffix that will be automatically appended to all CSS styles that affect this module. The use of a specified suffix makes it possible for you to style this module individually.

- **Feed URL:** The address of the feed. Typically this begins with `http://`. This field is required.

- **RTL Feed:** If your feed reads right to left, set this option to Yes.

- **Feed Title:** Controls whether to display the title of the feed, as supplied by the source of the feed.

- **Feed Description:** Controls whether to display the description of the feed, as supplied by the source of the feed.

- **Feed Image:** Controls whether to display the image associated the feed, as supplied by the source of the feed.

- **Items:** Specify an integer value to control the number of feed items that will be displayed in the module. The default is 3.

- **Item Description:** Controls whether to display the description of the Feed Item, as supplied by the source of the feed.

- **Word Count:** Specify an integer value to control the length of the feed item shown. Set the value to zero to show the entire item.

To add a Feed Display module to your site, follow these steps:

1. **Log in to the admin system of your site.**

2. **Access the Module Manager. To do so, go to the Extensions menu and select the Module Manager option.** The Module Manager loads in your browser.

3. **Click the Administrator link.** The Administrator Module Manager loads in your browser.

4. **Click the New icon on the toolbar at the top of the Module Manager.** The New Module dialogue opens. (Refer to Figure 18.2.)

5. **Select the option Feed Display and then click the Next button.** The Feed Display Module dialogue loads in your browser.

6. **In the Title field, type a name for the module.** This field is required.

7. **Set the option enabled to Yes.**

8. **Set the position of the module.**

9. **Enter the address for the source of the feed in the field labeled Feed URL.**

10. **Select any additional options you wish; all other fields are optional.**

11. **Click the Save icon on the toolbar at the top right to save your new module.** The dialogue closes and returns you to the Administrator Module Manager.

Note

Although adding feeds to the admin system may be a useful way to keep your administrators up-to-date with critical information — like the Joomla! Security Newsfeed — never forget that the Feed Display module draws its content from outside your server and that sometimes waiting on the feed data may result in delays in the loading of the admin interface.

Footer module

The Footer module in the admin system displays the Joomla! copyright information together with a link to check for system updates. Although there is a Footer module in the Administrator Module Manager, and the module is enabled, it does not appear because it has been assigned to an invalid module position, Footer. The default Khepri admin template does not include a module position named Footer. Figure 18.8 shows the output of the Footer module.

Note

The copyright notice you see at the bottom of the pages is coded into the Khepri admin template; it is not generated by the Footer module.

Note

The system name for this module type is mod_footer.

The module parameters section contains only one option. Caching allows you to exempt a specific module from the site's caching, as set in the Global Configuration. Select the option No Caching to prevent the contents of this module from being cached. The default setting is Use Global.

FIGURE 18.8

The output of the Footer module, in this case displayed in the Title Module Position.

Footer module

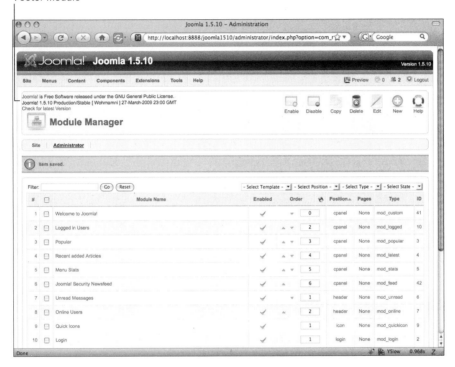

To add a Footer module to your site, follow these steps:

1. **Log in to the admin system of your site.**

2. **Access the Module Manager. To do so, go to the Extensions menu and select the Module Manager option.** The Module Manager loads in your browser.

3. **Click the link Administrator.** The Administrator Module Manager loads in your browser.

4. **Click the New icon on the toolbar at the top of the Module Manager.** The New Module dialogue opens. (Refer to Figure 18.2.)

5. **Select the option Footer and then click the Next button.** The Footer module dialogue loads in your browser.

6. **In the title field, type a name for the module.** This field is required.

7. **Set the option Enabled to Yes.**

8. **Set the position of the module.**

9. Select any additional options you wish; all other fields are optional.

10. Click the Save icon on the toolbar at the top right to save your new module. The dialogue closes and returns you to the Administrator Module Manager.

Item Stats module

The Item Stats module will display a list of all the menu items in your system, together with links to the individual menus. The default system includes one Item Stats module. The module is named Menu Stats and is assigned to the Cpanel Module Position, as shown in Figure 18.9. The module output appears on only the Control Panel.

Note

The system name for this module type is mod_stats.

The module parameters section contains only one option — Caching. This control allows you to exempt a specific module from the site's caching, as set in the Global Configuration. Select the option No Caching to prevent the contents of this module from being cached. The default setting is Use Global.

FIGURE 18.9

The Item Stats module, shown here as it appears on the Control Panel in the default installation.

Item Stats module

To add an Item Stats module to your site, follow these steps:

1. **Log in to the admin system of your site.**

2. **Access the Module Manager.** To do so, go to the Extensions menu and select the Module Manager option. The Module Manager loads in your browser.

3. **Click the link Administrator.** The Administrator Module Manager loads in your browser.

4. **Click the New icon on the toolbar at the top of the Module Manager.** The New Module dialogue opens. (Refer to Figure 18.2.)

5. **Select the option Item Stats and then click the Next button.** The Item Stats Module dialogue loads in your browser.

6. **In the Title field, type a name for the module.** This field is required.

7. **Set the option Enabled to Yes.**

8. **Set the Position of the module.**

9. **Select any additional options you want; all other fields are optional.**

10. **Click the Save icon on the toolbar at the top right to save your new module.** The dialogue closes and returns you to the Administrator Module Manager.

Latest News module

The Latest News module is somewhat misnamed, because it shows not the latest news items, but rather the most recently added articles. The module output shows a list of the ten most recent items, along with the creation date and time and the name of the author, as shown in Figure 18.10. The names of the articles are clickable and open the articles in editing view.

The default system includes one Latest News module. The module is named Recently Added Articles, and is assigned to the Cpanel module position, as shown in Figure 18.10. The module output appears on only the Control Panel.

Note

The system name for this module type is mod_latest.

The module parameters section contains three controls:

- **Order:** Provides two options for ordering the articles. The choices are Recently Added First and Recently Modified First.

- **Authors:** The Authors combo box provides a filter for the list, in this case based on the identity of the author of the articles. The options are: Anyone, Added or modified by me, and Not added or modified by me.

- **Caching:** This control allows you to exempt a specific module from the site's caching, as set in the Global Configuration. Select the option No Caching to prevent the contents of this Module from being cached. The default setting is Use Global.

FIGURE 18.10

The Latest News module, shown here in the default configuration, appearing on the Control Panel in the Cpanel module position.

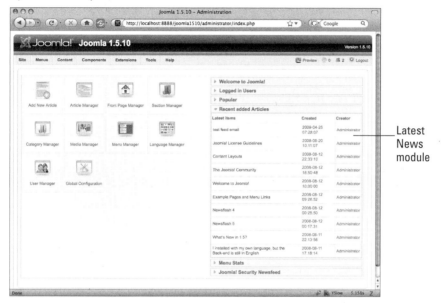

To add a Latest News module to your site, follow these steps:

1. Log in to the admin system of your site.

2. **Access the Module Manager. To do so, go to the Extensions menu and select the Module Manager option.** The Module Manager loads in your browser.

3. **Click the link Administrator.** The Administrator Module Manager loads in your browser.

4. **Click the New icon on the toolbar at the top of the Module Manager.** The New Module dialogue opens. (Refer to Figure 18.2.)

5. **Select the option Latest News and then click the Next button.** The Latest News Module dialogue loads in your browser.

6. **In the Title field, type a name for the module.** This field is required.

7. Set the option Enabled to Yes.

8. Set the position of the module.

9. Select any additional options you wish; all other fields are optional.

10. Click the Save icon on the toolbar at the top right to save your new module. The dialogue closes and returns you to the Administrator Module Manager.

Tip

This module is particularly useful in sites that have multiple administrators or multiple content creators because it allows you to see at a glance what has been changed.

Logged In Users module

The Logged In Users module displays a list of all the users of the system that are currently logged in. The list includes the user's name with a link to their data in the User Manager, an indication of their Group membership, the time of their last activity on the site, and an option to force the user to log out. In the default system there is one Logged In Users module. The module is named Logged in Users and is assigned to the Cpanel Module Position. The output appears on only the Control Panel, as shown in Figure 18.11.

Note

The system name for this module type is mod_logged.

The module parameters section contains only one control — Caching. This control allows you to exempt a specific module from the site's caching, as set in the Global Configuration. Select the option No Caching to prevent the contents of this module from being cached. The default setting is Use Global.

To add a Logged in Users module to your site, follow these steps:

1. **Log in to the admin system of your site.**

2. **Access the Module Manager. To do so, go to the Extensions menu and select the Module Manager option.** The Module Manager loads in your browser.

3. **Click the link Administrator.** The Administrator Module Manager loads in your browser.

4. **Click the New icon on the toolbar at the top of the Module Manager.** The New Module dialogue opens. (Refer to Figure 18.2.)

5. **Select the option Logged in Users and then click the Next button.** The Logged in Users Module dialogue loads in your browser.

6. **In the Title field, type a name for the module.** This field is required.

7. **Set the option Enabled to Yes.**

8. **Set the position of the module.**

9. **Select any additional options you wish; all other fields are optional.**

10. **Click the Save icon on the toolbar at the top right to save your new module.** The dialogue closes and returns you to the Administrator Module Manager.

FIGURE 18.11

The Logged in Users module in action, here shown assigned to the Cpanel module position on the Control Panel.

Logged in Users module

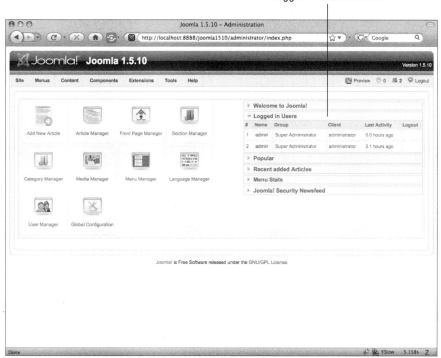

Cross-Reference

Turn to Chapter 11 for an extended discussion of user management.

Login Form module

The Login Form module supplies the Login Form used to access the administration system. The default system includes one Login Form module, named Login. The module is assigned to the Login module position and appears only on the admin entry page, as shown in Figure 18.12. This module is essential for the system and cannot be disabled.

Note

The system name for this module type is mod_login.

FIGURE 18.12

The output of the Login Form module, seen here on the admin entry page.

Login Form module

The module parameters section contains two controls:

- **Caching:** This control allows you to exempt a specific module from the site's caching, as set in the Global Configuration. Select the option No Caching to prevent the contents of this module from being cached. The default setting is Use Global.

- **Encrypt Login Form:** This parameter allows you to enable SSL for log-in process. Although this is more secure, if your server does not have SSL enabled, this option does not work.

To add a Login Form module to your site, follow these steps:

1. **Log in to the admin system of your site.**

2. **Access the Module Manager. To do so, go to the Extensions menu and select the Module Manager option.** The Module Manager loads in your browser.

3. **Click the link Administrator.** The Administrator Module Manager loads in your browser.

4. **Click the New icon on the toolbar at the top of the Module Manager.** The New Module dialogue opens. (Refer to Figure 18.2.)

5. **Select the option Login Form, and then click the Next button.** The Login Form Module dialogue loads in your browser.

6. **In the Title field, type a name for the Module.** This is a required field.

7. **Set the option Enabled to Yes.**

8. **Set the Position of the Module to Login.**

9. **Select any additional options you wish;** all other fields are optional.

10. **Click the Save icon on the toolbar at the top right to save your new module.** The dialogue closes and returns you to the Administrator Module Manager.

Tip

This is one of the system's modules that is better left untouched. There are no real options here, other than to enable SSL.

Online Users module

The Online Users module can be used to display the number of visitors who are currently viewing the front end of your web site.

Note

Although the descriptive text for this item says it displays the number of "Back-end Users that are logged in" this is not actually accurate — the module shows the number of front-end visitors. The number of back-end visitors that are logged in is shown on the User Status module that appears on the top right of the screen of all admin pages.

This module exists in the default system and although it is enabled, it is assigned to an inactive module position, Header. The default Khepri admin template does not include a module position named Header. The default module is named simply Online Users. Figure 18.13 shows the output of the module.

Note

The system name for this module type is mod_online.

The module parameters section contains only one option, Caching, and it is permanently set to Never. This option cannot be changed.

FIGURE 18.13

The Online Users module published to the Status module position.

To add an Online Users module to your site, follow these steps:

1. **Log in to the admin system of your site.**

2. **Access the Module Manager. To do so, go to the Extensions menu and select the Module Manager option.** The Module Manager loads in your browser.

3. **Click the link Administrator.** The Administrator Module Manager loads in your browser.

4. **Click the New icon on the toolbar at the top of the Module Manager.** The New Module dialogue opens. (Refer to Figure 18.2.)

5. **Select the option Online Users and then click the Next button.** The Online Users module dialogue loads in your browser.

6. **In the Title field, type a name for the module.** This is a required field.

7. **Set the option Enabled to Yes.**

8. **Set the position of the module.**

9. **Select any additional options you wish; all other fields are optional.**

10. **Click the Save icon on the toolbar at the top right to save your new module. The dialogue closes and returns you to the Administrator Module Manager.**

Tip

The Online Users module makes a nice addition to the admin interface and shows you information that is not readily available elsewhere. The most logical place to assign it is to the Status module position; unfortunately, due to the way the template is constructed, the only place you can put it is to the right of the existing User Status module, crammed up against the right hand frame of the page. If you try to place the module to the left of the User Status icons, the template forces the display to expand to take up two lines, which is not very aesthetically pleasing.

Popular Articles module

The Popular Articles module displays a list of the ten most frequently viewed articles on your web site. The module shows the name of the article, the created date and time, and the number of hits the article has received during its lifetime. You can click an article's title to open the article in editing view.

The default system includes one Popular Articles module. The module is named Popular and is assigned to the Cpanel module position, as shown in Figure 18.14. The module output only appears on the right side of the Control Panel; due to the module assignment it does not show on the internal pages.

Note

The system name for this module type is mod_popular.

The module parameters section contains only one option, Caching, and it is permanently set to Never. This option cannot be changed.

To add a Popular Articles module to your site, follow these steps:

1. **Log in to the admin system of your site.**
2. **Access the Module Manager. To do so, go to the Extensions menu and select the Module Manager option.** The Module Manager loads in your browser.
3. **Click the link Administrator.** The Administrator Module Manager loads in your browser.
4. **Click the New icon on the toolbar at the top of the Module Manager.** The New Module dialogue opens. (Refer to Figure 18.2.)
5. **Select the option Popular Articles and then click the Next button.** The Popular Articles module dialogue loads in your browser.
6. **In the Title field, type a name for the module.** This field is required.
7. **Set the option Enabled to Yes.**
8. **Set the position of the module.**
9. **Select any additional options you wish; all other fields are optional.**
10. **Click the Save icon on the toolbar at the top right to save your new module.** The dialogue closes and returns you to the Administrator Module Manager.

FIGURE 18.14

The output of the Popular Articles module, shown here in the default Cpanel module position on the Admin Control Panel.

Popular Articles module

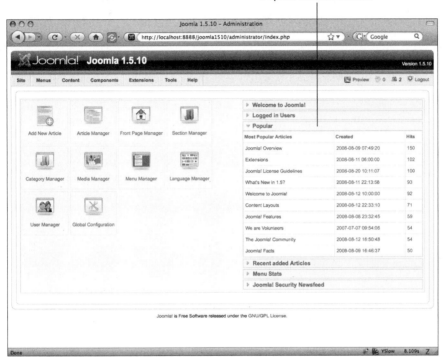

Quick Icons module

The Quick Icons module produces the shortcut icons that show on the left-hand side of the Control Panel, as shown in Figure 18.15. The default system includes one instance of the Quick Icons module. The module is assigned to the Icon module position holder. The Icon module position appears only on the Control Panel page and does not appear on the internal admin system pages.

Note

The system name for this module type is mod_quickicon.

The module parameters section contains only one control, Caching. This control allows you to exempt a specific module from the site's caching, as set in the Global Configuration. Select the option No Caching to prevent the contents of this module from being cached. The default setting is Use Global.

FIGURE 18.15

The Quick Icons module, shown here in the default position on the Control Panel.

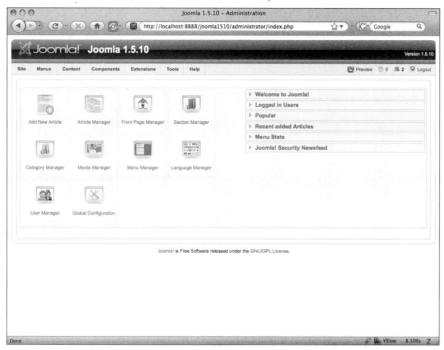

To add a Quick Icons module to your site, follow these steps:

1. Log in to the admin system of your site.

2. **Access the Module Manager. To do so, go to the Extensions menu and select the Module Manager option.** The Module Manager loads in your browser.

3. **Click the link Administrator.** The Administrator Module Manager loads in your browser.

4. **Click the New icon on the toolbar at the top of the Module Manager.** The New Module dialogue opens. (Refer to Figure 18.2.)

5. **Select the option Quick Icons and then click the Next button.** The Quick Icons module dialogue loads in your browser.

6. **In the Title field, type a name for the module.** This field is required.

7. Set the option Enabled to Yes.

8. Set the position of the module.

9. Select any additional options you wish; all other fields are optional.

10. **Click the Save icon on the toolbar at the top right to save your new module.** The dialogue closes and returns you to the Administrator Module Manager.

Note

As a practical matter, this module can only be displayed in the Icon module position. Although it is physically possible to assign it to the Title module position, that module position is not active on the Control Panel, hence the output does not appear on the Control Panel page. The only alternative for getting the Quick Icons on both the Control Panel and the internal pages is to create two instances of this module; assigning one to the default Icon position and another to the Title position.

Title module

The Title module displays the page title seen on many of the interior admin system pages. The default system includes one Title module named Title and assigned to the Title module position, as shown in Figure 18.16.

Note

The system name for this module type is mod_title.

FIGURE 18.16

The output of the Title module.

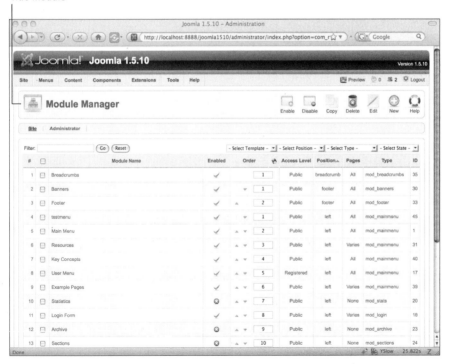

The module parameters section contains only one option, Caching, and it is permanently set to Never. This option cannot be changed.

To add a Title module to your site, follow these steps:

1. **Log in to the admin system of your site.**

2. **Access the Module Manager. To do so, go to the Extensions menu and select the Module Manager option.** The Module Manager loads in your browser.

3. **Click the link Administrator.** The Administrator Module Manager loads in your browser.

4. **Click the New icon on the toolbar at the top of the Module Manager.** The New Module dialogue opens. (Refer to Figure 18.2.)

5. **Select the option Admin Sub Menu and then click the Next button.** The Admin Sub Menu Module dialogue loads in your browser.

6. **In the Title field, type a name for the module.** This field is required.

7. **Set the option Enabled to Yes.**

8. **Set the position of the module.**

9. **Select any additional options you wish; all other fields are optional.**

10. **Click the Save icon on the toolbar at the top right to save your new module.** The dialogue closes and returns you to the Administrator Module Manager.

Toolbar module

The Toolbar module provides the icons seen at the top right of the admin system pages. The icons provide quick access to essential tasks throughout the system. The output of this module is essential for the site administrator.

The default system contains one instance of the Toolbar module; it is named Toolbar and is assigned to the Toolbar module position, as shown in Figure 18.17.

Note
The system name for this module type is mod_toolbar.

The module parameters section contains only one option, Caching, and it is permanently set to Never. This option cannot be changed.

FIGURE 18.17

The Toolbar module, shown here assigned to the default Toolbar module position.

Toolbar
module

To add a Toolbar module to your site, follow these steps:

1. Log in to the admin system of your site.

2. Access the Module Manager. To do so, go to the Extensions menu and select the Module Manager option. The Module Manager loads in your browser.

3. Click the link Administrator. The Administrator Module Manager loads in your browser.

4. Click the New icon on the toolbar at the top of the Module Manager. The New Module dialogue opens. (Refer to Figure 18.2.)

5. Select the option Toolbar and then click the Next button. The Toolbar module dialogue loads in your browser.

6. In the Title field, type a name for the module. This field is required.

7. Set the option Enabled to Yes.

8. Set the position of the module.

9. Select any additional options you wish; all other fields are optional.

10. Click the Save icon on the toolbar at the top right to save your new module. The dialogue closes and returns you to the Administrator Module Manager.

Caution

This is one of the Administrator modules that is best left alone — changing this module's position assignment can result in the icons being inaccessible, thereby making it impossible for the administrator to make further changes to the system!

Unread Messages module

The Unread Messages module shows an icon indicating the number of unread messages that exist in the Private Messaging system. The icon is clickable and links to the admin system's Private Messaging Manager, as shown in Figure 18.18.

Cross-Reference

The Private Messaging system is discussed in more detail in Chapter 19.

This module exists in the default system and although it is enabled, it is assigned to an inactive module position, Header. The default Khepri admin template does not include a module position named Header. The default Module is named simply Unread Messages.

Note

The system name for this module type is mod_unread.

The module parameters section contains only one option, Caching, and it is permanently set to Never. This option cannot be changed.

To add an Unread Messages module to your site, follow these steps:

1. Log in to the admin system of your site.

2. **Access the Module Manager. To do so, go to the Extensions menu and select the Module Manager option.** The Module Manager loads in your browser.

3. **Click the link Administrator.** The Administrator Module Manager loads in your browser.

4. **Click the New icon on the toolbar at the top of the Module Manager.** The New Module dialogue opens. (Refer to Figure 18.2.)

5. **Select the option Unread Messages and then click the Next button.** The Unread Messages module dialogue loads in your browser.

6. **In the Title field, type a name for the module.** This field is required.

7. **Set the option Enabled to Yes.**

8. **Set the position of the module.**

9. **Select any additional options you wish; all other fields are optional.**

10. **Click the Save icon on the toolbar at the top right to save your new module.** The dialogue closes and returns you to the Administrator Module Manager.

FIGURE 18.18

The Unread Messages module, shown here assigned to the Toolbar module position.

Unread Messages module

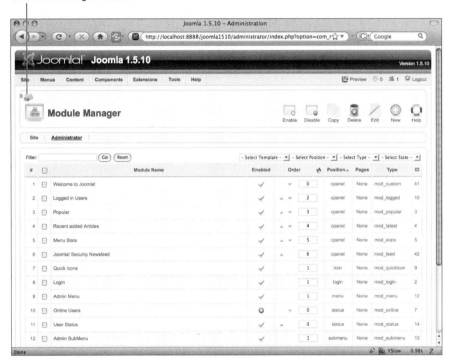

Tip

The Unread Messages module is redundant with the User Status module. The User Status module includes a mail messages icon that serves the exact same function as the Unread Messages module.

User Status module

The User Status module supplies the four icons seen at the top right of each admin system page. The four icons provide the following functions: a link to the preview function, an indication of how many messages the user has, an indication of the number of back-end users logged in, and a link to log out of the system.

The default system includes one instance of the User Status module. The module is named User Status and is defined to the Status module position, as shown in Figure 18.19.

Note

The system name for this module type is mod_status.

FIGURE 18.19

The output of the User Status module, shown in the default position.

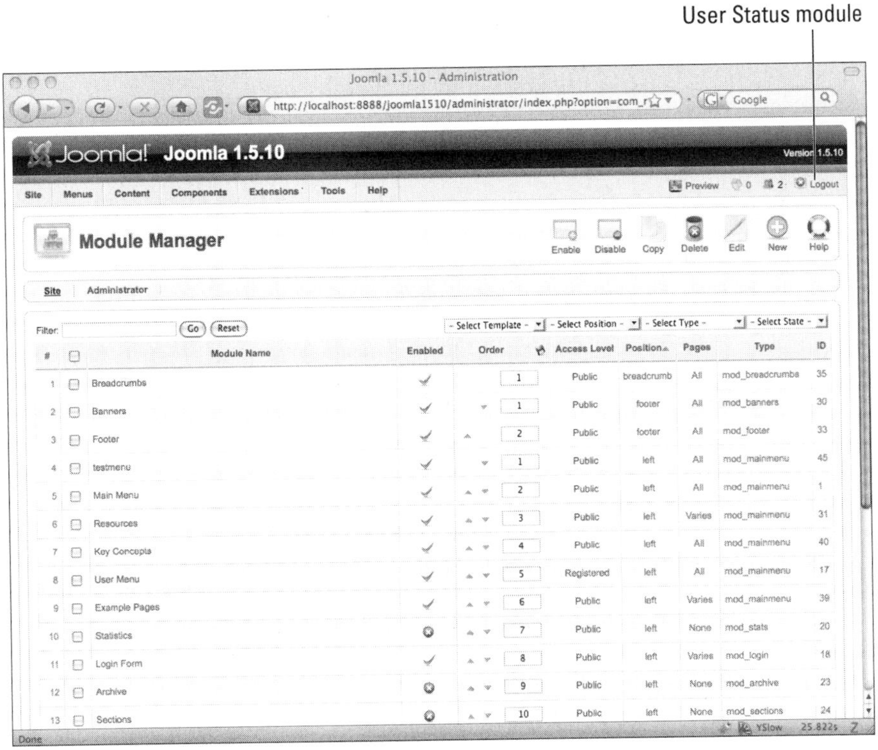

The module parameters section contains only one option, Caching, and it is permanently set to Never. This option cannot be changed.

To add a User Status module to your site, follow these steps:

1. **Log in to the admin system of your site.**

2. **Access the Module Manager.** To do so, go to the Extensions menu and select the Module Manager option. The Module Manager loads in your browser.

3. **Click the link Administrator.** The Administrator Module Manager loads in your browser.

4. **Click the New icon on the toolbar at the top of the Module Manager.** The New Module dialogue opens. (Refer to Figure 18.2.)

5. **Select the option User Status and then click the Next button.** The User Status module dialogue loads in your browser.

6. **In the Title field, type a name for the module.** This field is required.

7. Set the option Enabled to Yes.

8. Set the position of the module.

9. Select any additional options you wish; all other fields are optional.

10. **Click the Save icon on the toolbar at the top right to save your new module.** The dialogue closes and returns you to the Administrator Module Manager.

Summary

In this chapter, we have covered the use of the Administrator modules. You learned the following:

- How to use the Administrator Module Manager
- How to create, edit, and delete new Administrator modules
- The nature and uses of the core Administrator modules

Working with Plugins

Plugins are small, specialized pieces of code that typically run only when triggered by an event. Plugins are used as "helper" applications, providing bits of additional functionality or extending existing Joomla! functions.

The default Joomla! system includes 32 plugins. They provide a number of significant and useful functions, including login authentication, site search, search engine friendly URLs, and the WYSIWYG content editor. Although not all of the 32 plugins are enabled in the default configuration, the majority are in use by the system. Several of them are essential to the proper functioning of your Joomla! site and should only be disabled if you understand fully the implications and have planned accordingly.

Note

Plugins first appeared in Joomla! with the release of Version 1.5. Prior to version 1.5, the system used helper extensions called *mambots*. Although mambots and plugins are similar in function, they are not identical and cannot be interchanged.

Introducing the Plugin Manager

The Joomla! plugins are controlled through the Plugin Manager. The manager contains all the system plugins, together with any third-party plugins you may have installed. To view the plugins in your site, log in to the Admin system and go to the Extensions menu. Select the option Plugin Manager, and the Plugin Manager loads in your browser window, as shown in Figure 19.1.

FIGURE 19.1

The Plugin Manager, showing the plugins in Joomla! 1.5.x.

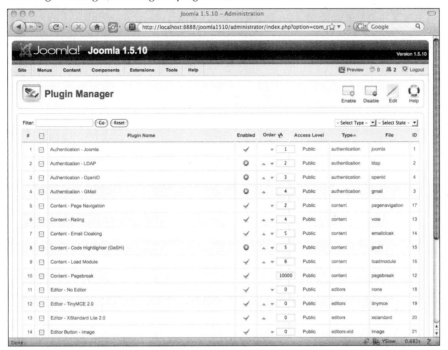

The toolbar at the top of the Plugin Manager provides quick access to the following functions:

- **Enable:** Select one or more plugins from the list and then click this icon to enable them.
- **Disable:** Select one or more plugins from the list and then click this icon to disable them.
- **Edit:** Select a plugin from the list and then click this icon to edit the plugin's details.
- **Help:** Click to access the online Help files related to the active screen.

Below the toolbar are three sorting and searching tools to help you filter the list of plugins:

- **The Filter field** on the left works like a search box. Type a word or phrase into the text box and then click Go. The page reloads and displays the results of the search. To clear the screen and return to a full listing, click the Reset button.
- **Select Type filter** located in the middle allows you to show the plugins by Plugin type. To reset this filter, change the combo box back to the default setting.
- **The Select State filter** on the far right allows you to filter and display the plugins according to whether they are published or unpublished. You can easily identify all the plugins that are currently active on the site. To reset this filter, change the combo box back to the default setting.

Tip

The Select Type filter and the Select State filter can be combined to further refine the view of the list of plugins.

The main content area of the screen contains a list of all the plugins in your site Plugins Manager. The columns provided are:

- **#** : An indexing number assigned by Joomla! This number cannot be changed.

- **Checkbox (no label):** Click in a checkbox to select a plugin; this is needed if you want to use several of the toolbar options.

- **Plugin Name:** This field displays the full name of the plugin. Click the name to edit the plugin's details.

- **Enabled:** A green checkmark in this column indicates that the plugin is published. The field shows a red X if the plugin is not published. Administrators can toggle between the two settings by clicking the icons.

- **Order:** The numbers in this field affect the ordering of the plugins on this list. Change the numbers and click the Save icon at the top of the column to reorder the plugins.

- **Access Level:** Displays the Access Level that has been specified for the plugin. You can click on the label to toggle between Public, Registered, and Special, or you can modify this by editing the settings inside the plugin.

- **Type:** The type of the plugin. Each plugin can be of only one type.

- **File:** The name of the plugin file. Note that each plugin has two files, a .php file and an .xml file. Do not change the value in this field.

- **ID:** The system-generated user ID number.

At the bottom of the screen, below the content area, is the Display # option. Change the value in the combo box control to alter the number of plugins that are displayed on the page. The default value can be altered by changing the List Length option on the Global Configuration Manager.

Cross-Reference

See Chapter 25 for a discussion on adding new plugins, and turn to Chapter 24 to see how to create plugins.

Editing and deleting plugins

Existing plugins can be edited from the Plugin Manager. To edit a plugin, either click the plugin name in the Plugin Manager, or select the plugin on the list and then click the Edit icon on the Plugin Manager toolbar. Regardless of which method you use, the system opens the Edit Plugin dialogue.

The Edit Plugin dialogue is identical to the New Plugin dialogue, with the same fields and requirements.

To make changes to a plugin, simply alter the desired fields in the Edit Plugin dialogue and then click the Save or Apply icon on the toolbar. Any changes you have made are applied immediately.

To delete one or more plugins, follow these steps:

1. Open the Plugin Manager.

2. Select one or more plugins.

3. Click the Delete icon.

Caution

Deleting Admin plugins is rarely appropriate. All the existing plugin types provide functional output in the default system. Some of the plugins are essential and the deletion of the plugin may make administering the site difficult. Note the Login plugin in particular, which cannot be disabled or deleted. In general, you should be cautious about deleting plugins because there is no confirmation dialogue — clicking the Delete icon immediately deletes the plugin!

Reviewing the Default Plugins

The workspace of each plugin dialogue is divided into two areas: Details and Parameters. The Details portions of all the plugin types are identical. There are few options associated with plugins, and those few that exist are found in the Parameters area of each plugin's workspace. A typical plugin workspace is shown in Figure 19.2.

The toolbar at the top of the plugin dialogue provides quick access to the following functions:

- **Save:** Click this icon to save your work and exit the plugin dialogue.

- **Apply:** Click to save your work without exiting from the plugin dialogue. This option lets you save without exiting the screen, and it useful in case you are interrupted or you otherwise want to save yet keep working on this screen.

- **Close:** Cancels the task and exits the Plugin Manager.

- **Help:** Displays the Help files related to the active screen.

The Details section of the workspace contains the following fields:

- **Name:** The name given to the plugin.

- **Enabled:** Select Yes to make the plugin active. The default state varies by plugin.

- **Type:** This identifier is set by the system and tells you the type of plugin. This cannot be changed.

- **Plugin File:** The name of the plugin file. Each plugin has two files associated with it; one .php and one .xml. Do not change the value in this field.

- **Access Level:** Choose from Public, Registered, or Special to set the access level for this plugin. Setting the plugin to a level higher than Public may result in some functionality working incorrectly for some site visitors.

- **Order:** Sets the order of the plugin relative to other enabled plugins of the same type. The order impacts the sequence in which plugins are activated and so may have impact on some functionality in limited circumstances. Do not change this from the default setting absent a compelling reason.

- **Description:** Joomla! provides this description text to help users understand the use of the plugin.

The Parameters section varies for each plugin. Details on the parameters for each plugin are discussed in the sections that follow.

FIGURE 19.2

A typical plugin dialogue, in this case, the Authentication - LDAP plugin. The Toolbar and Details sections are the same for all plugin types; the Parameters section varies by plugin type.

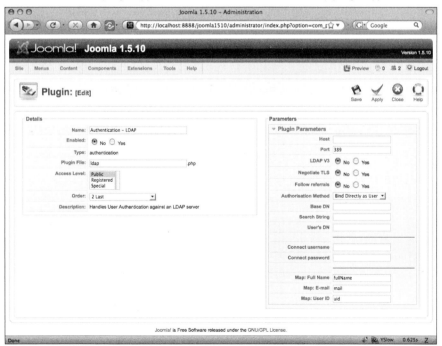

Authentication plugins

The Authentication plugins are responsible for handling the user authentication processes in Joomla! The system offers several alternative methods for handling authentication. The default method is the system-specific Joomla Plugin. Alternatives include Gmail, LDAP, and OpenID. In the default configuration only the Authentication - Joomla Plugin is active. If you want to use any of the alternative methods, you need to enable and configure the appropriate plugin from the Plugin Manager.

Note

The Authentication plugin files are located in the directory

```
plugins/authentication.
```

Joomla

The Authentication - Joomla Plugin provides the default Joomla! authentication scheme. This plugin is enabled in the default system and should not be disabled unless you have made provision for alternative authentication. The Authentication - Joomla Plugin dialogue is shown in Figure 19.3.

FIGURE 19.3

The Authentication - Joomla Plugin dialogue.

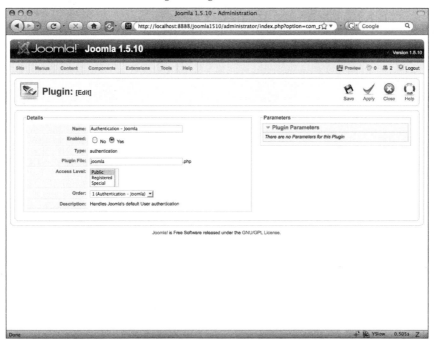

Note

The principal file for this plugin type is joomla.php.

No parameters are associated with this plugin.

Caution

Do not disable this plugin if you have not enabled an alternative Authentication plugin. Leaving the system with no active Authentication plugins causes problems.

LDAP

The Authentication - LDAP plugin allows you to configure your site to connect with an LDAP server. LDAP, or *Lightweight Directory Access Protocol*, is used in some systems to access directory systems over TCP/IP. The LDAP plugin is bundled with the Joomla! system but it is not enabled in the default configuration. If you want to use this plugin, you will need to enable it and set the configuration parameters. The plugin dialogue is shown in Figure 19.4.

Note

The principal file for this plugin is ldap.php.

FIGURE 19.4

The Authentication - LDAP Plugin dialogue.

The plugin Parameters section contains the following options:

- **Host:** Type into this field the URL of the LDAP server.

- **Port:** Set the Port to be used for the connection to the LDAP server. The default setting is 389.

- **LDAP V3:** Click Yes if your system is using LDAP V3.

- **Negotiate TLS:** Set to Yes to employ TLS encryption for traffic to and from the server.

- **Follow referrals:** Click Yes to set the LDAP_OPT_REFERRALS flag to yes.

- **Authorisation Method:** Sets the authorization method used in the LDAP connection. The default option is Bind Directly as User, and the alternative is Bind and Search.

- **Base DN:** Type here the Base DN of your LDAP server.

- **Search String:** Sets the query string to search for a user. This field supports multiple query strings, separated by semicolons.

- **User's DN:** This is only used if the Authorization Method Parameter is set to Bind Directly as a User. The field supports a string that dynamically matches the username typed by the user with the DN pattern of the user entry in LDAP.

- **Connect Username:** Set up the username needed to negotiate the DN phase of the connection. For an anonymous connection, leave this blank. If you enter a value here, you also need to complete the next field, Connect password.

- **Connect Password**: Set up the password needed to negotiate the DN phase of the connection. For an anonymous connection, leave this blank. The password is related to the Connect username.

- **Map: Full Name:** Enter the name of the LDAP attribute that contains the user's full name.

- **Map: E-mail:** Enter the name of the LDAP attribute that contains the user's e-mail address.

- **Map: User ID:** Enter the name of the LDAP attribute that contains the user's user ID.

Note

LDAP setup can be confusing, largely due to the number of options that exist on both sides of the equation — the LDAP server and the Joomla! CMS. There also exist several third-party extensions that can be added to your system to make LDAP more useful with features such as Single Sign On and Kerberos support. A good place to start is with this article in the Joomla! Community Magazine: http://community.joomla.org/magazine/article/507-developer-ldap-from-scratch-sam-moffett.html

OpenID

OpenID is an authentication protocol of growing popularity. Users who have a valid OpenID account can use their OpenID username to gain access to any site that supports login with OpenID. The Joomla! system includes an OpenID Authentication Plugin, but it is not enabled in the default system. If you want to enable OpenID on your site, you need to enable the plugin and configure the parameters. The plugin's dialogue is shown in Figure 19.5.

The Authentication - OpenID Plugin dialogue.

Note
The principal file for this plugin is openid.php.

Note
The plugin supports the newer OpenID 2.0.

GMail

The GMail Authentication plugin allows users to log in to your Joomla site using their GMail I.D. The Joomla! system includes the GMail Authentication plugin but it is not enabled in the default system. If you want to enable your site to accept logins with GMail credentials, then you need to enable the plugin and follow the following outlined steps . The plugin's dialogue is shown in Figure 19.6.

Note
The principal file for this plugin is gmail.php.

FIGURE 19.6

The Authentication - GMail Plugin dialogue.

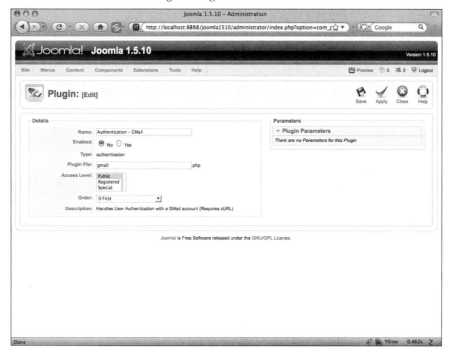

There are no parameters associated with this plugin.

To use GMail for authentication on your site the user must follow these steps:

1. Create a user account on the Joomla! site with the same name as the GMail user account.

2. Log out of Joomla!

3. The user can now log back in to the site using their GMail identity.

Note

You must have cURL installed on your server to use the GMail Authentication plugin. To learn more about cURL, visit, `http://curl.haxx.se/.`

Content plugins

The Content plugins provide various enhancements to the Joomla! articles. With the exception of the GeSHI Code Highlighter plugin, all are enabled and are used by the default system. Few parameters exist for this group of plugins.

Note

The Content plugin files are located in the directory `plugins/content`.

Page Navigation

The Page Navigation Plugin supplies the back, next and numbered page features you see in certain content areas of the site. This plugin is enabled by default. The plugin's dialogue is shown in Figure 19.7.

Note

The principal file for this plugin is pagenavigation.php.

The plugin Parameters section contains only one option: Position. The default setting is Below, which results in the Page Navigation being displayed below the article text. Set it to Above to move the display to the top, over the article text.

FIGURE 19.7

The Content - Page Navigation plugin dialogue.

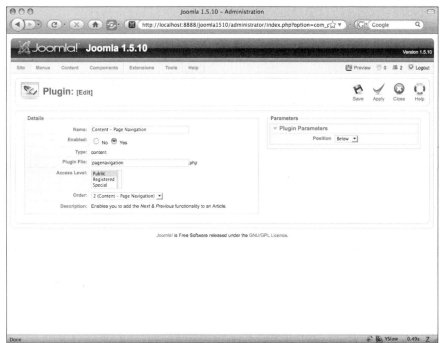

Note

If you want to hide this feature on your articles, it is not necessary to disable to the plugin, although that is one option. The easiest way to control this feature is through the site's Global Configuration and through the parameters associated with menu items.

Rating

The Ratings plugin enables the article ratings functionality in Joomla! This plugin is enabled by default. The plugin's dialogue is shown in Figure 19.8.

Note

The principal file for this plugin is vote.php.

There are no parameters associated with this plugin.

FIGURE 19.8

The Content - Rating plugin dialogue.

Note

If you want to hide this feature on your articles, it is not necessary to disable to the plugin, athough that is one option. The most flexible way to control this feature is through the site's Global Configuration and through the parameters associated with menu items.

Email Cloaking

The Email Cloaking plugin provides your site with a measure of protection against SPAM spiders and bots that try to harvest unprotected e-mail addresses from web sites. The plugin works by hiding e-mail addresses in content items. This plugin is enabled by default. The plugin's dialogue is shown in Figure 19.9.

Note

The principal file for this plugin is emailcloak.php.

FIGURE 19.9

The Content - Email Cloaking Plugin dialogue.

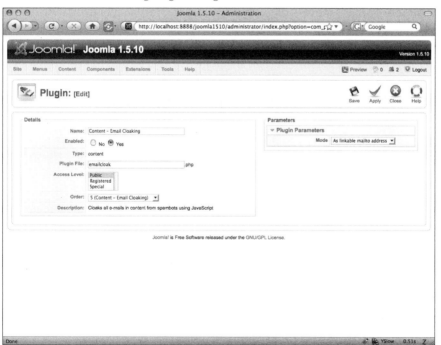

The plugin Parameters section contains only one control: Mode. This parameter determines the techniques used to hide the e-mail address. The default, As linkable mailto address, uses JavaScript to hide the e-mail address from spiders and bots, yet still allow the address to be functional and clickable. The other options, Non-linkable Text, simple converts the e-mail address to text and strips out any link to the e-mail functionality.

Tip

If you want to disable cloaking selectively, you can do so by inserting anywhere in the article the following tag

```
{emailcloak=off}
```

Code Highlighter (GeSHi)

The Code Highlighter Plugin adds GeSHI style formatting to any code you display to visitors on your site. This plugin is useful where your articles on your site include samples of code displayed in the article for viewers to see. GeSHI makes the code more readable by adding standardized code formatting to the text. This plugin is disabled by default; if you want to use it you must enable it. The plugin's dialogue is shown in Figure 19.10.

FIGURE 19.10

The Content - Code Highlighter (GeSHi) Plugin dialogue.

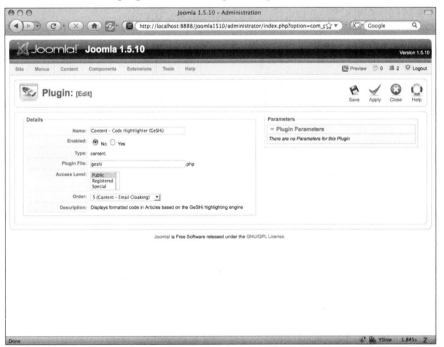

Note

The principal file for this plugin is geshi.php.

There are no parameters associated with this plugin.

Load Module

The Load Module plugin enables you to add modules inside of the content area of articles. This plugin exists in the default system and is enabled. The plugin's dialogue is shown in Figure 19.11.

Cross-Reference

See Chapter 7 for more on working with modules inside of articles.

Note

The principal file for this plugin is loadmodule.php.

FIGURE 19.11

The Content - Load Module plugin dialogue.

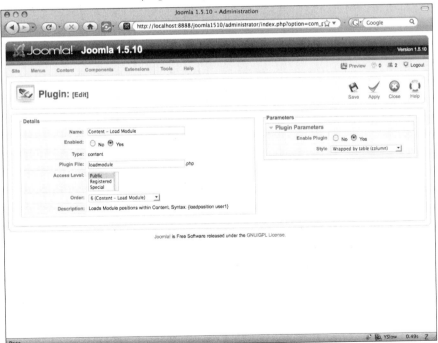

The plugin Parameters section contains two options:

- **Enable Plugin:** Set this control to Yes to enable the plugin. Note that this control is redundant with the Enabled control in the Details area; both must indicate the plugin is enabled for it to work properly.

- **Style:** This control allows you to specify how the system handles the styling of the module position. The options are: Wrapped by table (column); Wrapped by table (horizontal); Wrapped by Divs; Wrapped by Multiple Divs; No wrapping (raw output).

Tip

Managing the styling of modules inserted inside of articles can be a challenge. If you are uncertain which style approach is best for your purposes, try the various options, viewing the source code of the resulting article containing the module. In this way you can find the approach that works best for you and provides you with the selectors you need to style the module appropriately.

Pagebreak

The Pagebreak plugin enables the easy creation of multipage articles and article tables of contents. The plugin is enabled by default. The plugin's dialogue is shown in Figure 19.12.

FIGURE 19.12

The Content - Pagebreak Plugin dialogue.

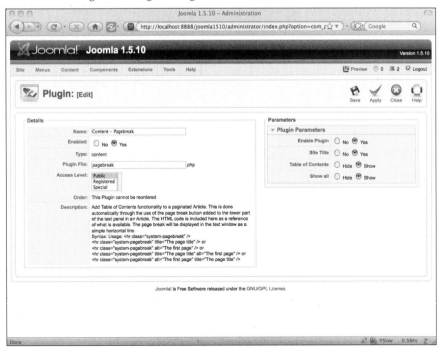

Note

The principal file for this plugin is pagebreak.php.

The plugin Parameters section contains the following options:

- **Enable Plugin:** Set this control to Yes to enable the plugin. Note that this control is redundant with the Enabled control in the Details area; both must indicate the plugin is enabled for it to work properly.

- **Site Title:** Determines whether the titles you set for the individual pages of the article are added to the Site Title tag. Set the control to Yes to enable this feature.

- **Table of Contents:** Set this control to Show to display a table of contents for the multi-page article.

- **Show All:** Set the control to show to display a link to in the table of contents that will show all the pages together on one page.

Cross-Reference

See Chapter 5 for a more complete discussion on how to create multipage articles and tables of contents.

Editor plugins

The Editor plugins add various content item- editing options to the system. This family of plugins provides the WYSIWYG editor functionality and the plain text editor functionality. Two of the three options, including the popular TinyMCE WYSIWYG editor are enabled by default.

Caution

You must have at least one of the Editor plugins installed to access your content items in the admin system.

The question of which editor, if any, will be used throughout the site is determined by the settings in the Global Configuration Manager. The options that appear on that screen are the result of enabling the various plugins.

Cross-Reference

Working with the various editors to create and edit content is discussed in detail in Chapter 6.

Note

The Editor plugin files are located in the directory `plugins/editors`.

No Editor

The No Editor plugin supplies the basic text editor option for content items. There is no WYSIWYG editor associated with this option. If the system is set to No Editor, then content creation is done in a plain text interface, where the content creator needs to add HTML tags to achieve formatting; it is the most basic editing option in Joomla! The plugin's dialogue is shown in Figure 19.13.

Note

The principal file for this plugin is none.php.

There are no parameters associated with this plugin.

Note

If you have the TinyMCE editor enabled, users can still edit the HTML of the article by clicking on the HTML button on the TinyMCE toolbar.

TinyMCE 2.0

The TinyMCE plugin enables the powerful TinyMCE WYSIWYG editor. TinyMCE is enabled by default both in the Plugins section and in the Global Configuration Manager. The plugin's dialogue is shown in Figure 19.14.

Note

The principal file for this plugin is tinymce.php.

FIGURE 19.13

The Editor - No Editor plugin dialogue.

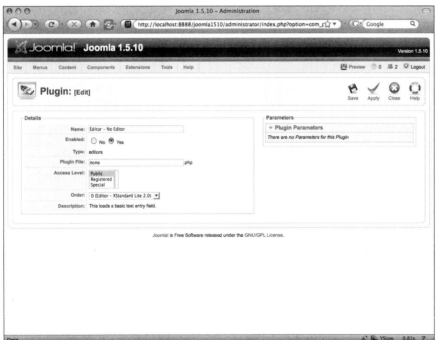

FIGURE 19.14

The Editor - TinyMCE 2.0 Plugin dialogue.

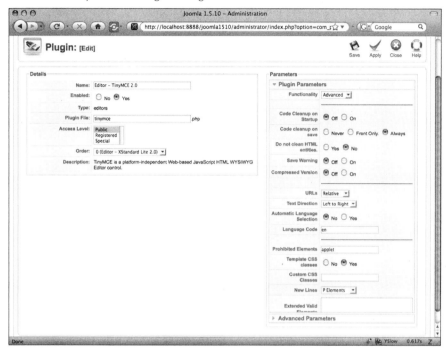

The Parameters section of the TinyMCE plugin provides a large number of configuration and customization options. The parameters are divided into two categories, labeled Plugin Parameters and Advanced Parameters.

The Plugin Parameters include:

- **Functionality:** The two options here allow you to select either a very basic editor or a more complex and full-featured version. The default setting is Advanced, which gives the user access to the full toolbar and all available options.

- **Code Cleanup on Startup:** If set to Yes, this option causes the Editor to clean up messy or defective HTML tags when the Editor first loads. The default is Off.

- **Code Cleanup on Save:** This parameter causes the Editor to clean up messy HTML when the article is saved. The options here are Never, Front Only, and Always. The default is Always. The Front Only option cleans only the tags used in Articles contributed through the front end of the web site.

- **Do not clean HTML entities:** Set this Parameter to Yes to force the Editor to skip cleaning up HTML. The default setting is No.

- **Save Warning:** Set to Yes to cause the system to warn you if you attempt to cancel without saving. The default option is No.

- **Compressed Version:** Set to Yes to use compression for the Editor. This causes the Editor to load more quickly. The default setting is No. Note that some problems have been reported when this option is used with Internet Explorer.

- **URLs:** Choose from either Absolute or Relative to control whether URLs to pages inside your site include the `http://` and primary domain prefix.

- **Text Direction:** Specify whether the text reads right-to-left or left-to-right.

- **Automatic Language Selection:** This control is only used where the site has multiple language packs installed. If none are installed, set this to the default No.

- **Language Code:** If the Automatic Language Selection Parameter is set to No, then enter into this field the default language to be used in the interface.

- **Prohibited Elements:** List in this field any HTML elements you want to be automatically cleaned out of articles. The default value for this field is applet, which prevents applets from being inserted into articles.

- **Template CSS classes:** Set this to Yes to let the Editor use the style selectors from the template's CSS file. Note that this can be overridden by the following parameter.

- **Custom CSS Classes:** Use this field to specify a particular Cascading Style Sheet to be used by the Editor. If a value is entered in this field it will override the settings in the previous Parameter, Template CSS classes.

- **New Lines:** This control allows you to specify whether the Editor will treat a new line in an article as a P (paragraph) element or a BR (line break) element.

- **Extended Valid Elements:** If you want to be able to use additional HTML tags, beyond those defined in the default Editor, then enter them in this field.

The Advanced parameters include:

- **Toolbar:** This control specifies whether the Editor's toolbar appears above or below the text editing window.

- **Horizontal Rule:** Show or hide the horizontal rule button on the toolbar.

- **Smilies:** Show or hide the Smilies button on the toolbar.

- **Table:** Show or hide the Table button on the toolbar.

- **Style:** Show or hide the CSS Style button on the toolbar.

- **Layer:** Show or hide the Layer button on the toolbar.

- **XHTMLxtras:** Show or hide the additional XHTML features on the toolbar.

- **Template:** Show or hide the Template button on the toolbar.

- **Directionality:** Show or hide the Directionality button on the toolbar.

- **Fullscreen:** Show or hide the Fullscreen button on the toolbar.

- **HTML Height:** Type an integer value in this field to set the height of the HTML editing pop-up window. The value is measured in pixels.

- **HTML Width:** Type an integer value in this field to set the width of the HTML editing pop-up window. The value is measured in pixels.

- **Preview:** Show or hide the Preview button on the toolbar.

- **Element Path:** Set the parameter to On to enable the display of the Element Path immediately below the editing window. The Element Path is an aid to accessibility and makes it simpler to navigate through the styling in the editing window, one element at a time.

- **Insert Date:** Show or hide the Insert Date button on the toolbar. Note the next parameter is related.

- **Date Format:** The date format to be used by the Insert Date command. The default is %Y-%m-%d, which means Year-Month-Day

- **Insert Time:** Show or hide the Insert Time button on the toolbar. Note the next parameter is related.

- **Time Format:** The time format to be used by the Insert Time command. The default is %H:%M:%S, which means Hour:Minute:Second.

XStandard Lite 2.0

The XStandard Lite plugin enables your Joomla! site to function with the XStandard WYSIWYG editor. In addition to enabling this plugin, you need to download and install the XStandard editor files; the actual editor is not included in the default Joomla! system. The XStandard editor is a standards-compliant editor that produces clean and accessible XHTML markup. The plugin's dialogue is shown in Figure 19.15.

Note

The principal file for this plugin is xstandard.php.

The plugin Parameters section contains only two options:

- **Editor Mode:** This control sets the default mode that will be displayed when the editor is launched. The three options are WYSIWYG, Source, or Screen Reader. Source provides text editor functionality, while Screen Reader shows you how the article will appear when viewed by a Screen Reader; it is not possible to edit in Screen Reader mode.

- **Word Wrap:** Turn word- wrapping on or off.

Tip

Download the files for the XStandard Lite 2.0 editor from

```
http://xstandard.com/
```

FIGURE 19.15

The Editor - XStandard Lite 2.0 Plugin dialogue.

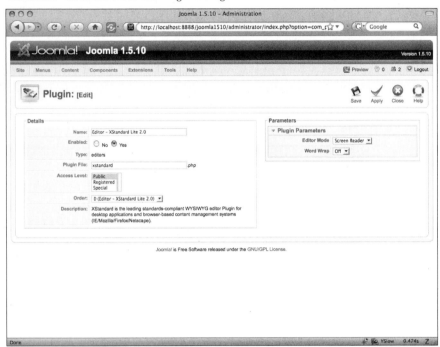

Joomla! 1.6

The XStandard editor is not bundled with Joomla! 1.6, hence this plugin does not exist in the default system.

Editors XTD plugins

The Editors XTD plugins are a set of utilities that extend the functionality of the content editors and the content items. The three plugins enable the three buttons that you see below the content editing window when creating or editing an article.

Note

The Editors XTD Plugin files are located in the directory `plugins/editors-xtd`.

Image

The Image Plugin displays the Image button below the editing window. Clicking the button produces a window that allows you to insert and configure images inside of content items. The plugin's dialogue is shown in Figure 19.16.

Note

The principal file for this plugin is image.php.

There are no parameters associated with this plugin.

Tip

The Image button is redundant to controls that exist on the TinyMCE and XStandard WYSIWYG editors. If you have either of these editors enabled, then you may want to disable the Image plugin.

Pagebreak

The Pagebreak plugin enables the Pagebreak button that appears below the content editing window. Clicking the button inserts a page break into an article, thereby turning a single-page article into a multipage article. The plugin's dialogue is shown in Figure 19.17.

Note

The principal file for this plugin is pagebreak.php.

FIGURE 19.16

The Editor Button - Image Plugin dialogue.

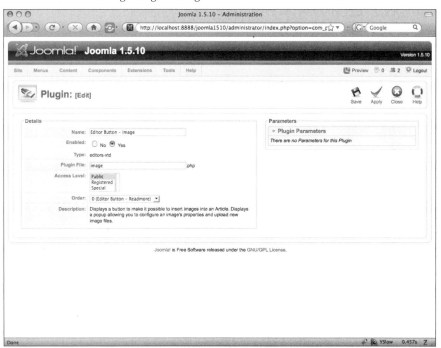

FIGURE 19.17

The Editor Button - Pagebreak Plugin dialogue.

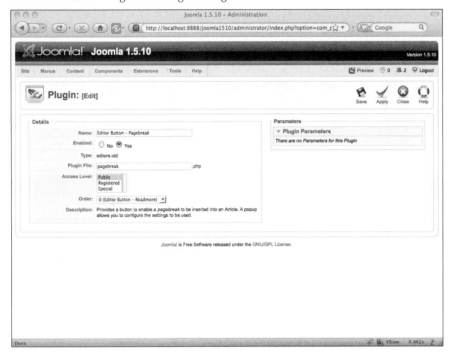

There are no parameters associated with this plugin.

Tip

The TinyMCE editor also provides pagebreak functionality. If you have enabled TinyMCE, you may want to consider disabling this control, as it is redundant.

Readmore

The Readmore plugin displays the Read more button below the content editing box. Clicking the button allows you to separate the first portion of the article from the remainder and shows a Read more link that leads the viewer to the full article. The plugin's dialogue is shown in Figure 19.18.

Note

The principal file for this plugin is readmore.php.

There are no parameters associated with this plugin.

FIGURE 19.18

The Editor Button - Readmore Plugin dialogue.

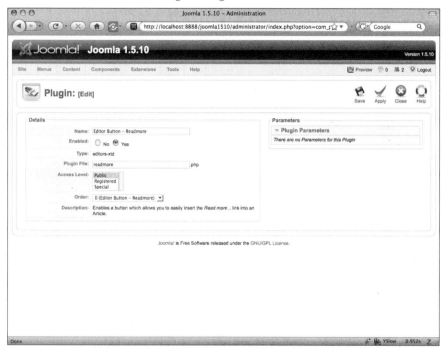

Search plugins

The Search group of plugins enables the site search functionality. Different plugins enable the indexing and searching of different types of content — articles, web links, contacts, categories, sections, and news feeds. All the plugins in the default installation are enabled. Disabling a particular plugin results in the related content being excluded from the search results.

Note

The Search plugin files are located in the directory `plugins/search`.

Content

The Content plugin enables the indexing and searching of articles on your site. The plugin's dialogue is shown in Figure 19.19.

Note

The principal file for this plugin is content.php.

FIGURE 19.19

The Search - Content Plugin dialogue.

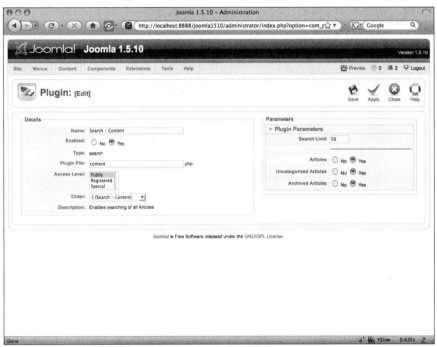

The Plugin Parameters section contains the following options:

- **Search Limit:** Type an integer value in this field to specify the maximum number of search results to return.

- **Articles:** Set the Parameter to No to exclude articles from the search results. The default setting is Yes.

- **Uncategorized Articles:** Set the parameter to No to exclude uncategorized articles from the search results. The default setting is Yes.

- **Archived Articles:** Set the parameter to No to exclude archived articles from the search results. The default setting is Yes.

Weblinks

The Weblinks plugin enables the indexing and searching of web link items. The plugin's dialogue is shown in Figure 19.20.

FIGURE 19.20

FIGURE 19.20

The Search - Weblinks Plugin dialogue.

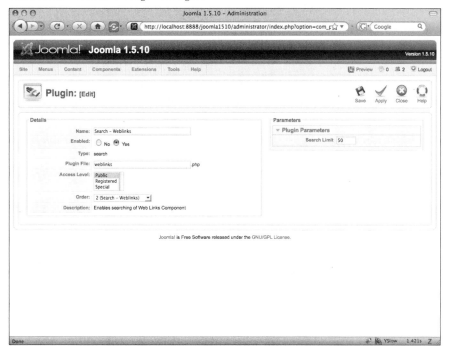

Note

The principal file for this plugin is weblinks.php.

The Plugin Parameters section contains only one option: Search Limit. Type an integer value in this field to specify the maximum number of search results to return.

Tip

Disable this plugin to exclude web links from the search results.

Contacts

The Contacts Plugin enables the indexing and searching of the contacts in your site. The plugin's dialogue is shown in Figure 19.21.

Note

The principal file for this plugin is contacts.php.

FIGURE 19.21

The Search - Contacts Plugin dialogue.

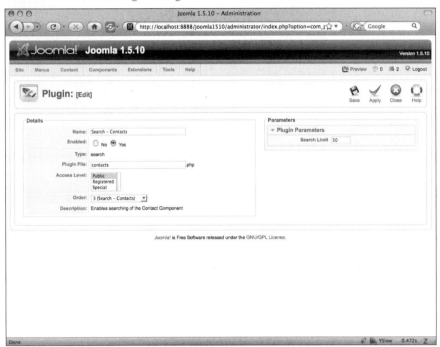

The Plugin Parameters section contains only one option: Search Limit. Type an integer value in this field to specify the maximum number of search results to return.

Tip

Disable this plugin to exclude contacts from the search results.

Categories

The Categories Plugin enables the indexing and searching of the Categories content. The plugin's dialogue is shown in Figure 19.22.

Note

The system name for this plugin is categories.php.

The Plugin Parameters section contains only one option: Search Limit. Type an integer value in this field to specify the maximum number of search results to return.

Tip

Disable this plugin to exclude categories content from the search results.

Joomla! 1.6

There is no Categories plugin in Joomla! 1.6.

Sections

The Sections plugin enables the indexing and searching of the sections content. The plugin's dialogue is shown in Figure 19.23.

Note

The principal file for this plugin is sections.php.

The Plugin Parameters section contains only one option: Search Limit. Type an integer value in this field to specify the maximum number of search results to return.

FIGURE 19.22

The Search - Categories Plugin dialogue.

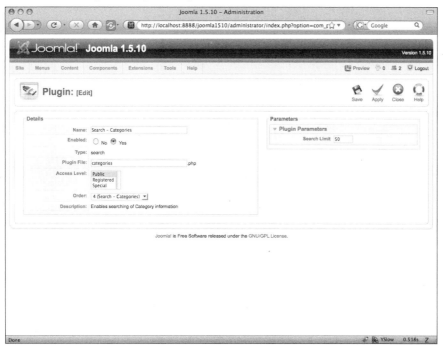

FIGURE 19.23

The Search - Sections Plugin dialogue.

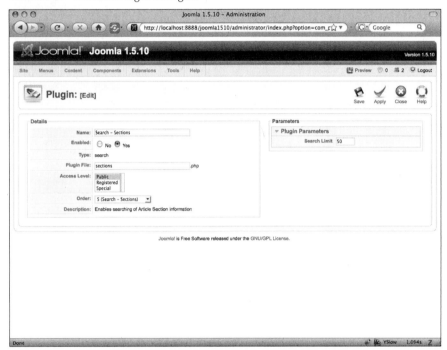

Tip

Disable this plugin to exclude sections content from the search results.

Newsfeeds

The Newsfeed Plugin enables the indexing and searching of News Feed items. The plugin's dialogue is shown in Figure 19.24.

Note

The principal file for this plugin is newsfeeds.php.

The Plugin Parameters section contains only one option: Search Limit. Type an integer value in this field to specify the maximum number of search results to return.

Tip

Disable this plugin to exclude News Feeds from the search results.

FIGURE 19.24

The Search - Newsfeeds Plugin dialogue.

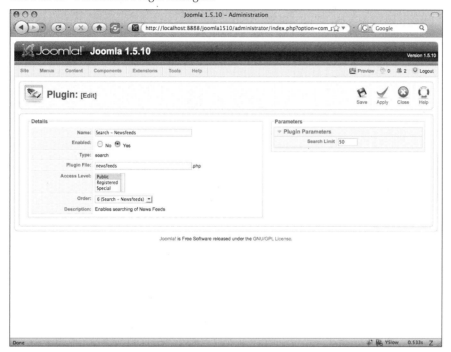

System plugins

The System plugins provide a variety of global system functions, from caching to debugging. Of the seven Plugins in this category only three are published. The other four plugins (Debug, Legacy, Cache and Log) provide functions that not all users may want or need.

Note

The System plugin files are located in the directory `plugins/system`.

SEF

The SEF Pplugin enables the use of Search Engine Friendly URLs in the articles on your site. This plugin is independent from the Search Engine Friendly option in the Global Configuration Manager. The plugin is enabled in the default installation. The plugin's dialogue is shown in Figure 19.25.

Note

The principal file for this plugin is sef.php.

FIGURE 19.25

The System - SEF Plugin dialogue in Joomla! 1.5.x.

No parameters are associated with this plugin.

Debug

The Debug plugin is used to display information about the system that is intended to be of use in debugging a site. When active, the Debug plugin outputs the information at the bottom of the screen in your browser. The Debug plugin is disabled in the default configuration and should only be turned on during development or when you are trying to solve a problem with your site and need access to this information. The plugin's dialogue is shown in Figure 19.26.

Note
The principal file for this plugin is debug.php.

The Plugin Parameters section contains the following options:

- **Display Profiling Information:** When set to Yes, includes the time profiling information in the debugging output.

- **Display SQL query log:** When set to Yes, includes the SQL query log in the debugging output.

- **Display memory usage:** When set to Yes, includes the memory usage data in the debugging output.

- **Display loaded language files:** When set to Yes, includes information on the loaded language file(s) in the debugging output.

- **Display undefined language strings:** This control determines whether to display undefined language strings in the debugging output. There are four options here: No, All Modes, Diagnostic Mode, and Designer Mode. Diagnostic mode displays the string and the file location; Designer mode displays the string in a format that makes it easy to cut and paste it into the .ini language file. The next parameter is related to this control

- **Strip Key Prefix:** When the preceding parameter, Display undefined language strings, is set to All Modes or Designer Mode, this parameter can be used to strip the prefix from the string. To use this parameter, specify the prefix you want to strip out in the field provided.

FIGURE 19.26

The System - Debug plugin dialogue.

Legacy

The Legacy plugin lets you use extensions that require Joomla's legacy mode. Typically this plugin is used to run extensions that were developed for the previous version of Joomla. The plugin is disabled by default. The plugin's dialogue is shown in Figure 19.27.

Note

The principal file for this plugin is legacy.php.

Joomla! 1.6

There is no Legacy plugin for Joomla! 1.6.

The Plugin Parameters section contains only one option: Use Legacy URL Routing. This control allows you to maintain the previous system's URL generation and routing.

Tip

Don't enable this unless it is specifically required by a third-party extension. Note also that this plugin is not sufficient by itself to make an extension created for Joomla 1.x work with Joomla 1.5.

FIGURE 19.27

The System - Legacy plugin dialogue in Joomla! 1.5.x.

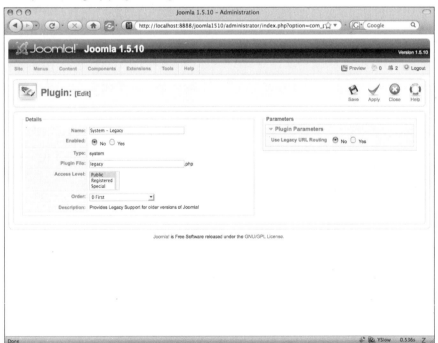

Cache

The Cache plugin enables page caching on your Joomla! site. This parameter is independent of the caching controls contained in the Global Configuration Manager. By default, this plugin is disabled. To use it on your site, you need to enable and configure it. The plugin's dialogue is shown in Figure 19.28.

Note

The principal file for this plugin is cache.php.

The Plugin Parameters section contains two options:

- **Use Browser Caching:** This control allows you to tap into the local caching function of the viewer's browser, assuming the browser permits this to occur.

- **Cache Lifetime:** Type an integer value in this field to specify the time in minutes that the page will be cached. The default value is 15.

FIGURE 19.28

The System - Cache Plugin dialogue.

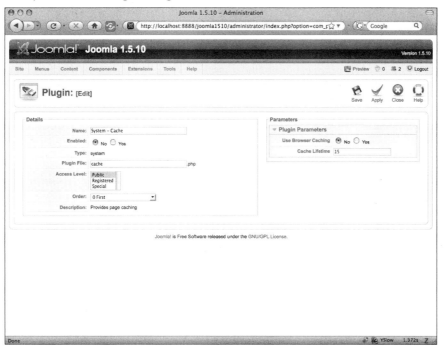

Caution

As of Joomla 1.5.9, the Cache plugin was still experiencing some problems with sites that require login for front-end visitors. It is also problematic with functions like the Random Image module, where it causes the same image to be displayed until the cache expires. Accordingly, use this plugin with some caution. If it is enabled, remember also to clean your cache if you update your site or delete or install items.

Log

The Log plugin provides optional system logging. When enabled, the plugin maintains a log file of web site activity. By default, this plugin is disabled. The plugin's dialogue is shown in Figure 19.29.

Note

The principal file for this plugin is log.php.

There are no parameters associated with this plugin.

FIGURE 19.29

The System - Log Plugin dialogue.

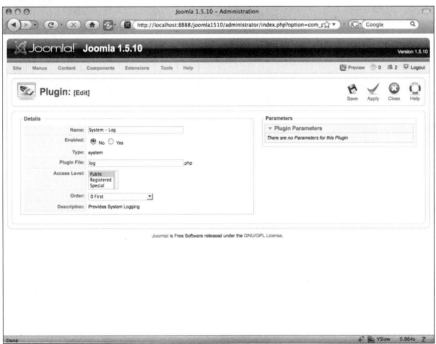

Tip

The Log plugin is a great aid to debugging a site; however, if it is not needed it should be disabled because it does generate additional load on the server.

Remember Me

The Remember Me plugin supplies the functionality that allows the web site to remember a visitor and thereby avoid prompting them to login again. This plugin is enabled by default. The plugin's dialogue is shown in Figure 19.30.

Note

The principal file for this plugin is remember.php.

There are no parameters associated with this plugin.

FIGURE 19.30

The System - Remember Me plugin dialogue.

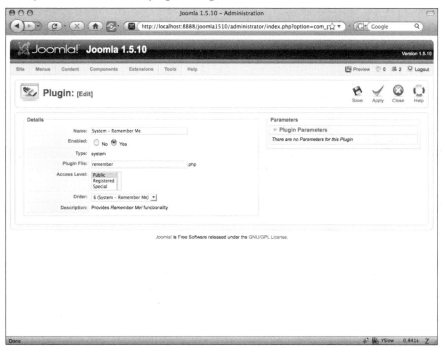

Tip

If site security or the preservation of personal data and identity is paramount for your site, then this plugin should be disabled, thereby removing the possibility that the site will enable an unauthorized person to use an authorized account.

Backlink

The Backlink plugin is intended to aid with the processing of legacy Joomla 1.0 style URLs. If your site has been upgraded from Joomla 1.0.x to Joomla 1.5.x, this plugin will help assure that the old links to your pages will continue to work with the new site. This plugin is disabled by default, if you want to use it, then enable and configure it. The plugin's dialogue is shown in Figure 19.31.

Note

The principal file for this plugin is backlink.php.

Joomla! 1.6

There is no Backlink plugin in Joomla! 1.6.

FIGURE 19.31

The System - Backlink plugin dialogue.

The Plugin Parameters section contains the following options:

- **Search Query Strings:** Set to Yes to enable the system to map Joomla 1.0 query strings to the appropriate URL in your site.

- **Search SEF:** Set to Yes if you want your site to use Joomla 1.0 style SEF URLs, with redirects to the correct new pages.

- **Attempt Legacy SEF:** Set to Yes to use Joomla 1.0 style SEF URLs linked to your new content items.

User - Joomla! plugin

The User - Joomla! Plugin is used by the system to handle user synchronization. This is an essential plugin and is enabled in the default configuration. The plugin's dialogue is shown in Figure 19.32.

Note

The User plugin files are located in the directory `plugins/user`.

The Plugin Parameters section contains only one option: Auto-create Users. Set this control to Yes to allow the system to auto-create users.

FIGURE 19.32

The User - Joomla! plugin dialogue.

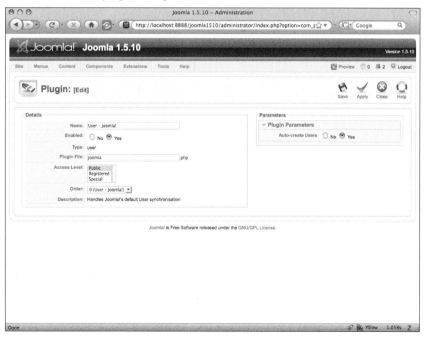

Caution

Disabling this plugin will result in users being unable to log in to the site!

XML-RPC plugins

XML-RPC is a protocol for remote procedure call that is based in XML. The XML-RPC plugins in Joomla! are provided to enable you to connect to your Joomla! site using any application consistent with either of the APIs provided by the plugins.

Note

The XMLRPC plugin files are located in the directory `plugins/xmlrpc`.

Joomla! 1.6

This plugin type does not exist in Joomla! 1.6.

Joomla

The Joomla XML-RPC Pplugin supplies the Joomla XML-RPC API. This plugin is disabled by default. The plugin's dialogue is shown in Figure 19.33.

FIGURE 19.33

The XMLRPC - Joomla Plugin dialogue.

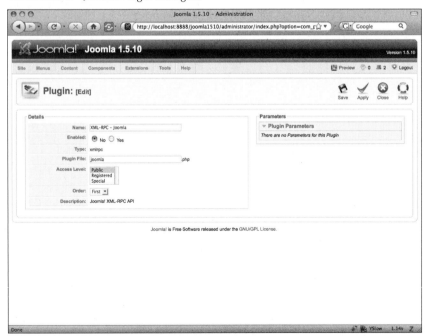

Note

The principal file for this plugin is joomla.php.

There are no parameters associated with this plugin.

Blogger API

The Blogger API Plugin allows you to post content to your Joomla! site using any application that supports the Blogger API. The plugin is disabled by default; you will need to enable it and configure it before using it. The plugin's dialogue is shown in Figure 19.34.

Note

The principal file for this plugin is blogger.php.

The Plugin Parameters section contains two options:

- **New posts:** Select from the combo box the category you want new posts to be assigned to. This field is required.

- **Edit posts:** Select from the combo box the section you want new posts to be assigned to. This field is required.

FIGURE 19.34

The XMLRPC - Blogger API Plugin dialogue.

Summary

In this chapter, we have covered the use of the Joomla! plugins. You learned the following:

- How to use the Plugin Manager
- How to edit and delete plugins
- The nature and uses of the core Administrator plugins
- How to configure the parameters of the default plugins

Part IV

Customizing and Extending the System

Customizing Joomla! Templates

O ne of the joys of working with the Joomla! system is the ease with which you can create an attractive web site. Unlike many other content management systems that lock you into a standardized, cookie-cutter approach to site design, Joomla! has great flexibility. You can create virtually any look and feel you want. Moreover, the widespread popularity of Joomla! has resulted in a large number of pre-existing templates being available in the market, often for little or no cost.

This chapter takes you through the basics of understanding how Joomla! templates work and then digs in more deeply to explain how you can customize an existing template or how you can even go further and build your own from scratch.

Discovering How the Templates Work

The Joomla! template files are responsible for what is seen on the screen by your visitors. When a visitor to your Web site clicks on a link, it sets off a process that culminates in the production of a web page inside their browser. The final step in that process is the rendering of the page inside the template. Though some elements, for example, modules and components, have their own templates that control the look and feel of a particular bit of output, all of those various elements are brought together inside the template.

Cross-Reference

In Chapter 21 there is a discussion of how to control and override the output elements generated by the modules and components.

As you can see in the next section, a template is a set of files; it is not one single item. The various parts of the template work together to format the final page output. Typically the template works as a frame, providing all the outer dressing and decoration you see on the page, while the content inside that frame is produced by the various functional elements of the site. All of the text and the colors on the screen are also controlled by the template, via the template's CSS files.

While some modules and components may influence on the site's look and feel, the template has the final say in the site output. This creates an opportunity for you; by gaining fluency in controlling the template you are able to tailor the site output to suit your needs.

Note

If you are new to Joomla! templates, one of the key concepts you need to grasp is that designing templates is very different from designing traditional Web pages. Where in a traditional Web page design you have to fix everything on each page inside a separate file, in Joomla! template design you are creating the outer shell only, the structure inside of which you will call other output for display. That one template is then used for multiple pages.

Exploring the Default Templates

The Joomla! default distribution includes a set of templates to help you get started. These templates may be sufficient for your needs, or they may serve as a base for your customization efforts. Regardless, they offer a great set of examples of what can be done from the system and provide you with an opportunity to learn. In Joomla! 1.5.x, there are three front-end templates and one back-end template:

- Front-end templates
  - Beez
  - JA_Purity
  - RHUK_Milkyway (this is selected as the default)
- Back-end template
  - Khepri

Beez

The Beez template is included in the default Joomla! 1.5.x distribution. More than any of the other default templates, Beez makes heavy use of CSS formatting and provides a number of overrides. The overrides are specifically designed to replace the table-based presentation of the core's modules and components.

The template is shown in Figure 20.1.

FIGURE 20.1

The Beez template, shown with the sample data installed.

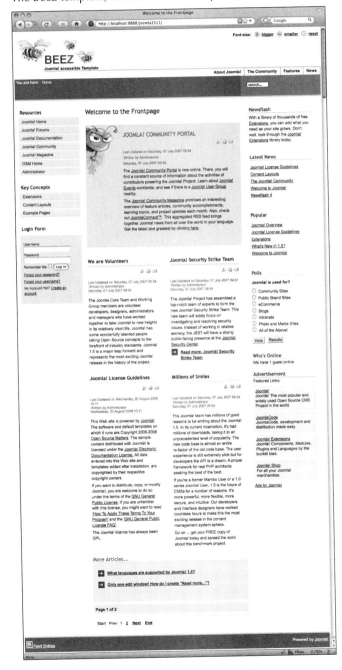

The Beez template includes the following attributes and features:

- The template's files are located at /templates/beez.
- The CSS files are located at /templates/beez/css
- The overrides are located at /templates/beez/html.
- The template provides overrides for the following:
  - Content component
  - Contact component
  - Newsfeeds component
  - Polls component
  - Search component
  - User component
  - Weblinks component
  - Latest News module
  - Login module
  - Newsflash module
  - Poll module
  - Search module
- The template overrides the default module chrome at /templates/beez/html/modules.php
- The template overrides the default pagination styling at /templates/beez/html/pagination.php
- The template does not include any parameters.
- The template includes ten module position holders:
  - left
  - right
  - top
  - breadcrumb
  - user1
  - user2
  - user3
  - user4
  - debug
  - syndicate

Note

In assessments of compliance with accessibility standards, this template performed the best of all the default templates. See Chapter 26 for more information.

Tip

For additional information above the Beez template, including a guide to the CSS, visit the dedicated page on the Joomla! docs site at

```
http://docs.joomla.org/Beez
```

JA_Purity

The JA_Purity template is included as part of the Joomla 1.5.x distro. The template is highly configurable and includes a large number of parameters that enable you to set the template's width, color scheme, and many other elements. One of the key features of this template is the ability to create easily drop-down menus. Of all the default templates, JA_Purity allows for the most flexibility without having to modify code.

The template is shown in Figure 20.2.

The JA_Purity template includes the following attributes and features:

- The template's files are located at `/templates/ja_purity`.
- The CSS files are located at `/templates/ja_purity/css`.
- The overrides are located at `/templates/ja_purity/html`.
- The Beez template provides overrides for the following:
  - Content component
  - Banners module
  - Login module
- The template overrides the default module chrome at `/templates/ja_purity/html/modules.php`.
- The template overrides the default pagination styling at `/templates/ja_purity/html/pagination.php`.
- The template provides the following parameters:
  - **Logo type:** Select whether the template displays an image or text. The default option is image. The image file is `/templates/ja_purity/images/login.gif`. If you select the text option for this parameter, you can enter the text you want to appear in the parameter that follows.
  - **Logo text:** Type the text you'd like to appear in the logo space on the template. This is only relevant if you have selected the option text in the parameter above.

- **Slogan:** Type the slogan text you want to appear under the logo on the template.

- **Horizontal Navigation Type:** Select whether the horizontal menus, if any, use Suckerfish or JAMoo Menu. Suckerfish is largely CSS dependent. JAMoo Menu relies on JavaScript. The default selection is Suckerfish.

Note

Simply setting this parameter is not sufficient to create horizontal drop-down menus. As discussed in the section on the drop-down menus, additional steps must be taken.

- **Font size:** Select the default font size for the text on the site.

- **Template Width:** Select how the width of the template will be calculated. The options are

  - **Auto (fluid):** The width of the template will automatically flex to fill the screen.

  - **Narrow Screen:** Sets the template to a fixed width compatible with 800 x 600 screen display settings.

  - **Wide Screen:** Sets the template to a fixed width compatible with 1024 x 768 screen display settings.

  - **Specified in percentage (fluid):** The width of the template will be flexible and determined by a percentage value entered in the next parameter.

- **Specified in pixels:** The width of the template will be a fixed value determined by the integer value entered in the next parameter. If you select either of the specified values, you will need to enter an integer value in the next parameter to provide that value. The default option is specified in percentage.

  - **Specified width:** If you have selected either of the specified options in the parameter immediately preceding, type an integer in this field to set the value to used.

  - **Header Themes:** Select from the combo box one of three header themes or select none to supply your own.

  - **Background Themes:** Select from the combo box one of three background themes or select none to supply your own.

  - **Primary Elements:** The Primary Elements parameter controls a number of text decoration variables, including the color of link text color and module titles. Select your preferred color from the combo box or select none to specify your own via the template's CSS.

  - **Right modules collapsible function:** Enable to allow modules assigned to the right column to expand and collapse (vertically).

  - **Default status:** If the parameter above is set to Enable, use this parameter to set the default value for the column.

  - **Exclude Modules:** If you have elected to enable the Right modules collapsible function, you can exempt individual modules from this control by typing their element ID here.

FIGURE 20.2

The JA_Purity template, shown with the sample data installed.

The template includes 12 module position holders:

- hornav
- breadcrumbs
- banner
- top
- user1
- user2
- user3
- user4
- user5
- footer
- syndicate
- debug

Tip

For additional information above the JA_Purity template, including a guide to the CSS, visit the dedicated page on the Joomla! docs site at

```
http://docs.joomla.org/Ja_purity
```

RHUK_Milkyway

The rhuk_milkyway template is the first thing you see when you log in to a new Joomla! installation; it is the system's default template. Though it has only a few configurable parameters, Milkyway is a solid all-purpose template.

The template is shown in Figure 20.3.

The RHUK_Milkyway template includes the following attributes and features:

- The template's files are located at /templates/rhuk_milkyway.
- The CSS files are located at /templates/rhuk_milkyway/css.
- The overrides are located at /templates/rhuk_milkyway/html.

- The Milkyway template provides an override for the Login module.

- The template overrides the default Module Chrome at `/templates/rhuk_milkyway/html/modules.php`.

- The template overrides the default pagination styling at `/templates/rhuk_milkyway/html/pagination.php`.

- The template includes the following parameters:

  - **Color Variation:** Select one of the six primary color variations from the combo box.

  - **Background Variation:** Select one of the six background color variations from the combo box.

  - **Template Width:** Select an option for controlling the width of the template.

- The template includes eleven module position holders:

  - breadcrumb
  - left
  - right
  - top
  - user1
  - user2
  - user3
  - user4
  - footer
  - debug
  - syndicate

Khepri

Joomla! is bundled with a single, dedicated template for use in the admin system. Khepri is tailored for use by administrators. The template is designed to be lightweight, fast, and easy to use. Few parameters are available for this template.

The template is shown in Figure 20.4.

FIGURE 20.3

The RHUK_Milkyway template, shown with the sample data installed.

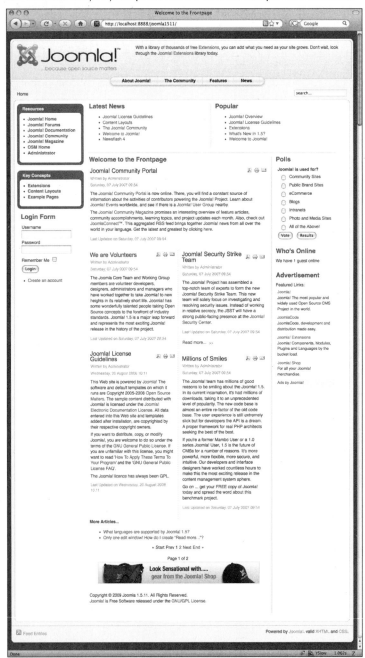

FIGURE 20.4

The Khepri template.

The Khepri template includes the following attributes and features:

- The template's files are located at /administrator/templates/khepri.
- The CSS files are located at /administrator/templates/khepri/css.
- The overrides are located at /administrator/templates/khepri/html.
- The Khepri template does not provides any override for the system's modules or components.
- The template overrides the default module chrome at /administrator/templates/ khepri/html/modules.php.

- The template overrides the default pagination styling at `/administrator/templates/khepri/html/pagination.php`.
- The template includes the following parameters:
  - **Use Rounded Corners:** Select the look for the corners of the page.
  - **Show Site Name:** Show or hide the site name on the header.
  - **Header Color:** Select one of three colors for the site header.

- The template includes five module position holders:
  - status
  - menu
  - title
  - toolbar
  - submenu

Tip

Looking for more help with the default templates? There is a dedicated support form at

`http://forum.joomla.org/viewforum.php?f=466`

Finding the Module Positions on a page

There are times when it is useful to be able to identify quickly the module positions that are active on the page you see in your browser. Although you can always look up the names of the positions in the template's XML file, preview the template in Template Manager, or open up the template's code and look where the module positions holders have been inserted, sometimes you just want to see where they are on the rendered page with the published items in place. To do this, follow these steps:

1. Open the page in your browser and look at the URL that appears in the browser's address bar.
2. If there are no parameters displayed at the end of the URL, append "?tp=1" to the URL and click refresh. The module positions will be outlined and lightly shaded, with the name of the position appearing in red.
3. If there are parameters at the end of the URL, append "&tp=1" to the URL and click refresh. The module positions will be outlined and lightly shaded, with the name of the position appearing in red.

Note that this shows you all active module positions, regardless of whether there is anything published to them; the one exception is if the template has made the appearance of module positions conditional and that condition is not being met.

Knowing the Parts of a Template

As noted earlier, a template is actually a collection of files that work together. In this section, I outline the basic files that are needed and their roles in the system. Note that some templates are more complex than others and may include a large number of additional files. The discussion of the default templates in the next section demonstrates the variance that can occur with various approaches to template design.

Directory structure

All front-end templates are kept inside the directory /templates, located at the root of the Joomla! installation. All back-end templates are kept in /administrator/templates. Inside the appropriate directory, each template will have its own directory names for the template. By way of example, the default RHUK_Milkyway template's files are found at /templates/rhuk_milkyway.

Inside the individual template's directory you typically find:

- **A /css directory** containing the CSS files needed by the template
- **An /html directory** containing overrides, if any
- **An /images directory** containing any images specifically needed by the template

The template may also have other directories, as defined by the template developer.

The key files

At a minimum, a Joomla! 1.5.x template includes the following files:

- component.php
- index.php
- template.css
- templateDetails.xml
- template_thumbnail.png

Each of these key files is discussed in detail in the following sections.

component.php

The component.php file has a very narrow and specific purpose; it provides the display of printer-friendly pages.

Here are the contents of this file, taken from the default RHUK_Milkyway template:

```
<head>
<jdoc:include type="head" />
<link rel="stylesheet" href="<?php echo $this->baseurl ?>/templates/
    rhuk_milkyway/css/template.css" type="text/css" />
<?php if($this->direction == 'rtl') : ?>
<link rel="stylesheet" href="<?php echo $this->baseurl ?>/templates/
    rhuk_milkyway/css/template_rtl.css" type="text/css" />
<?php endif; ?>
</head>
<body class="contentpane">
<jdoc:include type="message" />
<jdoc:include type="component" />
</body>
</html>
```

This file is standardized from template to template. The only lines that change from template to template relate to the path of the CSS files.

Note

The preceding code example omits the preliminary tag, comments, access control, and doctype declaration. Please see the file included in the distribution to view the file in its entirety.

index.php

The `index.php` is the key file in the template. This file contains the HTML formatting for the page layout and the statements that include the component and module output. The file provides a standard document head and then outlines the page's div structure and places all the element position holders on the page. Elements are positioned on the page through the use of jdoc:include statements.

Here is a snippet from the default RHUK_Milkway template's `index.php`, showing the placement of two module position holders:

```
<div id="search">
<jdoc:include type="modules" name="user4" />
</div>
<div id="pathway">
<jdoc:include type="modules" name="breadcrumb" />
</div>
```

The preceding code places on the page the user4 and breadcrumb module position holders. To enable easy styling of the elements inside those module positions, the user4 module position holder is wrapped in a div with the id search, and the user4 module position holder is wrapped in a div with the id pathway.

The include statements use the syntax jdoc:include type="nameoftype" The available jdoc include types are:

- component <jdoc:include type="component" /> This is used only once in the template to set the placement of the main content area for the page.

- head <jdoc:include type="head" /> This is used only once in the template to set the style, script, and meta elements inside the template's <head> area.

- installation <jdoc:include type="installation" /> This is only used in the Joomla! installer template and should not appear in your site or admin template's index.php file.

- message <jdoc:include type="message" /> This is used only once in the template. It is placed inside the <body> area where you want system messages to appear on the page.

- module <jdoc:include type="module" name="modulename" /> This is used to place a single module on the page. Additional attributes to control the layout and appearance may be available.

- modules <jdoc:include type="modules" name="modulepositionname" /> This is used to place the module position holders in the template. Additional attributes to control the layout and appearance may be available.

Note

Module position holders must not only be placed into the index.php **file but must also be declared in the**

templateDetails.xml file.

An index.php file may or may not make use of all the available types; however, it will certainly use at least the head, component, message, and modules types, as these are the minimum needed to construct a usable template.

Tip

The code for the index.php **file is too long for convenient inclusion in the text. Nonetheless, I strongly recommend reviewing the** index.php **files included in the default Joomla! distribution to familiarize yourself with what happens in this key template file.**

template.css

The styling of templates is handled by cascading style sheets. Although a template is very likely to have multiple CSS files, the key file is the template.css, which is located inside the template's /css directory. This file determines the page width and margins, the placement of the elements on the page, and the look of the fonts, backgrounds, borders, and so on.

Note

If you are looking for a listing of the various Joomla! core CSS styles, there are two lists that are maintained and updated: http://forum.joomla.org/viewtopic.php?t=125508 and http://docs.joomla.org/Template_reference_material.

templateDetails.xml

This file contains information that is needed by the Joomla! installer and the Template Manager. It also includes the definition of the template parameters for the Template Manager and the declaration of the module position holders for use by the Module Manager.

The contents of `templateDetails.xml` file from the default RHUK_Milkyway template are typical:

```xml
<?xml version="1.0" encoding="utf-8"?>
<!DOCTYPE install PUBLIC "-//Joomla! 1.5//DTD template 1.0//EN"
    "http://www.joomla.org/xml/dtd/1.5/template-install.dtd">
<install version="1.5" type="template">
<name>rhuk_milkyway</name>
<creationDate>11/20/06</creationDate>
<author>Andy Miller</author>
<authorEmail>rhuk@rockettheme.com</authorEmail>
<authorUrl>http://www.rockettheme.com</authorUrl>
<copyright></copyright>
<license>GNU/GPL</license>
<version>1.0.2</version>
<description>TPL_RHUK_MILKYWAY</description>
<files>
<filename>index.php</filename>
<filename>templateDetails.xml</filename>
<filename>template_thumbnail.png</filename>
<filename>params.ini</filename>
<filename>images/arrow.png</filename>
<filename>images/indent1.png</filename>
<filename>images/indent2.png</filename>
<filename>images/indent3.png</filename>
<filename>images/indent4.png</filename>
<filename>images/index.html</filename>
<filename>images/mw_box_blue_bl.png</filename>
<filename>images/mw_box_blue_br.png</filename>
<filename>images/mw_box_blue_tl.png</filename>
<filename>images/mw_box_blue_tr.png</filename>
<filename>images/mw_content_b_l.png</filename>
<filename>images/mw_content_b_r.png</filename>
<filename>images/mw_content_b.png</filename>
<filename>images/mw_content_t_l.png</filename>
<filename>images/mw_content_t_r.png</filename>
```

```
<filename>images/mw_content_t.png</filename>
<filename>images/mw_footer_blue_b_l.png</filename>
<filename>images/mw_footer_blue_b_r.png</filename>
<filename>images/mw_footer_blue_b.png</filename>
<filename>images/mw_footer_separator.png</filename>
<filename>images/mw_header_b.png</filename>
<filename>images/mw_header_blue_t_l.png</filename>
<filename>images/mw_header_blue_t_r.png</filename>
<filename>images/mw_header_blue_t.png</filename>
<filename>images/mw_header_l_b.png</filename>
<filename>images/mw_header_r_b.png</filename>
<filename>images/mw_header.jpg</filename>
<filename>images/mw_joomla_logo.png</filename>
<filename>images/mw_line_grey.png</filename>
<filename>images/mw_menu_active_bg.png</filename>
<filename>images/mw_menu_cap_l.png</filename>
<filename>images/mw_menu_cap_r.png</filename>
<filename>images/mw_menu_normal_bg.png</filename>
<filename>images/mw_menu_separator.png</filename>
<filename>images/mw_readon.png</filename>
<filename>images/mw_shadow_blue_l.png</filename>
<filename>images/mw_shadow_blue_r.png</filename>
<filename>images/spacer.png</filename>
<filename>css/index.html</filename>
<filename>css/template.css</filename>
<filename>css/template_rtl.css</filename>
<filename>css/editor.css</filename>
<filename>css/ieonly.css</filename>
</files>
<positions>
<position>breadcrumb</position>
<position>left</position>
<position>right</position>
<position>top</position>
<position>user1</position>
<position>user2</position>
<position>user3</position>
<position>user4</position>
<position>footer</position>
<position>debug</position>
<position>syndicate</position>
</positions>
<params>
<param name="colorVariation" type="list" default="white" label="Color
   Variation" description="Color variation to use">
<option value="blue">Blue</option>
<option value="red">Red</option>
```

```
<option value="green">Green</option>
<option value="orange">Orange</option>
<option value="black">Black</option>
<option value="white">White</option>
</param>
<param name="backgroundVariation" type="list" default="blue"
    label="Background Variation" description="Background color
    variation to use">
<option value="blue">Blue</option>
<option value="red">Red</option>
<option value="green">Green</option>
<option value="orange">Orange</option>
<option value="black">Black</option>
<option value="white">White</option>
</param>
<param name="widthStyle" type="list" default="fax" label="Template
    Width" description="Width style of the template">
<option value="fax">Fluid with maximum</option>
<option value="medium">Medium</option>
<option value="small">Small</option>
<option value="fluid">Fluid</option>
</param>
</params>
</install>
```

The preceding code provides the following key information:

- The initial descriptive information for the Installer and the Template Manager
- The declaration inside the `<files>` tags of all the files in the package for the installer
- The declaration inside the `<positions>` tags of all the module position holders for the Module Manager.
- The declaration inside the `<param>` tags of the template parameters that are available in the Template Manager.

Note
The preceding code example is shown in its entirety.

template_thumbnail.png
This file is the thumbnail image of the template that is shown inside the Template Manager. It is generally 206 x150 pixels in size. Although the system supports .jpg, .gif. and .png, the preferred format is .png.

Introducing the Template Manager

All of the system's templates, both front-end and back-end, are managed from within Joomla's Template Manager. To access the Template Manager, click on the option Template Manager under the Extensions menu. Clicking on the Template Manager option displays the output shown in Figure 20.5.

The toolbar at the top of the Template Manager provides quick access to the following functions:

- **Default:** Select a template then click this icon to set the template as the default for your site.

- **Edit:** Select a template from the list then click this icon to edit the template's details.

- **Help:** Click to access the online Help files related to the active screen.

FIGURE 20.5

The Template Manager interface.

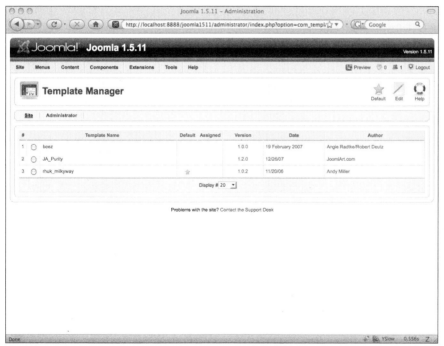

Below the toolbar there are two links: Site shows you the Site Templates. Administrator shows you the Administrator Templates.

The main content area of the screen contains a list of all the templates in your Joomla! site. The columns provided are:

- **#:** An indexing number assigned by Joomla! This cannot be changed.
- **Checkbox (no label):** Click in a checkbox to select a template; this is needed if you wish to use any of the toolbar options, referenced in the preceding list.
- **Template Name:** This field displays the name of the template. Click the name to edit the template's details. Move your mouse over the template's name to open a thumbnail view of the template.
- **Default:** A yellow star in this field indicates that the template is selected as the site's default template. Only one template can be the default template.
- **Assigned:** A green checkmark in this column indicates that the template is assigned to pages on the site. Click the name of the template to open the editing dialogue and view the pages it is assigned to. When the field is blank, the template is not assigned to any pages on the site. This is used to give a different look to each page in your site.
- **Version:** The version number of the template.
- **Date:** The date the template was created.
- **Author:** The author of the template.

Finally, at the bottom of the screen, below the content area, is the Display # option. Change the value in the combo box control to alter the number of templates that are displayed on the page. The default value can be altered by changing the List Length option on the Global Configuration Manager.

Editing templates

Clicking the name of a template in the Template Manager opens the Template Editing dialogue, as shown in Figure 20.6. The Template Editing dialogue enables you to accomplish several tasks:

- Preview the template's module position holders.
- Assign the template.
- Edit the template's HTML.
- Edit the template's CSS.

The toolbar at the top of the Template Editing dialogue provides quick access to the following functions:

- **Preview:** Click this icon to open a view of the template in a pop-up window. The template shown in the pop-up window has the module position holders marked for your reference.

- **Edit HTML:** Click this icon to open the template HTML Editor.

- **Edit CSS:** Click this icon to open the template CSS Editor.

- **Save:** Click this icon to save your work and exit the Template Editing dialogue.

- **Apply:** Click to save your work without exiting from the Template Editing dialogue. This option lets you save without exiting the screen and is useful in case you are interrupted or you otherwise wish to save yet keep working on this screen.

- **Close:** Cancels the task and exits the Template Editing dialogue.

- **Help:** Displays the Help files related to the active screen.

The workspace in this dialogue is broken down into three sections, Details, Menu Assignment, and Parameters. The Details section contains the following fields:

- **Name:** This displays the name of the template. It is not editable.

- **Description:** Displays a short description of the template. This is not editable.

FIGURE 20.6

The Template Editing dialogue, showing the default RHUK_Milkyway Template.

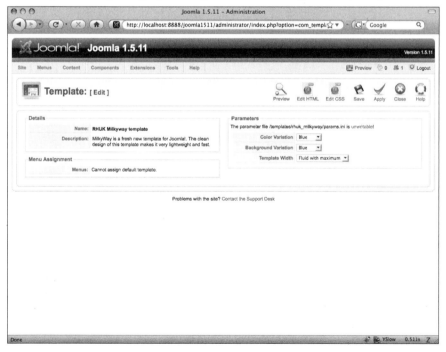

The Menu Assignment section contains the following fields:

- **Menus:** Select None to leave this template unassigned. Choose Select from List to enable the template to be assigned to pages on the site. After you click this option, you will need to select the pages from the box below.

- **Menu Selection:** The pages listed here are eligible for template assignment. Click on one or more to assign the template to those pages. Note that the pages that appear here are the Items from all of the site's various menus.

The contents of the Parameters section vary from template to template. The choices you have here, if any, are set by the template developer.

Editing the template's HTML

Once inside the Template Editing dialogue, you can click the Edit HTML option to view and edit the HTML of the template. Clicking the Edit HTML icon on the top right toolbar opens the dialogue shown in Figure 20.7.

FIGURE 20.7

The RHUK_Milkyway Template shown in the Edit HTML dialogue.

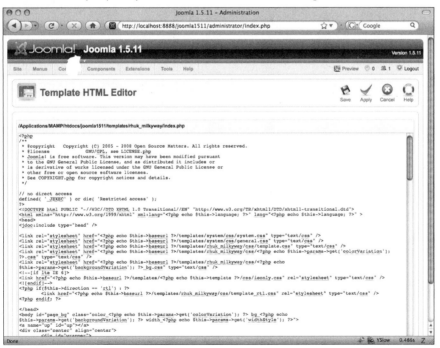

The window shows the template's `index.php` file. From this window, you can modify the code in the file and save the changes.

The toolbar at the top of the Edit HTML dialogue provides quick access to the following functions:

- **Save:** Click this icon to save your work and exit the HTML Editing dialogue.
- **Apply:** Click to save your work without exiting from the HTML Editing dialogue. This option lets you save without exiting the screen and is useful in case you are interrupted or you otherwise wish to save yet keep working on this screen.
- **Cancels:** Cancels the task and exits the HTML Editing dialogue.
- **Help:** Displays the Help files related to the active screen.

Editing the template's CSS

The Template Manager also enables you to edit the various CSS files associated with your templates. When you are inside the Template Editing dialogue, you can click on the Edit CSS icon to view a list of all the CSS files for the template, as shown in Figure 20.8.

FIGURE 20.8

The CSS selection screen.

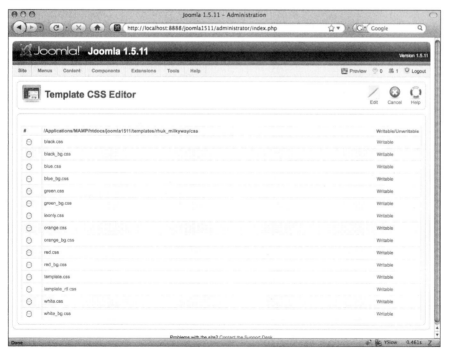

The right column of the CSS selection screen indicates whether the individual CSS files are editable. If the column indicates that the file is not editable, you will need to change the file permissions before you can use the Template Manager's Edit CSS tool.

On the CSS selection screen, select the CSS file you want to edit and click the Edit icon. The Edit CSS dialogue loads in your window, as shown in Figure 20.9.

The toolbar at the top of the Edit CSS dialogue provides quick access to the following functions:

- **Save:** Click this icon to save your work and exit the CSS Editing dialogue.
- **Apply:** Click to save your work without exiting from the CSS Editing dialogue. This option lets you save without exiting the screen and is useful in case you are interrupted or you otherwise wish to save yet keep working on this screen.
- **Cancels:** Cancels the task and exits the CSS Editing dialogue.
- **Help:** Displays the Help files related to the active screen.

FIGURE 20.9

The Edit CSS dialogue.

Setting the default template

The default template appears on all pages where another template is not specifically assigned. When no templates are assigned to any pages, the default template is shown throughout the site. The site can have only one default template.

To change the default template, follow these steps:

1. **Log in to the admin system of your site.**

2. **Access the Template Manager by selecting the option Template Manager under the Extensions menu.** The Template Manager loads in your browser.

3. **Click the radio button next to the template you want to make the default template.**

4. **Click the Default icon on the top right tool bar.** A yellow star appears in the Default column by the template of your choice. The new template will immediately become active as the site's default template.

Assigning templates

If you want to use more than one template on your site, you can do so by assigning one or more templates to specific pages on the site. The Edit Template dialogue provides you with the tools to perform this task. There is no limit to the number of templates you can use; if you wanted, you could use a different template for each section or even each page of your site.

Cross-Reference

See Chapter 22 for a discussion of how to add new Extensions, including templates, to your Joomla! site.

To assign a template to a specific page, follow these steps:

1. **Log in to the admin system of your site.**

2. **Access the Template Manager by selecting the option Template Manager under the Extensions Menu.** The Template Manager loads in your browser.

3. **Click the name of the template you want to assign.** The Template Editing dialogue opens.

4. **Click the option Select from List.**

5. **Click on the names of one or more pages in the box next to the label Menu Selection.**

6. **Click the Save icon on the top right tool bar.** The template immediately becomes active for the pages you have selected and the Template Editing dialogue closes, returning you to the Template Manager.

Tip

If you want to make a page eligible for template assignment, the page must have a Menu Item associated with it; or else the default template will be assigned to the page.

Caution

If you use multiple templates on your site, make note of the fact that any module and component overrides created for one template will not be available for the other templates. You must, in other words, duplicate the overrides across multiple templates if you want them to be available throughout the site.

Customizing Templates

If you have a found an existing template that is close to what you need for your site, the fastest path to having your site up and running may be through customizing an existing template. Some templates, like the JA_Purity template, come with a number of parameters that make it possible for the site administrator to customize the look and feel; others require you to make changes to the code of the template.

This section looks at the most common template customization requests.

Tip

Customizing an existing template is one of the easiest ways to learn Joomla! templating.

Working with template parameters

The easiest way to modify a template is to work with the template parameters. The problems here are twofold: First, and most importantly, not all templates provide parameters for your use and second, sometimes the parameters don't address your specific needs. Regardless, this is a good place to start because if there is a parameter that suits your needs, your work can be done in moments.

To check if your template has parameters, simply open the Template Manager and click the name of the template. If there are any parameters available, they will show in the right column of the Template Editing dialogue. (Refer to Figure 20.6.)

To modify the template parameters, follow these steps:

1. **Log in to the admin system of your site.**
2. **Access the Template Manager by selecting the option Template Manager under the Extensions menu.** The Template Manager loads in your browser.
3. **Click the name of the template you want to check.** The Template Editing dialogue opens.
4. **Select the parameter options you want in the right-hand column.**
5. **Click the Save icon on the top-right tool bar.** The changes are immediately visible on the template. The Template Editing dialogue will close, returning you to the Template Manager.

Making a copy of a template

As a first step to any of the customizations discussed in this chapter, I would strongly recommend that you make a copy of the template you want to modify and work off the copy. Leave the original template intact so you can use it as a reference in case you run into difficulties. Creating and working off a copy also has the added advantage of segregating your changes from the core and making your changes portable. When it comes time to upgrade your site, you can keep your changed files separate and intact. You can also take your changed files and install them on a different site if you so desire. There are a number of steps to this process, so the best approach is to look at an example.

To make a copy of the default RHUK_Milkyway Template, follow these steps:

1. Access the Joomla! installation on your server via FTP or your web host control panel's file manager.

2. Make a copy of the RHUK_Milkyway Template, located at `/templates/rhuk_milkyway`

3. Give your copy of the directory a unique name.

4. Edit the `templateDetails.xml` file to change the template name and description tags, plus any other details you want to modify.

5. Delete from the XML file all invalid resource references. To do this, open the `templateDetails.xml` file and go through the files listed inside the <files> tag, comparing the files listed with the contents of the template's `/images` and the `/css` directories. Delete from the `templateDetails.xml` file references to any file that is not present in the `/images` or `/css` directories.

6. Update all internal links in the template files, changing references to RHUK_Milkyway to the name of your new template directory.

7. Zip up the template directory.

8. Log in to the admin system of your Joomla! site.

9. Open the Extensions Installer by clicking on the option Install/Uninstall under the Extensions Menu.

10. Click Browse. A pop-up window opens.

11. Locate the zipped archive containing your new template and click Open.

12. The pop-up will close and the name of the archive will be displayed in the Package File text field.

13. Click Upload File & Install. The system will attempt to install the template. If successful you will see a confirmation message.

Note that while steps 7 through 12 are a best practices approach, you don't necessarily need to perform those steps if you have duplicated the folder and made changes to the xml file. If you refresh the template page in the back end, you will see a selection available with the name of your new template.

Changing the logo

Perhaps the most common template customization request seen on the Joomla! forums is to change the default template's logo. All the default templates display the Joomla! logo on the template header. The procedure varies somewhat depending upon the template with which you are working.

Here is how to make the change to each of the Joomla! 1.5.x default templates:

Beez

Follow these steps to change this default template:

1. Save your logo as a .gif file, using the name logo.gif.

2. Access your Joomla! location on your server via FTP or your web host's file manager.

3. Go to the directory `/templates/beez/images`.

4. Rename the existing `/templates/beez/images/logo.gif` **file.** (You are essentially creating a backup of logo.gif.)

5. Copy your logo.gif file to the directory **/templates/beez/images**. Your new logo now appears on your template.

Note

The default logo measures 300 x 97 pixels. Ideally, your replacement logo will be the same size. If it is not, you may have to adjust the code in the `index.php` file to account for the new logo dimensions.

Note

You could also replace the logo with an image file of a different name by editing the file name in the code of the `index.php` file.

JA_Purity

Follow these steps to change this default template:

1. Save your logo as a .gif file, using the name logo.png.

2. Access your Joomla! location on your server via FTP or your web host's file manager.

3. Go to the `directory /templates/ja_purity/images`.

4. Rename the existing `/templates/ja_purity/images/logo.png` **file.**

5. Copy your logo.png file to the `directory /templates/ja_purity/images`. Your new logo now appears on your template.

Note

The default logo measures 208 x 80 pixels. Ideally, your replacement logo will be the same size. If it is not, you may have to adjust the CSS styling to account for the new logo dimensions.

Note

You could also replace the logo an image file of a different name by making changes to the `template.css` file. See the next section for an example.

RHUK_Milkway

Follow these steps to change this default template:

1. Save your logo as a .gif file, using the name mw_joomla_logo.png.

2. Access your Joomla! location on your server via FTP or your Web host's file manager.

3. Go to the directory `/templates/rhuk_milkyway/`images.

4. Rename the existing `/templates/rhuk_milkyway/images/mw_joomla_logo.png` file.

5. Copy your mw_joomla_logo.png file to the directory `/templates/rhuk_milkyway/images`. Your new logo now appears on your template.

Note

The default logo measures 298 x 75 pixels. Ideally, your replacement logo will be the same size. If it is not, you may have to adjust the CSS styling to account for the new logo dimensions.

Note

You could also replace the logo with an image file of a different name by making changes to the `template.css` file. See the next section for an example.

Khepri

Eliminating or substituting the logo inside the Khepri admin template is significantly more complicated, due to the way the header image has been created. The author of Khepri has embedded the logo into the background image. Accordingly, replacing the logo means reworking the header image. To complicate matters further, the header image uses a two-tone effect and has rounded corners. This makes replacing or substituting the logo more complicated to execute graphically.

Tip

Arguably, it is easier to simply replace the entire header image than to try to rework what is there now.

If you want to rework the header, you will need to modify several files. First, however, you need to identify which files you should replace, as the Khepri header is offered in three different color schemes.

To find your images, look inside /administrator/templates/images. Inside that directory there are three sub-directories, one for each header color scheme: h_cherry, h_green, h_teal. The default color scheme is green; therefore the default header images are inside the directory h_ green. Each of the three color header directories contains files of the same name and function:

- j_header_left_rtl.png: The left corner of the header when text orientation is set right-to-left.

- j_header_left.png: The left corner of the header when text orientation is set to left-to-right (this is the default for most languages).

- j_header_middle.png: The middle portion of the header image. This is the portion that is repeated to allow the header image to expand to fit different screen resolution settings.

- j_header_right_rtl.png: The right corner of the header when text orientation is set right-to-left.

- j_header_right.png: The right corner of the header when text orientation is set to left-to-right (this is the default for most languages).

Before you begin the following five steps, you need to identify which pieces of the header you need to change. Create your new header images with the same names and file formats of the pieces you want to replace.

Tip

You will only need to modify those pieces that are used for your text orientation. If you want to replace the header entirely with one of your own design, you must replace three files and you must remember that the j_header_middle.png file must be able to be repeated to allow for smooth expansion of the header image for different display resolutions.

Follow these steps:

1. Access your Joomla! location on your server via FTP or your web host's file manager.

2. Go to the directory /administrator/templates/khepri/**images.**

3. Open the directory of the header images you wish to modify.

4. Rename the existing files inside the directory.

5. Copy your new files to the directory. Your new logo will now appear on your template.

Modifying the CSS

The CSS files are largely responsible for the appearance of your site. Although the extent of the role played by the CSS depends on the way the developer created the template, you can be certain that at the very least you can control your site's page dimensions, font colors, and sizes. You can achieve a significant amount of template customization by working with the template's CSS. In the preceding examples, logo replacement was handled by substituting graphics files. However, both the JA_Purity and the RHUK_Milkyway templates place the logo on the page through the use of a

CSS selector; for those two templates you can also change the logo by modifying the CSS. Working with the CSS has several advantages over substitution of the graphics file. First, you do not have to name your logo to match the default logo. Similarly, you do not have to rename the old logo to preserve it. Second, by working with the CSS, you can adjust the height, width, and margin attributes to account for differences in graphic file dimensions.

By way of example, look at the RHUK_Milkyway template. The `index.php` file includes the following line:

```
<div id="logo"></div>
```

This seemingly empty tag actually is responsible for the placement of the logo on the page. If you open RHUK_Milkyway's `template.css` file, you can identify the selector responsible:

```
div#logo {
position: absolute;
left: 0;
top: 0;
float: left;
width: 298px;
height: 75px;
background: url(../images/mw_joomla_logo.png) 0 0 no-repeat;
margin-left: 30px;
margin-top: 25px;
}
```

By altering this selector you can change the logo on your template. Follow these steps:

1. **Use FTP or your web host's file manager to upload your new logo to your Joomla! site installation. Put the image in the directory** /templates/rhuk_milkyway/images.

2. **Log in to the admin system of your site.**

3. **Access the Template Manager by selecting the option Template Manager under the Extensions menu.** The Template Manager loads in your browser.

4. **Click the name of the rhuk_milkyway template.** The Template Editing dialogue opens.

5. **Click the Edit CSS icon on the top-right toolbar.** The Template CSS selecting window opens.

6. **Click the radio button next to the file named template.css.**

7. **Click the Edit icon on the top-right toolbar.** The CSS editing dialogue opens.

8. **Find the selector div#logo.** Change the image name in this line of the selector to reflect the name of your new logo image file: `background: url(../images/mw_joomla_logo.png) 0 0 no-repeat`.

9. **Adjust the width and height values, if necessary.**

10. **Click the Save icon on the top-right tool bar.** The changes to the CSS are saved, and the CSS Editing dialogue closes, returning you to the Template Editing dialogue.

Using class suffixes

The Joomla! system provides the administrator with the option to add class suffixes to a number of items in the system. Page class suffixes, Module class suffixes, and Menu class suffixes are all examples of the Class Suffix option in action. The purpose of all these options is the same, that is, to give you the opportunity to make the styling specific to that item by appending to the existing class the suffix of your choice.

To take advantage of this feature you need to both specify the suffix for the item and then create the CSS styling that goes with it. You have two options for setting the value of the suffix. First, if you simply type a label into the provided class suffix field, the value will be appended directly to the existing class, thereby removing the old class from application to the item and also creating a new class that you can style. Alternatively, if you enter a space then type in the label, the system behaves differently: Instead of replacing the old class with a new one, the system leaves the old class and adds a new class with the same name as your label. Both the old class and the new class will be applied to the item.

By way of example, if the item was originally styled with a class named "moduleheading" and you add the Module Class suffix "_blue" then the styling for the item would look like this: class="moduleheading_blue". If instead you add the Module Class suffix " blue" (that is, a space " " plus the word "blue"), the code would be class="moduleheading blue".

The final step to complete the process would be to add the appropriate selector to your `template.css`.

You can learn more about class suffixes at `http://docs.joomla.org/Tutorial:Using_Class_Suffixes_in_Joomla!_1.5`

Tip
If you are new to working with CSS, there are a number of good resources online at the official Joomla! documentation site. A good place to start is here:

```
http://docs.joomla.org/Discover_your_template_css-styles_and_learn_how_to_
    change_them
```

Controlling the Appearance of Menus

The Joomla! system provides menu styling options as part of the parameters for the menu modules. You can also style the menus through the use of the system's CSS selectors. The following section looks at the default styling options.

Cross-Reference
The creation of menus, menu items, and sub-menus is discussed further in Chapter 8.

Using the default options

As discussed in Chapter 17, Joomla's menu modules provide basic control over the formatting of the menus. The parameters for menu modules include four default menu styles. The selection of the menu style has implications for the available CSS styling for the menu.

- **List:** The default menu style. This style creates the menu as a plain unordered list <ul>, where each Menu Item is a separate List Item <li>. This gives you the most flexibility for controlling menu layout and allows for the use of tools like the Suckerfish menu system . When this style is selected, the #menu id is applied to the <ul>.

- **Legacy - Vertical:** This style is intended to create a style compatible with the old Joomla 1.0 vertical menu style. When this style is selected, the class .mainlevel is applied to each link in a table. The table is set to 100% width (Note that using tables is generally frowned upon in the CSS community. UL and LI tags are worth learning to style if you want your web site to keep up with the latest standards.

- **Legacy - Horizontal:** This style is intended to create a style compatible with the old Joomla 1.0 horizontal menu style. When this style is selected, the class .mainlevel is applied to each link in a table. The table is set to 100% width.

- **Legacy - Flat List:** This style is intended to create a style compatible with the old Joomla 1.0 flat list menu style. This option is one option for creating horizontal menus, as seen in the Top Menu on the default site with the sample data installed. When this style is selected, the #menu id is applied to the <ul>.

The module's Advanced Parameters also include options to create specific CSS selectors for the menu and the ability to add a module class suffix or a menu class suffix.

Note
The use of Module Chrome can also make adding your own CSS styling to menus easy. See the discussion of Module Chrome in the following section.

Creating drop-down menus

Joomla! does not support drop-down menu styles in the default system. The reason for this is purely practical: Drop-down functionality has a number of variables, from placement to spacing to drop-down style to how to handle multiple tiers. Drop-down menus invariably require a bit of tailoring to fit a particular template.

If you want to use drop-down menus, you need to consider either a template that includes drop-downs, or a third party extension. If you want to use drop down menus with the default templates, your best choice is the JA_Purity template, as it includes support for drop-down menus.

To convert the main menu in the JA_Purity template to a horizontal drop-down menu, follow these steps:

1. Log in to the admin system.

2. **Open the Module Manager by selecting the option Module Manager under the Extensions menu.** The Module Manager loads in your browser window.

3. **Click on the name of the Main Menu Module.** The Module Editing window opens.

4. Change the Position to hornav.

5. Change the Menu Style to List.

6. Set the Parameter Always show sub-nav items to Yes.

7. Delete any values in the Menu Class Suffix and the Module Class Suffix.

8. **Click the Save button on the top-right toolbar.** The changes are saved, the Module Editing window closes and you are returned to the Module Manager.

Tip

You can also create drop-down menus with a number of third party extensions. One of the most common combinations is the Extended Menu Module combined with the Suckerfish drop-down. There is a good discussion of this on the official Joomla! docs site at

```
http://docs.joomla.org/Creating_a_CSS_Drop_down_Menu
```

Also note that you can style any type of UL using only CSS. Son of Suckerfish is one of the most commonly used CSS drop-down menus. It can be found at

```
http://htmldog.com/articles/suckerfish/dropdowns/
```

Cross-Reference

Chapter 22 includes reference to several third-party extensions that can enhance menu presentation.

Working with Module Chrome

Joomla! allows for control over the output of modules via either CSS or through the use of Module Chrome. While CSS control is limited to what can be achieved through manipulation of the selectors set in place in the module view, chrome opens up the possibility for you to define your own styling. You have the option either to create your own custom styles or to use a default set of module chrome styles.

The standard module chrome options are:

- **none:** Raw output with no styling or formatting added and no module title output
- **table:** Output the module in a table

- **horz:** Output the module as a table wrapped inside a table (a nested table)

- **xhtml:** Output the module wrapped in divs

- **rounded:** Output the module in nested divs that support the use of rounded corners

- **outline:** Output the module wrapped in the Module Position Preview wrapper

Note

For a breakdown of exactly what the effect of each of these has on the code output, please refer to these pages on the Official Joomla! docs site:

`http://docs.joomla.org/What_is_module_chrome%3F` and **http://docs.joomla.org/Core_module_chrome_CSS**

The module chrome styles are defined inside the `index.php` file, by adding the `style` attribute to the PHP includes that place the module position holders. By way of example, look at the following lines of code, taken from the default RHUK_Milkyway template's `index.php` file:

```
<div id="leftcolumn">
<?php if($this->countModules('left')) : ?>
<jdoc:include type="modules" name="left" style="rounded" />
<?php endif; ?>
</div>
...
...
<td width="170">
<jdoc:include type="modules" name="right" style="xhtml"/>
</td>
```

These two snippets show the default module chrome options in action. The first snippet shows the jdoc:include statement with the style attribute set to "rounded." The second shows the same attribute set to "xhtml." As a result of these attributes, all modules assigned to the Left position will use the tags for the rounded style in their output. In contrast, all modules assigned to the Right position will use the tags for the xhtml style in their output.

While the default styles add a great deal of flexibility there may be times when you need to achieve even more specific styling. In those cases where you cannot get what you need from the default module chrome styles, you can create your own custom module chrome.

To see custom module chrome in action, look at the default JA_Purity template. Note the following lines of code from the JA_Purity `index.php` file:

```
<div id="ja-col2">
<jdoc:include type="modules" name="right" style="jarounded" />
  </div>
```

531

The code uses the same syntax as above, but the style attribute is set to a custom value, in this case "jarounded." The value of jarounded is set by way of a function that is placed in the template's `modules.php` file. Here is the corresponding code from JA_Purity's `modules.php` file:

```php
function modChrome_jarounded($module, &$params, &$attribs)
{
<div class="jamod module<?php echo $params->get('moduleclass_sfx');
    ?>" id="Mod<?php echo $module->id; ?>">
<div>
<div>
<div>
<?php if ($module->showtitle != 0) : ?>
<?php
if(isset($_COOKIE['Mod'.$module->id])) $modhide = $_
    COOKIE['Mod'.$module->id];
else $modhide = 'show';
?>
<h3 class="<?php echo $modhide; ?>"><span><?php echo $module->title;
    ?></span></h3>
<?php endif; ?>
<div class="jamod-content"><?php echo $module->content; ?></div>
</div>
</div>
</div>
</div>
}
```

This function enables the jarounded custom style for use in the template. Note how the code sets out the formatting that will be used, calling the module output inside the div.jamod-content. The function is a normal PHP function and can use any regular PHP code. The available module properties are determined by what properties that particular module possesses. In this example, the key output properties used are: $module->title and $module->content.

Note

It is also possible to specify custom attributes and parameters by way of the `modules.php` file. Module parameters are accessed using the `$params` object. Additional attributes require the creation of an `$attribs` array. While these techniques are very powerful and add a great deal of flexibility, they also require some fluency with PHP. Learn more at

```
http://docs.joomla.org/Applying_custom_module_chrome
```

To add custom module chrome to your template, follow these steps:

1. Create a new blank file. Name it modules.php and place it inside your template's /html directory.

2. Make sure the file has both an opening and closing PHP tag.

3. Add the following code at the top of the file, inside the opening tag: defined ('_JEXEC') or die ('Restricted access').

4. Add the following to create your function. Substitute the name of your function for the value STYLENAME in this example code:

```
function modChrome_STYLENAME( $module, &$params, &$attribs )
{
  /* add the chrome for the Module output here
 must include <?php echo $module->content; ?> to output the
 content. */
}
```

5. Save the file.

6. Open the template's index.php file.

7. For each module position where you want the custom chrome to appear, add the attribute style="STYLENAME" to the jdoc:include statements used to create the module position holder, e.g., `<jdoc:include type="modules" name="right" style="STYLENAME" />`.

8. **Save the file.** The new module chrome appears, formatting the output of the modules in the affected module position.

Overriding Pagination Formatting

Many Joomla! pages include pagination controls. These are the controls that allow the user to set the number of items per page and to use links at the bottom of lists to navigate between pages or items. Pagination overrides are kept in a dedicated file named `pagination.php` and placed in the `/html` directory.

There are four functions available:

- **pagination_item_active:** The links to the pages other than the current active page.

- **pagination_item_inactive:** The current page that is active; typically this is not linked.

- **pagination_list_footer:** Responsible for the output of the control setting the number of items to display per page.

- **pagination_list_render:** Controls the display of the list of links to the other pages, including the Start, End, Previous, and Next links.

By way of example, look at the RHUK_Milkyway template. First, the template's `pagination.php` file provides the following override for the formatting of the output control setting the number of items per page:

```
function pagination_list_footer($list)
{
$html = "<div class=\"list-footer\">\n";
$html .= "\n<div class=\"limit\">".JText::_('Display
    Num').$list['limitfield']."</div>";
$html .= $list['pageslinks'];
$html .= "\n<div class=\"counter\">".$list['pagescounter']."</div>";
$html .= "\n<input type=\"hidden\" name=\"limitstart\" value=\"".$lis
    t['limitstart']."\" />";
$html .= "\n</div>";
return $html;
}
```

Next, the template's `pagination.php` file provides the following override for the formatting of the links that appear at the bottom of pages:

```
function pagination_list_render($list)
{
// Initialize variables
$html = "<span class=\"pagination\">";
$html .= '<span>&laquo;</span>'.$list['start']['data'];
$html .= $list['previous']['data'];
foreach( $list['pages'] as $page )
{
if($page['data']['active']) {
$html .= '<strong>';
}
$html .= $page['data'];
if($page['data']['active']) {
$html .= '</strong>';
}
}
$html .= $list['next']['data'];
$html .= $list['end']['data'];
$html .= '<span>&raquo;</span>';
$html .= "</span>";
return $html;
}
```

Finally, the template's `pagination.php` file provides the following overrides for handling the formatting of the active and inactive page links that appear at the bottom of pages:

```
function pagination_item_active(&$item) {
return "<a href=\"".$item->link."\" title=\"".$item-
    >text."\">".$item->text."</a>";
```

```
}
function pagination_item_inactive(&$item) {
return "<span>".$item->text."</span>";
}
```

The most efficient way to add pagination overrides to your template is to copy the `pagination.php` file from either the default RHUK_Milkyway template or the default Beez template. Use that code as your starting point. Save the copied code to your own `pagination.php` file inside your template's `/html` directory. Make any changes you need to your new file and you're done. If there is a `pagination.php` file in the active template's directory, the system will detect it automatically and use it in preference to the default styling.

Creating a New Template

This section looks at the minimum requirements to set up a basic template. With these basics in place, you have a solid foundation from which you can expand the template and introduce more advanced features as needed.

Creating the structure

As a first step to creating your own template, you need to set up the necessary directory structure and name properly the directories and files. By way of example, I am going to create a new Joomla! 1.5.x template named "Balinese."

Follow these steps to get started:

1. **Create a new directory inside** `/templates` and name it `/balinese`.

2. **Inside the** `/templates/balinese` **directory, create two new sub-directories:** `/css` **and** `/images`.

3. **Use your HTML editor to create the following empty files:** `index.php`, `templateDetails.xml`, `template.css` and `component.php`.

4. **Place the files** `index.php`, `component.php` and `templateDetails.xml` **inside** `/templates/balinese`.

5. **Place the file** `template.css` **inside the** `directory /templates/balinese/css`.

With the steps above completed, you now have the structure in place to meet the minimum requirements for a new template. The next step is to add the code to the files.

Creating the index.php file

The `index.php` file is responsible for placing all the output on the page. The code below sets all the key elements in place, but without any styling; you can add the styling later with CSS.

Open the `index.php` file you created earlier and add the code specified below:

Inside the <head>

Begin your file by adding the following code:

```php
<?php defined( '_JEXEC' ) or die( 'Restricted access' );?>
<!DOCTYPE html PUBLIC "-//W3C//DTD XHTML 1.0 Transitional//EN"
    "http://www.w3.org/TR/xhtml1/DTD/xhtml1-transitional.dtd">
<html xmlns="http://www.w3.org/1999/xhtml"
    xml:lang="<?php echo $this->language; ?>" lang="<?php echo $this-
    >language; ?>" >
```

The first line of the above enhances your site security by prohibiting direct access of the code. The next statement provides the doctype for the pages. The final line declares the language used by the site.

```html
<head>
<jdoc:include type="head" />
<link rel="stylesheet" href="<?php echo $this->baseurl ?>/templates/
    system/css/system.css" type="text/css" />Should there be an
    explanation of each of this line?
<link rel="stylesheet" href="<?php echo $this->baseurl ?>/templates/
    system/css/general.css" type="text/css" />Explanation of this
    line?
<link rel="stylesheet" href="<?php echo $this->baseurl ?>/
    templates/<?php echo $this->template?>/css/template.css"
    type="text/css" />
</head>
```

Note the `jdoc:include` statement at the top of the <head>. That include statement brings in the page title, meta information and system JavaScript. The following lines include the various minimum stylesheets.

Inside the <body>

Add the following lines immediately following the close of the <head> tag:

```html
<body>
<jdoc:include type="modules" name="top" />
<jdoc:include type="modules" name="breadcrumb" />
<jdoc:include type="modules" name="left" />
<jdoc:include type="modules" name="right" />
<jdoc:include type="modules" name="top" />
<jdoc:include type="modules" name="user1" />
<jdoc:include type="modules" name="user2" />
<jdoc:include type="modules" name="user3" />
<jdoc:include type="modules" name="user4" />
<jdoc:include type="message" />
```

```
<jdoc:include type="component" />
<jdoc:include type="modules" name="bottom" />
</body>
</html>
```

The preceding code places in your template all the essential elements, though without any styling. All the module position holders are set (type="modules"), as is the component output (type="component") and the system messages (type="message").

Tip

The User3 module position holder has emerged as a de facto standard for menu placement. While it is not necessary to use this module position for that purpose, you may want to consider it, as many other templates do so.

Creating the template.css file

The easiest way to get started with your CSS is to copy the styles of one of the default templates and then clean it up to suit your needs.

Creating the templateDetails.xml file

The templateDetails.xml needs to include all the data necessary for the Joomla! installer as well as the module positions. As our template does not include any parameters, there are none declared in the code.

Open the templateDetails.xml file you created earlier and add the following specified code:

```
<?xml version="1.0" encoding="utf-8"?>
<!DOCTYPE install PUBLIC "-//Joomla! 1.5//DTD template 1.0//EN"
  "http://dev.joomla.org/xml/1.5/template-install.dtd">
<install version="1.5" type="template">
        <name>Balinese</name>
        <creationDate>2009-06-01</creationDate>
        <author>Bob Author</author>
        <authorEmail>bob@theauthor.com</authorEmail>
        <authorUrl>http://www.theauthor.com</authorUrl>
        <copyright></copyright>
        <license>GNU/GPL</license>
        <version>1.0.0</version>
        <description>Bare Bones Template</description>
        <files>
                <filename>index.php</filename>
                <filename>component.php</filename>
                <filename>templateDetails.xml</filename>
                <filename>template_thumbnail.png</filename>
                <filename>css/template.css</filename>
```

```
        </files>
        <positions>
                <position>breadcrumb</position>
                <position>left</position>
                <position>right</position>
                <position>top</position>
                <position>user1</position>
                <position>user2</position>
                <position>user3</position>
                <position>user4</position>
                <position>bottom</position>
        </positions>
</install>
```

Note that the list of module positions in this file matches up with the module position holders placed in the index.php file.

Creating the component.php file

The component.php file is standardized. To create yours, simply copy the code from one of the default templates and paste it into the component.php file you created earlier, and then alter the following lines of code:

```
<head>
<jdoc:include type="head" />
<link rel="stylesheet" href="<?php echo $this->baseurl ?>/templates/
    rhuk_milkyway/css/template.css" type="text/css" />
<?php if($this->direction == 'rtl') : ?>
<link rel="stylesheet" href="<?php echo $this->baseurl ?>/templates/
    rhuk_milkyway/css/template_rtl.css" type="text/css" />
<?php endif; ?>
</head>
```

Working with template parameters

Adding parameters to a template can greatly enhance the flexibility of the template. Template parameters allow the site administrator to adjust the appearance or behavior of the template from within the Template Manager, without having to make changes to the code. The JA_Purity template included in the default Joomla! site distribution is a great example of how that works.

Perhaps not surprisingly, template parameters are most commonly used by designers who have built their templates for sale or for general release. Parameters are rarely included in templates by developers who are building for their own uses.

If you are interested in learning more about how to add parameters to your templates, there is a series of articles dedicated to this topic on the official Joomla! docs site. Start with http://docs.joomla.org/Introduction_to_template_parameters

Change the code to point to your `template.css` file, as shown next:

```
<head>
<jdoc:include type="head" />
<link rel="stylesheet" href="<?php echo $this->baseurl ?>/templates/
    balinese/css/template.css" type="text/css" />
<?php if($this->direction == 'rtl') : ?>
<link rel="stylesheet" href="<?php echo $this->baseurl ?>/templates/
    balinese/css/template_rtl.css" type="text/css" />
<?php endif; ?>
</head>
```

Save your changes and you are done — you have the framework for a fully functional Joomla! template. All that remains to be done is to set the styling you prefer by adding CSS styling to your `index.php` file.

Packaging the template files

Templates need to be archived for installation. To package the template, simple zip up all the files. The process is really that simple. Once zipped up, it can be installed with Joomla!'s automated Installer. You can use any of the most common archive formats, including .zip, .tar.gz, and .tar. bz2.

Note

In addition to the files discussed in the preceding section,, you should also include a thumbnail image of the template. The image should be 206 x 150 pixels. The recommended file format is .png. The file should be named `template_thumbnail.png`.

Working With the Admin Template

The appearance of the admin system of Joomla!, just like the front end of the site, is controlled by a template. The default Joomla! 1.5.x system provides only one option for the admin template, the Khepri template., shown in Figure 20.10.

The admin system provides only limited options for customization, but there are ways to squeeze a bit more out of Khepri and the admin interface as a whole. Here are some ideas for how you can tweak the admin interface; some are based on template modifications, others on changes to the Administrator modules. Figure 20.11 shows Khepri's appearance after the implementation of these minor changes.

- Use Khepri's Parameters to customize the color of the header.
- Use the Parameters to remove the words "Joomla 1.x.x" from the Header. If you remove the site name, the Header shows the word "Administration" in place of the site name.
- Use the Parameters to square off the corners of the workspace.

- Unpublish any unnecessary Administrator Modules in the right column of the Control Panel. The Welcome to Joomla! message is a likely candidate for deletion, so is the Menu Items Module. Alternatively, you can change the text in the Welcome to Joomla! Module to something else; if you are a developer, this is a good place to drop in your contact details and branding.

- Use the Module Manager to re-order the Administrator Modules that appear in the right column of the Control Panel; putting the Joomla! Security Newsfeed at the top is a good way to raise your site users' awareness of security announcements.

FIGURE 20.10

The Control Panel of the admin interface after the changes.

FIGURE 20.11

An interior admin page, after the changes listed above. Note the header is gone and the footer is customized to provide clients a link the developer's support site in the event of problems.

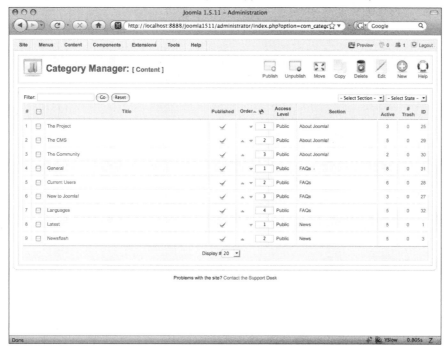

Cross-Reference

Managing the Administrator modules is discussed in Chapter 17.

- Edit the Khepri template code to remove the footer message or customize the message to your purposes.

- Create your own branded header, as discussed earlier in this chapter, or

- Edit the Khepri template code to eliminate complete the graphical header. This will decrease the page size and improve page loading speeds (slightly!). To make this change, remove these lines from immediately below the opening <body> tag:

```
<div id="border-top" class="<?php echo $this->params->get('headerColo
    r','green');?>">
        <div>
                <div>
```

```
                        <span class="version"><?php echo    JText::_
('Version') ?> <?php echo  JVERSION; ?></span>
                        <span class="title"><?php echo $this->params-
>get('showSiteName') ? $mainframe->getCfg( 'sitename' ) :
JText::_('Administration'); ?></span>
            </div>
        </div>
</div>
```

Tip

Don't forget to make a copy of the template if you want to customize it. The copy makes it easier to preserve your changes in the face of updates or upgrades!

Note

The Joomla! Extensions Directory has a separate category dedicated to extensions that are intended to enhance the admin interface.

```
http://extensions.joomla.org/extensions/administration/admin-interface
```

Summary

In this chapter, I covered the basics of customizing the Joomla! templates. You learned the following:

- How the templates work
- How to use the Template Manager
- The characteristics of the default templates
- How to customize the templates
- How to create new templates
- How to work with the appearance of the menus
- How to work with module chrome
- How to override the pagination controls

Customizing Joomla! Functionality

J oomla! is extensible and customizable by design. The system's various components, modules, and plugins are easily identified and can be targeted for customization. This chapter focuses on the basics of customizing those key elements.

Components, the system's most complex element, employ the Model-View-Controller architecture that cleanly segregates the business logic from the presentation layer. Although the MVC architecture helps make the planning and creation of new components simpler, component creation remains a challenging and sometimes complex task suited more to experienced programmers.

Modules are the most commonly modified element in the system. Managing the customization of modules is relatively easier than working with components and can be done by anyone with basic programming skills and an awareness of the system requirements and architecture.

Plugins tend to be focused on providing narrow and sometimes esoteric functonality. And although creating a plugin may require more knowledge of the underlying Joomla! framework, the Joomla! system includes plugin templates that make the creation of new plugins an easy task.

In this chapter, I take you through the key elements and anatomy of components, modules, and plugins and discuss how to approach customizing them to suit your needs. Along the way, I also look at overriding the output of the system's components and modules.

IN THIS CHAPTER

Understanding basic principles

Using the right tools

Discovering the Joomla! API

Working with components

Working with modules

Working with plugins

Understanding Basic Principles

Customizing the functionality of the Joomla! CMS means modifying or creating components, modules, and plugins. As you have seen in previous chapters, modules and components have varying roles on the front end and on the back end of your site. Plugins are enabling applications that provide extended functionality for other elements of the system.

Customization of Joomla's functionality varies widely in difficulty. You are most likely to make customization to modules. Modules are often self-contained and are relatively easy to work with. Plugins tend to be highly specialized and more often the provenance of a developer who needs to add some enabling functionality to a new component. Components are by far the most complex of these various extensions and often have both front-end and back-end elements that have to be considered when you are engaged in customization. Given the complexity of component architecture, and the key role that components play in the system, component customization is by far the more difficult task.

As a general rule, modifications to the core files should be undertaken reluctantly. The textbook approach is to create a new version of the component, module, or plugin and make your modifications to that code; you can then install your new extension and manage it independently of the core. Modifications made to core files can be more difficult to maintain when it comes time to update or upgrade your site. Modifications made to the core can also be troublesome if site maintenance is taken over by someone other than the developer. In either case, unless the changes are well-documented, they can be easy to miss and hard to replicate.

Using the Right Tools

As with any type of work, the right tools can make the job significantly easier. Although the selection of an individual tool kit is a personal and subjective decision, a few tools are clear winners, and there are a few that have been tailored specifically to work with Joomla!

Tools you need to customize a Joomla! site

In broadest and most basic terms, customizing a Joomla! site requires access to the following tools:

- **Web Browser:** You should have access to all of the most common browsers for testing purposes, but for development purposes the Firefox browser is the tool of choice. The existence of a number of add-ons that extend the functionality of Firefox have pushed Firefox into the forefront for developers. Several of these addons are discussed below. Firefox can be downloaded free of charge from www.mozilla.com

- **An editing program:** Many editing programs are available, and everyone seems to have their own favorites. Many people use Adobe's Dreamweaver, although I do not think that it is the easiest program or the best choice for working with PHP. Mac and Linux users, in particular, may find other choices preferable to Dreamweaver. Dreamweaver is a commercial application.

- **An FTP client:** Again, there are a multitude of choices here and many people have their own favorites. If you are using the Firefox browser, the FireFTP add-on gives you an effective FTP client that works directly from inside the browser. Download this add-on for free at `https://addons.mozilla.org/en-US/firefox/addon/684`

  While the items listed above may technically be all that you need (a number of developers get by with just these), if you want to do more, you can use other options. A popular choice among more sophisticated developers is the Eclipse Integrated Development Environment (IDE). Eclipse provides not only a powerful authoring environment, but also includes professional-quality debugging tools, integration with Subversion, and a variety of utilities that can make your work easier. Download the Eclipse IDE free of charge from `http://www.eclipse.org`

Tip

If you are not familiar with Eclipse, you may want to start with the the Joomla! docs article entitled "Setting up your workstation for Joomla! development."

```
http://docs.joomla.org/Setting_up_your_workstation_for_Joomla!_development
```

Tip

If you are looking to do a bit of quick work to the presentation layer, say, merely adding a bit of JavaScript to a template, or modifying the CSS, you don't need anything more than your browser. You can use Joomla's built-in Template Editor function to make changes to templates or their related CSS file. For a discussion of the Template Editor, see Chapter 20.

Useful extensions that aid customization

You can extend your Joomla! site, your Firefox browser, or your Eclipse workstation. Here's a list of popular add-ons and extensions that can make customization of your Joomla! site easier:

- **Firebug:** This add-on for Firefox provides a number of aids to Web development. With Firebug installed, you can click on an element on the screen and view the code that produces it, the CSS that styles it, and a variety of related information. Firebug is particularly useful when working on the presentation layer of a site. The YSlow and PageSpeed addons discussed in this list integrate with Firebug. Download the Firebug addon free of charge at `https://addons.mozilla.org/en-US/firefox/addon/1843`

- **FireFTP:** As mentioned, the FireFTP add-on is an FTP client that runs from inside Firefox as a new tab in the browser window.

- **Phing:** This Eclipse extension is designed to ease packaging, deploying, and testing applications. This works very well with extension development and helps provide an easy way to manage multiple changes and versions to your custom extensions. Download Phing for the Eclipse IDE free of charge at `http://phing.info`.

- **Web Developer:** This Firefox addon is targeted more at Web designers than programmers. It offers many of the same functions as Firebug and offers a toolbar that gives quick access to many options. Download the Web Developer addon for the Firefox browser free of charge at `https://addons.mozilla.org/en-US/firefox/addon/60`

- **YSlow or PageSpeed:** These add-ons for the Firefox browser help identify performance issues on web pages. These are diagnostic tools that help you identify bottlenecks, large files, and slow spots in your pages. Download the YSlow addon for the Firefox browser free of charge at `https://addons.mozilla.org/firefox/addon/5369`. Download PageSpeed free of charge at `http://code.google.com/speed/page-speed/download.html`.

Tip

The Joomla! Extensions Directory has a separate category containing a list of Developer Tools. Visit

`http://extensions.joomla.org/extensions/tools/development-tools`

Discovering the Joomla! API

The Joomla! CMS is an application built on top of the Joomla! framework. The framework is documented in the Joomla! API. Joomla! also relies on several third-party libraries, and some overlap exists between the Joomla! API and portions of some of these libraries.

Note

Where possible, you should always give preference to the Joomla! API calls, instead of calling third-party libraries directly.

Those users who want to create new extensions for Joomla!, or who want to contribute to the Joomla! development efforts, need to spend some time and become acquainted with the Joomla! API. The dedicated API web site is `http://api.joomla.org/`. The contents of that site are automatically generated by the phpDocumentor package and are based upon an analysis of the Joomla! source code.

Additional documentation can be found at the Joomla! Documentation Wiki at `http://docs.joomla.org/`. There is also a manually produced API reference at `http://docs.joomla.org/Framework`. All of these resources are worth at least a quick glance for those interested in creating Joomla! extensions.

Note

Although the Joomla! API is a useful resource, it can always use improvement. If you want to help out, you can contribute to the Joomla! API Reference Project. There's no need to join a working group or seek permission; simply sign up on the site and jump in. The documentation can always use further explanation, examples, corrections, and amplifications.

`http://docs.joomla.org/API_Reference_Project`

Working with Components

Components are at the heart of the Joomla! system. The main content area of each page is generated by a component, and many of the site's modules are dependent in some way on components for their data. Components are the most complex element of the system to customize. Many issues are involved, from the presentation of data to the manipulation of the database. A complete discussion of component development is worthy of a book of its own, and a full discussion of the topic is beyond the scope of this one chapter.

The following sections demonstrate how to execute simple modifications to a component and introduce the basic concepts that underlie the creation of new components.

Knowing the elements of a component

The system's components are divided into two categories: Site components and Administrator components. The front-end Site components are located in the directory /components. The back-end Administrator components are located in the directory /administrator/components. All components use the same naming convention: com_componentname.

With Joomla! 1.5, the project adopted the MVC Component architecture. That is, components are built around the creation of models, views, and controllers. Understanding the MVC concept is key to understanding how to work with Joomla! components.

Model-View-Controller is a software design pattern that helps developers plan an application and then organize the code into a consistent and logical framework. The segregation of the application into models, views, and controllers makes it easy to separate the business logic of the application from the presentation of the data. The key advantage of this approach is that you can work with the presentation of the data without having to make changes to the underlying application's logic.

Looking at each of the three elements in turn shows the following:

Models

The model provides routines to manage and manipulate the data for the application. In most cases, the data is pulled from the database, although other data sources can be used. The Joomla! framework provides the abstract class JModel.

Views

The view portion of the application renders the data. The view does not modify the data; it only displays what is retrieved. The view is technically part of the site's presentation layer and includes one or more templates that provide the formatting of the data. Note that views can display data from multiple models. The Joomla! framework provides the abstract class JView.

Controllers

The controller reacts to actions, triggers the retrieval of data from the model, and passes the data to the view for display. The role of the controller is to associate the model with the view. The Joomla! framework provides the abstract class JController.

The anatomy of a typical component

Joomla! 1.5's Polls component provides a simple example of the typical Joomla! component architecture.

The Polls component has both a front-end and a back-end element. The front-end component provides the polls output that appears in the main content area of the page. A separate Polls module is connected to this component to provide the Poll form you see in the sidebar module position in the default configuration. The back-end Polls component provides the admin interface that allows for the creation and management of your Polls data. The back-end component is located at /administrator/components/com_polls. The front-end component can be found at /components/com_poll.

The front-end Component directory contains the following:

- /assets
- controller.php
- index.html
- /models
- poll.php
- router.php
- /views

Note

You can see in this list the elements that correspond to the MVC architecture: The

/models directory, the /views directory, and the controller.php file.

The key file is poll.php. This is the first file called when the component is in use and is responsible for loading the proper controller, in this case the file controller.php.

The controller.php file defines the controller class and functions needed for this component. The controller file automatically loads the model that has the same name as the view and pushes the data to the view.

The /models directory contains the model for our component. The key file for the model is /models/polls.php, and a generic index.html file. The polls.php file specifies the class PollModelPoll, which sets out our model behavior and extends the system's JModel class. In the case of the Polls component, the model queries the database to extract the number of hits, voters, and the related date information.

The /views directory contains the files for the component's view:

- index.html
- /poll

In the Joomla! system, each view has its own directory. In the case of the Polls component, there is only one view, named poll, hence the presence of the sub-directory /poll. The /poll directory contains the following files:

- index.html
- metadata.xml
- /tmpl
- view.html.php

The key file for the view is the view.html.php file. The view file pushes the data to the template, which is located inside the /tmpl directory. The key functionality in this file is the class PollViewPoll, which extends the system's JView class.

Note

The metadata.xml **file is included in this view to give a title and a description to the view.**

The last piece of the puzzle is formatting of the final component output. This is done through the use of template files. Each view has a separate directory, named /tmpl, that contains the template files. The contents of the /tmpl directory for the poll view are:

- default_graph.php
- default.php
- default.xml
- index.html

The poll view uses two templates, default.php and default_graph.php. The default. php is the primary file and calls the default_graph.php file in the course of rendering the output. These two files contain the HTML needed to format the data on the screen.

Note

The final file, default.xml, **has no role in the actual data output. It only provides the name and description information for the page layout that is displayed during the Menu Item Type selection.**

The /assets directory contains a collection of various graphical elements and CSS for the use of the component:

- `blank.png`
- `index.html`
- `poll_bars.css`
- `poll.png`

Note

The Polls component also contains several files that are not unique to the component. Each of the directories listed above includes an `index.html` file. These files serve no purpose other than to block persons from accessing the directory index by typing into their browsers the URL of the directory. If a user enters the directory path as an URL, he is served the `index.html` file, which displays only a blank page. You can see these files in all the directories of your Joomla! installation. Also note the `router.php`. This file is not specific to the Polls component. It is used frequently throughout the Joomla! components to help with the creation of URLs.

Overriding component output

The Joomla! system allows you override the output of components by creating one or more new view templates and inserting them into your active template directory. This approach to overriding component output allows you to leave the core files untouched; all your changes are made to a new file which is segregated from the core component files. This system has the added advantage of making it easy to keep up with your modifications; no matter how many components you override, all the changed filed are all kept in one place.

By way of an example, I am going to make modifications to the two templates that control the output of the default Poll component. To override the templates, follow these steps:

1. Copy the files `/components/com_poll/views/poll/tmpl/default.php` and `/components/com_poll/views/poll/tmpl/default_graphs.php`

2. Open your active template directory and place the copied file inside a sub-directory named `/html/com_poll/poll`. For example, if you are using the default rhuk_milkyway template, you will create these two files: `/templates/rhuk_milkyway/html/com_poll/poll/default.php` and `/templates/rhuk_milkyway/html/com_poll/poll/default_graph.php`

3. Make your changes to the new files.

4. Save your changes. The new templates will now override the original templates and be displayed on the site.

Note

I have copied two template files only because I need to make changes to both of them. If you only need to change one, just copy one.

To show this process in more detail, here are the code changes made to the Poll component's template files.

Both the default Poll component and the Poll module provide a link to the results of the poll. The results of the poll are shown in the main content area of a dedicated page; it is the output that appears on that page that I want to change. If you look at the default output, you will see that the results page includes:

- A Page Title, which is the same as the Poll question
- A combo box listing the Poll question
- The Poll question
- The answer choices
- A Summary of the poll activity.

Figure 21.1 shows the default Poll component's results page output.

FIGURE 21.1

The results page produced by the default Poll component. Note the Poll question appears three times on the page!

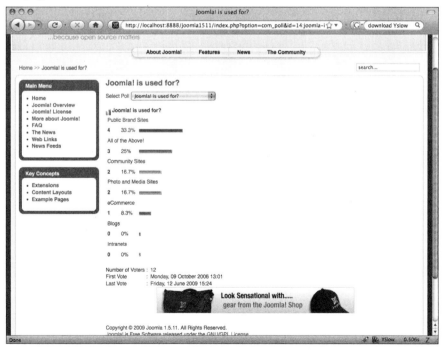

I find the default formatting to be redundant and less than optimal for sites that plan to display the output of only one poll. There are no parameters that allow you to get rid of the repetition of the Poll question, so I am going to modify the view to eliminate the redundancies. I also clean up the results layout a bit to display the results on one line, rather than one two lines per result. To do this, I must modify both the templates in the view, as follows.

First, the key file for the poll view is `default.php`, which looks like this:

```php
<?php // no direct accessdefined('_JEXEC') or die('Restricted
   access');?>
<?php JHTML::_('stylesheet', 'poll_bars.css', 'components/com_poll/
   assets/'); ?>
<form action="index.php" method="post" name="poll" id="poll">
<?php if ($this->params->get( 'show_page_title', 1)) : ?>
<div class="componentheading<?php echo $this->escape($this->params-
   >get('pageclass_sfx')); ?>">
   <?php echo $this->escape($this->params->get('page_title')); ?>
</div>
<?php endif; ?>
<div class="contentpane<?php echo $this->escape($this->params-
   >get('pageclass_sfx')); ?>">
   <label for="id">
        <?php echo JText::_('Select Poll'); ?>
        <?php echo $this->lists['polls']; ?>
   </label>
</div>
<div class="contentpane<?php echo $this->escape($this->params-
   >get('pageclass_sfx')); ?>">
<?php echo $this->loadTemplate('graph'); ?>
</div>
</form>
```

This file contains the code that places the combo box containing the Poll question on the page. To remove that from the output, delete these lines:

```php
<div class="contentpane<?php echo $this->escape($this->params-
   >get('pageclass_sfx')); ?>">
   <label for="id">
        <?php echo JText::_('Select Poll'); ?>
        <?php echo $this->lists['polls']; ?>
   </label>
</div>
   Note: these are lines 13-18
```

I've gone ahead and deleted the `div` that wrapped the combo box as it would be empty without the combo box. Keeping it in the code would serve no purpose.

Next, I need to open up the other template file to take care of the remaining items on my list. The other file is `default_graph.php`. This file is called for display in the last lines of the `default.`

php file (`<?php echo $this->loadTemplate('graph'); ?>`) and it is this template that supplies the results and the graphics that go with them. This file is significantly longer; I do not show it all here as I want to focus on only the code being modified.

The Poll question and the accompanying image are controlled by these lines of code:

```
<thead>
<tr>
<th colspan="3" class="sectiontableheader">
<img src="<?php echo $this->baseurl; ?>/components/com_poll/assets/
    poll.png" align="middle" border="0" width="12" height="14" alt="" />
<?php echo $this->escape($this->poll->title); ?>
</th>
</tr>
</thead>
    Lines 5-12 in the file.
```

The preceding code creates a row in the table that shows the small graph image and the Poll question. By deleting these lines I remove those items from the output.

Next, I want to change the formatting to show the Poll results on a single line. In the default configuration the results for each poll choice are shown on two lines. Here is the default code in question:

```
<?php foreach($this->votes as $vote) : ?>
    <tr class="sectiontableentry<?php echo $vote->odd; ?>">
        <td width="100%" colspan="3">
            <?php echo $vote->text; ?>
        </td>
    </tr>
    <tr class="sectiontableentry<?php echo $vote->odd; ?>">
        <td align="right" width="25">
            <strong><?php echo $this->escape($vote->hits); ?>
</strong> 
</td>
        <td width="30" >
            <?php echo $this->escape($vote->percent); ?>%
</td>
        <td width="300" >
            <div class="<?php echo $vote->class; ?>"
style="height:<?php echo $vote->barheight; ?>px;width:<?php echo
$vote->percent; ?>%"></div>
</td>
    </tr>
<?php endforeach; ?>
```

To affect this change, I need to change the preceding code, as follows:

```
<?php foreach($this->votes as $vote) : ?>
    <tr class="sectiontableentry<?php echo $vote->odd; ?>">
        <td width="150">
```

```
                   <?php echo $vote->text; ?>
         </td>
     <td align="right" width="25">
                   <strong><?php echo $this->escape($vote->hits); ?>
     </strong> 
     </td>
         <td width="30" >
                   <?php echo $this->escape($vote->percent); ?>%
         </td>
         <td width="300" >
                   <div class="<?php echo $vote->class; ?>"
     style="height:<?php echo $vote->barheight; ?>px;width:<?php echo
     $vote->percent; ?>%"></div>
         </td>
         </tr>
     <?php endforeach; ?>
```

Save these changes and you are done. Your new templates now override the original templates and can be displayed on the site. The result of these two changes can be seen in Figure 21.2.

FIGURE 21.2

The results page produced by the default Poll component.

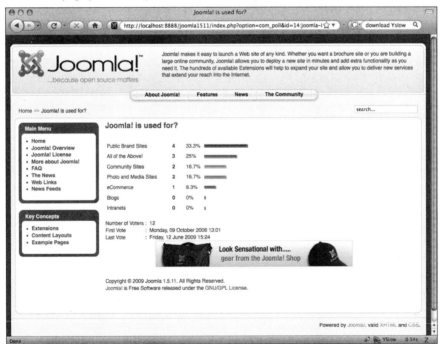

Creating a new component

Although a complete tutorial on creating new Joomla! components is beyond the scope of this text, you should be aware of some basic principles. In the sections that follow, I go through some of the most important issues. If you want to explore this topic in more detail, there are a number of excellent resources on the topic in the official Joomla! Developer documentation.

Note

To help get you started, the Joomla documentation site includes an excellent tutorial called Tutorial: Developing a Model-View-Controller Component. Start with Part 1 at

```
http://docs.joomla.org/Tutorial:Developing_a_Model-View-Controller_
    Component_-_Part_1.
```

Minimum requirements

Defining the minimum requirements for developing a component is difficult because the requirements are defined by the extent and nature of the functionality of the component you are building. Even the ideal of providing a model, a view, and a controller is merely advisory, rather than compulsory. Moreover, your component may not need both a front end and a back end; many components exist in one place only. The best advice is to define what you need the component to do, and then look at the most efficient way to get it done. If the component can benefit from a proper MVC architecture you should use it; if it cannot, then do only what is needed.

Note

The other factor to consider is whether you want to distribute the component. If you want to release the component for others to use, you should follow the MVC framework.

Tip

If you're looking for a quick start, you might want to check out the Joomla! Component Creator, a non-commercial tool available for download at the Joomla! Extentions Directory.

```
http://extensions.joomla.org/extensions/tools/development-tools/7627/details
```

Registering a component

Registering your component in the database is a quick way to make it visible in the back-end admin interface, so you can turn it on and off and work with it during development.

Note

Registering a component is optional; you can achieve the same thing by setting up the installer information in the XML file and using the Joomla! Extension Installer to handle this automatically. However, because you are likely to be writing and revising your component, you may want to register it at the very beginning of the process, so you can see the impact of your changes and manipulate the component more easily during development.

Registering a component is simply entering a record for the component into the `jos_components` table in your site's database. You can accomplish this process either by running an SQL query or by accessing phpMyAdmin and entering the information manually. To register a new component using phpMyAdmin, do the following:

1. **Access phpMyAdmin on the server where your Joomla! installation is located.**

2. **Select the name of your database from the list on the left.** The database information loads in the screen.

3. **From the list of tables on the left side of the screen, select the option jos_components.** The jos_components table summary information displays on the right side of the screen.

4. **Click the Insert tab.** The Insert dialogue loads.

5. **Type the name of your new component in the field marked name.**

6. **In the field labeled link, type option=com_componentname, where the string componentname represents the machine-friendly name of your component.**

7. **In the field labeled admin_menu_link, type option=com_componentname, where the string componentname represents the machine-friendly name of your component.**

8. **In the field labeled admin_menu_alt, type a short description for your component.**

9. **In the field labeled option, type com_componentname, where the string componentname represents the machine-friendly name of your component.**

10. **In the field labeled admin_menu_img, type js/ThemeOffice/component.png.**

11. **Click the button labeled Go.** The system now creates a new row ino the table containing your component information.

After your component is registered, you will be able to access it from the Joomla! admin system where you can easily assign it to the front end and view your work in progress.

Packaging a component

Proper packaging may not be a concern if your component is only intended for your own use, but if you intend to give your component to others, or you want to install it again elsewhere, you should create a proper installation package for the component. Proper packaging allows you to manage component installation through Joomla's default Extension Installer.

Packages are archives that contain all the necessary elements of a component, along with an XML file containing the information needed by the Joomla! Installer. The XML file must include the information needed both to install and to uninstall the component as well as the information needed for adding any menu items needed for the back-end admin interface for your component. The installation package must also contain any SQL scripts needed to set up the database properly.

Caution
Make sure that your XML file is created in UTF-8 format.

Given the wide number of variables related to component installers, and the fact that configuration is very dependent upon the component itself, you should refer to the Installer API when it comes time to create a Component Installation Package. The Installer API is located at: `http://docs.joomla.org/Using_the_installer_API_to_support_package_installation`

Working with Modules

Modules are the most commonly modified pieces of the Joomla! core. Modules are easy to customize and are even relatively easy to create from scratch. This section covers the elements of a typical module, customization of a module, and module creation.

Understanding the elements of a typical module

The system's modules are divided into two categories: Site modules and Administrator modules. The front-end Site modules are located in the directory `/modules`. The back-end Administrator modules are located in the directory `/administrator/modules`.

The easiest way to see all the elements of a typical module is to look at an example. The default system's Login module is typical of Site modules throughout the system. The Login module supplies a Login form for front-end users, along with links to the Password Reset and Username Reminder functions. If front-end user registration is enabled in the Global Configuration Manager, then the module also includes a user registration link labeled Create an account.

The Login module is a Site module and is located at `modules/mod_login`. The contents of the directory are:

- `helper.php`
- `index.html`
- `mod_login.php`
- `mod_login.xml`
- `/tmpl`
- `default.php`
- `index.html`

The mod_modulename.php file

The `mod_modulename.php` is the principle functional file for the module. This file is the first thing called by the system when the module is needed. It contains the initialization routines and includes the `helper.php` file. It will also call the template that will display the module output.

By way of example, here is the `mod_login.php` file:

```
// no direct access
defined('_JEXEC') or die('Restricted access');
// Include the syndicate functions only once
require_once (dirname(__FILE__).DS.'helper.php');
$params->def('greeting', 1);
$type     = modLoginHelper::getType();
$return   = modLoginHelper::getReturnURL($params, $type);
$user =& JFactory::getUser();
require(JModuleHelper::getLayoutPath('mod_login'));
```

The code first prevents direct access to the file, a simple and common security precaution used throughout the Joomla! system. Next the code includes the functions specified in the `helper.php` file.

The helper.php file

The file `helper.php` contains one or more classes that are used to retrieve the data that is displayed by the module.

The contents of the Login Form module's `helper.php` are typical:

```
defined('_JEXEC') or die('Restricted access');
class modLoginHelper
{
function getReturnURL($params, $type)
{
if($itemid =  $params->get($type))
{
$menu =& JSite::getMenu();
$item = $menu->getItem($itemid);
$url = JRoute::_($item->link.'&Itemid='.$itemid, false);
}
else
{
// stay on the same page
$uri = JFactory::getURI();
$url = $uri->toString(array('path', 'query', 'fragment'));
}
return base64_encode($url);
}
function getType()
{
$user = & JFactory::getUser();
return (!$user->get('guest')) ? 'logout' : 'login';
}
}
```

The file defines the helper class `modLoginHelper`, which includes two functions to help set the return URL and determine the user's status for the purpose of displaying either the logout or the login button.

The XML file

The `mod_modulename.xml` file is also a required module file. The XML file helps the Joomla! Installer determine what it needs to copy to install the module properly, and it also tells the Module Manager about the module, including not only basic identification information but also which parameters, if any, are available for module configuration.

The `mod_login.xml` file follows:

```xml
<?xml version="1.0" encoding="utf-8"?>
<install type="module" version="1.5.0">
    <name>Login</name>
    <author>Joomla! Project</author>
    <creationDate>July 2006</creationDate>
    <copyright>Copyright (C) 2005 - 2008 Open Source Matters. All
    rights reserved.</copyright>
    <license>http://www.gnu.org/licenses/gpl-2.0.html GNU/GPL
    </license>
<authorEmail>admin@joomla.org</authorEmail>
    <authorUrl>www.joomla.org</authorUrl>
    <version>1.5.0</version>
    <description>DESCLOGINFORM</description>
    <files>
        <filename module="mod_login">mod_login.php</filename>
    </files>
    <params>
        <param name="cache" type="list" default="1" label="Caching"
    description="Select whether to cache the content of this module">
<option value="0">Never</option>
        </param>
        <param name="@spacer" type="spacer" default="" label=""
    description="" />
        <param name="moduleclass_sfx" type="text" default=""
    label="Module Class Suffix" description="PARAMMODULECLASSSUFFIX"
    />
        <param name="pretext" type="textarea" cols="30" rows="5"
    default="" label="Pre-text" description="PARAMPRETEXT" />
<param name="posttext" type="textarea" cols="30" rows="5"
    label="Post-text" description="PARAMPOSTTEXT" />
        <param name="login" type="menuitem" default=""
    disable="separator" label="Login Redirection URL" description="PARAM
    LOGINREDIRECTURL" />
<param name="logout" type="menuitem" default="" disable="separator"
    label="Logout Redirection URL" description="PARAMLOGOUTREDIRECT
    URL" />
```

```
            <param name="greeting" type="radio" default="1"
        label="Greeting" description="Show/Hide the simple greeting
        text">
                    <option value="0">No</option>
                    <option value="1">Yes</option>
            </param>
            <param name="name" type="list" default="0" label="Name/
        Username">
        <option value="0">Username</option>
                <option value="1">Name</option>
            </param>
            <param name="usesecure" type="radio" default="0"
        label="Encrypt Login Form" description="Submit encrypted login
        data (requires SSL)">
        <option value="0">No</option>
                    <option value="1">Yes</option>
            </param>
        </params>
    </install>
```

The opening lines set out the type of file "module" and the associated Joomla! version number "1.5.0" Immediately following is a series of tags that indicate:

- Module's name
- Author's name
- Creation date
- Copyright
- Module's license agreement terms
- Author's e-mail
- Author's web site URL
- Module's version number
- A short description

The remainder of the code defines the parameters that appear to the site administrator inside the Module Manager.

The Module template

The /tmpl directory contains the template for the module. The template file takes the data that has been generated by the primary module file and displays it on the page. The key file that defines the module output is default.php, listed below.

```
<?php // no direct access
defined('_JEXEC') or die('Restricted access'); ?>
<?php if($type == 'logout') : ?>
```

```
<form action="index.php" method="post" name="login" id="form-login">
<?php if ($params->get('greeting')) : ?>
<div>
<?php if ($params->get('name')) : {
echo JText::sprintf( 'HINAME', $user->get('name') );
} else : {
echo JText::sprintf( 'HINAME', $user->get('username') );
} endif; ?>
    </div>
<?php endif; ?>
    <div align="center">
        <input type="submit" name="Submit" class="button"
    value="<?php echo JText::_( 'BUTTON_LOGOUT'); ?>" />
    </div>
    <input type="hidden" name="option" value="com_user" />
    <input type="hidden" name="task" value="logout" />
    <input type="hidden" name="return" value="<?php echo $return; ?>"
    />
</form>
<?php else : ?>
<?php if(JPluginHelper::isEnabled('authentication', 'openid')) :
$lang->load( 'plg_authentication_openid', JPATH_ADMINISTRATOR );
$langScript =    'var JLanguage = {};'.
' JLanguage.WHAT_IS_OPENID = \''.JText::_( 'WHAT_IS_OPENID' ).'\';'.
'JLanguage.LOGIN_WITH_OPENID = \''.JText::_( 'LOGIN_WITH_OPENID'
    ).'\';'.
'JLanguage.NORMAL_LOGIN = \''.JText::_( 'NORMAL_LOGIN' ).'\';'.
' var modlogin = 1;';
$document = &JFactory::getDocument();
$document->addScriptDeclaration( $langScript );
JHTML::_('script', 'openid.js');
endif; ?>
<form action="<?php echo JRoute::_( 'index.php', true, $params-
    >get('usesecure')); ?>" method="post" name="login" id="form-
    login" >
    <?php echo $params->get('pretext'); ?>
    <fieldset class="input">
    <p id="form-login-username">
        <label for="modlgn_username"><?php echo JText::_
    ('Username') ?></label><br />
        <input id="modlgn_username" type="text" name="username"
    class="inputbox" alt="username" size="18" />
    </p>
    <p id="form-login-password">
        <label for="modlgn_passwd"><?php echo JText::_('Password')
    ?></label><br />
        <input id="modlgn_passwd" type="password" name="passwd"
    class="inputbox" size="18" alt="password" />
    </p>
```

```php
<?php if(JPluginHelper::isEnabled('system', 'remember')) : ?>
<p id="form-login-remember">
        <label for="modlgn_remember">
<?php echo JText::_('Remember me') ?>
</label>
        <input id="modlgn_remember" type="checkbox" name="remember"
    class="inputbox" value="yes" alt="Remember Me" />
    </p>
    <?php endif; ?>
    <input type="submit" name="Submit" class="button" value="<?php
    echo JText::_('LOGIN') ?>" />
    </fieldset>
    <ul>
        <li>
<a href="<?php echo JRoute::_( 'index.php?option=com_user&view=reset'
    ); ?>">
        <?php echo JText::_('FORGOT_YOUR_PASSWORD'); ?></a>
</li>
<li>
<a href="<?php echo JRoute::_( 'index.php?option=com_
    user&view=remind' ); ?>">
<?php echo JText::_('FORGOT_YOUR_USERNAME'); ?></a>
</li>
<?php            $usersConfig = &JComponentHelper::getParams( 'com_
    users' );              if ($usersConfig-
    >get('allowUserRegistration')) : ?>
<li>
<a href="<?php echo JRoute::_( 'index.php?option=com_
    user&view=register' ); ?>">
<?php echo JText::_('REGISTER'); ?></a>
</li>
<?php endif; ?>
</ul>
<?php echo $params->get('posttext'); ?>

<input type="hidden" name="option" value="com_user" />
<input type="hidden" name="task" value="login" />
<input type="hidden" name="return" value="<?php echo $return; ?>"/>
<?php echo JHTML::_( 'form.token' ); ?>
</form>
<?php endif; ?>
```

This file plays the key role in the display of the module output. The majority of the code in this file is HTML used to create the various form fields needed by this module. The PHP supplies the logic and the variables that relate to the language strings and the URL paths.

Two forms are on this page. The first form provides the Logout button that appears when a user is logged in to the system. The second form is the Login Form that is displayed when a user is not logged in to the system. The file uses PHP to establish an If/Else relationship between the two forms; showing the first form if a user is logged in. If the user is not logged in, the second form is displayed.

Note

The root module directory and the /tmpl directory both contain an index.html file. This file serves no purpose other than to block persons from accessing the directory index by typing into their browsers the URL of the directory. If a user enters the directory path as an URL, they will be served the index.html file, which displays only a blank page. You will see these files used throughout the directories of your Joomla! installation.

Overriding module output

The Joomla! system allows you override the output of a module by creating a new view template and inserting it into your active template directory. This approach to overriding module output allows you to leave the core files untouched; all your changes are made to a new file that is segregated from the core module files. This system has the added advantage of making it easy to keep up with your modifications; no matter how many modules you override, all the changed files are all kept in one place.

By way of an example, I am going to make a very basic modification to the output of the default Joomla! 1.5.x Login module. To override the default template controlling the output of the Login module, follow these steps:

1. Copy the file /modules/mod_login/tmpl/default.php.

2. Open your active template directory and place the copied file inside a sub-directory named /html/mod_login. For example, if you are using the default rhuk_milkyway template, you will create this: /templates/rhuk_milkyway/html/mod_login/default.php.

3. Make your changes to the new file.

4. Save your changes. The new template will now override the original template and be displayed on the site.

To show this process in more detail, here are the code changes made to the Login module's template file.

As noted in the discussion of the module in Chapter 17, the Login module includes links to the Password Reset and Username Reminder functions, as shown in Figure 21.3. Those links are hard coded and cannot be disabled through the use of the Module parameters of the Global Configuration options. In this example, I eliminate those from the module.

FIGURE 21.3

The default display of the Login Form module. Note the password and username links below the form.

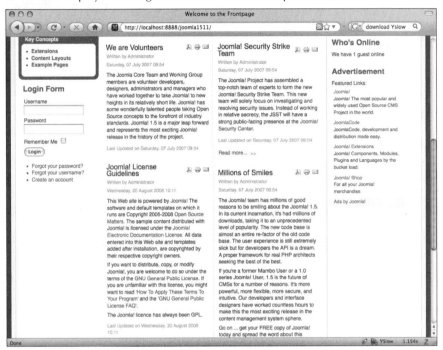

If you open the new template file created in the preceding steps, `/templates/rhuk_milkyway/html/mod_login/default.php`, you see the following lines at the bottom of the second form:

```
<ul>
        <li>
<a href="<?php echo JRoute::_( 'index.php?option=com_user&view=reset'
   ); ?>">
        <?php echo JText::_('FORGOT_YOUR_PASSWORD'); ?></a>
</li>
<li>
<a href="<?php echo JRoute::_( 'index.php?option=com_
   user&view=remind' ); ?>">
<?php echo JText::_('FORGOT_YOUR_USERNAME'); ?></a>
</li>
<?php        $usersConfig = &JComponentHelper::getParams( 'com_
   users' );        if ($usersConfig-
   >get('allowUserRegistration')) : ?>
<li>
```

```
<a href="<?php echo JRoute::_( 'index.php?option=com_
    user&view=register' ); ?>">
<?php echo JText::_('REGISTER'); ?></a>
</li>
<?php endif; ?>
</ul>
```

The code sets out an unordered list containing three list items. The first item generates a link to the Password Reset function. The second item generates the link to the Username Reminder function. The final item generates the User Registration link. For this example, I am going to eliminate the first two items.

Here's how the same lines of code will look after modification:

```
<ul>
        <?php            $usersConfig = &JComponentHelper::getParams
    ( 'com_users' );            if ($usersConfig-
    >get('allowUserRegistration')) : ?>
<li>
<a href="<?php echo JRoute::_( 'index.php?option=com_
    user&view=register' ); ?>">
<?php echo JText::_('REGISTER'); ?></a>
</li>
<?php endif; ?>
</ul>
```

Note that I simply deleted the two list items embedding the links I wanted to eliminate. I have not touched the UL tag that wrapped them, nor have I cut out any of the code related to the User Registration function. This modification will remove the two links, as shown in Figure 21.4. Aside from the cosmetic change, the User Registration function works normally.

Cross-Reference

See also Chapter 20 for a discussion of how to impact module output appearance by working with the module chrome.

Save this file and the change is done. Your new override will take precedence over the original template — and, importantly, you have accomplished this without making any changes to the original module.

Tip

If you don't want to cut the code out of your template file, then simply wrap it in comment tags to remove it from processing. Note also that the best practice is to use PHP comment tags, not HTML comment tags.

The modified Login Form module.

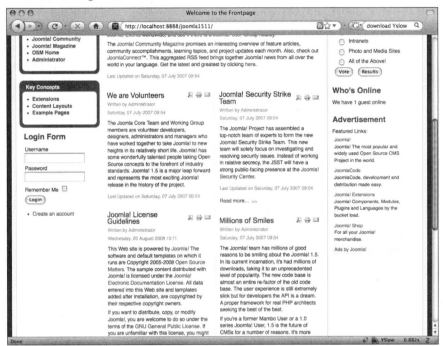

Creating a new module

A detailed tutorial on all the aspects of module creation is outside the scope of this chapter, but you should understand the basics of creating a new module. If you want to explore this topic in more detail, you can find a number of excellent resources on the topic in the official Joomla! Developer documentation.

Note

To help get you started, the Joomla documentation site includes a basic module tutorial called Creating a Hello World Module for Joomla 1.5 at

```
http://docs.joomla.org/Tutorial:Creating_a_Hello_World_Module_for_
    Joomla_1.5.
```

Tip

Don't forget that the Joomla! core includes the module type Custom HTML. That is a blank module that allows you to insert whatever content you wish. If you need only to create a module to hold content, there may be no reason for you to go through the process of coding a new module; instead, try creating a new module by using the Module Manager and select the type named Custom HTML. Use of the Custom HTML module is discussed in Chapter 17.

Minimum requirements

Make sure that you follow the naming requirements for the module elements:

- The naming convention for module directories is: mod_modulename. For front-end modules, the directory should be placed inside the /modules directory at the root of your site. For back-end administrator modules, the directory is placed inside /administrator/modules. All module files must be located inside the module directory.

- The primary module file must be named mod_modulename.php.

- The naming convention for the module's XML file is mod_modulename.xml.

- The Helper file should be named simply helper.php.

- The Template file should be named default.php and placed inside a subdirectory named /tmpl.

Caution

Make sure your XML file is created in UTF-8 format.

Tip

If you're looking for a quick start, you might want to check out the Joomla! Module Generator Wizard, a non-commercial tool available for download at the Joomla! Extentions Directory.

```
http://extensions.joomla.org/extensions/tools/development-tools/3379/
    details.
```

Registering a module

Registering your module in the database is a quick way to get it to appear in the back-end admin system so you can turn it on and off, assign it to pages and positions, and work with the parameters during development.

Note

Registering the module at this stage is optional; you can achieve the same thing by setting up the installer information in the XML file and using the Joomla! Extension Installer to handle this automatically. However, because you are likely to be writing and revising your module, you may want to register it at the very beginning of the process so you can see the impact of your changes and manipulate the module more easily during development.

Registering a module is simply entering a record for the module into the jos_modules table in your site's database. You can accomplish this process either by running an SQL query or by accessing phpMyAdmin and entering the information manually. To register a new module using phpMyAdmin, do the following:

1. Access phpMyAdmin on the server where your Joomla! installation is located

2. **Select the name of your database from the list on the left.** The database information loads in the screen.

3. **From the list of tables on the left side of the screen, select the option jos_modules.** The jos_modules table summary information displays on the right side of the screen.

4. **Click the Insert tab.** The Insert dialogue loads.

5. **Type the name of your new module in the field marked title.**

6. **Type the value 1 for the field ordering.**

7. **Type left for the field marked position.**

8. **Type the value 1 for the field published.**

9. **Type mod_modulename for the field labeled module, where the string (what is strong?) "modulename" is the name of your new module.**

10. **Click the button labeled Go.** The system creates a new row in the table containing your module information.

After your module is registered, you can access it from the Joomla! admin system where you can easily assign it to the front end and view your work in progress.

Packaging a module

Proper packaging may not be an issue if your module is only intended for your own use, but if you intend to give your module to others, or if you want to install it again elsewhere, you should go ahead and create a proper installation package for the module. Proper packaging allows you to manage module installations through Joomla's default Extension Installer.

Packages are archives that contain all the necessary elements of a module, along with an XML file containing the information needed by the Joomla! Installer. The XML file must be modified to include a list of all the files that need to be installed. You already have an XML file for your module, so you can simply add in the declarations needed by the Installer. Each file is listed inside the element <filename>. All filename elements are wrapped by the tag <files>.

Looking at an example makes this simpler. Using the filenames listed earlier in this section, the mod_modulename.xml file would be modified to include the following lines of code:

```
<files>
    <filename>mod_modulename.php</filename>
    <filename>help.php</filename>
<filename>index.html</filename>
    <filename>/tmpl/default.php</filename>
<filename>/tmpl/index.html</filename>
</files>
```

Note that it is not necessary to list directories, because the system will automatically creates a directory for the module, and the tag <filename>/tmpl/default.php<filename> results in the automatic creation of the sub-directory /tmpl. Declaring the mod_modulename.xml file is also not necessary.

Note

In the example list of files, I have included the index.html documents that you would want to create to protect direct access to the directories. Don't forget to create and include these. Simply copy an existing one from the Joomla! core for use in your module.

After this change is made to the XML file all you need to do is zip up the files and name the archive something descriptive, preferable mod_modulename_version.zip.

Note

Although I have used the .zip format for this example, you can use your preferred archive format: .zip, .gz, .tar, .tar.gz.

Caution

Make sure that you are careful about what you zip up into the archive. Do not accidentally include system files generated by your local machine. This an easy mistake to make and it can sometimes cause problems for module installation.

Working with Plugins

Joomla! plugins are helper applications that work by detecting and responding to events. Technically they are observer classes that look to a global event dispatcher. The result is that you, as a developer, are able to create a plugin that executes some bit of code when an event occurs. This is most useful to you as a way to supplement your work on a component or module.

Note

For discussion of how to use a plugin with another extension, see

```
http://docs.joomla.org/Tutorial:Using_plugins_in_your_own_extension.
```

Plugin architecture

Joomla 1.5 added the observer class JPlugin, and plugins follow the Observer design pattern. When you create a plugin, you extend the observer class JPlugin to observe Joomla's observable class, the JEventDispatcher object. Put another way, creating a plugin is a two-part process whereby you create a class to extend JPlugin, and then write a method for each event you want the plugin to handle.

Note

Joomla! includes a variety of core events. For a complete list, organized into groups and listed alphabetically, see

```
http://docs.joomla.org/Tutorial:Plugins.
```

Creating a new plugin

The system includes a number of plugins, all organized into eight categories and kept in the directory /plugins. Plugins require, at a minimum, two files: pluginname.php and pluginname. xml. The PHP contains the primary code, while the XML contains the descriptive information needed for the plugin to be recognized and used by Joomla!

Given that most plugins are relatively small and narrowly-tailored units of code, it is unlikely you will be modifying existing plugins. If you want to make changes, simply create a new plugin and add it to the system.

Your first step will be to determine how you will classify the plugin. The default classifications in Joomla! 1.5.x are:

- Authentication
- Content
- Editors
- Editors-xtd
- Search
- System
- User
- xmlrpc

Pick the classification that best fits your new plugin, as your plugin files will go into that directory inside the /plugins folder on the server.

Note

If you want to step outside the default plugin classification schema you can create your own classification by adding another subdirectory inside the /plugins directory.

The structure of the plugin files is best shown by looking at examples. Joomla! makes this easy. Inside each of the plugin directories in the Joomla! core, you will find example files that can serve as a template to help jumpstart your work creating new plugins. Inside the /plugins/content directory you can find example.php and example.xml. The essence of that PHP file, without the comment lines, is as follows:

```
jimport( 'joomla.plugin.plugin' );
class plgContentExample extends JPlugin
```

```
{
function plgContentExample( &$subject, $params )
   {
        parent::__construct( $subject, $params );
   }
function onPrepareContent( &$article, &$params, $limitstart )
   {
        global $mainframe;
   }
function onAfterDisplayTitle( &$article, &$params, $limitstart )
   {
        global $mainframe;
        return '';
   }
function onBeforeDisplayContent( &$article, &$params, $limitstart )
   {
        global $mainframe;
        return '';
   }
function onAfterDisplayContent( &$article, &$params, $limitstart )
   {
        global $mainframe;
        return '';
   }
function onBeforeContentSave( &$article, $isNew )
   {
        global $mainframe;
        return true;
   }
function onAfterContentSave( &$article, $isNew )
   {
        global $mainframe;
        return true;
   }
}
```

Look at what happens in the code:

- The first line uses the `jimport` function to import Joomla's general plugin library, JPlugin.
- The second line sets out the class `plgContentExample` as an extension of JPlugin. Note the naming convention here as it is mandatory: plgNameofdirectoryNameofplugin.
- What follows afterwards are seven methods, each tied to a specific event. Note the naming convention: The name of the method is the same as the event that triggers it.

- The example plugin, above, does nothing. It is intended as a template for your use. You would add your plugin action code inside whichever method is appropriate, after the line global $mainframe;

- For a breakdown of the various parameters listed in the preceding code, see the discussion on creating a content plugin at http://docs.joomla.org/How_to_create_a_content_plugin

Note

To learn more about when events are triggered, view the API Execution Order page at

http://docs.joomla.org/API_Execution_Order.

The XML file is even simpler. It is reproduced in its entirety:

```xml
<?xml version="1.0" encoding="utf-8"?>
<install version="1.5" type="plugin" group="content">
    <name>Content - Example</name>
    <author>Joomla! Project</author>
    <creationDate>July 2007</creationDate>
    <copyright>Copyright (C) 2005 - 2008 Open Source Matters. All
    rights reserved.</copyright>
    <license>http://www.gnu.org/licenses/gpl-2.0.html GNU/GPL</
    license>
    <authorEmail>admin@joomla.org</authorEmail>
    <authorUrl>www.joomla.org</authorUrl>
    <version>1.0</version>
    <description>An example content plugin</description>
    <files>
            <filename plugin="example">example.php</filename>
    </files>
    <params/>
</install>
```

This file's key function is to provide the information necessary for installation of the plugin, though it can also be used to activate parameters that can be set by the administrator from inside the Plugin Manager. Key points to note about the contents of this file: The <install> tag declared at the outset tells the system the type of file that is being installed, in this case a plugin, and the group to which it belongs, in this case, content.

Caution

Make sure your XML file is created in UTF-8 format.

Tip

The official Joomla! documentation sites contain three good, clear tutorials on creating plugins:

http://docs.joomla.org/How_to_create_a_content_plugin, http://docs.joomla.org/How_to_create_a_search_plugin, and http://developer.joomla.org/tutorials/184-how-to-create-a-joomla-plugin.html.

Registering a plugin

Registering your plugin in the database is a quick way to get it into the back end, so you can turn it on and off and work with the parameters during development.

Note

Registering your plugin is optional; you can achieve the same thing by setting up the installer information in the XML file and using the Joomla! Extension Installer to handle this automatically. However, because you are likely to be writing and revising your plugin, you may want to register it at the very beginning of the process, so you can see the impact of your changes and manipulate the plugin more easily during development.

The process of registering a plugin involves simply entering a record for the plugin into the jos_plugins table in your site's database. You can accomplish this process either by running an SQL query or by accessing phpMyAdmin and entering the information manually. To register a new plugin using phpMyAdmin, do the following:

1. **Access phpMyAdmin on the server where your Joomla! installation is located.**

2. **Select the name of your database from the list on the left.** The database information loads in the screen.

3. **From the list of tables on the left side of the screen, select the option jos_plugins.** The jos_plugins table summary information displays on the right side of the screen.

4. **Click the Insert tab.** The Insert dialogue loads.

5. **Type the full name of your new plugin in the field marked title.** Note that the standard full name is section - plugin Name, e.g., Content - Email Cloaking.

6. **In the field labeled element, type the machine-friendly name for the plugin.**

7. **In the field marked folder, enter the classification type for the plugin**

8. **Type the value 1 for the field published.**

9. **Click the button labeled Go.** The system now creates a new row in the table containing your plugin information.

After your plugin is registered, you can access it from the Joomla! admin system where you can view your work in progress.

Packaging a plugin

Proper packaging may not be an issue if your plugin is only intended for your own use, but if you intend to give your plugin to others, or you want to install it again elsewhere, you should go ahead and create a proper installation package for the plugin. Proper packaging allows you to manage plugin installation through Joomla's default Extension Installer.

Packages are archives that contain all the necessary elements of a plugin, along with an XML file containing the information needed by the Joomla! installer. The XML file must be modified to include a list of all the files that need to be installed. Because you already have an XML file for your plugin, you can simply add in the declarations needed by the Installer. Each file is listed inside the element <filename>. All filename elements are wrapped by the tag <files>.

Looking at an example makes this simpler. Looking at the `example.xml` file listed earlier in this section, you will note the following lines of code:

```
<files>
    <filename plugin="example">example.php</filename>
</files>
```

Note that it is not necessary to list the directory for the plugin files because the system automatically places the plugin in the proper directory according to its group attribute in the installer tag. Declaring the `example.xml` file is also not necessary.

After this change is made to the XML file, all you need to do is zip up the files and name the archive something descriptive, preferable `plg_pluginname-version.zip`.

Note

Although this example uses the .zip archive format, you can use your preferred archive format: .zip, .gz, .tar, .tar.gz.

Caution

Make sure that you are careful about what you zip up into the archive. Do not accidentally include system files generated by your local machine. This is an easy mistake to make, and it can sometimes cause problems for plugin installation.

Summary

In this chapter, we have covered the basics of customizing the functionality of the Joomla! system. You learned the following:

- Useful tools for working with Joomla! code
- The elements of component architecture
- How to modify components
- The elements of a typical module
- How to modify modules
- How to create new modules
- The elements of plugins
- How to create new plugins

Extending Your Site

O ne of the strengths of the Joomla! system is the ready availability of a large number of extensions. You can find a Joomla! extension for just about any purpose you can imagine.

An extension can be something as simple as a plugin that improves your search, to something as complex as a complete ecommerce catalog management and shopping cart functionality. Extensions can simply enhance existing functionality or add completely new functionality; they can also be purely aesthetic in the case of templates.

This chapter covers how to find extensions and how to install and uninstall them. This chapter also takes a look at some of the most popular extensions.

Finding Extensions

Joomla! extensions can be found in a number of locations, from the developers' web sites to various extension directories. Two officially maintained directories are JoomlaCode and the Joomla! Extensions Directory. The Joomla! Extensions Directory is shown in Figure 22.1.

The JoomlaCode site serves as a code repository and distribution point for non-commercial extensions. The site hosts over 2,000 extensions, organized into categories and sub-categories that can be browsed or searched. JoomlaCode does not include reviews or ratings and can be tough to use. The structure of the site makes it a challenge to find things, unless you already know what you are looking for!

FIGURE 22.1

The official Joomla! Extensions Directory web site. Note the directory tree at the bottom of the page.

Authoring
Authors (12)
Content Submission (26)
Planned Content (7)

Bridges
Authentication bridges (14)
CRM bridges (6)
Forum bridges (8)
Mailing & Newsletter bridges (21)
Photo Gallery bridges (7)
Wiki integration (7)

Calendars & Events
Birthdays & Historic events (8)
Calendars (12)
Clocks (40)
Countdown (9)
Events (28)
Events Registration (9)
Festivities (16)

Clients
CRM (8)
Help Desk (17)
Live support (14)
Online Status (13)

Communication
Bookmark & Recommend (24)
Chat (29)
Forum (8)
Forum add-ons (23)
Instant Messaging (15)
Mailing & Distribution Lists (5)
Newsletter (12)
PMS (7)
Shoutbox (16)
SMS (2)

Communities & Groupware
Communities (18)
Genealogy (6)
Members lists (11)
Membership (10)
Personal Life (6)
Profiles (12)
Project & Task Management (16)
Ratings & Reviews (19)
Social Bookmarking (56)
User Management (17)
Wiki (2)

RSS Syndicate (23)

Core Enhancements
Content Management (19)
Date & Time (24)
Embed & Include (10)
File Management (12)
Installers (6)
Mobile (10)
Multiple Sites (8)

Directory & Documentation
Bibliography (3)
Directory (18)
Downloads (29)
FAQ (11)
Glossary & Dictionary (20)
Portfolio (16)
Thematic Directory (25)
Weblinks (12)

e-Commerce
Affiliate Carts (12)
Auction (13)
Billing & Invoices (7)
Donations (36)
Paid Access and Content (18)
Payment Gateway (6)
Payment systems (12)
Shopping Cart (15)

Edition
Code Display (13)
Custom Code in content (20)
Custom Code in Modules (22)
Editor Buttons (29)
Editors (12)
Replace (4)

Phoca Gallery extensions (7)
PUArcade extensions (27)
Remository Extensions (8)
RSGallery2 extensions (11)
SEF Service Map extensions (9)
Seyret extensions (7)
sh404SEF extensions (11)
SOBI2 extensions (49)
VirtueMart extensions (144)
Xmap Extensions (15)

External Contents
Alerts & Awareness (9)
Audio & Radio Channels (16)
Automatic Articles (6)
Directories Search (17)
News Channels (5)
Photo Channels (19)
RSS Readers (28)
Social Blogging (22)
Social Channels (21)
TV & Movies Channels (10)
Video Channels (31)
Weather (26)
Web Search (19)
Widgets & Documents (21)

Financial
Calculators (6)
Currency & Exchange (20)
Graphs and Charts (5)
Stock Market (20)

Hosting & Servers
Data Conversion (14)
Database Management (14)
Hosting (4)
Servers (16)

Languages
Automatic translations (21)
Multi-lingual Content (17)
Translations for Joomla (83)

Miscellaneous
Development (27)
Religion (19)

Multimedia
Audio Players & Gallery (41)
Multimedia Display (10)
Shoutcast & Podcasts (7)
Streaming & Broadcasting (3)
Video Players & Gallery (27)
Virtual Reality & 3D (5)

SEF (18)
SEO & Metadata (44)
Site Analytics (29)
Site Traffic Statistics (16)
Visitors (36)

Sports & Games
Board & Table Games (8)
Game Servers (3)
Games (25)
Sports (9)
Sports Scores (16)
Tips & Bets (11)
Virtual worlds (5)
World of Warcraft Game (8)

Structure & Navigation
Articles Listing (40)
Menu Systems (90)
Multi Categorization (6)
Sections & Categories (16)
Site Links (29)
Site Map (14)
Site Navigation (17)
URL Redirection (18)

Style & Design
Accessibility (10)
Browsers & Web Standards (11)
Design (14)
Flash Management (12)
Modules presentation (11)
Popups & iFrames (35)
Print & PDF (9)
Scripts (12)
Tabs & Slides (25)
Templating (19)
Tips & Notes (28)
Titles (9)
Typography (27)

Tools
Database tools (9)
Design Tools (15)
Development Tools (13)
Edition Tools (2)
Icon Packs (10)
Site management tools (21)
Standalone Servers (6)

Vertical Markets
Booking & Reservation (19)
Books & Libraries (13)
Education (13)
Food & Beverage (6)
Real Estate (11)
Taxes & Mortgages (8)
Vehicles (15)

http://extensions.joomla.org/extensions/multimedia/streaming-&-broadcasting

Note

The Joomla! Extensions Directory is located at

```
http://extensions.joomla.org.
```

The most popular and easiest to use source of Joomla! extensions is the Joomla! Extensions Directory. The site lists nearly 4,500 extensions that can be downloaded and installed on your Joomla! site. The Joomla! Extensions Directory was purpose-built by the Joomla! team to provide a browsable directory of extensions. Each extension is classified and described. Information includes user reviews and ratings as well as indications of download volume and popularity, as shown in Figure 22.2. The additional information and feedback provided with the listings is invaluable, given the large number of options you face.

All the extensions on the Joomla! Extensions Directory are released under the open source GPL license. The majority of the extensions are free of charge, although some are commercial. The listings in the extensions directory identify the developer or company behind the extension and provide links to the developer's web site and to support and documentation resources, if any.

The Joomla! Extensions Directory is organized like most directories, with a tree of categories and subcategories that can be browsed topically. You can also browse the extensions based on ratings, views, and popularity, or you can view the newest or most reviewed extensions. Additionally, the site includes both a basic and an advanced search functionality at the top right of each page. The advanced search is particularly useful because it allows you to filter by version compatibility.

Caution

Make sure that you download only extensions that are compatible with your version of Joomla! Extensions written for Joomla! 1.0 are typically not compatible with Joomla! 1.5. The versions they are compatible with are shown in the heading of each extension.

Note that unlike JoomlaCode, the Joomla! Extensions Directory does not host any of the downloads. Therefore, when you click to download an extension, you are taken to a different site. Sometimes, the downloads are hosted on JoomlaCode, but many other times the files are hosted on the developer's Web site. Note also that some developers may require you to register on their site before you can download the Extension files.

FIGURE 22.2

A typical listing on the Joomla! Extensions Directory.

FIGURE 22.2 (continued)

Finding Joomla! templates

Both JoomlaCode and the Joomla! Extensions Directory contain a wide variety of components, modules, plugins, toos, l and language packs; however, neither of the official sites includes templates for your Joomla! site. As a direct result of this omission, a large number of template providers have jumped in to fill the gap. Following is a list of some of the more popular template sites. The list includes both commercial and noncommercial templates, but you should note that many of the sites that offer free templates typically expect promotional exposure on your site by means of links back to their web sites on the template.

Dream Template

www.dreamTemplate.org

Dream template provides more than 4,000 web designs. They provide designs only, not ready to use Joomla! templates, so you will have to do the conversion work yourself before you can use them in Joomla! Prices vary widely, depending largely on whether you want exclusive rights to the design.

Open Source Web Design

www.oswd.org

This site is home to over 2,000 web designs, all free of charge. They provide designs only, not ready to use Joomla! templates. Although many designs are here and it is all free of charge, site activity has been very low over the last couple of years and the catalog is starting to look rather dated.

Template Monster

www.Templatemonster.com

With a catalog of over 12,000 designs, Template Monster is perhaps the largest of the commercial template providers. Template Monster includes more than 200 ready-to-use Joomla! templates. Prices vary widely, depending largely on whether you want exclusive rights to the design.

Rocket Themes

www.rockettheme.com

This group specializes in ready to use Joomla! and phpBB templates. The number of designs is more limited, but the templates themselves are some of the most flexible and functional Joomla! templates in the market. They have recently introduced templates tailored for the VirtueMart e-commerce system for Joomla!

Working with the Extension Manager

Extensions are managed through the admin system, by way of the Extension Manager. The manager enables you to install, uninstall, enable, and disable all the extensions on your site.

Introducing the Extension Installer

In Joomla! 1.5.x, access the Extension Installer by going to the Extensions menu and selecting the option Install/Uninstall. The Extensions Installer interface loads in your browser, as shown in Figure 22.3.

FIGURE 22.3

The Joomla! 1.5.x Extension Installer interface.

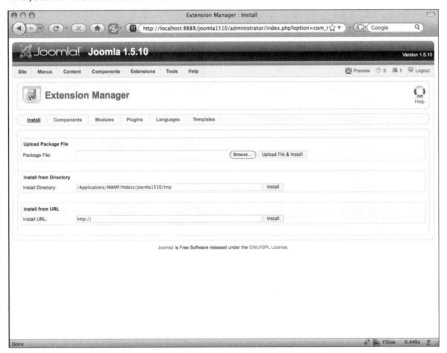

The toolbar at the top of the Extension Manager provides access to only one icon, the Help icon, which you can click to view the online Help files related to this screen.

Six links are below the toolbar:

- **Install** shows you the Install screen.
- **Components** shows you the components installed on your system.
- **Modules** shows you the modules installed on your system.
- **Plugins** shows you the plugins installed on your system.
- **Languages** shows you the language packs installed on your system.
- **Templates** shows you the templates installed on your system.

Joomla! 1.6

The Extension Manager has been revised and simplified in Joomla! 1.6. The changes begin with the Extensions menu. Gone is the option Install/Uninstall, replaced with the more descriptive term Extension Manager. Clicking on the Extension Manager takes you to the Extension Installer dialogue. The dialogue in Joomla! 1.6 serves exactly the same purpose as it did in 1.5. Note that the links below the toolbar have been simplified from six links to five links. The new links are Install, Update, Manage, Discover, and Warnings.

Going over the Extension Packages dialogue

In Joomla! 1.5.x, each type of extension is the subject of a different interface, as shown in Figure 22.4.

The toolbar at the top of the Extension Manager provides quick access to the following functions:

- **Uninstall:** Select one or more extensions from the list, then click this icon to uninstall it.
- **Help:** Click to access the online Help files related to the active screen.

Below the toolbar are the same six links as on the Install screen.

Below the links and above the list of templates you will note the system-generated reminder message that only certain templates can be removed; those that are necessary for the system to function cannot be uninstalled.

FIGURE 22.4

The Joomla! 1.5.x Extension Packages interface, showing the templates; this screen is typical of all the individual extension packages in Joomla! 1.5.x.

The main content area of the screen contains a list of all the templates in your Joomla! site. The columns provided are:

- **#:** An indexing number assigned by Joomla! This cannot be changed.
- **Checkbox (no label):** Click in a checkbox to select a template; this is needed if you want to use several of the toolbar options, referenced in the preceding section.
- **Template:** This field displays the full name of the template.
- **Client:** Indicates whether the template is intended for the front-end site or the back-end admin system.
- **Version:** The Version number of the template. This is set by the template developer and cannot be changed.
- **Date:** The Creation Date of the template. This is set by the template developer and cannot be changed.
- **Author:** The name of the Author of the template. This is set by the template developer and cannot be changed.
- **Compatibility:** Indicates which version of Joomla! the template was built for.

Finally, at the bottom of the screen, below the content area, is the Display # option. Change the value in the combo box control to alter the number of templates that are displayed on the page. The default value can be altered by changing the List Length option on the Global Configuration Manager.

Installing extensions

The Extension Installer interface, (refer to in Figure 22.3), provides three alternative methods for installing extensions for your site. The three methods are:

- Install from a package file
- Install from a directory
- Install from an URL

You only need to use one method to install an extension, and you will likely use the same method for the life of your site. The selection of method is largely a by-product of the nature and location of the extension files you need to install.

Installing from a Package File

This is the normal way to install an extension. Most users find that this method handles all their needs. To install a new extension from a package file, follow these steps:

1. **Download the extension's archive file to your local computer.**

2. **Log in to the admin system.**

3. **Access the Extensions Installer dialogue by clicking on the option Install/Uninstall under the Extensions menu.** The Extensions Installer loads in your browser window.

4. **Click the Browse button.** The File Upload dialogue opens.

5. **Locate the extension's archive file on your local computer. Click on it and then click the Open button.** The pop-up menu closes, and you should see the name of the extension archive file in the Package File: field.

6. **Click Upload File and Install.** The system attempts to install the extension and if successful, you can see a confirmation message.

Installing from a directory

Installing from a directory is used when you need to unarchive the files before you move them to the server, or if you have been given the files in unarchived form. To install a new extension from a directory, follow these steps:

1. **Download the extension's archive file to your local computer.**

2. **Unarchive the files locally.**

3. **Log into your server by FTP or via your web host file manager.**

4. **Move the extension directory and files up to your server, noting the location.** A safe place to put this is the tmp folder.

5. **Log in to the admin system of your Joomla! site.**

6. **Access the Extensions Installer dialogue by clicking on the option Install/Uninstall under the Extensions menu.** The Extensions Installer loads in your browser window.

7. **Type name address of the directory on the server that contains the extension files into the field label Install Directory.**

8. **Click the Install button.** The system attempts to install the wxtension and if successful, you will see a confirmation message.

Installing from an URL

Installing from a URL is used in situations where you can access the archive file directly on another server and do not need to download it to your local machine first. You can use this, for example, to install archives directly from the JoomlaCode web site. To install a new extension from a URL, follow these steps:

1. **Locate the extension's archive file on the remote computer, noting the URL.**

2. **Log in to the admin system.**

3. **Access the Extensions Installer dialogue by clicking on the option Install/Uninstall under the Extensions menu.** The Extensions Installer loads in your browser window.

4. **Type the extension archive file's URL into the field labeled Install URL.**

5. **Click the Install button.** The system attempts to install the extension and if successful, you will see a confirmation message.

Uninstalling extensions

To uninstall an extension in Joomla! 1.5.x, follow these steps:

1. **Log in to the admin system.**

2. **Access the Extensions Installer dialogue by clicking on the option Install/Uninstall under the Extensions Menu.** The Extensions Installer loads in your browser window.

3. **Click the link to the relevant Extensions Manager screen.** For example, to uninstall a module, click on the modules link. The Extension Manager loads in your browser.

4. **Click the radio button next to the name of the extension you want to uninstall.**

5. **Click the Uninstall icon on the top-right of the toolbar.** A pop-up menu appears, with a prompt for confirmation.

6. **Click OK.** The menu closes, and the system will uninstall the Extension. If successful, you will see a confirmation message.

Joomla! 1.6

Uninstalling an extension in Joomla! 1.6 is slightly different, due to a change in labels and controls. The Uninstall icon is now located on the Manage dialogue, inside the Extension Manager. In all other regards, the process is the same.

Caution

Deleting an extension is permanent and cannot be undone. Uninstalling will also typically wipe out any data on the extension from the database. If you want to use the extension again, you must reinstall it.

Finding the Right Extension for the Job

Perhaps one of the most daunting parts of using extensions is finding the right tool for the job. Thousands of extensions are available and sometimes you are faced with multiple options that appear to achieve your goals. Although there really is no substitute for downloading things and trying them out yourself, in this chapter I provide a list of extensions that are a good starting point for addressing common needs.

Note that I am not endorsing one particular extension over another, but rather simply listing resources to help you get started. The list includes both commercial and noncommercial extensions. Note also that this list was created for Joomla! 1.5.x and that you must always be certain that the extensions you download and install on your site are compatible with your version of the core.

Caution

The rate of change in the open source world can be daunting. Developers change, projects fork, some projects get abandoned. It's impossible to say what will be here in 12 months' time. One thing is certain: The extensions provided in this list will change over time. You should always keep this in mind when you are selecting extensions, and if business risk is an issue for you, then you need to do your own research and consider carefully which extensions you adopt.

Improving content management

The extensions listed here all expand upon Joomla!'s default Content Management functionality. The list includes both extensions to enhance existing articles as well as several powerful tools for changing the nature of the articles and the article-editing functionality.

AllVideos Reloaded

```
http://joomlacode.org/gf/project/allvideos15/
```

This component enables the embedding and displaying of videos on your web site. The component comes in multiple parts: a content plugin, an editor plugin, a system plugin, and a module. Once installed, you can display video files either inside of articles or inside module positions, or as a pop-up window inside a lightbox. The most recent version also includes a utility to convert various video formats in .flv (flash video) files. This extension is non-commercial.

Attachments for Content articles

`http://joomlacode.org/gf/project/attachments/`

This extension makes it easy to add attachments to your articles. The attachments can be viewed or downloaded by your site visitors. The extension combines a component for uploading and managing attachments and a plugin for adding attachments to the site articles. This extension is non-commercial.

Content Templater

`www.nonumber.nl/contentTemplater`

Content Templater is a powerful extension that enables the creation of predefined, reusable templates for your articles. If your site has multiple administrators, the use of content templates is one of the best ways to maintain a consistent appearance throughout the site. The extension allows you to create multiple templates that appear inside the editor where they can be selected by the person creating the article. The templates extend beyond content layout to include other common attributes, including the title, alias, publishing settings, and so on. This extension is non-commercial.

Custom Properties

`www.solidsystem.it/index.php/english/Custom-Properties/`

The Custom Properties extension provides a way to attach tags to your articles. Once you have tagged your articles, you can then use the tags as aids to organization and navigation. Custom Properties really adds a lot of flexibility to the Joomla! content hierarchy, as the extension makes it possible to associate multiple tags with a single article and to search and view the articles by those tags. Elements included in the extension give you the option to provide a dedicated search by tag and an option to generate a tag cloud. This extension is non-commercial.

JCE

`www.joomlacontenteditor.net`

JCE is a WYSIWYG editor for your Joomla! site. If you are looking for an alternative to the default editor, JCE is one option. The editor is extendable, allowing you to add in a file manager, a media manager, and an image manager. This is a non-commercial extension; however, some of the enhancements offered for this extension do incur a fee.

JomComment

`http://azrul.com/products/jom-comment.html`

JomComment enables user comments for your articles. The system is Ajax-based, thereby avoiding page reloads, and supports templates and SPAM prevention. You can also configure the system to require that comments be moderated and approved prior to appearing on your site. An additional module is available that allows you to display the most recent comments on the site in a module position. This is a commercial component.

JoomlaFCK Editor

www.joomlafckeditor.com

JoomlaFCK Editor is a port of the popular FCK Editor package. FCK is a powerful and easy-to-use WYSIWYG editor that gives you a strong alternative to Joomla's default editor. The editor includes image uploading and management functions and a wide array of formatting tools and options. This extension is non-commercial.

K2

http://k2.joomlaworks.gr

K2 bills itself as the ultimate content construction kit for Joomla. It presents a major change in the way content items are handled in your Joomla! site. By using this extension, you can create custom content types with custom fields. This makes it possible for you to break out of the restrictions of the default Joomla! 1.5.x three-tier content hierarchy and the limited content types. The extension also supports tagging as well as the inclusion of a variety of media formats. K2 is non-commercial.

Labels

http://jxtended.com/products/labels.html

Labels provide a way to tag your Joomla! articles and contacts. The labels can be used to impose organization on your site and to enhance user navigation. Using labels, you can assign one article to multiple classifications. The labels can then be used as the basis for lists of articles or they can be displayed independently as a Tag Cloud. This extension is commercial.

MetaMod

www.metamodpro.com

The MetaMod extension enhances module management. It allows you to add additional rules and logic for displaying modules on your pages. You can set start and end dates for module publication and can trigger module display according to the appearance of text or metadata in an item. It also has geo-location filtering, making it possible to show visitors different content, based upon their IP address. One of the more useful features is the ability to hide modules after a user has logged in. This extension is non-commercial.

News Show Pro

http://tools.gavick.com

News Show Pro is a content display extension that allows you to display articles in a wide variety of formats using a combination of modules. The extension make displaying multiple items on one page in a variety of formats easy and lessens the burden of ongoing management. Configuration options allow you to display articles vertically or horizontally and to sort them and control their appearance by a variety of criteria. This extension is noncommercial.

Improving administration

The extensions listed in this section are all intended to make managing the administration of your Joomla! site easier. They provide functionality you may well get already from other external tools, but with these extensions you are able to do the job directly from within the Joomla! admin system, thereby savings yourself time and effort.

eXtplorer

http://joomlacode.org/gf/project/joomlaxplorer/

eXtplorer is a file and FTP management component. It enables you to browse and manage files from within your Joomla! admin interface without the necessity of using an external FTP or file management client. You can search, browse, upload, and download files on your server and you can create and extract archives and manage file permissions. This extension is non-commercial.

Joomla! Tools Suite

http://joomlacode.org/gf/project/jts/

The Joomla! Tools Suite extension is intended to be installed independently of Joomla! in order to provide you with a fallback in the case of problems with the site and to allow you to assess and monitor the site's health. Features include post-installation health checks, installation assessment, security-auditing, core-file modification auditing, file-system auditing, extension-reporting, and database-auditing facilities. This extension is non-commercial.

JoomlaPack

www.joomlapack.net

JoomlaPack is a back-up component for Joomla! It creates a full backup of a site in a single archive and can be restored by any Joomla!-capable server, thereby providing not only basic back-up facility, but also an aid for site migration. It is flexible and customizable. This extension is non-commercial.

Enhancing search

Joomla! search sometimes needs a little help. Here are two extensions that enhance the site search experience.

JXtended Finder

http://jxtended.com

Finder is an advanced search engine for Joomla!, giving you a more powerful alternative to the default search functionality. In addition to full text search, the extension also enables a variety of filters, including custom-defined filters. This extension is commercial.

PixSearch

`http://labs.pixpro.net`

The PixSearch module creates an Ajax-based search box that searches as you type and displays results immediately in a pop-up window. The search is similar to that seen on a number of sites and in the Mac OSX Spotlight search feature. This is a non-commercial extension, but it does require registration.

Enhancing menus and navigation

Although the most recent version of Joomla! provides more flexibility in the menu layouts, these two extensions make it easy to create great looking menus in a variety of formats and styles.

Extended Menu

`http://de.siteof.de/extended-menu.html`

Extended Menu extends the functionality of Joomla's MainMenu module. You will still have to use CSS to achieve the styling, but the configuration options make it very easy to change the menu orientation and to split and reorder the menus. The extension also enhances the ability to work with parent-child menu item relationships. This extension is non-commercial.

swMenu

`www.swmenupro.com/`

swMenu is a set of menu creation and management extensions. You can create and integrate unlimited menu modules and achieve a wide variety of styling. Commercial and non-commercial versions are available on the developer's site.

Building complex forms

The default Joomla! system offers extremely limited options for form creation. The extensions listed here address this issue by providing the ability to create complex forms on your Joomla! site.

bfForms

`www.forms-for-joomla.com`

An AJAX admin interface makes it easy to create complex forms. The extension supports unlimited forms and fields and is Smarty Templates-enabled. Forms created with this extension support the Akismet and Mollom anti-SPAM systems, as well as IP banning and blacklists. Submit buttons and validation are also configurable. This is a commercial extension.

ChronoForms

www.chronoengine.com

ChronoForms is a great choice for those with HTML skills who want more control over their forms. By using this extension, you can create the form in your favorite HTML editor and then copy and paste it into the ChronoForms component. There is also a drag-and-drop form creation interface for those who don't want to do the work in HTML. The extension also gives you the ability to create database tables and connect those to forms, thereby allowing you to capture form data in the database. This extension is a non-commercial component, but does include a back link to the developer's site. You can remove the back link for a fee.

RSform!Pro

www.rsjoomla.com/joomla-components/joomla-form.html

RSForm! Pro is an AJAX-enabled form builder. The extension supports a wide variety of fields and input types and allows you to create forms without any HTML knowledge. Data gathered with the forms can be exported to CSV format. This is a commercial extension.

Adding a gallery

Galleries are one of the most requested extensions to Joomla! Perhaps then it is not surprising that a large number of options are available in this area. The following list includes both full-featured galleries and simple slideshow components.

Expose

www.gotgtek.net/15/

Expose creates Flash-based slideshows. The size is adjustable and the resulting slideshow is search engine friendly. The component includes album management and various configuration options that allow you to create attractive slideshows. This extension is non-commercial.

Frontpage Slideshow

www.joomlaworks.gr/content/view/24/28/

Frontpage Slideshow creates JavaScript and CSS-based slideshows. One of the most powerful features of this extension is the ability to integrate text with images to create PowerPoint-type slides. Configuration options give you a great deal of control over the timing, display triggers, and transitions. This extension is a commercial extension.

Phoca Photo Gallery

www.phoca.cz/phocagallery/

The Phoca Component provides an image gallery that also includes slideshow functionality. The extension provides a large number of options for controlling the catalog categories and the images they contain. Images can be displayed by using a variety of techniques, including light-boxes, slideshows, or standard page views. The gallery supports images and videos and is search engine friendly. A number of modules and themes are available to extend the functionality of this Component. This extension is non-commercial.

RokSlideshow

`www.rocketwerx.com/products/rokslideshow/overview`

RokSlideshow is a JavaScript-powered slideshow module. The extension provides a choice of six customizable transition types and 30 wipe and push transitions. You can add titles, captions, and control font size and colors. This extension is non-commercial.

RSGallery2

`http://joomlacode.org/gf/project/rsgallery2/`

RSGallery provides an easy to customize gallery component. The extension's use of a separate template system means that you can modify the presentation significantly without hacking the core files. The extension includes not only image and category management but also a slideshow functionality. RSGallery supports image download and integrates well with Community Builder. This extension is non-commercial.

Adding a directory

If you want to create a categorized listing of companies, products, or other items or services, then these directory extensions can help you create a professional and functional site.

Mosets Tree

`www.mosets.com/tree/`

The Mosets Tree Extension enables the creation of a Yahoo! style directory on your site. The system provides all the features you normally associate with online directories including unlimited categories and subcategories, the ability to browse the listings, and the ability to search for listings. Listing fields are customizable, and the extension supports the creation of custom fields. This extension is used to power the official Joomla! Extensions Directory. This extension is a commercial extension.

SOBI2

`www.sigsiu.net/`

The SigSiu Online Business Index Extension allows you to create complex directories. The directory listings can be maintained by either the site administrator or by the registered users. The system offers a number of fields for listings and it is possible to create custom fields. The core extension is non-commercial but some of the additional modules are commercial.

Adding a forum

Threaded discussion forms have moved way past the old bulletin board format. Joomla! has several excellent forum extensions. Here are two of the best.

ccBoard

`http://codeclassic.org`

The ccBoard forum provides complete forum functionality with a wide variety of options. You can create moderated or unmoderated forums, and allow guest postings or force user registration. The extension also supports user karma, bad word filtering, SPAM filters, and more. This extension is non-commercial.

Kunena

`www.kunena.com`

The Kunena extension is a fork of the popular Fireboard Forum component. This full-featured forum supports all common features, including threaded discussions, multiple categories, user management, moderation, avatars, and much more. This extension is non-commercial.

Adding a file exchange

File exchanges provide a way for you to exchange documents or other files with your site visitors.

DocMan

`www.joomlatools.eu`

DocMan is a document management and file exchange extension. You can manage documents and files in multiple categories and subcategories and give users permission to upload, download, or edit documents. The system supports multiple group permissions that allow you to show specific files to only specific groups. A search system is integrated. This extension is non-commercial.

Remository

`www.remository.com`

Remository is a file repository that can be used to organize files for upload or download. The system supports nested categories and includes an optional search plugin.

Managing multilingual content

While the language packs in Joomla! enable the system messages to work in multiple languages, they do nothing about the articles and other content. If you want to display a fully multilingual site you need to install a multilingual content extensions to help you manage the translations. The dominant extension is Joom!Fish.

Cross-Reference

For a discussion of working with the Language Manager and the language packs, see Chapter 11.

Joom!Fish

www.joomfish.net

The Joom!Fish Extension enables multilingual content management on your Joomla! site. With this extension you can run your front-end content in multiple languages and allow users to switch easily between languages. The newest version supports routing to assist with your search marketing efforts and to build consistency into the URL structures. The core extension is free of charge but some enhancements are now commercial.

Enhancing SEO

Joomla! provides SEF URLs as part of the Global Configuration options, but for those of you who want to do more, you should consider these extensions.

Cross-Reference

For a discussion of creating a search engine friendly site, see Chapter 27.

Artio JoomSEF

www.artio.net/en/joomla-Extensions/joomla-seo-sef-component-artio-joomsef

This SEF Extension rewrites your Joomla! URLs to be search engine friendly. The extension handles multilingual sites and works with both the Apache web server and the IIS web server. The system allows you to customize the URL strings and supports multiple URL formats. JoomSEF goes beyond just SEF URLs, adding in support for expanded metatags and customizable error pages. This is a non-commercial extension but does include a back link to the developer's site. The back link can be removed for a fee.

Sh404SEF

http://Extensions.siliana.com

This extension generates search engine friendly URLs and also provides management for titles and meta tags. Additional plugins are available for this extension to provide support for many other common extensions, like VirtueMart, Fireboard, and Community Builder. This extension is non-commercial.

Xmap

`http://joomla.vargas.co.cr`

Xmap is based on Joomap The two extensions are very similar and both produce front-end user site maps and XML site maps. You should review both to determine your preference. This extension is non-commercial.

Extending user management

If you want to break out of the limited Joomla! 1.5.x user manager and group access privileges, you need to look at installing a third-party extension. Similarly, if you are integrating other software systems that require login access, you should consider a third-party extension to provide single login for your users.

JACLPlus

`www.byostech.com`

JACLPlus enables you to break out of the default Joomla! Access Control Rules and create custom groups and permissions. This system also included the ability to assign users to multiple groups. Note that this extension requires that your server use the Zend Optimizer. This extension is commercial.

Jfusion

`http://jfusion.org`

If your site integrates additional systems that require login, Jfusion allows your users to log in only one time to access all systems. Systems supported include phpBB, Vbulletin, Magento, SimpleMachines Forum, and Moodle. This extension is non-commercial.

JUGA

`www.dioscouri.com`

JUGA provides enhanced access control to Joomla! articles and components. It also enables you to create unlimited numbers of user groups and control user assignment within groups. One of the key features allows you to hide menu items and modules based on a user's group membership. The extension has a dual licensing scheme with the basic version non-commercial. Basic version, however, lacks many of the key features. A complete version is available for a fee.

Adding Web 2.0 functionality

Web 2.0 functionality is widely in demand. This section lists several extensions that help build community and stimulate user interaction.

AddThis Social Bookmarking

`www.informationmadness.com/cms/index.php?option=com_content&task=view&id=600&Itemid=1`

Integrates the AddThis social bookmarking button to your site. This extension is non-commercial.

Community Builder

`www.joomlapolis.com/`

Community Builder is an entire suite of components and modules that enable you to turn Joomla! into a community web site with user pages and a high degree of user interactivity. Many modules and plugins are available for Community Builder and integration of the extension is widely supported by other common extensions. This extension is non-commercial, but it does require registration to download.

JReviews

`www.reviewsforjoomla.com/`

JReviews is a powerful extension that lets you create a reviews and ratings web site with Joomla! The system is customizable and can even be used as an alternative method for handling your Joomla! content items, with custom structure and fields. This extension is commercial.

MyBlog

`www.azrul.com`

MyBlog provides greatly enhanced blogging functionality for Joomla! The default Joomla! system allows you to create blog-type layouts, but MyBlog gives you true blogging functionality with a wide range of common features. It includes RSS feeds, Technorati pings, Trackbacks, and support for multiple bloggers. MyBlog integrates with both Community Builder and JomSocial. This extension is commercial.

Plugin Googlemaps

`http://joomlacode.org/gf/project/mambot_google1/`

Plugin Googlemaps is a Joomla! plugin that integrates Google Map functionality. It enables users to view Google Maps and also includes support for KML files and marker placement. Directions are integrated and can appear in pop-up menus or in lightbox. This extension is non-commercial.

Tweetme

`www.herdboy.com/support/viewtopic.php?f=4&t=14`

Tweetme is a simple extension that adds a Tweet This button to your articles and items. This extension is non-commercial.

Improving Ad Management

If you want to run ads on your site at anything more than a basic level, you need to look to an extension to provide you with greater functionality than Joomla!'s basic Banner Manager.

AdSense Module

www.joomlaspan.com/Free-Extensions/Google-AdSense-Related-Modules/index.php

The AdSense module allows you to place single or multiple Google AdSense units on the pages of your Joomla! site. The extension supports the various Google options as well as the ability to randomize ad colors and to block ads from being displayed to certain IP addresses. This extension is non-commercial.

Easy AdSense for Joomla

www.wzcreativetechnology.com

Easy AdSense allows you to run one or more Google AdSense units on your pages. This simple extension provides control over all key variables plus the ability to block an unlimited number of IPs and to use alternative messages when ads are not displayed. This extension is non-commercial.

iJoomla Ad Agency

www.ijoomla.com/ijoomla-ad-agency/ijoomla-ad-agency/index

iJoomla Ad Agency is a full-featured banner and ad management system for Joomla! You can run single ads, campaigns, or packages. The system also supports breaking pages into zones for the purpose of managing ads and rates. It supports a wide range of ad formats and sizes. This extension is commercial.

Summary

In this chapter, we have taken a look at how to find and install extensions for your Joomla! site, as well as a look at some of the most popular extensions. You learned the following:

- How the find extensions
- How to install and uninstall extensions
- Some of the most popular extensions

Implementing e-Commerce with VirtueMart

I f you want to create an online catalog or sell products on your Joomla! site, you can do so easily by installing the VirtueMart system. VirtueMart turns your Joomla! site into a powerful and full-featured e-commerce system.

VirtueMart can either be added to an existing site, or you can obtain an all-in-one installer that provides Joomla! plus VirtueMart and a selection of additional extensions. Once installed, you can configure the extension to handle multiple products and categories and support a wide range of shipping and payment options.

This chapter examines how to obtain and install VirtueMart, together with the basics of setting up a store and populating it with products.

Introducing VirtueMart

VirtueMart is an open source ecommerce plugin for the Joomla! Content Management system. VirtueMart can be used either as a simple catalog management system, or as a catalog with a shopping cart that enables online transaction capability. The system interfaces with all the most common shipping programs and payment gateways to give a turnkey ecommerce solution for Joomla! users. Figure 23.1 shows the default interface.

The VirtueMart project has been around for a number of years, indeed longer than Joomla!, and is the most popular ecommerce plugin for Joomla! The VirtueMart team has created a full-featured system that provides all the most common functionality one expects from an online shopping site.

FIGURE 23.1

The front-end of the default VirtueMart package with the sample data installed.

Who Uses VirtueMart?

Here's a sampling of some of the companies and brands that use VirtueMart.

- Bauman College: www.baumancollege.org/
- Cuisine Solutions: www.cuisinesolutions.fr
- Cycle Taiwan Shop: http://shop.cycletaiwan.com
- Grand Living: www.grandliving.se/
- HD AV: http://hdav.co.uk/
- Ink Bags: www.inkbags.com/
- Nelson Events: www.nelsonevents.co.uk/
- Sejwix: http://sejwix.co.uk/
- Power Balance: www.powerbalanceshop.de/
- The Untouchables: www.untouchables.co.uk

Note

You can test drive a live VirtueMart installation at the demo site the project maintains. The demo site allows you to check out both the front end and the back end of the system. View it online:

```
http://virtuemart.net/index.php?option=com_content&task=view&id=145&Itemid=97.
```

Features

The default VirtueMart system supports a wide range of features for both site visitors and administrators. Note that these features are in addition to the standard Joomla! site features and further, that you can extend your VirtueMart site by adding extensions to the installation.

For visitors

Front-end visitors, or *shoppers* as they are referred to in the system, have access to a number of features that enable finding items and tracking of their orders.

- Quick search for products with filters for features and discounts
- Manage your account (registered users only)
- Manage your shipping details (registered users only)
- View your order history (registered users only)
- Pick your preferred currency
- View and rate products

- Automatic notifications when product is back in stock
- Browse and sort products by relevance, price, newest additions, and so forth

For site administrators

Site administrators can manage the catalog and the users. The VirtueMart system is intended to cover all the most common needs of an online shop manager, including currencies, taxes, shipping, discounts, and order management.

- Unlimited number of products and categories
- Multiple images per product
- Catalog management only, or catalog plus shopping cart
- Customizable product attributes
- Group shoppers to show different prices and payment options
- Handles downloadable products
- Support multiple currencies and multiple payment gateways
- Flexible pricing
- Support SSL connections
- Supports multiple delivery methods and shipping modules
- Supports multiple discount systems and "specials"
- Set stock levels and show product availability
- Supports multiple tax calculations
- Order status management
- Shop statistics

Note

VirtueMart, like Joomla! itself, is extendable. The VirtueMart site includes an Extension directory with more than 150 entries. Browse the directory at http://extensions.virtuemart.net/

Finding an appropriate use for VirtueMart

VirtueMart is intended to be used for two purposes:

- Online catalog management
- Online sales

It is equally well suited to either task, and typically these two functions are combined into one site; that is, the system is used to manage an online catalog from which items are sold.

VirtueMart is capable of handling either physical or virtual products, meaning that you can either carry inventory that is physically delivered, or you can provide digital products that are delivered by download directly from the site.

Obtaining and Installing VirtueMart

The first step to setting up your online store is to obtain the VirtueMart code. There are multiple versions of the package available, so make sure you obtain the proper version for the version of Joomla! you have installed. You should obtain the VirtueMart installer package from only the VirtueMart site, `www.virtumart.com` or from the JoomlaCode site, as shown in Figure 23.2.

Tip

You can also find the official VirtueMart packages at JoomlaCode.org

```
http://joomlacode.org/gf/project/virtuemart/
```

Creating a fresh installation

If you want to create a fresh installation, you probably want to obtain the all-in-one installer that bundles Joomla! with VirtueMart and additional related extensions. This package is created by VirtueMart and is called the eCommerce Bundle.

The VirtueMart eCommerce Bundle is a package of Joomla! plus the VirtueMart components and modules, all rolled up into one convenient unified installer. If you are creating a fresh installation, this is the easiest way to get VirtueMart up and running.

Caution

Because the eCommerce Bundle is maintained by VirtueMart, not the Joomla! team, you will need to make sure your Joomla! installation is up-to-date. Immediately after installation you should check if there are any upgrades or patches for the Joomla! Code, and if so, get them installed without delay.

FIGURE 23.2

The VirtueMart.com downloads page. Note the various packages available.

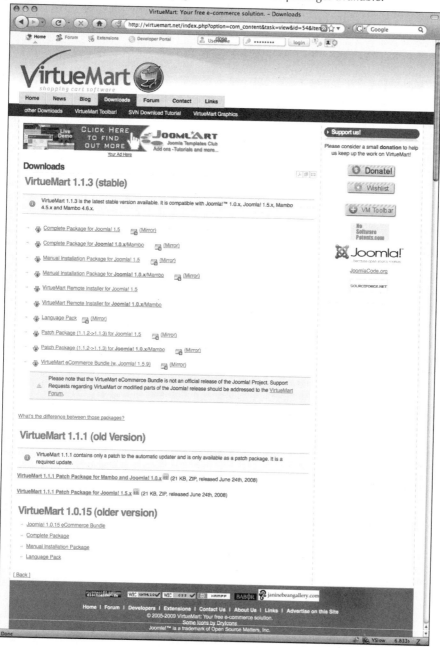

The VirtueMart eCommerce Bundle includes the following core files that are consistent with the default Joomla! distribution:

- **Core Joomla! Components**

  - VirtueMart component: The key VirtueMart extension.

  - Custom QuickIcons component: Third-party extension that provides a replacement for the standard Joomla! Control Panel Quick Icons.

  - eXtplorer component: Third party extension that provides a file manager you can use from within your Joomla! admin interface.

  - JCE component: Third-party extension that provides an alternative WYSIWYG editor. Note that this editor is enabled as the default editor in the VirtueMart eCommerce Bundle.

- **Core Joomla! Modules**

  - JA News module: Third-party extension that provides a functionality similar to Joomla's Newsflash module. Though this is included in the bundle, it is not enabled by default.

  - JA Slideshow module: Third-party extension that provides a basic slideshow inside a module position. Though this is included in the bundle, it is not enabled by default.

  - JA VM Product Slideshow: Third-party extension that provides a rotating slideshow of products drawn from one or more categories. This is enabled in the default configuration at the top of the home page.

  - Product Scroller module: This VirtueMart module displays a scrolling list of products inside a module position. It is included with the bundle but disabled in the default configuration.

  - Products module: This VirtueMart module displays a list of product categories inside a module position. It is included with the bundle but disabled in the default configuration.

  - VirtueMart module: This all-purpose VirtueMart module can be configured to display a number of items, from lists of categories to search boxes to login forms. Numerous configuration options let you control the output. This is enabled in the default system and assigned to the left-hand column.

  - All-In-One module: This VirtueMart module can display the latest products, featured products, top ten products, or random products in one module using tabs. It is included with the bundle but disabled in the default configuration.

  - Cart module: This VirtueMart module is a mini-cart that has a link to the full cart page. The module is enabled in the default configuration.

  - Currencies module: This VirtueMart module displays a list of currencies and allows your visitors to select the currency for prices.

  - Featured Products module: This VirtueMart module displays the products you have marked as being on special.

- Latest Products module: This VirtueMart module displays the most recent products.

- Manufacturers module: This VirtueMart module displays a list of manufacturers, with a link to all products by the manufacturer.

- Random Product module: This VirtueMart module randomly displays a product from your store or from a specific category.

- Search module: This VirtueMart module displays a search form for your store.

- Top Ten module: This VirtueMart module displays the top ten most popular products, in terms of sales.

- CustomQuickIcons module: This administrator module enables the display of the output of the Custom Quick Icons component. It is set to display on the control panel.

- JCE QuickIcon module: This administrator module enables the display of icons for the JCE component's administration control panel.

- **Core Joomla! Plugins**

  - VirtueMart Product Snapshot plugin: Enables you to place products inside of articles. For guidance on the syntax, read the comments inside the file /plugins/content/vmproductsnapshots.php

  - Editor - JCE 1.5.1 plugin: Enables the JCE WYSIWYG content editor.

  - VirtueMart Extended Search plugin: Enables search of the VirtueMart products.

  - System - VM Mainframe plugin: This plugin renders the VirtueMart CSS and JS on non-VirtueMart pages.

- **Core Joomla! Templates**

  - js_larix template: The default template in the bundle.

  - js_jamba template: An optional template included with the bundle.

The installation process applicable the VirtueMart eCommerce bundle is identical to installation process for the Joomla! core.

Cross-Reference

See Chapter 2 for a full explanation of how to install the Joomla! core files on your server.

Tip

Note that the bundle installer includes the option to install sample data. If this is your first time to work with VirtueMart, installing the sample data is recommended as a way to grasp the system's capabilities and see various modules in action.

Note

The technical requirements for VirtueMart are consistent with the requirements for Joomla!

Integration with an existing site

If you already have an existing and properly functioning Joomla! site, you can add VirtueMart into the site using one of three installation techniques:

- Complete Package
- Remote Installer
- Manual Installation Package

Installing the Complete Package

The installation download package labeled Complete Package by VirtueMart contains all the components and various modules needed to install VirtueMart on an existing Joomla! site. To use this package, you must extract the contents, and then upload and install them one by one.

The Complete Package contains:

- The VirtueMart component, ready to install, in .zip format
- A modules directory that contains the following modules, ready to install, all in .zip format:
  - Product Scroller module: This VirtueMart module displays a scrolling list of products inside a Module position. Included with the Bundle but disabled in the default configuration.
  - Products module: This VirtueMart module displays a list of product categories inside a module position. Included with the Bundle but disabled in the default configuration.
  - VirtueMart module: This all-purpose VirtueMart module can be configured to display a number of items, from lists of categories, to search boxes, to login forms. Numerous configuration options let you control the output. This is enabled in the default system and assigned to the left-hand column.
  - All-In-One module: This VirtueMart module can display the latest products, featured products, top ten products or random products in one module using tabs. Included with the bundle but disabled in the default configuration.
  - Cart module: This VirtueMart module is a mini-cart that has a link to the full cart page. The module is enabled in the default configuration.
  - Currencies module: This VirtueMart module displays a list of currencies and allows your visitors to select the currency for prices.
  - Featured Products module: This VirtueMart module displays the products you have marked as being on special.
  - Latest Products module: This VirtueMart module displays the most recent products.
  - Manufacturers module: This VirtueMart module displays a list of manufacturers, with a link to all products by the manufacturer.
  - Random Product module: This VirtueMart module randomly displays a product from your store or from a specific category.

- Search module: This VirtueMart module displays a search form for your store.
- Top Ten module: This VirtueMart module displays the top ten most popular products, in terms of sales.
- A plugins directory that contains two plugins.

- An installation guide in .pdf format

To install this version of VirtueMart, follow these steps:

1. **Download the Complete Package.**

2. **Unzip the archive locally.** You can see the contents described.

3. **Log in to the admin system of your Joomla! site.**

4. **Click on the option Install/Uninstall, under the Extensions menu.** The Extensions Installer dialogue opens in your browser.

5. **Click the Browse button next to the Upload Package File field.** The file upload dialogue opens.

6. **Find and select the file com_virtuemart_x.x.x.zip. Click the Open button.** The file upload dialogue closes and the name of the file appears in the field next to the label Package File.

7. **Click Upload File & Install.** The system will now install the component. If successful, you will see a confirmation message, as shown in Figure 23.3.

8. **If you want to add the sample data, click the Install Sample Data button, or else click the button labeled Go Directly to Shop.** The component populates the database accordingly and then take you to the Store Control Panel and a confirmation message.

9. **You must next install the main VirtueMart Module. Click on the option Install/ Uninstall, under the Extensions menu.** The Extensions Installation Manager opens in your browser.

10. **Click the Browse button next to the Upload Package File field.** The file upload dialogue opens.

11. **Find and select the file mod_virtuemart_x.x.x.zip. Click the Open button.** The file upload dialogue closes and the name of the file appears in the field next to the label Package File.

12. **Click Upload File & Install.** The system now installs the module. If successful, you will see a confirmation message.

13. **Repeat the installation process for any additional modules or plugins you desire.**

14. **Access the Module Manager by selecting the option Module Manager under the Extensions menu.** The Module Manager loads in your browser.

15. **Enable all VirtueMart modules.**

16. **Access the Plugins Manager by selecting the option Plugin Manager under the Extensions menu.** The Plugin Manager loads in your browser.

17. **Enable all VirtueMart plugins.**

FIGURE 23.3

The VirtueMart component installation confirmation screen.

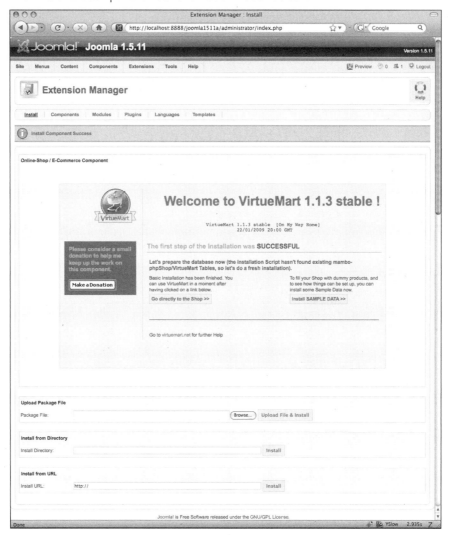

Installing by using the Remote Installer

The Remote Installer is a utility component that enables you to easily install the basic VirtueMart package without first having to download the package to your local machine. Given the large size of the VirtueMart installation files, the Remote Installer can save you a bit of time.

To use the Remote Installer, follow these steps:

1. Download the Remote Installer Component package.

2. Log in to the admin system of your Joomla! site.

3. **Click on the option Install/Uninstall, under the Extensions menu.** The Extensions Installer dialogue opens in your browser.

4. **Click the Browse button next to the Upload Package File field.** The file upload dialogue opens.

5. **Find and select the Remote Installer package you downloaded earlier. Click the Open button.** The file upload dialogue closes, and the name of the file appears in the field next to the label Package File.

6. **Click Upload File & Install.** The system installs the component. If successful, you will see a confirmation message.

7. **Access the component by clicking on the option Download VirtueMart under the Components menu.** The VirtueMart Getter / Downloader script loads in your browser.

8. **Click the Download Component button.** The system attempts to contact the remote server, download the Component Installer and extract it on your server. If successful you can see a confirmation message on a new screen in your browser.

9. **On the new screen in your browser, click the Install button.** The system attempts to install the VirtueMart component on your server. If successful, you see a confirmation message; refer to Figure 23.3.

10. **If you want to add the sample data, click the Install Sample Data button, or else click the Go Directly to Shop button.** The component populates the database accordingly and then takes you to the Store control panel where it will display a confirmation message.

11. **You must next install the main VirtueMart module. Access the component by clicking on the option Download VirtueMart under the Components menu.** The VirtueMart Getter / Downloader Script loads in your browser.

12. **Click the Download module button.** The system attempts to contact the remote server, download the Module Installer and extract it on your server. If successful you see a confirmation message on a new screen in your browser.

13. **On the new screen in your browser, click the Install button.** The system attempts to install the VirtueMart component on your server. If successful, you will see a confirmation message.

Note

The Remote Installer only sets up the basic component and module. If you want to install the additional modules and plugins, you need to use the Extension Manager's Installer function to add them to your system.

Installing the Manual Installation package

The Manual Installation package is not installable through the Joomla! Extensions Installer. This package must be unpacked and then moved to the appropriate directories manually, via FTP or your web hosting control panel's file manager. This option is provided for those whose server configuration blocks the use of Joomla's default installer.

The complete Manual Installation Package contains the same components, modules, and plugins as the Complete Package, outlined earlier, but the files are in a different format. Where, in the Complete Package, the various components, modules, and plugins are bundled in archives, in the Manual Installation Package they are unpacked. When extracted, the contents of the archive show you a set of directories:

- `/administration`
- `/components`
- `/modules`
- `/plugins`

The directory structure provides you with guidance as to where on the server you should copy the directory contents.

To install the VirtueMart Manual Installation package, follow these steps:

1. **Download the Manual Installation Package.**
2. **Unzip the archive locally.** You can see the contents.
3. **Access your Joomla! installation on your server.**
4. **Copy the contents of the VirtueMart /components directory to your Joomla! installa-tion's** `/components` **directory.**
5. **Copy the contents of the VirtueMart /modules directory to your Joomla! installation's** `/modules` **directory.**
6. **Copy the contents of the VirtueMart** `/plugins/content` **directory to your Joomla! installation's /plugins/content directory.**
7. **Copy the contents of the VirtueMart** `/plugins/search` **directory to your Joomla! installation's** `/plugins/search` **directory.**
8. **Copy the contents of the VirtueMart** `/administrator/components` **directory to your Joomla! installation's** `/administrator/components` **directory.**
9. **Log into the admin system of your Joomla! site.**
10. **Go to this URL:** `www.your domain.com/administrator/index.` `php?option=com_virtuemart`. You should see a confirmation page.

11. **If you want to add the sample data, click the Install Sample Data button, or click the Go Directly to Shop button.** The component populates the database accordingly and then takes you to the Store control panel where it displays a confirmation message.

12. **Access your Joomla! database installation; typically this is done through phpMyAdmin.**

13. **Import into your database the file virtuemart.installation.addons.joomla1.5.sql, which is located inside the** /administration/components/com_virtuemart/ sql **directory.** If successful, you see a confirmation message.

14. **Access the Module Manager by selecting the option Module Manager under the Extensions menu.** The Module Manager loads in your browser.

15. **Enable all VirtueMart modules.**

16. **Access the Plugins Manager by selecting the option Plugin Manager under the Extensions menu.** The Plugin Manager loads in your browser.

17. **Enable all VirtueMart Plugins.**

The installation process is now complete and you should be able to access all the features of VirtueMart.

Reviewing the VirtueMart Control Panel

When you access the VirtueMart component you will first see the default VirtueMart control panel, as shown in Figure 23.4. The control panel is intended to give you quick access to the most common functionalities needed by a shop administrator.

Note at the top left, above the VirtueMart logo, two texts links labeled Simple Layout and Extended Layout. The default view is the Simple Layout. Clicking the Extended Layout link radically changes the interface, as shown in Figure 23.5. If you are doing extensive work on the Shop, you are likely find the Extended Layout to be more usable. Keep in mind that the Extended Layout is geared toward administratrators and the simple layout is the layout you would probably want to display to your users who prefer a less cluttered interface.

FIGURE 23.4

The Joomla! control panel with the VirtueMart Bundle installed. This is the Simple Layout interface.

FIGURE 23.5

View of the VirtueMart Administration Panel in Extended Layout view.

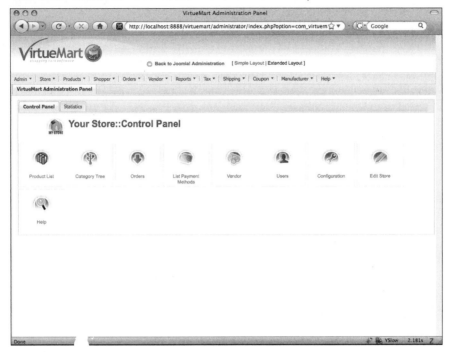

Configuring VirtueMart

Immediately after installation you can configure the Shop to suite your needs. Configuration is a lengthy process and can be time-consuming, particularly if you have not yet thought through the options you want to use for your Shop. Note that the decisions you make during the initial configuration can be modified at a later time.

To begin, click the Configuration icon on the VirtueMart Control Panel.

Global Store configuration

The Global Store configuration opens to display a set of seven tabs:

- Global
- Security
- Site

- Shipping
- Checkout
- Downloads
- Feed Configuration

Each tab is discussed in detail in the following sections.

Global tab

Clicking the Configuration icon on the VirtueMart control panel displays the Configuration screen. The default tab displayed is the Global tab, as shown in Figure 23.6.

The Global tab's workspace is divided into seven areas:

- Global
- Price Configuration
- Frontend Features
- Tax Configuration
- User Registration Settings
- Core Settings
- Logfile Configuration

The Global area includes the following options:

- **Shop is offline?:** Check this box to take the Shop offline. This causes the message entered in the parameter immediately below to be displayed to visitors who click on the link to the Shop. Note that this is does not take the entire site offline, just the Shop portion of the site. If you want to take the entire site offline, use the controls in Joomla's Global Configuration Manager.

Cross-Reference
Joomla!'s Global Configuration Manager is discussed in Chapter 4.

- **Offline Message:** Enter into this text field the message you want visitors to see when the Shop is offline. This is only visible when the parameter immediately above is checked.
- **Use only as catalogue:** Check this box to disable all shopping cart functionalities. (for example, add to cart and buy now buttons.)

FIGURE 23.6

The Global tab of the Configuration Manager.

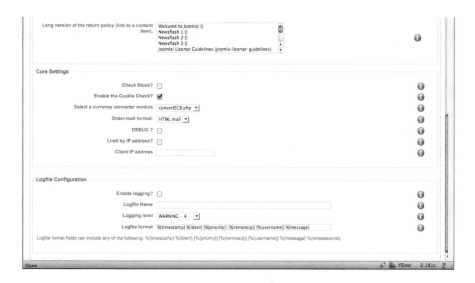

The Price Configuration area includes the following options:

- **Show Prices:** Check this box to show prices with the products.

- **Member group to show prices to:** If you want to only show prices to certain groups of users, select them here. To show the price information to all visitors, select Public Front-end.

- **Show "(including XX% tax)" when applicable?:** If your prices include tax (that is, tax is not extra), then check this box to show users the text "including xx% tax" alongside the price information for the product.

- **Show the price label for packaging?:** Use this when products are sold in multiples of units and the pricing is based upon the purchase of a set package of units.

The Frontend Features area includes the following options:

- **Enable content mambots / plugins in descriptions?:** Allows the Joomla! system plugins to parse the content of the product descriptions. This is useful for providing dynamic content in the product or category descriptions.

- **Enable Coupon Usage:** Check this box if you want to accept coupons on your site. This allows customers to fill in coupon numbers to get discounts on products.

- **Enable Customer Review/Rating System:** Check this box to enable User Reviews and Ratings of Products.

- **Auto-Publish Reviews?:** Check this box to publish automatically any user reviews without requiring prior administrator approval.

- **Comment Minimum Length:** The minimum required number of characters for a valid comment.

- **Comment Maximum Length:** The maximum number of characters for a valid comment.

- **Enable Affiliate Program?:** Check this box to enable affiliate tracking on the front end. Use this if you have planned to add affiliates in the back-end system.

The Tax Configuration area includes the following options:

- **Virtual Tax:** Check to include tax for all items, even virtual products.

- **Tax mode:** Select the basis for calculating tax: Vendor address, shipping address, or European Union mode.

- **Enable multiple tax rates?:** Check this option if you need to be able to input different tax rates for different types of products.

- **Subtract payment discount before tax/shipping?:** Check to calculate the tax on the discounted price, rather than on the pre-discounted price.

Note
Taxes rates can be configured under the Tax menu.

The User Registration Settings area includes the following options:

- **User Registration Type:** Select your preferred method for handling user registration: Normal Account Creation forces users to select a username and password; Silent registration automatically creates a username and password and sends the information to the user at the address they enter during the transaction; Optional registration lets the user decide whether they want to register; the No registration option neither provides nor requires registration.

- **Show the "Remember me" checkbox on login?:** Check this to allow users the option to have the system "remember" them; typically not a good option if you are using SSL.

- **Joomla!: User registrations allowed?:** This option reflects the values set in the Joomla Global Configuration Manager. Click the Update link to change this setting.

- **Joomla!: New account activation necessary?:** This option reflects the values set in the Joomla Global Configuration Manager. Click the Update link Update to change this setting.

Note

User, or Shoppers as they are commonly referred to in VirtueMart, can be grouped using the Shopper Groups function under the Shopper menu.

- **Must agree to Terms of Service on EVERY ORDER?:** Check this box to require the user to agree to Terms of Service on every order, even if during the same session as a previous order.

- **Show information about "Return Policy" on the order confirmation page?:** Check to show the Return Policy information on the order confirmation page. This will cause the text input in the parameter immediately below to be shown on the order confirmation page.

- **Legal information text (short version):** Input the legal or returns policy copy you want to display on the order confirmation page. This will be displayed if the parameter above is checked.

- **Long version of the return policy (link to a content item):** After you have created a new article containing your full return policy, you can select the article from the list of articles that appear in this box. The system will then generate a link to this article for users to read the full policy.

The Core Settings area includes the following options:

- **Check stock?:** Check this box if you want to restrict orders to no more than the number of items in inventory.

Note

Inventory levels for a product are set when creating or editing a product.

- **Enable the Cookie Check?:** Check to have system verify if the user's browser is set to accept cookies; if so, cookies will be used to persist data and improve the user friendliness of the site.

- **Select a currency converter module:** Select from the currency converter plugins installed on your site. By default there is only one, convertECB, which fetches the data for the currency converter from the European Central Bank.

Note

The currency converter module is only needed if you offer shoppers their choice of currencies. The currencies option is set in the Store Information panel, which is accessed by clicking on the sub-menu Edit Store under the Store menu.

- **Order--mail format:** Select either HTML or text only e-mails format for e-mails sent by the system.

- **DEBUG?:** Check to enable Debugging. Note this will cause debugging info to be displayed at the bottom of pages.

- **Limit by IP address:** Check to limit the display of the debugging information to a specific IP address. If this is checked, enter the IP address in the Client IP address field.

- **Client IP address:** Enter the IP address you want to see the debugging address. This is only relevant if the previous parameter is checked.

The Logfile Configuration area includes the following options:

- **Enable logging?:** Check to enable logging. If unchecked the Joomla! system default logging can still apply.

- **Logfile Name:** Enter the path to the logfile. Only applicable if the box above is checked.

- **Logging level:** Set the cut off level for logging issues. Only relevant if logging is enabled.

- **Logfile format:** Set your preferred logfile format. Only relevant if logging is enabled. Note the syntax is explained below the field.

Security tab

The Security tab includes a number of parameters related to establishing the security levels for your site. Clicking on the tab labeled Security will display the screen shown in Figure 23.7.

FIGURE 23.7

The Security tab of the Configuration Manager.

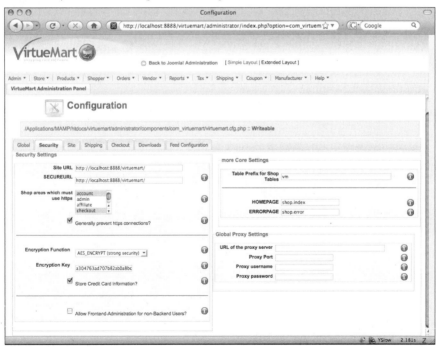

The Security tab's workspace is divided into three areas:

- Security Settings
- More Core Settings
- Global Proxy Settings

The Security Settings area includes the following options:

- **Site URL:** This field should show the site URL that resulted from the installation process. You can alter this if necessary, but an incorrect value will cause problems!
- **SECUREURL:** Enter the secure URL to be used for the site (https).
- **Shop areas which must use https:** Select from the combo box one or more areas of the site that must use secure https protocol.
- **Generally prevent https connections?:** When checked, the system will steer the user out of https URLs when the visitor is viewing pages where https is not needed. This improves site performance.
- **Encryption Function:** If you want to use encryption on the site, select AES_ENCRYPT.
- **Encryption Key:** System-created encryption key. It is generally not necessary for you to change this value.
- **Store Credit Card Information:** Check if you want the system to store the users' credit card information in the database. This will be encrypted, but you should not select this option if you do not need the data.
- **Allow Frontend-Administration for non-Backend Users?:** Check if you want to allow any of the front-end registered user groups to manage the shop. Do not select this if you do not intend to allow this level of access to the Shop.

The More Core Settings area includes the following options:

- **Table Prefix for Shop Tables:** The default value for the database table prefix is vm. Changing this value can crash your site, so do not do this unless you know what you are doing!
- **HOMEPAGE:** The Shop's default home page. Typically you do not want to alter this unless you have created a special home page.
- **ERRORPAGE:** The Shop's error page. Typically you do not want to alter this unless you have created a special error page.

The Security Settings area includes the following options:

- **URL of the proxy server:** This value will be used by the Shop server to connect to the Internet when needed. Typically this field is left blank as this will be handled automatically by your server.
- **Proxy Port:** The port used for the connection with the proxy server. Typically this field is left blank as this will be handled automatically by your server.

- **Proxy username:** If the proxy requires authentication, enter the username here. Typically this field is left blank as this will be handled automatically by your server.

- **Proxy password:** If the proxy requires authentication, enter the password here. Typically this field is left blank as this will be handled automatically by your server.

Site tab

The Site tab includes a number of options related to the display of the catalog pages, including the sort order of products and the page template. To view these parameters, click on the Site tab. The page that loads is similar to what is shown in Figure 23.8.

FIGURE 23.8

The Site tab of the Configuration Manager.

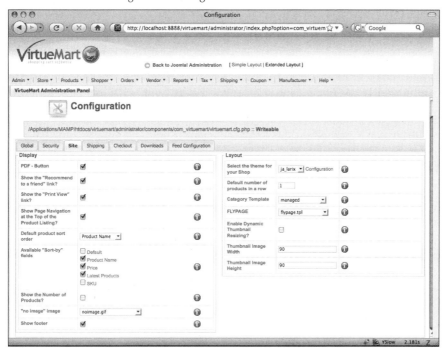

The Site tab's workspace is divided into two areas:

- Display
- Layout

The Display area includes the following options:

- **PDF - Button:** Check to show a PDF button on pages, thereby allowing user's to save Shop page as a PDF.

- **Show the Recommend to a friend link?:** Check to display the Recommend to a Friend link on Shop pages.

- **Show the Print View link?:** Check to display a Print link for the Shop pages.

- **Show Page Navigation at the Top of the Product Listing?:** Check to display page navigation at the top of Product Listings on the front-end.

- **Default product sort order:** Select the default product display sort order from the combo box.

- **Available Sort-by fields:** Check the fields you want to appear as sort options for site users.

- **Show the Number of Products?:** Check to display a product count to users.

- **"no image" Image:** Select the image you want to display when the product being viewed has no image of its own.

- **Show footer:** Check to display the Powered by VirtueMart footer on the front-end.

The Layout area includes the following options:

- **Select the theme for your Shop:** Choose the theme for the Shop from the combo box. Clicking on the Configuration link opens the Theme Settings Parameters dialogue, discussed below.

- **Default number of products in a row:** Set the number of products to appear in each row.

- **Category Template:** The system provides eight default category layouts. Select the one you prefer from the combo box. The Category Templates are kept in the `com_virtuemart/themes/default/templates/browse` directory.

- **FLYPAGE:** A flypage is a product details page. The system provides eight default layouts. Select the one you prefer from the combo box. The product templates are kept in the `com_virtuemart/themes/default/templates/product_details` directory.

Note

Category page layout selections set in the Global Configuration can be overridden for individual categories on the Category Editing dialogue.

- **Enable Dynamic Thumbnail Resizing?:** If you want the system to automatically create thumbnails for you, check this box. Images will be resized to match the measurements you specify in the parameter fields immediately below.

- **Thumbnail Image Width:** Set the thumbnail image width in pixels. Only applicable if you have enabled dynamic resizing.

- **Thumbnail Image Height:** Set the thumbnail image height in pixels. Only applicable if you have enabled dynamic resizing.

Clicking on the Configuration link next to the theme selection combo box opens up the VirtueMart system's Theme Settings parameters dialogue. It contains the following parameters:

- **Product List Style:** Select from the combo box the style of the listing of products on the page.
- **Show the Feed Icon?:** Hide or show a feed icon for the pages of the Shop.
- **Show the Add-to-cart Button on the product list?:** Hide or show the Add to cart button on the product list pages.
- **Show Vendor Link?:** Hide or show a link to the vendor pages.
- **Show Manufacturer Link?:** Hide or show a link to the manufacturer pages.
- **Show Availability Information?:** Hide or show whether product is available.
- **Show additional Pathway on the Product Page?:** Hide or show the path information on the product page.
- **Open Product Images in a LightBox?:** Select Yes to pop up the product image in a light-box. Set to No to show product image on the page.
- **Customer Checkout in a popup:** Set to Yes to use a pop-up for the checkout process. Set to No to load the checkout process on the pages.
- **Use Ajax to add, update or delete products from the cart?:** Set to use Ajax to update the cart; this can improve performance as it decreases the number of page reloads.
- **Show featured products on frontpage?:** Set to Yes to show featured products on the homepage of the Shop.
- **Show the latest products on the frontpage?:** Set to Yes to show latest products on the homepage of the Shop.
- **Number of recent products to Display?:** Enter an integer value here to set the number of items to show as recent items.

Shipping tab

This tab lists the various default shipping options bundled with VirtueMart. Select all the ones you want to appear as options for users at checkout, or add other shipping methods via the Store form. The Shipping tab is shown in Figure 23.9.

Note

If you do not want to use shipping, you must deselect all the options here and choose a checkout process that does not include Shipping Method selection. The checkout process parameter is on the Checkout tab.

FIGURE 23.9

The Shipping tab of the Configuration Manager.

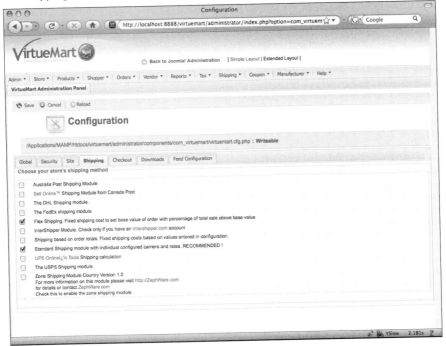

Checkout tab

The Checkout tab enables you to configure the checkout process for your shoppers, as shown in Figure 23.10.

The first option on this tab is labeled Enable the Checkout Bar. Leave this checked to display a progress bar to your site visitors as they move through the checkout process.

FIGURE 23.10

The Checkout tab of the Configuration Manager.

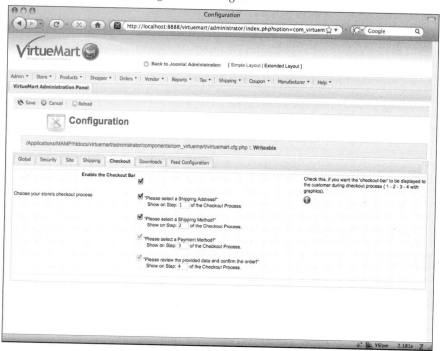

The four checkboxes immediately below establish the steps in the checkout process. The default process involves four steps:

- Please select a Shipping Address
- Please select a Shipping Method
- Please select a Payment Method
- Please review the provided data and confirm the order.

If you want to remove any of these from the process, simply deselect them. You can also re-order the steps by changing the numbers in the boxes to reflect your preference in the numerical order of the steps. If you do not want to use Shipping process on your site, disable the top two boxes.

Downloads tab

The Downloads tab is provided to allow you to set up your Shop for selling downloads, as shown in Figure 23.11. If you do not want to enable downloads on your site, simply uncheck the top parameter and move on to the next tab.

The Download tab of the Configuration Manager.

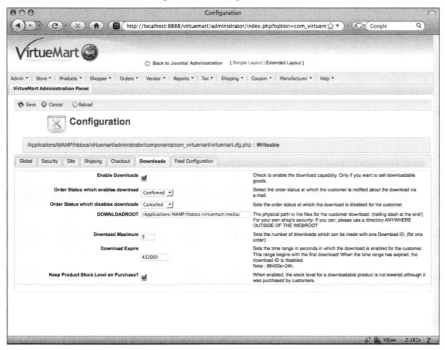

The Downloads tab includes the following options:

- **Enable Downloads:** Check to enable download transactions.

- **Order Status which enables downloads:** Use this combo box to determine what order status setting causes the system to notify the user of the information needed to complete the download.

- **Order Status which disables downloads:** Use this combo box to determine which order status setting results in disabling of the download.

- **DOWNLOADROOT:** Enter into this field the path where the download files will be kept on the server.

- **Download Maximum:** Set the maximum number of downloads that can be done with one download code.

- **Download Expire:** Enter a value, in seconds, for the lifespan of the download code; beyond this time the code is invalid.

- **Keep Product Stock Level on Purchase?:** Check this box to remove downloads from the stock level count.

Feed Configuration tab

The Feed Configuration tab, shown in Figure 23.12, controls all the parameters associated with the RSS feeds for your Shop. If you do not want to enable feeds for your Shop, disable the first option; all other choices on this page are dependent upon the Product Feed being enabled.

FIGURE 23.12

The Feed Configuration tab of the Configuration Manager.

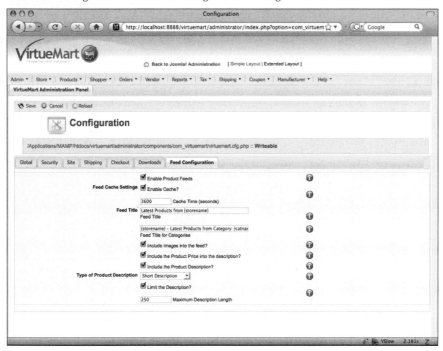

The Feed Configuration tab includes the following options:

- **Enable Product Feeds:** Check this box to enable the feeds functionality.

- **Enable Cache?:** Check to enable caching of feed data.

- **Cache Time:** Enter a time, in seconds, before the product feed cache is refreshed. Note this is only relevant if the Parameter, Enable Cache, is checked.

- **Feed Title:** Enter a title for the feed. This is seen by subscribers to the feed.

- **Feed Title for Categories:** Enter a title for feeds of individual Categories. This is seen by subscribers to the feed.

- **Include Images into the feed?:** Check to include images with the feed output. This is seen by subscribers to the feed.

- **Include the Product Price into the description?:** Check to include the product price in the feed output. This is seen by subscribers to the feed.

- **Include the Product Description?:** Check to include the product description in the feed output. This is seen by subscribers to the feed.

- **Type of Product Description:** Select from the combo box with a short description or the full item description for inclusion in the feed output. This is seen by subscribers to the feed.

- **Limit the Description?:** Check to force a maximum word count on the feed output. If this is checked, you can set the maximum length in the next parameter.

- **Maximum description Length:** Enter an integer value here to set a maximum word count for the length of the description in the feed output. This is dependent upon the checkbox above be selected.

Setting the Store Information

The second key step to getting your Store up and running is to supply the data requested in the Store Information dialogue. Clicking on the Edit Store option on the VirtueMart Control Panel displays the Store Information dialogue.

The Store Information page workspace is divided into the following six areas, as shown in Figure 23.13.

- Store
- Contact Information
- Store Information
- Currency Display Styles
- Description
- Terms of Service

FIGURE 23.13

The Store Information dialogue.

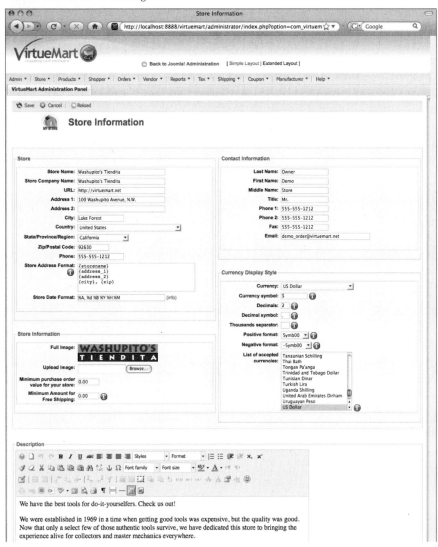

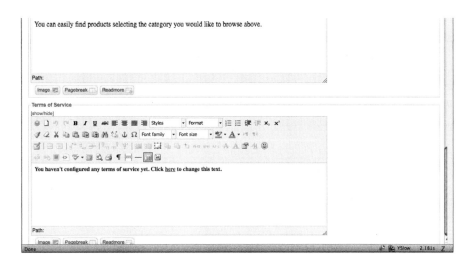

The Store area includes the following options:

- **Store Name:** This is the name of the store that will be displayed on the site. This is a required field.

- **Store Company Name:** This is for the proper name of your business entity. This is displayed in some correspondence and is used by the system as the default vendor. This field is required.

- **URL:** Your Shop's URL, as you want it to appear in correspondence.

- **Address 1:** Address field for your physical location. This is displayed in some correspondence.

- **Address 2:** Alternate field for address information. This is displayed in some correspondence.

- **City:** The city where your business is physically located. This is displayed in some correspondence.

- **Country:** The country where your business is physically located. This is displayed in some correspondence.

- **State/Province/Region:** The State, Province, or Region where your business is physically located. This is displayed in some correspondence.

- **Zip/Postal Code:** The Zip or Postal Code of your business. This is displayed in some correspondence.

- **Phone:** Enter the telephone number you want associated with the Store.

- **Store Address Format:** Input the variables you want to display in the order you want to display them. Hover the mouse over the info symbol underneath the label for a list of the available variables.

- **Store Date Format:** Set the date format used by the Store. Click the info link to the right of the text field for more information on the options available here.

The Contact Information area includes the following options:

- **Last Name:** The last name of the person you want listed as the contact for the Store.

- **First Name:** The first name of the person you want listed as the contact for the Store.

- **Middle Name:** The middle name of the person you want listed as the contact for the Store.

- **Title:** The title of the person listed as the contact for the Store.

- **Phone 1:** The phone number of the person listed as the contact for the Store.

- **Phone 2:** An alternate phone number for the person listed as the contact for the Store.

- **Fax:** A fax number for the person listed as the contact for the Store.

- **Email:** The e-mail address of the person listed as the contact for the Store.

Caution

You must change this e-mail address; if you don't, all correspondence concerning the store will be directed to the VirtueMart.com address provided by default!

The Store Information area includes the following options:

- **Full Information:** Displays the current logo image associated with the store. Upload your own image using the following field.

- **Upload Image:** Use this field to upload the logo of your choice for the Store.

- **Minimum purchase order value for your store:** Set a minimum purchase order value, if you want to use one.

- **Minimum Amount for Free Shipping:** Set a minimum order value to trigger free shipping, if you want to offer this option.

The Currency Display Styles area includes the following options:

- **Currency:** Select your primary currency from the combo box.

- **Currency symbol:** Set the symbol you want to display with the currency.

- **Decimals:** Enter an integer value to specify the number of decimals displayed with the price.

- **Decimal symbol:** Enter the character you want to use to separate the decimal in the price.

- **Thousands separator:** Enter the character you want to use to separate thousands units in the price.

- **Positive format:** Select from the combo box the format for positive numbers.

- **Negative format:** Select from the combo box the format for negative numbers.

- **List of accepted currencies:** Select the currency options you want to offer to Store users. Note that every currency you select here will be available at checkout! If you do not want to offer users their choice of currency, select only your default currency.

The Description area includes a text field with a WYSIWYG editor bar. Enter into this field the descriptive text or images you want to display to visitors when they arrive to the Store.

The Terms of Service text field is provided to allow you to enter the text for your Store's Terms of Service.

Working with products and categories

The VirtueMart system is capable of supporting a wide range of product attributes. By default, you can classify products by manufacturer, vendor, type, or category. For larger shops, the various options are useful, but for a small shop sometimes they are a bit overwhelming. To work in the simplest configuration, you need only create products. That said, as a Shop owner, if you have more than just a few products, you may find that product management is significantly improved if you also create categories for grouping your products. Categories are not required but they are very useful.

The following sections cover the basics of creating categories and products. The information covered is sufficient to get your Store started. If you need additional classifications for your products, such as manufacturer or type, you can always add them later.

Overview of the Category Manager

Categories are used for the grouping of products. The system supports the creation of both parent and child categories, allowing you to create a logical organization for your site. Categories make organizing the products easier on both the front end and the back end and make it easier for your users to find things quickly.

To get started adding categories to your Shop, either click the Category Tree icon on the VirtueMart Control Panel or click on the option labeled List Categories under the Products menu. In either case, you can see the Category Tree, as shown in Figure 23.14.

The toolbar at the top of the Category Tree provides the following functions:

- **New:** Click to add a new category.

- **Publish:** Select one or more categories from the list and then click this icon to publish them.

- **Unpublish:** Select one or more categories from the list and then click this icon to unpublish them.

- **Remove:** Select one or more categories from the list and then click this icon to delete them.

FIGURE 23.14

The Product Category Tree, shown here with the sample data installed.

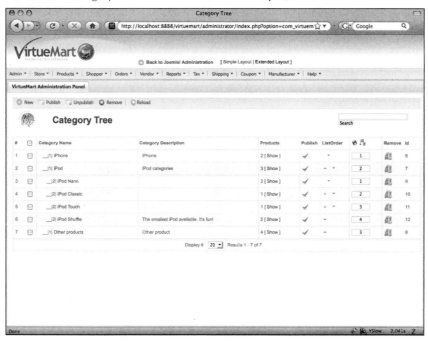

The main content area of the screen contains a list of all the categories in your Shop. The columns provided are:

- **#:** An indexing number assigned by the system. This number cannot be changed.

- **Checkbox** (no label): Click in a checkbox to select a category; this is needed if you want to use several of the toolbar options.

- **Category Name:** This field displays the name of the category. Click on the name to edit the category's details.

- **Category Description:** This field displays the description of the category.

- **Products:** The number of products in the category. Click the Show link to view them.

- **Publish:** A green checkmark in this column indicates that the category is active. The field will show a red X if the category is disabled. Administrators can toggle between the two settings by clicking the icon shown.

- **List Order:** Click the up and down arrows to move the category up or down in the order.

- **Order** (no label): Enter numerical values to indicate the sequence of display for the categories; then click the save icon to save the changes.

- **Remove:** Click to delete a category.

- **ID:** The system-generated user ID number.

At the bottom of the screen, below the content area, is the Display # option. Change the value in the combo box control to alter the number of categories that are displayed on the page. The default value can be altered by changing the List Length option on the Global Configuration Manager.

Creating a new category

Click the New icon at the top of the Category Tree page to add a new product category to your Shop. Clicking on the icon displays the New Category dialogue, as shown in Figure 23.15.

FIGURE 23.15

The New Category dialogue.

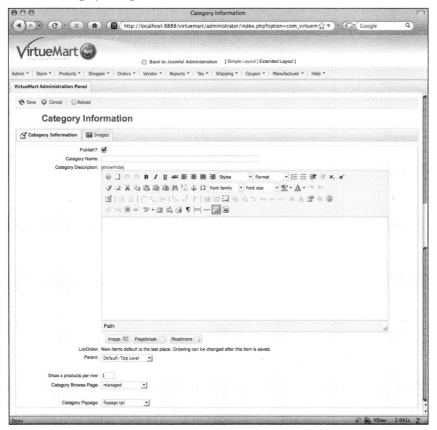

The toolbar at the top of the Global Configuration Manager provides the following functions:

- **Save:** Click to save any changes you've made. After saving, the system exits the New Category dialogue and returns you to the Category Tree.

- **Apply:** Click this icon to save your work without exiting from the New Category dialogue.

- **Cancel:** Cancels the task, exits the New Category dialogue and returns you to the Category Tree.

The New Category dialogue provides two tabs — Category Information and Images. The Category Information tab includes the following fields:

- **Publish:** An indexing number assigned by Joomla! This cannot be changed.

- **Category Name:** Enter a name for the category.

- **Category Description:** Enter a short description for the category.

- **List Order:** You cannot control this at the time of category creation; new categories default to the bottom of the list. If you want to alter the order after creation, you can do so from the Category Tree interface or by editing the category.

- **Parent:** If you want to create a sub-category, choose the Parent Category from the combo box.

- **Show x products per row:** Enter an integer value to specify the number of products shown per row. Note the settings you choose here will override those specified in the VirtueMart Global configuration.

- **Category Browse Page:** Select one of the system's templates for the category browse page layout. Note the settings you choose here will override those specified in the VirtueMart Global configuration.

- **Category Flypage:** Select one of the system's templates for the product page layout. Note the settings you choose here will override those specified in the VirtueMart Global configuration.

The Image tab is divided into two areas, Full Image and Thumbnail. Both areas include the same fields, all of which are optional:

- **Full Image:** Click Browse to upload an image for the category. This will be used as the large category image.

- **Image Action:** Select the Auto-Create Thumbnail? option if you want the system to create a thumbnail of the image. Click none if you do not want a thumbnail created.

- **URL:** Associate an URL with the image.

To create a new category, follow these steps:

1. **Log in to the admin system on your site.**

2. **Access the VirtueMart component by clicking on VirtueMart under the Components menu.** The VirtueMart Control Panel loads in your browser.

3. **Select the Category Tree icon on the Control Panel.** The Category Tree loads in your browser.

4. **Click the New icon on the toolbar at the top of the Category Tree.** When you click that icon, the New Category dialogue opens. (Refer to Figure 23.15.)

5. **In the Name field, type a name for this category.** This is the only required field.

6. **Add additional information or optional settings as you see fit.**

7. **Click the Save icon on the toolbar at the top right to save your new category.** The dialogue closes and returns you to the Category Tree.

Editing and deleting categories

Existing product categories can be edited from the Category Tree. To edit a category, click on the category name in the Category Tree; the system opens the Edit Category dialogue.

The Edit Category dialogue is identical to the New Category dialogue, with the same fields and requirements as discussed in the previous section.

To make changes to a category, simply alter the desired fields in the Edit Category dialogue, then click the Save or Apply icon on the toolbar. Any changes you have made are applied immediately.

To delete one or more categories, follow these steps:

1. Open the Category Tree.

2. Select one or more categories.

3. Click the Remove icon.

Caution

Deleting a category is permanent and cannot be undone. Note, however, that a category cannot be deleted if there are sub-categories assigned to that category. If you wish to delete the category, you need to first delete or move any sub-categories to another category. Note that if there are products assigned to the category you are removing, they will be deleted, unless they are also members of another category.

Overview of the Product List

To view all the products in your Shop, click the Product List icon on the VirtueMart Control Panel, or select the option Product List from the Products menu. Either option displays the Product List as shown in Figure 23.16.

The toolbar at the top of the Product List provides the following functions:

- **Add Attribute:** Select one or more products from the list, then click this icon to add an attribute specific to the selected product(s).

- **List Prices:** Select one or more products from the list, then click this icon to add multiple prices to the selected product(s).

- **Add Product Type:** Select one or more products from the list, then click this icon to add a Product Type relevant to the selected product(s).

- **New:** Click to add a new product.

- **Publish:** Select one or more products from the list, then click this icon to publish them.

- **Unpublish:** Select one or more products from the list, then click this icon to unpublish them.

- **Remove:** Select one or more products from the list, then click this icon to delete the product(s).

FIGURE 23.16

The Product List page, shown here with the sample data installed.

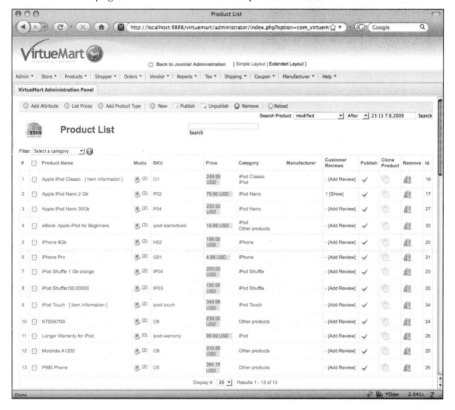

Below the icons and above the list of products are several sorting and searching tools to help you manage long lists of products:

- The Filter field on the left sorts the view by Product Category. The page reloads and displays all the products in the selected category. To clear the screen and return to a full listing, change the selection to the default Select a category.

- The Search box in the middle of the screen is a free text search field. Type in the search query and then press the Return key or click the Search button to view the results. To clear the screen and return to a full listing, enter a blank space and press Return or click the Search button.

- The Search Product boxes at the top right allow you to construct a more advanced search query with multiple criteria. The first box allows you to choose from one of three criteria: modified, with price modified, without price. This is then combined with the second combo box to put an additional condition on the search. There are two options on this combo box: before and after. Set the limiting criteria in these two boxes then enter a date in the text field. Click Search to see the results. To clear the screen and return to a full listing, enter a blank space and press Return or click the Search button.

The main content area of the screen contains a list of all the products in your Shop. The columns provided are:

- **#:** An indexing number assigned by Joomla! This cannot be changed.

- **Checkbox** (no label): Click in a checkbox to select a product; this is needed if you want to use several of the toolbar options.

- **Product Name:** This field displays the full name of the product. Click on the name to edit the product's details.

- **Media:** Shows the number of images associated with the product. Clicking on the value opens a pop-up window that lists the images. Note that a large image plus a thumbnail of the large image counts as two images, not one.

- **SKU:** The SKU of the product.

- **Price:** The base price of the product. Click to pop-up a window that lets you view all prices for all groups. You can also edit the price in the pop-up window.

Note
If you use the pop-up window to edit the price of a product you will need to refresh the Product List page to see the new value displayed.

- **Category:** A list of the categories to which the product is assigned.

- **Manufacturer:** The manufacturer associated with the product.

- **Customer Reviews:** If the product has any reviews, this column shows the number of reviews and a link to show to reviews. If there are no reviews, the column shows an Add a Review link. Clicking on either link takes you to the Product Reviews page.

- **Publish:** A green checkmark in this column indicates that the contact is active. The field will show a red X if the contact is disabled. Administrators can toggle between the two settings by clicking the icon shown.

- **Clone Product:** Click to create a duplicate product entry. This can make it simpler to add new products.

- **Remove:** Click to delete the product.

- **ID:** The system-generated user ID number.

At the bottom of the screen, below the content area, is the Display # option. Change the value in the combo box control to alter the number of contacts that are displayed on the page. The default value can be altered by changing the List Length option on the Global Configuration Manager.

Creating a new product

To add a new poduct to your Shop, click the New icon on the top-right toolbar of the Product List, or click the Add Product option under the Products menu. In either case you see the New Product dialogue, as shown in Figure 23.17.

The toolbar at the top of the New Product dialogue provides the following functions:

- **Save:** Click this icon to save your work, create a new product, and exit the New Product dialogue.

- **Apply:** Click to save your work and create a new product without exiting from the New Product dialogue. This option lets you save without exiting the screen and it useful in case you are interrupted or you otherwise want to save yet keep working on this screen.

- **Cancel:** Cancels the task and exits the New Product dialogue.

The New Product dialogue includes six tabs:

- Product Information
- Display Options
- Product Status
- Product Dimensions and Weight
- Product Images
- Related Products

FIGURE 23.17

The New Product dialogue, showing the product Information tab.

The first tab is the Product Information tab, which contains the following fields. (Refer to Figure in 23.17.)

- **Publish:** Check this box to publish the product.
- **SKU:** Enter into this field an alphanumeric value to use for tracking the product in the system. Typically this is called a Stock Keeping Unit - an SKU. This field is required.

- **Name:** Enter a name for the product. This field is required and will be shown on the front end of the site.

- **URL:** You have the option of associating a URL with the product.

- **Vendor:** The vendor with which the product is associated. If you have no vendors in your system, the product will automatically be associated with your Store company name.

- **Manufacturer:** The manufacturer with which the product is associated.

- **Categories:** Select one or more categories to associate with the product.

- **Product Price (Net):** Set the price for the default Shopper Group. Use the combo box on the right to select the currency.

- **Product price (Gross):** The Gross Product Price is the Net Price plus the tax. This should be set for the default Shopper Group.

- **VAT id:** The ID of the tax rate you want applied to the product.

- **Discount Type:** If you want to use a discount, select a type from the combo box.

Note

You can add new Discount Types using the Add Product Discount link under the Products menu.

- **Discounted Price:** If you want to use a set discounted price, rather than an automatic calculation, enter the value in this field. If a value is entered in this field, it will override the Discount Type Parameter, set above.

- **Short Description:** Enter text here to be displayed on the overview page for the product.

- **Product Description:** Enter the text of the full product description here.

Tip

The Short Description is what shoppers see when they are browsing categories or viewing search results. The text entered in the Product Description field is displayed to shoppers on the Product details page.

Clicking on the tab labeled Display Options displays the screen shown in Figure 23.18.

The Display Options tab contains the following fields:

- **Use Parent Settings:** Check this box to force any child products to use the formatting options of the parent product.

- **List:** Select the options here for List display, if desired. Note that the Child Class Suffix option makes it possible to add a suffix string that will be added to the CSS of the child products. This makes it possible for you to specify CSS styling for the child products. Selecting one of the options in this parameter enables the List Style parameter, immediately below.

- **List Style:** Select options for your List display. Note this is dependent upon the List parameter being selected.

- **Extra IDs:** If you want to display other products, enter their IDs here.

- **Quantity:** Select the formatting you want to use for the Quantity box for this Product. Note that selecting one of these values enables the Drop Down Box Values parameter, below.

- **Drop Down Box Values:** Set the high and low values and the increment for your Quantity box. Note this parameter is only active if the previous Quantity parameter is selected.

FIGURE 23.18

The Display Options tab.

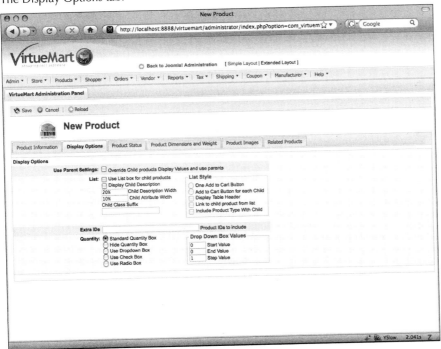

Clicking on the tab labeled Product Status displays the screen shown in Figure 23.19:

FIGURE 23.19

The Product Status tab.

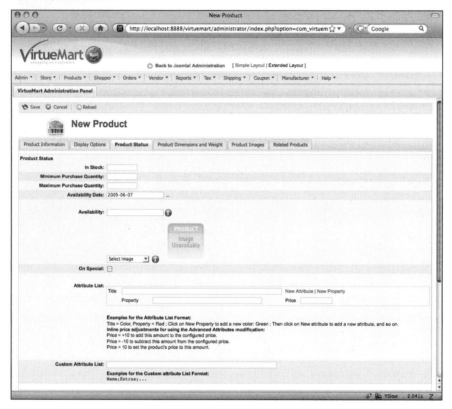

The Product Status tab contains the following fields:

- **In Stock:** Set the number of items in stock. This is used for the shipping and inventory functions and will prohibit Shoppers from ordering more than you have.

- **Minimum Purchase Quantity:** Enter an integer value for minimum purchase quantity for this product.

- **Maximum Purchase Quantity:** Enter an integer value for maximum purchase quantity for this product.

- **Availability Date:** When the quantity set above will be available for purchase.

- **Availability** (Text field and Image field): You can use either text to indicate Product Availability or an Image. If you want to use text, enter in the field next to the label Availability. If you prefer to use an image, select one from the combo box below the text field.

- **On Special:** Checking this box marks the product as being on special and displays it as a featured product.

- **Attribute List:** This field sets up the Product Attribute options that will be shown to the Shopper as choices available with this product. Enter the attribute and property and price and then click the New Attribute link to add. Click New Property to add additional properties to the Attributes List.

Tip

Only use the Attribute List option to list attributes that are not tied to the quantity of the products available. If, for example, you have one quantity of red shirts, but a different quantity of blue shirts, you should enter them as two different products.

- **Custom Attribute List:** Enter manually custom attributes here using your own labels.

Tip

The syntax for the attribute options, above, is rather complicated, so make sure you read the tip text below the fields for guidance in formatting your Attribute List. Note that you can also add attributes to products after creation by using the Add Attribute option on the Product List page, or by editing the product.

Clicking on the tab labeled Product Dimensions and Weight displays the screen in Figure 23.20:

FIGURE 23.20

The Product Dimensions and Weight tab.

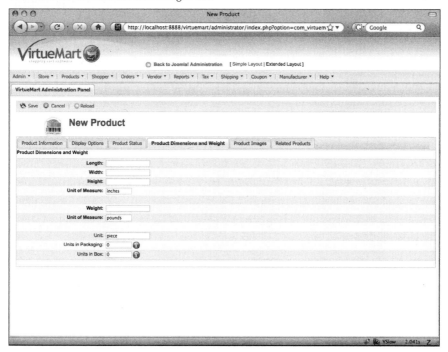

The Product Dimensions and Weight tab contains the following fields:

- **Length:** Enter a numerical value for the length of the product. This is used in calculating shipping.
- **Width:** Enter a numerical value for the width of the product. This is used in calculating shipping.
- **Height:** Enter a numerical value for the height of the product. This is used in calculating shipping.
- **Unit of Measure:** Select the unit of measure used in the dimensions parameters, above. This is used in calculating shipping.
- **Weight:** Enter a numerical value for the weight of the product. This is used in calculating shipping.

- **Unit of Measure:** Select the unit of measure used for the weight parameter, above. This is used in calculating shipping.

- **Unit:** Enter the descriptive label to be used for the units of the product. The default is piece.

- **Units in Packaging:** How many units of this product fit in one package. This is used in calculating shipping.

- **Units in Box: How many units of this product fit in one box.** Typically this is a multiple of the value entered for the Packages parameter, immediately above. This is used in calculating shipping.

Clicking on the tab labeled Product Images displays the screen shown in Figure 23.21:

FIGURE 23.21

The Product Images tab.

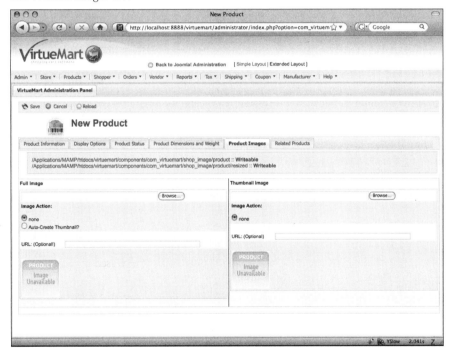

The Product Images tab is divided into two areas, Full Image and Thumbnail Image. They contain the same fields:

- **Full Image:** Click Browse to upload an image for the product. The image loaded under the heading Full Image will be used as the large product image. The image loaded under the heading Thumbnail Image will be used as the product thumbnail image.

- **Image Action:** Select the Auto-Create Thumbnail? option if you want the system to create a thumbnail of the image. Click none if you do not want a thumbnail created.

- **URL:** Associate an URL with the image.

Clicking on the tab labeled Related Products displays the screen shown in Figure 23.22.

FIGURE 23.22

The Related Products tab.

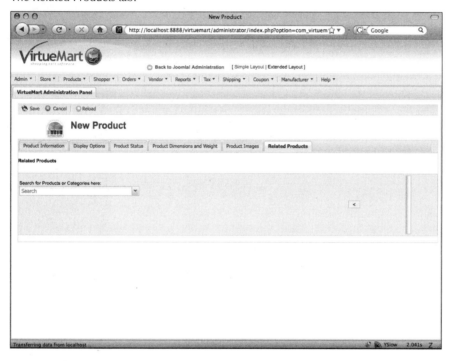

The Related Products tab is provided to allow you to identify related or similar products that can be displayed for cross-selling purposes. This is an optional step. If you do not intend to offer a related items functionality, skip this. If you want to use it, select the Product Categories from the box on the left and then the products on the right.

To create a new product, follow these steps:

1. **Log in to the admin system on your site.**

2. **Access the VirtueMart Component. To do so, go to the Components menu and select the option VirtueMart.** The VirtueMart Control Panel loads in your browser.

3. **Click on the Products menu on VirtueMart Control Panel.** The Products menu expands to show the sub-menu.

4. **Click on the sub-menu option Add Product.** The New Product dialogue will appear in your browser.

5. **In the SKU field, type an alphanumeric value to help identify the product.** This field is required.

6. **In the Name field, type a name for the product.** This field is required.

7. **Add additional information or optional settings as you see fit.**

8. **Click the Save icon on the toolbar at the top right to save your new product.** The dialogue closes and displays instead a summary of the product.

Editing and deleting products

Existing products can be edited from the Product List. To edit a product, click on the product name on the product list; the system opens the Edit Product dialogue.

The Edit Product dialogue is identical to the New Product dialogue, with the same fields and requirements as discussed in the previous section.

To make changes to a product, simply alter the desired fields in the Edit Product dialogue and then click the Save or Apply icon on the toolbar. Any changes you have made are applied immediately.

To delete one or more products, follow these steps:

1. Open the Product List.

2. Select one or more products.

3. Click the Remove icon.

Administering the Store

In addition to enabling the front-end display of a catalog and the processing of sales, VirtueMart includes a number of features that are intended to make administering an online Shop easier. The back office feature of VirtueMart is one of the areas where the system has seen significant improvements over the years and it now contains a number of useful features.

Tracking orders

After a shopper places an order, the system will create a record for the Shop owner. To view all orders, click on the List Orders option under the Orders menu. The Order List appears in your browser, as shown in Figure 23.23.

The screen shows all orders, whether pending, cancelled, or completed, along with additional information for at-a-glance viewing of the transaction history of the Shop. Key functionality includes:

- Clicking on the Order Number takes you to the Order Details page, which shows complete order information and allows you to edit key data.
- Clicking on the Name entry opens the User Details page. The User Details page includes information about the user as well as their order history.
- Clicking the icon in the Print View column opens a print-friendly version of the order, which is useful both for internal record-keeping and for sending a copy to the customer.
- The Status combo box allows you to change the status of the order.
- The Update column automatically notifies the customer of changes to the order status, if you so desire.
- To Delete an order, click the icon in the Remove column.

FIGURE 23.23

The List Orders screen.

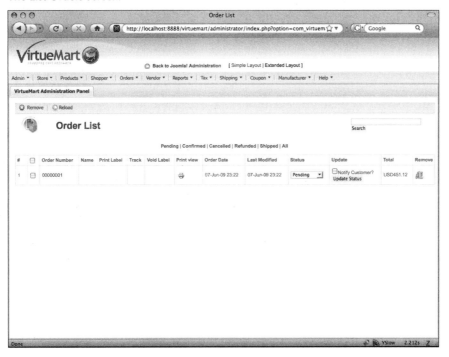

Generating reports

VirtueMart provides two different snapshots of activity in the system: The Statistics tab and the Reports feature. The Statistics tab is accessed from the VirtueMart Control Panel. Clicking on the tab displays a summary of the Shop — number of customers, products, and orders, as shown in Figure 23.24.

FIGURE 23.24

The Statistics tab.

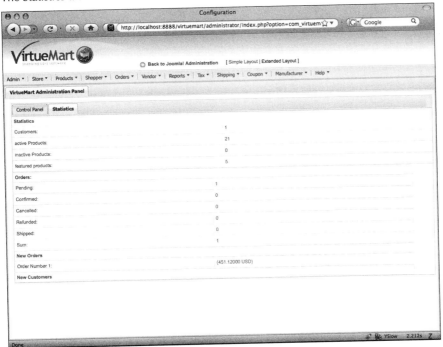

The Reports feature is access by clicking on the Reports option under the Reports menu. VirtueMart's ability to generate reports is somewhat limited and is focused on transactions. It can be tailored to display activity data by date range and can include not only orders, but also a summary of the products sold, as shown in Figure 23.25.

FIGURE 23.25

The VirtueMart Reports function.

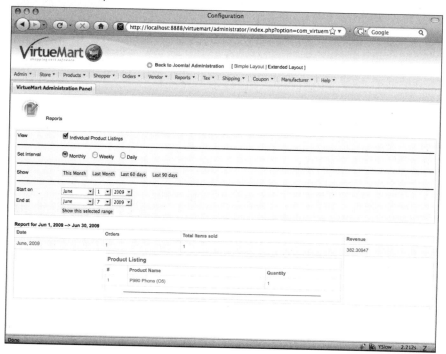

Summary

In this chapter, we have taken a look at the basics of setting up e-commerce on your Joomla! site with the VirtueMart extension. You learned the following:

- How the download and install VirtueMart
- How to set VirtueMart's Global Configuration
- How to set up a Shop
- How to create product categories
- How to add new products to the Shop
- How to track orders

Creating a Community Site with JomSocial

S ocial networking and Web 2.0 functionality are two of the most significant trends in web site development in the last few years. The basic
Joomla! system provides little in the way of true social networking
functionality. JomSocial, a commercial extension to the Joomla! system, has
stepped in to fill the gap with a powerful and extensible suite of extensions
that enable you to turn a basic Joomla! site into a full-featured social networking site.

JomSocial comes with a large number of modules and plugins and a fairly
complex presentation. Configuration of the site's many options can be challenging and time-consuming. This chapter looks at what's involved in
obtaining and installing JomSocial, and then steps you through the basics of
configuring a JomSocial site.

Introducing JomSocial

JomSocial is a complex extension for Joomla! comprised of a number of elements that provide an assortment of functionalities typically associated with
creating a social networking Web site. By installing JomSocial on your existing Joomla! site, you can offer site visitors a full range of social networking
tools and activities, thereby greatly enhancing the interactivity and stickiness
of your site. Figure 24.1 shows the front end of the basic JomSocial package.

FIGURE 24.1

The front end of the basic JomSocial package, shown here with all modules activated.

JomSocial is a commercial extension and is relatively new. It is built to integrate with a number of other extensions that provide community-related functionality, like threaded discussion forums. While you can use the system to create a Facebook-type site, you can also do a lot more with it, as the example sites in the "Who uses JomSocial" sidebar demonstrates.

Who uses JomSocial?

Here's a sampling of some of the companies and brands that use JomSocial.

- Barkley and Paws: `http://www.barkleyandpaws.com/`
- CMS Market: `http://www.cmsmarket.com/`
- LDS Online Community Gathering: `http://www.ldstribe.com/`
- Linux.com: `http://www.linux.com/`
- qAachen: `http://www.qaachen.de/`

Tip

JomSocial is a complicated system with a large number of options and configuration choices. The initial setup of a JomSocial site can take a bit of time and the creation of an attractive site requires planning and good template selection. Don't try deploying this on a live site without first working through it in detail on a development server.

If you'd like to see more examples, visit the JomSocial Showcase, which maintains a collection of JomSocial sites. Go to `www.jomsocial.com/overview/showcase.html`

Note

You can test drive a live JomSocial installation at the demo site the project maintains. The demo site allows you to check out both the front-end and the back-end of the system. View it online at

`www.jomsocial.com/community.html`

The default JomSocial system supports a wide range of features for both site visitors and administrators. Note that these features are in addition to the standard Joomla! site features and that you can further extend your JomSocial site by installing additional extensions.

Figuring out features for visitors

Front-end visitors have access to a number of features and functionalities. The front-end activity is all focused around the user profiles and interaction with other users and groups.

- User profiles with user pages
- User points
- Photo and video galleries
- Support for Facebook connect
- Buddy system
- Private messaging between users
- Activity stream

- Installable applications
- Groups
- Search

Features for site administrators

The JomSocial administration system covers the management of users, groups, and applications. Key features include:

- Customizable user fields
- Smooth integration with other popular extensions
- Customizable page templates
- User Points management
- User mass mail
- Applications management
- Group management

Note

JomSocial , like Joomla!, is extendable. The JomSocial site includes a small but growing extensions directory. Browse the directory at `www.jomsocial.com/addons.html`

Obtaining and Installing JomSocial

The first step to building your community site is to obtain the JomSocial code. As this is a commercial product, the only place to obtain the code is through the official JomSocial Web site, `www.jomsocial.com`. The software can be purchased online and downloaded immediately; it will be delivered in an archive file that must be extracted prior to installation.

After you extract the JomSocial installation package, you find the following:

- The JomSocial component, ready to install, in .zip format
- A zipped modules directory that must be unpacked prior to installation
- A zipped apps directory that must be unpacked prior to installation
- An installation guide in .pdf format

Installing the JomSocial component

The only thing you absolutely have to install to get JomSocial up and running is the component. After the component is installed you can decide what further applications and modules you want to include in your site.

To install the core JomSocial component, follow these steps:

1. Download the installation archive.

2. Unzip the archive locally.

3. Log in to the admin system of your Joomla! site.

4. **Click on the option Install/Uninstall, under the Extensions menu.** The Extensions Installation dialogue opens in your browser.

5. **Click the Browse button next to the Upload Package File field.** The file upload dialogue opens.

6. **Find and select the file com_JomSocial_x.x.x.zip, where x.x.x represents the version number of your JomSocial installer. Click the Open button.** The file upload dialogue closes, and the name of the file appears in the field next to the label Package File.

7. **Click Upload File & Install.** The system now installs the component. If successful, you will see a confirmation message, as shown in Figure 24.2.

FIGURE 24.2

Step 1 of the JomSocial component installation; the start screen.

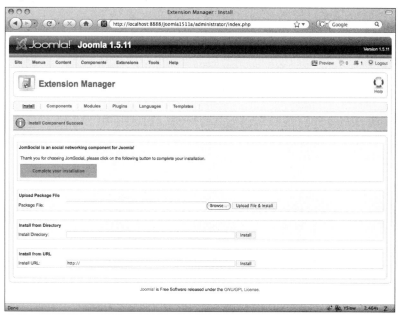

8. **Click on the button marked Complete your Installation.** A new page loads as the JomSocial installer does a quick system check to make sure your server is configured to handle the system, as shown in Figure 24.3. If all is okay, the Install button will be active. If not, address the issues indicated.

9. **Click the Install button.** The system installs all the necessary elements and displays a progress indicator. When it reaches 100%, a confirmation message is displayed, as shown in Figure 24.4.

10. **Click the Next button.** The installer closes and you are taken to the JomSocial control panel.

FIGURE 24.3

Step 2 of the JomSocial component installation; the system check screen.

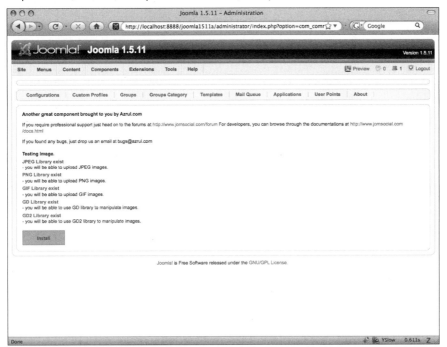

FIGURE 24.4

Step 3 of the JomSocial component installation; the final confirmation screen.

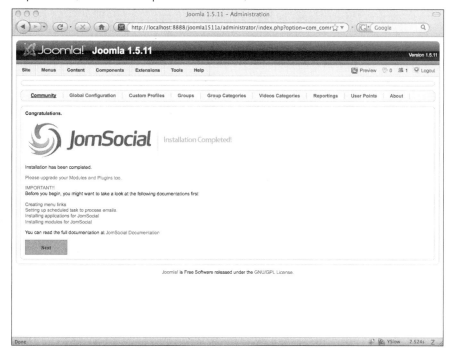

Installing the JomSocial modules

In addition to the core JomSocial component, your installation package also includes a set of optional modules. The modules expand the functionality of the site and give you more choices for displaying data and community activity. Like any Joomla! module, a JomSocial module is controlled through the Module Manager. The modules are assigned to appear on the front end of the site through module positions and page assignments.

Cross-Reference

Assigning modules is covered in Chapter 17.

In the JomSocial installation archive, the modules directory is compressed. Before you can begin to install the modules, you must unpack the directory labeled `module_unzip_first_xxxx.zip`, where xxxx represents the version number of your JomSocial installer.

After you extract the JomSocial Modules directory, you can find the following, all ready to install, in .zip format:

- **Active Groups Module:** Displays a list of the most active groups on the site.
- **Activity Stream Module:** Shows a stream of posts and other activity on the site.
- **Hello Me Module:** Displays statistics relevant to the user, including new messages and friend requests.
- **JomSocial Connect Module:** Shows data about the FaceBook Connect functionality.
- **Latest Group Discussions Module:** Displays a list of the most recent groups discussion posts.
- **Latest Group Wall Module:** Displays most recent wall postings
- **Latest Members Module:** Lists the most recent members.
- **Online Users Module:** A Who's Online-type module, showing the names and avatars of the members that are currently authenticated on the site.
- **Photo comments module:** Displays the most recent comments on photos.
- **Statistics Module:** Shows statistics about the site activity levels.
- **Top Members Module:** Displays a list of the top members, based up on their karma points.
- **Video comments module:** Displays the most recent comments on videos.

JomSocial modules are installed like any other Joomla! module. Don't forget that once installed you have to enable the module before it can be used.

Cross-Reference
Installing new modules is covered in Chapter 22.

Installing the JomSocial apps

In addition to the core JomSocial component, your installation package also includes a set of optional apps, or applications. The apps expand the functionality of the site and assist with the integration of other components, like the Fireboard forum, phpBB, or MyBlog.

Note
Though JomSocial calls them applications, these are actually what Joomla! calls plugins, and like other Joomla! plugins, the JomSocial apps are controlled using the Plugin Manager.

Tip
A number of these plugins are only used where you have installed certain third-party extensions to the site. Where those extensions have not been installed, you should disable, or uninstall completely the related plugins to help keep your site secure and decrease maintenance overhead.

In the installation archive, the Apps directory is compressed. Before you can begin to install the apps, you must unpack the directory labeled `apps_unzip_first_xxxx.zip`, where xxxx represents the version number of your JomSocial installer.

After you extract the JomSocial apps directory, you will find the following, all ready to install, in .zip format:

- **All Video:** This plugin is used for integration of JomSocial with the AllVideoPlugin. Enables the use of AllVideos tags inside JomSocial content items.
- **Article Activity:** Enables the JomSocial system to recognize the posting of an article in Joomla! as an event to be shown in JomSocial.
- **Author Link:** Links the name that appears as the author of an article to their profile in JomSocial.
- **Delete User:** Enables deletion of users. Note that this Plugin is automatically installed by the primary JomSocial Component installer.
- **Event List:** This plugin is used for integration of JomSocial with the EventList component. Allows the user to display events information inside their profile.
- **Feeds:** Enables the user to display RSS feeds inside their profile.
- **Fireboard:** This plugin is used for integration of JomSocial with the Fireboard forum.

Note
The Fireboard plugin also supports the Kunena forum extension.

- **Friends Location:** Enables the display of the physical location of all a user's friends using Google Maps.
- **Groups:** Shows which groups the user is a member of.
- **Input:** This is a system plugin that is responsible for stripping html tags and replacing new lines with html <br /> tags in posts.
- **Invite:** Enables users to invite friends.
- **JomComment:** This plugin is used for integration of JomSocial with the JomComment component. Enables the display of comments in the user's profile.
- **JomSocialConnect:** Aids in integration with Facebook Connect.
- **Latest Photo:** Enables display of the latest photos uploaded.
- **My Articles:** Enables the listing of all articles by the user on their profile.
- **My Blog:** This plugin is used for integration of JomSocial with the MyBlog extension. Enables display of user's blogs in their profile.
- **MyBlogToolbar:** Enables connection with the MyBlog extension.
- **My Google Ads:** Enables users to put their own Google Ads in their profiles.

Note

Users need to omit the <script> tags when they input their Google Ads code.

- **Nice Talk:** This plugin is used for integration of JomSocial with the Nice Talk discussions extension.
- **phpBB:** This plugin is used when you have also installed the phpBB forum on your site. It links phpBB forum posts with the user's profile.

Note

At the time of writing this plugin only supported phpBB integration via the ROKBridge phpBB forum bridge.

- **Seyret:** This plugin is used for integration of JomSocial with the Seyret Extension. Enables display of videos from Seyret.
- **System:** This plugin is not used by the system and can be disregarded.
- **Twitter:** Enables users to synch and show their Twitter feed in their profile.
- **Walls:** Sets up a Facebook-like wall functionality that enables users to comment on each others' profiles. Note that this plugin is automatically installed by the primary JomSocial component installer.
- **Word Filter:** Enables filtering of bad words.

JomSocial apps are installed like any other Joomla! plugin. Don't forget to enable the plugins. You can't use them until you do.

Cross-Reference

Installing new Plugins is covered in Chapter 22.

Note

The Apps Delete User and Walls and Invite are redundant; though you will find them in the Apps directory, they are installed automatically by the JomSocial installer during the initial installation of the primary JomSocial component; there is no point in trying to install them again and the system will display an error message if you try.

Overview of the JomSocial Control Panel

When you access the JomSocial component you will first see the default JomSocial control panel, as show in Figure 24.5, below. The control panel is intended to give you quick access to the most common functionalities needed by a site administrator.

FIGURE 24.5

The JomSocial control panel.

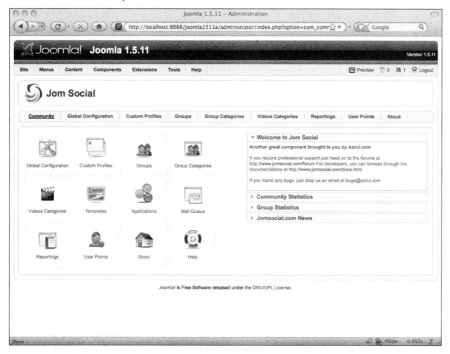

The work area is largely similar to the default Joomla! control panel. There is a navigation bar and below the bar on the left is a set of Quick Icons that act as accelerators and allow you to access key functions in one click. Below the navigation bar on the right side is a set of panels that can unfold to show you summary information for your JomSocial installation.

The navigation bar includes nine options:

- **Community:** Clicking on this option shows you the JomSocial control panel.
- **Global Configuration:** Click to access JomSocial's Global Configuration panel. (I discuss this in detail in the next section).
- **Custom Profiles:** Click to view and customize the list of the user profile fields.
- **Groups:** Click to view and administer groups.
- **Group Categories:** Click to view and manage group categories.
- **Videos Categories:** Click to view and manage video categories.
- **Reportings:** Click to view a list of the available reports.

- **User Points:** Click to administer the User Points system. This screen allows you to set the point values associated with each activity.

- **About:** Click to view information about the system.

The Quick Icons provide access to the same choices as above, plus the following additional accelerators:

- **Templates:** Click to view and manage the JomSocial templates.

- **Applications:** This icon really does nothing — it takes you to a page with a link to the applications, which are in reality plugins, and can be accessed directly under the Joomla! Plugins Manager under the Extensions menu.

- **Mail Queue:** Click to view a history of the mail queue.

- **Help:** Click to open the JomSocial.com documentation pages in a new window. Note that you have to be connected to the Internet for this to work properly.

The panels on the right provide:

- **Welcome to JomSocial:** This panel contains a standard welcome message from the JomSocial team. This panel is open by default, but if it is closed you can click on the title to open it again.

- **Community Statistics:** Click the title of this panel and it will open up to display basic statistics about the JomSocial users and applications.

- **Groups Statistics:** Click the title of this panel and it will open up to display basic statistics about the JomSocial groups.

- **Jomsocial.com News:** Click the title of this panel to display output from the Jomsocial.com newsfeed.

Configuring JomSocial

Immediately after installation you want to configure the component to suit your needs. To begin, click the Configuration icon on the JomSocial control panel. The Global Configuration opens to display a set of five links:

- Site
- Media
- Layout
- Network
- Facebook Connect

Each link is discussed in detail in the following sections.

The Site tab

Click on the Site link on the Global Configuration screen to see the Site tab, as shown in Figure 24.6. The tab provides access to an assortment of configuration options that affect the JomSocial installation as a whole.

The Site tab of the JomSocial Global Configuration Manager.

The Site tab's workspace is divided into 12 areas:

- Groups
- Reportings
- Privacy
- Time Offset
- Frontpage
- SEO
- Messaging
- Walls
- Registrations
- My Blog Integrations
- Advance Search
- Cron Process

The Groups area includes the following options:

- **Enable Groups:** Click Yes to enable the groups functionality on the front-end.
- **Moderate groups creation:** Click Yes if you want group creation to be moderated by the site administrator. If you click No, the groups will be automatically created immediately without the need of administrator approval.
- **Allow Group Creation:** Click Yes to allow new groups to be created by site users.

Note
Groups can only be created on the front end of the site. There is currently no admin function for creation of groups.

- **Enable Discussion Utility:** Click Yes to enable the discussions functionality for the Groups.

The Reportings area includes the following options:

- **Enable Reporting:** Click Yes to set the system to gather data for generating reports.
- **Execute default task when reach:** Enter an integer value in the field to trigger the creation of a new report. When the value is reached, the report will be automatically generated and available for view on the Reports tab.
- **Send notification e-mails to:** Enter an e-mail address if you want the system to send a notification e-mail when a report is created.
- **Allow guests to report:** Click Allow to give site visitors the option to use access the reports.

- **Predefined text (separated by a new line):** Enter here a list of options you want front-end users to see when they want to report a post. This is typically a list of classifications of problems, like "spam" or "inappropriate," and so forth.

The Privacy area includes the following options:

- **Default Privacy Profile:** Select from the options to determine who can see the users' profiles. Friends is the most restrictive; Public the least.
- **Default Friends Privacy:** Select from the options to determine who can see the users' friends. Self is the most restrictive; Public the least.
- **Default Photos Privacy:** Select from the options to determine who can see the users' photos. Self is the most restrictive; Public the least.
- **Receive System e-mails:** Set the default option for whether the user receives e-mail from the system.
- **Receive e-mails for messaging:** Set the default option for whether the user receives e-mail notifications of new messages.

Note
Any of the above privacy settings can be overridden by the individual user in their preferences.

- **Allow applications?:** Click Yes to allow the user to access and choose Applications.

The Time Offset parameter allows you to set the default time for the site. Set this to match your local GMT offset. The Frontpage area enables you to set the page title for the JomSocial front page. The SEO Parameter includes a combo box that allows you to select the format for the page URLs of the pages inside the JomSocial portion of your site.

The Messaging area includes the following options:

- **Enable messaging:** Set to Yes to enabling the user messaging feature of JomSocial.
- **Limit number of new messages:** Enter an integer value to set an upper limit on how many messages a user can send per day through the system.

The Walls area includes the following options:

- **Lock walls in profile to friends only:** Setting this parameter to Yes means that only a user's friends can interact with the user's wall. Setting it to No leaves to wall open to anyone.
- **Lock walls in groups to group members only:** Setting this parameter to Yes means that only group members can interact with the group's wall. Setting it to No leaves to wall open to anyone.

The Registrations area includes the following options:

- **Enable Terms & Conditions:** Click Yes to require new users to agree to the Terms and Conditions, which are set in the next parameter.

- **Terms & Conditions:** Enter the text for the Terms & Conditions for your users. Note this parameter is only relevant if the preceding parameter is set to Yes.

The My Blog Integrations parameter is only relevant if you have the My Blog extension installed. Setting this parameter to Yes will show the blog icon in the user profile.

Tip
To integrate fully the MyBlog Extension, you should also install and enable the JomSocial MyBlog plugin.

The Advance Search option allows you to enable the Advanced Search option for users.

The Cron Process option allows you to trigger e-mail sending on page load. If set to No, e-mail will not be processed until the next Cron run.

The Media tab

Click on the Media link on the Global Configuration screen to see the Media tab, as shown in Figure 24.7.

The Media tab's workspace is divided into Photos and Videos.

The Photos area includes the following options:

- **Enable Photos:** Set to Yes to enable user's to upload photos to their accounts.

- **Path to uploaded photos:** This field allows you the option to set your preferred path for the images.

- **Maximum photo upload size:** Enter an integer value to limit the size of files the user can upload.

- **Image Magick Path:** Enter a path to the server's Image Magick application, if any.

- **Use flash uploader:** Click Yes to enable the Flash uploader for users.

Tip
The Flash uploader makes it easier to upload multiple images, but is of course, Flash dependent.

FIGURE 24.7

The Media tab of the Configuration Manager.

The Videos area includes the following options:

- **Enable videos:** Set this parameter to Yes to allow users to display videos on their profiles.

- **Enable videos upload:** Set this parameter to Yes to allow users to upload videos to their profiles.

- **Delete original videos:** Enable this option to force the system to automatically delete original videos once they are converted into the appropriate format.

- **Videos Root Folder:** Enter your preferred path for the storage of video files.

- **Maximum video upload size:** Enter an integer value to set an upper limit on the file size of videos uploaded by the users.

- **FFMPEG Path:** Set the absolute path to the FFMPEG binary. This is needed to allow JomSocial to convert videos to Flash video (.flv) files.

- **FLVTool2 Path:** Set the absolute path to the FLVTool2 binary. This is needed to enable Flash video metadata injections.

- **Video Quantizer Scale:** Enter an integer value to set the video quality. 1 is the best; 31 is the worst. JomSocial recommends the values 5, 9, or 11.

- **Videos Size:** Select the preferred video display dimensions from the combo box.

- **Custom Command:** This field is provided to allow advanced users to enter custom commands for the FFMPEG utility.

- **Video Player License Key:** Enter the license key provided by JomSocial. It is not necessary, but failing to enter a key value will result in JomSocial's logo appearing as a watermark on the converted video.

- **Video Debug:** Set to Yes to view debugging information. This should normally be set to No.

The Layout tab

Click on the Layout link on the Global Configuration screen to see the Layout tab, as shown in Figure 24.8.

The Layout tab of the Configuration Manager.

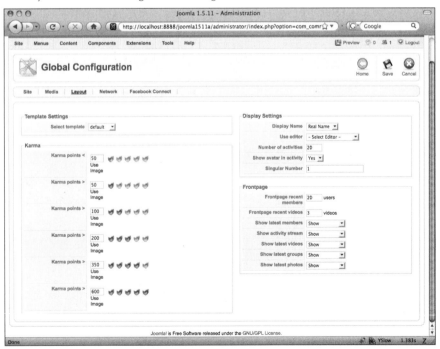

The Layout tab's workspace is divided into four areas:

- Template Settings
- Karma
- Display Settings
- Frontpage

The Template Settings provides the Select template combo box. Select from the list in the combo box the default template set for want to use for the JomSocial pages of your site.

The Karma area let's you specify the amount of karma points each user will receive for performing certain acts. This is intended as an incentive to get users to complete their profiles.

The Display Settings area includes the following options:

- **Display Name:** Select from the combo box one of the formatting options for displaying the user's name on the site.
- **Use editor:** Select from the combo box the WYSIWYG editor you want to make available to users, if any.

Note

The WYSIWYG Editor settings are inherited from the settings in Joomla's Global Configuration Manager.

- **Number of activities:** Enter an integer value to specify the number of activities to display on the front page.
- **Show avatar in activity:** Select Yes to display an avatar with the activity.
- **Singular Number:** Set the value you consider to be singular. The default is 1 and there is probably no reason why you would want to change this.

The Frontpage area includes the following options:

- **Frontpage recent members:** Enter an integer value to specify the number of members to display on the frontpage, most recent first.
- **Frontpage recent videos:** Enter an integer value to specify the number of videos to display on the frontpage, most recent first.
- **Show latest members:** The combo box allows you to show or hide a list of the latest members to all site visitors or to limit the view to only other members, most recent first.
- **Show activity stream:** The combo box allows you to show or hide a list of the activity stream to all site visitors or to limit the view to only other members.
- **Show latest videos:** The combo box allows you to show or hide a list of the latest videos to all site visitors or to limit the view to only other members, most recent first.

- **Show latest groups:** The combo box allows you to show or hide a list of the latest groups to all site visitors or to limit the view to only other members, most recent first.

- **Show latest photos:** The combo box allows you to show or hide a list of the latest photos to all site visitors or to limit the view to only other members, most recent first.

The Network tab

Click on the Network link on the Global Configuration screen to see the Network tab, as shown in Figure 24.9.

FIGURE 24.9

The Network tab of the Configuration Manager.

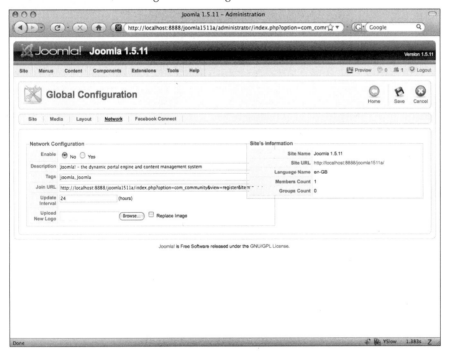

The Network tab's workspace is divided into two areas:

- Network Configuration
- Site's Information

The Network Configuration area includes the following options:

- **Enable:** Click Yes to enable the system to report information about your site to the JomSocial network.

- **Description:** Enter a description for your site. This description is used to describe your site in the JomSocial network.

- **Tags:** Type the tags you want associated with your site.

- **Join URL:** Enter the direct URL for your site where new visitor's can register.

- **Update Interval:** Set in hours how frequently your site information is updated in the JomSocial Network.

- **Upload New Logo:** Click the Browse button to upload an image that you want to be associated with your site.

The Site's Information area shows the information that describes your site.

Note

The JomSocial Network is created and maintained by the JomSocial team. The Network is simply a way to raise awareness of your site and drive community membership. If your site targets a closed or private community, you will not want to enable this feature.

The Facebook Connect tab

Click on the Facebook Connect link on the Global Configuration screen to see the Facebook Connect tab, as shown in Figure 24.10.

The Facebook Connect tab's workspace is divided into the following areas:

- API Configurations
- Imports

The API Configuration area includes the following options:

- **API Key:** Type here the API key you obtain from Facebook.

- **Application Secret:** Type the Application Secret you obtain from Facebook.

The Imports area includes the following options:

- **Import facebook profile on first sign up:** Set to Yes to allow the system to query Facebook when a user first signs up. The system will attempt to extract the user's information from their Facebook account.

- **Add Facebook watermarks on avatar:** If set to Yes the system will show the user's Facebook avatar along with a watermark.

- **Automatically re-import user profile upon login:** Set to Yes to have the system query Facebook for user profile updates each time the user logs in.

- **Automatically re-import user avatar upon login:** Set to Yes to have the system re-import the user's avatar from Facebook each time the user logs in.

- **Update user status:** Set to Yes to have the system import the user's status from Facebook each time they log in.

FIGURE 24.10

The Facebook Connect tab of the Configuration Manager.

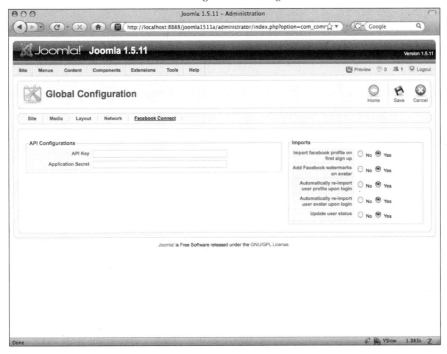

To set up Facebook Connect with JomSocial, you first need to create a new application in Facebook in order to obtain the necessary API keys.

To create a new application in Facebook, follow these steps:

1. **Access the Facebook developers page at** www.facebook.com/developers. **You need to log in and accept the disclaimer to Facebook to see this page.**

2. **At the top right of the page is a button labeled Set Up New Application. Click that button.** The Create Application page loads in your browser.

3. Type a name for the Application. (ie: jomsocial link)

4. Click Agree to the Facebook Terms.

5. **Click Save Changes.** The Edit application page loads in your browser.

6. Copy the API Key and the Secret; you will need to input those inside JomSocial.

7. Type a description for your site in the Description field.

8. **Click the Authentication tab on the left side of the page.** The Authentication page shows in the browser.

9. Select both Installable to? options, Users and Facebook Pages.

10. Enter your site's URL in the two fields on this page.

11. **Click the Connect tab on the left side of the page.** The Connect page shows in your browser.

12. Enter your site's full URL in all the fields marked Connect URL and Account Reclamation URL.

13. Enter the Base Domain, that is, your domain with the "http://www." in the Base Domain field.

14. Complete any other fields you want; the other values are optional.

15. **Click the Save Changes button.** A confirmation and summary page appears.

16. Access your JomSocial Global configuration page.

17. **Click the Facebook Connect tab.** The Facebook Connect page loads in your browser.

18. Paste the Facebook application's API key into the appropriate field. Paste the Secret string into the Secret field.

19. **Click the Save button on the toolbar.** The information is saved and you are returned to the Site tab.

After the Facebook Connect application is set up and associated with your site, the users of your site will be able to populate and update their profile with the data in their Facebook profile.

Note
The use of the Facebook Connect functionality is up to the user; they will have to authorize your site to access to their Facebook data.

Administering the Community

Administering a community site is a significant challenge. As the success of your site is largely dependent upon your ability to inspire and retain membership, you need to think carefully about how much information you require from users (you don't want to discourage them from registering) and about the opportunities you provide for networking and interaction with other members (you want to inspire them to interact). The JomSocial system gives you options for controlling both user profiles and for managing the use of groups for your members.

Working with users

The JomSocial user function integrates with and supplements the core Joomla! user management system. The two registration processes co-exist in the system; the JomSocial registration does not replace the default Joomla! registration. JomSocial gives you to ability to gather significantly more information from your visitors. You can create and manage a selection of custom fields.

Tip

Only users that register through the JomSocial registration link are taken through the custom fields. Therefore you will probably want to unpublish the default Joomla! login module to avoid confusion and the possibility that people might bypass your JomSocial registration path. The Hello Me application provides quick links to registration and login pages.

JomSocial also provides a basic incentives system for your visitors. The User Points functionality credits the users with points, based upon their completion of certain actions on the site. The more they participate, the greater their point totals. The point totals and the triggers are configurable.

Creating custom profiles

The default JomSocial user configuration includes a number of custom fields. The field data goes into building the User Profiles that appear on the front end of the site. You can view the profile fields by clicking on the Custom Profiles option inside the JomSocial control panel. The Custom Profiles Manager loads in your web browser, as shown in Figure 24.11.

The Custom Profiles Manager gives you the ability to modify the existing fields, set the required fields, and to create new fields.

The toolbar at the top of the Custom Profiles Manager provides quick access to the following functions:

- **Home:** Click this link to return to the JomSocial control panel.
- **Publish:** Select one or more fields from the list, then click this icon to publish them.
- **Unpublish:** Select one or more fields from the list, then click this icon to unpublish them.
- **Delete:** Select one or more fields from the list, then click this icon to delete them.
- **New Field:** Click to add a new Custom Profile field.

FIGURE 24.11

The Custom Profiles Manager.

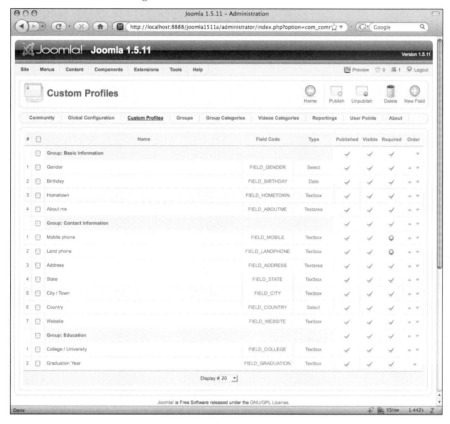

Below the toolbar is the main JomSocial navigation menu.

The main content area of the screen contains a list of all the Custom Profile fields in your site. The columns provided are:

- **#:** An indexing number assigned by Joomla! This cannot be changed.
- **Checkbox** (no label): Click in a checkbox to select a field; this is needed if you want to use several of the toolbar options.
- **Name:** This field displays the full name of the field as displayed to the user. Click on the name to edit the field details.
- **Field Code:** Shows the machine-friendly name of this field.
- **Type:** Indicates the type of input field supplied with this field.

- **Published:** A green checkmark in this column indicates that the field is active. The field will show a red X if the field is disabled. Administrators can toggle between the two settings by clicking on the icon shown.

- **Visible:** A green checkmark in this column indicates that the field is visible. The field shows a red X if the field is disabled. Administrators can toggle between the two settings by clicking on the icon shown.

- **Required:** A green checkmark in this column indicates that the field is required. The field shows a red X if the field is optional. Administrators can toggle between the two settings by clicking on the icon shown.

- **Order:** The numbers in this field affect the ordering of the fields on this list. Change the numbers and click the Save icon at the top of the column to re-order the fields.

Finally, at the bottom of the screen, below the content area, is the Display # option. Change the value in the combo box control to alter the number of fields that are displayed on the page. The default value can be altered by changing the List Length option on the Global Configuration Manager.

To create a new custom field, follow these steps:

1. **Access the Custom Profiles Manager.**
2. **Click the New Field icon on the toolbar at the top right of the page.** The New Field dialogue opens in a lightbox.
3. **Type a name for the field; note this will also be used as the field's data label.** This is the only required field.
4. **Select the other options you desire.**
5. **Click Save.** The field is created and the window closes.

Note

Unfortunately in the release that was available at this time this was written, it was only possible for the administrator to view the user data through the default Joomla! User Manager. The User Manager does not show the custom fields data; it only shows the standard Joomla! user data. If you want to mine the extended JomSocial user data you will need to do it by exporting it directly from the database using phpMyAdmin. There is also a paid extension on the JomSocial site which allows you to export the info in csv form.

Setting up user points

JomSocial includes a user incentive system that awards users points for performing any of a number of tasks. As a site administrator, you can specify the actions that merit points and the number of points associated with each action. You can also disable this function completely, if that is your preference.

Tip

Use the points function to create categories of members based on participation levels, or to award prizes or other incentives.

User points are administered by clicking on the User Points link in the JomSocial control panel; once you click, the User Points Manager appears in your browser, as shown in Figure 24.12. The User Points Manager gives you the ability to modify the points calculations, set the access level for the awards and publish or unpublish specific points rules.

The User Points Manager.

The toolbar at the top of the User Points Manager provides quick access to the following functions:

- **Home:** Click this link to return to the JomSocial control panel.
- **Rule Scan:** Click this to force the system to update the list of User Point rules.

- **Publish:** Select one or more rules from the list, then click this icon to publish them.
- **Unpublish:** Select one or more rules from the list, then click this icon to unpublish them.

Below the toolbar is the main JomSocial navigation menu.

The main content area of the screen contains a list of all the User Point rules in your site. The columns provided are:

- **#:** An indexing number assigned by Joomla! This cannot be changed.
- **Checkbox** (no label)**:** Click in a checkbox to select a rule; this is needed if you want to use several of the toolbar options, previously referenced.
- **User Rule:** This field displays the full name of the rule. Click on the name to edit the rule details.
- **Rule Descriptions:** This column provides a short summary description of the rule.
- **Plugin:** The name of the plugin that supports this rule.
- **User Access:** Shows the user level that this rule applies to.
- **Points:** Displays the number of points associated with the activity.
- **Published:** A green checkmark in this column indicates that the rule is active. The field will show a red X if the rule is disabled. Administrators can toggle between the two settings by clicking on the icon shown.

Finally, at the bottom of the screen, below the content area, is the Display # option. Change the value in the combo box control to alter the number of rules that are displayed on the page. The default value can be altered by changing the List Length option on the Global Configuration Manager.

To modify a User Points rule, follow these steps:

1. **Access the User Points Manager.**
2. **Click on the name of the rule you want to modify.** The User Award dialogue opens in a lightbox.
3. **Make the changes you desire.**
4. **Click Save.** The field is modified and the window closes.

Working with groups

JomSocial provides groups for users to join. Groups are typically created to allow users with common interests to interact. In the default configuration, groups can be created by your site's members. If your site has a large number of active members, it is conceivable that a significant number of groups could arise. To help keep things organized, JomSocial provides a categories function for the classification of groups.

Group categories are created by the site administrator using the Group Categories Manager. By default, the system includes a basic set of five categories. You can keep the defaults, delete them, or modify them to suit your needs. You can also create new categories from the Group Categories Manager.

To access the Group Categories Manager, click on the menu link label Group Categories inside the JomSocial Control Panel. The Group Categories Manager loads in your browser, as shown in Figure 24.13.

The Group Categories Manager.

The toolbar at the top of the Group Categories Manager provides quick access to the following functions:

- **Home:** Click this link to return to the JomSocial control panel.
- **Delete:** Select one or more categories from the list, then click this icon to delete the category(s).
- **New:** Click to add a new category.

Below the toolbar is the main JomSocial navigation menu. The main content area of the screen contains a list of all the group categories in your site. The columns provided are:

- **#:** An indexing number assigned by Joomla! This cannot be changed.
- **Checkbox** (no label): Click in a checkbox to select a category; this is needed if you want to use several of the toolbar options, previously referenced.
- **Name:** This field displays the full name of the category. Click on the name to edit the category's details.
- **Groups:** The number of groups in this category.
- **Members:** The number of users in the groups in this category.

Finally, at the bottom of the screen, below the content area, is the Display # option. Change the value in the combo box control to alter the number of categories that are displayed on the page. The default value can be altered by changing the List Length option on the Global Configuration Manager.

To create a new category, follow these steps:

1. **Access the JomSocial control panel and click on the Group Categories link.** The Group Categories Manager loads in your browser.
2. **Click the New icon on the top right toolbar.** The New Category dialogue opens in a pop-up window.
3. **Type a name for the category.** This is the only required field.
4. **Add a description if you so desire.**
5. **Click the Save button.** The new category is created and the window closes.

Tip

For additional help with JomSocial, visit their site. There is an Online User Guide at www.jomsocial.com/
docs/User_guide **and additional Developer Documentation at** www.jomsocial.com/docs/Developer

Summary

In this chapter, we have taken a look at the basics of adding social networking functionality to your Joomla! site by adding the JomSocial extension. You learned the following:

- Where to get JomSocial
- How to install the basic JomSocial system
- How to install the various extensions bundled with JomSocial
- How to set JomSocial's Global Configuration
- How to set up a custom profile fields
- How to create groups and categories
- How to set up Facebook Connect

Part V

Site Maintenance and Management

Keeping Your Site Secure and Up to Date

S ite security and change managements are two critical issues for site owners and administrators. This chapter looks at security best practices for Joomla! and provides advice and tips on how to set up your Joomla! site in a secure manner and thereafter keep it secure.

Keeping your site patched and up to date is one of the keys to maintaining your site's integrity and protecting it against hackers. Accordingly, this chapter also discusses basic back up and upgrade processes. Management of upgrades and patches can be time consuming, particularly for complex sites with numerous extensions. Accordingly, adoption of a formalized process for handling these recurrent issues is your best bet for decreasing your site management overhead.

Security Best Practices

Creating and maintaining a secure web site requires attention to a variety of issues. The process starts at server setup and continues throughout the life of the site. There is no such thing as a site you can create and forget; no such thing as a site that takes care of itself. To keep your site safe you must take affirmative steps and you must develop an awareness of the issues. Although you cannot protect yourself from every conceivable threat, you can reduce the vulnerability of your site to a manageable level with a reasonable amount of effort.

Caution
The single most important factor in maintaining the integrity of your site over time is the creation and maintenance of a backup and recovery process.

Securing the Joomla! core

Security is not one single thing; it is a process, a set of steps that need to be taken to achieve a result. The process begins with your server settings and the Joomla! core files. If you fail to make this base level of the system secure, then additional steps are at the very least of limited effectiveness, at the very worst pointless.

Tip
The first step toward assuring your site's integrity is also one of the easiest: Only install the most recent version of the Joomla! core file packages found at the official download site, JoomlaCode.org. Do not download and install core file archives from other sites, because you cannot be certain of their origins, completeness, or integrity.

Protecting directories and files

You can take several steps to enhance the security of the directories and files on your server. The first step is adjusting the permissions to be as strict as possible without impairing use of the site. Write-protect your critical directories. As a general rule, set the directory permissions to 755 and the file permissions to 644 using either FTP or the options in the Global Configuration Manager. Note that this is best done after you have fully completed your installation of the core and all extensions. It is possible that you may have to make these setting more permissive if you need to install extensions in the future.

Cross-Reference
The file permissions controls in the Global Configuration Manager are discussed in Chapter 4.

Tip
There's a good discussion of how to set file permissions and what they all mean on the Joomla! docs site at

```
http://docs.joomla.org/Security_and_Performance_FAQs#How_do_UNIX_file_
permissions_work.3F
```

There are a number of other steps you may want to consider taking; however, you should note that each of these has a trade-off, either in terms of increased admin overhead or other limitations:

- **Move the configuration.php file outside of the public HTML directory on your server and rename it:** Place a new `configuration.php` file in the public HTML directory pointing to the new file. Make sure your new file is not writable in order to avoid it being overwritten by the Global Configuration Manager. Note that making this change forces you to modify the new configuration file manually, rather than by using the Global Configuration Manager. For more information on how to set this up, see `http://docs.joomla.org/Security_and_Performance_FAQs`

- **Use .htaccess to block direct access to critical files:** Note this is only applicable to servers using the Apache web server and web hosts that allow you to modify .htaccess. Make sure you back up your old .htaccess file before you try this in case you experience problems and need to restore the old file.

- **Change the default log path:** Hackers sometimes look to the log files as a way to identify what extensions you have installed, in hopes of finding an extension that has a known vulnerability they can exploit. To help deter this bit of information-fishing, alter the log path settings in the Global Configuration Manager.

- **Change the default temp directory:** The contents of the temp directory can also provide information you may not want to disclose about your site. You can alter the temp directory settings in the Global Configuration Manager.

- **Use SEF URL rewriting:** Joomla!'s default URLs often carry with them information that indicates the extensions used on the site. The default URLs provide another source of information for those who might be looking for vulnerable URLs. Implement an SEF URLs extension to avoid this problem. In addition to providing search engine benefits, the SEF URL writing will obscure your original URLs and mask this information.

Cross-Reference

Working with the Global Configuration Manager is discussed in detail in Chapter 4.

Protecting from unauthorized access

Humans are your most common point of security policy failure. Admin passwords should be changed often. The default username that is produced for the administrator during the installation process should also be changed immediately after the system is set up. Leaving the default username as "admin" gives a hacker one half of the answer to the puzzle he needs to solve to gain access to your site. Passwords should always be as secure as practicable.

When the Joomla! creates your first user account, it always gives it the same ID number, 62. As a result, this means that hackers have a place to start trying to gain access to your site; they know the userID of your super administrator account. In order to shut down this avenue of attack, create a new super administrator user and delete the default account.

Cross-Reference

Creating and deleting users is covered in Chapter 10.

In addition to controlling the access to your admin system, you need to be sensitive to the access issues that relate to your database. If you have control over the access privileges to the user accounts on your MySQL database, make sure that all accounts are set with limited access.

If you want to go further, you may want to vary from the default database prefix used by the Joomla! installer. During the installation process you are given the choice of whether to use the default prefix, jos_, or to set your own. If you want to increase the security of your site, select the option to designate your own prefix. By varying from the default setting, you make it more difficult for a hacker to compromise your database.

Cross-Reference

Setting the database table prefix is covered in the discussion of Joomla! installation in Chapter 2.

Caution

A good administrator password should be at least seven characters in length and employ a combination of upper- and lowercase letters, numbers, and nonalphanumeric characters. Never, under any circumstances, use words that can be found in the dictionary! This is common sense: "4tG~9fU#ss3" is a lot harder to crack than "tinytoons."

Removing unnecessary files

If you don't need it now and you don't intend to use it, get rid of it. Logical targets for deletion include:

- Unused templates
- Extensions you have installed then decided not to use
- Unused applications you have installed on your server
- Archive files copied to your server during the course of installation
- The installation directory

Tip

As mentioned in Chapter 3, don't simply rename the installation directory, delete it.

- Another candidate for deletion in Joomla! 1.5.x is the system's XML-RPC server. If you are not using this functionality, delete it. It is located in the Joomla! root in the directory named xmlrpc/.

Another good idea is to disable all unused core components that cannot be uninstalled. Disabling unneeded core components shuts down one more avenue of attack and has the added advantage of cleaning up the administration interface.

To disable a core component in Joomla! 1.5.x, follow these steps:

1. **Access the admin system of your site.**
2. **Click on the InstallUnistall option under the Extensions menu.** The Extensions Installer dialogue opens in your browser.
3. **Click on the Components link.** The Components dialogue opens in your browser.
4. **Indentify the components you want to disable and then click on the green arrow in the Enabled column.** The Enabled column indicator changes to show a red X, and the component is now disabled.

Maintaining a sensible server setup

In an ideal world, we would all have our own dedicated servers where we could control every aspect of the system. In the real world, shared hosting is the reality for many users. Shared hosting, although certainly more cost effective than a dedicated host, involves trade-offs in terms of security and access privileges.

Your goal should be to make the host setup as secure as possible, regardless of whether it is dedicated or shared. Exactly what you are permitted to do with your server varies, but you should consider the following:

- **Use Secure FTP, if available:** Doing this helps avoid the possibility that someone can determine your username and password while you are in the process of a file transfer.

- **If possible, use PHP 5:** While both PHP 4 and 5 are supported by Joomla!, PHP 5 is the superior solution, and PHP 4 is being phased out.

- **Make sure your server does not have Register Globals enabled:** Joomla! does not need it and it is a security risk.

- **If the mod_security module is installed on your Apache web server, use it:** It acts as an embedded web application firewall and provides significant protection against many common attacks. Learn more about how to use it at www.modsecurity.org/.

  - **Turn safe mode off:** Safe mode is not necessary for Joomla! and may cause problems with some extensions.

  - **Set Magic Quotes GPC to On:** Set this option to On.

  - **Don't use PHP allow_url_fopen:** Set this option to Off.

- **Use PHP open_basedir:** Set this option to On.

Tip

Contracting with a web host solely on the basis of price is a bad idea. Moreover, as competition has increased in the hosting space, it is becoming more of a commodity business and price points have narrowed. Instead of simply taking the cheapest host, make your selection based on service levels, quality of hardware, access privileges, software installed, and backup policies.

Securing third-party extensions

From a security perspective, every extension you install on your Joomla! site increases the risk you face. Each extension comes with its own set of files and potential vulnerabilities. Moreover, the fact that extension quality varies wildly is a serious issue for site owners, and each extension you install brings with it a need for due diligence and ongoing maintenance. Given these issues, the first point of concern for site owners should be the issue of trust: Do you trust that the developer is capable of producing solid, secure code and do you trust this developer to keep it patched and keep users abreast of risks as they arise? Never forget that, just like the core files, extensions have to be maintained, patched, and upgraded.

The wide variety of Joomla! extensions means that you have choices. Accordingly, before you decide to adopt a particular extension, you need to do your research. Not only should you be concerned with whether it works and looks like you want it to, but also you need to be convinced that the extension is of good quality and comes from a reputable source. There are no guarantees; it is up to you to do your homework and make a judgment call. Visit the developer's site. Is it professional? Is it up to date? If this is a project-based extension, check for levels of project activity and issues that have been reported but remain unfixed. Extensions listed on the Joomla! Extensions Directory include ratings and reviews — read them!

Tip

Joomla! maintains a Vulnerable Extensions List. You should always check this before making a final decision on the adoption of a particular extension. The list is maintained at

```
http://docs.joomla.org/Vulnerable_Extensions_List.
```

Next, before you install a new extension on a live site, test it locally. Check to make sure it installs cleanly and without error messages. Test all the various functionalities, regardless of whether you intend to use them all. It's also a good idea to check and see if the extension comes with a README file; if it does, read it!

Finally, before installing the new extension on your live site, back up the live site. That way, if a problem occurs you can roll back and restore from the backup.

If at some point in time you decide that the extension is no longer necessary and you uninstall it, make sure that the extension has uninstalled cleanly and has not left any files on your server. Often, extensions leave directories and files behind on your server, despite being uninstalled.

Keeping Up With Security Notices

Things change. New vulnerabilities are discovered and new exploits are created to take advantage of them. Sometimes the rate of change is quite impressive, and it becomes a challenge to keep up and maintain all aspects of your site. The Joomla! Security Strike Team was formed by the community as an attempt to address the dynamic nature of threats to the Joomla! system. As new issues are discovered, the community reports them to the Strike Team. The team formulates responses, works to learn more and, when needed, get patches out to the users.

Keeping up with the announcements from the Joomla! Security Strike Team is one of the ways you can stay informed of important news that may impact your Joomla! site. Important notices are always published on the home page of Joomla.org. In addition, the default Joomla! 1.5.x system includes in the control panel an RSS feed from the Joomla! Security Strike Team, as shown in Figure 25.1. Of course, if you rely on these default notifications, you only discover new alerts when you visit Joomla.org or when you log into your Joomla! installation. If you want more immediate notices, then you should consider either subscribing to the RSS feed with a separate news reader or joining the mailing list so that notifications are sent to you by e-mail. The URLs for both services are included in the Table 25.1.

FIGURE 25.1

FIGURE 25.1

The admin system's control panel includes by default the Joomla! Security Newsfeed.

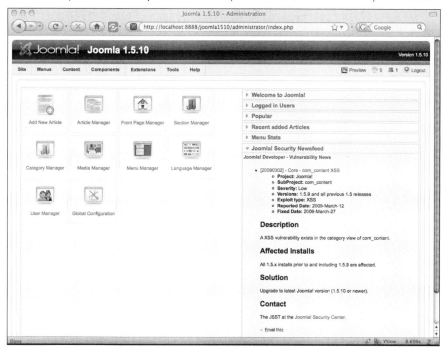

The channel you prefer to use for alerts is entirely up to you, but the simple fact is that the only way to keep your site secure is to keep it — and its extensions — up to date. When new versions are released, do not delay in upgrading. New releases require immediate action. If you fail to upgrade your site after a security release is announced and your site is subsequently hacked, you really have no one to blame but yourself.

The Joomla! team and community have created and maintain a number of useful security resources. Table 25.1 lists the resources.

TABLE 25.1	

Joomla! Security Resources

Name of resource	URL
Security Checklist: Getting Started	`http://docs.joomla.org/Security_Checklist_1_-_Getting_Started`
Security Checklist: Hosting and Server Setup	`http://docs.joomla.org/Security_Checklist_2_-_Hosting_and_Server_Setup`
Security Checklist: Testing and Development	`http://docs.joomla.org/Security_Checklist_3_-_Testing_and_Development`
Security Checklist: Joomla Setup	`http://docs.joomla.org/Security_Checklist_4_-_Joomla_Setup`
Security Checklist: Site Administration	`http://docs.joomla.org/Security_Checklist_5_-_Site_Administration`
Security Checklist: Site Recovery	`http://docs.joomla.org/Security_Checklist_6_-_Site_Recovery`
Joomla Security Strike Team Contact Form	`http://developer.joomla.org/security/contact-the-team.html`
Security and Performance FAQs	`http://docs.joomla.org/Security_and_Performance_FAQs`
Automatic Email Notification System	`http://feedburner.google.com/fb/a/mailverify?uri=JoomlaSecurityNews`
Security RSS Feed	`http://feeds.joomla.org/JoomlaSecurityNews`
Joomla! 1.5 Security Forum	`http://forum.joomla.org/viewforum.php?f=432`
Vulnerable Extensions List	`http://docs.joomla.org/Vulnerable_Extensions_List`
Security Announcements for Joomla! Developers	`http://developer.joomla.org/security/news.html`
Joomla! Developers Security Articles and Tutorials	`http://developer.joomla.org/security/articles-tutorials.html`

Managing Site Maintenance

Whenever a new patch or update is released, you need to get it installed on your site without delay. Sometimes, particularly in the case of extensions, the patch can be a small matter; in other cases, particularly in the case of a new version release, installation of the new files can entail a significant amount of work. In either event, having an established process for dealing with the upgrades is useful as it helps avoid the possibility that you will miss something during the upgrade, only to discover problems later on.

Before you begin any significant maintenance process, you should make sure that you have a current backup of your site. If something goes wrong, you need to be able to roll the site back to the previous version. While it may be time consuming to follow this advice, it is worth it. Trust me, you aren't doing this for the 99 times out of 100 that you don't have a problem; you are doing it for the one time that you do! If you are dealing with your personal site this may be simply a matter of inconvenience, but if you are handling a client or an employer's site, it is unprofessional not to take the appropriate precautions to protect their site and their data.

Taking a site offline

Prior to undertaking any major upgrade on a live site you should take the site offline, that is, hide it from public view. Joomla! makes it possible to take a site offline with one click, while still retaining access to the admin system. After the site is offline, you can perform whatever maintenance you need and check your work prior to putting the site back live.

To take your site offline, follow these steps:

1. Log in to the admin system of your site.

2. Access the Global Configuration Manager either by clicking on the Global Configuration icon on the control panel or by clicking on the Global Configuration link under the Site Menu. The Global Configuration Manager loads in your browser, as shown in Figure 25.2.

3. Click the Yes option next to the label Site Offline.

4. Adjust the Offline Message text, if you so desire.

5. Click the Save icon. The system takes the front end of the site offline and displays the Offline Message to site visitors.

To put the site back online, follow these steps:

1. Log in to the admin system of your site.

2. Access the Global Configuration Manager by either clicking on the Global Configuration icon on the control panel or by clicking on the Global Configuration link under the Site Menu. The Global Configuration Manager loads in your browser. (Refer to in Figure 25.2).

3. Click the No option next to the label Site Offline.

4. Click the Save icon. The system puts the front end of the site back online.

FIGURE 25.2

The Site Settings of the Global Configuration Manager.

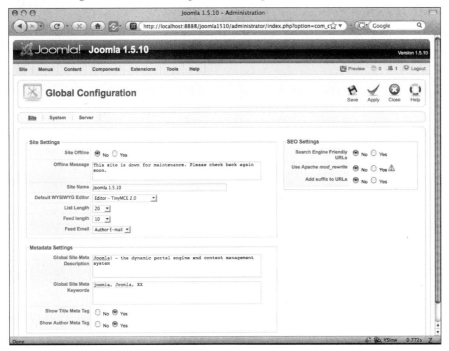

Backing up your site

Backing up a Joomla! site involves making copies of the files on the server and the data in your database. A complete backup encompasses both elements.

Tip

In terms of best practices, it is a good idea to maintain at all times the two most recent full backups of your site. This provides you with protection in the event the most recent backup is corrupted or incomplete. If your site is large, maintaining multiple full backups can take up a lot of space. If space is an issue, then maintain an incremental back-up regimen that backs up only your changed files.

The question of how frequently you need to back up your site is best answered with reference to the frequency with which your site changes. If your site changes daily, then perhaps daily backups are in order. If you site changes only sporadically, then weekly backups will probably do the job.

Make sure that you don't keep all your backups in one location. If there is a fire or other problem that results in the loss of one backup, you want to increase your chances that the second copy is protected. If your web hosting contract provides for back-up services, make sure you periodically download the files to keep a copy locally as your failsafe.

To make a complete backup of your site, you will need to access the files on the server and make a copy of them. Typically this is done by FTP or through your web hosting control panel's file manager. You also need to use a tool such as phpMyAdmin to make a copy of the database for the site. As an alternative to using multiple tools and doing this manually, you can install additional extensions to your Joomla! site to enable this from within the admin interface. As discussed in Chapter 22, several tools can help you create and manage your backups.

Restoring from a backup

Manually restoring the files on your server is a simple process; you only need to copy your back-up files onto the server, replacing the files that are there. If you have used full backups this is a one-step process. If you are using incremental backups you, first you need to copy the full backup and then copy the incremental back-up files.

Manually restoring your database is slightly more complicated, because you need to use phpMyAdmin to import the back-up files to overwrite the existing database tables.

Just like creating back ups, restoring from a back up can be undertaken manually, but the process can be made much simpler through the use of any of several third-party extensions.

Tip
If you have never tried to restore a site from a backup, I highly recommend that you try the process once before you deploy your site. The process is not difficult, but you don't want to be doing it for the first time on a live site that you need to get working again!

Regaining access to your admin account

Sometimes a site administrator loses his password, or a hack attempt results in the loss of the administrator's password. If you have access to the Password Reset functionality on the Login Form, you can try to use it to get a new password. If that does not work, then you need to go to the database to solve the problem. Although you cannot recover a lost admin password, you can reset it in the database and thereby gain access to the account.

Passwords are stored in the database along with the user data. The passwords are not human-readable, because they are stored as MD5 hashed values, as shown in Figure 25.3.

FIGURE 25.3

The jos_users table, as viewed from phpMyAdmin. Note the password field, showing the password as an MD5 hashed value.

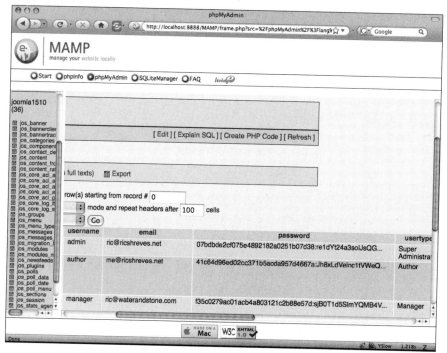

By way of example, follow these steps to reset a user's password to the value "admin":

1. **Use phpMyAdmin to access the database on your server.**

2. **Select the database for your Joomla! site from the combo box on the left side of the page.** The list of database tables in the database is displayed in the left column, below the combo box.

3. **Click on the table named jos_users in the list of tables.** The users table screen shows on the right side of the page.

4. **Click on the Browse button on the top toolbar.** The screen shows all of the users that are set up for this site.

5. **Find the user whose password you want to change. Click the Edit icon next to the user's name.** The Edit screen is displayed.

6. **Copy this value exactly: 21232f297a57a5a743894a0e4a801fc3 — this is the MD5 hash value that equates to the string "admin." Paste this value into the field names password.**

7. **Click the Go button.** phpMyAdmin saves the new value for the password and return you to the users table.

The value entered into the password field in the preceding example changes the user's password to "admin." The user should now be able to log in to the site by typing their username along with the password "admin." They should change their password immediately to their preferred value.

Upgrading a Joomla! Installation

One thing is certain: At some point during the life of your Joomla! site you will find the need to go through the process of upgrading your site. Indeed, odds are you will need to go through this process numerous times. Accordingly, I recommend that you adopt a process for handling upgrades in order to avoid disruption to the site and downtime.

The first step to any upgrade is identifying the version you are currently running, and then identifying the proper upgrade package for your installation. To find the version of your current site, follow these steps:

1. **Log in to the admin system of your site.**

2. **Access the System Info page by clicking on the System Info link under the Help menu.** The System Info page loads in your browser, as shown in Figure 25.4.

3. **Look at the line labeled Joomla! Version — this is the version of Joomla! installed on your site.**

After you know your current version, you can identify and download the proper upgrade package from JoomlaCode.org.

Cross-Reference
Finding and obtaining the Joomla! core files from JoomlaCode.org is covered in Chapter 2.

Next, before you begin the actual upgrade, make a full backup of your existing site. Set this aside in the event that something goes wrong and you need to restore your site. After the backup is done, you can proceed with the actual upgrade process.

FIGURE 25.4

The System Info page, in this example showing a site with a Joomla! Version 1.5.10 installed.

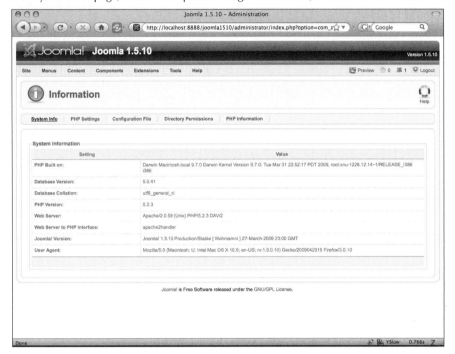

Follow these steps:

1. Unpack the upgrade archive on your local machine.

2. Take your site offline, as discussed earlier in this chapter.

3. Move the files to your server using either FTP or your web hosting control panel's file manager; note the cautions outlined in the "Upgrade issues" sidebar.

4. If database changes are required, follow the instructions given with the upgrade and make the changes.

5. Test the changes.

6. If all is well, put the site back online, as discussed earlier in this chapter.

Tip

Official Joomla! upgrade instructions can always be found at

```
http://docs.joomla.org/Upgrade_Instructions.
```

Upgrade Issues

Due to the wide variance in systems, servers, and upgrades, you may cover all the various issues that may result in the process of an upgrade. You should take note of the following key issues:

- A Joomla! upgrade package will only cover the core files; extensions will need to be upgraded separately.

- For complex sites, it is best to test the upgrade first on a local or development installation. If all goes well, then you can roll out the upgrade to the live site.

- Installing upgrade files on your server involves overwriting the old files. If you have installed third-party templates and other extensions, take special care you do not erase them! Moreover, if you have modified any of the core files, make certain you have identified the changes so that you can apply the changes to the new files.

Tip

The official Joomla! forums include a section dedicated to Upgrades and Migration. Visit

```
http://forum.joomla.org/viewforum.php?f=430.
```

Summary

In this chapter, we have taken a look at Joomla! security and site maintenance issues. You learned the following:

- How to help secure your Joomla! installation
- How to back up and restore your site files and database
- How to install patches and upgrades to your site

Managing Performance and Accessibility

The performance and accessibility of your site should be common concerns for all web site owners. This chapter looks at how Joomla! can be optimized for better performance and how the accessibility can be improved through good management of templates and content items.

Although it may initially appear that no positive relationship between performance tuning and web site accessibility exists, the opposite is true. Many of the items that improve the performance of a Web site are also consistent with improving the accessibility of a Web site. Indeed, the bells and whistles that many site owners include in their sites can limit both the site's performance and its accessibility.

Understanding Cache Management

Cache files are temporary files created and stored on the server that help to cut down on server load and improve performance times. When a file is cached, the server can display the cached value instead of going through the effort of calling up the information from out of the database and assembling it for display. When site traffic is heavy, the efficiency gained through caching can result in dramatic performance improvements.

Joomla! supports both global site caching and the ability to control caching for individual modules. You can also set the length of the time things are cached, which tells the system how long to hold something before refreshing it. In some situations, for example when you install an updated component, you may want to dump your cached data in order to force the system to update the information in the cache. The Joomla! admin system gives you the ability to flush the cache either completely or selectively.

The Joomla! cache management controls are split between the Global Configuration Manager, the System - Cache plugin, and the individual module parameter controls. In the sections that follow, all three options are discussed, as well as how to clean and purge your site's cache.

Tip

If you are looking for more cache control, consider installing a third party extension to expand this functionality. The Joomla! Extensions Directory includes a sub-category dedicated to enhanced caching: `http://` `extensions.joomla.org/extensions/site-management/cache`

Setting the Site cache

In the default configuration, caching is turned off. The global site caching settings are located in the Global Configuration Manager, as shown in Figure 26.1.

FIGURE 26.1

The Joomla! 1.5.x Global Configuration Manager's System tab, showing the Cache Settings.

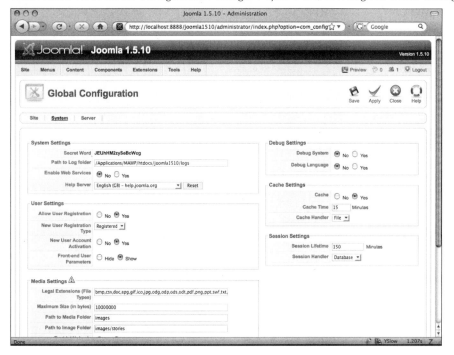

To enable caching, follow these steps:

1. **Log in to the admin system of your site.**

2. **Access the Global Configuration Manager by either clicking on the Global Configuration icon on the Control Panel or by clicking on the Global Configuration link under the Site menu.** The Global Configuration Manager loads in your browser.

3. **Click the System link.** The System tab opens in your browser.

4. **Set the Cache option to Yes.**

5. **Click the Save icon.** The system enables caching.

Tip

The default cache time is 15 minutes. Setting the Cache Time option in the Global Configuration Manager to longer times results in improved performance, but it also means that the site will be serving older content. The decision of what is the right cache time for your site balances on the trade-off between performance and time-liness. If your content changes frequently, the cache time value should be low. If your content changes rarely, then you can safely set it to a higher value.

Setting the System – Cache

The System - Cache plugin provides another global caching alternative, in this case, page caching. The plugin is disabled by default. Access the plugin by going to the Plugin Manager under the Extensions menu. Clicking on the option named System - Cache will open the plugin for editing, as shown in Figure 26.2.

To enable page caching, follow these steps:

1. **Log in to the admin system of your site.**

2. **Access the Plugin Manager by clicking on the Plugin Manager link under the Extensions menu.** The Plugin Manager loads in your browser.

3. **Click the System - Cache plugin.** The Plugin Editing dialogue opens in your browser.

4. **Set the Enabled option to Yes.**

5. **Click the Save icon.** The system enables page caching.

Note

You can also enable browser-side caching for your site's pages by setting the Use Browser Caching Plugin parameter to Yes.

FIGURE 26.2

The System - Cache plugin.

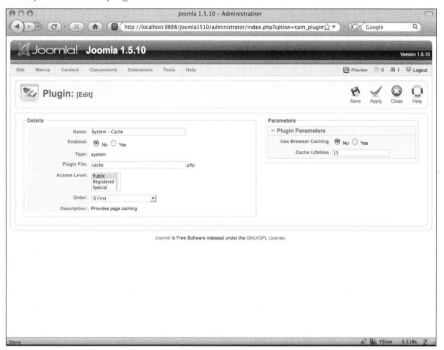

Caution

Page caching is the most aggressive form of caching offered by the default Joomla! system. You should test your site after enabling page caching, testing in particular the impact on front-end functionalities such as the Random Image module, the Newsflash module, and the log in and log out process. If you have installed any third-party extensions, make sure that you also test those after enabling the System - Cache plugin. If you observe problems, disable the plugin and test again.

Setting the module cache

Because the cache serves up "old" content, that is, content that has been stored rather than produced live, some items should not be cached. Banner and image rotators, login functionalities and the like are typically excluded from caching. In those situations where you want to exempt items from the global cache settings, or you want to change the length of time the information for a certain module is cached, then you can do so by managing the module cache settings.

Module cache controls are located in the parameters section of each module. Note that not all modules provide this option; those that do will typically place this control in the Advanced Parameters tab, as shown in Figure 26.3.

FIGURE 26.3

A typical module cache setting, in this case for the Random Image module.

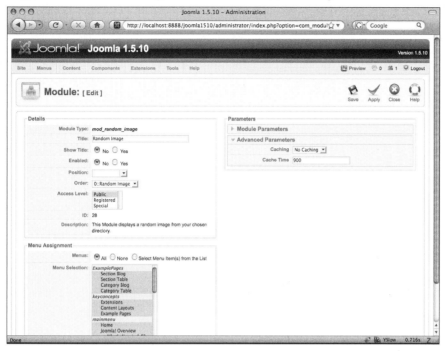

In the default Joomla! 1.5.x system, caching is disabled in the following modules:

- Banners (the Advertisement module only in the sample data)
- Feed Display
- Newsflash
- Random Image
- Related Items
- Statistics
- Wrapper

Caching is not an option for the following modules:

- Breadcrumbs
- Login
- Syndicate
- Who's Online

Module caching parameters typically include two options for users. You can choose to use the Global Cache settings, as defined in the Global Configuration Manager, or to exempt the module from that setting. The second option is to set the cache time for the module, though this option is not available for all modules.

Cleaning the cache

Cleaning the cache wipes out the cached files and forces the system to refresh the cached information. If you have updated an important content item, or installed a new module or component, you will probably want to clean the cache and get the updated information showing on the site.

Joomla! includes a cache cleaner that is accessed from within the admin system. Simply click on the option Clean Cache under the Tools menu. The Cache Manager will load in your browser, as shown in Figure 26.4.

FIGURE 26.4

The Cache Manager - Clean Cache Admin screen, in this case showing the Site tab.

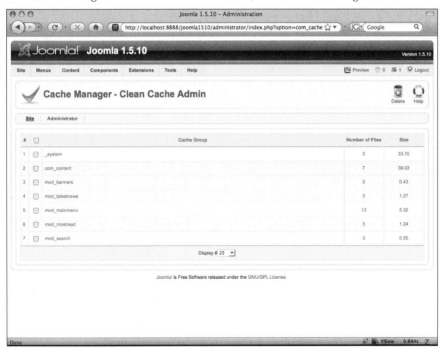

The toolbar at the top of the Cache Manager - Clean Cache Admin screen provides quick access to the following functions:

- **Delete:** Select one or more items from the list, then click this icon to delete the items. In this context, deleting an item means deleting only the cached files.

- **Help:** Click to access the online help files related to the active screen.

Below the toolbar are two links: Site shows you the Site items that are cached. Administrator shows you the Administrator items that are cached.

The main content area of the screen contains a list of all the cached files for your site. The columns provided are:

- **#:** An indexing number assigned by Joomla! This number cannot be changed.

- **Checkbox (no label):** Click in a checkbox to select an item; this is needed if you want to selectively delete items from the cache.

- **Cache Group:** The type of item being cached. Note that the name here reflects the name of the subdirectory where the cached item is kept on the server.

- **Number of Files:** The number of files in the cache group.

- **Size:** The total size of the files cached in this group.

Finally, at the bottom of the screen, below the content area, is the Display # option. Change the value in the combo box control to alter the number of items that are displayed on the page. The default value can be altered by changing the List Length option on the Global Configuration Manager.

To clean up your site's cached files, follow these steps:

1. **Log in to the admin system of your site.**

2. **Click on the Clean Cache option under the Tools menu.** The Cache Manager - Clean Cache Admin screen loads in your browser.

3. **Select the checkbox next to the items you want to delete, or click the top checkbox to select them all.**

4. **Click the Delete icon.** The system immediately deletes the cache files.

Note

Using the Clean Cache option deletes both the current cache as well as the expired cache files. If you only want to free up some server space by cleaning the expired cache files, you can either use this option, or the Purge Expired Cache option discussed next.

Purging the expired cache

The system's caching mechanism retains expired cache files on the server. When you use the Clean Cache option, you clean both the current cache and the expired cache files. The system also provides you with a separate option to clean up, or purge, the expired cache files, leaving the current cache files intact.

To use this alternative cache cleaning tool, click on the option Purge Expired Cache under the Tools menu. The Cache Manager - Purge Cache Admin screen opens in your browser, as shown in Figure 26.5

The Cache Manager - Purge Cache Admin screen.

The toolbar at the top of the Cache Manager provides quick access to the following functions:

- **Purge Expired:** Click this icon to instigate the purge.
- **Help:** Click to access the online help files related to the active screen.

The main content area of the screen contains only the instruction text and a warning that the process may take a while.

To purge the expired cache files, follow these steps:

1. **Log in to the admin system of your site.**
2. **Click on the Purge Expired Cache option under the Tools menu.** The Cache Manager - Purge Cache Admin screen loads in your browser.
3. **Click the Purge Expired icon.** The system immediately deletes the cache files.

Note

Using the Purge Expired Cache option has the advantage of not causing a dip in the front-end site performance. If your site sees heavy traffic, using the Clean Cache option can cause a performance dip because the system must rebuild the cache after you force it dump the files. Purge Expired Cache only kills off the expired files, leaving the current cache files untouched. Typically this is only an issue if your site has numerous users active at the time you decide to clean the cache.

Improving Content Performance

Everything that is on the pages of your web site has an impact on the site's performance. If you build large pages with large files, the page loads more slowly than a smaller, lighter page. While the pages your Joomla! site generates from components are largely beyond your control, you can have a significant impact on your articles pages. If you work smart and keep in mind the need to build lean pages, you can serve web pages to your visitors more quickly and also reduce the burden on your server. Never forget, it all adds up. If you have multiple visitors on your site simultaneously, the page each is viewing contributes to the load. Saving a few kilobytes in file size here and there can add up quickly.

The following sections explain the issues you should consider when creating content for your site.

Avoid large files

Large file size is most commonly an issue with graphical files inserted into articles. Optimize your images to keep file sizes down to reasonable levels. As image file size is at least partially a byproduct of the physical dimensions of the image files (width and height), it is hard to say what is right for your site; however, a reasonable goal is to keep your images under 50K in size. If your images are too large to achieve that goal without a loss in quality, you may want to consider whether you need to display large images on the page, or perhaps you should consider whether a better course would be to display a smaller image, a thumbnail, that is clickable to open a larger image. Note also that for the web, image resolution of 72 dpi is sufficient; anything higher is overkill and unlikely to be reflected in the user's monitor.

Tip

If you are using the Firefox web browser, two free add-ons can help you diagnose and solve performance problems. The YSlow and Firebug add-ons include tools that help you identify the sizes of all the files on any particular web page. This is a great way to identify problem areas and bottlenecks. YSlow also provides suggestions
for improving performance. Get both extensions from `https://addons.mozilla.org`.

Save images in the right format

Closely related to avoiding large files is this issue: Use the correct image format for the content you
need to display. The most common formats for web use are .jpg (or .jpeg), .gif and .png. Use .jpg
for photos and anything that requires smooth transition from color to color or large amounts of
detail. Use .gif or .png for anything that is primarily large blocks of color or black and white. For
example, photos are best saved as .jpgs. A chart or a graphical illustration is best served as a .gif or
.png. Given a choice between .png and .gif, I prefer .png as it produces a smaller file and is copy-
right-free. Choose .gifs if you need animation, as .png does not support this, or if the file is very
small, in which case .gif often produces a smaller file.

Tip

.png files can be created either interlaced or non-interlaced. Interlaced files provide progressive rendering; that
is, they render little by little on the screen, starting out fuzzy and getting clearer. Avoid interlaced .pngs. They are
larger in size, and they confuse some users. Also, note that there are two types of .png: 8-bit and 24-bit. The
24-bit offers full transparency whereas the 8-bit .png offers the same type of transparency as a transparent .gif.

Don't resize images

Upload your image in the actual size that it will be displayed. Do not, in particular, upload files
larger than what is needed and then force them to resize into a smaller display. Forcing the images
to a new size not only fails to save file size, as the file size remains constant, but it also forces the
system to do additional work to resize the image dimensions.

Keep your code clean

If you are copying and pasting text into your WYSIWYG editor, pay careful attention to the code
that results. Although the Joomla! system does its best to eliminate unneeded tags and redundant
code, look at it yourself and make sure that no redundant tags and inline style definitions have
found their way into your page formatting. One of the worst culprits for producing redundant
code is text copied from older versions of Microsoft Word. The clean-up option on the default
WYSIWYG browser can help, but a manual check is always the best solution. Note also that valid
code renders faster, so it is always a good idea to validate your HTML and CSS.

Cross-Reference

The clean-up code option is detailed further in the discussion of WYSIWYG editors in Chapter 6.

Avoid tables

To the extent practicable, use cascading style sheets (CSS) instead of tables to format your page layouts. Tables slow things down, as the whole table needs to be assembled before the contents are rendered. Tables also have implications for accessibility. Complex tabular data may require the use of tables, but as a general rule, CSS is the better way to go.

Note
If you are not familiar with CSS, a good starting point is the W3C site. www.w3.org/MarkUp/Guide/Style.

Use image rotators conservatively

Image rotators are modules that provide a rotating image inside a module position on your page. A popular technique you see on many web sites today is the use of a rotating image on the header of the page. The rotator works like a slideshow, displaying a series of images as the visitor is looking at the page. The problem is that many of the extensions that provide this functionality require all the images to load before the rotation occurs. Therefore, a large amount of data is loaded for the page, some of which may be completely pointless as the user has already clicked and moved on before the image displays. If you have to use an image rotator, keep the image sizes small and do not load too many images into the sequence; three images in rotation perform much better than four, five, or six images. If front page performance is a key concern, keep image rotators off the front page.

Use wrappers (iframes) reluctantly

Wrappers are used to display a web page inside of your web page. This means that the wrapper contents have to be fetched and displayed inside your page. By definition, this increases the number of HTTP requests that have to be made to complete the page, thereby increasing the loading time of the page. Where the Web page you are wrapping is located on another server, the display of the wrapper content depends upon the performance of the remote system and upon the quality of your connection to that server. All of these factors add up to a greater risk of disruption and to increases in page loading time. If, on the other hand, the wrapped content is kept on your server, the risk decreases dramatically, but the delay factor remains. If front page performance is a key concern, keep wrappers off the front page.

Cross-Reference
Working with Wrappers is discussed in Chapter 7.

Limit use of animation

Animation files tend to be larger in size and must load in their entirety before they function properly. Accordingly, limit the use of animation on your page to keep page file size down.

Limit use of flash

Flash files can be quite large in size, and they keep your visitors waiting as they spool in to play. If you must use Flash on your pages, use only Flash elements inside the page, rather than using Flash for the entire page content area. Also plan your Flash so that there are not long delays for your viewers.

Don't stream video until requested

If you want to give users access to video files, do not stream the video until requested by the user. While this does mean that users who want to view the video have to wait for it, it does not force all the users to endure slow page loading while a file they may never view eats up their bandwidth.

Tuning Joomla! Performance

This section looks at various techniques you can use to tweak the performance of your Joomla! site. Not all of these suggestions are suitable for your site, but certainly some of them are applicable.

Use server-side compression

Joomla! supports the server side compression protocol GZIP. If your server supports GZIP, enable this option in the Global Configuration Manager as it can result in some significant performance improvements. The GZIP page compression options are located on the Server tab in the Global Configuration Manager.

Cross-Reference
See Chapter 4 for more information on using the Global Configuration Manager.

If you don't use it, disable it

Disable all components, modules, and plugins that you are not using. Even if you are not displaying the output on the page, the system is likely doing at least some of the processing associated with the feature.

Cross-Reference
As discussed in Chapter 25, unneeded components, modules, templates, and plugins can also have site security implications!

Minify your CSS and JavaScript

Minification is the process of reducing the size of CSS selectors and JavaScript by reducing unnecessary spaces and characters. Although minifying a single selector saves only a small amount, it all adds up, and minifying the entire CSS can result in a meaningful savings. This is a tedious manual process, so if you want to employ this technique I suggest that you use one of the many tools designed to make this easier. Run a Google search for "minify CSS" and "minify JavaScript" for lists of options.

Tip
The Joomla! Extensions Directory also lists several extensions that can compress your CSS and JavaScript.

Tip
If you use javascripts like mootools or jquery, consider linking to Google's hosting of those files. They then become cached once you have loaded it once.

Be careful with Google Analytics

Google Analytics, though a wonderful and useful service, can slow down your site. Every page that includes the Google Analytics code increases your load time as the Google Analytics script causes the system to wait while it contacts the Google servers. The impact of this varies greatly depending on the time of day, the traffic on your site, and the location of your servers.

Be selective about your template

Your template developer can have a significant impact on your Jomla! site performance. Many of the lovely templates I see in circulation rely heavily upon images to achieve their look and feel. The size of the templates and the number of HTTP requests they generate are not optimal. Select your template carefully. Look at the file size and the quality of the code. You want to select templates that use CSS, not tables, and those that prefer system text to image usage. Be particularly careful of templates that use images for the menus, rather than system text and CSS. Not only do these templates have a negative impact on site performance, but they also tend to be less than optimal from the perspective of both SEO and accessibility.

Be selective about extensions

Some third-party extensions are incredibly resource-intensive. When you are comparing components, modules, or plugins, use YSlow to compare the impact on your page performance and check resource usage on your server. Don't forget that small differences in performance can balloon into big differences when the site experiences spikes in traffic.

Skip live stat reporting

Components or modules that produce live, real-time statistics on your site can be significant drains on site performance. If you don't have a compelling need for real-time statistics, skip them.

Disable SEF URLs

Though this may not be an option for many of you, if your goal is performance above all else, disable the SEF URLs option. The conversion of your native URLs into aliases causes a performance hit.

Optimize your database

One of the main performance bottlenecks for any content management system is the database server. To improve performance, you should periodically optimize the database tables. Optimization is performed from within phpMyAdmin. To learn more about this process, visit the MySQL web site: `http://dev.mysql.com/doc/refman/5.0/en/optimize-table.html`.

Enhancing Accessibility

Accessibility refers to the extent to which the largest number of users with different physcial capabilities are able to gain access to the contents and functionalities of your web site. The topic is often a point of focus in discussions concerning persons with disabilities and their rights to access. The right to access has been the subject of legislation in North America and in other jurisdictions and is widely considered to be an issue of best practices in web design. In the U.S., the right is codified in Section 508 of the Federal law. In web design circles, the standards are outlined by the World Wide Web Consortium's Web Content Accessibility Guidelines, also known as WCAG.

Note

The Section 508 guidelines can be found at `http://www.section508.gov`. The WCAG guidelines can be found at `http://www.w3.org/TR/WCAG10/`.

Creating an accessible web site can be a challenge. Although basic levels of compliance can be achieved with a modicum of work, the more stringent requirements impose many limitations upon the way that content can be displayed and on the way the functionality behaves. Before you begin work on a site, determine what level of compliance is necessary, because the limitations imposed by the standard will impact template and extension selection. Going forward, awareness of the required standard will inform your content management decisions and the ways in which your content creators work.

Tip

One of the best resources for information on web site accessibility is the Web Accessibility Initiative from the W3C. The site includes a lot of information about how to build accessible sites as well as links to tools that can help you test your site's compliance with various standards. Visit WAI at `http://www.w3.org/WAI`.

Joomla! and accessibility

The default Joomla! system comes with three templates. All three produce valid CSS and XHTML, but the degree of their compliance with various accessibility standards is less clear.

I set out to test all three of the Joomla! 1.5.x default templates for compliance with entry level accessibility standards. Because accessibility testing tools tend to give conflicting results, I employed three different testing tools: EvalAccess, Fujitsu's Web Accessibility Inspector, and worldspace. All three tools support testing for WCAG 1.0, so I focused on this standard, rather than the U.S.-specific Section 508 standard. For this test, I installed the sample data and tested the home page only. See Table 26.1, Table 26. 2, and Table 26.3 for the results for the tests.

TABLE 26.1

Testing the Default Templates for Accessibility with EvalAccess

Template	WCAG 1.0 Priority 1
Beez	0 violations, 114 minor problems
JA_Purity	0 violations, 135 minor problems
rhuk_milkyway	0 violations, 126 minor problems

TABLE 26.2

Testing the Default Templates for Accessibility with Fujitsu's Web Accessibility Inspector

Template	WCAG 1.0 Priority 1
Beez	0 violations, 7 minor problems
JA_Purity	0 violations, 22 minor problems
rhuk_milkyway	0 violations, 19 minor problems

TABLE 26.3

Testing the Default Templates for Accessibility with worldspace

Template	WCAG 1.0 Priority 1
Beez	0 violations, 10 minor problems
JA_Purity	0 violations, 5 minor problems
rhuk_milkyway	0 violations, 5 minor problems

Although they vary, the results consistently show that all three templates pass the entry level WCAG standard for creating accessible web sites.

Taking these tests a littler further, I disabled the JavaScript in the browser and retested all three. The sites remain navigable with JavaScript disabled. Both Beez and JA_Purity provide a font size switcher to improve readability. The switcher allows users to increase, or decrease the font size by clicking the icons on the header of each page. The switcher functionality relies on JavaScript and as a result these tools are lost when the JavaScript is disabled. Interestingly, the Beez Template detects whether JavaScript is active and if it is not, it hides the font resizer icons. JA_Purity unfortunately does not, leaving the icons visible even though they have no function.

Note

The Joomla! admin system requires JavaScript to function properly.

Next, I checked all three templates for usability with a text-only browser emulator. Beez performed best, with a logical structure, jump links appropriately placed, and an aesthetically useful layout. JA_Purity also performed fairly well, though the page organization was less logical. The laggard in this test was the rhuk_milkyway template, which suffered from bad layout, poor content structure, and a lack of jump links to help users jump to the key spots on the page.

For one final test, I disabled the colors on the screen. All three templates remained quite usable, though Beez remained visually more consistent.

In conclusion, on the whole the Beez template performs better in accessibility measures. The worldspace testing tool was the only one that indicated poorer performance by the Beez template. Looking at the potential errors reported by worldspace, the issues related to the use of color to highlight URL links, a minor point in light of the fact that Beez uses both color and text style (underline) to indicate the presence of a hyperlink.

This analysis shows that the basic Joomla! system is capable of performing well in basic accessibility scenarios. The errors displayed during the testing process also emphasized the vital role of templates and the importance of creating accessible content as the content items themselves were the source of many of the minor problems reported.

Note also that the impact of extensions on accessibility can be substantial. If you are concerned with creating and maintaining a compliant site, then you can retest the site after installing each of the extensions.

Tip

Several extensions are designed to improve Joomla's accessibility. The Joomla! Extensions Directory provides a specific category for these extensions: `http://extensions.joomla.org/extensions/style-&-design/accessibility`**.**

Improving template accessibility

The results of the testing in the previous section demonstrates the key role that templates play in Joomla! accessibility. The performance in text-only mode also demonstrates the importance of creating logical template structures with appropriate HTML tags. The creation of accessible templates is a broad topic, but certain basic principles need to be followed. I cover these in the next sections.

Support semantic structure

The H tags in HTML were intended to allow the people who create content to impose hierarchical ordering on that content. The proper use of these tags makes it easy for users — and search engines — to determine the information structure and the relationship between the various parts of the document. When designing the site's CSS selectors, make sure that you provide for the use of H tags in proper sequence by your content managers.

Avoid tables

By now, avoiding tables should be well established. Tables are not optimal and should be avoided. The exception to this general rule is complex tabular data. If you must use tables, use the TH element to make the table headings separate from the data.

Don't rely on JavaScript

A number of users are working on browsers that have the JavaScript disabled. If you build your template so that it relies on JavaScript for functionality, you need to make sure that the template degrades gracefully and that alternatives are provided. Always test to make sure that the page is navigable with only a keyboard.

Use system fonts for your nav menus

Use of image files for your navigation can cause accessibility problems unless you consistently provide for text alternatives. Note that use of images is also disadvantageous because they decrease the search engine friendliness of the site while increasing the page file size.

Use a suitable color scheme

Make sure that your color selection maintains an appropriate level of contrast for viewers with visual acuity problems. Also remember to test your system in black and white to make sure that it remains navigable with the colors turned off.

Order elements on the screen logically

Place the page elements in a logical order inside your code. If the visitor views the site without the benefit of the CSS, the logical structure you have created in the code helps to maintain the integrity of the page. The use of *skip to* or *jump* links can also help make the page more navigable and enable users to jump to interim points on the page.

Make sure your text resizes

Use proper CSS coding to assure that text can be resized by the user's browser; typically this means using ems or percentages for font size in the CSS.

Use jump links

Jump links should be placed at the top of the page to allow visitors to jump directly to key content or functionality.

Make forms accessible

Forms need to be usable by all visitors. If necessary, use assistive technologies.

Provide alternatives to applets and plugins

If the page requires the use of an applet or plugin, provide a text link to the download of the applet or plugin, or provide an alternative for the display of the content.

Avoid requiring timed responses

Avoid forms or other functions that require timed responses. If this is unavoidable, make sure that it is clear that there is a time limit, make the limit generous, and make sure that the time markers are clearly communicated to the user.

Creating accessible content

If the developer has done a good job of creating an accessible template and you have assembled accessible components, you have half of the problem solved. Unfortunately, if your content creators aren't mindful of what accessibility means and how to create accessible content, the entire previous effort may have been wasted! Creating accessible content items is a key success factor. Following these tips in the next sections can help keep your content items accessible by the widest audience of users.

Use headings correctly

Just as the developer should make sure that the CSS provides the formatting to support the creation of semantic content, the content manager must make sure that headings are used properly to convey the structure of the content. Do not use strong, bold, or italic tags to make headings stand out, rather use the proper H tags.

Use lists correctly

Do not use the ordered list and unordered list tags for purposes other than the creation of lists inside content items.

Use alt image attributes

The alt attribute for images allows you to provide text equivalents for images. If a visitor has the images turned off in their browser, proper use of the image alt attribute can help the user better understand the role the images play on the page and help improve understanding of the content.

Summarize graphs and charts

Provide a summary of graphical and chart data along with the chart or use the longdesc attribute to link to a separate description and data set.

Summarize multimedia

Provide summaries or transcripts of multimedia or use the longdesc attribute to link to a separate description and data set.

Testing accessibility

As a web developer or a site owner, you need to be able to test your site to identify accessibility issues. Table 26.4 lists several free tools that can be used online or downloaded and run locally. In addition to the tools listed here, the Web Developer Toolbar add-on for the Firefox browser also provides a number of useful pieces of information and links to testing resources.

TABLE 26.4

Free Tools for Testing

Tool	URL
EvalAccess 2.0	http://sipt07.si.ehu.es/evalaccess2/index.html
Web Accessibility Inspector	http://www.fujitsu.com/global/accessibility/assistance/wi/
worldspace	http://worldspace.deque.com/wsservice/eval/checkCompliance.jsp
wave	http://wave.webaim.org

For a complete and maintained list of accessibility testing tools, visit `www.w3.org/WAI/ER/tools/complete`

Summary

In this chapter, we looked at Joomla! performance and accessibility issues. You learned the following:

- How to manage your Joomla! site's various caching options
- How to improve performance of your site
- The role of templates and content items in accessibility
- How to improve accessibility of templates
- How to improve accessibility of articles

CHAPTER 2

Making a Site Search Engine Friendly

I f I build it, they will come — or so goes the old way of thinking. On today's web that sort of thinking is the recipe for failure. The amount of noise and competition is nothing short of spectacular, and it can easily drown out your site, even if the quality of your content is excellent. If you want to get traffic and you want to be seen, you need to make an effort to create a search engine friendly site and you need to engage in at least some basic search engine optimization.

Joomla!, like most content management systems, faces some challenges to create a truly search engine friendly site. You will hear some commentators say that you cannot achieve good search engine optimization (SEO) with a CMS, but that view is not entirely correct. You can create a search engine friendly site; however, you may not achieve the level of optimization that a highly trained SEO specialist can get from a pure HTML web site. That said, given the competitiveness of search marketing these days, your use of a CMS is not likely to be fatal to your SEO goals. Effective site optimization should be only one part of your broader search-marketing campaign.

This chapter looks at various SEO techniques that can be applied using only the default Joomla! features. Of course, if you want to do more — and those of you who really want to be competitive must do more — there are numerous third-party extensions that can be added to your site to address various SEO issues.

Creating Search Engine Friendly URLs

The default Joomla! system produces messy URLs. A default URL contains query strings and other characters that are hard for humans and search engines to read. Accordingly, the first step of any effort to make Joomla! more search engine friendly is to get rid of the messy URLs and get your system to use search engine friendly (SEF) URLs.

What is a search engine friendly URL? Generally speaking, a search engine friendly URL is a human friendly URL. The default Joomla! system produces a URL that looks something like this:

```
http://www.joomla1510.com/index.php?option=com_content&view=article&
id=27:the-joomla-community&catid=30:the-community&Itemid=30
```

This is not search engine friendly because some search engines will choke on the odd characters and query strings. It is also not human friendly because it is long, hard to remember, and even harder to type accurately. URLs like this are even difficult to e-mail because their length often forces a line break and causes people to make mistakes when they cut and paste the URL into their browsers.

A better URL would look like this:

```
http://www.joomla1510.com/the-community
```

The URL above is a search engine friendly, and human friendly, URL.

These two example URLs are real. They actually point to the same page in the Joomla! sample data, in this case the article entitled "The Joomla! Community." The first example is the default Joomla! system's URL formulation for the article; the second example shows what you can achieve by simply enabling the SEF URLs feature in the Joomla! system.

The process for enabling SEF URLs depends on the Web server being used on your Web host. SEF URLs are simplest to enable on the Apache web server, but they are dependent upon the mod_rewrite package being installed and your ability to create a .htaccess file. This is not as hard as it may sound because mod_rewrite is typically installed on most common systems and Joomla! actually bundles in the default distro a .htaccess file that is ready to go — all you have to do is rename it.

If you are running Apache, all you need to do to enable SEF URLs on your Joomla! site is to follow these steps:

1. **Access the files of your Joomla! installation on the server.**
2. **Find the file htaccess.txt. Create a duplicate of it and rename the new file to .htaccess.** You can exit the server; you are done here.

Creating your own URL aliases

In the preceding SEF URLs example, the last part of that URL, the-community, is referred to as the alias. It is possible to achieve a degree of control over the alias created by Joomla!

Sections, categories, articles, and individual menu items include options to set a specific alias. During the creation or editing of a section, category, article, or menu item you can specify an alias for the system to use to construct the SEF URL. This is done by typing the string you want to use into the field named Alias. Note that the alias field will only accept lowercase letters, numbers, and the hyphen character; it will not accept spaces, uppercase letters, or unusual characters. If you do not specify an alias, the system will automatically convert the item's title into an alias.

Pay attention when creating aliases in order to avoid creating multiple, conflicting aliases. This is primarily an issue where you are setting the alias for an article, and then linking directly to the article from a menu. In this case, the menu item will also have an alias field. You should try to make the article alias and the menu item alias consistent, for simplicity's sake. Note that where there is a menu item linking directly to an article, the menu item alias will take precedence of a conflicting article alias.

Note also that sections and categories have aliases. If you are linking directly into the section or category list pages, then you will need to pay attention to those aliases, as well.

In some cases, use of SEF URLs in Joomla! will result in the creation of duplicate article content. If you are concerned about this and want to avoid it, you must manage closely and carefully the aliases between the articles and the menu items.

Note

On some servers, once you rename the file to .htaccess the file disappears in the file structure. (It doesn't really disappear, the file is still there just "hidden" from the file view.)

3. **Log into the admin system of your Joomla! site.** The Control Panel loads in your browser.

4. **Click on the shortcut icon labeled Global Configuration.** The Global Configuration Manager loads in your browser.

5. **On the right side of the site page is a section named SEO Settings. Set the option Search Engine Friendly URLs to Yes.**

6. **Set the option Use Apache mod_rewrite to Yes.**

7. **Click the Save icon.** The system will save your changes and enable SEF URLs.

Caution

You must use the .htaccess file provided by Joomla! Do not attempt to create your own or modify the file, unless you have experience with this process. Definitely do not try this on a live site without first testing it!

If your site is using Microsoft's IIS web server, instead of the Apache web server, the process is different and more involved. Note that the process requires you to install the ISAPI filter on the server. This filter is unlikely to be an option available to you if you are on a shared web host. Accordingly, I have not described the steps here in detail. If you have access to your IIS installation, or you can convince your web host, then it is possible to set up SEF URLs on IIS. To learn more about this process, please see the dedicated page on this topic on the Joomla! documentation site at `http://docs.joomla.org/IIS6_and_SEF_URLs_using_Joomla_1.5x`.

Note

The Joomla! SEF URLs functionality is enabled by the plugin named System - SEF. This plugin must be enabled for SEF URLs to work. Although it is enabled by default, if you are having problems, check the Plugin Manager to assure it is enabled in your system. The plugins and the Plugin Manager are discussed in Chapter 19.

Creating Custom Error Pages

You can create custom pages to handle common errors, such as 404 (page not found) errors. This step is optional, and while it has little direct benefit for search marketing, it is very helpful for your site visitors. It can help keep visitors on your site and can improve the perception that the site is professional and useful.

Error pages in Joomla! 1.5.x are handled by this file: `/templates/sytem/error.php`. You can override the default file copying it to your default template directory and then making your changes on the copy; if there is an `error.php` file in the active template directory, it will be shown instead of the default system file. If you want to work on the styling of the file, you also need to copy the CSS file, `/template/system/css/error.css` and move it to your default template directory. Remember to update the `error.php` file to point to the new location of the CSS.

Tip

There is a page dedicated to SEO and SEF tips on the Official Joomla! Documentation Web site. Visit `http://docs.joomla.org/SEF`.

Working with Metadata and Page Titles

A site's metadata and page titles also play a role in search engine optimization. Key metadata fields, like the description and keywords fields, are sometimes used by search engine spiders to classify your content and in some cases for the description that is associated with your site in the search results output. Page titles not only appear on the browser for the users, but also are indexed by the search engines and appear in the search results.

Setting the metadata

Joomla! provides both global and individual article metadata options. The default system does not, unfortunately, provide options for individual component metadata. Global metadata is controlled in the Global Configuration Manager. Article metadata is controlled by the metadata parameters inside the Article Editing dialogue.

Cross-Reference
See Chapter 4 for more information on Global Configuration Manager, and turn to Chapter 5 to find more on working with article parameters.

Note that article metadata overrides and takes precedence over the global metadata. Where metadata has been specified in the article's parameters it will appear inside the code for that page, in place of the global metadata. Where no article metadata has been specified, the default global metadata will appear in the page's code.

The default system only supports four metadata fields:

- Description
- Keywords
- Robots
- Author

If you want to add expanded metadata sets either edit the template files to add additional metadata fields into the head of the template or consider adding a third-party extension that provides this facility.

Cross-Reference
For a discussion of modifying the default template files, please see Chapter 20.

Setting the page titles

By default, the value you specify for the title field of an article becomes not only the title you see on the page above the article's text, but also the resulting web page title. The web page title appears on the title bar of the browser and is also displayed as the page title in the search results of most of the popular search engines, including Google.

Many search engine specialists believe that the page title has a direct impact on the site's search engine effectiveness. Unfortunately, the default Joomla! configuration does not give you much flexibility. Page titles are generated dynamically, so it is not possible to specify a consistent value for them, absent hacking the core files, as noted later in this section. Moreover, displaying the same value for the title of the text and for the title of the resulting web page may restrict your ability to create optimal page titles that are in line with your search marketing efforts.

You can use a work-around for this problem. Doing so requires the creation of menu items in which you specify and override the default Page Title display function.

It works like this: Where a menu item is used to link to an article, you can specify the page title in the menu item's system parameters. The page title value in that menu item parameter will take precedence over the title specified in the article. When configured properly, you can specify the title that goes with the text when you create the article, yet specify the title that goes with the web page when you create the menu item.

To set this up in Joomla! 1.5.x, follow these steps. Note for this example I assume that you already have an article set to display the article title (the default setting) and that there is an existing menu item linking to that article:

1. **Access the admin system of your site.**

2. **Click the name of the menu where the menu item you want to change is located.** The Menu Item Manager opens.

3. **Click on the name of the menu item you want to change.** The Menu Item Editing dialogue opens in your browser.

4. **Click on Parameters (System).** The Parameters box expands to reveal the options.

5. **In the field labeled page title, type whatever you want to appear as the page title for the target of the menu item.**

6. **Set the value of the parameter named Show Page Title to No.**

7. **Click the Save icon.** The system saves your changes, closes the Menu Item Editing dialogue, and returns you to the Menu Item Manager.

This example results in the title given to the article showing above the text of the article, but the page title given in the menu item will be used for the web page title tag. Note that if you set the menu item parameter named Show Page Title to Yes, then the string you entered in the menu item Page Title parameter would be used as both the web page title tag and as the title above the article text.

To extend this technique a bit further, if you need to specify page title tags for pages that are not linked to any menu, you can build a menu whose only purpose is to assist you with the management of page title tags. To do this, you can create a menu, and then create menu items for each page, specifying in each menu item the page title you desire. The key is to leave the menu module unpublished. If you do not publish the menu module for the menu, then the visitors cannot see the menu or the items it contains, but the page title functionality can still be used to the site administrator to manage the title tag for one or more of the site's pages.

Note
The approaches discussed work equally well on menu items that link to components.

Tip

It is possible to add static text to the existing page title tag, but you have to modify the Joomla! core files to make this happen. Adding static text to the title tag would allow you to specify text that will appear as part of the page title string on all the pages of the site. To make this modification to the system, you must edit the file: `libraries/joomla/document/html/renderer/head.php` **to modify the line of code, that generates the title tag output:** `$strHtml .= $tab.'<title>'.htmlspecialchars($document->getTitle()).'</title>'.$lnEnd;`

Summary

This chapter has covered the basics of search engine optimization of your Joomla! web site. You learned the following:

- How the enable search engine friendly URLs
- How to override the default Joomla! error page template
- How to control site and article metadata
- How to create effective page titles

Part VI

Appendixes

The Directory Structure of a Joomla! Installation

A complete Joomla! installation includes a large number of directories and files. The directories and files reside on your server, typically, though not necessarily, in the public directory of your hosting account.

Figure A.1 shows is a view of the default installation of Joomla! 1.5.10, with all the key directories expanded to give you the big picture of what is installed on your server. See Appendix B for a map of the locations of the key files and directories that you might need to locate during the customization of your site.

APPENDIX A
Understanding Joomla! installation

FIGURE A.1

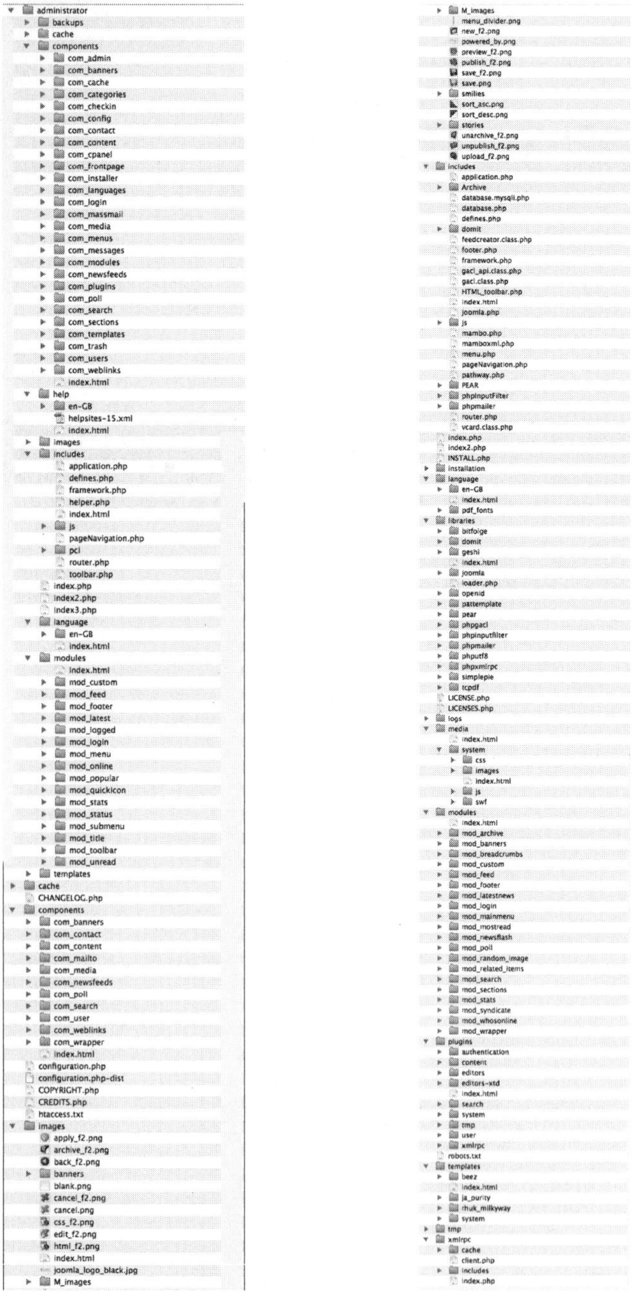

administrator
- backups
- cache
- components
  - com_admin
  - com_banners
  - com_cache
  - com_categories
  - com_checkin
  - com_config
  - com_contact
  - com_content
  - com_cpanel
  - com_frontpage
  - com_installer
  - com_languages
  - com_login
  - com_massmail
  - com_media
  - com_menus
  - com_messages
  - com_modules
  - com_newsfeeds
  - com_plugins
  - com_poll
  - com_search
  - com_sections
  - com_templates
  - com_trash
  - com_users
  - com_weblinks
  - index.html
- help
  - en-GB
    - helpsites-15.xml
    - index.html
- images
- includes
  - application.php
  - defines.php
  - framework.php
  - helper.php
  - index.html
  - js
  - pageNavigation.php
  - pcl
  - router.php
  - toolbar.php
  - index.php
  - index2.php
  - index3.php
- language
  - en-GB
  - index.html
- modules
  - index.html
  - mod_custom
  - mod_feed
  - mod_footer
  - mod_latest
  - mod_logged
  - mod_login
  - mod_menu
  - mod_online
  - mod_popular
  - mod_quickicon
  - mod_stats
  - mod_status
  - mod_submenu
  - mod_title
  - mod_toolbar
  - mod_unread
- templates
- cache
- CHANGELOG.php
- components
  - com_banners
  - com_contact
  - com_content
  - com_mailto
  - com_media
  - com_newsfeeds
  - com_poll
  - com_search
  - com_user
  - com_weblinks
  - com_wrapper
  - index.html
- configuration.php
- configuration.php-dist
- COPYRIGHT.php
- CREDITS.php
- htaccess.txt
- images
  - apply_f2.png
  - archive_f2.png
  - back_f2.png
  - banners
  - blank.png
  - cancel_f2.png
  - cancel.png
  - css_f2.png
  - edit_f2.png
  - html_f2.png
  - index.html
  - joomla_logo_black.jpg
  - M_images

- M_images
  - menu_divider.png
  - new_f2.png
  - powered_by.png
  - preview_f2.png
  - publish_f2.png
  - save_f2.png
  - save.png
  - smilies
  - sort_asc.png
  - sort_desc.png
  - stories
  - unarchive_f2.png
  - unpublish_f2.png
  - upload_f2.png
- includes
  - application.php
  - Archive
  - database.mysqli.php
  - database.php
  - defines.php
  - domit
  - feedcreator.class.php
  - footer.php
  - framework.php
  - gacl_api.class.php
  - gacl.class.php
  - HTML_toolbar.php
  - index.html
  - joomla.php
  - js
    - mambo.php
    - mamboxml.php
    - menu.php
    - pageNavigation.php
    - pathway.php
  - PEAR
  - phpInputFilter
  - phpmailer
    - router.php
    - vcard.class.php
  - index.php
  - index2.php
  - INSTALL.php
- installation
- language
  - en-GB
  - index.html
  - pdf_fonts
- libraries
  - bitfolge
  - domit
  - geshi
  - index.html
  - joomla
  - loader.php
  - openid
  - pattemplate
  - pear
  - phpgacl
  - phpinputfilter
  - phpmailer
  - phputf8
  - phpxmlrpc
  - simplepie
  - tcpdf
  - LICENSE.php
  - LICENSES.php
- logs
- media
  - index.html
  - system
    - css
    - images
    - index.html
    - js
    - swf
- modules
  - index.html
  - mod_archive
  - mod_banners
  - mod_breadcrumbs
  - mod_custom
  - mod_feed
  - mod_footer
  - mod_latestnews
  - mod_login
  - mod_mainmenu
  - mod_mostread
  - mod_newsflash
  - mod_poll
  - mod_random_image
  - mod_related_items
  - mod_search
  - mod_sections
  - mod_stats
  - mod_syndicate
  - mod_whosonline
  - mod_wrapper
- plugins
  - authentication
  - content
  - editors
  - editors-xtd
  - index.html
  - search
  - system
  - tmp
  - user
  - xmlrpc
  - robots.txt
- templates
  - beez
  - index.html
  - ja_purity
  - rhuk_milkyway
  - system
- tmp
- xmlrpc
  - cache
  - client.php
  - includes
  - index.php

A Guide to the Location of Key Files

O ne of the first steps in customizing your Joomla! site is figuring out where to go to find the files you need to change. Table B.1 shows the locations of the items that are most commonly modified by site owners.

The table's contents provide the locations of the key files used by the front-end components and modules, as well as the locations of the language packs, the default images, and perhaps most importantly, the front-end and admin Templates and CSS files.

Note that the location given is the path to the files on your server, relative to directory where you have placed your Joomla! installation.

TABLE B.1

Key Files

Item	Location
Components (front-end output)	
Banner	components/com_banners
Contacts	components/com_contact
Newsfeeds	components/com_newsfeeds
Polls	components/com_poll
Weblinks	components/com_weblinks
Site Modules (front-end output)	
Archive module	modules/mod_archive
Banners module	modules/mod_banners
Breadcrumbs module	modules/mod_breadcrumbs
Custom HTML modules	modules/mod_custom
Feeds module	modules/mod_feed
Footer module	modules/mod_footer
Latest News module	modules/mod_latestnews
Login module	modules/mod_login
Menu modules	modules/mod_mainmenu
Most Read module	modules/mod_mostread
News Flash module	modules/mod_newsflash
Poll module	modules/mod_poll
Random Image module	modules/mod_random_image
Related Items module	modules/mod_related_items
Search module	modules/mod_search
Sections module	modules/mod_sections
Stats module	modules/mod_stats
Syndicate module	modules/mod_syndicate
Who's Online module	modules/mod_whosonline
Wrapper module	modules/mod_wrapper
Language Files	
English (default en-GB language pack)	language/en-GB

Item	Location
Site Templates	
Beez template	`templates/beez`
Purity template	`templates/ja_purity`
Milkyway template	`templates/rhuk_milkyway`
CSS (front-end)	
Stylesheets	`templates/[active template/css`
Admin Template	
Khepri	`administrator/templates/khepri`
CSS (admin system)	
Stylesheet	`administrator/templates/khepri/css`
Image Files	
Banner ads	`images/banners`
Smilies	`images/smilies`
System images	`images/`
	`images/M_images`
Images shown in Media Manager	`images/stories`
Configuration file	`configuration.php`

Installing XAMPP

XAMPP is a unified software package that bundles all the necessary elements for creating a fully functional server environment. The system includes not only the basics, like the Apache web server, the MySQL database, and the PHP language support, but also useful tools such as phpMyAdmin.

XAMPP is cross-platform compatible and can be installed on Windows, Linux, or Mac. This Appendix provides a step-by-step guide to installing XAMPP on a Windows machine.

At the conclusion of this process you will have a functional server on your Windows machine that allows you to run Joomla! locally.

Follow these steps to acquire the XAMPP installation package and get it set up on your local machine.

1. **Connect to the Internet and open your browser.**

2. **Direct your browser to** `www.apachefriends.org` The web page loads in your browser.

3. **Click on the main menu choice XAMPP.** The XAMPP page loads.

4. **Click the links XAMPP for Windows.** The XAMPP for Windows page loads.

5. **Click the download link.** The page jumps to the Download packages list.

6. **Click the Installer option.** A new window opens and goes to Sourceforge.net's downloads page.

7. **Select the download link next to the option XAMPP Windows.** A new page loads listing the available download packages.

8. **Select the option xampp-win32-1.7.1-installer.exe.** The download should begin automatically.

9. **A pop-up menu prompts you to save the file. Click OK.** The software installer downloads to your computer. After it is complete, you can move to the next step.

10. **Locate the downloaded archive (.zip) package on your local machine.**

11. **Double-click on the archive package.** The software unpacks and leaves a new file on your desktop.

12. **Double-click on the new file.** Select the language you prefer. Click OK. The installer takes you to the next screen.

13. **Click Next.** The installer will advance to the next screen. Select the installation location. Click the Next button. The installer takes you to the next screen.

Tip

Installing this application outside your programs directory is the best choice.

14. **Change any setting you require on the Options page.** All choices are optional. Click Install. The installer takes you to the next screen and completes the installation.

15. **Click Finish. The installer closes.**

The installation is complete and the software is ready to run.

To begin, simply start XAMPP from under Start ⇨ Programs ⇨ XAMPP. Use the start/stop buttons to control the servers.

To create a new web site, simply copy the files into a directory placed inside the /htdocs directory. You can then access your new site by opening the URL in your browser, as follows:
`http://localhost/sitedirectoryname`

Installing MAMP

MAMP is a unified software package that bundles all the necessary elements for creating a fully functional server environment. The system includes not only the basics, like the Apache web server, the MySQL database, and the PHP language support, but also useful tools like phpMyAdmin.

MAMP is cross-platform compatible and can be installed on Windows, Linux, or Mac. This Appendix provides a step-by-step guide to installing MAMP on a Windows machine.

At the conclusion of this process you will have a functional server on your Mac that allows you to run Joomla! locally.

Follow these steps to acquire the MAMP installation package and get it set up on your local machine.

1. **Connect to the Internet and open your browser.**

2. **Direct your browser to** `http://www.mamp.info.` The web page loads in your browser.

3. **Click on the main menu choice Downloads.** The Downloads page loads.

4. **Click to download the software package named MAMP.**

5. **A new window opens and goes to Sourceforge.net's downloads page.** The download should begin automatically.

6. **A pop-up menu prompts you to save the .dmg file. Click OK.** The software installer downloads to your computer. After it is complete, you can move to the next step.

> **APPENDIX D**
>
> **Installing MAMP**

7. **Locate the downloaded archive (.zip) package on your local machine.**

8. **Double-click on the archive package.** The software unpacks and leaves a new .dmg file on your desktop.

9. **Double-click on the .dmg file.** The file opens a new window showing the installer icon.

10. **Drag the MAMP icon into the applications directory shown in the installer window.** The system immediately begins to copy all the necessary files to your computer's applications directory. Confirmation that it is complete is signified by a beep.

11. **Close the installer window.**

12. **Eject the installation disk by dragging it to the trash.**

The installation is complete and the software is ready to run.

To run the servers, simply double-click on the MAMP icon inside the new MAMP directory. The MAMP controller opens. If the servers fail to start when you open the application, click the Start Servers button. You should see two green lights, one for the Apache server, another for the MySQL server. You need two green lights to use the application! When both green lights light, the system automatically opens the MAMP welcome page in a browser window. Note this page contains links to all the information and utilities you need, including the phpMyAdmin tool. Typically this page URL is `http://localhost:8888/MAMP/?language=English`.

To shut down the servers, click the Stop Servers button.

To create a new web site, simply copy the files into a directory placed inside the /applications/ MAMP/htdocs directory. You can then access your new site by opening the URL in your browser, as follows: `http://localhost:8888/sitedirectoryname`.

Additional Online Help Resources

The popularity of Joomla! has created a significant demand for help resources and supplemental information. The system itself includes Help files, but for those seeking more assistance, the official Joomla! project maintains a number of rich informational sites with documentation, tutorials, and more. Whether you are a developer, a designer, or a site administrator, there are Joomla! help resources designed specifically to help you.

The Help Files inside Joomla!

For site administrators, one of the most useful features of Joomla! is the ability to display context-sensitive help information inside the admin system. Virtually every screen in the admin system has a Help icon on the top-right toolbar. Clicking the icon opens a window containing the Help files that are relevant to that specific page.

By default, the help file information you see within the administration system of your site is drawn from the online Joomla! help site, `www.help.joomla.org`. Joomla's approach to providing help information inside the admin interface via Help files that are hosted online is a sensible solution. When the online files are updated, users can access the most recent data immediately, without having to download any additional files. The use of the online Help files is, however, dependent upon you having a connection to the Internet. Although most web sites will have a connection to the Internet, if the Joomla! installation is located on a local network, access to the online Help files may not be practical or even possible.

You can change the default Help files setting by accessing the Global Configuration Manager and changing the URL associated with the Help files. The setting is located on the System tab, under the label Help Server. Note that the system does provide default options for Help files in alternative languages. At the time this was written the choices included English, Spanish, Italian, Hungarian, German, Dutch, and Catalan — a list that is certain to grow. If you want to set up your own Help files locally, rather than rely on the default online files, you can set up a local Help server. The process is rather complicated. If you want to create a local Help server, please refer to the instructions online at the Joomla! Docs site, `http://docs.joomla.org/Setting_up_a_local_help_server`.

Online Help and Support Resources

Joomla! is one of the best documented open source systems. In addition to a complete set of documents for site administrators, there are tutorials, examples, and documents for designers and developers. Table E.1 covers some of the highlights of the official online resources.

TABLE E.1

Name	Location
The Absolute Beginners Guide to Joomla	`http://docs.joomla.org/Beginners`
The Official Joomla! Documentation Site	`http://docs.joomla.org`
The Official Joomla! Forum	`http://forum.joomla.org/`
The Joomla! Developers Documentation	`http://docs.joomla.org/Developers`
The Joomla! Administrators Documentation	`http://docs.joomla.org/Administrators`
The Joomla! Web Designers Documentation	`http://docs.joomla.org/Web_designers`
The Joomla! API	`http://api.joomla.org/`
Joomla! Developers Tutorials	`http://developer.joomla.org/tutorials.html`
Joomla! 1.5 Template Tutorials	`http://docs.joomla.org/Joomla!_1.5_Template_Tutorials_Project`

There is also a wide variety of unofficial help resources, some more authoritative than others. One good source of information is the Scribd.com site. Scribd is a document-sharing site that includes a collection of Joomla! related documents and presentations. The Open Source CMS group on Scribd is a good place to start: `www.scribd.com/groups/groups/746618`.

Using Community Support Options

Joomla! is a community-driven open source project, meaning that all the project administrators, designers, and developers are unpaid volunteers. A surprising number of persons participate in the forums, both to provide assistance for solving common problems and to enjoy the company of others with similar interests. The forums are the primary resource for community support.

You can access the official Joomla! Community Forums at `http://forum.joomla.org`. The forums are incredibly active, with well over 200,000 members and more than 1.5 million posts.

Anyone is free to browse the forums and read the information and conversations posted there. If you want to post on the forums, you need to register. Registration is free and requires you to disclose only very basic information. I highly recommended that you register on the forums: Because there is very valuable information and because the community is so large, your chances of getting your question answered quickly is very high.

The first time you visit the forum, take a few moments to read the FAQs and the Rules; you can find links to both resources at the top of every page on the forum. If you want to post a question on the forum, first run a search to determine whether the question has been asked previously. Odds are that if you are having a problem, someone else has experienced it before and the issue has been discussed on the forums. As a matter of courtesy, check and see if it has been asked and answered before you raise the issue yet again.

Discussions on the forums are organized topically, with separate discussion areas set aside for languages other than English. Make sure that you take a look around and get a feel for what goes where prior to posting; you can greatly increase your odds of getting a responsive answer if you post your question in the right area!

Finding Commercial Support

Despite the popularity of the Joomla! system, commercial support is not widely available at this time. Although dedicated professional support providers may be lacking, you may be able to arrange for some level of support from your developer. Posting a request for commercial support on the Joomla! forums is another option that frequently turns up someone who is willing to provide assistance for a fee.

Index

A

Absolute Position control, TinyMCE editor, 122
accelerators, 121
access levels, 40, 263–267
accessibility, 714–719
Activate parent control, Menu module, 387
Active column
    Category Manager, 81
    Section Manager, 75
Active Groups module, 660
Activity Stream module, 660
ad management extensions, 598
Add Filter link, JoomlaCode site, 17
Add Long Quotation control, XStandard Lite editor, 127
Add suffix to URLs option, Global Configuration Manager, 59
add-ons. *See* extensions
AddThis Social Bookmarking extension, 597
admin interface. *See* back end
Admin Menu module, 426–427
Admin SubMenu module, 428–429
admin system access, 46
administration extensions, 590
Administrator link
    Cache Manager, 707
    Module Manager, 420
    Template Manager, 516
Administrator modules, 45, 419–452. *See also names of specific Administrator modules*
administrator template. *See* Khepri template
Administrator user group, 250
administrators, 21, 656, 695–697
AdSense Module extension, 598
Advanced Settings section
    Database Configuration screen, 28
    FTP Configuration screen, 29
aliases, URL, 723
Align Center control
    TinyMCE editor, 121
    XStandard Lite editor, 127
Align Fully control, TinyMCE editor, 121

Align Left control
    TinyMCE editor, 121
    XStandard Lite editor, 127
Align Right control
    TinyMCE editor, 121
    XStandard Lite editor, 127
All option, Module Manager, 421
All Video plugin, 661
All-In-One module, VirtueMart, 605, 607
Allow User Registration setting, Global Configuration Manager, 61
AllVideos Reloaded extension, 587
Alternative Read more: text option, New Article dialogue, 101
Always show submenu items option, Menu module, 386
-AMP packages, installing Joomla! on, 22
anchors, 121
animation, 711–712
Apache web server
    configuration requirements, 20
    enabling SEF URLs, 59
API Configuration area, JomSocial, 673
applets, 718
Apply icon, New User dialogue, 251
Apply option, Global Configuration Manager, 56
`apps_unzip_first_xxxx.zip` directory, 661
archive files, extracting, 24
archive formats, 18, 569
Archive function
    Article Manager, 91
    Front Page Manager, 237
Archive module, 117–118, 377
Archived Article List menu item type, 171–172
Archived Articles parameter, Content plugin, 478
Archived Content module, 362–365
archives, defined, 40
archiving articles, 7, 115–118
Article Activity plugin, 661
Article Editing dialogue, Article Manager, 50, 108, 277
Article Editing icon, 147
Article editing screen, 105

Index

Index

Index

Index

Index

Index

Index

Receives System E-mails field, New User dialogue, 253

Recent Added Articles option, Control Panel, 48

Recently Added Articles module, 436

Recommended Settings list, 25

Redirect Manager, 52

redirecting user after login or logout, 262–263

Redo control

    TinyMCE editor, 121

    XStandard Lite editor, 128

Registered access level, 40, 264–265

Registered user group, 249

registering components, 555–556

Registrations area, JomSocial, 668

Related Articles module, 400–402

Related Products tab, VirtueMart, 648–649

Remember Me plugin, 489–490

Remository extension, 594

Remote Installer, VirtueMart, 609–610

Remove column, VirtueMart, 635, 640

Remove Formatting control, TinyMCE editor, 123

Remove function

    Front Page Manager, 237

    VirtueMart, 633

Remove Long Quotation control, XStandard Lite editor, 127

Reportings area, JomSocial, 666–667

reports, VirtueMart, 651–652

Required column, JomSocial, 678

resizing text, 717

Resources option, Menus menu, 51

restoring

    articles from Trash, 113–114

    backups, 695

    menu items from Trash, 221–223

Restrict Uploads setting, Global Configuration Manager, 62

RHUK_Milkyway template, 504–505, 523, 525–527

Right modules collapsible function option, JA_Purity template, 502

Right to Left control, TinyMCE editor, 122

Robots field, Article Editing dialogue, 102

Rocket Themes, 581

RokSlideshow extension, 593

rounded option, Module Chrome, 531

RSform!Pro extension, 592

RSGallery2 extension, 593

RSS feeds, 143

RSS syndication icon, 152

RTL Feed control, Feed Display module, 374, 432

RTL Feed field, New News Feed dialogue, 328

Rule Descriptions column, JomSocial, 680

Rule Scan function, JomSocial, 679

S

sample data, 30, 33

Save FTP Password option, FTP Configuration screen, 29

Save Warning parameter, TinyMCE plugin, 472

Scope field, New Section dialogue, 76

Screen Reader option, XStandard editor, 128

Screen Reader Preview control, XStandard Lite editor, 127

Scroll Bars parameter, Who's Online module, 416

Scrollbars option, Wrapper menu item type, 214

Search box, VirtueMart, 639

Search button as image parameter, Search module, 405

Search button, Search module, 404

Search by Tags parameter, Banner module, 299, 366

Search Engine Friendly (SEF) plugin, 483–484

Search Engine Friendly (SEF) URLs, 8, 59, 714, 722–724

search engine optimization. *See* SEO

search enhancement extensions, 590–591

Search Limit parameter, Content plugin, 478

Search module, 7, 402–405, 606, 608

Search option, Components menu, 52

Search plugins, 477–483

Search Product box, VirtueMart, 639

Search Query Strings parameter, Backlink plugin, 491

Search SEF parameter, Backlink plugin, 491

Search String option, LDAP plugin, 460

Secret Word setting, Global Configuration Manager, 61

Section Blog Layout menu item type, 181–184

Section ID parameter

    Latest News module, 379

    Most Read Content module, 389

Section Layout menu item type, 184–186

Section Manager, 51, 73–79

Section Name option

    Article Editing dialogue, 101

    Article Manager, 97

    Internal Link - Articles menu item types, 169

Section parameter

    Section Blog Layout menu item type, 184

    Section Layout menu item type, 185

Section Title Linkable option

    Article Editing dialogue, 101

    Article Manager, 98

    Internal Link - Articles menu item types, 169

sections

    copying, 77–78

    deleting, 78–79

    editing, 78–79

    relationship with categories and articles, 72

    restricting access to, 265

Index

Index